6.75

D1030630

PUBLIC PAPERS OF THE PRESIDENTS

OF THE UNITED STATES

R
353.03p

PUBLIC PAPERS OF THE PRESIDENTS

OF THE UNITED STATES

Dwight D. Eisenhower

1955

Containing the Public Messages, Speeches, and

Statements of the President

JANUARY 1 TO DECEMBER 31, 1955

38023

PUBLISHED BY THE
OFFICE OF THE FEDERAL REGISTER
NATIONAL ARCHIVES AND RECORDS SERVICE
GENERAL SERVICES ADMINISTRATION

U.S. GOVERNMENT PRINTING OFFICE: 1959

For sale by the Superintendent of Documents, U.S. Government Printing Office
Washington 25, D.C. - Price $6.75

FOREWORD

THERE HAS BEEN a long-felt need for an orderly series of the Public Papers of the Presidents. A reference work of this type can be most helpful to scholars and officials of government, to reporters of current affairs and the events of history.

The general availability of the official text of Presidential documents and messages will serve a broader purpose. As part of the expression of democracy, this series can be a vital factor in the maintenance of our individual freedoms and our institutions of self-government.

I wish success to the editors of this project, and I am sure their work through the years will add strength to the ever-growing traditions of the Republic.

Dwight D. Eisenhower

PREFACE

IN THIS VOLUME are gathered most of the public messages and statements of the President of the United States that were released by the White House during the year 1955. A similar volume, covering the year 1957, was published early in 1958 as the first of a series. The President's foreword is reprinted from that volume.

Immediate plans for this series call for the publication of annual volumes soon after the close of each new calendar year, and at the same time undertaking the periodic compilation of volumes covering previous years. Volumes covering the years 1955 through 1958 are now available.

This series was begun in response to a recommendation of the National Historical Publications Commission (44 U.S.C. 393). The Commission's recommendation was incorporated in regulations of the Administrative Committee of the Federal Register issued under section 6 of the Federal Register Act (44 U.S.C. 306). The Committee's regulations, establishing the series, are reprinted at page 886 as "Appendix D."

The first extensive compilation of the messages and papers of the Presidents was assembled by James D. Richardson and published under Congressional authority between 1896 and 1899. It included Presidential materials from 1789 to 1897. Since then, there have been various private compilations, but no uniform, systematic publication comparable to the *Congressional Record* or the *United States Supreme Court Reports*.

For many years Presidential Proclamations have been published in the *United States Statutes at Large*. The Federal Register Act in 1935 required that Proclamations, Executive Orders, and some other official Executive documents be published in the daily *Federal Register;* but the greater part of Presidential writings and utterances still lacked an official medium for either current publication or periodic compilation. Some of them were interspersed through the issues of the *Congressional Record* while others were reported only in the press or were generally available only in mimeographed White House releases. Under these circumstances it was difficult to remember, after a lapse of time, where and in what form even a major pronouncement had been made.

CONTENT AND ARRANGEMENT

The text of this book is based on Presidential materials issued during the calendar year 1955 as White House releases and on transcripts of news conferences. Where available, original source materials have been used to protect against substantive errors in transcription. A list of the White House releases from which final selections were made is published at page 863 as "Appendix A."

During this year the White House began the practice of filming the news conferences and of allowing direct quotation of the President's answers (see editorial note to Item 18, page 185).

Proclamations, Executive Orders, and similar documents required by law to be published in the *Federal Register* and *Code of Federal Regulations* are not repeated. Instead, they are listed by number and subject under the heading "Appendix B" at page 877.

The President is required by statute to transmit numerous reports to Congress. Those transmitted during 1958 are listed at page 884 as "Appendix C."

The items published in this volume are presented in chronological order, rather than being grouped in classes. Most needs for a classified arrangement are met by the subject index. For example, a reader interested in veto messages sent to Congress during 1955 will find them listed in the index under "veto messages."

The dates shown at the end of item headings are White House release dates. In instances where the date of the document differs from the release date that fact is shown in brackets immediately following the heading. Other editorial devices, such as text notes, footnotes, and cross references, have been held to a minimum.

Remarks or addresses were delivered in Washington, D.C., unless otherwise indicated. Similarly, statements, messages, and letters were issued from the White House in Washington unless otherwise indicated.

The planning and editorial work for this volume were under the direction of David C. Eberhart of the Office of the Federal Register, assisted by Warren R. Reid and Mildred B. Berry. The index was prepared by Dorothy M. Jacobson. Frank H. Mortimer of the Government Printing Office developed the typography and design.

WAYNE C. GROVER
Archivist of the United States

FRANKLIN FLOETE
Administrator of General Services

October 15, 1959

CONTENTS

Page

FRONTISPIECE—Picture of the President taken in his office at the White House, July 25, 1955.

FOREWORD V

PREFACE VII

LIST OF ITEMS XIII

PUBLIC PAPERS OF DWIGHT D. EISENHOWER . . I

Appendix A—White House Press Releases, 1955 . . 863

Appendix B—Presidential Documents Published in the Federal Register, 1955 877

Appendix C—Presidential Reports to the Congress, 1955 . 884

Appendix D—Rules Governing This Publication . . 886

INDEX 889

LIST OF ITEMS

Page

1   Memorandum Concerning the Government Employees Incentive Awards Program. January 1, 1955   1

2   Statement by the President on the Death of President Remon of Panama. January 3, 1955   2

3   Letter to the Secretary of Defense on National Security Requirements. January 5, 1955   2

4   Annual Message to the Congress on the State of the Union. January 6, 1955   7

5   Special Message to the Senate Transmitting Mutual Defense Treaty Between the United States and the Republic of China. January 6, 1955   30

6   Special Message to the Congress on the Foreign Economic Policy of the United States. January 10, 1955   32

7   Message to the Congress Transmitting the President's First Semiannual Report on Activities Under the Agricultural Trade Development and Assistance Act. January 10, 1955   40

8   Special Message to the Congress on Federal Personnel Management. January 11, 1955   41

9   Special Message to the Congress on Postal Pay and Rates. January 11, 1955   46

10   The President's News Conference of January 12, 1955   54

11   Remarks at Luncheon Meeting of the Association of American Colleges. January 13, 1955   69

Page

12   Special Message to the Congress on National Security
     Requirements. January 13, 1955   72

13   Special Message to the Congress on Career Incentives
     for Military Personnel. January 13, 1955   78

14   Letter to the President of the Senate and to the
     Speaker of the House of Representatives Approving
     Certain Virgin Islands Corporation Activities. Janu-
     ary 13, 1955   84

15   Cablegram to Dr. Albert Schweitzer on the Occasion
     of His 80th Birthday. January 13, 1955   85

16   Statement by the President on United Nations Nego-
     tiations With Communist China for Release of
     American Airmen and Other Personnel. January
     14, 1955   85

17   Annual Budget Message to the Congress: Fiscal Year
     1956. January 17, 1955   86

18   The President's News Conference of January 19,
     1955   185

19   Annual Message Presenting the Economic Report to
     the Congress. January 20, 1955   200

20   Letter to Representative Auchincloss on the Second
     Anniversary of the President's Inauguration. Janu-
     ary 20, 1955   205

21   Special Message to the Congress Regarding United
     States Policy for the Defense of Formosa. January
     24, 1955   207

22   Remarks on Receiving Statue Presented by Ambassa-
     dor Krekeler on Behalf of the German People. Janu-
     ary 25, 1955   212

List of Items

Page

23 Toasts of the President and President Magloire of
Haiti. January 26, 1955   214

24 Statement by the President Upon Signing the Joint
Resolution on the Defense of Formosa. January 29,
1955   215

25 Special Message to the Congress Recommending a
Health Program. January 31, 1955   216

26 The President's News Conference of February 2,
1955   223

27 Message Recorded for the New York USO Defense
Fund Dinner. February 3, 1955   237

28 Message to the Boy Scouts of America. February
6, 1955   238

29 Letter to the Governors Concerning Uniform State
Legislation on Absentee Voting Rights of Members
of the Armed Services. February 7, 1955   239

30 Letter to Chan Gurney, Acting Chairman, Civil
Aeronautics Board, on the West Coast-Hawaii Case.
February 7, 1955   242

31 Special Message to the Congress Concerning Federal
Assistance in School Construction. February 8, 1955   243

32 Message to Nationwide Meetings in Support of the
Campaign for Radio Free Europe. February 8, 1955   250

33 The President's News Conference of February 9,
1955   251

34 Message to Meetings of the Nationwide Clinical
Conference on Heart Ailments. February 9, 1955   264

Page

35 Remarks at Luncheon Meeting of the Republican National Committee and the Republican National Finance Committee.   February 17, 1955   265

36 Exchange of Messages Between the President and President Chiang Kai-shek of the Republic of China. February 18, 1955   271

37 Letter to Emil Sandstrom, League of Red Cross Societies, on Completion of the Flood Relief Program in Europe.   February 19, 1955   272

38 Remarks Recorded for the "Back-to-God" Program of the American Legion.   February 20, 1955   273

39 Special Message to the Congress Regarding a National Highway Program.   February 22, 1955   275

40 Letter Extending Greetings to the Brotherhood Dinner of the National Conference of Christians and Jews.   February 22, 1955   281

41 The President's News Conference of February 23, 1955   282

42 Exchange of Messages Between the President and His Imperial Majesty the Shah of Iran.   February 23, 1955   295

43 Remarks at the Annual Breakfast of Masonic Leaders.   February 24, 1955   296

44 Message to the Inter-American Investment Conference Held in New Orleans.   February 28, 1955   299

45 Remarks Recorded for the Opening of the Red Cross Campaign.   February 28, 1955   300

List of Items

		Page
46	Message to the Pope on the Occasion of His 79th Birthday. March 2, 1955	301
47	The President's News Conference of March 2, 1955	302
48	Letter to His Majesty Bao Dai, Chief of State of Viet-Nam. March 3, 1955	315
49	Statement by the President Concerning Offer of Food Supplies to Albania. March 4, 1955	316
50	Special Message to the Congress on the Extension of the Renegotiation Act of 1951. March 4, 1955	318
51	Letter to General Omar N. Bradley, Chairman, President's Commission on Veterans' Pensions, Concerning a Study of Veterans' Benefits. March 5, 1955	320
52	Remarks to Distinguished Service Cross Recipients and Commanders Who Participated in the Seizure of the Remagen Bridge. March 7, 1955	323
53	Remarks to Students Attending the International School of Nuclear Science and Engineering, Argonne National Laboratory. March 10, 1955	324
54	Message to the Prime Ministers of the Seven Nations Signatory to the Protocols Establishing the Western European Union. March 10, 1955	325
55	Letter to George A. Garrett, President, Federal City Council, Concerning the Redevelopment of Southwest Washington. March 10, 1955	328
56	The President's News Conference of March 16, 1955	329
57	Statement by the President Announcing the Appointment of Harold Stassen as Special Assistant to the President for Disarmament Studies. March 19, 1955	343

List of Items

Page

58 Remarks at 11th Annual Washington Conference of the Advertising Council. March 22, 1955 — 345

59 The President's News Conference of March 23, 1955 — 350

60 Remarks to Representatives of the American Voluntary Societies Cooperating in the United States Escapee Program. March 25, 1955 — 366

61 Joint Statement Following Discussions With Prime Minister Scelba of Italy. March 28, 1955 — 367

62 The President's News Conference of March 30, 1955 — 368

63 Statement by the President on the Death of Joseph Pulitzer and Robert R. McCormick. April 1, 1955 — 381

64 Letter to the President of the Senate and to the Speaker of the House of Representatives Concerning the Inter-American Highway. April 1, 1955 — 382

65 Statement by the President on the Retirement of Sir Winston Churchill, Prime Minister of the United Kingdom. April 5, 1955 — 384

66 Statement by the President on the Appointment of Anthony Eden as Prime Minister of the United Kingdom. April 6, 1955 — 385

67 Memorandum to the Director of the Office of Defense Mobilization Relating to the Buy American Act. April 7, 1955 — 385

68 Remarks to the Easter Egg Rollers on the South Grounds of the White House. April 11, 1955 — 386

69 Statement by the President on the Mutual Security Program. April 11, 1955 — 386

List of Items

Page

70 Remarks at The Citadel, Charleston, South Carolina. April 12, 1955   388

71 Letter to the Chairman of the Joint Committee on Atomic Energy on the Proposed Agreement for Cooperation With NATO on Atomic Information. April 13, 1955   391

72 Special Message to the Congress on United States Membership in the Proposed Organization for Trade Cooperation. April 14, 1955   393

73 Telegram to Senator Thurmond Saluting James F. Byrnes as a Great American. April 16, 1955   399

74 Letter to Secretary Dulles Regarding Transfer of the Affairs of the Foreign Operations Administration to the Department of State. April 17, 1955   399

75 Statement by the President on the Death of Albert Einstein. April 18, 1955   403

76 Special Message to the Congress on the Mutual Security Program. April 20, 1955   404

77 Citation Presented to Dr. Jonas E. Salk and Accompanying Remarks. April 22, 1955   414

78 Citation Presented to the National Foundation for Infantile Paralysis and Accompanying Remarks. April 22, 1955   415

79 Address at the Annual Luncheon of the Associated Press, New York City. April 25, 1955   416

80 Letter to Harvey S. Firestone, Jr., Upon Accepting Honorary Chairmanship of the United Service Organizations. April 26, 1955   424

List of Items

Page

81 The President's News Conference of April 27, 1955   425

82 Special Message to the Congress Concerning a Program for Low Income Farmers. April 27, 1955   440

83 Remarks to the Committee for a National Trade Policy Following Congressional Action on the Proposed Trade Agreements Extension Act. April 28, 1955   442

84 Remarks at the Cornerstone-Laying Ceremony for the American Federation of Labor Building. April 30, 1955   443

85 Remarks at the Annual Meeting of the United States Chamber of Commerce. May 2, 1955   446

86 Special Message to the Congress on United States Participation in the International Finance Corporation. May 2, 1955   449

87 Citation and Remarks at Presentation to Field Marshal Pibulsonggram of Thailand of the Legion of Merit, Degree of Chief Commander. May 2, 1955   453

88 Remarks at the Governors' Conference Dinner. May 2, 1955   454

89 Statement by the President on Approving a Proposed Agreement With Turkey for Cooperation in the Peaceful Uses of Atomic Energy. May 3, 1955   457

90 The President's News Conference of May 4, 1955   459

91 Letter to the President of the Senate and to the Speaker of the House of Representatives on Revision of the Philippine Trade Agreement. May 5, 1955   475

List of Items

Page

92 Remarks at the Dedication of the Washington Hebrew Congregation Temple.   May 6, 1955   476

93 Remarks to Delegates to the General Assembly of the Organization of World Touring and Automobile Clubs.   May 10, 1955   479

94 Remarks at the Republican Women's National Conference.   May 10, 1955   480

95 The President's News Conference of May 11, 1955   486

96 Statement by the President Concerning Community and State Conferences on Education.   May 11, 1955   500

97 Message Recorded for Use in Conjunction With Observance of Armed Forces Day.   May 12, 1955   501

98 Message to President Koerner of Austria on the Signing of the Treaty Restoring Austrian Independence.   May 15, 1955   502

99 Remarks of the President During Secretary Dulles' Television Report on His European Visit.   May 17, 1955   503

100 The President's News Conference of May 18, 1955   505

101 Memorandum to Federal Agencies Directing Participation in a National Civil Defense Exercise. May 18, 1955   519

102 Veto of Postal Field Service Compensation Bill. May 19, 1955   520

103 Remarks to the President's Committee on the Employment of the Physically Handicapped.   May 23, 1955   522

Page

104 Remarks at a Dinner Sponsored by the District of Columbia Republican Women's Finance Committee. May 23, 1955 — 524

105 Remarks to the National Association of Radio and Television Broadcasters. May 24, 1955 — 527

106 Letter to Ross Rizley, Chairman, Civil Aeronautics Board, Regarding the States-Alaska Case. May 25, 1955 — 531

107 Special Message to the Congress Transmitting Conventions and Recommendations Adopted at Geneva by the International Labor Conference. May 26, 1955 — 532

108 Remarks at Dedication of the Armed Forces Institute of Pathology, Walter Reed Medical Center. May 26, 1955 — 535

109 Special Message to the Congress Recommending Amendments to the Refugee Relief Act. May 27, 1955 — 538

110 Citation and Remarks at Presentation of the National Security Medal to J. Edgar Hoover. May 27, 1955 — 542

111 Statement by the President on Safe Driving. May 27, 1955 — 544

112 The President's News Conference of May 31, 1955 — 544

113 Statement by the President on the Polio Vaccine Situation. May 31, 1955 — 559

114 Message to the Senate Transmitting the Austrian State Treaty. June 1, 1955 — 563

List of Items

Page

115 Remarks on Acceptance of a Palestinian "Lamp of Freedom" From the United Jewish Appeal. June 3, 1955 — 565

116 Veto of Bill for Relief of Kurt Glaser. June 3, 1955 — 566

117 Remarks at the United States Military Academy Alumni Luncheon, West Point, New York. June 6, 1955 — 569

118 Address at the Graduation Ceremonies, United States Military Academy, West Point, New York. June 7, 1955 — 572

119 The President's News Conference of June 8, 1955 — 578

120 Statement by the President Upon Signing the Postal Field Service Compensation Act. June 10, 1955 — 592

121 Address at the Centennial Commencement of Pennsylvania State University. June 11, 1955 — 593

122 Joint Statement Following Discussions With Chancellor Adenauer of Germany. June 14, 1955 — 600

123 Statement by the President on Proposed Agreements With Belgium, Canada, and the United Kingdom for Cooperation on the Civil Uses of Atomic Energy. June 15, 1955 — 601

124 Letter to William Randolph Hearst, Jr., Regarding His Appointment to the President's Committee for Traffic Safety and Its Advisory Council. June 18, 1955 — 603

125 Letter to T. S. Petersen Requesting Him To Serve on the President's Committee for Traffic Safety. June 18, 1955 — 604

XXIII

List of Items

Page

126   Address at the Tenth Anniversary Meeting of the United Nations, San Francisco, California. June 20, 1955   605

127   Remarks to the National Association of Television and Radio Farm Directors. June 21, 1955   611

128   Remarks to the National 4–H Conference. June 21, 1955   613

129   Statement by the President Upon Signing the Trade Agreements Extension Act. June 21, 1955   615

130   Memorandum to Federal Agencies on the Community Chest Campaign. June 22, 1955   615

131   Remarks at the Vermont State Dairy Festival, Rutland, Vermont. June 22, 1955   616

132   Remarks at a Breakfast for Vermont Women Representatives of Dairy and Agricultural Organizations, Chittenden, Vermont. June 23, 1955   620

133   Remarks at the State Capitol, Concord, New Hampshire. June 23, 1955   621

134   Remarks at the Belknap Lodge Picnic Grounds, Laconia, New Hampshire. June 23, 1955   623

135   Remarks at the Lincoln High School, Lincoln, New Hampshire. June 24, 1955   624

136   Remarks at Ceremonies Commemorating the Discovery of the Old Man of the Mountain, Franconia Notch, New Hampshire. June 24, 1955   626

137   Remarks at Lancaster, New Hampshire. June 25, 1955   630

Page

138   Remarks at Jefferson, New Hampshire. June 25, 1955   631

139   Remarks at the Hansen Ski Jump Area, Berlin, New Hampshire. June 25, 1955   632

140   Letter to Helen Keller on the Occasion of Her 75th Birthday. June 26, 1955   634

141   Remarks at the Fawn Presentation Ceremonies, Rangeley, Maine. June 27, 1955   634

142   Remarks at the Skowhegan Fairgrounds, Skowhegan, Maine. June 27, 1955   635

143   Remarks at the Dow Air Force Base, Bangor, Maine. June 27, 1955   638

144   Remarks on Presentation of the Distinguished Service Medal to General Ridgway, and Accompanying Citation. June 28, 1955   639

145   Message to the Congress Transmitting Final Report of the Commission on Intergovernmental Relations. June 28, 1955   641

146   The President's News Conference of June 29, 1955   643

147   Veto of Bill To Prohibit Publication by the Government of the United States of Predictions as to Apple Prices. July 1, 1955   662

148   Joint Statement Following Discussions With Prime Minister U Nu of Burma. July 3, 1955   663

149   The President's News Conference of July 6, 1955   665

150   Message to the Congress Transmitting the Second Semiannual Report Under the Agricultural Trade Development and Assistance Act. July 12, 1955   681

List of Items

Page

151 Remarks to American Field Service Students. July
12, 1955   682

152 Letter Accepting the Resignation of Mrs. Oveta
Culp Hobby, Secretary of Health, Education, and
Welfare. July 13, 1955   684

153 Remarks Following the Acceptance of the Resignation of Secretary Hobby. July 13, 1955   685

154 Letter to Secretary Wilson Marking the Third Anniversary of Operation Skywatch. July 13, 1955   687

155 Special Message to the Congress Upon Signing the
Department of Defense Appropriation Act. July
13, 1955   688

156 Message to the Congress Transmitting the Ninth
Annual Report on United States Participation in the
United Nations. July 15, 1955   690

157 Statement by the President Upon Signing the Public
Works Appropriation Act. July 15, 1955   696

158 Statement by the President Upon Signing the Act
Providing for a Highway Bridge Across Lake
Texoma. July 15, 1955   698

159 Statement by the President Upon Signing Bill for
the Relief of the Highway Construction Company.
July 15, 1955   699

160 Letter to the Chairman, House Committee on Ways
and Means, Concerning United States Membership in the Organization for Trade Cooperation.
July 15, 1955   700

161 Radio and Television Address to the American
People Prior to Departure for the Big Four Conference at Geneva. July 15, 1955   701

List of Items

Page

162 Remarks at the Keflavik Airport, Iceland. July 16, 1955   706

163 Remarks Upon Arrival at the Airport in Geneva. July 16, 1955   707

164 Opening Statement at the Geneva Conference. July 18, 1955   707

165 Remarks at the Research Reactor Building, Palais des Nations, Geneva. July 20, 1955   712

166 Statement on Disarmament Presented at the Geneva Conference. July 21, 1955   713

167 Statement on East-West Contacts Delivered at the Geneva Conference. July 22, 1955   716

168 Memorandum to Federal Agencies on the United Fund and Community Chest Campaigns. July 22, 1955   719

169 Letter to Prime Minister Maung Nu Concerning the Gift of the Burmese People. July 22, 1955   720

170 Closing Statement at the Final Meeting of the Heads of Government Conference at Geneva. July 23, 1955   721

171 Remarks on Leaving Geneva. July 23, 1955   723

172 Statement by the President Upon Signing Bill Concerning Mineral Claims Filed on Public Lands. July 23, 1955   724

173 Remarks at Washington National Airport on Returning From Geneva. July 24, 1955   724

174 White House Statement Following Bipartisan Meeting on the Geneva Conference. July 25, 1955   725

List of Items

Page

175   Radio and Television Address to the American People on the Geneva Conference. July 25, 1955   726

176   The President's News Conference of July 27, 1955   731

177   Remarks at the Ceremony Marking the Issuance of the Atoms for Peace Stamp. July 28, 1955   744

178   Statement by the President on Congressional Action Regarding a Nationwide System of Highways. July 28, 1955   746

179   Statement by the President Regarding Release of United States Airmen by Communist China. August 1, 1955   746

180   Special Message to the Congress Recommending Changes in Act Relating to Construction of Irrigation Systems on Federal Projects by Local Agencies. August 1, 1955   747

181   Remarks to Members of the Bull Elephants Club. August 2, 1955   748

182   Statement by the President Upon Signing the Mutual Security Appropriation Act. August 2, 1955   753

183   Citation and Remarks at Presentation of the Medal of Freedom to Robert B. Anderson. August 3, 1955   754

184   Statement by the President Upon Signing Bill Relating to the Red River Flood Control Project. August 3, 1955   755

185   The President's News Conference of August 4, 1955   757

186   Letter to the Treasurer of the United States Appointing Her Chairman of the Interdepartmental Savings Bond Committee. August 4, 1955   767

List of Items

Page

187   Memorandum to Federal Agencies Concerning the Voluntary Payroll Savings Plan for the Purchase of U.S. Savings Bonds. August 4, 1955   768

188   Citation Accompanying the Distinguished Service Medal Presented to Admiral Robert B. Carney. August 4, 1955   769

189   Memorandum of Disapproval of Bill Concerning Term of Office of Subversive Activities Control Board Members. August 6, 1955   770

190   Exchange of Letters Between the President and Chancellor Adenauer of Germany on the Geneva Conference. August 6, 1955   771

191   Message to the United Nations Conference on the Peaceful Uses of Atomic Energy at Geneva. August 8, 1955   772

192   Statement by the President Upon Signing the Reserve Forces Act of 1955. August 9, 1955   775

193   Statement by the President Upon Signing H.R. 7684 Authorizing Salary Payment to an Interim Appointee to the Atomic Energy Commission. August 10, 1955   777

194   Statement by the President Upon Signing the Housing Amendments of 1955. August 11, 1955   777

195   Statement by the President on the Death of Ambassador John E. Peurifoy and His Son. August 12, 1955   780

196   Memorandum of Disapproval of Bill for the Relief of the E. J. Albrecht Company. August 12, 1955   780

List of Items

Page

197 Memorandum of Disapproval of Bill To Change the
Military Record of Stephen Swan Ogletree. August
12, 1955   782

198 Memorandum of Disapproval of Bill Amending the
Internal Revenue Code of 1954. August 12, 1955   785

199 Memorandum of Disapproval of Bill To Reconvey
to Former Owners Certain Lands Acquired for
Reservoir Projects in Texas. August 12, 1955   787

200 Memorandum of Disapproval of Bill for the Relief
of Fred P. Hines. August 12, 1955   789

201 Memorandum of Disapproval of Bill To Amend the
Civil Service Retirement Act. August 12, 1955   789

202 Statement by the President Upon Signing Bill
Amending the Agricultural Trade Development and
Assistance Act. August 12, 1955   791

203 Letter to Maj. Gen. John S. Bragdon Appointing
Him as Special Assistant to the President To Coordinate Public Works Planning. August 12, 1955   792

204 Exchange of Messages Between the President and
Chancellor Adenauer on the Air Force Disaster in
Germany. August 13, 1955   794

205 Memorandum of Disapproval of Bill Extending the
Domestic Minerals Purchase Programs. August
14, 1955   795

206 Statement by the President Upon Signing Bill Concerning Public Transit Services in the District of
Columbia. August 14, 1955   797

xxx

List of Items

Page

207 Presidential Statement Upon Signing Order Pre-
scribing a Code of Conduct for Members of the
Armed Forces While in Combat or Captivity.
August 17, 1955   798

208 Remarks on the Hurricane-Flood Disaster in the
Northeastern States. August 22, 1955   798

209 Remarks Following a Meeting With the Governors
of Flood-Stricken States at Bradley Field, Hartford,
Connecticut. August 23, 1955   800

210 Address at the Annual Convention of the American
Bar Association, Philadelphia. August 24, 1955   802

211 Statement by the President Concerning New York
Meeting of the United Nations Subcommittee on
Disarmament. August 29, 1955   810

212 Statement by the President: Labor Day. September 5, 1955   810

213 Remarks at the Breakfast Meeting of Republican
State Chairmen, Denver, Colorado. September
10, 1955   811

214 Telegram to the President of the United States
Chamber of Commerce on Assistance Given Flood
Disaster Areas. September 12, 1955   819

215 Statement by the President on the Occasion of the
Jewish New Year. September 16, 1955   820

216 Message to President Ruiz Cortines on the Anniversary of the Independence of Mexico. September
16, 1955   820

217 Message Prepared for the Conference on Fitness of
American Youth. September 18, 1955   821

List of Items

Page

___ Editor's Note Regarding the President's Illness   822

218 Message Opening the United Community Campaigns of America. October 2, 1955   822

219 Letter to the Columbus Citizens' Committee in New York City. October 11, 1955   823

220 Letter to Nikolai Bulganin, Chairman, Council of Ministers, U.S.S.R. October 12, 1955   824

221 Statement by the President on Observance of Farm-City Week. October 17, 1955   825

222 Letter to Governor Roberts of Rhode Island on the Recommendations of the New England Governors' Conference. October 18, 1955   826

223 Letter to Governor Roberts of Rhode Island on the Establishment of Atomic Reactor Generating Plants in New England. October 18, 1955   829

224 Statement by the President on the 14th Anniversary of the Civil Air Patrol. October 19, 1955   830

225 Letter to the Vice President Concerning the Conference on Equal Job Opportunity. October 22, 1955   831

226 Letter to the Vice President and the Cabinet Regarding the Task of Secretary Dulles at Geneva. October 23, 1955   832

227 Statement by the President on the Foreign Ministers Meeting at Geneva. October 26, 1955   833

228 Message to the National Industrial Conference Board on the Peaceful Uses of Atomic Energy. October 27, 1955   834

List of Items

Page

229 Letter to President Ruiz Cortines of Mexico on the Hurricane-Flood Disaster in Tampico. October 28, 1955 835

230 Telegram Welcoming President Castillo-Armas of Guatemala Upon His Arrival in Washington. October 31, 1955 836

231 Message to His Majesty Haile Selassie I on the 25th Anniversary of His Reign. November 3, 1955 837

232 Telegram on the Dedication of the International Brotherhood of Teamsters New Building. November 3, 1955 838

233 Message to K. Voroshilov, Chairman of the Presidium of the Supreme Soviet, U.S.S.R., on the National Anniversary of the Soviet Union. November 7, 1955 838

234 Statement by the President on the Hostilities Between Egypt and Israel in Violation of the General Armistice Agreement. November 9, 1955 839

235 Remarks on Leaving Denver, Colorado. November 11, 1955 840

236 Remarks Upon Arrival at the Washington National Airport. November 11, 1955 841

237 Remarks Upon Arrival in Lincoln Square, Gettysburg, Pennsylvania. November 14, 1955 842

238 Letter to Mrs. Martin P. Durkin on the Death of Her Husband. November 14, 1955 843

239 Message to Rabbi Abba Hillel Silver on the Near East Situation. November 15, 1955 843

Page

240 Message to the Sultan of Morocco on the Anniversary of His Accession to the Throne. November 18, 1955 844

241 Message to King Haakon VII of Norway on the 50th Anniversary of His Reign. November 24, 1955 845

242 Remarks for the White House Conference on Education. November 28, 1955 846

243 Statement by the President on Observance of Safe Driving Day. November 30, 1955 849

244 Letter Accompanying Medallion for Presentation to Sir Winston Churchill on His 81st Birthday. November 30, 1955 850

245 Telephone Broadcast to the AFL–CIO Merger Meeting in New York City. December 5, 1955 851

246 Statement by the President on Early Mailing of Christmas Gifts and Greetings. December 10, 1955 855

247 White House Statements Following Meetings With Republican Leaders of the Senate and the House of Representatives. December 12, 1955 855

248 White House Statement Following Bipartisan Conference on Foreign Affairs and National Defense. December 13, 1955 858

249 Statement by the President: Bill of Rights Day. December 14, 1955 859

250 Remarks Broadcast for the Pageant of Peace Ceremonies in Washington. December 18, 1955 860

Dwight D. Eisenhower

1955

1 ¶ Memorandum Concerning the Government Employees Incentive Awards Program.
January 1, 1955

[Released January 1, 1955. Dated December 28, 1954]

To Heads of Executive Departments and Agencies:

The vast complexity of modern government demands a constant search for ways of conducting the public business with increased efficiency and economy. I am firmly convinced that employees of the Federal Government can, through their diligence and competence, make further significant contributions to the important task of improving Government operations. Wide participation by Federal employees in this task is essential if we are to derive full benefit from the ingenuity and inventiveness that exist in the Federal Service. This participation can be obtained only if all levels of management and supervision understand its importance, encourage it, and insure that it is promptly and properly recognized.

A means for adequately recognizing those employees who contribute to improved government operations, was provided by the Government Employees Incentive Awards Act passed by the 83rd Congress. This Act was a part of the Administration's legislative program on personnel management. Under it the Civil Service Commission was given general responsibility for the administration of a government-wide incentive awards program. The Commission has authorized each of you to establish and operate an incentive awards program within broad principles and guide lines. I am relying upon you to provide personal leadership for the incentive awards program in your agency.

I am looking forward to personal participation in the program through the provision in the Act for a Presidential award for employees rendering exceptionally meritorious service. The necessary instructions for submitting recommendations for this award are now being prepared.

DWIGHT D. EISENHOWER

NOTE: This memorandum was released at Augusta, Ga.

2 ¶ Statement by the President on the Death of President Remon of Panama.   *January* 3, 1955

I WAS GRIEVED to learn of the tragic assassination of President Jose Antonio Remon of Panama.   A firm friend, President Remon was held in great respect by the government of our nation. Only last year he and Senora Remon were visitors at the White House.

To Senora Remon, to the new President Guizado and his associates in the Panamanian Government, and to the people of Panama, I extend my personal sympathies as well as the sincere condolences of the people of the United States.

3 ¶ Letter to the Secretary of Defense on National Security Requirements.   *January* 5, 1955

Dear Mr. Secretary:

Responding to your request I shall, in this note, briefly summarize the views on our general needs in military strength, including personnel, that I expressed verbally to you and the Joint Chiefs of Staff in December.   Needless to say, these convictions on how best to preserve the peace were formed after earnest consideration of the oral and written views of our military advisers.

In approaching this problem, we should keep ever before us the realization that the security of the United States is inextricably bound up with the security of the free world.   For this reason, one of our tasks is to do everything possible to promote unity of understanding and action among the free nations so that each may take its full and proper part in the cooperative process of establishing a lasting and effective security.

Certain considerations, applying more specifically to our own country's military preparations, are these:

First, the threat to our security is a continuing and many-sided one—there is, so far as we can determine, no single critical "danger date" and no single form of enemy action to which we could soundly gear all our defense preparations. We will never commit aggression, but we must always be ready to defeat it.

Second, true security for our country must be founded on a strong and expanding economy, readily convertible to the tasks of war.

Third, because scientific progress exerts a constantly increasing influence upon the character and conduct of war, and because America's most precious possession is the lives of her citizens, we should base our security upon military formations which make maximum use of science and technology in order to minimize numbers in men.

Fourth, due to the destructiveness of modern weapons and the increasing efficiency of long-range bombing aircraft, the United States has reason, for the first time in its history, to be deeply concerned over the serious effects which a sudden attack could conceivably inflict upon our country.

Our first objective must therefore be to maintain the capability to deter an enemy from attack and to blunt that attack if it comes—by a combination of effective retaliatory power and a continental defense system of steadily increasing effectiveness. These two tasks logically demand priority in all planning. Thus we will assure that our industrial capacity can continue throughout a war to produce the gigantic amounts of equipment and supplies required.

We can never be defeated so long as our relative superiority in productive capacity is sustained.

Other essential tasks during the initial period following a possible future attack would require the Navy to clear the ocean lanes, and the Army to do its part in meeting critical land situations. Our forces in NATO and elsewhere could be swiftly engaged. To maintain order and organization under the conditions that would prevail in attacked areas of our country would of itself constitute a major challenge. Improved Reserve programs would help greatly—in fact might prove the decisive margin—in these as in other major tasks.

To provide for meeting lesser hostile action—such as local aggression not broadened by the intervention of a major aggressor's forces—growing reliance can be placed upon the forces now being built and strengthened in many areas of the free world. But because this reliance cannot be complete, and because our own vital interests, collective security and pledged faith might well be involved, there remain certain contingencies for which the United States should be ready with mobile forces to help indigenous troops deter local aggression, direct or indirect.

In view of the practical considerations limiting the rapid deployment of large military forces from the continental United States immediately on outbreak of war, the numbers of active troops maintained for this purpose can be correspondingly tailored. For the remainder we may look primarily to our Reserves and our mobilization base, including our stockpile of critical materials.

All these capabilities have a double value—they serve our aim in peacetime of preventing war through their deterrent effect; they form the foundation of effective defense if aggressors should strike.

Both in composition and in strength our security arrangements must have long-term applicability. Lack of reasonable stability is the most wasteful and expensive practice in military activity. We cannot afford intermittent acceleration of preparation and expenditure in response to emotional tension, inevitably followed by cutbacks inspired by wishful thinking. Development of sound, long-term security requires that we design our forces so as to assure a steadily increasing efficiency, in step with scientific advances, but characterized by a stability that is not materially disturbed by every propaganda effort of unfriendly nations.

It is, of course, obvious that defensive forces in America are maintained to defend a way of life. They must be adequate for this purpose but must not become such an intolerable burden as to occasion loss of civilian morale or the individual initiative on which, in a free country, depends the dynamic industrial effort which is the continuing foundation of our nation's security.

It is at this point that professional military competence and political statesmanship must join to form judgments as to the minimum defensive structure that should be supported by the nation. To do less than the minimum would expose the nation to the predatory purposes of potential enemies. On the other hand, to build excessively under the impulse of fear could, in the long run, defeat our purposes by damaging the growth of our economy and eventually forcing it into regimented controls.

It is for the reasons so briefly touched upon above that I have decided to present to the Congress, on behalf of the Administration, a program which has been under development during the past two years. That program contemplates an active personnel strength of the Armed Forces at June 30, 1955, of approximately 3,000,000, within which the Air Force will be increased to about 975,000.

Experience will determine to what extent the personnel strengths set for June 1955 can be further reduced. It would not be wise at this time to fix rigid targets for 1956. As a goal, I suggest a strength of the order of 2,850,000—with any further material reductions dependent upon an improved world situation. To reach such figures without injuring our combat strength will require continuing close scrutiny of all defense elements, with particular emphasis on administrative overhead.

Essential to this entire program is economy in operation. If we are to support active and effective forces of the order indicated over a period which may last for decades, we must practice a strict austerity in day-to-day operations. This is an insistent and constant mission of every responsible official, military and civilian, in the Defense Department.

In this time of rapidly developing technology and frequent changes in the world situation, we should in our efforts for peace and security continuously re-shape our programs to changing conditions and avoid fixed or frozen ideas. The threat of modern war calls for constant modernization.

Since your request to me and this reply both deal with matters on which our citizenry ought to be as fully informed as considerations of security permit, I am directing the public release of the two documents.

Sincerely,

DWIGHT D. EISENHOWER

NOTE: Secretary Wilson's letter of January 3, 1955, follows:

Dear Mr. President:

For nearly two years we have discussed the various problems relating to the armed services and in particular the need for the conservation and proper utilization of our manpower, both military and civilian. Just before Christmas you again discussed the question of personnel strengths with me and the Joint Chiefs of Staff.

I have found so much value in the views underlying your decisions as to the personnel strengths of the armed services that I wonder if you would give me the gist of them in written form. I should like very much to have them available during the next year to guide me in my consideration of those matters and to be able to make them available to all of the interested people who are considering this problem.

With great respect, I am

Faithfully yours,

CHARLES E. WILSON

For the President's message to the Congress on national security requirements, see Item 12, below.

4   ¶ Annual Message to the Congress on the State of the Union.   *January* 6, 1955

[Delivered in person before a joint session]

Mr. President, Mr. Speaker, Members of the Congress:

First, I extend cordial greetings to the 84th Congress.   We shall have much to do together; I am sure that we shall get it done—and, that we shall do it in harmony and good will.

At the outset, I believe it would be well to remind ourselves of this great fundamental in our national life: our common belief that every human being is divinely endowed with dignity and worth and inalienable rights.   This faith, with its corollary—that to grow and flourish people must be free—shapes the interests and aspirations of every American.

From this deep faith have evolved three main purposes of our Federal Government:

First, to maintain justice and freedom among ourselves and to champion them for others so that we may work effectively for enduring peace;

Second, to help keep our economy vigorous and expanding, thus sustaining our international strength and assuring better jobs, better living, better opportunities for every citizen;

And third, to concern ourselves with the human problems of our people so that every American may have the opportunity to lead a healthy, productive and rewarding life.

Foremost among these broad purposes of government is our support of freedom, justice and peace.

It is of the utmost importance, that each of us understand the true nature of the struggle now taking place in the world.

It is not a struggle merely of economic theories, or of forms of government, or of military power.   At issue is the true nature of man.   Either man is the creature whom the Psalmist described as "a little lower than the angels," crowned with glory and honor, holding "dominion over the works" of his Creator; or man is a soulless, animated machine to be enslaved, used and consumed by the state for its own glorification.

It is, therefore, a struggle which goes to the roots of the human spirit, and its shadow falls across the long sweep of man's destiny. This prize, so precious, so fraught with ultimate meaning, is the true object of the contending forces in the world.

In the past year, there has been progress justifying hope, both for continuing peace and for the ultimate rule of freedom and justice in the world. Free nations are collectively stronger than at any time in recent years.

Just as nations of this Hemisphere, in the historic Caracas and Rio conferences, have closed ranks against imperialistic Communism and strengthened their economic ties, so free nations elsewhere have forged new bonds of unity.

Recent agreements between Turkey and Pakistan have laid a foundation for increased strength in the Middle East. With our understanding support, Egypt and Britain, Yugoslavia and Italy, Britain and Iran have resolved dangerous differences. The security of the Mediterranean has been enhanced by an alliance among Greece, Turkey and Yugoslavia. Agreements in Western Europe have paved the way for unity to replace past divisions which have undermined Europe's economic and military vitality. The defense of the West appears likely at last to include a free, democratic Germany participating as an equal in the councils of NATO.

In Asia and the Pacific, the pending Manila Pact supplements our treaties with Australia, New Zealand, the Philippines, Korea and Japan and our prospective treaty with the Republic of China. These pacts stand as solemn warning that future military aggression and subversion against the free nations of Asia will meet united response. The Pacific Charter, also adopted at Manila, is a milestone in the development of human freedom and self-government in the Pacific area.

Under the auspices of the United Nations, there is promise of progress in our country's plan for the peaceful use of atomic energy.

Finally, today the world is at peace. It is, to be sure, an insecure peace. Yet all humanity finds hope in the simple fact that for an appreciable time there has been no active major battlefield on earth. This same fact inspires us to work all the more effectively with other nations for the well-being, the freedom, the dignity, of every human on earth.

These developments are heartening indeed, and we are hopeful of continuing progress. But sobering problems remain.

The massive military machines and ambitions of the Soviet-Communist bloc still create uneasiness in the world. All of us are aware of the continuing reliance of the Soviet Communists on military force, of the power of their weapons, of their present resistance to realistic armament limitation, and of their continuing effort to dominate or intimidate free nations on their periphery. Their steadily growing power includes an increasing strength in nuclear weapons. This power, combined with the proclaimed intentions of the Communist leaders to communize the world, is the threat confronting us today.

To protect our nations and our peoples from the catastrophe of a nuclear holocaust, free nations must maintain countervailing military power to persuade the Communists of the futility of seeking their ends through aggression. If Communist rulers understand that America's response to aggression will be swift and decisive—that never shall we buy peace at the expense of honor or faith—they will be powerfully deterred from launching a military venture engulfing their own peoples and many others in disaster. This, of course, is merely world stalemate. But in this stalemate each of us may and must exercise his high duty to strive in every honorable way for enduring peace.

The military threat is but one menace to our freedom and security. We must not only deter aggression; we must also frustrate the effort of Communists to gain their goals by subversion.

To this end, free nations must maintain and reinforce their cohesion, their internal security, their political and economic vitality, and their faith in freedom.

In such a world, America's course is clear:

We must tirelessly labor to make the peace more just and durable.

We must strengthen the collective defense under the United Nations Charter and gird ourselves with sufficient military strength and productive capacity to discourage resort to war and protect our nation's vital interests.

We must continue to support and strengthen the United Nations. At this very moment, by vote of the United Nations General Assembly, its Secretary-General is in Communist China on a mission of deepest concern to all Americans: seeking the release of our never-to-be-forgotten American aviators and all other United Nations prisoners wrongfully detained by the Communist regime.

We must also encourage the efforts being made in the United Nations to limit armaments and to harness the atom to peaceful use.

We must expand international trade and investment and assist friendly nations whose own best efforts are still insufficient to provide the strength essential to the security of the free world.

We must be willing to use the processes of negotiation whenever they will advance the cause of just and secure peace to which the United States and other free nations are dedicated.

In respect to all these matters, we must, through a vigorous information program, keep the peoples of the world truthfully advised of our actions and purposes. This problem has been attacked with new vigor during the past months. I urge that the Congress give its earnest consideration to the great advantages that can accrue to our country through the successful operations of this program.

We must also carry forward our educational exchange program. This sharing of knowledge and experience between our citizens and those of free countries is a powerful factor in the development and maintenance of true partnership among free peoples.

To advance these many efforts, the Congress must act in this session on appropriations, legislation, and treaties. Today I shall mention especially our foreign economic and military programs.

The recent economic progress in many free nations has been most heartening. The productivity of labor and the production of goods and services are increasing in ever-widening areas. There is a growing will to improve the living standards of all men. This progress is important to all our people. It promises us allies who are strong and self-reliant; it promises a growing world market for the products of our mines, our factories, and our farms.

But only through steady effort can we hope to continue this progress. Barriers still impede trade and the flow of capital needed to develop each nation's human and material resources. Wise reduction of these barriers is a long-term objective of our foreign economic policy—a policy of an evolutionary and selective nature, assuring broad benefits to our own and other peoples.

We must gradually reduce certain tariff obstacles to trade. These actions should, of course, be accompanied by a similar lowering of trade barriers by other nations, so that we may move steadily toward greater economic advantage for all. We must further simplify customs administration and procedures. We must facilitate the flow of capital and continue technical assistance, both directly and through the United Nations, to less developed countries to strengthen their independence and raise their living standards. Many another step must be taken in and among the nations of the free world to release forces of private initiative. In our own nation, these forces have brought strength and prosperity; once released, they will generate rising incomes in these other countries with which to buy the products of American industry, labor and agriculture.

On January 10, by special message, I shall submit specific recommendations for carrying forward the legislative phases of our foreign economic policy.

Our many efforts to build a better world include the maintenance of our military strength. This is a vast undertaking. Major national security programs consume two-thirds of the entire Federal budget. Over four million Americans—servicemen and civilians—are on the rolls of the defense establishment. During the past two years, by eliminating duplication and over-staffing, by improved procurement and inventory controls, and by concentrating on the essentials, many billions of dollars have been saved in our defense activities. I should like to mention certain fundamentals underlying this vast program.

First, a realistic limitation of armaments and an enduring, just peace remain our national goals; we maintain powerful military forces because there is no present alternative—forces designed for deterrent and defensive purposes alone but able instantly to strike back with destructive power in response to an attack.

Second, we must stay alert to the fact that undue reliance on one weapon or preparation for only one kind of warfare simply invites an enemy to resort to another. We must, therefore, keep in our armed forces balance and flexibility adequate for our purposes and objectives.

Third, to keep our armed forces abreast of the advances of science, our military planning must be flexible enough to utilize the new weapons and techniques which flow ever more speedily from our research and development programs. The forthcoming military budget therefore emphasizes modern airpower in the Air Force, Navy and Marine Corps and increases the emphasis on new weapons, especially those of rapid and destructive striking power. It assures the maintenance of effective, retaliatory force as the principal deterrent to overt aggression. It accelerates the continental defense program and the build-up of ready military reserve forces. It continues a vigorous program of stockpiling strategic and critical materials and strengthening our mobilization base. The budget also contemplates the strategic concentration of our strength through redeployment of certain forces. It provides for reduction of forces in certain categories and their expansion in others, to fit them to the military realities of our time. These emphases in our defense planning have been made at my personal direction after long and thoughtful study. In my judgment, they will give our nation a defense accurately adjusted to the national need.

Fourth, pending a world agreement on armament limitation, we must continue to improve and expand our supplies of nuclear weapons for our land, naval and air forces, while, at the same time, continuing our encouraging progress in the peaceful use of atomic power.

And fifth, in the administration of these costly programs, we must demand the utmost in efficiency and ingenuity. We must assure our people not only of adequate protection but also of a defense that can be carried forward from year to year until the threat of aggression has disappeared.

To help maintain this kind of armed strength and improve its efficiency, I must urge the enactment of several important measures in this session.

The first concerns the selective service act which expires next June 30th. For the foreseeable future, our standing forces must remain much larger than voluntary methods can sustain. We must, therefore, extend the statutory authority to induct men for two years of military service.

The second kind of measure concerns the rapid turnover of our most experienced servicemen. This process seriously weakens the combat readiness of our armed forces and is exorbitantly expensive. To encourage more trained servicemen to remain in uniform, I shall, on the thirteenth of this month, propose a number of measures to increase the attractions of a military career. These measures will include more adequate medical care for dependents, survivors' benefits, more and better housing, and selective adjustments in military pay and other allowances.

And third—also on January 13—I shall present a program to rebuild and strengthen the civilian components of our armed forces. This is a comprehensive program, designed to make better use of our manpower of military age. Because it will go far in assuring fair and equitable participation in military training and service, it is of particular importance to our combat veterans. In keeping with the historic military policy of our Republic, this program is designed to build and maintain powerful civilian reserves immediately capable of effective military service in an emergency in lieu of maintaining active duty forces in excess of the nation's immediate need.

Maintenance of an effective defense requires continuance of our aggressive attack on subversion at home. In this effort we have, in the past two years, made excellent progress. FBI investigations have been powerfully reinforced by a new Internal Security Division in the Department of Justice; the security activities of the Immigration and Naturalization Service have been revitalized; an improved and strengthened security system is in effect throughout the government; the Department of Justice and the FBI have been armed with effective new legal weapons forged by the 83rd Congress.

We shall continue to ferret out and to destroy Communist subversion.

We shall, in the process, carefully preserve our traditions and the basic rights of our citizens.

Our civil defense program is also a key element in the protection of our country. We are developing cooperative methods with State Governors, Mayors, and voluntary citizen groups, as well as among Federal agencies, in building the civil defense organization. Its significance in time of war is obvious; its swift assistance in disaster areas last year proved its importance in time of peace.

An industry capable of rapid expansion and essential materials and facilities swiftly available in time of emergency are indispensable to our defense. I urge, therefore, a two-year extension of the Defense Production Act and Title II of the First War Powers Act of 1941. These are cornerstones of our program for the development and maintenance of an adequate mobilization base.

At this point, I should like to make this additional observation.

Our quest for peace and freedom necessarily presumes that we who hold positions of public trust must rise above self and section—that we must subordinate to the general good our partisan, our personal pride and prejudice. Tirelessly, with united purpose, we must fortify the material and spiritual foundations of this land of freedom and of free nations throughout the world. As never before, there is need for unhesitating cooperation among the branches of our government.

At this time the executive and legislative branches are under the management of different political parties. This fact places both parties on trial before the American people.

In less perilous days of the past, division of governmental responsibility among our great parties has produced a paralyzing indecision. We must not let this happen in our time. We must avoid a paralysis of the will for peace and international security.

In the traditionally bipartisan areas—military security and foreign relations—I can report to you that I have already, with the leaders of this Congress, expressed assurances of unreserved cooperation. Yet, the strength of our country requires more than mere maintenance of military strength and success in foreign affairs; these vital matters are in turn dependent upon concerted and vigorous action in a number of supporting programs.

I say, therefore, to the 84th Congress:

In all areas basic to the strength of America, there will be—to the extent I can insure them—cooperative, constructive relations between the Executive and Legislative Branches of this government. Let the general good be our yardstick on every great issue of our time.

Our efforts to defend our freedom and to secure a just peace are, of course, inseparable from the second great purpose of our government: to help maintain a strong, growing economy—an economy vigorous and free, in which there are ever-increasing opportunities, just rewards for effort, and a stable prosperity that is widely shared.

In the past two years, many important governmental actions helped our economy adjust to conditions of peace; these and other actions created a climate for renewed economic growth. Controls were removed from wages, prices and materials. Tax revisions encouraged increased private spending and employment. Federal expenditures were sharply reduced, making possible a record tax cut. These actions, together with flexible monetary and debt management policies, helped to halt inflation and stabilize the value of the dollar. A program of cooperation and partnership in resource development was begun. Social security and unemployment insurance laws were broadened and strengthened. New laws started the long process of balancing farm production with farm markets. Expanded shipbuilding and stockpiling programs strengthened key sectors of the economy, while improving our mobilization base. A comprehensive new housing law brought impressive progress in an area fundamental to our economic strength and closed loopholes in the old laws permitting dishonest manipulation. Many of these programs are just beginning to exert their main stimulating effect upon the economy generally and upon specific communities and industries throughout the country.

The past year—1954—was one of the most prosperous years in our history. Business activity now surges with new strength. Production is rising. Employment is high. Toward the end of last year average weekly wages in manufacturing were higher than ever before. Personal income after taxes is at a record level. So is consumer spending. Construction activity is reaching new peaks. Export demand for our goods is strong. State and local government expenditures on public works are rising. Savings are high, and credit is readily available.

So, today, the transition to a peacetime economy is largely behind us.

The economic outlook is good.

The many promising factors I have mentioned do not guarantee sustained economic expansion; however, they do give us a strong position from which to carry forward our economic growth. If we as a people act wisely, within ten years our annual national output can rise from its present level of about $360 billion to $500 billion, measured in dollars of stable buying power.

My Budget Message on January 17, the Economic Report on the 20th of this month, and several special messages will set forth in detail major programs to foster the growth of our economy and to protect the integrity of the people's money. Today I shall discuss these programs only in general terms.

Government efficiency and economy remain essential to steady progress toward a balanced budget. More than ten billion dollars were cut from the spending program proposed in the budget of January 9, 1953. Expenditures of that year were six and a half billion below those of the previous year. In the current fiscal year, government spending will be nearly four and a half billion dollars less than in the fiscal year which ended last June 30. New spending authority has been held below expenditures, reducing government obligations accumulated over the years.

Last year we had a large tax cut and, for the first time in seventy-five years a basic revision of Federal tax laws. It is now clear that defense and other essential government costs must remain at a level precluding further tax reductions this year. Although excise and corporation income taxes must, therefore, be continued at their present rates, further tax cuts will be possible when justified by lower expenditures and by revenue increases arising from the nation's economic growth. I am hopeful that such reductions can be made next year.

At the foundation of our economic growth are the raw materials and energy produced from our minerals and fuels, lands and forests, and water resources.   With respect to them, I believe that the nation must adhere to three fundamental policies: first, to develop, wisely use and conserve basic resources from generation to generation; second, to follow the historic pattern of developing these resources primarily by private citizens under fair provisions of law, including restraints for proper conservation; and third, to treat resource development as a partnership undertaking—a partnership in which the participation of private citizens and State and local governments is as necessary as Federal participation.

This policy of partnership and cooperation is producing good results, most immediately noticeable in respect to water resources. First, it has encouraged local public bodies and private citizens to plan their own power sources.   Increasing numbers of applications to the Federal Power Commission to conduct surveys and prepare plans for power development, notably in the Columbia River Basin, are evidence of local response.

Second, the Federal Government and local and private organizations have been encouraged to coordinate their developments. This is important because Federal hydroelectric developments supply but a small fraction of the nation's power needs.   Such partnership projects as Priest Rapids in Washington, the Coosa River development in Alabama, and Markham Ferry in Oklahoma already have the approval of the Congress.   This year justifiable projects of a similar nature will again have Administration support.

Third, the Federal Government must shoulder its own partnership obligations by undertaking projects of such complexity and size that their success requires Federal development.   In keeping with this principle, I again urge the Congress to approve the development of the Upper Colorado River Basin to conserve and assure better use of precious water essential to the future of the West.

In addition, the 1956 budget will recommend appropriations to start six new reclamation and more than thirty new Corps of Engineers projects of varying size. Going projects and investigations of potential new resource developments will be continued.

Although this partnership approach is producing encouraging results, its full success requires a nation-wide comprehensive water resources policy firmly based in law. Such a policy is under preparation and when completed will be submitted to the Congress.

In the interest of their proper conservation, development and use, continued vigilance will be maintained over our fisheries, wildlife resources, the national parks and forests, and the public lands; and we shall continue to encourage an orderly development of the nation's mineral resources.

A modern, efficient highway system is essential to meet the needs of our growing population, our expanding economy, and our national security. We are accelerating our highway improvement program as rapidly as possible under existing State and Federal laws and authorizations. However, this effort will not in itself assure our people of an adequate highway system. On my recommendation, this problem has been carefully considered by the Conference of State Governors and by a special Advisory Committee on a National Highway Program, composed of leading private citizens. I have received the recommendations of the Governors' Conference and will shortly receive the views of the special Advisory Committee. Aided by their findings, I shall submit on January 27th detailed recommendations which will meet our most pressing national highway needs.

In further recognition of the importance of transportation to our economic strength and security, the Administration, through a Cabinet committee, is thoroughly examining existing Federal transportation policies to determine their effect on the adequacy of transportation services. This is the first such comprehensive review directly undertaken by the Executive Branch of the government in modern times. We are not only examining major

problems facing the various modes of transport; we are also studying closely the inter-relationships of civilian and government
requirements for transportation. Legislation will be recommended to correct policy deficiencies which we may find.

The nation's public works activities are tremendous in scope.
It is expected that more than $12 billion will be expended in 1955
for the development of land, water and other resources; control
of floods, and navigation and harbor improvements; construction
of roads, schools, and municipal water supplies, and disposal of
domestic and industrial wastes. Many of the Federal, State and
local agencies responsible for this work are, in their separate
capacities, highly efficient. But public works activities are closely
inter-related and have a substantial influence on the growth of the
country. Moreover, in times of threatening economic contraction, they may become a valuable sustaining force. To these
ends, efficient planning and execution of the nation's public works
require both the coordination of Federal activities and effective
cooperation with State and local governments.

The Council of Economic Advisers, through its public works
planning section, has made important advances during the past
year in effecting this coordination and cooperation. In view of
the success of these initial efforts, and to give more emphasis and
continuity to this essential coordination, I shall request the Congress to appropriate funds for the support of an Office of Coordinator of Public Works in the Executive Office of the President.

A most significant element in our growing economy is an agriculture that is stable, prosperous and free. The problems of our
agriculture have evolved over many years and cannot be solved
overnight; nevertheless, governmental actions last year hold great
promise of fostering a better balance between production and
markets and, consequently, a better and more stable income for
our farmers.

Through vigorous administration and through new authority
provided by the 83rd Congress, surplus farm products are now
moving into consumption. From February 1953 through Novem-

ber 1954, the rate of increase of government-held surpluses has been reduced by our moving into use more than 2.3 billion dollars' worth of government-owned farm commodities; this amount is equal to more than seven percent of a year's production of all our farms and ranches. Domestic consumption remains high, and farm exports will be higher than last year. As a result of the flexibility provided by the Agricultural Act of 1954, we can move toward less restrictive acreage controls.

Thus, farm production is gradually adjusting to markets, markets are being expanded, and stocks are moving into use. We can now look forward to an easing of the influences depressing farm prices, to reduced government expenditures for purchase of surplus products, and to less Federal intrusion into the lives and plans of our farm people. Agricultural programs have been redirected toward better balance, greater stability and sustained prosperity. We are headed in the right direction. I urgently recommend to the Congress that we continue resolutely on this road.

Greater attention must be directed to the needs of low-income farm families. Twenty-eight per cent of our farm-operator families have net cash incomes of less than $1,000 per year. Last year, at my request, careful studies were made of the problems of these farm people. I shall later submit recommendations designed to assure the steady alleviation of their most pressing concerns.

Because drought also remains a serious agricultural problem, I shall recommend legislation to strengthen Federal disaster assistance programs. This legislation will prescribe an improved appraisal of need, better adjustment of the various programs to local conditions, and a more equitable sharing of costs between the States and the Federal Government.

The prosperity of our small business enterprises is an indispensable element in the maintenance of our economic strength. Creation of the Small Business Administration and recently enacted tax laws facilitating small business expansion are but two of many important steps we have taken to encourage our smaller enterprises. I recommend that the Congress extend the Small Business Act of 1953 which is due to expire next June.

We come now to the third great purpose of our government— its concern for the health, productivity and well-being of all our people.

Every citizen wants to give full expression to his God-given talents and abilities and to have the recognition and respect accorded under our religious and political traditions. Americans also want a good material standard of living—not simply to accumulate possessions, but to fulfill a legitimate aspiration for an environment in which their families may live meaningful and happy lives. Our people are committed, therefore, to the creation and preservation of opportunity for every citizen to lead a more rewarding life. They are equally committed to the alleviation of misfortune and distress among their fellow citizens.

The aspirations of most of our people can best be fulfilled through their own enterprise and initiative, without government interference. This Administration, therefore, follows two simple rules: first, the Federal Government should perform an essential task only when it cannot otherwise be adequately performed; and second, in performing that task, our government must not impair the self-respect, freedom and incentive of the individual. So long as these two rules are observed, the government can fully meet its obligation without creating a dependent population or a domineering bureaucracy.

During the past two years, notable advances were made in these functions of government. Protection of old-age and survivors' insurance was extended to an additional ten million of our people, and the benefits were substantially increased. Legislation was enacted to provide unemployment insurance protection to some four million additional Americans. Stabilization of living costs and the halting of inflation protected the value of pensions and savings. A broad program now helps to bring good homes within the reach of the great majority of our people. With the States, we are providing rehabilitation facilities and more clinics, hospitals, and nursing homes for patients with chronic illnesses. Also with the States, we have begun a great and fruitful expansion in the restoration of disabled persons to employment and useful lives. In the areas of Federal responsibility, we have made historic progress in eliminating from among our people demeaning practices based on race or color.

All of us may be proud of these achievements during the past two years. Yet essential Federal tasks remain to be done.

As part of our efforts to provide decent, safe and sanitary housing for low-income families, we must carry forward the housing program authorized during the 83rd Congress. We must also authorize contracts for a firm program of 35,000 additional public housing units in each of the next two fiscal years. This program will meet the most pressing obligations of the Federal Government into the 1958 fiscal year for planning and building public housing. By that time the private building industry, aided by the Housing Act of 1954, will have had the opportunity to assume its full role in providing adequate housing for our low-income families.

The health of our people is one of our most precious assets. Preventable sickness should be prevented; knowledge available to combat disease and disability should be fully used. Otherwise, we as a people are guilty not only of neglect of human suffering but also of wasting our national strength.

Constant advances in medical care are not available to enough of our citizens. Clearly our nation must do more to reduce the impact of accident and disease. Two fundamental problems confront us: first, high and ever-rising costs of health services; second, serious gaps and shortages in these services.

By special message on January 24, I shall propose a coordinated program to strengthen and improve existing health services.

This program will continue to reject socialized medicine. It will emphasize individual and local responsibility. Under it the Federal Government will neither dominate nor direct, but serve as a helpful partner. Within this framework, the program can be broad in scope.

My recommendations will include a Federal health reinsurance service to encourage the development of more and better voluntary health insurance coverage by private organizations. I shall also recommend measures to improve the medical care of that group of our citizens who, because of need, receive Federal-State public assistance. These two proposals will help more of our people to meet the costs of health services.

To reduce the gaps in these services, I shall propose:

New measures to facilitate construction of needed health facilities and help reduce shortages of trained health personnel;

Vigorous steps to combat the misery and national loss involved in mental illness;

Improved services for crippled children and for maternal and child health;

Better consumer protection under our existing pure food and drug laws; and, finally,

Strengthened programs to combat the increasingly serious pollution of our rivers and streams and the growing problem of air pollution.

These measures together constitute a comprehensive program holding rich promise for better health for all of our people.

Last year's expansion of social security coverage and our new program of improved medical care for public assistance recipients together suggest modification of the formula for Federal sharing in old age assistance payments. I recommend modification of the formula where such payments will, in the future, supplement benefits received under the old age and survivors insurance system.

It is the inalienable right of every person, from childhood on, to have access to knowledge. In our form of society, this right of the individual takes on a special meaning, for the education of all our citizens is imperative to the maintenance and invigoration of America's free institutions.

Today, we face grave educational problems. Effective and up-to-date analyses of these problems and their solutions are being carried forward through the individual State conferences and the White House Conference to be completed this year.

However, such factors as population growth, additional responsibilities of schools, and increased and longer school attendance have produced an unprecedented classroom shortage. This shortage is of immediate concern to all of our people. Positive, affirmative action must be taken now.

Without impairing in any way the responsibilities of our States, localities, communities, or families, the Federal government can and should serve as an effective catalyst in dealing with this problem. I shall forward a special message to the Congress on February 15, presenting an affirmative program dealing with this shortage.

To help the States do a better and more timely job, we must strengthen their resources for preventing and dealing with juvenile delinquency. I shall propose Federal legislation to assist the States to promote concerted action in dealing with this nationwide problem. I shall carry forward the vigorous efforts of the Administration to improve the international control of the traffic in narcotics and, in cooperation with State and local agencies, to combat narcotic addiction in our country.

I should like to speak now of additional matters of importance to all our people and especially to our wage earners.

During the past year certain industrial changes and the readjustment of the economy to conditions of peace brought unemployment and other difficulties to various localities and industries. These problems are engaging our most earnest attention. But for the overwhelming majority of our working people, the past year has meant good jobs. Moreover, the earnings and savings of our wage earners are no longer depreciating in value.

Because of cooperative relations between labor and management, fewer working days were lost through strikes in 1954 than in any year in the past decade.

The outlook for our wage earners can be made still more promising by several legislative actions.

First, in the past five years we have had economic growth which will support an increase in the Federal minimum wage. In the light of present economic conditions, I recommend its increase to ninety cents an hour. I also recommend that many others, at present excluded, be given the protection of a minimum wage.

Second, I renew my recommendation of last year for amendment of the Labor Management Relations Act of 1947 to further the basic objectives of this statute. I especially call to the attention of the Congress amendments dealing with the right of economic strikers to vote in representation elections and the need for equalizing the obligation under the Act to file disclaimers of Communist affiliation.

Third, the Administration will propose other important measures including occupational safety, workmen's compensation for longshoremen and harbor workers, and the "Eight Hour Laws" applicable to Federal contractors. Legislation will also be proposed respecting nonoccupational disability insurance and unemployment compensation in the District of Columbia.

In considering human needs, the Federal Government must take special responsibility for citizens in its direct employ. On January 11 I shall propose a pay adjustment plan for civilian employees outside the Postal Field Service to correct inequities and increase individual pay rates. I shall also recommend voluntary health insurance on a contributory basis for Federal employees and their dependents. In keeping with the Group Life Insurance Act passed in the 83rd Congress, this protection should be provided on the group insurance principle and purchased from private facilities. Also on January 11 I shall recommend a modern pay plan, including pay increases, for postal field employees.

As part of this program, and to carry forward our progress toward elimination of the large annual postal deficit, I shall renew my request for an increase in postal rates. Again I urge that in the future the fixing of rates be delegated to an impartial, independent body.

More adequate training programs to equip career employees of the government to render improved public service will be recommended, as will improvements in the laws affecting employees serving on foreign assignments.

Needed improvements in survivor, disability, and retirement benefits for Federal civilian and military personnel have been extensively considered by the Committee on Retirement Policy for Federal personnel. The Committee's proposals would strengthen and improve benefits for our career people in government, and I endorse their broad objectives. Full contributory coverage under old-age and survivors' insurance should be made available to all Federal personnel, just as in private industry. For career military personnel, the protection of the old-age and survivors' insurance system would be an important and long-needed addition, especially to their present unequal and inadequate survivorship protection. The military retirement pay system should remain separate and unchanged. Certain adjustments in the present civilian personnel retirement systems will be needed to reflect the additional protection of old-age and survivors' insurance. However, these systems also are a basic part of a total compensation and should be separately and independently retained.

I also urge the Congress to approve a long overdue increase in the salaries of Members of the Congress and of the Federal judiciary to a level commensurate with their heavy responsibilities.

Our concern for the individual in our country requires that we consider several additional problems.

We must continue our program to help our Indian citizens improve their lot and make their full contribution to national life.

Two years ago I advised the Congress of injustices under existing immigration laws. Through humane administration, the Department of Justice is doing what it legally can to alleviate hardships. Clearance of aliens before arrival has been initiated, and except for criminal offenders, the imprisonment of aliens awaiting admission or deportation has been stopped. Certain provisions of law, however, have the effect of compelling action in respect to aliens which are inequitable in some instances and discriminatory in others. These provisions should be corrected in this session of the Congress.

As the complex problems of Alaska are resolved, that Territory should expect to achieve statehood. In the meantime, there is no justification for deferring the admission to statehood of Hawaii. I again urge approval of this measure.

We have three splendid opportunities to demonstrate the strength of our belief in the right of suffrage. First, I again urge that a Constitutional amendment be submitted to the States to reduce the voting age for Federal elections. Second, I renew my request that the principle of self-government be extended and the right of suffrage granted to the citizens of the District of Columbia. Third, I again recommend that we work with the States to preserve the voting rights of citizens in the nation's service overseas.

In our determination to keep faith with those who in the past have met the highest call of citizenship, we now have under study the system of benefits for veterans and for surviving dependents of deceased veterans and servicemen. Studies will be undertaken to determine the need for measures to ease the readjustment to civilian life of men required to enter the armed forces for two years of service.

In the advancement of the various activities which will make our civilization endure and flourish, the Federal Government should do more to give official recognition to the importance of the arts and other cultural activities. I shall recommend the establishment of a Federal Advisory Commission on the Arts within the Department of Health, Education and Welfare, to advise the Federal Government on ways to encourage artistic endeavor and appreciation. I shall also propose that awards of merit be established whereby we can honor our fellow citizens who make great contribution to the advancement of our civilization.

Every citizen rightly expects efficient and economical administration of these many government programs I have outlined today. I strongly recommend extension of the Reorganization Act and the law establishing the Commission on Intergovernmental Relations, both of which expire this spring. Thus the Congress will assure continuation of the excellent progress recently made in improving government organization and administration. In this connection we are looking forward with great interest to the reports which will soon be going to the Congress from the Commission on Organization of the Executive Branch of the Government. I am sure that these studies, made under the chairmanship of former President Herbert Hoover with the assistance of more than two hundred distinguished citizens, will be of great value in paving the way toward more efficiency and economy in the government.

And now, I return to the point at which I began—the faith of our people.

The many programs here summarized are, I believe, in full keeping with their needs, interests and aspirations. The obligations upon us are clear:

To labor earnestly, patiently, prayerfully, for peace, for freedom, for justice, throughout the world;

To keep our economy vigorous and free, that our people may lead fuller, happier lives;

To advance, not merely by our words but by our acts, the determination of our government that every citizen shall have opportunity to develop to his fullest capacity.

As we do these things, before us is a future filled with opportunity and hope. That future will be ours if in our time we keep alive the patience, the courage, the confidence in tomorrow, the deep faith, of the millions who, in years past, made and preserved us this nation.

A decade ago, in the death and desolation of European battle-fields, I saw the courage and resolution, I felt the inspiration, of American youth. In these young men I felt America's buoyant confidence and irresistible will-to-do. In them I saw, too, a devout America, humble before God.

And so, I know with all my heart—and I deeply believe that all Americans know—that, despite the anxieties of this divided world, our faith, and the cause in which we all believe, will surely prevail.

DWIGHT D. EISENHOWER

NOTE: This is the text of the document which the President signed and transmitted to the Senate and the House of Representatives (H. Doc. 1, 84th Cong., 1st sess.).

The Address as reported from the floor appears in the Congressional Record (vol. 101, p. 94).

5 ¶ Special Message to the Senate Transmitting Mutual Defense Treaty Between the United States and the Republic of China. *January* 6, 1955

To the Senate of the United States:

With a view to receiving the advice and consent of the Senate to ratification, I transmit herewith the Mutual Defense Treaty between the United States of America and the Republic of China, signed at Washington on December 2, 1954.

I transmit also for the information of the Senate a document containing statements made by the Secretary of State and the Chinese Minister for Foreign Affairs on the occasion of the initialing of the Treaty on December 2, 1954, together with a joint statement regarding conclusion of negotiations for the

Treaty issued simultaneously in Washington and Taipei on December 1, 1954.

There is further transmitted for the information of the Senate the report made to me by the Secretary of State regarding the Treaty.

Finally, there are transmitted for the information of the Senate texts of notes exchanged by the Secretary of State and the Minister for Foreign Affairs of the Republic of China on December 10, 1954 which, while not a part of the Treaty, express agreed understandings as to certain phases of its implementation.

The Mutual Defense Treaty between the United States of America and the Republic of China is defensive and mutual in character, designed to deter any attempt by the Chinese Communist regime to bring its aggressive military ambitions to bear against the treaty area.

This Mutual Defense Treaty, taken in conjunction with similar treaties already concluded with Japan, Korea, the Philippines, and Australia and New Zealand, reinforces the system of collective security in the Pacific Area. It is also complementary to the action taken in the signing of the Southeast Asia Collective Defense Treaty at Manila on September 8, 1954.

I recommend that the Senate give early and favorable consideration to the Treaty submitted herewith, and advise and consent to its ratification.

DWIGHT D. EISENHOWER

NOTE: The text of the treaty and the documents submitted with this message are printed in Senate Executive A (84th Cong., 1st sess.).

The treaty was ratified by the Senate on February 9, entered into force March 3, and was proclaimed by the President on April 1, 1955.

6   ¶ Special Message to the Congress on the
Foreign Economic Policy of the United States.
January 10, 1955

To the Congress of the United States:

For the consideration of the Congress, I submit my recommendations for further developing the foreign economic policy of the United States. Although largely based upon my Special Message to the Congress of March 30, 1954, these proposals are the product of fresh review.

The nation's enlightened self-interest and sense of responsibility as a leader among the free nations require a foreign economic program that will stimulate economic growth in the free world through enlarging opportunities for the fuller operation of the forces of free enterprise and competitive markets. Our own self-interest requires such a program because (1) economic strength among our allies is essential to our security; (2) economic growth in underdeveloped areas is necessary to lessen international instability growing out of the vulnerability of such areas to Communist penetration and subversion; and (3) an increasing volume of world production and trade will help assure our own economic growth and a rising standard of living among our own people.

In the world-wide struggle between the forces of freedom and those of communism, we have wisely recognized that the security of each nation in the free world is dependent upon the security of all other nations in the free world. The measure of that security in turn is dependent upon the economic strength of all free nations, for without economic strength they cannot support the military establishments that are necessary to deter Communist armed aggression. Economic strength is indispensable, as well, in securing themselves against internal Communist subversion.

For every country in the free world, economic strength is dependent upon high levels of economic activity internally and high levels of international trade. No nation can be economically self-sufficient. Nations must buy from other nations, and in order to pay for what they buy they must sell. It is essential for the security of the United States and the rest of the free world that the United States take the leadership in promoting the achievement of those high levels of trade that will bring to all the economic strength upon which the freedom and security of all depends. Those high levels of trade can be promoted by the specific measures with respect to trade barriers recommended in this message, by the greater flow of capital among nations of the free world, by convertibility of currencies, by an expanded interchange of technical counsel, and by an increase in international travel.

From the military standpoint, our national strength has been augmented by the over-all military alliance of the nations constituting the free world. This free world alliance will be most firmly cemented when its association is based on flourishing mutual trade as well as common ideals, interests and aspirations. Mutually advantageous trade relationships are not only profitable, but they are also more binding and more enduring than costly grants and other forms of aid.

Today numerous uneconomic, man-made barriers to mutually advantageous trade and the flow of investment are preventing the nations of the free world from achieving their full economic potential. International trade and investment are not making their full contribution to production, employment and income. Over a large area of the world currencies are not yet convertible.

We and our friends abroad must together undertake the lowering of the unjustifiable barriers to trade and investment, and we must do it on a mutual basis so that the benefits may be shared by all.

Such action will add strength to our own domestic economy and help assure a rising standard of living among our people by opening new markets for our farms and factories and mines.

The program that I am here recommending is moderate, gradual and reciprocal. Radical or sudden tariff reductions would not be to the interest of the United States and would not accomplish the goal we seek. A moderate program, however, can add immeasurably to the security and well-being of the United States and the rest of the free world.

TRADE AGREEMENT AUTHORITY

I request a three-year extension of Presidential authority to negotiate tariff reductions with other nations on a gradual, selective and reciprocal basis. This authority would permit negotiations for reductions in those barriers that now limit the markets for our goods throughout the world. I shall ask all nations with whom we trade to take similar steps in their relations with each other.

The three-year extension of the Trade Agreements Act should authorize, subject to the present peril and escape clause provisions:

1. Reduction, through multilateral and reciprocal negotiations, of tariff rates on selected commodities by not more than five percent per year for three years;

2. Reduction, through multilateral and reciprocal negotiations, of any tariff rates in excess of fifty percent to that level over a three-year period; and

3. Reduction, by not more than one-half over a three-year period, of tariff rates in effect on January 1, 1945, on articles which are not now being imported or which are being imported only in negligible quantities.

THE GENERAL AGREEMENT ON TARIFFS AND TRADE

For approximately seven years the United States has cooperated with all the major trading nations of the free world in an effort to reduce trade barriers. The instrument of cooperation is the General Agreement on Tariffs and Trade. Through this Agreement the United States has sought to carry out the provisions and purpose of the Trade Agreements Act.

The United States and thirty-three other trading countries are now reviewing the provisions of the Agreement for the purpose of making it a simpler and more effective instrument for the development of a sound system of world trade. When the current negotiations on the revision of the organizational provisions of the General Agreement are satisfactorily completed, the results will be submitted to the Congress for its approval.

CUSTOMS ADMINISTRATION AND PROCEDURE

Considerable progress has been made in freeing imports from unnecessary customs administrative burdens. Still more, however, needs to be done in the three areas I mentioned in my message last year: (1) the simplification of commodity definitions, classification and rate structures; (2) improvement in standards for the valuation of imports; and (3) further improvement of procedures for customs administration.

An important step toward simplification of the tariff structure was taken by the Congress last year with the passage of the Customs Simplification Act which directs the Tariff Commission to study the difficulties of commodity classification of imports. The interim report of the Tariff Commission to be made by next March 15 should help enable the Congress to determine whether further legislative steps should then be taken or should await submission of the final report.

The uncertainties and confusion arising from the complex system of valuation on imported articles cause unwarranted delays in the determination of customs duties. I urge the Congress to give favorable consideration to legislation for remedying this situation.

The improvement of customs administration requires continuous effort, as the Congress recognized by enacting the Customs Simplification Acts of 1953 and 1954. The Treasury Department in its annual report to the Congress will review the remaining reasons for delay or difficulty in processing imported articles through customs and will propose still further technical amendments to simplify customs procedures.

UNITED STATES INVESTMENT ABROAD

The whole free world needs capital; America is its largest source. In that light, the flow of capital abroad from our country must be stimulated and in such a manner that it results in investment largely by individuals or private enterprises rather than by government.

An increased flow of United States private investment funds abroad, especially to the underdeveloped areas, could contribute much to the expansion of two-way international trade. The underdeveloped countries would thus be enabled more easily to acquire the capital equipment so badly needed by them to achieve sound economic growth and higher living standards. This would do much to offset the false but alluring promises of the Communists.

To facilitate the investment of capital abroad I recommend enactment of legislation providing for taxation of business income from foreign subsidiaries or branches at a rate fourteen percentage points lower than the corporate rate on domestic income, and a deferral of tax on income of foreign branches until it is removed from the country where it is earned.

I propose also to explore the further use of tax treaties with the possible recognition of tax concessions made to foreign capital by other countries. Under proper safeguards, credit could be given for foreign income taxes which are waived for an initial limited period, as we now grant credit for taxes which are imposed. This would give maximum effectiveness to foreign tax laws designed to encourage new enterprises.

As a further step to stimulate investment abroad, I recommend approval by the Congress at the appropriate time of membership in the proposed International Finance Corporation, which will be affiliated with the International Bank for Reconstruction and Development. This Corporation will be designed to increase private investment in less developed countries by making loans without Government guarantees. Although the Corporation will not purchase stock, it will provide venture capital through investing in debentures and similar obligations. Its operation will cover a field not dealt with by an existing institution.

The Executive Branch will continue through our diplomatic representatives abroad to encourage a climate favorable to the private enterprise concept in investment.

We shall continue to seek other new ways to enlarge the outward flow of capital.

It must be recognized, however, that when American private capital moves abroad it properly expects to bring home its fair reward. This can only be accomplished in the last analysis by our willingness to purchase more goods and services from abroad in order to provide the dollars for these growing remittances. This fact is a further compelling reason for a fair and forward-looking trade policy on our part.

TECHNICAL COOPERATION

The United States has a vast store of practical and scientific know-how that is needed in the underdeveloped areas of the world. The United States has a responsibility to make it available. Its flow for peaceful purposes must remain unfettered.

United States participation in technical cooperation programs should be carried forward. These programs should be concerned with know-how rather than large funds. In my budget message next week, I shall recommend that the Congress make available the funds required to support the multilateral technical cooperation programs of the United Nations. The bilateral programs of the United States should be pressed vigorously.

INTERNATIONAL TRAVEL

The United States remains committed to the objective of freedom of travel throughout the world. Encouragement given to travel abroad is extremely important both for its cultural and social importance in the free world, and for its economic benefits. Travel abroad by Americans provides an important source of dollars for many countries. The Executive Branch shall continue to look for ways of facilitating international travel and shall continue to cooperate with private travel agencies.

One legislative action that would be beneficial in this field is the increase of the present duty-free allowances for tourists from $500 to $1,000 exercisable every six months. I recommend the passage of such legislation.

TRADE FAIRS

International trade fairs have been of major importance to foreign countries for many years, and most of the trading nations have strengthened the promotional aspects of their industrial displays in many fairs with a central exhibit designed to emphasize the industrial progress and achievement of the nation.

Soviet and satellite exhibits, for example, have been costly, well-planned and housed in expensive structures designed to convey the impression that the USSR is producing on a large scale for peace and is creating a paradise for workers.

The United States, which has a larger volume of international trade than any other nation, until recently has been conspicuous by its absence at these trade fairs. American visitors and participants have pointed out the failure of their Government to tell adequately the story of our free enterprise system and to provide effective international trade promotion cooperation.

As a result, I have undertaken an international trade fair program under the direction of the Department of Commerce. Since the inauguration of this program in August, participation has been authorized in eleven fairs to be held before June 30. Sixteen additional fairs are being considered for exhibition purposes in the latter part of the year. The first fair in which the United States presented a central exhibit is that at Bangkok, which opened December 7, 1954. At it our exhibit was awarded first prize. Over 100 American companies supplied items for inclusion in it.

I shall ask the Congress for funds to continue this program.

CONVERTIBILITY

Convertibility of currencies is required for the development of a steadily rising volume of world trade and investment. The achievement of convertibility has not been possible in the post-war period due to dislocations caused by the war, inflation and other domestic economic difficulties in many countries, which have contributed to an imbalance in international trade and payments. However, steady progress, particularly by western European countries, is being made toward our mutual objective of restoring currency convertibility. The foreign economic program proposed here will make an important contribution to the achievement of convertibility.

AGRICULTURE

No single group within America has a greater stake in a healthy and expanding foreign trade than the farmers. One-fourth to one-third of some major crops, such as wheat, cotton and tobacco, must find markets abroad in order to maintain farm income at high levels.

If they are to be successful, programs designed to promote the prosperity of agriculture should be consistent with our foreign economic program. We must take due account of the effect of any agricultural program on our foreign economic relations to assure that it contributes to the development of healthy, expanding foreign markets over the years.

CONCLUSION

The series of recommendations I have just made are all components of an integrated program, pointing in a single direction. Each contributes to the whole. Each advances our national security by bringing added strength and self-sufficiency to our allies. Each contributes to our economic growth and a rising standard of living among our people.

DWIGHT D. EISENHOWER

NOTE: The President's special message to the Congress of March 30, 1954, referred to in the opening paragraph of this message, is printed in House Document 360 (83d Cong., 2d sess.).

7 ¶ Message to the Congress Transmitting the President's First Semiannual Report on Activities Under the Agricultural Trade Development and Assistance Act. *January* 10, 1955

To the Congress of the United States:

I transmit herewith my first semi-annual report on the activities carried on under Public Law 480, 83rd Congress, as required by that Law.

Public Law 480 is an expression by Congress of its determination to deal with the abundance of our agricultural production in a constructive way. Despite the problems created by this abundance, we may be thankful we live in a land which is able to produce plentifully rather than one which suffers the affliction of food shortages.

The enclosed report includes the dollar value of the foreign currency for which commodities exported pursuant to Section 102(a) of the Act have been sold, as well as the estimated order of magnitude of the total country programs which have been generally agreed on but not fully negotiated, together with the cost to the Commodity Credit Corporation of such sales. The report also contains a summary of the policies and operating techniques evolved for the administration of the Act during the first six months of its existence.

DWIGHT D. EISENHOWER

NOTE: The report is printed in House Document 62 (84th Cong., 1st sess.).

8　¶ Special Message to the Congress on Federal
Personnel Management.　*January* 11, 1955

To the Congress of the United States:

The Eighty-Third Congress made an outstanding record in
progressive personnel legislation for the benefit of the Government and its employees.　Among other steps forward, the new
laws improved overtime pay practices, established a Government-
wide incentive awards program, removed restrictive controls on
appointments, authorized group life insurance and extended the
benefits of the unemployment insurance system to Federal workers.　These changes have taken us a long way toward the goal of
combining the best practices of private employers with the special
demands of public service.

I am now recommending the enactment of legislation to improve other aspects of Federal personnel management, including
adjustments in basic pay scales, group health insurance, employee
training, personnel practices affecting Government employees
stationed overseas, and increased travel allowances.　Specific legislative proposals for carrying out these recommendations will be
submitted shortly by the Civil Service Commission, the State
Department and the Bureau of the Budget.　Their purpose will
be to bring the average governmental remuneration into line with
prevailing non-governmental standards.　I earnestly urge favorable consideration of them by the Congress.

ADJUSTMENTS OF PAY SCALES

Pay adjustments are needed (1) to recognize more fully the
differences between the duties and responsibilities of positions of
varying levels, (2) to relieve as far as possible, under the present
ceiling, the increasing compression between the lower and higher
salaries, and (3) to take into account the decline in the real
income of many Federal employees.

The inequities and deficiencies existing in the present pay

scales of the Classification Act of 1949, as amended, should be corrected. Similar adjustments should also be made in the pay schedules provided for employees subject to the Foreign Service Act of 1946, as amended, and employees in the Veterans Administration Department of Medicine and Surgery who are subject to Public Law 293, the 79th Congress, as amended.

In a separate message submitted to the Congress today, I am recommending appropriate pay adjustments covering employees of the Postal Field Service.

The recommended changes for the Classification Act group provide for an upward adjustment of pay rates for each grade, except that no change is recommended at this time in the ceiling pay rate of $14,800. Emphasis is placed upon a greater and more meaningful differential between pay scales of successive grades. The proposal recognizes the fact that, in general, compensation rates in the lower grades of the Classification Act are fairly well in line with those prevailing outside the Federal Government while rates in the middle and upper grades have lagged behind.

Insofar as possible, adjustments in the Foreign Service and Veterans Administration pay schedules should parallel the dollar amounts of pay adjustments provided for Classification Act employees at similar levels.

For Classification Act employees, the recommended pay adjustments would add an additional $202,000,000 or approximately 5 percent to present payroll costs. Even though the correction of inequities in the middle and upper pay levels is a primary objective of the Classification Act pay adjustments, 45.5 percent of the cost results from additional pay proposed for the lowest five grades. Only 4.5 percent will be applied in the highest five grades. The proposed pay schedules are presented in an appendix to this message.

Proposed changes for employees subject to the Foreign Service Act and those in the Department of Medicine and Surgery of the Veterans Administration, which are incorporated in the comprehensive proposal, will add approximately $8,500,000 to the cost, making the over-all total approximately $210,000,000.

The Classification Act of 1949, as amended, sets a ceiling on the number of positions that can be placed in grades 16, 17, and 18. Without regard to this ceiling, nineteen other statutory authorities permit or require the establishment of additional positions in these three highest grades. The Classification Act limitation coupled with this complex array of other authorizations seriously hampers our ability to meet the changing needs of the Government. These conditions prevent sound pay administration and handicap the Federal Service in recruiting and retaining top level personnel. Therefore, I am recommending the removal of this ceiling, and urge the consolidation of all existing authorities.

GROUP HEALTH INSURANCE

As another means for strengthening the Federal Service, I propose for the consideration of the Congress a contributory system of voluntary health insurance for civilian employees in all branches of the Government and their dependents.

This contributory system has been designed to meet the requirements of the Federal service and to take into account the experience of private employers. The system would permit employees to choose either a standard plan of uniform benefits or an approved plan operating in an individual community when more suitable to employees in that location. It is proposed that the Government contribute approximately one-third the cost of the insurance for the employees and their dependents. It is estimated that the annual cost to the Government will be approximately $55,000,000.

Under the standard plan, a comprehensive set of uniform benefits will be offered, including reimbursement for the costs of hospitalization, surgery, and other personal health services. The newest health insurance features, such as major medical or catastrophe coverage, are included. Appropriate provisions will be made for the continuance of substantial protection for employees and their dependents after they retire in the future—a valuable feature inasmuch as health insurance protection is frequently beyond the reach of those at the older ages.

Where the standard plan is not desired, provision is also made for employees in the various localities to purchase, with Government contributions, approved plans of health insurance especially suited to their needs.

All types of insurers are to be utilized under orderly processes established and supervised by the Civil Service Commission. This contributory system has been developed through the cooperative efforts of representatives of employee groups, insuring organizations and the leaders among the professions in the field of health.

EMPLOYEE TRAINING

Attainment of the greatest possible efficiency in governmental operations is a major goal of this Administration. Achievement of this goal requires the effective use of training facilities outside as well as within Government to maintain a high level of competence in the Federal civilian career service.

Most civilian agencies of Government do not have comprehensive and adequate training programs, chiefly because there is no general statutory authority to use outside training facilities. Although it is clearly in the Government's interest to do so, many agencies now cannot send employees to private laboratories, industrial plants, universities, or state agencies for critically needed training in the use of new methods, techniques and machines.

A comprehensive training program should be authorized that will (1) permit Government agencies to use outside facilities for training required to meet operating needs when it is in the Government's interest, (2) consolidate in one law the training authorities now carried in many separate statutes, and (3) permit the establishment of Government-wide policies and effective controls on the use of outside training facilities.

OVERSEAS PERSONNEL MANAGEMENT

At present many different Government agencies conduct a wide variety of governmental functions in the territories and foreign countries ranging from such activities as postal service and aid to veterans to such newer operations as economic and military aid and technical development programs. The development of sound personnel practices has not always been able to keep pace with the necessarily accelerated growth of Federal operations overseas.

The Civil Service Commission is now taking action, in cooperation with the Federal agencies concerned, to extend the competitive service to those operations overseas that should be included within the regular civil service system. This will be done in the near future and does not require new legislation.

The State Department already has under way an action program designed to improve personnel administration in both its overseas and departmental activities at home. This program results from the recommendations made by a committee of distinguished citizens appointed by the Secretary of State in March, 1954. Certain features of the program will require new legislation in the form of amendments to the Foreign Service Act of 1946. These are now in preparation by the State Department.

There is also a need for improvements in certain conditions affecting all United States citizens employed overseas. Such matters as allowances, leave, housing, retirement, and health, and medical care as well as the whole range of problems posed by the management of alien personnel, require attention. As a first step, the Civil Service Commission will propose for consideration by the Congress comprehensive recommendations on allowances and leave for overseas personnel.

TRAVEL ALLOWANCES

The per diem allowance of $9.00 for civilian employees who travel on official business was established in 1949. Since that time the cost of lodging, meals, and incidental expenses has increased. It is not fair to ask Government employees to defray part of their official travel and subsistence expenses from their personal funds. Recommendations soon will be submitted to the Congress for an appropriate increase in the present rate.

The various measures, described in this message, are essential to the further improvement of the Federal career service. I earnestly urge that the necessary legislation be enacted by the Congress.

DWIGHT D. EISENHOWER

NOTE: This message, together with the appended proposed pay sched- ules, is published in House Document 66 (84th Cong., 1st sess.).

9   ¶ Special Message to the Congress on Postal Pay and Rates.   *January* 11, 1955.

To the Congress of the United States:

The Post Office Department, in its daily operations, affects the entire life of the Republic from the family home to the great industry. A vast business-type enterprise within Government, the Post Office Department, consequently, requires a continuing vigilance that its methods, practices and policies assure the most efficient possible service to the public. The measures recommended in this message are designed to that end.

Last August 23 in announcing my disapproval of H.R. 7774, "An Act to Increase the Rates of Compensation of Classified, Postal and Other Employees of the Government, and for Other Purposes", I expressed a purpose to continue to encourage the enactment of legislation to correct obvious distortions in the pay scales of the postal service and to provide for a more proper and effective relationship between pay and work performed.

I also pointed out the necessity of adequate postage rates in order to check a deficit in the operation of the Post Office Department which, since World War II, has reached the staggering total of more than four billions of dollars.

An increase in the average wage of Postal employees along with correction of the serious inequities in the salary structure is an essential step in bringing the wage scale into line with non-governmental standards and in furthering the progressive personnel program to which the Administration is committed. The increase must be accompanied by a salary plan which will place the wages for postal service positions in proper relationship to each other so that inequities will be eliminated, incentive for advancement offered and the principle of higher pay for more difficult and responsible work followed.

In order to accomplish these objectives, the Postmaster General will submit to the Congress a new postal salary plan along with a five percent increase in basic salary rates. This plan will include reasonably detailed descriptions of the series of key positions to which the great majority of postal employees are assigned. A rate range for each of these positions will be recommended, and together this series of rate ranges will make up a related, uniform and equitable salary schedule.

The Congress will be asked to include the key position descriptions and their appropriate salary ranges in the legislation, thus assigning specific wage rates to the bulk of the positions common to all offices of the Postal Service.

The Post Office Department should then be granted the authority to allocate the remaining positions, held by the relatively few employees whose work is not covered by a key position, to the proper level in the salary schedule on the basis of a comparison of the duties and responsibilities of these positions with the duties and responsibilities of the key positions.

In the allocation of the positions other than the key positions to the proper salary level an appeal procedure will be provided. Further, to insure that the salary plan will not work to the disadvantage of any employee, the legislation proposed will incorporate a guarantee against reduction of salary so long as the employee occupies the same or a position comparable to that which he held at the time of the installation of the plan.

This legislation would eliminate the inequities inherent in the present inflexible system which requires assignment of all employees to a limited number of job titles, in many cases having no relation to the work actually performed. The present practice of paying salaries to some employees on the basis of the number of cubic feet in the area they supervise, or solely in relation to the number of employees under their direction, would be replaced by a system requiring that salaries be based on the actual duties and responsibilities of the position.

Under this plan, postmasters of the nation would receive salaries commensurate with the volume of work and the level of the responsibility of their offices rather than solely on the basis of cash receipts which presently govern their compensation. This practice results in discrimination against those holding offices where incoming mail represents most of the business volume.

The total cost of wage adjustments in the Postal Service is estimated at $129,000,000 a year. I recommend adoption of legislation incorporating these proposals.

The 83rd Congress authorized appropriations to be made for the furnishing of uniforms or the payment of an annual allowance to employees, including those of the Post Office Department, required by law or regulation to wear a prescribed uniform while on official duty. This measure, when Congress makes funds available, will benefit Post Office employees by an estimated $13,500,000 a year.

I am recommending in another special message today a health insurance plan to round out the federal personnel benefits program enacted by the 83rd Congress. This program already has provided group life insurance, unemployment compensation, elimination of restrictions on permanent promotions and reinstatements, adjustment of the statutory limit on the number of career employees, elimination of arbitrary restrictions on accumulation of annual leave, and a liberalized incentive awards system.

I wish to reaffirm my position that sound fiscal management requires consideration of revenues as well as costs. To this end, I am requesting that Congress also consider legislation to adjust postal rates to provide needed revenue.

The combined postal deficits of the 156 years of our history as a nation, up to 1945, are far less than the losses sustained in the last nine years. The anomaly of this situation is that the period which has witnessed this record-breaking deficit in the operations of the postal service has also been a decade of unprecedented national prosperity. Employment, production and use of the mails have been at an all time high and yet postal deficits have occurred year after year. Clearly it is time to reaffirm the need for sound fiscal management of the Post Office Department and to develop a positive program towards this end.

In fiscal 1954 the Post Office Department received revenues of $2,268,000,000 for services performed at a cost of $2,667,000,000, thus leaving a deficit of $399,000,000 in its operation. The services performed by the Post Office Department are of measurable value to the recipients. When the rates of postal services fail to provide sufficient revenues to meet the total cost of the service, the difference must be made up by general tax revenues.

A practice of this kind is neither equitable nor reasonable; it is neither good business nor good government. Even if a case could be made for regarding the postal patron and the taxpayer as one and the same, prudence and good sense would compel us to face the fact that it is far more efficient to collect the necessary revenues in direct exchange for services at the post office window than by the more costly methods of general taxation.

The Post Office is constantly working to reduce the deficit by improving the efficiency of its operations. During the last two years substantial progress has been made in organization, mail handling, transportation, mechanization, record keeping, and accounting methods. The Postmaster General has also taken the initiative in increasing rates and fees within his jurisdiction.

As a result of these measures there has been a recent reversal of the postwar trend of ever increasing postal deficits. These are the operating deficits for each of the last five years:

Fiscal Year	Operating Deficit
1950	$589, 500, 000
1951	$551, 500, 000
1952	$727, 000, 000
1953	$618, 800, 000
1954	$399, 100, 000

The large deficits in the postwar years are, in part, a direct consequence of the same inflationary increases in costs which all business operations have faced. Private business has increased prices of goods and services to offset increased costs of production. The Post Office operates in the same economic climate as private business. It must meet rising costs in very much the same way.

Since 1945, the largest part of the increase in postal expenditures is accounted for by salary increases legislated by Congress as follows:

Date	Public Law	Annual Increase in Cost to Post Office Department
July 1, 1945	134	$178, 767, 000
July 1, 1945	106	786, 000
Jan. 1, 1946	381	$190, 631, 000
July 1, 1946	390	684, 000
Nov. 1, 1949	{ 428 500 }	$112, 489, 000
Nov. 1, 1949	429	278, 000
July 1, 1951	204	$248, 600, 000
July 8, 1951	201	1, 100, 000

These wage adjustments, combined with an expansion in the number of postal employees necessary to handle the greater volume of mail, have resulted in an increase in total salary costs from $858,000,000 in 1945 to $2,002,000,000 in the last fiscal year.

The increases in wages and other costs since the end of World

War II have affected all classes of mail. It is desirable that the rates governing each class of mail be advanced in fair proportion. The Committees of Congress responsible for postal rate legislation will, of course, want to consider carefully the specific rates for each class of mail. The Postmaster General will soon submit to Congress, in addition to his views on increases in postal pay, detailed recommendations for raising postal rates to more reasonable levels. I wish to emphasize at this time a few of the major considerations which seem to me important in raising rates.

1. First-class mail has always provided by far the greater part of postal revenues. In 1933 the revenue contribution of first-class mail was more than 55 percent of total Post Office revenues. In the last fiscal year first-class mail provided only 40 percent of such revenues although the proportion of first class volume to the total volume was only three percentage points lower than in the earlier year. The failure of this type mail to maintain its revenue contribution is a major factor in the present postal deficit. There is, therefore, an urgent need to increase the rate of postage of first-class mail.

Postal rates are payments made by users of the mails for services received. The rate established for each service should reflect the value of that service in terms of speed, priority of handling, and the privileges incorporated in each class of mail. If these factors are taken into consideration in rate-making, the revenue contribution of first-class mail is clearly inadequate.

The privacy, security and swift dispatch of letter mail; the priority of service at all times, in all places; and the intrinsic value of such mail are factors which are pertinent to postal rate-making in addition to the cost factor.

But the present 3 cent rate for first-class letter mail has not been increased in almost a quarter of a century. During this period the costs of all goods and services have almost doubled. I am convinced that the American people will understand, appreciate, respect and support Congressional action to provide for a long-overdue rate increase on letter mail which will go far towards balancing the postal budget.

2. The revenues derived from second-class mail are clearly inadequate. These rates which apply to newspapers and magazines should be increased until such matter makes a fair and reasonable contribution to postal revenues. The Postmaster General will recommend a two-step increase in second-class rates which will enable publishers to adjust more readily to the proposed rate changes.

3. Third-class mail consists largely of advertising matter. In fiscal year 1954 the revenue contribution of such mail fell substantially below the cost of providing this service and was a major factor contributing to the postal deficit. The rates of postage on such matter should be increased so that the users of this class of mail pay a proportionately fair share of postal revenues.

In view of the recurring fiscal problems of the Post Office Department, and of the heavy burden which postal deficits continue to impose on the Federal treasury, I strongly recommend to Congress the formal adoption of a policy which will ensure that in the future the Post Office Department will be essentially self-supporting.

Certain services which are performed by the Post Office, such as those for the blind, are a part of general welfare services. The cost of such services should not be borne by users of the mails. Expenditures for them, and for services performed for the Government, should be identified and met by direct appropriation.

If the Post Office is successfully to meet the challenge of the future its prices must be sufficiently flexible to reflect changes in costs and the developing needs of a dynamic economy. It is my belief that an independent Commission entrusted with the authority to establish and maintain fair and equitable postal rates can best provide this needed flexibility.

There are also other advantages. Such a Commission, guided

by policies laid down by the Congress, would have the time and facilities to make thorough analytical studies before prescribing rate changes.   A Commission well versed in the economics of modern pricing practices can continuously appraise and re-appraise the soundness of the postal rate structure.   Legislation to secure these ends should be enacted by Congress.

With these views in mind I recommend to Congress the adoption of a temporary increase in postal rates as an interim measure, and the establishment and activation within the interim period of a permanent Commission to prescribe future rate adjustments under broad policy guidance of Congress.

Let me reiterate—the financial problems of the postal service result, in large measure, from lack of a positive program leading towards a well-defined fiscal goal.   I am, therefore, recommending to Congress the following five-point program for the Post Office Department:

1. Approval of the new salary plan and a 5 percent increase in basic salary rates.

2. Adoption by Congress of the policy that henceforth the Post Office Department shall be self-supporting.

3. Separation of those postal costs to be paid by the patron from those costs which should be paid by general taxation.

4. Establishment by Congress of a permanent Commission authorized to prescribe postal rate adjustments under policy guidance of Congress.

5. Enactment by Congress of an interim rate bill which will, pending activation of the Rate Commission, provide immediate revenue to meet proposed pay increases and reduce the postal deficit.

Approval of this program will be in the public interest for it will further assure efficient service by the Post Office Department.

Dwight D. Eisenhower

NOTE: The President's message on a health program for Federal personnel appears as Item 25, below.

10 ¶ The President's News Conference of
January 12, 1955.

[This is a complete transcript of the news conference of this date. No
portion of the conference was released for broadcasting or direct quotation
at that time.]

THE PRESIDENT. Please be seated.

I don't think I have had a chance to say Happy New Year to
you, which I say now.

There is only one short announcement. We have been reading
in the papers about this trouble in Costa Rica, and I am informed
that the commission set up by the Organization of American
States, which has been successful in the past in settling disputes,
left about 6:18 this morning for the scene of the trouble.

So, of course, we will have nothing to say about it here until
that investigation is complete and the report is made.

All right, we will go to questions.

Q. Marvin L. Arrowsmith, Associated Press: Mr. President,
do you see any need for any basic revision of the security program
under which the Agriculture Department found Wolf Ladejinsky
a security risk after the State Department had cleared him, and
under which the Foreign Operations Administration then gave
him full security clearance and a new sensitive job?

THE PRESIDENT. Well, Mr. Arrowsmith, you state certain
things in your question that I am not exactly sure are exactly
right. For example, did they put him in a particularly sensitive
job? I am not sure.

In anything as delicate as is this security program, when the
effort is to make certain that the Government is served by the
finest people you can get, and where, at the same time, you don't
want to take unnecessary risks of damaging the reputations of
people who are, many reasons to believe, honest and sincere, it is
a delicate operation and judgments will differ.

Now, as you know, responsibility is placed by law upon the

heads of the departments. In this case, on the evidence available, one department believed that the best interests of Government would be served by not hiring this man. Others differ.

Obviously, it was a case where the evidence was of a kind that was not conclusive, apparently, to the other people.

I have not been through this evidence in detail. I have seen the summarized reports of it.

Now, this is one reason we have set up in the Department of Justice a separate special group under Mr. Tompkins, I believe his name is, to specialize in these matters and to be available as an adviser. He can't take the responsibility; that belongs to the Department head, but he can be a special adviser and counsel in these delicate cases.

I would be the last to say that the program we have devised is perfect. Of course, it isn't. It has been made by humans, and it is bound to have its imperfections.

These are difficult matters. Now, we constantly seek ways to improve. I know of no subject that takes so much time on the part of the entire Cabinet, both individually and collectively, as trying to get this thing absolutely straightened out.

Now, while perfection will not be obtained, improvement will always be obtained; that is about all I can tell you.

Q. Merriman Smith, United Press: Mr. President, I am sure you are aware that Vice President Nixon has been attacked and criticized by certain political elements since the election for the manner in which he conducted himself during the 1954 congressional campaign.

We are aware, too, that you wrote Mr. Nixon a congratulatory letter in late October.

I wonder how you feel about these recent criticisms of the Vice President?

THE PRESIDENT. I think here, Mr. Smith, I have a right to ask *you* one question. [*Laughter*]

Is your question based upon an actual reading of Mr. Nixon's speeches or what you have learned from what the critics say about his speeches? In other words, have you read his speeches in detail?

Q. Mr. Smith: Yes, sir. My question was based on the Democratic criticism of him, not as to what he said, not as to the content of his speeches.

THE PRESIDENT. Well, I know this—I am going to give you just a few facts: I think it was before this body that once I found it necessary to say, and I know I have said it elsewhere, that I don't consider any party other than the Communists in the United States to be a party of treason; that there are just as many patriots and loyal and wonderful Americans in one of the great parties as in the other. So any sweeping condemnation of any party, certainly I have never made, and I have never heard of Mr. Nixon making them.

On the contrary, he has assured me time and again he has never by any implication tried to condemn an entire party. He has talked about certain individual cases and the way they were handled administratively, and he has questioned good judgment but never loyalty.

Now, exactly what these criticisms are trying to do, I am not so certain; but just as I defend and believe in the loyalty, the patriotism of some of the people that are possibly making the criticisms, I certainly believe in the loyalty and patriotism of Dick Nixon. I admire him.

So I would be loath to believe that he was guilty of indiscretions, although I do admit that in the heat of campaign, words, particularly if they are taken out of context, can be made the subject of possibly legitimate criticisms.

Q. Joseph C. Harsch, Christian Science Monitor: Mr. President, in your letter to Secretary Wilson about the new military budget you referred to the need for mobile forces, and you said we should "provide for meeting lesser hostile" acts in situations "not broadened by the intervention of a major aggressor's forces."

Could you enlarge for us your concept of what these mobile

forces would be like, the means for giving them mobility, their equipment and their weapons?

THE PRESIDENT. Well, I wouldn't attempt to describe in detail because there is no military situation that can be visualized entirely in advance, and the cure prescribed.

What we are trying to do around the world is to build up indigenous forces that can assure orderly government within the country and normally take care of any difficulty of rebellion, subversion, where there isn't major outside interference.

Consequently, the thought would be that if you were called upon by an established and friendly government to help out in some situation, that light forces, probably going in there by air, or fleet marine units in a nearby area could come in, and that would be sufficient to help out.

Now, I can't possibly describe to you in all details, because they would vary in severity from something of a very minor character on up. The fact of it is that you have got to have things ready to move—and ready to move rapidly.

I believe a stitch in time in this case is often one of those things that could save possibly very great disaster later.

Q. Mr. Harsch: Do you contemplate their using tactical atomic weapons, sir?

THE PRESIDENT. I would say, normally no, because I can't conceive of an atomic weapon as being a police weapon, and we were talking really more police action. Police are to protect and stop trouble, not just to cause destruction.

Now, nothing can be precluded in a military thing. Remember this: when you resort to force as the arbiter of human difficulty, you don't know where you are going; but, generally speaking, if you get deeper and deeper, there is just no limit except what is imposed by the limitations of force itself. But I would say, normally no, would be my answer.

Q. Joseph A. Loftus, New York Times: With respect to the security program, Mr. President, can you say, is there anything specific being done or under consideration to revise it?

THE PRESIDENT. To do what?

Q. Mr. Loftus: To revise it or make any changes in the processes.

THE PRESIDENT. No, other than the studies that come constantly from the group, that specialized group, that we have set up for watching, trying to improve, this thing; that is the place from where I would expect it.

Q. Chalmers M. Roberts, Washington Post and Times Herald: In connection with Mr. Harsch's question, in your state of the Union message, I believe it was, you have said that we should not have an undue reliance on one weapon, and you referred to flexibility of forces.

Yet the general assumption in Washington appears to be that our forces are moving towards making nuclear weapons conventional weapons. I think you have even used that phrase yourself.

When you were referring to not having undue reliance on one type of weapon, were you drawing a line between nuclear and non-nuclear or between strategic and tactical types of nuclear weapons?

THE PRESIDENT. No. I just said this: you cannot have too great a reliance on one kind of formation, one type of weapon, one kind of vehicle, or any other thing in an army. It has to be rounded, because you can't tell where is going to be the place you have to use your forces or the conditions under which you will have to use them.

At the same time, though, that I urged that, I did urge this: that our forces, their formation, their training, their doctrine, keep pace with what science is constantly giving to us—in fact, forcing upon us.

Now, you have got to be ready to do all of these things. And because this is so expensive, the only thing I say is, let's make certain that everything we do we need.

It is no crime, you know, as far as I can see, to try to be effective and efficient and economical. That is what we are trying to do.

Therefore, we must have what we need, and no more taken out, staying constantly in forces that are, after all, negative in their purpose; they are to protect what you have got, not to produce. So my whole effort is to keep the kind of forces that can meet our situations logically, particularly those that can threaten directly our vital interests.

I repeat again, which I have stated here so often, what is the thing today that, for the first time in our history, gives us legitimate cause for alarm as to our own safety? It is the advent of the atomic weapon, the weapon of great destructive force, and with means for delivering it.

Up until that time, the oceans had seemed to us such wonderful protective areas that we could well afford the, almost, the unpreparedness that has been our history from the Revolutionary War down to the Korean War.

We no longer can afford it. Now, that is all.

Q. Mr. Roberts: Sir, may I ask, as a military man would you say that it is possible to draw a distinction between strategic and tactical nuclear weapons?

THE PRESIDENT. As a matter of fact, I don't think it's possible to draw a sharp line even between strategy and tactics. I don't believe it is possible.

Every expert, everybody that has ever written on this subject, has had his own definition of strategy and his own definition of tactics.

They do merge, there is no sharp line. But I would say this: every military problem finally brings forward its own logical way of solving what you have to apply, when.

Now, war is a political act, so politics—that is, world politics—are just as important in making your decisions as is the character of the weapon you use.

I can't possibly stand here and, unless we take the world, construct for ourselves a logical military problem, could I give you my solution to that problem. I can't do it in the abstract. It is just impossible. But I do say you can draw no sharp line between tactical use of atomic weapons and strategic use.

Q. Clark R. Mollenhoff, Des Moines Register and Tribune: Mr. President, the Secretary of Agriculture, in commenting on the Ladejinsky case, branded Ladejinsky flatly as a member of two Communist front organizations, and as an economist, analyst, and investigator for Amtorg, the Russian trading agency.

THE PRESIDENT. Yes.

Q. Mr. Mollenhoff: If those facts are true, how can the FOA and the State Department clear this man, and Mr. Benson has not taken a backward step on his position? The other two departments have gone ahead, and these are facts that still stand on the record against the man.

THE PRESIDENT. Well, I am really not going to try to say what animated either side. I do say here are honest men approaching this problem. They have reached different answers, that is obvious.

One attached unquestionably more importance to a past association, particularly in Amtorg, than do the others, who say that is a long time in the past and the man has had a lot of chances to reform.

This man, by the way, I believe, wrote a book in which he was very severely critical of communism—in fact, condemned it; so you have got a nice balance in the case, and one believes one thing and the other believes another.

Q. Mr. Mollenhoff: Mr. President, in connection with that, the Agriculture Department stated that he had a high position in Amtorg, and set it out specifically. In the State Department loyalty investigation, security investigation, he denied this under oath. This would seem to me to raise a pretty serious question, if the Agriculture Department is correct.

THE PRESIDENT. Well, I will tell you: I know of nothing you can do with this except to go to the people responsible for the decisions directly and ask them the questions.

Q. Mr. Mollenhoff: Mr. President, will the White House make sure that we can get some of those answers?

THE PRESIDENT. I can't assure it. These people are responsible people, but you ought go and try it, I should think.

Q. Ray L. Scherer, National Broadcasting Company: Mr. President, it has been reported to us that you favor shifting the Presidential convention to September, thus making for a shorter campaign, which is the subject of considerable interest to a lot of people in this room. I wonder if you care to give us your views on that.

THE PRESIDENT. Well, now, this is what I said: they came to me—I mean the group, the chairman, I think it was—some weeks ago, and asked me what I would think about a later convention and shorter campaign. I said this at least: that if they would consult whoever was to be the candidate, I am sure he would favor it because he would have a shorter period in which he goes through an experience that only some of you who have traveled on one of those trains from beginning to end can have a faint idea—and it is only faint at that, I assure you. So I said that I really thought it was foolish to drag the thing out.

But they brought up to me other considerations. You still have your primaries by law early in the year; and now what's going to happen through this long year of uncertainty and conflicting ambitions?

I am sure it is one of those things I wouldn't be too positive about. My impression is that it would be well to have later conventions.

Q. Daniel L. Schorr, CBS News: Mr. President, were you aware, sir, in approving the idea of a late convention that you would be giving the impression that you will be the candidate?

THE PRESIDENT. Bosh! [*Laughter*]

Q. Cabell Phillips, New York Times: Mr. President, it wasn't clear from your answer to the earlier question as to whether Mr. Tompkins' unit in the Department of Justice has created a special group to study this security problem or whether it is just a part of their continuing study and responsibility.

THE PRESIDENT. It was set up as a special unit in the Attorney

General's Office to have this one problem; to study how to avoid, all right, anomalies like just have occurred; to see whether, through giving expert advice, and all the way through, they can be helpful to each of the departments which must themselves carry the responsibility.

Q. Mr. Phillips: May I also ask, sir, are you contemplating the appointment of a special commission of private citizens possibly to work with Senators and others in the Government to study this?

THE PRESIDENT. That has been proposed from the beginning; of course, we had something like that, you know, under Senator Bingham when I came in here, to this office.

It has been back and forth. I see no way right now in which such a commission could be helpful. Here is something that I know that honest men are studying every day, both collectively and individually, and if I do become convinced that such a commission is advisable, well then, of course, I will call on them. At this moment I don't see it.

Q. Richard L. Wilson, Cowles Publications: I would like to ask you for an elaboration of the remark you made earlier in which you said you had seen the summary of the Ladejinsky case, and I would like to ask you if you had formed any conclusion of your own as a result of reading this summary, and if so, what that conclusion was?

THE PRESIDENT. Well, it might be a little unfair to tell the details because it was so informal, but the summary of this was read to me by the Secretary of Agriculture, and as he read it to me, I said, "Well, that would scare me." I think those are the words that I said because he was talking about hiring a new man.

I didn't inquire into all of the circumstances, and it was my impression that both State and Agriculture felt the same way at that time, so I just said that. I never actually read it. I listened to it and just made that remark. I have never myself formed a judgment on this case because I just haven't time to take up the details of every one of these cases.

Q. Mr. Wilson: But you did feel, sir, that on the preliminary showing there was a reasonable doubt about Ladejinsky's security?

THE PRESIDENT. I thought there was some doubt about it.

Now, as I say, remember I hadn't studied the other side of the question. It was brought up here that certain things were so. For instance, I think at that moment I doubt I knew the man had written a book on the other side of the question.

Q. Sarah McClendon, El Paso Times: Mr. President, before you appoint the new Chairman of the Civil Aeronautics Board, would you be inquiring into his philosophy to see if he favors new entries in the field of commercial aviation and competition?

THE PRESIDENT. Well, I would certainly inquire into his general philosophy as to the relationship of government and free enterprise, but I would never really insult any individual by trying to ask him about his answers in advance to specific questions of every kind, whether he favors a route here or a route there.

If a man would give me an answer to a question like that, I should never appoint him, I assure you.

I would want to know what was his attitude toward efficient competition in this field, not just putting up competition in order to get another firm that the Government can pay money to because the law says they must be profitable.

Q. Alan S. Emory, Watertown Times: Mr. President, a Senate rules subcommittee, headed by Senator Jenner, in his recommendations a few days ago, recommended that newspapermen as witnesses before congressional committees be compelled to disclose their sources of information. I wonder if you had any comment on that?

THE PRESIDENT. Well, I have never heard of such a thing before. I guess I am mistaken. I understood that the courts have time and again upheld the right of newspaper people to withhold that, but I may be wrong. But I haven't any comment because I don't know enough about it to talk intelligently about it.

Q. Kenneth M. Scheibel, Gannett Newspapers: Mr. President, could you tell us your views now about the question of developing the Niagara power, whether you would favor private enterprise to develop that or a public body?

THE PRESIDENT. Well, I think it is a decision of New York State, as I understand it. That job has been turned over to New York.

Q. Mr. Scheibel: Well, inasmuch as the Federal Government must issue a license to any group which does it, might you have a preference?

THE PRESIDENT. Well, I don't think it makes any difference whether I do or not. I am not decisive in such a case. I haven't had a chance to study this particular one.

Generally speaking, I believe that the closer to the scene of action decision can be taken by that level of government, the better it is.

I would rather the State would make the decision than the Federal Government, because I believe they are right there.

Now, if we do have to approve the license, I believe that the CAB [FPC]—no, in that case the Congress reserved to itself the right to approve the license. Isn't that the one that they reserved? [*Confers with Mr. Hagerty*]. Well, it's Federal Power. I think the Congress reserved it to itself in that case, unless my memory is wrong.

But I do believe that when we have an established body like the CAB [FPC] that the CAB [FPC] working in cooperation with the State is better than to inject another Federal influence in the matter.

Q. Nat S. Finney, Buffalo Evening News: Mr. President, the Atomic Energy Commission sent the new schedule of its prices on uranium, and so forth, over to the Joint Committee on the Hill, as a classified document.

Senator Anderson, the new chairman of the committee, told me yesterday that he refused to receive it as a classified document, and sent it back, and is raising the question as to whether those prices should or should not be secret.

Can you throw any light on that problem?

THE PRESIDENT. Well, I will say this: as of now, the Chairman believes that the promiscuous publication of their price structure would almost necessarily be revealing of things that shouldn't be broadcast.

Now, obviously, both the committee, any bidding firms, any people that are properly cleared, must know about it; and I don't suppose that you could rate it, therefore, in the long run as the most delicate secret that the Government has.

I haven't discussed this thing in detail with the head of the Commission, and this is the first time I had heard that they didn't accept it. But if it has become a matter of argument, I think that Chairman Strauss will be in to see me, and we will reach a real conclusion on it.

Q. Mr. Finney: Mr. President, the debate has already started on the question of whether these prices are too high or too low, and we face the prospect of a public discussion, public debate over this question without any public knowledge of what the prices are.

THE PRESIDENT [*laughing*]. Well, I will have to take a look. You are bringing up one that I only knew that he did favor some restriction on it.

Q. Edward T. Folliard, Washington Post and Times Herald: Mr. President, it seems to me that there is still an unanswered question in connection with the Ladejinsky case. You have told how Secretary Benson read you a summary. You say, sir, that that scared you.

THE PRESIDENT. I didn't say "scared." I said, "Well, that would scare me," meaning that I would take a very jaundiced look at it.

Q. Mr. Folliard: I see. And that it did create a reasonable doubt in your mind?

THE PRESIDENT. Yes.

Q. Mr. Folliard: Now the question is: Did Mr. Stassen, in

hiring Ladejinsky, did he know about your state of mind, that is, that you had a reasonable doubt?

THE PRESIDENT. I don't know, Mr. Folliard. I assume that he did because in the conversations that these men must have had, certainly they would have said that the matter had been suggested to me. But that is the only time, I will say, that the matter has ever been brought to me directly.

I simply assure you, I am not going to go into those matters in detail, because it would break the back of any man if he tried to do that; these come up not only in such a highly publicized case as you are now talking about, but they come up every day.

This one happened to affect two departments, and for that reason was suggested to me.

Q. William H. Lawrence, New York Times: We have been under the impression that because State took one view and Agriculture took another, that Mr. Stassen had clearance from the White House, and by that, sir, I do not necessarily mean you——

THE PRESIDENT. No.

Q. Mr. Lawrence: Before he undertook to hire Mr. Ladejinsky.

THE PRESIDENT. He may have. I will tell you this, gentlemen: here is a difficult question to answer, and there are all stages of security and, let's say, sensitive positions.

If Mr. Stassen thought that this man could acceptably fill the position, that it was not so sensitive that he could damage the United States, and that this was a good thing for the Government, then I would uphold his right to do it.

But, remember this: he has to stand responsible, and, if something would turn up to show that his judgment was wrong, then he is the one that is held responsible. And remember this: each one of these heads of department is running an enormous organization. He himself has to work to find time to deal with these delicate cases; so, therefore, you have got to stand and back him up, which I do. In this case, I must say, it has created a situation that is certainly not easy to explain, but I do uphold the right of each to make his own decision in the matter.

Q. Paul Martin, Gannett Newspapers: Mr. President, in your discussions with Governor Dewey this week, did you talk about the possibility of him taking an appointment in the administration?

THE PRESIDENT. Well, I will tell you one thing, most of the time taken up between Mr. Dewey and me was his describing to me the joys of private life. [*Laughter*]

Q. Norman Carignan, Associated Press: Mr. President, there are reports that your brother, Dr. Milton Eisenhower, might make a speech some time soon in Texas on Latin American relations.

THE PRESIDENT. Yes.

Q. Mr. Carignan: I wonder if you could tell us about that.

THE PRESIDENT. Yes, that is correct. It is early February some time, and, of course, we have—[*confers with Mr. Hagerty*]— yes, Dallas Council of World Affairs. It is on the Latin American scene and situation in which, of course, my brother has taken a tremendous interest and remains, I think, very close to the State Department in discussing it.

Q. Charles S. von Fremd, CBS News: Mr. President, I would like to ask a question, sir, which I am not, in turn, asking for a yes or no answer. It has to do with whether or not you may be a candidate in '56, and I ask it for this reason: there have been a number of people, politicians, who have said that they believe you will run for one big reason, and that is the word "duty," that they feel that as a man who spent more than 40 years of his life serving his country, that it is unthinkable that you could again refuse another call to duty.

I wonder if you could comment on that and, possibly, give us your interpretation of the responsibility of duty.

THE PRESIDENT. Well, you put up the big question. I hope that I would never be sufficiently self-centered that I would fail to respond to a call to duty, but who is to define for any individual his duty in such a case as this?

I just can't say anything more at the moment. In one form or another, this question has kept popping at me about duty ever since 1943, June. I will never forget the day. [*Laughter*]

Now, I finally think that in such cases the individual has to determine what he believes to be best for the country, because he is the only one to make the decision. As I say, I hope I would never fail to do my duty, but I would certainly want to know in critical circumstances what is my duty.

Q. Robert G. Spivack, New York Post: Mr. President, in view of what has been said here this morning and in view of Secretary Benson's persistence in regarding Mr. Ladejinsky as a security risk, won't it be difficult for him to command the respect of the people of Viet-Nam in his new job?

THE PRESIDENT. Well, I doubt whether our newspapers are circulated there as widely as they are here. [*Laughter*] I doubt that that would be a serious matter.

Q. Mrs. May Craig, Maine Papers: Mr. President, I am a little confused by your remark about Governor Dewey. We understood he urged you to run again. Do I understand you that he was urging on you the joys of private life? [*Laughter*]

THE PRESIDENT. Well, I read in the paper that he did a lot of urging. I must say that he may have, I don't recall in detail.

Now, he may have said something that was taken for granted. But he did describe, as I say, at great length the joys of private life, and certainly he didn't do it in any terms where he seemed to be failing to commend it to me. [*Laughter*]

Q. Edward T. Folliard, Washington Post and Times Herald: Mr. President, so I won't be fretting over this for a week— [*laughter*]—would you tell us what happened in June 1943? Was that the beginning of the boom?

THE PRESIDENT. Well, I will tell you what happened. There was a man from the United States, a political figure, and I am not going to name him because he is still alive. We had just cleaned up northern Africa, and this man came in to me and said, "I hope you know that no American general can have a success of this scope and kind and fail to be considered for the

Presidency," and I kicked him out of the office. [*Laughter*]

Merriman Smith, United Press: Thank you, Mr. President.

NOTE: President Eisenhower's fifty-seventh news conference was held in the Executive Office Building from 10:33 to 11:06 o'clock on Wednesday morning, January 12, 1955. In attendance: 177.

11 ¶ Remarks at Luncheon Meeting of the Association of American Colleges.

January 13, 1955

Mr. Chairman and President of this distinguished audience:

I must first acknowledge and insist that my appearance today is really an ex officio one, because I do not presume that my short adventure, pleasant though it was, in the educational field, gives me the right to be here to talk to you. But as President it is a most pleasant duty and a truly great privilege to be able, on behalf of the Administration—the United States Government—to welcome this body here, to assure you of the interest with which we follow your work both collectively and in your individual capacities.

As to a message of substance, I doubt that I can say anything that you have not heard, that you will not hear, and possibly that each of you already understands better than I.

But it might be, nevertheless, of some significance that as the head of the Government charged with the responsibilities which were spoken of in the invocation, that by some simple statement I acknowledge clearly my appreciation of the importance of the work you people do—indeed, must do.

I am going to talk about education for a moment, not in its spiritual or its intellectual or its materialistic values and purposes. I want to talk about it, really, as a great cementing force by its promotion of understanding.

For example, we have a clear comprehension that we need to strengthen the spiritual bases of our free institutions. We know, also, that we need as never before, experts, technicians in the sciences, people to conduct the research in every kind of discipline that applies to our material world. But it certainly takes understanding, a deeper comprehension, than a true knowledge of either of these factors of human existence, to know how to put them together.

How do you combine idealism and realism and never be guilty just of weak compromise?

How do you establish for this nation great purposes, ideals that you are pursuing, and then manage other influences that come to bear and at least discolor or force a postponement of the achievement of those great ideals?

How do you cooperate with others in the international field, certain that we have a great task of leadership to do? There we must realize that if we try to plant our own methods, our own concepts of man's dignity and worth instantly into another area, all we do is incur resistance, indeed enmity. How do we bring about understanding? We cannot be content merely with studying our own history and seeing how we have developed. We cannot be content with a mere study of the history of others so far as it affects us directly, or as they come in contact with us through wars or trade agreements. We must understand their cultures, their histories, their aspirations, if we are to recognize—to be sympathetic even—to the decisions that they take that, sometimes now, are almost incomprehensible to us.

The great masses of people—the two and a half billions of people that make up the population of the world—are never going to grow closer together unless there is a promotion of understanding.

I think this is in a very large sense spiritual in character. Whence did we come? Why are we here? What is the true reason for our existence? And where are we going? For all of this, in the answers, we have the assistance—we have the faith—of the Christian ethic, or of our own particular religious convictions.

But others don't. Indeed, our greatest potential enemy in the world is the frank exponent of the doctrine of materialism, rejecting all of these values.

This is the kind of thing, it seems to me, that educators must concern themselves with, just as seriously as they do with mathematics and engineering and research and theology. The common questions of humanity must be comprehended to meet—and it must be an integrated answer—to meet the crying needs of the human race in the twentieth century.

Now I have only haltingly and possibly very roughly sketched out an idea that I think will portray to you my appreciation of your work. Consequently, you know how earnest I am when I say I could not wish anybody greater success than I do you people. In our schools, in our churches, indeed in our Government, in everything we do, we must find a way to supplement the efforts of the home to develop Americans of understanding, of great spiritual beliefs, intellectual capacity, and unexcelled collective material strength, in a prosperity that is so widely shared that we all march forward together.

That, is seems to me, is my rough idea of what I think you people have got to do, if the United States is going to attain that future that is surely hers by right and that, under God, she will attain.

Thank you very much.

NOTE: The President spoke at the Statler Hotel, Washington, D.C. His opening words referred to Rufus H. Fitzgerald, Chancellor of the University of Pittsburgh and President of the Association of American Colleges.

12　¶ Special Message to the Congress on
National Security Requirements.
January 13, 1955

To the Congress of the United States:

The military security of the United States requires armed
forces, disposed and alerted for instant action, quickly reinforce-
able by units ready for mobilization, assured an adequate pool of
trained manpower for necessary expansion.　Three elements are
necessary to this military posture—(1) active forces in the
strength and effectiveness necessary to meet, to repel and to
punish a first massive assault or to conduct a lesser operation that
does not require mobilization; (2) reserves so organized and
trained as units that they can be speedily mobilized to reinforce
the active forces in combat or to man defense operations at home;
(3) an unorganized reserve pool, adequate in training and numbers, to permit a quick general mobilization of all our military
strength.

Never, in peacetime, have we achieved this proper military
posture.　The penalties of our unreadiness have been manifold—in treasure, in blood, in the heartbreak of a mighty nation
buying time with the lives of men.　Now, in an uneasy peace, we
can and must move toward this proper posture—at tolerable
cost, with due regard for tradition, without disruption of human
plans or the material economy.

Korea and Indo-China are bitter reminders of the ever-
present threat of aggression.　The masses of armed men and the
vast array of war-making machines, maintained by the Soviets
and their satellites along the frontiers of the free world, sharpen
the reminders.

The first purpose of our defense planning remains the maintenance of a just, secure peace.　If, however, unwanted war should
come, it should find us ready with every resource at our command
to repel and defeat the enemy.　And, at home, we must have

forces trained for every emergency, should an aggressor be so criminally unwise as to attempt an atomic attack.

In seeking to attain these goals, we must remember that the active military forces are only the cutting edge of our nation's full strength. A vigorous economy, a strong mobilization base and trained citizens are the invincible elements in our military striking power.

But we cannot possibly keep armed and in uniform the total forces that might ultimately be required in all-out war. The inescapable burdens would endanger the liberties and the economic system we are determined to defend.

On the other hand, in case of a global war, the nation could not count on having time to marshal its strength while the enemy was engaged elsewhere. Unquestionably, the United States would be involved from the outset of such a conflict. We must be prepared.

The Defense Establishment, through the past two years, has concentrated on effectiveness, economy and efficiency within the active military forces. The result is a formidable assurance to any aggressor that we would react to attack, instantly and powerfully.

In the same period, exhaustive studies have been made on manpower—the key to a proper military posture. The recommendations herewith submitted, dealing with both the active and the reserve forces, are based on them.

In summary, I recommend (1) that the present statutory provisions authorizing the induction of young men by the Selective Service System for 24 months of training and service, scheduled to expire July 1, 1955, be extended until July 1, 1959; (2) that the existing special statutory provisions authorizing the registration and induction of doctors and dentists, also scheduled to expire on July 1, 1955, be extended until July 1, 1957; and (3) that legislation be enacted by the Congress to permit the strengthening of the reserve forces to meet essential mobilization requirements.

The extension of Selective Service is necessary because experience demonstrates that active Armed Forces of the size we must maintain cannot be raised by voluntary enlistments alone. The maximum number of volunteers will continue to be the recruiting goal of the services. But realistic estimates set the probable ceiling on voluntary forces, in the present economic situation, at a million and a half—more than 1,300,000 men short of the planned strength goal for the end of the Fiscal Year 1956.

Active force strengths are continually under review in the light of changing missions and technological improvement of weapons. A major purpose is economy in the use of men. But I see no reasonable prospect that the world situation or technological advances, in the next four years, will render the draft unnecessary. I earnestly recommend, consequently, that the extension be for four years. In the case of doctors and dentists I recommend that the extension be for another period of two years only. By that time it is expected that the medical personnel requirements of the Armed Forces can be met adequately by other means.

The term of service should be retained at the 24 month level established by the 82nd Congress after weighing the military efficiency and dollar-cost arguments involved. Those arguments, whose soundness was proved in the experience of the three past years, are now compellingly persuasive that shortening the term of service would seriously damage the combat readiness of our active forces.

The present operation of selective service is recognized by the American people as an equitable and necessary solution to a national problem. The calm planning for a call, the unquestioning acceptance of it, the smooth adjustment to a new way of life, manifested by millions of our young men and their families, evidences the maturity of their attitude toward the problem of national security.

Under the new National Reserve Plan, selective service and the reserve forces, in conjunction with our regular establishment, will fulfill our security needs with the least possible disruptive impact on the life of the individual citizen and the civilian economy. Flexibility is a primary characteristic of the Plan. Constant scrutiny and review of its operation by the Services will assure its increasing efficiency.

The reserve program has been the subject of extensive study in the Congress, in various government agencies and in the military services themselves over long periods of time. As in our active forces, we will rely as heavily as possible on voluntary service. To further this purpose, recent surveys indicate that certain improvements can be accomplished within the Services, without legislation, and steps have been taken to remedy existing deficiencies. I shall follow this action personally with particular attention to training for combat missions.

In addition, however, there is need for certain changes in present laws relating to the reserves. There are five principal areas where affirmative legislation is needed to provide the basis for a strengthened reserve plan.

First, present law divides reserve personnel into categories that do not lend themselves fully to strategic requirements. I recommend that this be altered so as to provide one group of reservists who can be organized into a force maintained in a high degree of readiness to meet immediate mobilization requirements, and a second non-organized group with prior service who would be called into military service by a selective process, if the need for their services should develop in a general mobilization.

The first group should be kept ready through training, through the constant flow of new men into the group, and through the screening from the group of combat veterans and persons of essential civilian skills in excess of military requirements whenever possible. This makes provision for meeting the essential manpower needs of defense supporting activities as well as those of the Armed Forces. Both these needs must be met if we are to realize our maximum national strength in time of emergency.

Second, present legislation does not make adequate provision for bringing young men directly into the reserve forces without either adversely affecting the readiness of the active forces or reducing the capability of the active forces to recruit long-term volunteers.

At present, the reserves are composed of older men who have completed their terms of active service. For example, less than 17 percent of the men now in the Army Reserves are under 24 years of age. I recommend that legislation be adopted by which physically fit young men between the ages of 17 and 19 may volunteer for six months' basic training, to be followed by active reserve participation for a period of nine and one-half years.

During the six-month period of training, these young men would receive pay at the reduced rate of $30 a month. The total numbers accepted in the basic-type training should be subject to quotas, fixed by the President, to avoid bringing the manpower pool down to an undesirably low level; on the other hand, if an adequate number do not volunteer for this program, authority should be given to induct the needed young men through the Selective Service System. Men so selected would be between the ages of 18½ and 19.

The six-months training program should be authorized for a term of four years, covering the same period as the requested extension of the draft. In connection with this program, the National Security Training Commission should serve in an advisory capacity to the Secretary of Defense and to the President as Commander-in-Chief.

Third, under present legislation, there is no assurance that the National Guard, which by law is in the first line of defense and dependent on voluntary enlistments, receives an adequate supply of young men with appropriate basic training. Young men who enlist in the National Guard receive no concentrated initial training of the type provided by the active services. I recommend that legislation be enacted by which the men enlisting in the National Guard receive basic training in the active services. There must be further assurance that the National Guard contain a hard core of men who have been schooled in leadership and technical military skills through longer periods of active training and service.

Primary emphasis on voluntary recruitment of personnel for the National Guard should continue. However, subject to constitutional limitations, the legislation should provide that in the event of failure to recruit the necessary numbers and quality of volunteer personnel, and at the request or approval of the Governor of a State, personnel completing training or service in the Active Forces may be assigned to the National Guard for their obligated period of reserve participation.

Fourth, I recommend that legislation be adopted to induce participation in reserve training by providing that men who have served less than two years may be recalled to active duty in order to maintain or restore proficiencies.

It is also contemplated that reservists who fail or refuse to participate in the reserve training that may be required of them and choose not to restore lost proficiencies, will be given other than an honorable discharge at the end of their period of military obligation. Such action, which will be taken in accordance with existing statutory authority and procedures, is based upon the concept that honorable military service includes complete fulfillment of all service obligations, reserve as well as active. I ask that the Congress reaffirm this concept which is already contained in the law.

Fifth, existing law does not permit states to maintain troops in addition to the National Guard. In view of the fact that the potential enemy possesses weapons of mass destruction and means for their delivery, it is a matter of urgent importance that there be no break between the time that National Guard units might be called into Federal service and the time that the states could raise additional forces to replace them. I therefore recommend that the Congress enact legislation which would permit the states to raise and maintain in time of peace organized militia forces which would take over the National Guard's domestic missions and support civil defense activities upon its withdrawal.

These five remedies are suggested as amendments to our existing legislative pattern, which is an essentially sound one. Through these amendments, certain broad objectives can be attained. To begin with, we will give each young man the maximum possible right of self-determination by offering him a choice of methods of meeting his military obligation. At the threshold of his career, he will understand his obligations, so that he can make definite plans for his future.

In addition, a more equitable sharing of the military obligations will be accomplished. The program will go far toward assuring combat veterans that they will not be called in an emergency until younger men who have not had combat duty are called, thus alleviating an inequity made apparent during the Korean conflict.

In sum, the program will constitute a substantial improvement in our present defense arrangements. It will make our determination evident to every would-be aggressor.

———

I believe that, under today's conditions, steps generally as outlined above represent the best available approach to the problem of military security. I earnestly urge that Congress promptly initiate its studies of the detailed measures necessary and that legislation incorporating the principles of the program be enacted.

Dwight D. Eisenhower

13   ¶ Special Message to the Congress on Career Incentives for Military Personnel.
January 13, 1955

To the Congress of the United States:

We are traditionally a peace-loving people with a heritage founded on the dignity of the individual. Because our defense planning is developed within this framework, we seek to man our armed forces with volunteers to the greatest extent possible. This is a basic objective.

To sustain our active forces at required levels of strength and efficiency, it is necessary to increase the present rate of voluntary enlistments. It is also necessary to induce volunteers, both officers and enlisted men, to continue in the service on a career basis in order to obtain maximum usefulness from the skills and leadership which are achieved after long and costly training. The increasing mechanization and complexity of defense forces make technical skills and a wide background of experience vastly more important than ever before.

The need for forces of the size now contemplated in our planning is obvious. The responsibilities and obligations imposed on us by our position of leadership in world affairs require that we stand prepared to shoulder the accompanying burdens.

PERSONNEL TURNOVER IN THE MILITARY SERVICES

But at this time when we must still maintain large forces under arms and alerted throughout the world, it is difficult to attract and retain volunteers, both enlisted and commissioned.

For example, only 11.6 percent of Army personnel reenlisted in 1954 compared with a rate of 41.2 percent in 1949. The other services, particularly the Marine Corps, have also experienced sharp drops in the rate of reenlistments and today the composite rate for all services is 20 percent.

Approximately one million enlisted men will become eligible for release from the military services during the coming year. Under present low reenlistment rates, it will be necessary to replace about 800,000 of these men.

The investment in this skilled manpower is enormous. For example, it costs approximately $3,200 to put one man through the normal course of basic training. It costs an additional $2,000 to $5,000 to train a man in the typical technical skills that are so essential in the military system of today. It costs $120,000 to train a jet pilot.

These are just a few indications of the expense associated with training alone. Moreover, the cost of equipment, transportation and other items goes up as the rate of personnel turnover increases.

The seriousness of the situation was recognized by the 83rd Congress when it substantially raised reenlistment bonuses.

REASONS FOR THE HIGH PERSONNEL TURNOVER

Field studies made by the Services have attempted to pinpoint reasons for the high personnel turnover rate. A very large portion of the military personnel surveyed expressed dissatisfaction with traditional service benefits such as PX facilities, dependents' medical care, family housing, death benefits for survivors and related items. Wherever administrative action can improve conditions, action is being taken by the Services. However, legislation is necessary for changes in most benefits and in the level of compensation.

Since 1949 there has been one increase in pay which, along with increases in allowances, amounted to an aggregate advance in compensation of 5.7 percent. Military pay, nevertheless, has fallen behind that of industry. In addition, supplementary pay practices, health, security and retirement benefits and bonus systems are now widespread throughout industry, and this fact tends to neutralize such advantage as the military services had in these fields.

EFFECTS OF HIGH TURNOVER RATE ON OPERATIONAL EFFICIENCY

While the high turnover in military personnel is costly in dollars, even more costly is the loss of experience and operational efficiency which results from it.

We are losing too many men trained in leadership and technical skills—the experienced hard core of a modern fighting force. To maintain required percentages of young officers we must obtain them from the service academies and from reserve training units.   A certain number should elect to continue a service career beyond the required minimum time.   Yet not enough of our younger officers currently continue in military service.   In 1954, 4,000 young Naval Reserve officers completed their obligated period of service.   Only 200 of these elected to remain in the career service.

As a result of the loss of younger officers, there is a noticeable shortage of officers and men in the services with intermediate levels of experience.   In the Army, for example, there are substantially fewer officers with 4 to 10 years service than with 10 to 15 years experience.   In the other services, a similar situation exists.   A large percentage of officers in the older age group who saw service in World War II and in Korea outnumbers a proportionately smaller group of younger officers.   We must not allow this trend to continue.

A continuing shrinkage in the rolls of young experienced commissioned and non-commissioned officers will blunt the battle readiness of our combat units.

HAZARDOUS AND SPECIAL DUTY

Peacetime military service has become more arduous, more dangerous and more disruptive of normal living habits.   The era of nuclear weapons and jet propulsion has drawn our services into new dimensions of hazard and uncertainty.   For example, jet flying is ranked by insurance companies as the most hazardous of all occupations.   Many young flyers find it impossible to secure insurance coverage and those who can get it must pay a sizable premium differential.

While we are in a peacetime situation, many men in the Strategic Air Command, the Air Defense Command, and various Naval units are on alert up to 60 hours per week, subject to sudden and prolonged absences from home and loved ones.   Airborne troops of the Army and submarine crews of the Navy are also exposed to discomforts and dangers not found in civilian pursuits.

CONCLUSIONS

The fundamental objectives to be attained by the proposed legislation are the attraction of young men to a military career and the retention of men in this career once they have chosen it. In addition, it is necessary to offer special attractions to men who undertake the particularly hazardous jobs that are becoming more important as weapons become increasingly complex.

These objectives require compensation which is more in line with that offered by private industry. They also require strengthening of traditional service benefits in recognition of the unusual difficulties facing the serviceman and his family. Servicemen frequently live in isolated areas and under circumstances that can be extremely trying. They are subject to frequent and long absences from their families, enforced on them by their defense missions.

Both pay and the non-pay benefits are important, varying with the status of the men we are trying to attract. At the present time, 60 percent of personnel on active duty are unmarried. These men are less likely to be attracted by deferred or family benefits than by an increase in pay.

So our problem is twofold. On the one hand we must attract more of the young, unmarried men into a military career. On the other, we must provide advantageous benefits for those who have families.

In proposing adjustments in pay I do not recommend that any across-the-board increase should be authorized. Such pay adjustments should foster career service. Specifically, no increase is proposed in the first two years for enlisted men, because this is the least valuable period of a man's service, and no increases are proposed in the first three years for officers. Our efforts should be directed at inducing men to stay on after those periods. For this reason, I consider it highly important that a schedule of selective adjustments be approved.

RECOMMENDATIONS

In summary, my recommendations are as follows:

(1) The compensation of military service personnel should be increased on a selective basis. The aggregate increase proposed would add approximately 6.7 percent to the present level of pay and allowances.

(2) Hazardous duty pay for airmen and submarine crews should be increased, also on a selective basis, and increases also should be made in the hazardous duty pay for parachute duty, demolition work, deep-sea diving and certain other specialties.

(3) Other non-pay benefits should be provided, including:

(a) A "dislocation" allowance for military personnel with dependents who are ordered to a new permanent duty station.

(b) An increase in the per diem allowance for temporary duty travel from $9 to $12, in keeping with a comparable proposal for civilian government employees.

(c) More housing for service families in areas where present facilities are insufficient and authority for reduced rentals where men and their families must live temporarily in substandard housing.

(d) Removal of existing inequities and provision for better medical care for military families.

(e) Equalization of survivor benefits according to rank for active and retired personnel.

These recommendations are vitally important to the welfare of our military people and to the sustained security of the nation. It is the objective of the Government that the size of the active military establishment shall be no greater than is consistent with the needs of national security. It shall always be our objective, in the present world situation, to maintain a military force that we can support for the many years that may be necessary to dispel the shadow of Communist threat. In my judgment, the measures herein presented will strengthen our security and preserve our way of life.

I urge that the Congress give early and favorable consideration to the recommendations I have herein submitted.

DWIGHT D. EISENHOWER

14   ¶ Letter to the President of the Senate and to the Speaker of the House of Representatives Approving Certain Virgin Islands Corporation Activities.   *January* 13, 1955

Sir:

In accordance with section 7(a) of the Virgin Islands Corporation Act (48 U.S.C. 1407f(a)) I hereby report my approval of the emergency undertaking by the Virgin Islands Corporation of certain activities of a type authorized by the Act, but not included in the budget program or subsequently approved by the Congress.

The activities undertaken are in connection with the management of the Federal properties in the Virgin Islands known as the Marine Corps Air Facility and the Naval Submarine Base. These properties had been transferred by the Navy to the Department of the Interior for operation and management under a revocable permit. The Department of the Interior had in turn leased the properties to the St. Thomas Development Authority, an instrumentality of the Municipality of St. Thomas and St. John, Virgin Islands. When serious mismanagement of the properties was brought to the attention of the Secretary of the Interior in June 1954, he terminated the lease and directed the Virgin Islands Corporation to assume responsibility for operation and maintenance. Immediate action was necessary to avoid further revenue losses and deterioration of Federal property.

Revenues from the operation of the property are expected to

be sufficient to pay all expenses of operation and to restore the property to good condition.

Respectfully yours,

DWIGHT D. EISENHOWER

NOTE: This is the text of identical letters addressed to the Honorable Richard M. Nixon, President of the Senate, and to the Honorable Sam Rayburn, Speaker of the House of Representatives.

15 ¶ Cablegram to Dr. Albert Schweitzer on the Occasion of His 80th Birthday. *January* 13, 1955

Dr. Albert Schweitzer
Lambarene
French Equatorial Africa

My cordial greetings and best wishes on your eightieth birthday. Your spirit and work have been an example and inspiration to all of us.

DWIGHT D. EISENHOWER

16 ¶ Statement by the President on United Nations Negotiations With Communist China for Release of American Airmen and Other Personnel. *January* 14, 1955

THE SECRETARY GENERAL of the United Nations has returned from his mission to Peiping. He has not yet formally reported but has indicated that his visit represented only a first stage in United Nations negotiations to achieve the release of the American airmen and other United Nations personnel detained in Red China. He believes that progress has been made and urges that restraint be exercised to permit of further efforts.

Quite naturally, the immediate reaction of all Americans to the Secretary General's announcement is disappointment. All of us are rightly aroused that our airmen have not long since been released by their Communist captors in accordance with the clear terms of the Korean Armistice.

We must never forget one fundamental thing: We want our airmen returned safely to their homes.

All Americans are united and dedicated to this cause. Truth and right are on our side. We must have faith in the community of nations and in the tremendous influence of world opinion.

It will not be easy for us to refrain from giving expression to thoughts of reprisal or retaliation. Yet this is what we must not now do. We must not fall into a Communist trap and through impetuous words or deeds endanger the lives of those imprisoned airmen who wear the uniform of our country.

They are fighting men, trained to discipline. We now owe them discipline from ourselves. We must support the United Nations in its efforts so long as those efforts hold out any promise of success.

17 ¶ Annual Budget Message to the Congress: Fiscal Year 1956. *January 17, 1955*

PART A

To the Congress of the United States:

I am transmitting to you today the Budget of the United States Government for the fiscal year 1956, which begins July 1, 1955.

The first part of this budget message summarizes the budget totals and highlights our policies and plans for next year, particularly as related to the fiscal situation. The second part presents summary tables and also contains my budget recommendations for each major Government activity.

The fiscal and budget story during this past year centers around the fact that we successfully made the adjustment from a wartime to a peacetime type of economy, a truly significant achievement. Aided by a proper fiscal policy, the inevitable dislocations of this adjustment, while difficult for some, have not been serious on the whole. Our present growing prosperity has solid foundations, free from the artificial stimulations of war or inflation. However, the peace in which we live is an insecure peace. We must be constantly on the alert. Along with the other free nations of the world we must continue to strengthen our defenses. At the same time to remain strong for what will apparently be a long period of uncertainty ahead, we must also progressively increase our prosperity and enhance our welfare.

The 1956 budget is based on this outlook. Total expenditures will be reduced. However, I am recommending somewhat increased expenditures in particular areas important to human well-being. Budget expenditures for the fiscal year 1956 are now estimated at 62.4 billion dollars, 1.1 billion dollars less than for the current year. All parts of the administration will continue to work toward further reductions during the year by eliminating nonessentials and by doing necessary things more efficiently.

We must maintain expenditures at the high level needed to guard our national security. Our economy is strong and prosperous but we should not dissipate our economic strength through inflationary deficits. I have therefore recommended to the Congress extension for 1 year of present excise and corporate income tax rates which are scheduled for reduction on April 1, 1955, under present law. If this is done, and employment and production increase as currently anticipated, we can expect budget receipts to rise 1 billion dollars over 1955, to a total of 60 billion dollars in the fiscal year 1956.

On the basis of these estimates of expenditures and receipts, the deficit will be reduced from the presently estimated 4.5 billion dollars in the fiscal year 1955 to an estimated 2.4 billion dollars in 1956. Thus we continue to progress toward a balanced budget.

BUDGET POLICIES

Three broad considerations of national policy have guided me in framing the budget for the fiscal year 1956.

First, we must defend our priceless heritage of political liberty and personal freedom against attack from without and under-mining from within. Our efforts to date have helped bring about encouraging results—cessation of fighting, new and stronger alliances, and some lessening of tensions. The grow-ing strength of the United States and its friends is a key factor in the improved outlook for peace. We must continue to build this strength. We must at the same time preserve our liberty at home by fostering the traditional initiative of the American peo-ple. We will increase the scope of private activity by continuing to take Government out of those things which the people can do better for themselves, and by undertaking on a partnership basis, wherever possible, those things for which Government action is necessary. Thus, people will be able to keep more of their earn-ings to use as they wish.

Second, the Government must do its part to advance human welfare and encourage economic growth with constructive actions, but only where our people cannot take the necessary actions for themselves. As far as possible, these steps should be taken in partnership with State and local government and private enterprise. We must do our part to provide the environment for our free enterprise system to keep employment high, to create new jobs, and to raise the standard of living. We must broaden the opportunity for individuals to contribute to the growth of our economy and enjoy the fruits of its productivity.

Third, we must maintain financial strength. Preserving the value of the dollar is a matter of vital concern to each of us. Surely no one would advocate a special tax on the widows and orphans, pensioners, and working people with fixed incomes. Yet inflation acts like a tax which hits these groups hardest. This administration has made a stable dollar and economy in Government operations positive policies from the top down. Expenditure reductions, together with a judicious tax program, effective monetary policy, and careful management of the public debt, will help to assure a stable cost-of-living—continuing our achievement of the past 2 years.

A liberal attitude toward the welfare of people and a conservative approach to the use of their money have shaped this budget. Our determination to keep working toward a balanced budget provides the discipline essential for wise and efficient management of the public business.

NEW AUTHORITY TO INCUR OBLIGATIONS

My recommendation for appropriations and other new authority to incur obligations for the fiscal year 1956 is 1.3 billion dollars more than the amount for the fiscal year 1955, primarily because of new requirements for our military services. However, it represents a reduction of 32.8 billion dollars from 1952, 21.7 billion dollars from 1953, and 4.2 billion dollars from 1954.

Fiscal year:	New authority to incur obligations (in millions)
1952	$91. 4
1953	80. 3
1954: As estimated, January 9, 1953	72. 2
Actual	62. 8
1955 estimated	57. 3
1956 recommended	58. 6

The new authority to incur obligations which I am recommending for our major national security programs is 2.4 billion dollars greater than in the fiscal year 1955. I am proposing a reduction in the total new authority for all other Government programs, although within this total, I am recommending selective increases.

Part of the reduction in 1955 of new authority for our major national security programs below the amount enacted for 1954 was possible because the military services improved their supply procedures, which resulted in larger use of existing stocks and reduction of the large backlog of unexpended balances. The accumulated unexpended balances of funds appropriated to all Government agencies in prior years are now on their way down to more reasonable levels and the continued downtrend in total unexpended balances will be less rapid in the future than in the fiscal year 1955.

Recommended new authority for 1956 is less than both the anticipated revenues and the estimated expenditures for that year. By holding the level of new authority lower than anticipated revenues, we can continue making progress toward balancing the budget. Likewise, as long as the amount of new authority is less than expenditures, we are continuing on the way toward lower levels of Government spending.

BUDGET EXPENDITURES

In the fiscal year 1956, net budget expenditures are estimated to be 11.9 billion dollars below actual spending in the fiscal year 1953. The record shows that this administration cut Government spending in 1954 by 6.5 billion dollars below 1953, and 10.1 billion dollars below the level estimated for 1954 on January 9, 1953. For 1955, an additional reduction of 4.3 billion dollars is now estimated and still another reduction in spending of 1.1 billion dollars is the present estimate for 1956. The fiscal year 1955 is only half completed and the beginning of 1956 is still 5½ months away. We shall continue working to improve efficiency and to reduce still further the totals now estimated for these years.

Fiscal year:	Expenditures (in billions)
1952	$65.4
1953	74.3
1954: As estimated, January 9, 1953	77.9
Actual	67.8
1955 estimated	63.5
1956 estimated	62.4

The stern requirements of our national defense dictate the largest part of our budget, and it is chiefly these requirements which prevent us from decreasing budget expenditures faster at this time. Further progress in reducing expenditures must result in large part from increasing efficiency and from finding better ways of doing the things that must be done. Future savings will be more difficult than those already accomplished. However, we expect to continue reducing the cost of Government.

Major national security.—Expenditures for major national security programs in the fiscal year 1956 are estimated at 40.5 billion dollars, 65 percent of total budget expenditures. This amount includes the cost of new legislation. I am proposing to establish an effective military reserve system and strengthen the career service. This budget provides for more expenditures by the Department of Defense for air power than ever before in peacetime history. New weapons for defensive and retaliatory action are being developed and produced in increasing quantities. High priority is being given to strengthening our continental defense system. Since military supplies are not being consumed in combat, the bulk of the military materiel being produced by our factories is adding to our capacity to defend ourselves. Our defense expenditures are now bringing about a steadily growing strength. Never in our peacetime history have we been as well prepared to defend ourselves as we are now.

We will deliver about the same amount of military equipment to friendly nations as in 1954 and 1955. New atomic energy plants will be placed in operation and more than in any previous year will be spent for peaceful applications of atomic energy. The dollar value of our stockpile of strategic materials is expected to reach 78 percent of the minimum objective, compared with 58 percent in 1954.

International affairs and finance.—Our international programs are closely related to national security. The conduct of our foreign affairs is crucial in preserving peace. We have materially contributed to the strengthening of friendly nations through the economic aspects of the mutual security program. Continuation of such assistance is urgently needed for some countries. Net expenditures for international affairs and finance are estimated to be 1.3 billion dollars, 88 million dollars lower than in the fiscal year 1955.

Keeping our own defenses strong and cooperating with our allies to increase their defenses will deter outside attacks on our freedom. We must at the same time look to the abiding sources of our internal strength—our faith in the power of free men, our individual initiative, and our competitive enterprise.

Commerce and manpower.—We are moving ahead in taking the Government out of business wherever this can properly be done. In addition to selling the Inland Waterways Corporation and liquidating the Reconstruction Finance Corporation, we have already sold or shut down a number of Department of Defense plants for processing scrap and manufacturing paint, clothing, and chlorine. Private industry is performing an increasing share, which has reached almost half, of major equipment overhauls for the Air Force. Most of the synthetic rubber plants have been sold to private purchasers, subject only to congressional approval. These actions not only serve to strengthen our system of private enterprise, but also in many cases reduce Government expenditures and increase tax receipts for cities, counties, and States as well as the Federal Government.

During the past year, legislation was enacted permitting private lenders to make mortgage money available on more liberal terms so that more people can buy their own homes. Local public agencies, aided by private investors, are being encouraged to start comprehensive urban renewal programs. Provision has been made for extension of unemployment insurance to 4 million more workers.

For the coming year, I am recommending that we start a 10-year program to modernize the interstate highway system in cooperation with State and local governments. I am also proposing that we step up aeronautical research, expand air navigation facilities, and help industry build more ships. These activities are important for our national security as well as for our growing economy. I firmly believe that as large a proportion as possible of the expenditures of the Government should be borne by those directly benefiting therefrom. The user charge principle should be further extended. I have recommended to the Congress that postal rates be increased to make the postal system self-supporting in the near future. With the enactment of this legislation, total net expenditures for commerce and manpower in the fiscal year 1956 are expected to be 2.2 billion dollars, 364 million dollars below 1955.

Natural resources.—An important policy of this Government is to encourage an increased sharing by State and local governments of our long-range development projects. For example, the State of New York and the Province of Ontario are now jointly developing the power resources of the St. Lawrence River without cost to the Federal Government. Under legislation passed last year the Markham Ferry project in Oklahoma and the Priest Rapids project in the State of Washington, both with large power developments, will be built by State or local units, with modest Federal contributions only for those purposes such as flood control which involve national responsibilities. This budget proposes the start of several new construction projects under such partnership arrangements. Thus, we are continuing to develop our natural resources at less cost to the Federal Government. Net budget expenditures of 953 million dollars in 1956 are estimated for natural resources, 180 million dollars less than in 1955.

Agriculture.—Greater freedom from Government direction and control of farming operations will be made possible in future years as a result of the new farm legislation enacted last summer. The flexible supports provided for therein will stimulate the consumption of farm products at home and abroad and will reduce Government expenditures for buying and storing surplus commodities. Greater private participation in the financing of loans to farmers has also been brought about by legislation enacted last year. By increased use of fully insured private loans, the need for direct Federal loans for farm ownership and for soil and water conservation has been reduced. A sound basis has also been provided through the new watershed protection legislation for greater cooperation between the Federal Government and States and local groups in the upstream flood prevention program. In addition, through strengthened agricultural research and educational work, farmers can better work out solutions for their own problems. These steps reduce the dependence of farmers on the Government, encourage farmers to take the initiative in adjusting production to demand, and provide the conditions under which farmers can maintain their incomes with less interference by the Government. The flexible support legislation will not greatly affect expenditures for the fiscal year 1956. Estimated net expenditures for agricultural programs in 1956 will be 2.3 billion dollars, 871 million dollars less than in 1955. This reduction is principally due to the anticipated smaller outlays for farm price supports resulting from acreage restrictions and increased sales.

Welfare, health, and education.—Our policy of partnership with State and local governments and with private enterprise is also enabling us to make significant contributions to human welfare. Our broadened programs of assistance for vocational rehabilitation and for construction of nonprofit hospitals and health centers will encourage greater State, local, and private activity in these fields. The extension of old-age and survivors insurance to 10 million more persons and the increased contribution and benefit rates enacted last year are in keeping with our tradition of self-reliance and will diminish dependence on charity. This budget includes appropriations for the health improvement program which I shall outline in a special message. Increases in some programs, principally for public health and vocational rehabilitation, will be offset by some reductions in other programs. Total expenditures for welfare, health, and education are estimated at 2.3 billion dollars in the fiscal year 1956, about the same as in 1955.

Veterans' services and benefits.—Expenditures for veterans' benefits continue to increase as a result of the growing number of veterans, now estimated at 21 million in civil life, becoming eligible for benefits. Legislation enacted last year raised compensation and pension benefits to our ex-servicemen and women. I have recently issued a proclamation ending the time period for acquiring further rights to readjustment benefits intended for veterans of the Korean conflict. Estimated net expenditures for veterans' programs will be 4.6 billion dollars, about 200 million dollars more than in 1955.

Interest and general government.—Expenditures for interest are estimated to amount to 6.4 billion dollars, 180 million dollars less than in 1955. In the field of general government, I recommend that we increase our expenditures for tax collection and management of Government property as further steps toward efficiency. I also recommend strengthening our law-enforcement agencies, particularly the Federal Bureau of Investigation. Finally, the Government should resume its payments as employer to the civil service retirement fund. As a result of these recommendations and anticipated increases in payments of certified claims, expenditures for general government purposes are expected to rise 344 million dollars to 1.6 billion dollars in the fiscal year 1956.

Special classification of expenditures.—The budget expenditures discussed above may be divided into four large groupings to show the ends for which we pay taxes and also the items which make our budgets big. These groupings are (1) the cost of civil operations and administration, (2) interest, (3) civil benefits to various parts of our society, and (4) the major cost of protection against war.

The expenditures for civil operations and administration of the Government have been obscured for many years by the large expenditures for defense and by the variety and complexity of the domestic and international programs. The cost of keeping the civil functions of the Government running for the fiscal year 1956 is estimated to be 2.3 billion dollars or about 4 percent of the net budget expenditures. This includes most of the expenditures

SPECIAL CLASSIFICATION OF NET BUDGET EXPENDITURES

[Fiscal years. In billions]

	1951 actual	1952 actual	1953 actual	1954 actual	1955 esti- mated	1956 estimated Amount	1956 estimated Percent
Current expenses for civil operations and administration.....	$1.9	$2.2	$2.3	$1.9	$1.9	$2.3	4
Interest............	5.7	5.9	6.6	6.5	6.6	6.4	10
Civil benefits........	11.5	12.2	13.4	11.6	13.3	12.0	19
Protection..........	25.6	46.0	52.0	47.9	41.7	41.5	67
Undistributed (reserves and adjustments)...	−.7	−.9	......	......	.1	.3	....
Total............	44.1	65.4	74.3	67.8	63.5	62.4	100

classified as general government plus the expenditures for repair, maintenance, and operation of Government civilian facilities, and for regulatory activities.

The fluctuation shown in the cost of civil operations arises primarily from the contribution made by the Federal Government, as employer, to the civil service retirement fund. This contribution was 321 million dollars in the fiscal year 1953 and 216 million dollars is proposed for 1956. No contributions were made during 1954 or 1955 pending a detailed review of all Federal retirement systems by a special commission. Increased funds are also provided for several departmental operations where there has been a longstanding backlog of work.

Decreasing interest rates during the past 12 months, together with a change in the timing of interest payments, have made possible a forecast for lower expenditures for interest in the fiscal year 1956.

The various civil benefit programs of the Government are estimated to amount to 12 billion dollars in the fiscal year 1956. Expenditures for veterans' benefits represent 38 percent of all civil benefits in that year. The variations in expenditures for farm price supports and mortgage purchases account for part of the changes in total benefit expenditures between the fiscal years 1953 and 1956.

The expenditures for protection, which account for two-thirds of total expenditures, include continental defense at home and mutual defense abroad. The total amount in the fiscal year 1956 consists of the 40.5 billion dollars for major national security programs and 1 billion dollars for economic and technical assistance under the mutual security program. In addition, many items of smaller size scattered through other parts of the budget, not included in this category, are related in varying degrees to protection. Examples are the Coast Guard and the Selective Service System.

TAX POLICY

Last year we made great progress in reducing tax burdens and improving the tax structure. Total tax reductions of 7.4 billion dollars became effective. This was the largest tax reduction in any single year in the country's history. It was made possible only by large cuts in Government expenditures. The basic tax law was revised to relieve hardships for millions of individuals and to reduce tax barriers to economic growth.

The budget would have been balanced for the current fiscal year if there had been no tax cuts. However, it was desirable to share the benefits from the large expenditure reductions. This enabled the people to have the extra money to spend for themselves which they retained because of the reduction in their taxes.

In view of the prospective deficit, we cannot afford to have any further loss of revenue this year through reductions in taxes. The corporate tax rate would be automatically reduced under existing legislation from 52 to 47 percent on April 1 with a revenue loss of about 2 billion dollars for a full year unless extended. Under existing law, the excise taxes on liquor, tobacco, gasoline, and automobiles would also be automatically reduced on April 1, with a revenue loss of 1 billion dollars unless appropriate legislation is enacted by the Congress extending them.

In the fiscal year 1956, there will be an automatic revenue reduction (as compared with 1955) of almost 2 billion dollars under existing law, wholly apart from any changes in tax rates. The principal reason is the completion of the plan adopted 5 years ago under which payments of corporate taxes have been moved forward into earlier fiscal years. Fortunately, this reduction in 1956 will be more than offset by increases in revenue due to the economic growth of the country.

Because we must keep our existing revenues intact, I have already recommended to the Congress in my State of the Union Message that existing rates on both excises and corporate incomes be extended for 1 year. Any other course of action would result in either (1) inadequate expenditures for national security, or (2) inflationary borrowing.

During the past year the Treasury Department has continued to examine possible changes in the tax laws concerning which no recommendations were made in the revision of the tax laws last year. As final conclusions are reached by the Department they will be sent to the Congress.

I have also directed the Secretary of the Treasury promptly to make recommendations for any other changes in the laws which may be found necessary to prevent anyone from avoiding his fair share of the tax burden.

The present tax take of nearly one-fourth of our national income is a serious obstacle to the long-term dynamic growth of the economy which is so necessary for the future. There must be the means for providing more and better jobs not only for those who are working today but also for the millions of young people who will come of working age in future years. The stimulus of further tax reductions is necessary just as soon as they can properly be made.

We must always make adequate provision for our security and other essential services, and further tax reductions can only be made as savings in governmental expenditures or increased revenues resulting from growth in our economy are in sight.

However, further tax reduction remains a firm goal of this administration, and our policy is directed to achieving both the savings in expenditures and the economic growth that will make such reductions possible.

I hope that tax reductions will be so justified next year. If so, I shall recommend a reduction in taxes to spread the relief fairly among all taxpayers in a way which will be the most effective to relieve individual tax burdens and to increase incentive for effort and investment.

DEBT MANAGEMENT

Debt management policy during the past year was keyed to Federal Reserve monetary policy to help assure the ready availability of money and credit needed to sustain a high level of business activity. The Treasury refrained under the special circumstances of 1954 from issuing long-term securities which would compete for long-term money available for the construction of new homes, for business expansion, or for new schools, highways, and hospitals at the State and local government level. At the same time, progress was made in improving the structure of the public debt by some extension of maturities through issuing more intermediate-term bonds. In each major Treasury financing during 1954, except for borrowing through tax anticipation securities, investors had the opportunity to buy securities longer than 1-year certificates. The result was a substantial reduction in the short-term debt.

On December 31, 1954, the public debt subject to the statutory limit was 278.3 billion dollars. We expect to be able to operate this fiscal year within the temporary debt limit of 281 billion dollars voted by the Congress last August. The increase beyond 275 billion dollars provided by this legislation is, however, temporary. The statutory limit will go back to 275 billion dollars on June 30, 1955. We anticipate that the heavy tax receipts during the remainder of this fiscal year will enable us to reduce the debt to within that figure by June 30, 1955.

At the start of the new fiscal year in July 1955 the debt will already be pressing against the legal limit. With the present seasonal pattern of tax collections, expenditures will exceed re-

38023

ceipts in the first 6 months of the fiscal year 1956 by about 8 billion
dollars. Thus, it will not be possible to pay the Government's
bills in that period without exceeding the 275 billion dollar limit.

We recognize that the statutory debt limit is valuable as an
expression of firm intent to maintain fiscal soundness. With present requirements for national security we have not yet been able
to achieve a balanced budget, even though we have made substantial progress toward it. Therefore, I have no alternative
but to ask the Congress to again increase the debt limit.

During the past 2 years, we have proved that a free, democratic
system can make the adjustment from war to peace without
serious economic disturbances. A major factor in this achievement has been the confidence of the people in the ability of the
Government to bring its financial affairs under control and to
conduct them in a responsible manner.

Our objective of being provident in financial matters has paid
and is still paying dividends in general well-being. We have reduced expenditures and eased the crushing load of taxation. We
have improved the structure of the public debt and provided a
favorable environment for sound monetary policy. We have encouraged private initiative by starting to take the Government
out of competition with private enterprise. We have made progress in housing and in protection against personal catastrophe.
We are developing our natural resources in partnership with the
State and local governments and with private initiative. These
steps are designed to assure high and rising employment, a growing prosperity, and a stable dollar.

This administration will continue to exercise the utmost care
in the manner in which it uses the taxpayers' money. It will continue to purchase what we must have for our security, well-being,
and prosperity with the fewest possible number of dollars. And
it will continue to administer the huge Government organization
more efficiently. It will put first things first and restrain spend-

ing to items of high priority. Our success thus far in reducing taxes, expenditures, and the deficit is the best evidence of the earnestness of our efforts.

With an indestructible faith in the destiny of this country, a faith equal to that of the founders who held that all men are Divinely endowed with inalienable rights; with full confidence that in the intelligent cooperation of free men is to be found the most effective way of solving group and national problems; with unshaken dedication to the pursuit of peace and justice at home and in the world, we shall continue to sustain our liberties and we shall meet and far surpass the objectives we now set for ourselves in promoting human welfare, happiness, and prosperity.

Dwight D. Eisenhower

Part B

[This second part of the budget message starts with three summary tables which are omitted.]

To the Congress of the United States:

This second part of my message contains further details regarding budget expenditures and new appropriations and my legislative recommendations. Major trust fund transactions are summarized. Expenditures are analyzed from two different points of view.

Purposes of expenditures.—From one point of view, budget expenditures serve four broad purposes. These were summarized on page 96. Four percent goes for keeping the civil functions of Government running. Another 10 percent is necessary to pay the interest charges on the Government debt. A somewhat larger proportion, 19 percent, is devoted to the costs of various programs combined under the heading of civil benefits. Some of these benefit particular groups or localities. Others are in the nature of more general benefits. Another 67 percent is for the major programs for protection against possible war.

That part of the expenditures of various agencies which is for current expenses of civil operations and administration is shown by agency in the following table:

CURRENT EXPENSES FOR CIVIL OPERATIONS AND ADMINISTRATION

[Fiscal years. In millions]

	1951 actual	1952 actual	1953 actual	1954 actual	1955 estimated	1956 estimated
Legislative branch............	$57	$58	$53	$55	$64	$65
The Judiciary................	25	27	27	28	30	33
Executive branch:						
Department of Agriculture...	101	89	96	139	138	139
Department of Commerce....	105	145	112	50	84	82
Department of Defense—Civil functions.................	56	58	81	52	59	60
Department of Health, Education, and Welfare.........	7	8	8	8	9	10
Department of the Interior...	111	119	127	125	150	150
Department of Justice.......	150	194	169	181	184	200
Department of Labor........	38	48	53	51	86	96
Post Office Department......	74	70	35	¹6	......	....
Department of State........	193	211	221	144	131	141
Treasury Department:						
Claims and judgments.....	98	76	137	213	163	250
Other...................	434	471	478	488	480	495
Civil Service Commission....	324	332	346	50	48	235
Economic Stabilization Agency......................	......	91	64	2	......	....
General Services Administration....................	96	163	162	147	148	153
Other....................	43	13	130	135	143	144
Total...................	1,911	2,174	2,299	1,872	1,916	2,251

¹ Since August 15, 1953, the cost of Government mail has been paid by the various agencies.

Expenditures for civil benefits are shown in the following table. These expenditures are partly for the acquisition of assets, which have varying degrees of recoverable value or permanency. Other expenditures are for long-range development, and for current aids and services to various groups.

The largest amount of benefits goes to veterans for compensation and pension payments, hospital and medical care, and readjustment benefits, including vocational training. The next largest current expense for benefits is for public assistance grants to States. Current expenses for agriculture consist of losses realized in disposition of commodities acquired under price support programs, payment for the removal of surplus commodities, administrative expenses of loan programs and other aids to farmers.

EXPENDITURES FOR CIVIL BENEFITS

[Fiscal years. In millions]

	1951 actual	1952 actual	1953 actual	1954 actual	1955 estimated	1956 estimated
Federal assets (loans, construction, major equipment, and additions to commodity inventories).................	$1,771	$2,905	$4,672	$2,840	$3,323	$2,013
Long-range development:						
State, local, and private assets (roads, airports, schools, and soil conservation)....	961	1,023	1,124	1,022	1,131	1,302
Expenditures for education, training, health, and research and development...	1,178	566	602	586	667	754
Current expenses for aids and services:						
Agriculture................	905	463	305	540	995	750
Business:						
Post Office..............	521	670	624	307	267	[1] 15
Other..................	288	371	310	341	483	522
Labor.....................	203	209	215	216	272	348
Home owners and tenants...	−160	−129	−123	−116	−92	−48
Veterans..................	4,515	4,710	4,178	4,185	4,347	4,536
Public assistance...........	1,186	1,178	1,330	1,438	1,445	1,420
Other aids................	141	186	176	209	420	371
Total..................	11,509	12,153	13,413	11,570	13,259	11,984

[1] Based on proposed increases in postal rates and postal pay.

Most of the postal deficit for 1954 and 1955 has been included among benefits to private business since the Post Office Department's analysis shows that it arises principally from inadequate second- and third-class mail rates. The proposed rate increase will practically absorb the postal deficit in 1956.

Expenditures for protection, as shown in the next table, likewise include the acquisition of Federal assets, of varying degrees of permanent value, from airbases to aircraft, tanks, trucks, and bombs. Such expenditures also include long-range development, and current expenses. The last mentioned is primarily the cost of military pay and operations. Protection also includes a substantial amount of military equipment and economic and technical assistance furnished under the mutual security program, of which a significant amount goes to Korea and other Far Eastern countries.

EXPENDITURES FOR PROTECTION

[Fiscal years. In millions]

	1951 actual	1952 actual	1953 actual	1954 actual	1955 estimated	1956 estimated
Federal assets (construction, plant and major equipment, and stockpiling)	$6,099	$15,059	$21,438	$19,914	$16,762	$16,934
Long-range development (research and development)	915	1,285	1,617	1,616	1,546	1,649
Current expenses (military pay, operations, maintenance, administration, and military aid abroad)	15,293	27,505	27,219	24,994	22,336	23,625
Current expenses of economic assistance abroad	3,320	2,154	1,705	1,339	1,029	1,017
Unallocated reduction in estimates (Department of Defense)	......	......	......	......	......	−1,750
Total	25,626	46,002	51,979	47,863	41,673	41,475

Controllability of expenditures.—The preceding analysis has indicated the broad purposes of expenditures. It is important that we also consider our budget from another point of view. About one-fourth of the total expenditures can be classified as permitting little or no administrative discretion through the budget process. The level of these expenditures depends upon the provisions of the legislation which authorized the programs and on other factors independent of Executive control.

SUMMARY OF NET BUDGET EXPENDITURES INDICATING
CONTROLLABILITY

[Fiscal years. In millions]

Description	1953 actual	1954 actual	1955 estimated	1956 estimated
Major national security programs.......	$50,274	$46,522	$40,644	$40,458
Major programs not readily subject to administrative discretion through the budget process:				
Veterans' compensation, pensions, and selected benefit programs.........	3,383	3,297	3,512	3,680
Veterans' unemployment compensation	26	82	131	150
Grants to States for public assistance..	1,330	1,438	1,445	1,420
Payment to railroad retirement fund for military service credits........	33	35	....	....
Agricultural price support (Commodity Credit Corporation)..............	1,943	1,526	2,159	[1] 1,142
Removal of surplus agricultural commodities.......................	82	178	113	180
Conservation of agricultural land resources.........................	273	171	190	212
Federal-aid highway grants..........	509	531	600	680
Grants to States for unemployment compensation and employment service administration................	202	203	195	245
Payment to the unemployment trust fund.............................	....	....	64	87
Claims and relief acts...............	129	213	163	250
Payments to Federal employees' retirement funds......................	321	31	30	217
Unemployment compensation for Federal employees....................	....	....	33	40
Legislative and the Judiciary.........	88	87	102	116
Interest..........................	6,583	6,470	6,558	6,378
Total......................	14,902	14,262	15,295	14,797
All other..........................	9,098	6,988	7,565	7,153
Total budget expenditures........	74,274	67,772	63,504	62,408

[1] For comparability with prior years, includes expenditures (127 million dollars) from appropriations to reimburse Commodity Credit Corporation.

For example, interest depends upon the size of the public debt and the interest rates. Expenditures for veterans' benefits depend upon the benefit rates and the number of eligible veterans. Expenditures for agricultural price supports are affected by such factors as the weather, the level of world prices, and the ability of foreign purchasers to pay dollars. Grants to States are made under formulas fixed in legislation and vary with State participation and general economic conditions. Expenditures for relatively uncontrollable programs will be 14.8 billion dollars in the fiscal year 1956. This will be 498 million dollars less than in 1955. Increases for grants under the Federal-Aid Highway Act of 1954, veterans' benefits, payment of claims, and resumption of the Government's contribution to the civil service retirement and disability fund are more than offset by the decreases expected for agricultural price supports and interest on the public debt.

Expenditures for major national security programs will decline 186 million dollars in the fiscal year 1956. All other Government expenditures are estimated to decline 412 million dollars. Although these latter expenditures are only 11 percent of the total, they include the great majority of the individual appropriation items in the budget. Between the fiscal years 1953 and 1956, these expenditures are estimated to be reduced by 1.9 billion dollars. Included in this total are expenditures for international affairs and finance, and for most of the regular operations of the Government such as enforcing laws, collecting taxes, promoting health, postal service, and civil public works.

Major trust funds.—The budget receipts and expenditures which I have so far discussed reflect only transactions of funds which belong to the Federal Government. In addition, the Federal Government engages in extensive transactions with funds which it does not own but holds in trust for others. The following table summarizes the receipts, expenditures, and balances for the major trust funds. These include the trust funds for veterans' life insurance, old-age and survivors' insurance, railroad retirement, Federal employees retirement, and unemployment compensation. The total receipts and expenditures of the many smaller trust funds which are not included in the table have amounted to about one-half billion dollars annually in recent years.

SUMMARY OF RECEIPTS, EXPENDITURES, AND BALANCES OF MAJOR TRUST FUNDS

[Fiscal years. In millions]

	1954 actual	1955 estimated	1956 estimated
Balance in funds at start of year...........	$43,057	$44,924	$46,449
Receipts...............................	8,698	9,343	10,882
Expenditures..........................	6,832	7,819	8,245
Balance in funds at close of year...........	44,924	46,449	49,087

The accumulated balances of these funds will increase substantially from 43.1 billion dollars at the beginning of the fiscal year 1954 to an estimated 49.1 billion dollars at the close of 1956. Most of these balances are invested in special issues of United States Government securities. Receipts of these trust funds include interest on such investments, payroll taxes paid by employers and employees, and premiums paid by veterans for life insurance. Expenditures are primarily for the payment of benefits. Additional information on these funds can be found in part III of the budget document.

Receipts from and payments to the public.—Transactions of trust funds and Federal funds are consolidated to show the total of the Federal Government's receipts from and payments to the public. This statement shows the total flow of funds for the year and is one measure of the inflationary or deflationary impact of Federal fiscal transactions on the national economy; it is not a substitute for the regular budget statements.

RECEIPTS FROM AND PAYMENTS TO THE PUBLIC, EXCLUDING BORROWING

[Fiscal years. In millions]

	1954 actual	1955 estimated	1956 estimated
Cash receipts from the public..............	$71,636	$66,649	$68,793
Cash payments to the public..............	71,868	69,026	68,235
Excess of cash receipts...................	....	....	558
Excess of cash payments.................	232	2,377	....

MAJOR NATIONAL SECURITY

The major national security category of the budget includes not only the military functions of the Department of Defense, but also the development of atomic energy, the stockpiling of strategic and critical materials, and the portions of the mutual security program which consist of military assistance and direct forces support to other free nations.   These four major programs are the basic elements of our national security.   Other programs with smaller totals and relating to activities which are not so exclusively defense are included under other classifications of the budget. For example, the commerce and manpower section includes the Coast Guard, merchant marine, the Selective Service System, civil defense, aeronautical research, and promotion of defense production.

Expenditures for major national security programs in the fiscal year 1956 are estimated at 40.5 billion dollars.   This total is 186 million dollars below that for 1955, and 6.1 billion dollars below the actual 1954 amount.   Recommended new authority to incur obligations is greater than for 1955 but less than for 1954.   After the cessation of combat operations in Korea, we were able to reduce our 1955 military appropriations because the unobligated balances available were greater than required and the large stocks of supplies on hand permitted the military services to "live off the shelf" to a large degree without replacing the items consumed.

Recommendations in this budget for our major national security programs are based on the same philosophy which I recommended and the Congress adopted for the fiscal years 1954 and 1955.   I then proposed that we should plan and finance our national security program on a long-term basis that would maintain essential military strength over an indefinite period of time without impairing the basic soundness of the United States economy.   This budget continues the concept of no assumed fixed date of maximum danger.   Any other concept would lead to an inevitable let-down in strength and produce peaks and valleys in our defense spending and production.

It is essential that we, together with other nations of the free world, maintain a level of military strength which will effectively discourage any would-be aggressor from attacking. We cannot accept less. The effectiveness of our power to deter rests principally upon our capability to retaliate swiftly and decisively and upon our ability to defend ourselves against attack. The advent of nuclear weapons has profoundly affected our concepts of military strategy and tactics as well as our national security policies. Such weapons multiply many fold the striking power of any military force. This budget, therefore, continues the emphasis on the development and maintenance of effective nuclear-air retaliatory power of the Air Force and Naval aviation as the principal deterrent to military aggression. Such power is being supplemented by other military forces of great strength, flexibility, and mobility and by the forces of our allies.

In order to safeguard our striking power and resources, we are giving continued high priority to the accelerated development of continental defense programs.

Priority is also being given to the development and introduction into operating units of new weapons and techniques adapted to the radically changed conditions imposed by the potential of nuclear warfare. This budget also provides for continued improvement in mobilization reserve stocks and for the cost of expanding and strengthening our military manpower reserves as outlined in my special message on this subject.

The complexity of modern military equipment and the revolution in military concepts in this atomic age put an extra premium upon military leadership, skill, and training. Unfortunately, much of our investment in developing trained manpower is being lost, as too many servicemen are rejecting a military career for the attractions they expect from civilian life. My legislative proposals to meet these problems were set forth in my special message on military pay and incentives, and funds for them are provided in this budget.

MAJOR NATIONAL SECURITY

[Fiscal years. In millions]

Item	Budget expenditures (net)				
	1950 actual	1953 actual	1954 actual	1955 estimated	1956 estimated
Direction and coordination of defense.................	$10	$15	$12	$12	$12
Other central defense activities..................	199	394	452	488	588
Army defense activities......	3,983	16,242	12,910	8,900	8,850
Navy defense activities......	4,100	11,874	11,293	9,775	9,700
Air Force defense activities...	3,600	15,085	15,668	15,200	15,600
Proposed legislation.........	....	....	....	....	1,000
Unallocated reduction in estimates.................	....	....	....	....	−1,750
Subtotal, Department of Defense...............	11,892	43,610	40,336	34,375	34,000
Development and control of atomic energy, present program..............	550	1,791	1,895	2,050	1,910
Proposed legislation.......	....	....	....	....	90
Strategic and critical materials................	438	919	651	994	783
Mutual security (military):					
Military assistance, present program............	130	3,954	3,629	2,675	2,875
Proposed legislation.....	....	....	....	....	200
Direct forces support, present program.........	....	....	12	550	500
Proposed legislation.....	....	....	....	....	100
Subtotal, military assistance and support.	130	3,954	3,641	3,225	3,675
Total budget expenditures...	13,010	50,274	46,522	40,644	40,458

Item	1950 actual	1953 actual	1954 actual	1955 estimated	1956 recommended
Direction and coordination of defense....................	$11	$15	$13	$13	$13
Other central defense activities	180	540	778	645	627
Army defense activities......	4,392	15,221	12,777	7,788	7,303
Navy defense activities......	4,359	12,689	9,612	10,272	8,937
Air Force defense activities...	5,428	20,451	11,411	12,065	14,536
Proposed legislation.........	....	....	....	....	2,983
Reduction through transfers of prior year appropriations	....	....	....	....	−1,500
Subtotal, Department of Defense...............	14,370	48,916	34,590	30,783	32,899
Development and control of atomic energy...........	839	4,152	1,118	1,284	1,292
Strategic and critical materials	425	134	....	380	522
Mutual security (military):					
Military assistance, present program...........	1,359	4,096	3,192	1,144	....
Proposed legislation.....	....	....	....	....	1,400
Direct forces support, present program........	....	....	570	795	....
Proposed legislation.....	....	....	....	....	630
Subtotal, military assistance and support.	1,359	4,096	3,763	1,939	2,030
Total new obligational authority.................	16,993	57,298	39,471	34,386	36,742

Table header: *New obligational authority*

Department of Defense.—To maintain a strong military posture and assure that our national security policy will adequately support our foreign policy, our military planning must be kept flexible and dynamic. The structure of our military forces must be subjected to continuing review and adjusted to reflect the rapid technological advances of this nuclear and electronic age. A year ago, I approved a long-range plan for our military forces upon which the fiscal year 1955 budget was based. Recent reviews of our plans and policies have resulted in reaffirmation of most of the elements of this long-range plan, but with some changes in timing. Our current military plans, in turn, will be subjected to continuing review so that they—as well as our military equipment—will be kept up-to-date. It is important that we do not attempt to fix our minds or plans upon any particular set of numbers, for today's technological changes may make yesterday's numbers and concepts obsolete.

In my judgment, the military forces and programs upon which this budget is based are accurately adjusted to the national needs.

Under our current plans, the number of military personnel is scheduled to be reduced from the present level of approximately 3.2 million to about 3 million by June 30, 1955, and to something over 2.8 million by June 30, 1956, for an average of approximately 2.9 million personnel during the fiscal year 1956, compared with an average of 3.2 million during the fiscal year 1955. Within this figure, however, the Air Force personnel strength will be somewhat increased.

The cessation of hostilities and the buildup of the Republic of Korea forces have permitted us to withdraw five United States ground divisions from the Far East. We have thus increased the number of divisions in a central reserve of forces which can be deployed where and when needed. In addition, $1\frac{1}{3}$ Marine divisions will be withdrawn from the Far East in the near future, so that their capability as a highly trained, combat-ready, amphibious force may be available as part of the central reserve. United States military forces will be maintained at appropriate levels in the Far East, with emphasis on highly mobile naval and air units of unparalleled striking power.

The Army has devoted considerable effort to assessing the changes in Army organization and doctrine required to meet the conditions of the atomic battlefield. These studies are continuing, and it appears that the Army of the future will be organized into smaller, but more mobile and self-contained, units with greater fire power. The Navy will operate approximately 1,000 active ships—including 400 warships. The number of carrier air groups is to be increased from the present 16 to 17, and an additional attack carrier equipped with modern aircraft will be added to the fleet. The Navy will continue to maintain 15 anti-submarine warfare squadrons. The Marine Corps will maintain 3 combat-ready divisions and 3 air wings. The current level of approximately 10,000 Naval and Marine operating aircraft will be maintained. The Air Force is continuing its buildup toward a goal of 137 wings, and expects to have 130 wings in being by June 30, 1956—119 of which will be combat wings. The major units of all services will be supplemented by appropriate combat support units. All the services will continue their efforts to increase the proportion of military personnel assigned to combat units.

About two-thirds of the projected Department of Defense expenditures in the fiscal year 1956 will be devoted to air power and related programs—both offensive and defensive. Expenditures for these programs will be the largest in our peacetime history. The active aircraft inventory in combat and supporting units of the Air Force, Navy, and Marine air forces will increase from over 34,000 on June 30, 1954, to 36,000 on June 30, 1956, and will continue to increase in succeeding years toward the present objective of close to 40,000 aircraft. In addition, the Army will maintain 3,600 active aircraft, with more than a 20 percent increase during the next 2 years in the number of helicopters. The growth in our effective air power is far greater than these numbers indicate, for our aircraft continue to increase in size, speed, range, and striking power.

By the end of the fiscal year 1956, the total number of aircraft in combat units of the Air Force, Navy, and Marine Corps will be approximately one-fourth greater than at the beginning of the current fiscal year. The number of jet aircraft in such units will increase by more than one-third during the same period. The increasing modernization of our air power is shown by the fact that by June 30, 1956, the Air Force combat units will be almost 100 percent jet equipped. The proportion of jets in the combat units of the Marines and Navy will increase by approximately 15 percent over the beginning of the current fiscal year.

During the past year, continuing improvements have been made in the management and operations of the Department of Defense. The stock-fund principle, which has been applied in the Navy over a period of years, is now being broadly adopted by the Army and is being initiated in the Air Force. Stock funds have been extended to include 9.3 billion dollars in inventories. Major savings—particularly in the Army—are resulting from the extension of such property accounting and other businesslike management techniques. The Army is now beginning to account for its supplies in terms of dollar value, and is relating its needs and purchases to its inventories. Largely as a result of the Army's more efficient administration of the supplies and financial assets in its stock fund account, operating stocks are being reduced to lower but better-balanced levels. In addition, military installations with 1.6 billion dollars of annual transactions have been put on a businesslike basis through the use of industrial funds.

Military functions of the Department of Defense will require 32.9 billion dollars of new authority to incur obligations in the fiscal year 1956, including proposed legislation. The gross requirements to finance proposed legislation total 3 billion dollars, but I am recommending that 1.5 billion dollars of this be met with currently available funds which can be transferred as a result of actual and prospective savings and adjustments by the Department of Defense.

Total expenditures for military functions of the Department of Defense will be greater than the new obligational authority required. Expenditures have been estimated at 34 billion dollars despite the fact that the present estimates for the many individual Department of Defense programs add to a total of 35.75 billion dollars. The success of the Secretary of Defense to date in introducing improvements in planning and increased efficiency in operations leads him to believe that he will find more opportunities for savings and economies. It is not feasible for the Secretary to predict at this time what the possible savings, slippages, and program adjustments will be in each category of military expenditures but he expects that total expenditures will not exceed 34 billion dollars. Consequently, the anticipated savings and adjustments are shown as an unallocated reduction of 1.75 billion dollars, about 5 percent of the total estimated expenditures of the Department of Defense.

The estimated 34 billion dollars of expenditures for the fiscal year 1956 includes 1 billion dollars for proposed legislation. The total estimate is 375 million dollars lower than the current estimate of expenditures for the fiscal year 1955 and 6.3 billion dollars below expenditures in the fiscal year 1954.

DEPARTMENT OF DEFENSE COSTS BY MAJOR CATEGORIES

[Fiscal years. In millions]

Cost category	Budget expenditures				Recommended new obligational authority for 1956
	1953 actual	1954 actual	1955 estimated	1956 estimated	
Military personnel..........	$11,556	$10,961	$10,245	$10,295	$10,612
Operation and maintenance.	10,379	9,356	7,869	8,576	9,184
Major procurement and production..............	(17,123)	(15,958)	(12,627)	(12,718)	(9,524)
Aircraft...............	7,416	8,334	7,557	7,550	6,064
Ships.................	1,191	1,090	888	999	1,317
Other.................	8,516	6,534	4,182	4,169	2,143
Military public works.......	1,913	1,706	1,418	1,749	1,914
Reserve components........	522	584	705	927	1,037
Research and development..	1,412	1,385	1,307	1,369	1,370
Establishment-wide activities.	759	771	719	793	758
Working capital (revolving) funds...................	−54	−384	−515	−677	....
Unallocated reduction in estimates...................	....	....	....	−1,750	....
Reduction through transfers of prior year appropriations..	....	....	....	....	−1,500
Total................	43,610	40,336	34,375	34,000	32,899

Military personnel costs, which include the compensation of military personnel, family allowances, subsistence, clothing, and permanent-change-of-station transportation, will be approximately the same in 1956 as during the current fiscal year but about 6 percent below the fiscal year 1954. Although the number of military personnel is scheduled to decrease during the fiscal year 1956, the resulting decrease in expenditures will be more than offset by the added costs of the pay increase and other benefits proposed in my special message. I am again recommending legislation to provide medical care for dependents of members of our Armed Forces in both military and civilian medical facilities. Funds are included in this budget for this proposal. I will also recommend an extension of the Dependents Assistance Act and funds are included in this budget to cover these costs.

Continuing improvements in organization and management of the Department of Defense have resulted in significant savings in the costs of operating and maintaining posts, stations, airbases, aircraft, ships, and other military equipment during the past 2 years. The planned reduction in numbers of military personnel will permit further savings through appropriate reductions in the number of supporting establishments. Nevertheless, total expenditures for operation and maintenance will be greater in the coming fiscal year than during the fiscal year 1955, since the cost reductions will be more than offset by the increasing costs of operating and maintaining the modern equipment being provided for our forces, and for operating our expanding system of continental defense in which all services participate.

Major strides have been made during the past year in expanding the system for defense of continental United States against possible enemy attack. NIKE guided-missile battalions are rapidly being installed for the defense of key potential targets. A separate Continental Air Defense Command, reporting directly to the Joint Chiefs of Staff, has been established. It has operational control over continental defense forces, including (1) Air Force fighter interceptors and aircraft control and warning networks, (2) Army anti-aircraft and guided missile battalions, (3) Navy radar picket ships and air units in the contiguous radar system, and (4) additional forces from other Air Force, Navy, Marine Corps, and Air National Guard fighter and radar units when made available for air defense. Our radar screen is being expanded and existing gaps in coverage are being filled. Our Air Defense forces, as well as the Strategic Air Command and Naval air power, are being kept on an alert basis. A surprise enemy attack would find us with increasing readiness to resist attack and retaliate with devastating effect. These measures inevitably lead to increased operating costs for continental defense, which are now higher than ever before in our history and are still rising.

Expenditures for procurement and production of major items of equipment will continue at approximately the same level as during the current fiscal year and will constitute more than one-third of the total projected expenditures of the Department of Defense. Procurement of aircraft and guided missiles will continue at the same level as during the current year and will account for two-thirds of total major procurement expenditures. Shipbuilding expenditures will increase over the current fiscal year. This budget provides for an increased number of new shipbuilding starts. This continues the program I recommended in the 1955 budget to cope with the problem of "block obsolescence" of the fleet, which was largely built during World War II. Included in the proposed shipbuilding program for the fiscal year 1956 is a fifth carrier of the *Forrestal* class.

Appropriations enacted in prior years have permitted us to build our mobilization stocks of key military items to greater levels than ever before accumulated except in time of war. My recommendations in this budget will permit us to continue the accumulation of reserves of selected types of materiel. They also provide for our operating needs for newer weapons and equipment. As has been the policy of this administration in the past, maximum feasible reliance will also be placed upon keeping military production facilities in operation rather than on accumulating even larger reserve stocks of end-items.

Military construction expenditures during the fiscal year 1956 are expected to increase substantially over the 1955 level, reflecting progress in all Services on construction of bases. A substantial portion of the military public works projects proposed to be undertaken during the fiscal year 1956 are related to the continental defense program. In addition, this budget provides for essential increments to overseas construction programs now nearing completion and for rounding out the facilities needed for the approved military force levels. The program includes a portion of the family housing greatly needed at military installations. Limited provision is also made for replacing a small portion of substandard World War II construction which has passed the point of economical maintenance and operation.

In my special message I recommended urgently needed legislation to create a more effective military reserve. Expenditures for the reserve components are expected to increase markedly during the fiscal year 1956 as a result of this legislation. Reservists in drill pay status are estimated to increase from 697,000 as of June 30, 1954, to about 857,000 at the end of the current fiscal year and a little over 1,000,000 at the end of the fiscal year 1956. In addition, under the terms of the proposed new program, there will be approximately 50,000 reservists in drill pay status who will have completed 6 months' active duty training by the end of the fiscal year 1956.

This budget also provides for continuation of the present high level of research and development in the Department of Defense. Major emphasis is being placed on developments which will more effectively utilize nuclear energy in military operations. New equipment and techniques are being developed to provide the mobility needed to meet the changed requirements of nuclear warfare. We shall continue to concentrate on those programs which show the greatest promise of providing reliable new weapons and significant improvements in both our offensive and defensive capabilities under the conditions of modern warfare. It is my belief that increased returns in military research and development can best come from maintaining a stable high level program. Although this level of program utilizes, either through direct employment or on a contractual basis, about one-half the research scientists and engineers in the United States, it also permits a high level of nonmilitary research and development essential to an expanding economy.

Civil defense.—Civil defense is also an integral part of the overall program for defense of the continental United States against enemy attack. Although the major part of continental defense is in the military budget, expenditures by the Federal Civil Defense Administration are classified in the commerce and manpower section together with those for dealing with peacetime disasters.

The concept of civil defense adopted last year takes account of the destructive threat of modern weapons and places emphasis on improved warning of impending attack, to allow time for evacuation of potential target cities. Since this policy was announced, the Federal Civil Defense Administration has developed its plans more fully and individual cities have tested mass evacuation. I cannot stress too much that civil defense will succeed or fail in proportion to the willingness of American communities to meet the peril. The Federal Government is developing cooperative methods with State governors, mayors, and voluntary citizen groups, as well as among Federal agencies, in building the civil defense organization. In accordance with the Federal Civil Defense Act of 1950, the primary responsibility for civil defense rests with the States and their political subdivisions.

Development and control of atomic energy.—It is our purpose, working in concert with other nations, to banish the threat of atomic warfare which now confronts the world. Progress is being made toward establishing an international agency for cooperation in developing the peaceful uses of atomic energy, as I proposed to the United Nations on December 8, 1953. The budget of the Atomic Energy Commission for the fiscal year 1956 provides for greater expenditures than ever before on projects to develop peaceful applications of atomic energy. We shall continue unabated our efforts to assure that this great force will be used, not for war, but for the well-being of all mankind. Until such assurance can be achieved, however, we have no alternative but to strengthen further our most effective deterrent to armed aggression—the power of our nuclear weapons stockpile.

Despite a growing program, I am recommending for 1956 only a slight increase over 1955 in new authority to incur obligations because of the availability of large unobligated balances, due partly to savings in construction costs. Total expenditures in the fiscal year 1956 are estimated at 2 billion dollars, 50 million dollars less than in 1955.

Operating expenditures will rise in the fiscal year 1956 to the highest rate yet attained. They will increase from 1.2 billion dollars in 1955 to 1.5 billion dollars in 1956 principally because of an expected higher level of procurement of raw uranium ores and concentrates and because of greater production at the Commission's plants as new facilities are completed and placed in operation. The estimates assume continuing reductions in unit production costs.

Capital expenditures in the fiscal year 1956 will drop considerably as the large new production plants authorized in prior years approach completion. Recommended new construction will include: (1) plant improvements and other facilities to increase the efficiency and capacity of the production complex, (2) certain weapons research facilities, (3) a medical research center, (4) an international training school in reactor technology, and (5) developmental atomic reactor projects.

The national effort to develop industrial atomic power for peacetime uses will go forward with increased vigor. The Atomic Energy Act of 1954 makes possible substantial private activity and investment in the constructive applications of atomic energy. Construction of one large atomic powerplant jointly financed by the Government and industry is already underway. As I stated in my message of February 17, 1954, to the Congress, "It is essential that this program so proceed that this new industry will develop self-reliance and self-sufficiency." Accordingly, it is expected that industry will finance an increasingly larger share of the total national effort in developing power reactor technology. However, to speed progress in getting the new technology established, the Atomic Energy Commission in 1956 will expand substantially its program to develop industrial power reactors. Construction of several experimental reactors will be started in 1955 and 1956. Of these, one of the most significant is a power breeder, designed to produce more fissionable material than it consumes. Nearly 15 million dollars is included in the budget for this project.

Effective progress in military propulsion reactors will continue. The launching in 1954 of the first atomic submarine, the U.S.S. *Nautilus,* will be followed by the launching in 1955 of the U.S.S. *Sea Wolf,* an atomic submarine of different design. In addition, two atomic-powered attack type submarines have been financed by Department of Defense appropriations in the fiscal year 1955. My recommendations for the Department for 1956 include additional submarines of this type. In 1956, development work will proceed on improved types of submarine reactors, and on a reactor to power larger naval vessels. The Atomic Energy Commission and the Department of Defense will expand and accelerate research on atomic powered aircraft, and will continue development work on small transportable power reactors for military use.

The basic—as distinct from applied—research which is fundamental to progress in all aspects of nuclear energy will be pursued energetically and will entail somewhat higher expenditures in 1956, both in the Commission's own laboratories and through support of research in universities and other institutions.

I again recommend that the Congress approve legislation to allow the residents of Oak Ridge, Tennessee, and Richland, Washington, to purchase their homes and establish self-government, thus taking the Federal Government out of the business of owning and governing these communities.

Stockpiling of strategic and critical materials.—A new long-term stockpile level has been established to provide an additional measure of security over and above the minimum goals. Procurement of the additional minerals will generally be limited to instances where purchases at favorable prices will serve both to meet the long-term stockpile objectives and to maintain essential domestic production, as in the case of lead and zinc in the past 6 months.

Preliminary reviews of 50 minerals indicate that the new policy may eventually increase the inventories of materials by 3.3 billion dollars above the 6.5 billion dollars of minimum objectives. By the end of the fiscal year 1956, about 5.1 billion dollars of materials within the minimum objectives, and an additional 1.2 billion dollars toward the long-term objectives will be in inventory, compared with June 1954 levels of 3.8 billion dollars and 700 million dollars, respectively. In considerable measure, this progress is made possible under the Defense Production Act, discussed in the commerce and manpower section of this message.

Mutual security program.—Military assistance and direct forces support help other free nations to train and equip the modern armed forces which are necessary for our security as well as their own. Such assistance is an integral part of our own national security program for it helps to create, in crucial areas of the free world, essential military strength which bolsters our own forces. Because our allies generally provide the major portion of the costs of maintaining the forces, this strength is being created at a relatively low cost to the United States taxpayer.

The military assistance and direct forces support programs are two parts of an integrated mutual security program which in its entirety is designed to provide other nations with the margin of outside assistance which they need to develop and maintain their political, military, and economic strength, which is in our interest. Other parts of this program are discussed in the international affairs and finance section of this message. I shall submit to the Congress proposals for necessary changes in the Mutual Security

Act. These will include my specific requests for authorization of appropriations for the fiscal year 1956. Total expenditures for mutual security are estimated at 4.7 billion dollars in the fiscal year 1956, including the provisions for a program in Asia. Recommended new authority to incur obligations is 3.5 billion dollars.

Organization for mutual security operations.—The organizational arrangements to carry on the mutual security program beyond the present fiscal year are now under careful study and I shall in the near future present to the Congress my recommendations regarding them.

MUTUAL SECURITY PROGRAM, MILITARY AND ECONOMIC

[Fiscal years. In millions]

	Expenditures			Recommended new obligational authority for 1956
	1954 actual	1955 estimated	1956 estimated	
Military:				
Military assistance:				
Present programs.......	$3,629	$2,675	$2,875	....
Proposed legislation.....	....	....	200	$1,400
Direct forces support:				
Present programs.......	12	550	500	....
Proposed legislation.....	....	....	100	630
Nonmilitary:				
Present programs.........	1,241	1,075	725	....
Proposed legislation.......	....	....	300	1,500
Total:				
Present programs......	4,882	4,300	4,100	....
Proposed legislation....	....	....	600	[1] 3,530

[1] Compares with new obligational authority of 4,725 million dollars in 1954 and 2,781 million dollars in 1955.

Military assistance.—The mutual military assistance proposed for the fiscal year 1956 will further help our allies to complete equipping and training the equivalent of more than 180 divisions, 551 combat vessels, 278 air squadrons, and related supporting units. Our assistance goes only for forces determined to be essential by our Joint Chiefs of Staff. It provides only the critical margin of training and equipment which the countries cannot provide for themselves. During the past 5 years we have delivered over 6,000 airplanes, almost 900 naval vessels of all types, 36,000 tanks and combat vehicles, nearly 200,000 transport vehicles, billions of rounds of ammunition, and many other items. Furthermore, specialized training courses have been conducted for officers and technicians from 32 countries.

Expenditures for military assistance in the fiscal year 1956 are estimated at 3.1 billion dollars as compared with 3.6 billion dollars in the fiscal year 1954, and an estimated 2.7 billion dollars in 1955. The decline in estimated expenditures from 1954 to 1955, and the subsequent increase projected for 1956, do not accurately reflect the probable rates of delivery of equipment to our allies during 1956. Actual deliveries are expected to continue in the fiscal years 1955 and 1956 at around the 3-billion dollar level which was attained in the fiscal year 1954. The fluctuations in expenditure estimates are due to a change in the method of financing wherein the Department of Defense finances the production of common type materiel, pending delivery to the mutual security program and subsequent reimbursement of Department of Defense appropriations.

Much of our mutual military assistance continues to strengthen our allies in the North Atlantic Treaty Organization, and I hope that we may soon begin furnishing certain items of military equipment which will be needed by the new German forces. To the extent that this materiel cannot be financed by the Federal Republic of Germany from its own resources, it will be financed from appropriations made for the mutual security program. The continuing growth of economic strength in Europe and completion of the financing of much of the capital equipment which was required for the initial rapid military buildup will make it possible to reduce military assistance for this area in the immediate future below the level of the last few years.

The military assistance program proposed for the fiscal year 1956 will include aid to Korea which, in previous years, was financed from regular Department of Defense appropriations.

We are also proposing the continuation of assistance designed to strengthen further the defenses of Formosa, Japan, and certain other countries in Asia which are presently receiving military assistance.

Expenditures in the fiscal year 1956 will be largely from appropriations made in previous years. At the same time, however, new authority of 1.4 billion dollars, which I am recommending, is needed to incur obligations in the fiscal year 1956 to finance in advance certain new requirements such as the Korean program.

Direct forces support.—The present Mutual Security Act distinguishes between military equipment and those supporting items which are necessary to make the soldiers and weapons effective. These supporting items, commonly referred to as direct forces support, include gasoline, tires, uniforms, medicines, rations, and similar items which all military forces consume every day.

For the fiscal year 1956 I propose that direct forces support be provided to only a few selected countries. These countries, primarily in Asia, are ones where our mutual security requires the maintenance of active forces larger than those which these countries could support from their own resources. In the fiscal year 1956 direct forces support for the armed forces of the Republic of Korea, which was formerly provided for in the Department of Defense budget, will be covered for the first time by the mutual security program.

Direct forces support will continue to be a significant part of the mutual security program for so long as the security of the free world requires that large military forces be maintained in Asia and the Near East. I recommend 630 million dollars of new obligational authority under proposed legislation for this purpose. Expenditures for this program from existing appropriations and from the proposed legislation are estimated at 600 million dollars in the fiscal year 1956, as compared with 550 million dollars in the fiscal year 1955.

INTERNATIONAL AFFAIRS AND FINANCE

During the past year the free world, despite some setbacks, has made heartening progress in building the strength and unity which are so important to our security.   In this hemisphere, in Europe, Asia, and Africa, the free nations acted together to strengthen their defenses against international communism, to widen economic cooperation, and to settle long standing disputes which have undermined free world unity.   In these developments the United States has played a vital role.

My program for the coming year is designed to consolidate these gains and to make further progress.   Particular emphasis will be laid on further strengthening the foreign service organization of the Department of State which carries the burden of foreign policy leadership and negotiations.   We are likewise placing emphasis on revision of our several international programs to give appropriate attention to the important trouble spots around the world today.

My budget recommendations for international affairs and finance reflect a coordinated plan for the conduct of foreign affairs, for the expansion of trade and investment, for mutual security economic assistance, and for foreign information.   Total net budget expenditures for the fiscal year 1956 are estimated at 1.3 billion dollars, as compared with 1.4 billion dollars for the current year.

Recommended new authority to incur obligations in the fiscal year 1956 amounts to 1.9 billion dollars, 291 million dollars more than for 1955.   Major items of this increase in new obligational authority result from increased emphasis on defense support and development assistance in Asia and reimbursement of the Commodity Credit Corporation for emergency assistance in the form of commodities furnished in previous years.

INTERNATIONAL AFFAIRS AND FINANCE

[Fiscal years. In millions]

| Program or agency | Expenditures | | | Recommended new obligational authority for 1956 |
	1954 actual	1955 estimated	1956 estimated	
Gross expenditures:				
Economic and technical development:				
International investment activities:				
International Finance Corporation (proposed legislation)...	....	....	$35	$35
Export-Import Bank (including Reconstruction Finance Corporation liquidation)........	$534	$334	335	....
Investment guaranties.........	4	6	7	....
Mutual security program (nonmilitary):				
Defense support and development assistance.............				
Technical cooperation........	1,241	1,075	725	....
Refugee and other aid (contributions to international agencies)				
Proposed legislation...........	....	....	300	1,500
Civil assistance programs, Department of Defense..............	87	30	6	3
Emergency commodity assistance, Department of Agriculture.....	74	124	177	[1] 79
Other assistance.................	3	6	9	9
Other refugee activities (Department of State)...............	1	9	15	16
Foreign information and exchange activities:				
United States Information Agency.	71	77	86	88
Department of State.............	20	18	21	22
Emergency fund for international affairs........................	....	4	1	....
Conduct of foreign affairs (Department of State and other)........	130	116	124	123
Total........................	2,166	1,800	1,841	[2] 1,876
Deduct applicable receipts:				
Export-Import Bank..............	434	376	425	....
Reconstruction Finance Corporation	9	....	....	....
Investment guaranties..............	2	4	4	....
Commodity Credit Corporation....	....	....	79	....
Net budget expenditures..............	1,720	1,420	1,332	....

[1] Appropriation to reimburse the Commodity Credit Corporation for commodity assistance provided in previous years.

[2] Compares with new obligational authority of $1,268 million in 1954 and $1,585 million in 1955.

International investment activities.—In my recent special message on foreign economic policy, I made recommendations which will enable us to expand foreign trade and investment. As a further step in providing capital to underdeveloped areas through stimulating private investment, the United States is participating with other members of the International Bank for Reconstruction and Development in working out proposals for an International Finance Corporation. Such a corporation, although it could not purchase stock, could provide venture capital by making special types of loans without government guaranties to private enterprises in less developed countries. This budget includes 35 million dollars as the United States' share of the corporation's capital of 100 million dollars.

Moreover, in keeping with legislation approved last year, the Export-Import Bank estimates an increase in direct loans and guaranties of private loans from 460 million dollars in the fiscal year 1955 to 665 million dollars in 1956. It is expected that a significant part of this increase will consist of guaranties of private loans which are not included in gross budget expenditures. New direct loans are expected to be authorized in the amount of 403 million dollars. The collections on old loans, including lend-lease and postwar reconstruction credits in Europe, will exceed disbursements against new direct loans, so that a net receipt of 90 million dollars to the Treasury is estimated in 1956.

Defense support and development assistance.—We anticipate that the trade and investment policies outlined above, and the marked advance in economic strength of many foreign countries over the past 2 years, will increasingly enable us to confine direct Government assistance for defense support and economic development abroad generally to two types of situations, both of which are related intimately to our own future security.

In the first place, we will find it necessary for some time to provide defense support to certain countries which have undertaken a military effort beyond the capacity of their own economies to support. This defense support includes consumption goods and capital equipment to support the general economy, as contrasted with direct forces support which provides assistance to the military forces of the country. In the second place, our national interest will require direct assistance to certain less developed countries where a rate of economic progress which would be impossible without such assistance is essential to their becoming and remaining strong and healthy members of the community of free nations capable of resisting Communist penetration and subversion.

Employment, production, and foreign exchange reserves in free European countries are generally increasing. Most of these countries can now strengthen their military establishments and at the same time improve their living standards without further United States defense support. In the fiscal year 1955, defense support has been limited to very few countries, and a similar situation is expected to prevail in 1956.

Latin America, an area with which we have well-established trade and investment relations, has a great need for capital for economic development. Nevertheless, if Latin American countries follow a policy of encouraging private investment, domestic and foreign, they should be able to continue to raise the capital needed for further economic growth. In those cases in which private or International Bank resources are not available or not appropriate for financing sound projects, the Export-Import Bank will welcome applications for loans. The new International Finance Corporation, when organized, can also help provide capital. Grants in Latin America have been necessary only in special situations such as in Bolivia and Guatemala.

In Asia, active warfare has only recently ceased and the free countries of this continent continue to face the threat of Communist subversion and external aggresssion. We therefore have been furnishing and propose to continue to furnish defense support to several countries including Korea, Formosa, Vietnam, Laos, and Cambodia. Some assistance in economic development has been extended to India.

Unless such support is provided, we may expect economic deterioration and dangerous reductions in the military defenses of the free world. Moreover, without such assistance, these countries, most of which border on Russia and Communist China, will not achieve the economic progress which is necessary to meet the threat of Communist subversion. The loss of northern Vietnam makes this support more imperative than ever.

In the Middle East and Africa, we have provided some grant and loan assistance to promote economic development and political stability, and will request funds to continue this type of assistance in the fiscal year 1956. This assistance has gone to Iran, Israel, Lebanon, Jordan, Egypt, and Libya.

My budget proposals for the mutual security program were developed on the assumption that all requirements for that program will be met from appropriations made for that purpose. Therefore if it becomes desirable to utilize foreign currencies accruing from sales of surplus agricultural commodities made under the Agricultural Trade Development and Assistance Act for mutual security purposes, mutual security appropriations will be used to reimburse the Commodity Credit Corporation for currencies so utilized.

Technical cooperation.—Over recent years, technical cooperation has become a continuing part of United States policy toward the rest of the world. American experts help the people in foreign countries, and foreign technicians come to the United States to observe our methods. As a result, millions of people are learning how to produce more food, to improve health and educational standards, and to operate modern industries more effectively. Agreements for technical cooperation are in effect in 68 countries and territories in Latin America, Asia, the Near East, and Africa.

In addition to these bilateral efforts, we have contributed to meeting the total cost of the United Nations technical assistance program, for which experts and financial contributions come from many nations. I am proposing new obligational authority to cover the total proposed contributions of the United States to this program for both calendar years 1955 and 1956.

Refugee and other foreign relief.—The 1953 Refugee Relief Act provides for the admission of 214,000 people beyond regular immigration quotas before December 31, 1956. Approximately 17,000 visas have been granted to date. Sufficient progress has been made on concluding agreements with other countries, organizing staff abroad, and completing arrangements with voluntary agencies in the United States to justify the expectation that the program can be completed in accordance with the provisions of the act. To accomplish this, I recommend an increase for the Department of State appropriation for the fiscal year 1956, and a supplemental appropriation for 1955.

I am also recommending continued United States support of those programs and international agencies through which funds have been made available for relief, rehabilitation, and resettlement of escapees, refugees, and other special groups. These agencies include the Intergovernmental Committee for European Migration, and the United Nations agencies for Palestine refugees, and for emergency aid to children. In addition, this budget makes provision for a small contribution to help the United Nations High Commissioner for Refugees take refugees out of camps and make them part of the local communities.

Foreign information and exchange activities.—The United States Information Agency has done a capable job of redirecting its work and is increasingly effective. It is carrying out its mission in 79 countries through local radio, press, films, and information centers. Its worldwide radio broadcasting is increasingly directed to the countries beyond the Iron Curtain. But the Soviet efforts to divide the United States from other nations of the free world by twisting our motives, as well as its efforts to sow fear and distrust, are mounting in tempo in many areas of the world. I believe it is of the highest importance that our program for telling the truth to peoples of other nations be stepped up to meet the needs of our foreign policy.

The Department of State's educational exchange program is primarily directed toward the exchange of educators, newsmen, labor and management officials, students and others who influence the formation of public opinion abroad. The sharing of ideas strengthens the community of interest so vital to our relations with other people. I recommend that these exchanges be increased, particularly with underdeveloped areas.

Conduct of foreign affairs.—A prerequisite to the achievement of all our international affairs and finance programs is dynamic, positive, and dedicated leadership by the Department of State.

This budget recognizes the essentiality of a stronger and better trained career corps of foreign service officers. We should also provide more adequate facilities for carrying out statutory consular functions. Finally, more comprehensive commercial, labor, and other economic data are necessary to assist American businessmen to increase their foreign investment and trade.

As a result of the recommendations of the Committee on Government Operations of the House of Representatives and a committee of distinguished citizens, we are starting a series of improvements in the foreign service. The foreign service will be expanded to cover departmental positions; officers will be rotated more regularly between United States and foreign posts; and training will be improved. Appropriations to initiate these reforms are recommended.

VETERANS' SERVICES AND BENEFITS

Expenditures for veterans' programs are now rising—reversing the decline from the peak in 1947 as World War II veterans completed their readjustment to civilian life. In the fiscal year 1956, the Federal Government will spend an estimated 4.6 billion dollars for a wide variety of aids to veterans, an increase of 9 percent over the actual outlays in 1954 and 5 percent over 1955. This increase will occur notwithstanding the savings made through improved management of the Veterans Administration, and the long-run outlook under present laws is for continued large increases in payments to veterans.

Three main factors account for this outlook. First, World War II, the Korean conflict, and large defense requirements have increased the present and potential veteran population tremendously. Twenty-one million veterans are now in civilian life, 5 times the number before World War II. An additional 3 million men and women now in the Armed Forces have acquired rights to wartime veterans' benefits by serving during the Korean emergency.

Second, the 3 million veterans of World War I are reaching age 65 and are qualifying for pensions in large numbers. A service-incurred disability is not required for these benefits.

Third, benefits for veterans who served during wartime or an emergency have been increased in scope and liberality. Last year, laws were enacted which will add more than 170 million dollars in estimated expenditures for veterans' benefits for the fiscal year 1956, principally for increased pension and compensation payments.

These facts require sober consideration. Our Government has a responsibility to provide generous assistance to those who have special needs arising from service in the Armed Forces, particularly war service. We must make sure that benefits which are provided to veterans and their survivors are timely and reach those who need them most. At the same time, we must bear in mind that Government policies designed to assist in the maintenance of a prosperous economy and to support social security, health, and other humanitarian programs are all of value to veterans as well as to other people. Since more than two-fifths of all adult males are entitled to veterans' benefits, expenditures for veterans are a budgetary problem of major interest to the whole population.

Our veterans' pension and compensation laws, in particular, are in need of constructive reconsideration. The non-service-connected pension system dates back to the Revolutionary War, and its principles require reexamination in the light of recent developments, including the nearly universal coverage of the old-age and survivors insurance system. The overall system of statutes and regulations governing eligibility and payment rates for service-connected compensation has not had a fundamental review for many years. It also needs to be reappraised in the light of the great improvement in medical and rehabilitation techniques and the actual economic situation of the many beneficiaries.

I am therefore appointing a Commission on Veterans' Pensions to study the entire structure, scope, and philosophy of our veterans' pension and compensation laws in relation to each other and to other Government programs. This budget includes 300,000 dollars for the continuation of the work of this Commission in the fiscal year 1956.

An especially complex and difficult problem exists in the field of survivor benefits for military personnel and veterans, where 4 different agencies now provide 5 major benefits. This problem has received extensive attention within the executive branch and from the Select Committee on Survivor Benefits of the House of Representatives. I hope that our mutual efforts will result in enactment of adequate and improved programs which will include full coverage for military personnel under our basic old-age and survivors insurance program and will properly relate benefits provided military personnel to those for veterans.

I have recently issued a proclamation terminating accrual of eligibility after January 31, 1955, for various benefits authorized for veterans who served during the Korean conflict. Few of those discharged during the fiscal year 1956 will be materially affected by this action. Studies will be undertaken to determine the need for measures to ease the readjustment to civilian life of men required to enter the Armed Forces for 2 years of service.

VETERANS' SERVICES AND BENEFITS

[Fiscal years. In millions]

Program or agency	Expenditures			Recommended new obligational authority for 1956
	1954 actual	1955 estimated	1956 estimated	
Gross expenditures:				
Readjustment benefits:				
Education and training..........	$546	$602	$587	$587
Loan guaranty and other benefits (Veterans Administration)......	76	38	40	40
Unemployment compensation (Department of Labor)............	82	131	150	150
Compensation and pensions........	2,482	2,679	2,800	2,800
Insurance and servicemen's indemnities...............	104	72	135	127
Hospital and medical care:				
Current expenses...............	724	688	710	716
Hospital construction...........	59	48	60	20
Other services and administration (Veterans Administration and other)........................	217	211	202	173
Total.....................	4,289	4,468	4,684	[1] 4,615
Deduct applicable receipts:				
Insurance programs (Veterans Administration)...................	4	9	16	....
Other services and administration (Veterans Administration, primarily canteen services)...........	29	28	29	....
Net budget expenditures.............	4,256	4,431	4,640	....

[1] Compares with new obligational authority of 4,272 million dollars in 1954 and 4,285 million dollars in 1955.

Readjustment benefits.—The Veterans' Readjustment Assistance Act of 1952 authorizes education and training, loan guaranty, and unemployment compensation benefits for veterans who served during the Korean conflict. Many World War II veterans are still eligible for loan guaranty benefits and some are still completing their education and training under the original "GI bill." In addition, special vocational rehabilitation aid is provided under other laws for veterans of both conflicts who were disabled in service.

The total estimated expenditures of 777 million dollars for all readjustment benefits in the fiscal year 1956 will be at about the same level as in the current year, and 10 percent higher than in 1954. The proportion of total readjustment benefits going to veterans of the Korean conflict has been increasing, and is expected to exceed 90 percent in the fiscal year 1956.

An average of 516,000 trainees is expected in the school, job, and farm training courses during the fiscal year 1956. One out of each 4 of the 4.7 million veterans eligible for these Korean conflict benefits will have participated in education or training by the end of the fiscal year 1956. The reservoir of potential enrollees is still large, considering that 1 out of each 2 World War II veterans received such benefits.

Budget expenditures under the loan guaranty program have declined sharply since the fiscal year 1954 because payments for the first year of interest on mortgages have ceased. It is expected that 467,000 loans totaling 5 billion dollars will be insured or guaranteed during the fiscal year 1956. Almost all of these loans will be for housing. The estimated 40 million dollars of expenditures in this category for 1956 includes 25 million dollars for acquisition of properties and losses on defaulted guaranteed loans. The other 15 million dollars is for tuition and supplies in the vocational rehabilitation program and grants of up to 10,000 dollars each for special housing for certain severely disabled veterans. Expenditures for the Veterans Administration direct housing loan program under present law and its proposed extension are included among aids for private housing in the commerce and manpower section of this message.

Federal unemployment compensation benefits of 26 dollars a week for a maximum of 26 weeks are payable through State agencies to veterans of the Korean conflict. Where the veteran who is insured under a State unemployment compensation system receives lower benefits from that system, the United States Department of Labor supplements the State benefit. Expenditures for this purpose are increasing as the number of eligible veterans rises.

In the fiscal year 1956 an estimated weekly average of 138,000 veterans will receive unemployment benefits, wholly or partly financed by the Federal Government.

These unemployment benefits were intended to assist veterans of the Korean conflict during their transitional period immediately following separation from military service. Possibly by inadvertence, the present provisions were so written that a veteran of the Korean conflict may apply for these benefits at any time up to January 31, 1960, no matter how many years have passed since his discharge. I recommend that the law be amended to limit the time for filing claims to 3 years after separation or enactment of the amendment, whichever is later.

Compensation and pensions.—The upward trend in total expenditures for veterans results mainly from the rise in compensation and pensions. Expenditures for this purpose are estimated to increase more than 300 million dollars from the fiscal year 1954 to 1956, to a total of 2.8 billion dollars. They will equal more than half of all payments from the old-age and survivors insurance system. On the basis of present laws and veteran population, the present annual rate of expenditures for veterans' pensions and compensation is expected to double in 3 or 4 decades.

The estimated expenditures of 2.8 billion dollars include 1.9 billion dollars in payments to nearly 2,486,000 families and veterans for death or disability resulting from service, and 859 million dollars for pension payments in 1,046,000 cases where death or disability was not connected with military service. During the fiscal year 1954, an average of 2,412,000 cases received about 1.7 billion dollars in death and disability compensation benefits, and 716 million dollars in pensions were paid in 902,000 cases. The expenditures for 1956 also include 17 million dollars for 110,000 burial awards and 26 million dollars in subsistence payments to disabled veterans during their vocational rehabilitation.

Insurance and servicemen's indemnities.—Payments for insurance and indemnity benefits go to families of personnel who die in military service. The increase in expenditures in the fiscal year 1956 reflects (1) a steady increase in indemnity benefits, and (2) an unusual increase in insurance expenditures resulting from recently declared deaths of servicemen who were previously reported missing during the hostilities in Korea.

Indemnity benefits of $92.90 a month are paid for 120 months to the family of each serviceman who dies while on active military service or within 120 days after separation. The benefits are reduced proportionately if the serviceman has any Veterans Administration insurance. Payments of 42 million dollars estimated for the fiscal year 1956 are 79 percent higher than in 1954.

While no new national service life insurance or United States Government life insurance has been issued since 1951, previously issued policies continue in force. Where deaths are caused by the hazards of war, or occur during military service while premiums have been waived, the Government reimburses the insurance trust funds for losses. The Government also pays benefits directly to certain policyholders. Budget expenditures for insurance losses are estimated at 93 million dollars in the fiscal year 1956, somewhat more than in 1954 and more than double the amount in 1955.

Hospital and medical care.—A rising patient load in the veterans' hospital and medical program will result in an increase in current expenses for the fiscal year 1956. The average number of patients in Veterans Administration and contract hospitals is expected to rise 4 percent above the 1955 level to 114,500. While the proportion of service-connected cases is slowly increasing as more veterans of the Korean conflict are treated, it is estimated that more than two-thirds of the expenditures in 1956 will still be for patients hospitalized or treated for ailments not connected with military service. The number of persons in Veterans Administration and State homes is estimated to be 25,700 in the fiscal year 1956. The workload for out-patient care to service-incurred dental and medical cases is expected to be about 14 percent below that in 1954, with a total of 2,340,000 examinations and treatments in 1956. About four-fifths of the estimated average employment of 171,000 in the Veterans Administration during the fiscal year 1956 will be in the hospital and medical programs.

The budget includes recommended new authority to incur obligations of 20 million dollars for construction and improvements at Veterans Administration facilities. Most of this is for modernization of existing structures. Expenditures for construction and improvements in the fiscal year 1956 are estimated at 60 million dollars, approximately the same amount as in 1954 and somewhat higher than in 1955. Expenditures will be greater than the recommended new appropriations because funds for three large new hospitals to be built in 1956 were appropriated in previous years.

Other services and administration.—The general operating expenses of the Veterans Administration are estimated to decline further in the fiscal year 1956, reflecting declining workloads in some parts of this agency, especially in the insurance programs, and better organization and management throughout the agency. Average employment in nonmedical activities in 1956 is estimated at 34,500, or 13 percent below the 1954 level.

Trust funds.—Nearly 6 million national service life insurance and United States Government life insurance policies, which provide more than 40 billion dollars of protection, continue in force. About 1 million of these policies are held by personnel still in the Armed Forces, largely on a waiver-of-premium basis. The remainder are held by veterans who pay premiums. As the special dividend payments to the policyholders declared in 1954 and earlier years are completed, the receipts of the insurance trust accounts begin to exceed their disbursements. The transactions in these, as well as other, trust funds are not included in the budget totals.

VETERANS' LIFE INSURANCE FUNDS

(Trust funds)

[Fiscal years. In millions]

Item	1954 actual	1955 estimated	1956 estimated
Balance in funds at start of year............	$6,613	$6,541	$6,574
Receipts:			
Transfers from general and special accounts.	72	31	81
Interest on investments..................	200	208	209
Premiums and other....................	426	414	406
Total............................	697	652	696
Expenditures:			
Dividends to policyholders..............	267	174	160
Benefits and other.....................	503	446	444
Total............................	769	620	604
Net accumulation (+) or withdrawal (−)	−72	+33	+92
Balance in funds at close of year............	6,541	6,574	6,665

WELFARE, HEALTH, AND EDUCATION

Major advances have been made in the past year in the fields of social security, health, and education, pursuant to recommendations which I made to the Congress. We have demonstrated that the well-being of our people can be strengthened without yielding to the dangers of centralized power in the Federal Government, and we shall continue firmly to resist any project which would seem to us to involve such dangers. We have found ways to provide greater human security and social opportunity, while restricting the Federal Government's role to that of assisting private action and State and local responsibility with research and technical assistance, social insurance, and grants-in-aid. We believe that these gains can be continued through cooperative action among all levels of American government together with private participation.

In the last Congress, old-age and survivors insurance was extended to 10 million more persons and benefits were improved. Vocational rehabilitation grants to the States have been stepped up toward the objective for 1959 of helping 200,000 people a year to rehabilitate themselves. We have undertaken to aid the construction of medical diagnostic and treatment centers, rehabilitation facilities, nursing homes, and chronic disease hospitals, as well as general hospitals.

To assist in the search for solution of the Nation's serious school problems, the White House Conference on Education was authorized. The Office of Education has been strengthened. Assistance to schools especially affected by Federal activities was extended.

In this budget, I recommend increased appropriations for certain activities, including health research and the training of health personnel, and basic scientific research. I am also proposing new legislation to help fill gaps in present programs for health care, public assistance, and old-age and survivors insurance, and to obtain better coordination among them. Estimates for new legislation include 3 million dollars for grants-in-aid to enable State, local, and private agencies to deal more effectively with juvenile delinquency. I am recommending the enactment of legislation to establish an Advisory Commission on Fine Arts within the Department of Health, Education, and Welfare, to provide recognition of the importance of the further development of our cultural heritage.

Budget expenditures for welfare, health, and education, including proposed legislation, are estimated at 2.3 billion dollars in the fiscal year 1956, a decrease of 4 million dollars from 1955. These figures do not include expenditures for health, education, and research which are classified among veterans' benefits or in the military, atomic energy, and other programs in other sections of the budget.

WELFARE, HEALTH, AND EDUCATION

[Fiscal years. In millions]

Program or agency	Budget expenditures (net)			Recommended new obligational authority for 1956
	1954 actual	1955 estimated	1956 estimated	
Promotion of public health:				
Present programs	$288	$292	$321	$335
Proposed legislation			17	52
Public assistance:				
Present program	1,439	1,447	1,402	1,402
Proposed legislation			20	20
Other welfare aids and services:				
School lunch program	84	84	68	68
Vocational rehabilitation	24	29	43	43
Indian health, education, and welfare	49	59	76	80
Other	106	77	80	83
Promotion of education:				
Assistance for schools in federally affected areas	184	224	173	89
Vocational education	25	31	31	31
Other educational aids	25	30	33	30
General-purpose research:				
National Science Foundation	6	10	21	31
Department of Commerce	17	35	27	27
Total	2,248	2,316	2,312	[1] 2,289

[1] Compares with new obligational authority of 2,190 million dollars in 1954 and 2,310 million dollars in 1955.

Promotion of public health.—This budget includes funds necessary to assist an expansion of existing services and initiate appropriate new measures which will carry out the objectives of a coordinated health program which I shall outline shortly in a special message to the Congress.

Under existing legislation, budget expenditures for public health are estimated at 321 million dollars in the fiscal year 1956. The principal expenditures are for grants to States for construction of hospitals and other health facilities, public health services, maternal and child health, and the control of various diseases; for research programs, including grants to universities and medical schools; and for operation of Public Health Service hospitals.

Significant items in the 29-million-dollar increase of expenditures over 1955 are for expansion of the research and training activities of the National Institutes of Health, including special emphasis on mental health; construction of more health facilities; an intensified attack on problems of air and water pollution; and strengthened enforcement of the food and drug laws.

I am recommending elsewhere in this message that the Atomic Energy Commission be authorized to build a new medical research center containing a nuclear reactor designed specifically for medical research and therapy. This will be a significant addition to the Nation's facilities for basic research in the field of health.

The new health legislation which I shall recommend will require budget expenditures of approximately 37 million dollars in the fiscal year 1956.

This legislation includes health reinsurance—the best method yet proposed for encouraging adequate health insurance coverage for our people. It includes also the part-year cost of a program of grants-in-aid for medical care for public assistance recipients, shown in the table under proposed legislation for public assistance. Other measures in the health program are designed to foster construction of more adequate medical facilities, training of nurses and other necessary medical personnel, and general improvement of key services in the States and local communities.

Public assistance.—The recent expansion of old-age and survivors insurance should gradually reduce the need for public assistance, with a consequent saving to all levels of Government in budget outlays for this purpose.

Further savings will result over the long run from amendments to public assistance legislation which I am recommending. The present grant-in-aid formula requires the Federal Government to pay each State 20 dollars of the first 25 dollars of average monthly old-age assistance benefits, and half of the next 30 dollars for any recipient. One of the proposed amendments would modify the public assistance law so that Federal grants can be adjusted downward to reflect gradually, by application to new cases, the number of old-age and survivor insurance beneficiaries who also need supplementary old-age assistance. By limiting to 50 percent the Federal share of old-age assistance for these future recipients of both types of benefits, this amendment would result in a more equitable sharing of costs between the State and Federal governments. The other amendment would encourage States to help needy individuals to become self-supporting or to care for themselves at home.

Other welfare aids and services.—Expenditures of 84 million dollars from the school lunch appropriation in the fiscal years 1954 and 1955 include about 67 million dollars for cash payments to States and nearly all of the rest is for commodities. The appropriation recommended for 1956 covers only the cash payments to the States and the costs of administration. In addition, contributions of surplus commodities, financed mainly from a permanent appropriation to the Department of Agriculture for this purpose, are expected to continue at a high level, so that the combined total of Federal cash payments and food donations will remain approximately the same in 1956 as in 1955. Moreover, the new school milk program authorized by the Agricultural Act of 1954 provides 50 million dollars a year in the fiscal years 1955 and 1956 to encourage increased consumption of milk by schoolchildren. Taken together, these various aids will make Federal support of the overall school lunch program the largest in our history. The expenditures for surplus commodities and school milk are classified under agriculture and agricultural resources.

This budget fully supports the enlarged vocational rehabilitation program enacted last year and will make possible the rehabilitation of 95,000 people in the fiscal year 1956.

The Congress last year provided for the transfer of Indian health services from the Department of the Interior to the Department of Health, Education, and Welfare, where they can be administered with other health programs. The appropriations recommended for the fiscal year 1956 will provide improved medical care for our Indian population.

Social insurance and retirement trust funds.—The Federal Government acts as trustee of three large, publicly sponsored retirement and insurance programs—old-age and survivors insurance, railroad retirement, and Federal employees' retirement. Contributions under these programs, including Federal payments, are collected in the respective trust funds and maintained separately from the budget accounts of the Government.

In connection with old-age and survivors insurance, I am recommending two legislative measures. One is the coordination of income and old-age insurance tax collection procedures to make reporting easier for wage earners and employers and at the same time to reduce Government costs for collecting taxes and paying benefits. The second is extension of this insurance to military personnel and to those Federal civilian personnel not now covered, as the basic part of improved systems of survivorship, disability, and retirement protection, with existing staff retirement systems retained as independent and separate entities. The military retirement pay system should remain unchanged. Certain adjustments in the present civilian personnel retirement systems will be needed.

Promotion of education.—We are all aware that our schools are passing through a period of extraordinary stress. School-age population is increasing faster than classroom space has been enlarged and qualified teachers recruited. In some communities, the available fiscal resources have been strained severely by efforts to meet these needs; in too many States and school districts, the financial support given to schools has not kept pace with recent increases in taxable resources.

The national problem is to find means of overcoming these difficulties within the present framework of responsibilities. In our system of government, the States and their subdivisions have

SOCIAL INSURANCE AND RETIREMENT FUNDS

(Trust funds)

[Fiscal years.   In millions]

Fund and item	1954 actual	1955 estimated	1956 estimated
Federal old-age and survivors insurance trust fund:			
Balance in fund at start of year................	$18,363	$20,040	$21,356
Receipts:			
Appropriation from general receipts...........	4,537	5,190	6,175
Deposits by States.........................	92	120	130
Interest and other.........................	451	464	494
Payments of benefits, construction and administrative expenses, and tax refunds..............	−3,405	−4,459	−4,968
Net accumulation.........................	1,675	1,315	1,831
Balance in fund at close of year................	20,040	21,356	23,187
Railroad retirement fund:			
Balance in fund at start of year................	3,183	3,418	3,538
Receipts:			
Appropriation from general receipts...........	638	600	625
Interest on investments......................	99	102	106
Payments of benefits, salaries, and expenses......	−502	−581	−590
Net accumulation.........................	235	121	141
Balance in fund at close of year................	3,418	3,538	3,679
Federal employees' retirement funds (Civil Service and Foreign Service):			
Balance in funds at start of year................	5,652	5,932	6,196
Receipts:			
Employee contributions.....................	430	444	502
Interest..................................	226	234	222
Transfer from budget accounts and other:			
Present law............................	35	34	5
Proposed legislation.....................	....	....	216
Payments of annuities and refunds, and expenses..	−411	−447	−489
Net accumulation.........................	280	265	456
Balance in funds at close of year...............	5,932	6,196	6,652

146

the privilege and the responsibility of providing free public education. The role of the Federal Government has wisely been confined to encouragement and special assistance. I am confident that the overwhelming majority of our people agree that there should be no dilution of that State and local responsibility.

I have called a White House conference this fall of representatives from all the States. Some local and State conferences of citizens and professional educators have already been held in preparation for this national assembly. Others will meet this spring and summer. These meetings will highlight possible long-range solutions to the problems and will place in better perspective the obligations and opportunities of the respective levels of government.

Concurrently, without impairment in any way of State, local, community, and family responsibility, the Federal Government should serve as an effective catalyst in dealing with the problem of classroom shortages. I shall send to the Congress, in February, a special message presenting an affirmative program.

The major Federal expenditure for promotion of education consists of grants to aid school construction and operation in districts where enrollment has grown significantly because of Federal operations. Last year, the Congress extended the temporary program of aid for construction for 2 years. To finance this extension, I am recommending an appropriation of an additional 70 million dollars for the current fiscal year and 24 million dollars for 1956.

The Congress also delayed a requirement that these school districts absorb a greater proportion of the operating costs resulting from increased enrollments. Primarily for this reason, a supplemental appropriation of 19 million dollars will be needed this year. In the fiscal year 1956, greater absorption of the increased enrollments by the local districts will reduce the assistance payments for operations 6 million dollars below 1955, to a total now estimated at 70 million dollars.

The budget recommendations provide for continuing the increase in vocational education grants which was enacted for 1955, and will permit the Office of Education to initiate a program of cooperative research as authorized by the last Congress.

General-purpose research.—Despite our tremendous technological strides in recent years, our national interest requires that we support a strong program of basic research and that we train a greater number of highly qualified scientists and engineers. Accordingly, this budget recommends increased National Science Foundation grants for basic research and for training more graduate students, college instructors, and high school science teachers. It includes also the remaining necessary financial support for United States participation in the International Geophysical Year, a worldwide scientific undertaking which will yield great long-range benefits to this country.

The budget estimates for the Department of Commerce include substantial expansion in the general scientific and technological work of the National Bureau of Standards as recommended by a committee of outstanding scientists.

Another aspect of general-purpose research is the statistical work of the Census Bureau. We do not have all the statistical information required in our dynamic economy. I am therefore recommending a governmentwide effort to improve statistics in those areas where our work has been most handicapped by incomplete information. Increases in appropriations are recommended for the Census Bureau for statistics on the labor force and for an intercensal survey on housing. At the same time, in other parts of the budget, increases are recommended for statistics on agriculture, production, construction, employment, and finance.

AGRICULTURE AND AGRICULTURAL RESOURCES

The basic agricultural legislation which I recommended and which the Congress enacted last year will help to promote a stable, prosperous, and free agriculture. By helping farmers solve many of their own problems we shall make possible reduced reliance on Government intervention such as production controls, and on Government spending for support of farm income. The Agricultural Act of 1954 and the Agricultural Trade Development and Assistance Act will facilitate readjustment of farm production, expansion of agricultural exports, and stimulation of domestic consumption of farm products. The Watershed Protection and Flood Prevention Act of 1954 provides a sound basis for Federal partnership with States and local groups in upstream flood prevention and soil and water conservation. The Farmers' Home Administration was given expanded authority to make loans for soil and water conservation, and a basis was provided for greater participation of private lenders in the financing of this and other loan programs.

My recommendations for agricultural programs in this budget will carry forward the broad objectives reflected in this new legislation. They will also continue the steps taken last year to place greater emphasis on research and educational activities. I have confidence in the ability and willingness of farmers to deal with many of their economic problems if given help through expanded agricultural research and advice in making use of the research results.

Gross expenditures for agriculture and agricultural resources in the fiscal year 1956 are estimated at 7.6 billion dollars. Receipts, estimated at about 5.4 billion dollars, consist mainly of collections on loans and sales of commodities. Net budget expenditures are estimated at 2.3 billion dollars in the fiscal year 1956, which is 871 million dollars less than estimated for 1955 and 298 million dollars less than in 1954. The reduction in net budget expenditures for 1956 is primarily due to anticipated smaller outlays for farm price supports.

New authority to incur obligations recommended for the fiscal year 1956 is 1.3 billion dollars, as compared with 2.6 billion dollars in 1955 and 4 billion dollars in 1954. The reduction in 1956 is accounted for almost entirely by the Commodity Credit Corporation. The Corporation's present borrowing authority, which was increased from 6.75 billion dollars to 10 billion dollars during the fiscal years 1954 and 1955, is now expected to be adequate to finance price support activities in the fiscal year 1956.

Stabilization of farm prices and farm income.—Establishment of the principle of flexible supports and provision for a gradual shift to modernized parity for the basic agricultural commodities in the legislation enacted last year will encourage farmers to adjust their production to realistic market prices in keeping with the current needs of the economy. Since the transition to the new basis for price supports will be gradual, the benefits for the agricultural economy and for the Nation will not be fully realized for several years.

Based on the best information now available, gross price support expenditures in the fiscal year 1956 are estimated at 4.2 billion dollars, 1.5 billion dollars less than the amount estimated for 1955. These gross expenditures do not represent losses; rather they are outlays for loans and commodities to be acquired during the year, and for redemption of certificates of interest in commodity loans previously sold to private lenders. A substantial part of these outlays will be recovered from collections on loans and sales of commodities in later periods. Receipts from commodity sales and collections on loans in 1956 are estimated at 3.2 billion dollars, resulting in net budget expenditures of 968 million dollars.

The decline in net price support expenditures anticipated in the budget will be brought about by two major factors. First, continuation of acreage restrictions, particularly on 1955 crop year cotton and wheat, and lower support levels on some commodities are expected to result in a lower volume of price support loans. Second, receipts from sales of such commodities as cotton, corn, and wool are expected to increase as our efforts to find new and expanded markets for agricultural products begin to show results. These factors will be offset in part by increased Commodity Credit

Agriculture and Agricultural Resources

[Fiscal years. In millions]

Program or agency	Gross expenditures 1954 actual	Gross expenditures 1955 estimated	Gross expenditures 1956 estimated	Net expenditures 1954 actual	Net expenditures 1955 estimated	Net expenditures 1956 estimated	Recommended new obligational authority for 1956
Stabilization of farm prices and farm income:							
Price support, supply, and purchase programs (CCC)	$4,220	$5,705	$4,176	$1,333	$1,934	$968	$2
International Wheat Agreement	59	106	142	59	106	84	57
Removal of surplus agricultural commodities	178	113	180	178	113	180	165
Sugar Act	66	61	61	66	61	61	62
Federal crop insurance	39	36	34	11	12	3	6
Agricultural adjustment programs	41	41	39	41	41	39	39
Financing farm ownership and operation:							
Farm Credit Administration	1,817	1,885	1,988	−74	22	37	28
Farmers' Home Administration [1]	191	178	172	191	178	172	172
Disaster loans and emergency feed	255	101	88	139	16	−39	42
Financing rural electrification and rural telephones [1]	217	217	233	217	217	233	238
Agricultural land and water resources:							
Agricultural conservation program	201	233	255	183	173	246	216
Soil Conservation Service, flood prevention and other	61	76	74	61	76	74	75
Research and other agricultural services	150	180	206	150	180	200	186
Total	7,497	8,934	7,647	2,557	3,130	2,259	[2] 1,288

[1] Net expenditures for the Farmers' Home Administration and for rural electrification and telephone loans do not reflect loan collections, since these collections go directly into miscellaneous receipts of the Treasury. In 1956, these collections are estimated at 152 million dollars and 112 million dollars, respectively.

[2] Compares with new obligational authority of 4,010 million dollars in 1954 and 2,630 million dollars in 1955.

Corporation expenditures to retire certificates of interest in prior-year crop loans sold to banks and private lenders, because a substantially smaller volume of new commodity loans will be available in 1956 than in 1955 to serve as a basis for certificates of interest. Also, funds of the Corporation will be used to provide for increased milk consumption by schoolchildren and members of the Armed Forces during 1955 and 1956 when supplies of dairy products are expected to be plentiful.

Expenditures in 1956 under the International Wheat Agreement are estimated to be lower than in 1955, but higher than in 1954. In the fiscal year 1954 a total of 119 million bushels of wheat was exported under this program. The average amount paid by the Government to cover the difference between the domestic price and the Wheat Agreement price was 48 cents per bushel. Larger exports under this program are expected in both 1955 and 1956.

In addition to exports under the Wheat Agreement, the Commodity Credit Corporation has offered to sell wheat in limited quantities for export at competitive world prices. Net costs to the Corporation of these additional exports in 1954 were 26 million dollars and are estimated at 59 million dollars in each of the fiscal years 1955 and 1956.

The Corporation may also sell surplus agricultural commodities for foreign currencies under the Agricultural Trade Development and Assistance Act. The law provides for a 3-year program with total cost to the Corporation to be reimbursed by appropriations limited to 700 million dollars. With due regard to the impact on world markets, we are moving ahead in an orderly manner in the negotiation of agreements, and it is expected that transactions completed during the fiscal year 1955 will account for a substantial part of the costs under this Act. Except for expenditures under the International Wheat Agreement, these expenditures for export programs are included in the total shown for the Commodity Credit Corporation.

The trade development act is helpful in marketing commodity

surpluses and tends to reduce current outlays under the regular price support program. However, it is unwise to rely upon this means as a final solution to our surplus problem. We must continue our efforts to restore a sound position for agriculture in world markets.

Financing farm ownership and operation.—The agricultural credit institutions supervised by the Farm Credit Administration make standard risk loans to farmers and their cooperatives on both a short- and long-term basis. Some of these loans are made with funds obtained through the federally owned intermediate credit banks. New loans of the Federal intermediate credit banks are estimated to be nearly 2 billion dollars in the fiscal year 1956, and will exceed loan collections by 40 million dollars. Receipts from other operations will reduce total net budget expenditures of the Farm Credit Administration to 37 million dollars.

The Farmers' Home Administration makes direct loans to farmers to supplement the credit services provided by private and cooperative credit agencies, and also insures loans by private lenders. By greater reliance on insured loans, the services of the Farmers' Home Administration can be increased without increasing budget expenditures. Under legislation enacted last year the interest rate on insured loans for farm ownership, farm housing, and other improvements has been set at a level that will attract a larger volume of funds from private lenders. Insured loans will also be used to finance an increase in soil and water conservation loans, which the new legislation has made available in all States. In addition, the Farmers' Home Administration can now take second mortgages as security for direct loans. This will permit private lenders to continue as first mortgage holders in the financing of farm ownership and development, thereby increasing the number of borrowers that can be served under that program.

Financing rural electrification and rural telephones.—The programs of the Rural Electrification Administration have brought about great advances for rural America, and this administration will continue to make loans available to meet all legitimate needs for rural electrification and telephones.

The need for electrification loans to provide initial connections of farm homes with central station service is much less than in earlier years. But this is more than offset by larger requirements for improvements of existing systems and for power generation. My budget recommendations, therefore, provide for a higher level of new electrification loans in 1956 than in the current fiscal year.

The rural telephone program is still in an early stage of development. Progress is being made in resolving the various problems involved in achieving adequate telephone service in rural areas. This budget makes provision for new loan authority sufficient to raise the level of telephone loans in 1956 to 80 million dollars, which is 5 million dollars higher than in 1955.

Agricultural land and water resources.—My recommendations for agricultural land and water resources for the fiscal year 1956 recognize the great importance to the Nation of soil and water conservation activities. The new watershed protection legislation enacted last year is a vital part of our conservation program. It provides a practical basis for partnership between the Federal Government and State and local groups in the planning and carrying out of a coordinated program for upstream flood prevention and soil and water conservation. This budget recommends an increase of 4 million dollars for 1956 to provide for the necessary Federal participation in watershed protection projects.

Under the forward authorization for the 1955 crop year agricultural conservation program, contained in the 1955 appropriation act, larger expenditures will be required for payments to farmers in the fiscal year 1956 than in 1955. This program assists farmers in applying sound soil conservation practices and in putting to proper use farm land diverted from its previous use through acreage allotments. Because the problems created by diverted acreage are expected to become progressively less pressing, I am recommending a forward authorization of 175 million dollars for the 1956 crop year as compared with the 250 million dollars provided for the current crop year.

Research and other agricultural services.—Additional research and educational work on problems of agricultural production, soil and water conservation, and marketing of farm products, can make important contributions to a more efficient and stable agriculture capable of meeting the needs of a growing population. These activities not only contribute directly to the solution of immediate problems of farmers, but also benefit consumers of farm products by more efficient production and marketing. The 1956 budget provides for an increase of 9 million dollars in expenditures for research and an increase of 6 million dollars for extension work. These additional amounts are needed to expand the Federal-State cooperative research and extension programs and to strengthen the basic agricultural research program carried on by the Federal Government.

As part of the coordinated plan to improve economic statistics of the Government, this budget includes added funds to strengthen the work of the Department of Agriculture in developing adequate farm income and production statistics. Expenditures for other agricultural services also include 10 million dollars in 1955 and 15 million dollars in 1956 for eradication of brucellosis in cattle. The necessary funds are to be made available by transfer from the Commodity Credit Corporation. This program is designed both to assist in stabilizing the dairy industry and to give added protection to the health of our citizens.

NATURAL RESOURCES

This administration believes that achievement of the resource development basic to the economic progress and security of the Nation requires encouragement of local public and private initiative and, where Federal participation is necessary, emphasis on the partnership aspects of essential cooperative arrangements with

State and local governments or with private enterprise. To the greatest extent possible, the responsibility for resource development, and its cost, should be borne by those who receive the benefits. In many instances private interests or State and local governments can best carry on the needed programs. In other instances Federal participation or initiative may be necessary to safeguard the public interest or to accomplish broad national objectives, where projects because of size or complexity are beyond the means or the needs of local public or private enterprise. The Federal Government must be willing and ready to bear the cost of improvements made for national purposes; but in all cases where the partnership principle logically applies there is automatically acquired a concern for economy and efficiency that is often lacking when no local contribution is required.

As a result of this partnership policy and the willingness of State, local, and private interests to undertake or cooperate in the development of our natural resources, it has been possible to reduce Federal expenditures for these programs since the fiscal year 1954. At the same time, we have strengthened our resource development programs.

The conservation and development of our natural resources will require estimated net Federal expenditures of 953 million dollars in the fiscal year 1956, as compared with 1.1 billion dollars in 1955 and 1.2 billion dollars in 1954. About two-thirds of the net expenditures in 1956 will be for flood control, irrigation, power and multiple-purpose river basin development. The other one-third will be largely for the management and development of the national forests, parks, and public lands, and for our fish and wildlife and mineral resources programs. Federal expenditures for natural resources, if wisely made in proper relation to local public and private efforts, are investments for the benefit of the Nation; in many cases they also result in receipts to the Treasury, thus often providing reimbursement in later years for part of the costs incurred.

NATURAL RESOURCES

[Fiscal years. In millions]

Program or agency	Gross expenditures			Net expenditures			Recommended new obligational authority for 1956
	1954 actual	1955 estimated	1956 estimated	1954 actual	1955 estimated	1956 estimated	
Land and water resources:							
Corps of Engineers: Flood control and multiple-purpose projects:							
Present programs.......	$416	$366	$363	$416	$366	$363	$371
Proposed legislation:							
Passamaquoddy Bay survey...............	.....	.....	1	.....	.....	1	1
Partnership projects...	.....	.....	10	.....	.....	10	10
Department of the Interior:							
Bureau of Reclamation: Irrigation and multiple-purpose projects:							
Present programs.....	199	168	177	196	165	174	180
Proposed legislation:							
Federal projects.....	.....	.....	5	.....	.....	5	7
Partnership projects.	.....	.....	10	.....	.....	10	10
Power transmission agencies................	53	48	41	53	48	41	25
Indian lands resources...	33	37	41	32	36	40	24
Bureau of Land Management and other.......	15	17	18	15	17	18	17
Tennessee Valley Authority.	409	431	250	238	214	2	28
Department of State......	7	5	4	7	5	4	2
Federal Power Commission.	4	4	5	4	4	5	5
Forest resources...........	117	121	115	117	121	115	116
Mineral resources:							
Present programs.........	41	47	46	37	43	42	40
Proposed legislation: Aid for anthracite mine drainage.	.....	2	3	.....	2	3	....
Fish and wildlife resources...	38	46	43	38	46	43	41
Recreational use of resources.	33	39	50	33	39	50	25
General resource surveys and other..................	27	26	26	27	26	26	26
Total................	1,391	1,358	1,209	1,213	1,133	953	[1] 929

[1] Compares with new obligational authority of 1,196 million dollars in 1954 and 967 million dollars in 1955.

Land and water resources.—Under the recommendations for the fiscal year 1956, the Federal Government will spend 673 million dollars for the development of land and water resources. A large share of this total—430 million dollars—is for continuation of work on 152 river-basin development projects and units under construction by the Bureau of Reclamation and the Corps of Engineers. Much of this work is multiple-purpose development for irrigation, flood control, navigation, and hydroelectric power. Construction on 37 of these projects will be virtually completed in 1956. Funds recommended for work underway in 1956 will maintain power generation schedules and continue nonpower projects at economical rates. Maintenance and operation activities will be at a level which will provide reasonable protection of the Federal investment.

My recommendations are intended to encourage States and local public and private groups to take the initiative in developing our valuable water resources with Federal cooperation where national interests are involved. This budget includes 20 million dollars under proposed legislation to enable the Bureau of Reclamation and the Corps of Engineers to participate, in 1956, in partnership water developments. Five million dollars of this amount is proposed for three multiple-purpose projects with power facilities in the Pacific Northwest. It is expected that local interests will install and operate the power facilities of the Cougar and Green Peter-White Bridge projects in Oregon and that the Corps of Engineers will build the flood control and other facilities in which there is a national interest. Non-Federal interests are also expected to build the Rocky Reach project in Washington, and the Corps of Engineers will assist in financing the nonpower facilities having national benefits. Assistance will be given to other partnership projects as specific proposals are developed. In addition, provision will be made for cooperation in authorized partnership projects, such as Priest Rapids in Washington and Markham Ferry in Oklahoma, when satisfactory arrangements have been completed.

I also recommend enactment of legislation authorizing the Bureau of Reclamation to undertake construction of two comprehensive river-basin improvements which are beyond the capacity of local initiative, public or private, but which are needed for irrigation, power, flood control and municipal and industrial water supply. These are the Upper Colorado River Basin development in the States of Colorado, Utah, Wyoming, Arizona, and New Mexico, and the Fryingpan-Arkansas development in Colorado. The Colorado River development will enable the Upper Basin States to conserve flood waters and to assure the availability of water and power necessary for the economic growth of the region. The total cost of these major developments is estimated at 1.1 billion dollars, with first-year expenditures of 5 million dollars. Sale of power generated at these developments will repay the power investment within 50 years and will make a contribution toward repayment of other investments.

In furtherance of the policy to move forward with needed water use and control projects, the 1956 budget provides for the starting of a number of new authorized Federal projects. For each authorized project recommended, planning has advanced to the stage where the project could be placed under construction early in 1956. Most of the projects are small or intermediate-sized developments, having a high degree of financial participation by local interests or a reasonable excess of benefits over costs. Some of them are essential to permit full functioning of Federal works already completed or under construction.

This budget makes provision for the Bureau of Reclamation to start construction on 5 new irrigation and water supply projects, and for the Corps of Engineers to begin work on 10 local flood protection projects, 2 flood control projects of broader scope, 8 projects for beach erosion control, and 14 navigation projects. It also provides for resumption of work which was suspended a few years ago on 1 local flood protection project and 1 navigation project. These add up to 39 new projects and 2 resumptions. In addition, 2 million dollars is recommended for the construction

of a number of small projects to be selected by the Secretary of
the Army, none of which may cost more than 150,000 dollars.
The total cost of all this new work is estimated at 347 million
dollars, of which expenditures of 23 million dollars are contemplated for the fiscal year 1956. The navigation projects included
in the above construction starts, at an estimated cost of 198 million
dollars, are discussed in the commerce and manpower section of
this message.

In the selection of reclamation projects, consideration has been
given to (1) more efficient use of present water supply and correction of adverse water supply conditions, and (2) the proportion
of the irrigation investment which will be repaid by the water
users. The new local flood protection works will provide benefits
primarily in highly urban and industrialized areas. The new flood
control projects are the Eagle Gorge Reservoir in Washington,
on which there will be substantial local contributions in related
work and cash, and the Old River Control project in Louisiana.
The latter project is essential to prevent the diversion of the Mississippi River to the Atchafalaya River channel, with resultant
disruption to the economy of the lower Mississippi River area.

Adequate collection and evaluation of basic data on topog-
raphy, minerals, soils, and water and weather conditions are
essential to provide a sound basis for water resources projects.
Current progress in collection of basic data will be continued. It
is also essential to prepare adequate project designs prior to construction to assure efficient construction and to safeguard the public investment. I am recommending increased funds for general
investigations by the Bureau of Reclamation to assure a proper
basis for project authorization. Advance planning of authorized
projects by the Corps of Engineers and the Bureau of Reclamation
will proceed at a rate which will permit early initiation of construction on projects in accordance with needs and budget policy.
This budget also provides 1 million dollars under proposed legislation for a survey to determine whether hydroelectric power can

be economically developed from the tremendous tides at Passamaquoddy Bay.

Expenditures of the Bonneville, Southeastern and Southwest-
ern Power Administrations in the fiscal year 1956 are in line with
the partnership policy whereby State, local, and private interests
participate in power development and transmission. The expenditure estimates also reflect the approaching completion of transmission systems for marketing power from Federal projects now
under construction.

In order to establish equity between the Federal Government
and other interests, I recommended in my 1955 budget message
enactment of legislation to provide that the Federal Government
make payments to non-Federal owners of water resources projects
when Federal hydroelectric power developments benefit from
these projects. Payments are now required from other licensees
deriving such benefits and I see no reason why the Federal Government should be exempted. I hope the Congress will amend
the Federal Power Act during this session to require such Federal
payments.

The Tennessee Valley Authority, in the fiscal years 1955 and
1956, will continue installation of steam electric and hydroelectric
generation units started in prior years. With construction on
some of the facilities nearing completion, gross expenditures of
the Authority are estimated to show a very substantial decrease
from 431 million dollars in 1955 to 250 million dollars in 1956.
Receipts from operations, largely from the sale of power, are
expected to increase from 217 million dollars to 248 million dollars. Thus, an approximate balance between expenditures and
receipts is estimated for 1956, with net budget expenditures of 2
million dollars.

No appropriations have been recommended for new power
generation units in the fiscal years 1955 or 1956 for the Tennessee
Valley Authority. After 600,000 kilowatts contracted for by the
Atomic Energy Commission with the Mississippi Valley Generating Company become available for replacing power furnished

the AEC by TVA, the scheduled capacity of the TVA system will provide for a substantial increase in loads through the calendar year 1958. The Tennessee Valley Authority is giving immediate attention to the possibilities of financing further expansion of its power system by means other than Federal appropriations. The Authority has been requested to complete its studies in time to permit consideration by the Congress at this session of any legislation that may be necessary. It is expected that the power needs for the system will be reexamined after the Congress has had an opportunity to consider legislation to provide for future financing.

Legislation will also be presented to the Congress to provide that an adequate rate of interest be paid to the Treasury on appropriated funds invested in power facilities of the Tennessee Valley Authority.

National forest and other public lands.—Forest and range lands managed by the Forest Service and the Bureau of Land Management provide valuable timber, range, and mineral resources. Receipts from these lands are estimated at 165 million dollars in 1956. Part of these receipts are appropriated for payments to the States and counties in which the lands are located. Increased expenditures are recommended in 1956 for construction of forest roads and trails, supervision of timber sales, and soil and moisture conservation work. As a result of Federal cooperative assistance in the past, States are now assuming greater responsibility for forest fire control on non-Federal lands and some reduction in Federal payments is proposed for 1956. Expenditures on Indian lands and resources will provide for management of forest and range lands at the current level, but some increases are recommended for soil and moisture conservation, maintenance of buildings and utilities, and construction of roads.

In the fiscal year 1955, the submerged lands of the Outer Continental Shelf were first offered for drilling for oil and gas under Federal leases. Receipts from these leases, deposited in the Treasury, are estimated at 147 million dollars in 1955 and

100 million dollars in 1956. Leasing of these lands will continue to provide substantial receipts in later years.

Urgent needs for maintenance and for improved services to the increasing number of visitors will require some increase in expenditures for our national parks, monuments, and historic sites. Employment of additional personnel to collect admission fees, together with the increase in fees put into effect during the current year, will result in increased receipts to the Treasury. Parkways, roads, and trails will be extended in 1956, pursuant to authority provided in the Federal Aid Highway Act of 1954.

Mineral resources.—During the past year, the Cabinet Committee on Minerals Policy has recommended, and I have approved, general guidelines for developing mineral resources in accordance with our national security needs. Case by case studies of individual mineral industries will be made to determine within the framework of our overall domestic and foreign economic policies the proper level of efficient domestic production necessary for our mobilization base. Where necessary, the various means available to the Government will be used to support essential parts of the mobilization base. The factfinding and research activities of the Geological Survey and the Bureau of Mines will contribute to this end.

I recommend legislation and a supplemental appropriation in the fiscal year 1955 to enable the Federal Government to cooperate with the State of Pennsylvania in providing facilities for surface water drainage in the anthracite coal region. This will afford protection against the flooding of valuable resources and the decrease in employment which would result if additional mines were closed.

COMMERCE AND MANPOWER

The basic principle underlying budget recommendations for programs in the field of transportation, housing, and business is that the national interest is best served by privately owned and operated industry, which is assisted by a minimum of Federal funds and Federal basic facilities operated at the lowest feasible cost and financed, where possible, by charges levied on the users of the services. Budget recommendations for manpower programs are designed to help the Nation's productive system function smoothly and efficiently, by providing economic safeguards for workers, by helping bring together jobseekers and jobs, and by fostering orderly labor relations and the amicable settlement of disputes.

In the past 2 years, in furtherance of these principles, we have strengthened our major commerce and manpower programs by placing increased reliance on expansion of private investment, by encouraging greater participation of State and local governments, and by providing for the extension of coverage of unemployment insurance. Wherever possible, Federal programs are being placed on a self-supporting basis. As a result, a large share of the Government's operations in these areas is being financed from program receipts, rather than from tax revenues.

After 30 years of discussion, the United States is joining with Canada in constructing the Saint Lawrence Seaway. A joint program is underway with industry to modernize our merchant fleet. Federal aids to States for highway construction have been increased. Positive steps have been taken to promote an economically sound system of air transportation with reduced reliance on Federal subsidies. The Post Office Department has made major improvements in service and substantially reduced its operating deficit. Limited attacks on urban blight through slum clearance have been expanded into a comprehensive urban renewal program. More private investment in housing is being encouraged by more liberal mortgage insurance, by the voluntary home mortgage credit program, and by permitting private investors to retire gradually the Government's investment in the secondary mortgage market. Meanwhile, other housing loans and Government-owned housing are being liquidated as rapidly as feasible. Our production capacity has been expanded to make possible speedier mobilization in case of future emergencies.

Provision has been made for extension of coverage of the Federal-State unemployment compensation system to 4 million more workers.

COMMERCE AND MANPOWER

[Fiscal years. In millions]

Program or agency	Gross expenditures 1954 actual	Gross expenditures 1955 estimated	Gross expenditures 1956 estimated	Net expenditures 1954 actual	Net expenditures 1955 estimated	Net expenditures 1956 estimated	Recommended new obligational authority for 1956
Provision of highways.....	$586	$659	$725	$586	$659	$725	$919
Merchant marine.........	236	228	198	153	209	192	235
Navigation aids and facilities...................	403	409	441	313	325	353	330
Promotion of aviation.....	275	274	283	275	274	283	284
Postal service:							
Present program........	2,686	2,741	2,811	312	268	294	295
Proposed pay and rate increases.............	.....	.....	−270	.....	.....	−270	−270
Other transportation and communication programs.	62	58	60	−28	36	42	37
Urban development and redevelopment:							
Present programs.......	37	86	145	22	56	94	4
Proposed legislation.....	.....	.....	.....	.....	.....	.....	200
Aids to private housing:							
Federal Housing Administration.............	125	143	130	−28	−42	−67	....
Federal National Mortgage Association......	563	813	338	−221	243	−193	....
Veterans Administration:							
Present programs.....	118	170	92	85	118	39	....
Proposed legislation...	.....	.....	90	.....	.....	90	100
Other...............	31	5	5	−16	−29	−29	....
Public housing programs..	658	570	604	−401	−85	34	96
Other housing and community facilities........	93	83	52	53	54	44	19
Civil defense and disaster relief.................	103	80	76	61	72	70	71
Promotion of defense production:							
Present programs.......	936	1,061	626	216	76	104	6
Proposed legislation.....	.....	.....	12	.....	.....	12	....
Business loans and guaranties:							
Present programs.......	131	50	11	−100	−38	−106	....
Proposed legislation.....	.....	.....	28	.....	.....	28	67

COMMERCE AND MANPOWER—Continued

[Fiscal years. In millions]

Program or agency	Gross expenditures			Net expenditures			Recommended new obligational authority for 1956
	1954 actual	1955 estimated	1956 estimated	1954 actual	1955 estimated	1956 estimated	
Other promotion or regulation of business.........	$33	$37	$37	$17	$21	$36	$36
Unemployment compensation and placement:							
Administration..........	211	204	254	209	203	253	257
Payment to Unemployment Trust Fund.....	.....	64	87	.....	64	87	87
Other labor and manpower programs:							
Present programs.......	67	65	66	67	65	66	66
Proposed legislation.....	.....	.....	4	.....	.....	4	5
Total................	7,355	7,800	6,908	1,577	2,550	2,186	[1] 2,846

[1] Compares with new obligational authority of 2,846 million dollars in 1954 and 3,381 million dollars in 1955.

The appropriations recommended in this budget will permit even greater progress in the fiscal year 1956 and later. In addition I am recommending legislation (1) to bring the interstate highway system up to modern standards in the next decade; (2) to make the postal system self-supporting; (3) to increase authority for mortgage insurance and urban renewal grants and to authorize contracts for additional public housing units; (4) to extend the Defense Production Act, the Small Business Act, and the veterans' housing loan program beyond their present expiration dates of June 30, 1955; and (5) to raise the minimum wage now provided under the Fair Labor Standards Act and modernize Federal workmen's compensation and other labor laws.

Gross expenditures for commerce and manpower, including proposed legislation, will be reduced from an estimated 7.8 billion dollars in the fiscal year 1955 to 6.9 billion dollars in 1956, primarily because of reduced purchases of mortgages by the Federal National Mortgage Association and lower spending for defense production activities. Assuming enactment of the recommended increase in postal rates, net budget expenditures for 1956 are estimated at less than 2.2 billion dollars, 364 million dollars below 1955.

Highways.—In the past decade and a half we have not kept pace with the rapidly growing needs for highways adequate for economic development and national security. I plan to send a special message to the Congress in the near future recommending a program of coordinated action by Federal, State, and local governments, to overcome major highway deficiencies. The additional budget expenditures, if any, required in the fiscal year 1956 would be relatively minor.

Budget expenditures for highways under present programs will continue to increase as a result of the enlarged program already provided in the Federal Aid Highway Act of 1954. Grants to States (including Federal administrative expenses) will amount to 680 million dollars, with an additional 45 million dollars of expenditures for highways in Federal forests, on public lands, and in Alaska.

Merchant marine.—To continue our program of helping to bring the merchant fleet up to date, I am recommending for the fiscal year 1956 new obligational authority for ship construction of 103 million dollars. These funds will: (1) continue the trade-in-and-build tanker program begun this year; (2) start orderly replacement of cargo ships built during or before World War II; (3) finance construction of two cargo ships and one tanker as prototypes for mass production in an emergency; (4) provide for the construction or conversion of four passenger-cargo ships; and (5) continue essential research and development work on ship design. The appropriation of 103 million dollars will be more than matched by private funds, resulting in total investment of about 225 million dollars in new ship construction. Together with the joint 400-million-dollar program now underway and with expanded naval construction in private yards, it should maintain a substantial nucleus of peacetime shipyard employment.

Payment of subsidies to American ship operators to offset lower

operating costs of foreign ships will require appropriations estimated at 115 million dollars in 1956. The rapid rise recently
in expenditures for this purpose and the possibility of continued
increases make it important to provide more effective budgetary
control over the level of subsidized operations. I am, therefore,
proposing in this budget to establish a limitation on new long-
term contracts to pay operating-differential subsidies. Such a
limitation will permit annual review by the President and the
Congress of the extent of our future subsidy commitments.

Navigation aids and facilities.—In accordance with legislation
enacted last May, the Saint Lawrence Seaway Development Corporation has been established to construct, operate, and maintain
that part of the new Seaway located in United States territory.
Construction is being pushed at maximum speed because of the
Seaway's importance to economic development and national
security. Almost one-quarter of the work is scheduled for
completion by the end of the fiscal year 1956.

The Corps of Engineers program for rivers and harbors gives
primary emphasis to inland waterways and to those navigation
projects needed to provide reliable access to important ports or to
relieve serious congestion for important established deep draft
traffic. The increase in expenditures from 108 million dollars
in 1955 to 135 million dollars in 1956 reflects mainly the normal
rate of progress on construction of projects started in 1955 and
the resumption of urgently needed maintenance of shallow draft
channels.

In addition, 14 new navigation projects and the resumption of
one project previously suspended are recommended in the fiscal
year 1956. These are projects which promise to yield benefits
relatively high in comparison to the construction costs involved
or which have substantial local participation. With 2 exceptions,
these are relatively small or intermediate-sized projects. Dredging of the Delaware River channel between Philadelphia and
Trenton is proposed, but specific recommendations will be sent
to the Congress only on the basis that provision be made for

adequate cost-sharing in some form. Appropriations are recommended to widen the Calumet-Sag Waterway in Illinois to make this vital channel adequate to handle present and steadily increasing traffic needs.

Although expenditures of the Coast Guard will continue to decline from 205 million dollars in 1955 to 193 million dollars in 1956, the basic aids provided for air and water commerce will be maintained at their current strength. In addition, the Coast Guard will again operate the ocean weather-station network for the Department of Defense.

Promotion of aviation.—We have made shifts in Federal aviation programs during the past 2 years in order to reduce assistance no longer required and to concentrate on those Federal aids which are indispensable to the continued rapid progress of aviation.

Since October 1953, when responsibility for subsidy payments to commercial air carriers was placed in the Civil Aeronautics Board, substantial progress has been made in decreasing the level of subsidies. Expenditures by the Civil Aeronautics Board for this purpose in 1955 are now estimated at 70 million dollars compared to 80 million dollars estimated a year ago; a further decline to 63 million dollars is anticipated for 1956. This trend is consistent with the recommendations made by the Air Coordinating Committee after a comprehensive study made at my request of our basic civil aviation policies. In addition, wherever possible, military mail is being carried by commercial airlines, thus not only eliminating Government competition with private business, but also helping to reduce subsidies to the private carriers.

The continuing growth of civil and military air traffic has increased congestion on the airways system—at times restricting aircraft operations in areas of heavy traffic. As a step to maintain high standards of safety and increase the regularity of flights, I am recommending increased appropriations for the Civil Acronautics Administration for expansion and improvement of air navigation facilities and for more radar traffic control equipment.

With the increasing maturity of civil aviation, the Federal Government soon should be able to reduce substantially its safety promotion and enforcement activities without affecting the present high level of safety. I have requested the early preparation of a plan, in cooperation with industry, to achieve this objective.

I again recommend incorporation of Washington National Airport to provide the administrative flexibility needed for efficient operation of this business-type enterprise.

The work of the National Advisory Committee for Aeronautics is of key significance in strengthening our military aircraft and guided missiles programs and in supporting our continued progress in the air. During recent years we have achieved spectacular success in flying at speeds well beyond the speed of sound. However, we have not yet overcome all problems of structural failure, engine malfunctioning, and lack of stability and control at high speeds. A more intensive effort in these fields is needed in order that the great improvements in performance now known to be possible can be realized in the actual production of military aircraft, engines, and missiles, which represent such an important and costly part of our defense program. For these reasons, I am recommending additional appropriations for both 1955 and 1956 to increase the Committee's research effort in fields of critical military importance.

Postal service.—Considerable progress is being made in providing better postal service to the American people at lower cost to the taxpayer. Movement of first-class mail has been expedited. Substantial investments have been made in capital improvements and in skilled personnel which are just beginning to pay dividends. Long-term leases are being negotiated which will permit acquisition of needed modern postal facilities. Promising experiments in new equipment are underway which, if successful, will revolutionize mail-handling techniques.

Largely because of these savings, the net expenditures of the Post Office under existing laws have been reduced to the lowest level in the last 8 years. The increased postal rates which I recommended in my special message to the Congress would add 400 million dollars to postal revenues. This would be enough to cover the recommended pay adjustments of 130 million dollars and reduce net expenditures to 24 million dollars in the fiscal year 1956. These steps, together with further major economies now in process, should cause the postal system to become self-supporting in the near future. As a long-run solution, an independent commission should be created to review future rate changes proposed by the Postmaster General in accordance with a basic formula laid down by the Congress.

Urban development and redevelopment.—Under the new urban renewal program authorized by the Housing Act of 1954, local public agencies, jointly with forward-looking private investors, are developing and executing plans to rebuild our major cities and prevent the decay which is making large urban areas unfit for sound economic investment or family life. The act strengthens the previous slum clearance program by (*a*) requiring localities as a condition of Federal aid to have a workable plan to eliminate substandard housing and neighborhood decay; (*b*) providing Federal grants and loans for neighborhood rehabilitation, as well as redevelopment projects; and (*c*) authorizing the Federal Housing Administration to insure mortgages on homes in blighted areas and to help finance new homes for families displaced by slum clearance.

By the end of the fiscal year 1956, an estimated 22 slum clearance projects will be completed, and 364 other slum clearance and urban renewal projects will be underway. Net expenditures will increase from 56 million dollars in 1955 to 94 million dollars in 1956, largely for capital grants to pay the Federal share of project costs. On the basis of experience thus far, private investment and local government expenditures for slum clearance and urban renewal projects will be about four to five times as great as the Federal capital grants.

Before the end of the current fiscal year, the present 500 million dollars in contract authority for capital grants will be committed. Accordingly, to permit the program to go forward without delay, I am recommending legislation to provide an additional 100 million dollars in capital grant authority in the fiscal year 1955, and 200 million dollars in each of the two subsequent fiscal years.

Federal Housing Administration.—The Federal Housing Administration is now authorized to insure larger loans with longer maturities, as well as loans to support the urban renewal program and to help servicemen buy homes. Thus, more of our people can buy their own homes. Because of the more liberal terms provided and the increased availability of mortgage credit, applications for mortgage insurance have risen substantially in recent months. On the basis of the present outlook, construction or purchase of almost 800,000 homes and improvement or repair of 1,500,000 other homes will be financed during the fiscal year 1956 by private lenders backed by Government insurance commitments.

The total private investment in both new and existing homes by homeowners and builders, underwritten by the Federal Housing Administration, in the fiscal year 1956 will amount to an estimated 8.3 billion dollars. To meet the expanding needs for mortgage insurance for the remainder of the fiscal year 1955 and through 1956, approximately 5 billion dollars in additional insurance authority will be required.

In recent months both legislative and administrative measures have been taken to eliminate abuses in insurance programs. The budget also includes additional funds to assure more adequate supervision. The increase in premium collections and other income will, however, more than offset the increased supervisory expenditures, and receipts are estimated to exceed expenditures by 67 million dollars in the fiscal year 1956, compared with 42 million dollars in 1955.

Federal National Mortgage Association.—Under the Housing

Act of 1954, the Federal National Mortgage Association was reconstituted to comprise financially separate activities for the secondary market, special assistance, and management and liquidating functions. Except for the initial transfer of the Government capital investment of 92 million dollars from the earlier association, the secondary market activity will be financed entirely from private funds and its operations are, therefore, not reflected in this budget. The purpose of this activity is to make sure that mortgage funds are available to meet normal needs in all parts of the Nation at market rates of interest. Private capital will be gradually substituted for the Government investment until the Government funds are fully repaid and the private owners take over responsibility for the program.

Expenditures and receipts for the other two activities are included in the budget totals. Under the special assistance program, the President can authorize limited purchases of mortgages (*a*) to meet acute housing needs of groups or areas unable to obtain private financing, or (*b*) to prevent a decline in housing activity. In the fiscal years 1955 and 1956, the Association expects to support the financing of about 90,000 housing units, primarily for the urban renewal program. This support will be mainly through commitments to purchase participations in private mortgages. Under the management and liquidating function, the Association will administer the 3.1 billion dollars of mortgages and undisbursed commitments outstanding at the beginning of the fiscal year 1955.

Primarily because of large purchases under previous commitments, expenditures by the Association will exceed receipts by 243 million dollars in the fiscal year 1955. In 1956, however, net receipts of 193 million dollars are anticipated.

Veterans' housing loans.—The Veterans Administration program of direct housing loans expires on June 30, 1955. These loans are made only where guaranteed private mortgages are not available or cannot be secured through the voluntary home mortgage credit program. I recommend legislation continuing this program until expiration of the veterans' loan guaranty program for World War II veterans on July 25, 1957. If permission is granted to use receipts from repayments, as well as from sales, new obligational authority of 100 million dollars should be adequate for the fiscal year 1956.

Public housing.—The aids contained in the Housing Act of 1954, and especially the aids to low-cost housing, will provide the opportunity for the private housing industry to satisfy, eventually, the housing requirements of families of all income groups. In the meantime, it is essential to continue a minimum amount of low-rent public housing construction to meet the critical needs of the lowest income families and to help provide a new place to live for families displaced by urban renewal and slum clearance operations. I recommend a 2-year authorization for contracts with local housing authorities to pay contributions for an additional 35,000 low-rent units each year. Funds necessary for this purpose have been included in this budget.

Liquidation of the emergency World War II public housing program is accelerating. By June 30, 1956, two-thirds of the 195,000 units owned by the Government at the end of 1954 will have been sold, transferred, or demolished. Meanwhile expenditures for the defense housing program started during the Korean emergency will be almost completed.

Gross expenditures for public housing programs, chiefly temporary construction loans to local authorities and annual contributions for completed projects, are estimated at 604 million dollars in 1956. Receipts, mostly from private refinancing of these Federal loans and rental and sale of emergency housing, will total an estimated 570 million dollars, leaving net expenditures of 34 million dollars.

Other housing and community facilities.—By the end of 1956, the Housing and Home Finance Agency will have approved 297 loans to finance construction of dormitory rooms for about 63,800 students and homes for 1,500 faculty and student families at colleges and universities throughout the Nation. In the past 2 years the Agency has helped to develop a private market for long-term dormitory revenue bonds, formerly rarely bought by private investors. The increasing success in attracting private funds is a major reason for the decline in net expenditures from 41 million dollars to 28 million dollars.

Civil defense and disaster relief.—Expenditures for civil defense are classified with expenditures for dealing with peacetime disasters in the commerce and manpower section, but the program is discussed in the major national security section of this message in view of its close relation to continental defense.

Promotion of defense production.—Gross expenditures for promotion of defense production are expected to decline from 1,061 million dollars in 1955 to 638 million dollars in 1956. Most of this reduction is in the synthetic rubber and tin programs. In accordance with the terms of the Rubber Producing Facilities Disposal Act, the estimates assume that these plants will be sold or leased before June 30, 1955. Most of these facilities have already been sold, subject to congressional approval. Moreover, since purchases of tin for the national stockpile have now been completed and world supplies are ample to meet current needs, no provision is made for continued operation of the Government tin smelter.

Gross expenditures under the Defense Production Act will continue at relatively high levels, primarily to meet previous commitments made to provide guaranteed markets, loans, or grants to producers of critical defense materials. Net expenditures will amount to only a fraction of gross disbursements, since most of the materials purchased are being sold to the stockpile of strategic and critical materials to meet its objectives, and to industry. The stockpile program is discussed in the major national security section of this message.

Under present law, the Defense Production Act expires on June 30, 1955. Since important gaps in our mobilization preparedness require continued Government encouragement, I recommend extension of the act with modifications for 2 years. No increase in the present borrowing authority of 2.1 billion dollars is anticipated at this time.

Business loans and guaranties.—Liquidation of business loans made by the Reconstruction Finance Corporation is well advanced. During the 3-year period from June 30, 1953, to June 30, 1956, business loans and commitments will have been reduced from 458 million dollars to about 53 million dollars through repayments, refinancing, and sales to private financial institutions.

Loans to small businesses by the Small Business Administration have been expanding substantially during the last year. Loans are made only if private credit on reasonable terms is not available, and more than two-thirds of the loans so far extended have been made jointly with private banks. The present authority expires on June 30, 1955, and I recommend its extension. Assuming continuance of the 1955 level of operations, about 1,200 new loans would be authorized in the fiscal year 1956, and additional appropriations of 67 million dollars would be required.

Labor placement and unemployment compensation administration.—Budget expenditures under existing law for administering the joint Federal-State program of employment services and unemployment insurance are estimated at 253 million dollars for the fiscal year 1956, 50 million dollars higher than in the current year. About 29 million dollars of this increase is nonrecurring and results from a change in the timing of funds advanced to the States; this does not affect the level of operations. The rest is largely for State-approved increases in salaries paid to the State employees who administer the program, and for improvements in the placement service.

Legislation enacted last year provides for transferring annually to the unemployment trust fund the excess of receipts from the Federal unemployment tax over operating costs of the program. The excess received during 1955, to be transferred in the fiscal year 1956, is estimated at 87 million dollars, an increase of 23 million dollars over the amount transferred this year. These funds are to be used to set up a reserve of 200 million dollars from which loans can be made to those States which deplete their own reserves for benefit payments.

The present law authorizing the recruiting of qualified workers from Mexico for seasonal farm employment in the United States expires December 31, 1955. However, the need for this service will continue and I shall recommend its extension. Accordingly, my budget recommendations, including proposed legislation, provide funds for the entire fiscal year 1956.

Other labor and manpower programs.—Industrial injuries have been significantly reduced through the efforts of both labor and management, but these injuries still cost us 40 million man-days every year. This is a heavy tax on our economic progress, as well as on the individual employees and employers. Workmen's compensation programs—an important facet of the industrial safety problem—have lagged behind other social insurance programs in recent years. Although workmen's compensation is predominantly a State program, the Federal Government can and should stimulate improvement—especially through studies and clearing house activities. The budget for the fiscal year 1956 provides for studies which will enable the Department of Labor to promote more effective safety programs and assist States in improving their workmen's compensation standards. In addition, I shall recommend legislation which, over the next few years, should aid the States in further developing industrial safety programs. Two million dollars are included for this purpose in 1956.

At present all workmen's compensation payments to Federal employees are provided from a single appropriation. To encourage better safety practices, I shall recommend legislation to shift the financing of some of these benefit payments to the employing Federal agency. Legislation will also be recommended to liberalize workmen's compensation benefits paid to longshoremen and harbor workers under laws administered by the Federal Government.

The apprentice training program of the Department of Labor

has contributed to improvement of the skill and versatility of thousands of workers. As our economy continues to expand, many more skilled workers are needed. Accordingly, the budget proposals provide for redirecting and improving Federal participation in these training activities.

As part of a governmentwide program to improve our economic statistics, this budget includes 1.5 million dollars for additional work during the fiscal year 1956 in the labor and manpower field, covering primarily statistics on employment and unemployment, and for basic data for mobilization and civil defense.

Unemployment trust fund.—The following table shows receipts and expenditures of the unemployment trust fund.

UNEMPLOYMENT TRUST FUND

[Fiscal years. In millions]

Item	1954 actual	1955 estimated	1956 estimated
Balance in fund at start of year...................	$9,246	$8,993	$8,785
Receipts:			
Deposits by States and railroad unemployment taxes.....................................	1,268	1,219	1,421
Interest.....................................	224	220	204
Transfer from general fund.....................	....	64	87
Payments: State and railroad withdrawals for benefits.	−1,745	−1,712	−1,594
Net accumulation (+) or withdrawal (−).......	−253	−209	+118
Balance in fund at close of the year..............	8,993	8,785	8,903

GENERAL GOVERNMENT

Net expenditures for general government activities are estimated at 1.6 billion dollars for the fiscal year 1956, an increase of 344 million dollars from the fiscal year 1955. The higher level of expenditures in 1956 reflects primarily (*a*) the proposed resumption of payments to the Civil Service Retirement Fund for the Government's share of the cost of current benefits for retired Federal civilian personnel and (*b*) substantially higher payments arising from claims against the Government. Other expenditures for general government cover in the main the costs of such basic Government services as making and enforcing laws, collecting taxes and customs, managing the public debt, and safeguarding and maintaining public buildings and records.

Special allowances are made in the reserves for proposed legislation of this budget for adjustments in the pay and benefits of civilian employees of the Government which I recommended recently in a special message to the Congress. The proposed benefits include a new system of contributory hospitalization and health insurance.

Legislative functions.—Expenditures for legislative activities are estimated to increase from 51 million dollars in 1955 to 63 million dollars in 1956, primarily because of construction of the new Senate Office Building.

Federal financial management.—To enable the Internal Revenue Service to make still more progress in equitable and effective enforcement of the revenue laws, I am recommending increased appropriations of 12 million dollars to extend the audit of tax returns. The improved enforcement should result in increased tax receipts from those who have not been paying their fair share. In addition, I am recommending legislation to reduce the frequency of information returns submitted by employers withholding income and social security taxes and to strengthen enforcement of these taxes. These amendments will not only cut down the reporting burden on private business, but will also increase budget receipts, especially in later years. Total expenditures for collection of taxes and customs, for administration of the public debt and for other Federal financial management are estimated at 450 million dollars for the fiscal year 1956.

Central property and records management.—The General Services Administration is making substantial and continuing economies in the governmentwide management of property and records. Central motor pools are planned for 15 cities, with important savings anticipated. Substantial reductions in office and warehouse space are continuing. As a result of examination

GENERAL GOVERNMENT

[Fiscal years. In millions]

Program or agency	Expenditures 1954 actual	Expenditures 1955 estimated	Expenditures 1956 estimated	Recommended new obligational authority for 1956
Legislative functions........................	$45	$51	$63	$50
Judicial functions...........................	29	33	34	33
Executive direction.........................	11	13	11	11
Federal financial management:				
Tax collection...........................	277	273	285	286
Customs collection, debt management and other.................................	171	164	165	164
Other central services:				
Central property and records management....	152	156	162	164
Civil Service Commission..................	16	15	17	17
Other....................................	16	21	21	24
Retirement for Federal civilian employees:				
Present programs.........................	34	32	2	2
Proposed legislation......................	......	......	216	216
Unemployment compensation for Federal civilian employees................................	......	33	40	40
Protective services and alien control:				
Federal Bureau of Investigation.............	75	79	91	88
Immigration and Naturalization Service.....	40	44	45	45
Other....................................	31	23	25	24
Territories, possessions, and District of Columbia:				
District of Columbia......................	13	25	34	32
Territories, possessions, and other...........	43	49	48	45
Other general government:				
Payment of claims and relief acts............	213	163	250	....
Weather Bureau..........................	26	25	29	33
Other....................................	20	23	32	30
Total.................................	1,212	1,225	1,569	[1] 1,305
Deduct applicable receipts....................	4	3	3	....
Net budget expenditures.....................	1,209	1,222	1,566	....

[1] Compares with new obligational authority of 1,041 million dollars in 1954 and 1,056 million dollars in 1955.

of Government real property holdings, the sales program of surplus real property will be accelerated, with the desirable result of returning this property to local tax rolls and increasing budget receipts.

In this budget, I recommend added funds for more adequate

repair and improvement of public buildings to protect the Government's investment. Estimated expenditures for central property and records management will therefore rise from 156 million dollars in 1955 to 162 million dollars in 1956.

To help meet the most critical needs for office space, construction of several general-purpose buildings has already been approved under the long-term lease-purchase contract authority provided by the Eighty-third Congress, and additional buildings will be considered as quickly as determinations of need and cost can be made. These buildings will be purchased through annual appropriations for rental payments.

Civil Service Commission.—Under the recent revisions of the Federal civil service rules, a substantially higher proportion of civilian employees will be on a competitive basis. The transition to this system will require additional funds for the Civil Service Commission for administering the necessary examining program, both in the continental United States and overseas.

Retirement for Federal civilian employees.—The civil service retirement and disability system should be financed on a more satisfactory basis. Employees now contribute 6 percent of pay, covering about one-half the currently accruing cost, and the Government is responsible for the rest of the cost. In the past the Government's share of payments to this fund has not been provided on a consistent basis and in the last 2 years appropriations have been deferred pending the report of the Committee on Retirement Policy for Federal Personnel. The Committee's report to the Eighty-third Congress establishes the necessity for a sound and lasting financial basis for the civil service retirement system.

Financing of the civil service system is a problem requiring careful consideration because of its importance to the Federal career service. For 1956 I am recommending a Government contribution of 216 million dollars which is estimated to be the difference in that year between the Government's share of current benefit disbursements and the interest earned on its part of the fund. This will serve to maintain at its present level the equity the Government already has built up in the fund through its past contributions.

Other budget expenditures for retired Federal civilian employees are estimated to decline from 32 million dollars in the fiscal year 1955 to 2 million dollars in 1956 because payments for cost-of-living increases under the act of July 16, 1952, will be made from the trust fund.

Unemployment compensation for Federal civilian employees.—Legislation enacted by the last Congress provides for the payment of unemployment compensation benefits to Federal civilian workers.   These payments are similar to those available to most workers in private industry and are being paid through existing State unemployment compensation agencies. Payments reimbursing the States for the cost of this program for the fiscal year 1955 are estimated at 33 million dollars, requiring a supplemental appropriation of 20 million dollars. Expenditures are estimated to rise in 1956 to 40 million dollars because for the first time the plan will be in operation for a full fiscal year.

Protective services and alien control.—Increased expenditures for protective services and alien control are recommended to strengthen the border patrol operations of the Immigration and Naturalization Service and to maintain the Federal Bureau of Investigation at its present effectiveness in the fiscal year 1956. The Bureau's work has been increased by added responsibilities for internal security. At the same time, its costs have risen because of recently enacted legislation providing premium pay for FBI agents for overtime and holiday work.

District of Columbia.—Under the new public works program authorized by the Congress last spring, Federal expenditures for the District of Columbia will increase to 34 million dollars in the fiscal year 1956. Of this amount, 22 million dollars represents the Federal Government's share in the costs of District government and public services; loans of 12 million dollars will be made to the District for construction of highways, sewers, and waterworks.

Weather Bureau.—To increase the effectiveness of the weather service, I am recommending replacement of certain obsolete facilities with modern observational equipment. This budget provides for the Weather Bureau to take over operation of 25 upper-air stations and perform certain other activities basic to civilian weather service which are now carried on by the Department of Defense. These proposals will carry out recommendations made by an advisory committee of eminent meteorologists. With the improved program, the expenditures of the Weather Bureau for the fiscal year 1956 are estimated at 29 million dollars, an increase of 4 million dollars over 1955.

Claims and relief acts.—Payments for claims and relief acts are estimated at 250 million dollars for the fiscal year 1956, an increase of 87 million dollars over the 1955 estimate. The increase consists entirely of higher payments for certified claims, which represent, in the main, bills presented for payment after the appropriation involved has lapsed. In the fiscal year 1955 certified claims are expected to be lower than in 1956 because claims which would otherwise have been paid from this account are being paid from certain Department of Defense appropriations which were extended by the Congress for 1 year.

INTEREST

The large interest payments by the Federal Government arise primarily from the tremendous increase in the public debt during World War II. In the fiscal year 1956 they account for about 10 percent of total budget expenditures. The size of the public debt and interest rates on the debt determine the general level of interest expenditures; variations may also occur from year to year from changes in interest payment provisions of specific securities.

Interest on the public debt.—Interest payments on the public debt in the fiscal year 1956 are estimated at 6.3 billion dollars.

INTEREST

[Fiscal years.   In millions]

Item	Budget expenditures (net)			Recommended new obligational authority for 1956
	1954 actual	1955 estimated	1956 estimated	
Interest on public debt....................	$6,382	$6,475	$6,300	$6,300
Interest on refunds of receipts...............	83	78	73	73
Interest on uninvested trust deposits...........	5	5	5	5
Total.................................	6,470	6,558	6,378	[1] 6,378

[1] Compares with new obligational authority of 6,470 million dollars in 1954 and 6,558 million dollars in 1955.

Although the debt has increased, interest payments are estimated to be 175 million dollars less than in the current year.   This decrease reflects primarily the reduction in the calendar year 1954 in interest rates on the outstanding debt.   Another reason for the decrease is the unusual concentration in 1955 of interest payments on part of the public debt refunded this year.   As an example of both reasons, in the fall of 1954, 7.5 billion dollars of 2⅝ percent certificates were refunded into a 1⅛ percent certificate and a 2⅛ percent bond.   A full year's interest was paid in the fiscal year 1955 on the maturing 2⅝ percent certificates; in addition, the first interest payment on the new 2⅛ percent bond will be due in 1955.   For these reasons interest payments in 1955 on this 7.5 billion dollar segment of the debt will be about 130 million dollars more than in 1956.

We have made progress in improving the structure of the public debt by lengthening the average maturity.   Nevertheless, the average interest rate on the debt has declined from 2.41 percent to 2.29 percent during the last 12 months.

In this message, we have stated our objectives and our proposals for the coming year.

In preparing this budget we have weighed the requirements of each element of our strength in order that we may allocate our resources according to the requirements of the whole. To each is apportioned the full measure required by relative need and permitted by available means. At the same time our awareness of the necessity for efficient, economical, and moral Government and the development of partnerships with State and local governments and with private enterprise permit reductions in total expenditures. A growing prosperity will result in increasing revenues and should make possible both a balanced budget and lower tax rates in the near future.

DWIGHT D. EISENHOWER

NOTE: As printed, the following have been deleted: (1) three summary tables setting forth new obligational authority and budget expenditures, by function and agency, and budget receipts; (2) references to special analyses appearing in the budget proper.

18 ¶ The President's News Conference of *January* 19, 1955.

[This is a complete transcript of the news conference of this date. Those portions of the President's replies which were not released for broadcasting or direct quotation at that time are enclosed in brackets.

[Television, newsreel, and newspaper camera equipment were present for the first time throughout a Presidential news conference. Candid photographs of the President were released. Portions of the film and sound track were released for broadcast that night over television and radio and were available for newsreels. The release of portions of news conferences for radio, television, and newsreel use continued until May 18, when the practice of releasing the entire conference began.

[The broadcasting and newsreel release of excerpts of the news conferences led to a major change in their treatment in the press. Heretofore it had been customary to state the President's replies in indirect discourse only. Beginning with the January 19 conference, direct quotation was authorized for those portions of the transcript corresponding to the released tape and film. With the conference of May 18 direct quotation of the entire transcript began.]

THE PRESIDENT. Please be seated.

Well, I see we are trying a new experiment this morning. I hope it doesn't prove to be a disturbing influence.

I have no announcements. We will go directly to questions.

Q. Robert E. Clark, International News Service: Mr. President, could you discuss the seriousness of the latest Communist attacks on Nationalist islands in the China Sea, in the light of our commitments to defend Formosa?

THE PRESIDENT. No military authority that I know of has tried to rate these small islands that are now under attack, or indeed the Tachens themselves, as an essential part of the defenses of Formosa and of the Pescadores, to the defense of which we are committed by the treaty that is now before the Senate for approval.

The two islands, I believe, that have been under attack are not occupied by Chinese National regulars. They have been occupied by irregulars or guerrillas.

Now, the Tachens themselves are a different proposition. They are occupied by a division of troops. They are of value, there is no denying that, they are of value as an outpost, an additional point for observation. They are not a vital element, as we see it, in the defense of the islands.

Exactly what is going to be the development there, I cannot foresee, so I won't try to speculate on exactly what we should do in that area. We don't even know, I think, at this moment—at least I wasn't informed this morning—what the Generalissimo's personal intentions are with respect to that particular region.

Q. Chalmers M. Roberts, Washington Post and Times Herald: Mr. President, in the light of this latest fight, would you consider that it would be useful to have a cease-fire between Communist China and Nationalist China if that could be arranged through the U.N. or by some other means?

THE PRESIDENT. Well, I should like to see the U.N. attempt to exercise its good offices, I believe, because wherever there is any kind of fighting and open violence in the world, it is always sort of a powder keg.

Whether the United Nations could do anything in this particular place, I don't know, because probably each side would insist that it was an internal affair; although from our viewpoint it might be a good thing to have them take a look at the problem.

Q. Merriman Smith, United Press: Mr. President, would it be possible for you, sir, to define or give us your impressions of Secretary Dulles' use of the word "forever" yesterday when he said that we would not wait forever for the release of our airmen by the Chinese Communists?

THE PRESIDENT. Well now, Mr. Smith, I didn't read the exact terms of his statement. I did not and, therefore, I don't know the context in which he was speaking.

I do know this: Mr. Dulles and I meet together more often, I think, than any other two individuals of this Government, at least in the Cabinet level, and we are in perfect accord as to our solution to these problems as they arise; so whatever he said, I am sure it was in keeping with the general policies and convictions he and I hold about this problem.

Q. Nat S. Finney, Buffalo News: Mr. President, in your state of the Union message, I believe you used the phrase "never to be forgotten men."

THE PRESIDENT. That is right.

Q. Mr. Finney: I wonder if you could give us a little better, a more complete insight as to what you had in mind in using that phrase?

THE PRESIDENT. Well, as long as there is an American unjustly imprisoned, I am going to continue to do my best to exert the influence that I think is available to us to secure his release, and to see that he gets justice.

Now, let us never forget, ladies and gentlemen, that the lives of these individuals are at stake as well as some academic concept of the exact right in this thing. And let us not forget this either: our own knowledge of our purity of motive in the world is not always shared sometimes even by those we know to be our friends; and it is idle to say that there cannot be misunderstandings on the other side as to our motives and intentions and ideas.

You will recall there were 25,000 prisoners escaped—North Koreans. They escaped into South Korea, and this created a very great difficulty at the time of the armistice negotiations.

Now, we thought we were right, but what did the other side think?

So you have these problems where we are certain that justice, decency, and right is on our side, but we also have the problem of convincing others that we are right and just and decent, and sometimes these things can create a lot of misapprehension and misunderstanding.

Q. Roscoe Drummond, New York Herald Tribune: Mr. President, do you think it is fair to conclude or do you conclude that the negotiations by Mr. Hammarskjold are a failure?

THE PRESIDENT. Well, I would never admit failure to anything as long as it is going on. I have understood from his report that this was one step in negotiations that he expects to carry forward. He is meeting with the Secretary of State at 11:00 this morning, and I assume that we will have a little bit clearer understanding of exactly what he means.

Now, the negotiations can never be a success until the Americans and allies unjustly held in China are returned to their homelands.

On the other hand, they are certainly not a failure as long as they are going on. That would be just as incomprehensible as to admit defeat in a battle as long as you have got one man on the firing line. I never would admit that, so I don't think we are defeated there.

Q. Laurence H. Burd, Chicago Tribune: Mr. President, can you give us any idea what you would consider a reasonable time for the U.N. to negotiate for the return of these prisoners?

THE PRESIDENT. No, I don't think I could guess. I think that the time factor would always have to be related to any progress that you can see or feel or believe in. So, as long as a man of the character and standing of Hammarskjold believes that he is making progress, I think that you would have to wait; because, I repeat, there is here involved a question of lives of people as well as our rights, the common understanding of the facts in the case—there are numerous things that are involved, and I think he ought to have a full chance to do what he can.

Q. May Craig, Maine Papers: Mr. President, in view of the Communist violation of the Korean truce, what compliance could we expect from a U.N. truce in the Formosa Straits?

THE PRESIDENT. Well, maybe the best answer to that might be my saying that is a good question. [*Laughter*]

But I think that is a problem forever in dealing with someone who shows a proclivity for acting like solemn agreements were scraps of paper, and it is what I think that we—Mr. Dulles and I—always mean when we say we want some confirmation in deeds, not just words. You will recall that in dealing with these questions in the past, when we have talked about the deeds that were necessary in the Far East, we have talked about withdrawal of troops in Korea that would remove the stigma placed upon Communist China by the United Nations in calling them an aggressor nation; in returning our prisoners; in abstaining from aggressive acts in Southeast Asia; in conducting itself as a civilized nation in the councils of the world.

Now, you begin to understand what we mean by deeds that give some belief that we may have confidence in the agreements we draw up with them. What you are doing is voicing a doubt, and I must say that all of us share it.

Q. Sarah McClendon, El Paso Times: Mr. President, the Congressmen on Capitol Hill say that if they can find a copy of the budget to read that they can't understand it. [*Laughter*] Particularly, they say, the military budget is couched in such general terms that they can't find where the money is to be spent.

Now, the justifications for these individual projects will go to two committees, appropriations committees, and not to the Members of Congress in general.

Is there anything you can do to tell these people who have to vote on this where the money is to be spent?

THE PRESIDENT. [It is my understanding that is what the committees of Congress are for, and that is what the people that appear before those committees are for.

[The national defense officials, from the Secretary on down to any level that the military committees and the appropriation committees want to call, will appear before them; and they will explain every single item in it. I can't be expected to take the details of a volume like that—I forget the number of pages—and explain that in detail to individuals anywhere.]

Q. Joseph A. Loftus, New York Times: Mr. President, will you comment on the proposal that Formosa and Red China be considered separate independent nations, and that there be an exchange of mutual security, and settle the problem that way?

THE PRESIDENT. [No, I don't think I will comment on it for the simple reason that that commenting would make it appear that my convictions were finally formed in this area.

[It is, of course, one of the possibilities that is constantly studied, but you can see that both sides to it might be very reluctant to have that proposal seriously considered.]

Q. John C. O'Brien, Philadelphia Inquirer: In your budget message you said you would not recommend an appropriation for the dredging of the upper channel of the Delaware River unless a cost-sharing plan was worked out. Now, some of the Congressmen from that area are pointing out that private industry has never before been assessed for a navigation project.

Now, my question is: is this a new Government policy or are there special reasons for cost-sharing in the Delaware River project?

THE PRESIDENT. [Well, there are two things, I think: one is that I do believe that when the Federal Government spends money that is mainly to the interests of the locality, we should find some way to make that locality participate.

[I did not, by any manner of means, specify the method by

which this partnership could be worked out. I suppose that the range of things that could be studied would be all the way from tolls, that is, from vessels actually using such a channel, to some direct participation in the original case. I do believe that we should, in these great projects, try to find a way that you get the local concern for economy or local benefits reflected in the appropriations the Federal Government makes.

[Admittedly, let us say, this is to the general welfare of the whole Nation; and if it is a new policy, I think it should have been considered long ago myself.]

Q. Mr. O'Brien: Mr. President, the only new feature, I think, is the assessment on industry, local contributions, which are somewhat different.

THE PRESIDENT. [That is what I say: I do believe there ought to be some way of participation, and I wouldn't say that it couldn't be by tolls. I do say that I feel that there should be some local participation by those who are going to profit directly and in a major way in these things.]

Q. Marvin L. Arrowsmith, Associated Press: Mr. President, as tomorrow is the second anniversary of your inauguration, I wonder if you would care to give us an appraisal of your first 2 years, and tell us something of your hopes for the next 2 or maybe even the next 6. [*Laughter*]

THE PRESIDENT. It looks like a loaded question. [*Laughter*]

Well, of course, I know of no way of evaluating the 2 years of this except to remind ourselves of certain things that have happened. I think I can say this without attempting to take either too much partisan credit or personal credit, because all of us realize that if these things have gone on, some of them have been participated in almost unanimously by both parties.

But, let us without any further explanation just take a look:

We were then fighting in Korea, and that war has been ended.

Iran was in such situation that we weekly thought we had possibly lost it or we would see it going under Communist influence unreservedly and finally.

There was a struggle going on between two of our friends, Britain and Egypt.

The Trieste situation was upsetting all our relations in the Mediterranean, and bade fair to create really serious trouble in those countries, particularly in Italy.

There was a growing difficulty in Central America, which finally flared up into the Guatemalan incident.

And at that moment it looked like we were probably approaching close to defeat in our efforts to get any kind of agreement in Western Europe.

Now, those things have been largely eliminated.

In addition, I believe that we have been successful in convincing all of the countries of the Mid-East that we are desperately trying to be friends with everybody, trying to make friends between ourselves and each of the nations concerned.

So I think that on the whole, in spite of a weakened situation in Indonesia [Indochina] and of the partial loss of Viet-Nam, that the foreign situation is more stable, generally speaking, looks better, and that is not by any means to say that it looks rosy.

At home, we started out, you will recall, with a definite economic program.

I am going to read one thing someone called to my attention this morning, because they said that I had been here 2 years. They pointed out that I said I was going to balance the budget quickly, and I want to read from the speech I made in Peoria, Illinois, October 2, 1952:

"A first and vital step is to eliminate the deficit from our national budget.

"Second, restore the incentive to expand production. A major step toward this end is to reduce Government spending and thereby permit lower taxation. Federal spending can be cut from the present rate of $81 billion a year.

"My goal, assuming that the cold war gets no worse, is to cut Federal spending to something like $60 billion within 4 years. Such a cut would eliminate the deficit in the budget."

Now, of course, you have seen the recent budget, and its estimate that there will still be a $2,400,000,000 deficit; but the budget itself, by coincidence, is $62,400,000,000, so I almost can claim credit for being a prophet.

If there could be found some way of eliminating that $2,400,-000,000, why, it would look like it would be in balance.

Now, in addition to that, controls have been removed from our economy.

There has been a new farm program set up which we have every reason to believe will bring about a better balance between production and markets.

We have brought about the transition from a war economy to a peace economy with, I think, almost an unprecedented easing of the situation and its impact upon our people and their several occupations and businesses.

There has been a reduction in taxes that is unprecedented for any single year in our history.

Now, along with that, we come to the moment, and we look ahead. We have an expanding economy. We have an economy and an industry, financial situation, that reflects the confidence and hope of our people, the belief of our people.

Now, I am not saying that the stock market itself, its rises and falls, is necessarily an index of what is going to happen in this country; but it does reflect that kind of confidence that we have tried in the past so hard to instill.

There is a greater production of houses in our country today than ever before in our history. We are even higher today than we were in 1953.

All the way along, consumer spending is going up, consumer savings are going up.

There is, of course, not a wholly satisfactory picture. There are industries in particular areas where there are still difficulties. We are working on them.

But the outlook, certainly from the standpoint of our internal economy, is good. I know of no better measure, if I may conclude here, Mr. Arrowsmith, than to say: how do people feel today as to the way they felt then?

Q. Clark R. Mollenhoff, Des Moines Register and Tribune: Mr. President, last week you told us that Secretary Benson had given you a one-sided version of this Ladejinsky case, and at that time you indicated that you personally could not look into all of these cases.

I wondered if, in light of that, you could tell us if you have any mechanism set up in the White House to protect yourself against misinformation or half information from Cabinet officers or other individuals, the types of thing that led Mr. Truman and Mr. Harding in so much trouble.

THE PRESIDENT. I think you are a little bit unfair in your interpretation of exactly what I said. I didn't say he deliberately gave me a one-sided picture. I said he gave me a memorandum of the facts, as he saw them; and the facts as he saw them, I said, would have disturbed me very badly.

Now, I also said that I trust the judgment of the people that I put in these important administrative positions. In spite of the fact that in this case two of these people have reached different conclusions, I believe that each has exercised his own judgment honestly; and I am not going to take unto myself making an investigation in this area, I assure you.

Q. Mr. Mollenhoff: Mr. President, I understood that you backed them in their right to make different judgments——

THE PRESIDENT. That is right.

Q. Mr. Mollenhoff: ——on these things.

I wondered, though, if you would feel there was something you should step in on where there was a difference on fact, as in a serious situation where one department would say a man was a member of two Communist front organizations, and the other department would make a flat statement that he was not?

THE PRESIDENT. [Well, what we had here, of course, was a simple thing. This was a case where the heads of two principal departments were involved, and they reached different conclusions.

[Normally, and under the orders that have been issued, it is expected that each individual, each head of department, will in his own field exercise his judgment; and that created rather a paradox.

[Now, arrangements have been made that when two departments reach different conclusions on these things, there will be coordination.]

Q. Robert J. Donovan, New York Herald Tribune: Mr. President, is that something new that you are telling us here now?

THE PRESIDENT. [No, I think it is not really new. I think it is a precautionary admonition, you might say, a piece of advice because it should be normal procedure in a well-run organization, and possibly it was overlooked here.]

Q. Mr. Donovan: May I rephrase this question just once more?

THE PRESIDENT. Yes.

Q. Mr. Donovan: Are there any specific new changes or studies in prospect in this matter?

THE PRESIDENT. Well, Mr. Donovan, I told you people several times I know of nothing that is engaging more attention all the time.

I have told you of the special department set up in the Attorney General's Office to which all the troublesome, particularly troublesome, matters can be referred for advice and counsel and, particularly, to which can be referred any case where there are differing views.

There has also been initiated by other groups—I believe by a university group in one case, I believe by the New York Bar Association—certain inquiries into these things. I assure you they will be assisted in the making of their inquiries into policy or into programs; they are not attempting to be judges in particular cases.

Q. Edward T. Folliard, Washington Post and Times Herald: Mr. President, to go back to the fighting in the Far East for a moment, the dispatches from Formosa say that the Chinese Reds may now storm the other islands off the coast, including the Tachens.

A United Press story from Formosa says there is an American detachment on one of the Tachen Islands.

If we may assume that that story is correct, would we leave that American detachment on any of those islands, in view of the fact that they may be attacked by the Chinese Reds?

THE PRESIDENT. Well, I would have to ask the commander on the spot what orders these individuals are under; whether they are still there or not, I don't know. Most of these units—[*confers with Mr. Hagerty*]—well, I think that is a technicality.

The fact is that I assume the commander has given his instructions under different circumstances as to what will occur, and it hasn't been brought to my attention; but Mr. Hagerty does say there are four or five men on one of the islands, I think.

Q. John Herling, Editors Syndicate: Mr. President, Secretary of Labor Mitchell has recommended to you that a career servant, Ewan Clague, be renominated as Commissioner of Labor Statistics, and that recommendation has been in the White House for several months. I wonder whether you have any knowledge of the situation?

THE PRESIDENT. [I will have to look it up. I don't recall the name.]

Q. Mr. Herling: Ewan Clague is the incumbent Commissioner.

THE PRESIDENT. [I don't recall the name; I will have to look it up.]

Q. Mr. Herling: Thank you, sir.

Q. William Theis, International News Service: Yesterday Secretary Wilson said he would favor nonstrategic trade with the Communist bloc countries. Does that bear your considered approval, or can you comment further on it?

THE PRESIDENT. Well, it certainly could not be said to carry my considered approval, although the subject, of course, has been discussed in this Government, in Congress, since—well, for 2 years.

There are two points, I think, that it is well to remember about trade: one, that trade is a process that takes place between two nations or two groups and, presumably, for the economic benefit of both.

If you trade something to me, you think that you are getting the benefit of the trade, and I think I am getting it.

But there is also this: trade is one of the greatest influences in the hands of the diplomat; and how he uses it, negatively or positively or in roundabout methods even, it is an influence to bring about and carry out the policies under which that country is operating.

Now, our policy is simple—to promote peaceful relationships in the world; and I would say we would never with anyone carry on trade unless we thought that that cause were gaining. Certainly under present conditions we do have complete embargoes with respect to certain countries, and so just some casual statement of that kind would not change our policy.

Q. Merriman Smith, United Press: Mr. President, when you referred, you said arrangements had been made that when two departments reached different conclusions on security cases, that there will be coordination. Could you tell us who does the coordinating? Are you referring to the unit in the Justice Department——

THE PRESIDENT. That is correct.

Q. Mr. Smith:——or does the White House——

THE PRESIDENT. That is correct. I have asked them in each case, before that case would have to be referred to me, that they first meet with this individual and try to accomplish that coordination.

Of course, I think if a similar case to the one to which you referred occurred in the future, and it couldn't be settled, well, they would bring it to me; but then there would be a complete report of investigation on both sides.

Q. Alice A. Dunnigan, Associated Negro Press: Mr. President, will the Government continue to permit naval vessels to visit ports where the crews must submit to segregation, racial segregation, as happened when the carrier Midway visited Capetown, South Africa, recently?

THE PRESIDENT. [You will have to go and ask the Secretary of Defense or the Secretary of the Navy, one of the two.

[What I know about that case has been brought to me by showing me a clipping out of the newspaper, and I don't know anything about it.]

Q. Martin S. Hayden, Detroit News: Mr. President, in your state of the Union message you promised or indicated there would be a positive Federal program to aid the construction of schools, but in the budget message we couldn't find any money for it. Will there be some actual expenditures?

THE PRESIDENT. Remember this, there has to be a new authorization in that regard. Now, there is a plan from Mrs. Hobby's office going to the Congress on 15 February. Remember this: there is a White House Conference called for November. It is a very broad educational conference, and nobody in this administration is going to get in the way of the findings of that to the extent of, let's say, vitiating the recommendations or trying to anticipate them. But what we are trying to do now, recognizing the acute shortage of schoolrooms, is to find a method of helping and assisting States and localities and districts to get this thing on the rails, knowing that we can't possibly in this way damage anything that will be done by this conference.

Q. John D. Morris, New York Times: A moment ago you read from a speech in which you outlined a 4-year program for balancing the budget.

THE PRESIDENT. Yes.

Q. Mr. Morris: I believe about 3 of those are up now. Could you say that is a promise to balance that next year?

THE PRESIDENT. [I thought someone had reminded me I had been here 2 years.]

Q. Mr. Morris: Well, this is the third budget, I believe, sir.

THE PRESIDENT. [Oh, no. The first budget had been prepared.

[We have been here 2 years, let's don't try to push me too hard.] [*Laughter*]

Q. Edward Milne, Providence Evening Bulletin: Mr. President, I would like to know, sir, your reaction to former Senator Harry Cain's strong criticism over the weekend of these employee security programs.

THE PRESIDENT. [Well, Mr. Cain, like everybody else, has his right to criticize.

[Again I say the system that he criticizes, I believe, is fairly well conceived. Certainly it is the best that we have been able to devise in view of the conflicting considerations that apply. And they are also sensitive considerations, sensitive on the side of the Government and sensitive on the side of the individual. In their application always there is human failure; I admit that, and I don't claim any kind of perfection.

[Now, so far as I know, Mr. Cain has not submitted to any responsible official in the executive department a summary of his objections or on what he bases his criticism. I did read part of his speech, and that is all I know about it.]

Q. Andrew F. Tully, Jr., Scripps-Howard: Mr. President, after 2 years in office, how do you like your job? [*Laughter*]

THE PRESIDENT. I don't think I will try to answer that one. Like everything else, there are not wholly unmixed blessings in such duties and responsibilities.

Merriman Smith, United Press: Thank you, Mr. President.

NOTE: President Eisenhower's fifty-eighth news conference was held in the Executive Office Building from 10:33 to 11:05 o'clock on Wednesday morning, January 19, 1955. In attendance: 218.

19 ¶ Annual Message Presenting the Economic Report to the Congress.   *January* 20, 1955

To the Congress of the United States:

I am herewith presenting my Economic Report, as required by Section 3 (a) of the Employment Act of 1946.

In preparing this Report, I have had the assistance and advice of the Council of Economic Advisers.   I have also had the advice of the heads of executive departments and independent agencies.

I present below, largely in the words of the Report itself, what I regard as its highlights.

SOURCES OF ECONOMIC PROGRESS

With production and employment now increasing on a broad front, the events of the past year have borne out the major conclusions of the Economic Report of January 1954 concerning the state of our economy and the policies needed to promote sound economic growth.

Economic well-being sustains our whole national life. A high and rising standard of living brings to more of our people the opportunity for continued intellectual and spiritual growth.

The main sources of our Nation's economic strength are its free institutions and the qualities of its people—their ambition, skill, enterprise, and willingness to make great efforts in their own behalf and in behalf of their families and communities.

The need of our times is for economic policies that, in the first place, recognize the proven sources of sustained economic growth and betterment, and in the second place, respect the need of people for a sense of security as well as opportunity in our complex, industrialized society.

A free economy has great capacity to generate jobs and incomes if a feeling of confidence in the economic future is widely shared by investors, workers, businessmen, farmers, and consumers.

Many factors favor a continuation of our vigorous economic growth. The population is increasing rapidly, educational levels are rising, work skills are improving, incomes are widely distributed, consumers are eager to better their living standards, businessmen are starting new enterprises and expanding old ones, the tools of industry are multiplying and improving, research and technology are opening up new opportunities, and our public policies generally encourage enterprise and innovation.

With wise management of the national household, our country can within a decade increase its production from the current annual level of about 360 billion dollars to 500 billion, or more, expressed in dollars of the same buying power.

In the future as in the past, increases in productivity and in useful employment opportunities will be the core of economic expansion.

The role of the Federal Government in the achievement of these goals is to create an atmosphere favorable to economic activity by encouraging private initiative, curbing monopolistic tendencies, avoiding encroachment on the private sector of the economy, and carrying out as much of its own work as is practicable through private enterprise. It should take its full part at the side of State and local governments in providing appropriate public facilities. It should restrain tendencies toward recession or inflation. It should widen opportunities for less fortunate citizens, and help individuals to cope with the hazards of unemployment, illness, old age, and blighted neighborhoods.

Last year the Government took many steps, both legislative and administrative, to encourage economic expansion. Fiscal and monetary measures fostered an expectation of improving economic conditions and encouraged people to maintain a high rate of expenditure. The opportunities of competitive enterprise were enlarged; economic ties with other countries were improved; the floor of personal and family security was strengthened; and additions were made to our public assets.

THE ECONOMY TODAY

The year 1954 was one of transition from contraction to recovery. The contraction reflected the efforts of businessmen to reduce inventories, and was aggravated by a large reduction in military expenditures.

The contraction was relatively mild and brief, because of a variety of timely public and private actions.

The Government cut taxes, the Federal Reserve System eased credit conditions, and the Treasury arranged its financing so as not to compete with mortgages and other long-term issues. A comprehensive program for encouraging private enterprise was submitted to the Congress. Apart from this, the decline in private incomes was automatically cushioned by increased payments of unemployment insurance and other benefits and by sharp cuts in taxes due the Government on the reduced incomes.

Consumers maintained a high rate of spending, businessmen kept capital expenditures at a high rate, builders stepped up their activities, trade unions conducted their affairs with a sense of responsibility, farmers recognized the dangers of piling up ever larger surpluses, private lenders made ample supplies of credit available on liberal terms, States and localities carried out large construction programs, and export demand remained strong.

Although manufacturing production fluctuated, total output was fairly stable, and disposable personal income reached record levels. But some industries and localities suffered from serious unemployment. The fortunes of most of them turned for the better when recovery got under way in the early autumn, and they will benefit from further general economic expansion.

Instead of expanding Federal enterprises or initiating new spending programs, the basic policy of the Government in dealing with the contraction was to take actions that created confidence in the future and stimulated business firms, consumers, and States and localities to increase their expenditures.

The vigor of the recent recovery, which has already made up half of the preceding decline in industrial production, suggests that economic expansion will probably continue during coming months. It holds out the promise that we shall achieve a high and satisfactory level of employment and production within the current year.

A further expansion of consumer spending may reasonably be expected; we are soon likely to experience some rebuilding of inventories; the decline of Federal spending next year will be less rapid than during the last two years; State and local expenditure will probably continue to expand; the outlook for housing and commercial construction continues to be good; there is a prospect that plant and equipment expenditures may turn upward, as the general economic advance proceeds; the outlook for export demand is brightened by the economic resurgence of an ever-widening area of the Free World.

It is essential to keep a close watch on financial developments; continued economic recovery must not be jeopardized by over-emphasis of speculative activity.

TOWARD SUSTAINED ECONOMIC GROWTH

The wise course for Government in 1955 is to direct its program principally toward fostering long-term economic growth rather than toward imparting an immediate upward thrust to economic activity.

Further efforts to reduce Federal expenditures, together with increasing revenues from a tax base growing as the economy expands, should make possible some additional general tax reductions next year. Progress could then also be made in further lowering tax barriers to the free flow of funds into risk-taking and job-creating investments.

Government should persist in its efforts to maintain easy entry into trade and industry, to check monopoly, and to preserve a competitive environment. Continued encouragement should be given to small and new businesses.

Scientific research and development activities in all their phases should continue to have the earnest support of the Federal Government.

Measures by ourselves and other nations to reduce existing barriers to international trade, payments, and investment will make the Free World stronger and aid our own economic growth.

Measures should be considered to extend personal security against the hazard of unemployment, to strengthen minimum wage legislation, to protect savings in credit unions, and to increase the President's discretionary authority to vary the terms of insured mortgage loans in the interest of economic stability.

A great ten-year program to modernize the interstate highway system should be authorized.

Our partnership policies of water resource development should be further implemented by appropriate Congressional and local action.

Action should be taken this year to help meet our Nation-wide needs for school construction. I shall shortly send to the Congress a special message that will deal with methods by which the Federal Government can appropriately assist in this vital field.

Support should be provided for an Office of Coordinator of Public Works Planning in the Executive Office of the President, and for a revolving fund for advances to the States and municipalities for public works planning.

CONCLUSION

Our Nation's recent history teaches that a foresighted Government can do much to help keep the economy stable, but experience affords no good basis for a belief that the Government can entirely prevent fluctuations.

We should harness the idealism as well as the intelligence of our generation to the practical end of facilitating the growth of private enterprise and of increasing the stability of our economy.

The Government will shoulder its full responsibility to help realize that goal.

DWIGHT D. EISENHOWER

NOTE: The message and the complete report (203 pages) are published in "Economic Report of the President, 1955" (Government Printing Office, 1955).

20 ¶ Letter to Representative Auchincloss on the Second Anniversary of the President's Inauguration. *January* 20, 1955

[Read at ceremonies held at the Capitol Hill Club by the Club's President, Representative Auchincloss]

Dear Jim:

Because it would be a great pleasure for both of us, Mrs. Eisenhower and I are disappointed that we cannot be at the Capitol Hill Club on January twentieth for the inaugural anniversary. For me, personally, the occasion would be an opportunity to discuss with my fellow members some thoughts that I feel are of interest to us all. But—at the risk of mixing a message of regret with a dissertation—I venture, in this note, to suggest a few of them.

This Administration is committed to a program of progressive moderation, liberal in its human concerns, conservative in its economic proposals, constructively dynamic and optimistic in its appraisal of the future. This program, I firmly believe, merits the endorsement and support of thinking, confident, forward-looking Americans.

For our country and the world, we seek establishment of international relationships characterized by order and justice, in which reason and truth are respected, under which men can live as neighbors at peace. Within the United Nations and in all our pacts for mutual security, our treaties of alliance, our proposals for trade, that purpose inspires our foreign policy.

For our national economy, we seek a dependable stability in our present assets, a vigorous expansion in our future growth. These can be best achieved, we believe, by giving the private citizen the greatest possible opportunity—consistent with the rights of others—to contribute to the development of the economy and to share in its abundance.

For individual Americans, we seek increase in their opportunity to enjoy good health, good schools, good homes; we seek a lessening in their fear of personal disaster and in the impact of hardships beyond their control. In this endeavor, we reject Federal domination over state and community, for we seek to strengthen—not to weaken—the historic self-reliance of our people.

The principles and purposes, sketchily outlined here, must be in my judgment the standard of the Republican Party through the coming months. Committed to them, we can and must work together to advance the legislative program now before the 84th Congress, for this program is their legislative expression.

Thereby we shall serve our Party and the Republic. We shall draw to our ranks men and women of action and wisdom who, in prayerful thought and dedicated effort, strive for an America worthy of their forebears' dream and fit for their children's living. Together—all of us—we shall achieve it.

Sincerely,

DWIGHT D. EISENHOWER

21 ¶ Special Message to the Congress Regarding United States Policy for the Defense of Formosa. *January* 24, 1955

To the Congress of the United States:

The most important objective of our nation's foreign policy is to safeguard the security of the United States by establishing and preserving a just and honorable peace.   In the Western Pacific, a situation is developing in the Formosa Straits, that seriously imperils the peace and our security.

Since the end of Japanese hostilities in 1945, Formosa and the Pescadores have been in the friendly hands of our loyal ally, the Republic of China.   We have recognized that it was important that these islands should remain in friendly hands.   In unfriendly hands, Formosa and the Pescadores would seriously dislocate the existing, even if unstable, balance of moral, economic and military forces upon which the peace of the Pacific depends.   It would create a breach in the island chain of the Western Pacific that constitutes, for the United States and other free nations, the geographical backbone of their security structure in that Ocean.   In addition, this breach would interrupt North-South communications between other important elements of that barrier, and damage the economic life of countries friendly to us.

The United States and the friendly Government of the Republic of China, and indeed all the free nations, have a common interest that Formosa and the Pescadores should not fall into the control of aggressive Communist forces.

Influenced by such considerations, our government was prompt, when the Communists committed armed aggression in Korea in June 1950, to direct our Seventh Fleet to defend Formosa from possible invasion from the Communist mainland.

These considerations are still valid.   The Seventh Fleet continues under Presidential directive to carry out that defensive mission. We also provide military and economic support to the Chinese Nationalist Government and we cooperate in every proper and feasible way with that Government in order to promote its security and stability. All of these military and related activities will be continued.

In addition, there was signed last December a Mutual Defense Treaty between this Government and the Republic of China covering Formosa and the neighboring Pescadores. It is a treaty of purely defensive character. That Treaty is now before the Senate of the United States.

Meanwhile Communist China has pursued a series of provocative political and military actions, establishing a pattern of aggressive purpose. That purpose, they proclaim, is the conquest of Formosa.

In September 1954 the Chinese Communists opened up heavy artillery fire upon Quemoy island, one of the natural approaches to Formosa, which had for several years been under the uncontested control of the Republic of China. Then came air attacks of mounting intensity against other free China islands, notably those in the vicinity of the Tachen group to the north of Formosa. One small island (Ichiang) was seized last week by air and amphibious operations after a gallant few fought bravely for days against overwhelming odds. There have been recent heavy air attacks and artillery fire against the main Tachen Islands themselves.

The Chinese Communists themselves assert that these attacks are a prelude to the conquest of Formosa. For example, after the fall of Ichiang, the Peiping Radio said that it showed a "determined will to fight for the liberation of Taiwan (Formosa). Our people will use all their strength to fulfill that task."

Clearly, this existing and developing situation poses a serious danger to the security of our country and of the entire Pacific area and indeed to the peace of the world. We believe that the situation is one for appropriate action of the United Nations under its charter, for the purpose of ending the present hostilities in that area. We would welcome assumption of such jurisdiction by that body.

Meanwhile, the situation has become sufficiently critical to impel me, without awaiting action by the United Nations, to ask the Congress to participate now, by specific resolution, in measures designed to improve the prospects for peace. These measures would contemplate the use of the armed forces of the United States if necessary to assure the security of Formosa and the Pescadores.

The actions that the United States must be ready to undertake are of various kinds. For example, we must be ready to assist the Republic of China to redeploy and consolidate its forces if it should so desire. Some of these forces are scattered throughout the smaller off-shore islands as a result of historical rather than military reasons directly related to defending Formosa. Because of the air situation in the area, withdrawals for the purpose of redeployment of Chinese Nationalist forces would be impractical without assistance of the armed forces of the United States.

Moreover, we must be alert to any concentration or employment of Chinese Communist forces obviously undertaken to facilitate attack upon Formosa, and be prepared to take appropriate military action.

I do not suggest that the United States enlarge its defensive obligations beyond Formosa and the Pescadores as provided by the Treaty now awaiting ratification. But unhappily, the danger of armed attack directed against that area compels us to take into account closely related localities and actions which, under current conditions, might determine the failure or the success of such an attack. The authority that may be accorded by the Congress would be used only in situations which are recognizable as parts of, or definite preliminaries to, an attack against the main positions of Formosa and the Pescadores.

Authority for some of the actions which might be required would be inherent in the authority of the Commander-in-Chief.

Until Congress can act I would not hesitate, so far as my Constitutional powers extend, to take whatever emergency action might be forced upon us in order to protect the rights and security of the United States.

However, a suitable Congressional resolution would clearly and publicly establish the authority of the President as Commander-in-Chief to employ the armed forces of this nation promptly and effectively for the purposes indicated if in his judgment it became necessary.   It would make clear the unified and serious intentions of our Government, our Congress and our people.   Thus it will reduce the possibility that the Chinese Communists, misjudging our firm purpose and national unity, might be disposed to challenge the position of the United States, and precipitate a major crisis which even they would neither anticipate nor desire.

In the interest of peace, therefore, the United States must remove any doubt regarding our readiness to fight, if necessary, to preserve the vital stake of the free world in a free Formosa, and to engage in whatever operations may be required to carry out that purpose.

To make this plain requires not only Presidential action but also Congressional action.   In a situation such as now confronts us, and under modern conditions of warfare, it would not be prudent to await the emergency before coming to the Congress. Then it might be too late.   Already the warning signals are flying.

I believe that the threatening aspects of the present situation, if resolutely faced, may be temporary in character.   Consequently, I recommend that the Resolution expire as soon as the President is able to report to the Congress that the peace and security of the area are reasonably assured by international conditions, resulting from United Nations action or otherwise.

Again I say that we would welcome action by the United Nations which might, in fact, bring an end to the active hostilities in the area.   This critical situation has been created by the choice of the Chinese Communists, not by us.   Their offensive military intent has been flaunted to the whole world by words and by deeds. Just as they created the situation, so they can end it if they so choose.

What we are now seeking is primarily to clarify present policy and to unite in its application. We are not establishing a new policy. Consequently, my recommendations do not call for an increase in the armed forces of the United States or any acceleration in military procurement or levels of defense production. If any unforeseen emergency arises requiring any change, I will communicate with the Congress. I hope, however, that the effect of an appropriate Congressional Resolution will be to calm the situation rather than to create further conflict.

One final point. The action I request is, of course, no substitute for the Treaty with the Republic of China which we have signed and which I have transmitted to the Senate. Indeed, present circumstances make it more than ever important that this basic agreement should be promptly brought into force, as a solemn evidence of our determination to stand fast in the agreed Treaty area and to thwart all attacks directed against it. If delay should make us appear indecisive in this basic respect, the pressures and dangers would surely mount.

Our purpose is peace. That cause will be served if, with your help, we demonstrate our unity and our determination. In all that we do we shall remain faithful to our obligations as a member of the United Nations to be ready to settle our international disputes by peaceful means in such a manner that international peace and security, and justice, are not endangered.

For the reasons outlined in this message, I respectfully request that the Congress take appropriate action to carry out the recommendations contained herein.

DWIGHT D. EISENHOWER

22 ¶ Remarks on Receiving Statue Presented by Ambassador Krekeler on Behalf of the German People. *January 25, 1955*

Mr. Ambassador, Mr. Carmichael, Ladies and Gentlemen:

It is indeed a great privilege to speak for the American people in accepting from the German people this product of a German artist and a gift of that entire nation.

We know that twice in our generation our two countries have been at war. What this gift symbolizes in a revolution of thinking—in the erasing of old enmities and a desire to cooperate among ourselves for the peaceful advancement of all nations—is going to be meaningful as long as this statue, this work of art, endures.

I think, for myself, I have a particular additional item of satisfaction in that I was, after all, the commander of the great forces from the West that swept over Germany in the most recent war. The fact that I am now privileged as the representative of our country to accept this, with feelings and mutual expressions of peaceful intent and purpose, is something that is very dear to me at this moment.

I hope, Mr. Ambassador, that you will express to President Heuss, and through him to all the people of Germany, the very great satisfaction we shall take in this, not only for its own sake as a great work of art, but because of what it symbolizes in the efforts that both nations and both peoples are now making to do our best to make this a peaceful world.

Thank you very much.

NOTE: The President spoke at the Natural History Building of the Smithsonian Institution, following the presentation by the German Ambassador of a bronze statue, "Laboring Youth." The President's opening words "Mr. Ambassador, Mr. Carmichael" referred to Dr. Heinz L. Krekeler, Ambassador from Germany, and Leonard Carmichael,

Secretary of the Smithsonian Institution.

The following letter from President Heuss, dated December 10, 1954, was read during the ceremonies by Ambassador Krekeler:

Mr. President:

During the years of Germany's deepest despair countless men and women in countries both near and far sent us gifts expressing their warmth of heart. These acts of humanity saved the lives of many Germans. Men and women, broken and exhausted, drew from them renewed courage to face life.

Among the nations who have helped in great-hearted fashion to mitigate the suffering in Germany, the United States of America occupies the foremost position. Numerous societies and organizations in your country have placed themselves in the service of brotherly love in a truly imposing effort that stands forth unrivalled in our time. Over and above this, innumerable American citizens have untiringly lent their aid by privately sending charitable gifts of every kind. Even today this flow of gifts from the United States has not spent itself and helps countless suffering human beings in Ger-

many, especially refugees and expellees who are still obliged to live in camps, to preserve their faith in a better future.

The German people cannot repay the debt of gratitude which accumulated during their years of anguish, but they can acknowledge it and attempt to make it manifest. This is to be done by means of art works created by our people and in many cases by men and women who themselves live in hard-pressed circumstances. All of my countrymen have gladly contributed to making these art works available in order that they may serve as symbols of their gratitude. Through these monuments we hope to find our way to the unknown benefactors in your country, so that each and every one of them will know that we have not forgotten his great-hearted act.

I ask your Excellency to accept this sculpture of a kneeling man by the sculptor Hermann Blumenthal as a modest token of the heartfelt gratitude which we bear to the people of the United States of America.

It is with pleasure, Mr. President, that I avail myself of this opportunity to assure you of my highest esteem.

THEODOR HEUSS

23 ¶ Toasts of the President and President Magloire of Haiti. *January 26, 1955*

My Friends:

It is a privilege to welcome to this country and to this house the President of Haiti and Mrs. Magloire. He comes from a Republic with which ours has a long record of friendship. We know that his visit can serve only to strengthen and to give fresh vigor and vitality to those ties.

We do trust that while they and their party are here in our country, they will find themselves in the midst of people that they feel are welcoming them to our shores, and extending to them the warm hand of hospitality.

When they go back home, we trust that they will have even a deeper affection than ever for this country and for our people—as we shall have for them.

So, as a token of our welcome to them, will you rise to drink, with me, a Toast to President and Mrs. Magloire.

NOTE: The President proposed this toast at a state dinner at the White House, at 9:50 p.m. President Magloire responded as follows:

Mr. President:

To the honor of being this evening the guest of one of the greatest military leaders that the United States has had, is added my profound satisfaction of being the spokesman of the whole Haitian nation, to express to the most qualified representative of this friendly country our profound gratitude for the generous assistance which comes to us from our powerful neighbors for the solution of the vital problem which we are facing.

I also take this opportunity to thank you, Mr. President, for the spontaneity with which you have come to our help at the time of the recent hurricane, which has caused so much damage in Haiti, and to beg you to accept our wishes for the continuing prosperity of the United States, and the arrival of this era of peace to the triumph to which you devote all your efforts.

To Mrs. Eisenhower, who represents with such dignity the American women, who beside their husbands work to make more beautiful and much stronger this land of liberty, I address in the names of Mrs. Magloire and myself, with our thanks, the cordial salute of the Republic of Haiti.

24 ¶ Statement by the President Upon Signing the Joint Resolution on the Defense of Formosa. *January* 29, 1955

I AM deeply gratified at the almost unanimous vote in the Congress of the United States on this joint resolution. To the members of the Congress and to their leaders with me here today I wish publicly to thank them for their great patriotic service.

By their vote, the American people through their elected representatives have made it clear to the world that we are united here at home in our determination to help a brave ally and to resist Communist armed aggression.

By so asserting this belief we are taking a step to preserve the peace in the Formosa area. We are ready to support a United Nations effort to end the present hostilities in the area, but we also are united in our determination to defend an area vital to the security of the United States and the free world.

NOTE: As adopted, the Joint Resolution is Public Law 4, 84th Congress (69 Stat. 7).

Two days earlier, on January 27, the White House announced that following a meeting of the National Security Council the President met with top Defense Department and military advisers to discuss the deployment of United States air and naval forces in the Formosa area. At that meeting, the release stated, the President made it clear that these forces were designed purely for defensive purposes and that any decision to use United States forces other than in immediate self-defense or in direct defense of Formosa and the Pescadores would be a decision which he would take and the responsibility for which he had not delegated.

25 ¶ Special Message to the Congress Recommending a Health Program. *January* 31, 1955

To the Congress of the United States:

Because the strength of our nation is in its people, their good health is a proper national concern; healthy Americans live more rewarding, more productive and happier lives. Fortunately, the nation continues its advance in bettering the health of all its people.

Deaths from infectious diseases have diminished. During the past year, important progress has been made in dealing with such diseases as rheumatic fever, high blood pressure, poliomyelitis and tuberculosis. Intensified research has produced more knowledge than ever before about the scourges of heart disease and cancer.

The 83rd Congress, during the last legislative session, supported dramatic new strides in vocational rehabilitation. By 1959, consequently, we should be restoring to useful lives most persons who become disabled and who can be rehabilitated and returned to employment. In human terms, this will be a heart-warming achievement.

The 1954 amendments to the Hospital Survey and Construction Act opened another new chapter in the national drive for better health. Under these amendments, further provision was made to help build health care facilities for the chronically ill; to aid in the construction of nursing and convalescent homes; to provide for more diagnostic and treatment centers for patients who do not need hospital care; and to help make centers available for the rehabilitation of the disabled.

These achievements represent a major gain for the immediate and future welfare of countless Americans—in the health of both mind and body. Recent advances do not, however, represent our full capacity to wage war on illness and disability throughout the land.

THE IMMEDIATE NEEDS

As a nation, we are doing less than now lies within our power to reduce the impact of disease. Many of our fellow Americans cannot afford to pay the costs of medical care when it is needed, and they are not protected by adequate health insurance. Too frequently the local hospitals, clinics, or nursing homes required for the prevention, diagnosis and treatment of disease either do not exist or are badly out of date. Finally, there are critical shortages of the trained personnel required to study, prevent, treat and control disease.

The specific recommendations that follow are designed to meet this three-fold deficiency.

MEETING THE COSTS OF MEDICAL CARE

For most Americans, insurance—private, voluntary insurance—provides a sound and effective method of meeting unexpected hazards which may be beyond the capacity of the individual to bear. Risk sharing through group action is in the best tradition of vigorous and imaginative American enterprise.

The Government should cooperate with, and encourage, private carriers in the improvement of health insurance. Moreover, a great many people who are not now covered can be given its protection, particularly in rural areas where group enrollment is at present difficult.

Existing health insurance can also be improved by expanding the scope of the benefits provided. Not all private expenditures for medical care can or should be covered by insurance; nevertheless, many policies offered today are too limited in scope. They are principally for hospitalized illness and for relatively short periods of time.

I recommend, consequently, the establishment of a Federal health reinsurance service to encourage private health insurance organizations in offering broader benefits to insured individuals and families and coverage to more people.

In addition, to improve medical care for the aged, the blind, dependent children, and the permanently and totally disabled who are public assistance recipients, I recommend the authorization of limited Federal grants to match State and local expenditures.

Reinsurance.—The purpose of the reinsurance proposal is to furnish a system for broad sharing among health insurance organizations of the risks of experimentation. A system of this sort will give an incentive to the improvement of existing health insurance plans. It will encourage private, voluntary health insurance organizations to provide better protection—particularly against expensive illness—for those who now are insured against some of the financial hazards of illness. Reinsurance will also help to stimulate extension of private voluntary health insurance plans to millions of additional people who do not now have, but who could afford to purchase, health insurance.

The Department of Health, Education, and Welfare has been working with specialists from the insurance industry, with experts from the health professions, and with many other interested citizens, in its effort to perfect a sound reinsurance program—a program which involves no Government subsidy and no Government competition with private insurance carriers. The time has come to put such a program to work for the American people.

I urge the Congress to launch the reinsurance service this year by authorizing a reasonable capital fund and by providing for its use as necessary to reinsure three broad areas for expansion in private voluntary health insurance:

1. health insurance plans providing protection against the high costs of severe or prolonged illness,

2. health insurance plans providing coverage for individuals and families in predominantly rural areas,

3. health insurance plans designed primarily for coverage of individuals and families of average or lower income against medical care costs in the home and physician's office as well as in the hospital.

Medical care for public assistance recipients.—Nearly 5 million persons in the United States are now receiving public assistance under State programs aided by Federal grants. Present arrangements for their medical care, however, are far from adequate. Special provision for improving health services for these needy persons must be made.

I recommend to the Congress, therefore, that it authorize separate Federal matching of State and local expenditures for the medical care needed by public assistance recipients. The separate matching should apply to each of the four Federally-aided categories—the aged, the permanently and totally disabled, the blind and children deprived of parental care.

STIMULATING THE CONSTRUCTION OF HEALTH FACILITIES

Many communities in the United States today lack the hospitals, clinics, nursing homes, and other modern technical facilities required for the protection of the people's health. In other communities, structures are antiquated or otherwise deficient in construction or equipment.

Present methods of financing are not always satisfactory in meeting this problem. Many sponsors and operators are unable to qualify for grants under the recently extended Hospital Survey and Construction Act. Sponsors of health facilities often find it difficult to obtain private capital for construction.

In other fields, Government insured loans have consistently helped produce the new construction required in the urgent national interests. The tested procedures developed by such successful Government guaranty programs as these should now be used to stimulate construction of additional health facilities.

I recommend, therefore, that the Congress authorize the Secretary of Health, Education, and Welfare to insure, for a small premium, mortgage loans made by private lending institutions for the construction of health facilities.

The continuing responsibility of the mortgagor and of the lending institution should be preserved by limiting the insurance to less than the face amount of the loan and by requiring that a mortgage loan, to be eligible for insurance, must be for less than the full value of the property. The authorizing legislation should, of course, include any needed safeguards against the encouragement of substandard or unsound projects.

HEALTH PERSONNEL NEEDS

Whether we look at health problems in terms of services for the community or for the individual—at problems of research, prevention or treatment of disease—we find that supplies of trained personnel are critically short.

The Administration's legislative program for this year therefore contains proposals addressed to crucial areas of personnel shortages. These particular areas, moreover, hold the key to other possible advances and improvements in health programs.

Two proposals are aimed at shortages in nurse personnel: First, I recommend a 5-year program of grants to State vocational education agencies for training practical nurses. Second, I recommend an expansion of Public Health Service operations to establish traineeships for graduate nurses in specialties such as nursing service administration, teaching and research.

In addition, my recommendations for the revision of the present public health grant programs include authority for the establishment of traineeships in all public health specialties, including mental health.

PUBLIC HEALTH PROGRAMS

The Public Health Service, the Children's Bureau of the Social Security Administration, and the Food and Drug Administration are skilled and vigilant guardians of our nation's health. All three of these agencies should be strengthened, and the programs of the Public Health Service and the Children's Bureau for aiding State health activities made more responsive to changes in State and local health needs. To this end, I urge the Congress to take the following steps:

1. Improve present grant-in-aid programs providing services for mothers, for crippled children and for children requiring special health services. Separate funds should be provided for extension and improvement of these activities and for special projects designed to develop improved medical care techniques both for mothers and for children.

2. Permit greater flexibility in the use by the States of Federal grant funds for public health services. The States could adapt their programs more effectively to their own needs if the separate Public Health Service grants were combined into a single, unified grant-in-aid structure. In addition, separate funds should be provided for extension and improvement of existing public health programs and for special projects looking to the development of improved techniques.

3. Step up research on air pollution. As a result of industrial growth and urban development, the atmosphere over some population centers may be approaching the limit of its ability to absorb air pollutants with safety to health. I am recommending an increased appropriation to the Public Health Service for studies seeking necessary scientific data and more effective methods of control.

4. Provide greater assistance to the States for water pollution control programs. As our population grows and demands for water increase, and as the use of chemicals expands, our water supply problems become more acute. Intensified research in water pollution problems is needed as well as continuing authority for the Public Health Service to deal with these matters. The present Water Pollution Control Act expires on June 30, 1956. This termination date should be removed and the Act should be strengthened.

5. Authorize the Public Health Service to establish traineeships for both graduate and specialized training in public health in order to increase the numbers of trained personnel.

6. Strengthen the Public Health Service Commissioned Corps by improving its status and its survivor benefits.

MENTAL HEALTH

Care for the mentally ill presents a special set of problems.

Only in the past few decades have we, as a people, begun to regard mental and emotional disorders as capable of specific diagnosis, alleviation, cure, and rehabilitation. We now know that effective preventive and control programs are possible in the field of mental health.

I recommend, therefore, new and intensified measures in our attack on mental illness. These are:

1. Strengthening of present aid to State and community programs for the early detection, control and alleviation of mental and emotional derangements;

2. Increased budgetary support for training activities which are now authorized, so as to increase the number of qualified personnel available for care of mental patients; and

3. Authorization of a new program of mental health project grants. Such projects would aim at improving the quality of care in mental institutions and the administration of the institutions themselves. They would also search out ways of reducing the length of stay and the necessity for institutional care in as many cases as possible.

JUVENILE DELINQUENCY

As a vital part of our attack on a serious health and social problem, I also recommend new grants to the States to enable them to strengthen and improve their programs and services for the prevention, diagnosis and treatment of delinquency in youth. There should be assistance for State planning, for coordination of all State and local agencies concerned with juvenile delinquency, for training of personnel, and for special research and demonstration projects.

INTERNATIONAL ASPECTS OF HEALTH

For half of mankind, disease and disability are a normal condition of life. This incalculable burden not only causes poverty and distress, and impedes economic development, but provides a fertile field for the spread of communism.

The World Health Organization of the United Nations is exerting forceful leadership in a cooperative world-wide movement toward better health. Its program merits adequate and growing financial support on the part of the United States. Our contribution to the World Health Organization should be raised, so that the effort to release men from the bondage of disease through international cooperation may be increased.

These recommendations to the Congress represent a broad and coordinated offensive against many of the problems which must be solved if we are to have better health for a stronger America. All the proposals recognize the primacy of local and State responsibility for the health of the community. They encourage private effort, with private funds. With the cooperation of the States and the medical profession, they can form the basis for better health for all.

DWIGHT D. EISENHOWER

26 ¶ The President's News Conference of *February 2, 1955.*

[This is a complete transcript of the news conference of this date. Those portions of the President's replies which were not released for broadcasting or direct quotation at that time are enclosed in brackets.]

THE PRESIDENT. Good morning; please sit down.

I have no announcements. We will go right to questions.

Q. Merriman Smith, United Press: Mr. President, have you had any indication from Generalissimo Chiang Kai-shek that he wants a public statement or some form of assurance from you or this Government that we consider Quemoy and Matsu part of the defense of Formosa?

THE PRESIDENT. Well, there are constantly, of course, conversations going on between our representatives and the Chinese Nationalists, and not always do our views exactly coincide; but I think that in view of the delicacy of this whole situation, one that in its main parts is before the United Nations, it is better to stand for the moment just on what we have said, at least publicly, let it go at that, and say no more for the moment.

Q. David P. Sentner, Hearst Newspapers: Mr. President, if I might presume to ask a question on the fringe of the situation, in Moscow a few days ago, Foreign Minister Molotov gave an interview to W. R. Hearst, Jr., and Kingsbury Smith of International News Service, and he indicated that the Soviet Government would be willing to take up with the Chinese Communist Government the question of a temporary cease-fire for the evacuation of the Tachens, if the United States made a request of the Kremlin for such a step.

Now, is there any communication on that subject or relating to it, under consideration?

THE PRESIDENT. First of all, I know nothing about that, but I do call attention to this: that it's the Chinese Nationalists that are occupying the Tachens and not the United States, and if there were any such request, I don't see how the United States could make it unilaterally.

Q. Alan S. Emory, Watertown Times: Mr. President, Senator Humphrey of Minnesota has introduced a resolution that would put Congress on record as backing U.N. efforts to reach a cease-fire in the Formosa controversy.

Senator George, the Chairman of the Foreign Relations Committee, says he thinks the administration favors such a plan, and he knows he does, and he thinks it would meet the approval of the American people.

Senator Knowland says that such resolution might constitute a blanket endorsement of appeasement.

I wondered how you felt about that, sir?

THE PRESIDENT. [I haven't thought about it; and I suppose

that here you have personalities reflecting their own convictions about such things.

[Any answer I give you now would be so much of a shotgun opinion I would rather think that one over. I had not noticed that before.]

Q. Mr. Emory: Well, sir——

THE PRESIDENT. [I really have nothing more to say about it.]

Q. Chalmers M. Roberts, Washington Post and Times Herald: Mr. President, could you enlighten us, sir, as to whether the 7th Fleet is under orders which include the doctrine of "hot pursuit" in case our planes or ships are attacked by Communist planes?

THE PRESIDENT. Frankly, I considered whether I would talk about such things this morning. And I repeat what I have said, I don't believe it is best to put out any specific blueprint on orders or instructions. I believe it is just best to leave it as it stands at the moment.

The United Nations is working on this, and I don't see how any statement of mine could do anything more than muddy the water.

Now, this is not any attempt to keep either you people or the American people in the dark, but this is an international situation. There is every kind of influence and crosscurrent involved, and I just think it is wise to say nothing.

Q. Richard L. Wilson, Cowles Publications: Mr. President, in spite of assurances which you have given, and in spite of statements which have been made in Congress, I think there is still a great deal of uneasiness in the country with respect to whether your policy will lead to fighting in the Far East. Could you discuss that subject again?

THE PRESIDENT. Well, certainly this: the purpose is to make certain that no conflict occurs through mistaken calculations on the other side as to our concern about Formosa and our determination to defend it.

We have been as exact as it seems possible to be, and we have certainly tried to avoid being truculent.   The purpose is honestly and hopefully to prevent war.

Q. Jack Norman, Fairchild Publications: Mr. President, there is talk now on Capitol Hill that there might have to be some compromises to get the reciprocal trade legislation through Congress; and I wanted to ask you, if it comes to a choice, would you give up your minimum wage recommendations or something else to get H.R. 1 through in its present form?

THE PRESIDENT. [Well, I don't see the relationship.]

Q. Mr. Norman: Well, some of the witnesses yesterday before the Ways and Means Committee were making the point, there is no point in hiking the minimum wage if we are going to lower the tariffs.

THE PRESIDENT. [So far as I am concerned, on both these points, I have expressed my recommendations.

[Now, as usual, I have to wait to see what Congress does; I couldn't predict in any degree whatsoever what would be my action thereafter.]

Q. Marvin Arrowsmith, Associated Press: Mr. President, General Ridgway told the House Armed Services Committee 2 days ago that he is against the projected cut in Army strength, and he said he believes that the proposed cut jeopardized national security to a degree.   How do you feel about that, and is there any possibility of the reduction order being rescinded?

THE PRESIDENT. Well, I assume that you are asking me the question so far as it affects the executive department.   My decision in this matter was not reached lightly; it was reached after long study of every opinion I could get, in consultation with every single individual in this Government that I know of that bears any responsibility whatsoever about it.

General Ridgway was questioned in the Congress as to his personal convictions; naturally, he had to express them.

His responsibility for national defense is, you might say, a special one, or, in a sense, parochial.   He does not have the overall responsibility that is borne by the Commander in Chief, and by him alone, when it comes down to making the recommendations to the Congress.

My recommendations, I repeat, were made from my best judgment of what is the adequate defense structure for these United States, particularly on the long-term basis. That decision has not been altered, and at this moment I don't see any chance of its being altered.

Q. Sarah McClendon, El Paso Times: Mr. President, in that same connection, your letter of January 5th to Mr. Wilson, I believe, mentioned that recent scientific and technological developments made it necessary for us not to use as many men as we might otherwise use.

Well, the Joint Chiefs of Staff, in their testimony before the House Armed Services Committee, don't agree with this. They say, no.

Will you have any further conferences with them on this?

THE PRESIDENT. I confer with the Joint Chiefs of Staff through their chairman several times a week, every week. I am never out of touch with them. I know their opinions, and I know exactly who agrees with me and who doesn't.

Now, they are entitled to their opinions, but I have to make the decisions.

Q. Lloyd M. Schwartz, Fairchild Publications: I would like to ask a question about procurement policy.

THE PRESIDENT. Procurement?

Q. Mr. Schwartz: Some manufacturers of silk cartridge cloths, which are vital to the defense program, say they have protested to you the award of contracts by the Army to manufacturers using yarns spun abroad, and they claim this endangers the mobilization base. I wondered whether you were considering that and, perhaps, some change in the regulations?

THE PRESIDENT. [I have no doubt, if they say that, that they have submitted the recommendation. If so, it has unquestionably been routed, as it would normally be, to the proper people. I have not personally seen it, so I couldn't comment on it.]

Q. Raymond P. Brandt, St. Louis Post-Dispatch: Several weeks ago you said you were going to consult with the Democratic leaders in Congress, and you had not decided on the mechanism.

Have the Cabinet officers consulted the Democratic leaders on legislation going up? And the reason I ask, there are two points: one is on your road program; two is on the cut in the Army.

THE PRESIDENT. I have personally talked to them about the structure of the Defense Establishment that I would recommend for this year, and as a long-term program. I personally did that.

Now, unquestionably, the Secretary of Defense and his people are in touch with them constantly.

As to the road program, I can't answer specifically except that I know the Secretary of the Treasury has at least talked with Senator Byrd to some extent about financing it.

Q. Mr. Brandt: The reason I asked is, when these messages go up or when the announcements were made, we get adverse comments from the Hill from the Democrats.

THE PRESIDENT. Well, I don't mean to say that everything we send up is agreed to in advance by the leaders of the other side.

As far as I know, we are certainly trying to avoid springing something on them that we know about. Again, I suppose, errors certainly can occur; but the purpose is to keep them informed of what is coming up.

Q. A. E. Salpeter, Haaretz (Tel Aviv): Going back to Formosa, it seems since the cease-fire, by nature, is a temporary arrangement, do you foresee the possibility of a permanent peaceful relationship between Formosa and the Red China regime?

THE PRESIDENT. [I just don't know. I think that only time will tell. It is something that we must take a step at a time and try to make advancement toward conditions that will promote peace.]

Q. Harry W. Frantz, United Press, South American Service: The Foreign Minister of Venezuela, in connection with the Formosan situation, has made a statement of friendship, moral and economic support toward the United States, which later was generally republished by the American Chamber of Commerce in Venezuela. If that has come to your attention, would you care to comment?

THE PRESIDENT. Well, it hadn't come to my attention. Of course, our hope is that through the Organization of Pan American States our general attitude toward this whole business of promoting peace and friendly relations in the world will have a solid foundation and agreement among our own American States. That is, I should say, one of the cornerstones of American policy.

Q. Robert G. Spivack, New York Post: Mr. President, the charge has been made that the censorship of the record of these press conferences before they are released to TV and radio means that only exchanges favorable to the administration and the Republican Party would be issued. Would you care to comment on that censorship?

THE PRESIDENT. I think that that is an item you can talk over with my technician, who is Mr. Hagerty. [*Laughter*]

I believe someone told me that for one of the press conferences we had, 28 minutes of it was released; I couldn't think there could be much room for censorship there.

Q. Clark R. Mollenhoff, Des Moines Register: Mr. President, both your Justice Department and Civil Service Commission have stated that they have advisory functions in coordinating your security program. However, they both state that their functions are purely advisory, and that they can't go beyond that in the event that some department head would want to disregard their advice.

In the light of that, I wondered what recourse there is in the administration for an employee who might have a security risk tag put on him by one department, and other departments might hold that he was not a security risk?

THE PRESIDENT. [Of course, it is understood that if two department heads differ on any subject—whether it is security, whether it is anything else that involves this Government—if that cannot be settled between them eventually, it must come to me; that is inherent in organization, and it is inherent in this problem.]

Q. Mr. Mollenhoff: Mr. President, I wondered if the individual cases, as such—though I was thinking in terms of the employee in this case who might have this security risk tag tied on him, and that would be rather serious in his eyes—and would he have any recourse though, could he come to you personally, was that what you meant?

THE PRESIDENT. [No, I don't think that he would come to me personally. I think the problem would. As quickly as two departments differ on anything, it must come to me if not settled otherwise.]

Q. Mr. Mollenhoff: All of those cases that are pending, then, will eventually be brought in?

THE PRESIDENT. [As a matter of fact, I have heard only of one case where two different departments were involved; I could be wrong. There may be more.]

Q. Mr. Mollenhoff: I wondered if in that case that would eventually be decided by that——

THE PRESIDENT. [That one would have, except that someone had taken it over. We agreed that each of them followed their own best judgment, the man was rehired, and it was a *fait accompli*. Of course, I didn't come into it, because it was done. And I approved it.]

Q. Nat S. Finney, Buffalo Evening News: Mr. President, do you have any plans to withdraw the Dixon-Yates contract?

THE PRESIDENT. I do not.

Q. Ethel Payne, Defender Publications: Sir, I wonder if you would care to comment on the coming Asian-African conference, and if you could——

THE PRESIDENT. Would I comment on what? I couldn't hear you.

Q. Miss Payne: The coming Asian-African conference; and could you tell us if we are going to send observers to that conference?

THE PRESIDENT. [As a matter of fact, I am not certain as to detail. Of course, any conference of that kind we follow with the greatest of interest,[1] but I don't even know whether we have been invited to send observers. It is a question you would have to ask the State Department; I am really not up on it.]

Q. Donald Irwin, New York Herald Tribune: Mr. President, it is nearly 3 months since you sent Judge Harlan's nomination to the Senate, and the Judiciary Committee has put off hearings until the 23d of February; and I wondered if you had any comment.

THE PRESIDENT. None, except that I continue to believe that Judge Harlan's qualifications for that post are of the highest; certainly they were the highest of any that I could find.

Q. Benjamin R. Cole, Indianapolis Star: Mr. President, could you tell us, sir, your feelings about the FHA cleanup? Is that nearly completed, sir, or do you feel that there is still more to be done there?

THE PRESIDENT. [I haven't had a report on it in the last couple of weeks. There was a report then that they hoped they were getting down to the final action in the case. I would hope so, because I personally think that FHA, and confidence in FHA, is of the utmost importance to the United States. So I would hope we get this cleaned up and really back to where it belongs in the respect of our people.]

Q. Frank van der Linden, Nashville Banner: Mr. President, in your budget message regarding TVA, you raised the possibility of some new method of financing the TVA steam plants. Would that include the issuance of bonds by TVA itself?

---

[1] On April 17, the White House released a statement by the Secretary of State following a meeting with the President in Augusta, Ga., at which time they discussed the Asian-African conference then opening in Bandung. Secretary Dulles noted that the President "expressed the hope that it will heed the universal longing of the peoples of the world for peace and that it will seek a renunciation of force to achieve national ambitions. The President hailed the Bandung Conference as providing an opportunity, at a critical hour, to voice the peaceful aspirations of the peoples of the world and thus exert a practical influence for peace where peace is now in grave jeopardy."

THE PRESIDENT. [I think there are a number of methods, but I would have to wait on the TVA recommendations. That is one reason for the appointment as the head of TVA of a man in whom I have the utmost confidence, his disinterest in this, studying what is the public, the national good, in the premises; so I would have to wait on their recommendations.]

Q. Mr. van der Linden: Sir, do you plan to submit a recommendation to Congress later, then?

THE PRESIDENT. [I don't, unless I can get something from him.]

Q. Roscoe Drummond, New York Herald Tribune: Mr. President, may I ask a further question about Judge Harlan? Do you think there is an inordinate delay in holding the hearings on Judge Harlan, and do you think that this delay could conceivably harm the functioning of the Court itself?

THE PRESIDENT. Report was made to me that the members of the Court naturally wanted to have a full Court as early as they could. So I moved as rapidly as I could to find a proper individual and recommended him to the Congress after the vacancy occurred as fast as I could.

Now, I think it is too bad that the delay seems to be necessary in the eyes of the committee; but on the other hand, I, as usual, don't intend to stand up and publicly criticize Congress for what it does. I personally think it is unfortunate that this delay has to occur.

Q. Mrs. May Craig, Maine Papers: Mr. President, have you reached any conclusion on revision of the United Nations Charter, which can be done soon, and would that include admitting any nation which applies?

THE PRESIDENT. [The only thing I know about it at this moment is that for some months it has been a matter of casual discussion between the Secretary of State and me. I know they are studying it and have a group set up to study, but I am sure there is no readiness to report whatsoever—no conclusion reached.]

Q. L. G. Laycook, Nashville Tennessean: Mr. President,

would you comment on the resolution adopted by the Joint Atomic Energy Committee last week urging cancellation of the Dixon-Yates contract?

THE PRESIDENT. No, I won't comment on it except it seemed to be drawn upon strictly party lines; that is the only thing I noted about it particularly.

Q. Lloyd M. Schwartz, Fairchild Publications: Mr. President, I wonder if you could give us your views on standby authority to freeze prices and wages. There have been reports of a decision that you would ask Congress for such authority.

THE PRESIDENT. I could give you a long speech now. One of the first subjects given to me in the War Department somewhere back along 1928 or '29 to study was this one.

I think I have conferred with literally hundreds of people in the United States, pro and con, on this subject. I really can't say that I think solution is vital, and I don't know whether there is any use of starting to talk on the subject unless you are going to talk for a half hour; I don't think you want me to do that.

I would say this: if Congress sees fit to do it, I not only can live with it, but I think in certain respects it would be advantageous.

On the other hand, the mere existence of that kind of authority has a certain psychological reaction on certain sections of our population who believe that it implies an intent to extend that kind of control to our economy in time of peace, and it also implies an intent to go your own way in time of war without consultation with the Congress.

Now, there are psychological values here against immediate—let's say—economic values in a crisis. I think that Congress can act probably fast enough so that no great damage will be done if the two branches of Government work together well.

It is not one of the factors in the legislation that we need to which I attach terrific importance.

Q. William V. Shannon, New York Post: Mr. President, in line with this earlier question about filming the news conferences, the principal point of the criticism is not how much is cut out, but that the television networks, unlike newspaper editors, don't have the power to decide what to use, and that is decided at the White House first, and they get the censored transcript. And some people feel it is more than a technical question, more a question of freedom of the press.

THE PRESIDENT. Well, let me say this: that no head of any broadcasting company has yet protested to me, and I can't very well make any answer until I get their protests and their reasons for it.

Q. Chalmers M. Roberts, Washington Post and Times Herald: Mr. President, in answering Mr. Wilson's question a while back, you said the purpose of your program in Formosa, in regard to the Formosa situation, was honestly and hopefully to prevent war.

Could you tell us whether, as of now, you feel as hopeful or more hopeful or otherwise than when you launched this program?

THE PRESIDENT. Well, I think at least we have made this stride, that we certainly have removed any doubt from anybody's mind, friend or potential foe, as to the determination of America to see that this great island barrier is maintained intact in the Pacific, that we are not going to let international communism get that spearhead extending into the Pacific and, therefore, extend its influence in that region.

Now, that has been made crystal clear in the resolution and to that extent ought to be helpful; because so many things happen in the international world through probing, through false conclusions that might be drawn from a successful probe, the thought that the victim will never react.

Here it is an attempt that has been made, at least in the field of intention, to make our purposes clear.

Q. Richard L. Wilson, Cowles Publications: Permit me to follow that up a bit. I think in one of your messages to Congress—I think it was the state of the Union message—you referred to a world stalemate, the possibility of it continuing. Do you think the element of stalemate is implied in the Far Eastern situation as it stands today?

THE PRESIDENT. Well, of that I can't be too sure. I used the word "stalemate" deliberately, Mr. Wilson, because it seems to me, we get so much in the habit of using terms or phrases, and then each of us attaches to the term or phrase his own meaning; for instance, this thing of coexistence: someone defines it with an adjective, and suddenly it is appeasement. To my mind, coexistence is, in fact, a state of our being as long as we are not attempting to destroy the other side.

I make it a very simple thing in my mind, but I find that others give additional interpretations that I don't mean at all.

Now, when I said "stalemate," I was trying to describe where neither side is getting what it desires in this whole world struggle, but they at least have sense enough to agree that they must not pursue it deliberately and through force of arms; that is all.

Q. Mr. Wilson: Do you think, sir, that that would be a good result from this present situation?

THE PRESIDENT. Well, you mean, in that one point?

Q. Mr. Wilson: Yes, yes, sir.

THE PRESIDENT. Well, again I say I don't believe I will comment on the one point at all.

Q. Paul Scott Rankine, Reuters: Mr. President, you referred to this great iron barrier being kept intact in the Far East. Could you be more specific about what the great iron barrier is?

THE PRESIDENT. [I didn't say "iron barrier," I said "island barrier." Well, of course, it's largely islands. There are, of course, a few bits of the mainland involved along the eastern coast, but you know where they are.

[What I mean is that we are making that the principal feature of our whole protective system in the region; that is all I mean.]

Q. Edward T. Folliard, Washington Post and Times Herald: Mr. President, you have used the term "miscalculation." You do not want Red China to miscalculate in this situation. Do you feel that wars have started as a result of a miscalculation or, to put it another way, do you feel that recent wars might have been avoided had something been said in advance to head off a miscalculation?

THE PRESIDENT. Well, of course, we don't want to get into a discussion of military history here, I think. But I do believe this: I believe World War I did start largely through miscalculation. A prince was murdered; there began to be an exchange of notes back and forth; and I believe that there was a miscalculation of what Russia, France, and Britain would do, and that created that war. The Second World War, I would rather doubt that. I think that you had a personality there that was so bent upon achieving certainly pan-European power, at least, that probably nothing would stop it. I feel that the Korean conflict started because of our failing to make clear that we would defend this small nation, which had just started, in a pinch.

Now, I don't mean to say—I am not trying to attach any blame to anybody here; but we were weak in forces, we were hopeful for peace—and I think it's logical to hope for peace—we took our forces out of there; and it became possibly the conviction of the Reds that they could take the country over without resistance.

Q. Douglass Cater, The Reporter Magazine: Mr. President, some of the Senators have criticized the recent resolution in that it leaves the islands that are in greatest peril in the greatest obscurity, namely, Matsu and Quemoy.

Do you feel there is a danger of miscalculation because there is not exact knowledge as to what our position towards them is to be?

THE PRESIDENT. [Well, I repeat, to be as exact as you can; but when it comes down to the tactical details of these things, you just simply cannot afford to be too specific. So again I say on that particular point, I shall comment no more.]

Q. Robert E. Clark, International News Service: Mr. President, one of General Ridgway's reasons for opposing a reduction in the strength of the Army is reportedly his belief that it would require ground troops, the use of our ground troops, to help defend Quemoy and the Matsus.

Is it your opinion that we could defend Formosa only with air and naval units without committing any ground forces?

THE PRESIDENT. Ground forces other than on Formosa, is that what you are talking about? We have small detachments on Formosa, training troops; we have had small detachments in some of the other places, training troops, and that sort of thing. But when it comes to committing land forces of the United States in this particular situation, there has been no recommendation of that kind made to me at all.

Merriman Smith, United Press: Thank you, Mr. President.

NOTE: President Eisenhower's fifty-ninth news conference was held in the Executive Office Building from 10:33 to 11:01 o'clock on Wednesday morning, February 2, 1955. In attendance: 194.

27 ¶ Message Recorded for the New York USO Defense Fund Dinner. *February* 3, 1955

My fellow Americans:

I welcome this opportunity to express my thanks and appreciation to all those of you, who, despite busy lives, never relax your efforts in backing up and helping the men and women in our Armed Services.

Today, we have the largest military establishment in our peacetime history. Men and women of that establishment are standing guard for us in many outposts of the world. In every kind of circumstance and condition they are performing onerous duties that the rest of us may enjoy security. But—and we thank God when we say it—young Americans are not exposed to gunfire today.

So, to some it may seem that special civilian attention to the morale of our Armed Services is no longer important. In fact, however, among troops in foreign stations it is often more difficult to maintain morale during peace than during war. Loneliness, all the penalties of separation from home, are far sharper then.

I know what the USO means to our Service personnel. More than just a Camp Show or a chance for an hour's diversion, more than just relaxation or warm hospitality, it means to the men and women in the Armed Services that they have a host of friends in the homes of America. No matter what part of the country a serviceman comes from, no matter what his race or religion, he wants to feel confident that what he is doing is important to other human beings, and that they are grateful for it.

Such assurance fortifies spirit and morale, strengthens the ties in heart and mind which unite the individual serviceman with his fellow citizens, which make him feel that he is part of America! He must have such assurance, if he is willingly and ably to perform the vitally important duties which our times and our nation's good demand of him.

I hope that people throughout America will be reminded of this fact through the work of the USO and the other United Defense Fund groups. This work must go forward, for the happiness of the individual man and woman in our Armed Services, for the furtherance of our country's security.

I congratulate all of you on your willingness to take an active part in this endeavor, and I wish you the fullest possible success.

NOTE: The dinner was held at the Sheraton-Astor Hotel, New York City.

28 ¶ Message to the Boy Scouts of America.
February 6, 1955

[Released February 6, 1955. Dated January 3, 1955]

To the Boy Scouts of America:

Boy Scout Week gives all of us an opportunity to honor the two million, seven hundred and sixty-five thousand boys and their nearly one million leaders who make up this great organization. Self-development and service to others, independence and good citizenship, a sense of brotherhood and responsiveness to spiritual values—these qualities which Scouting fosters mean much to America. To all Boy Scouts I extend congratulations on what they are achieving and on what they promise for our nation's future.

DWIGHT D. EISENHOWER

NOTE: This message marked the opening of Boy Scout Week and commemorated the 45th anniversary of the organization. The President serves as Honorary President of the Boy Scouts of America.

29 ¶ Letter to the Governors Concerning Uniform State Legislation on Absentee Voting Rights of Members of the Armed Services. *February 7, 1955*

[Released February 7, 1955. Dated February 2, 1955]

Dear Governor——————:

I am writing to you and to the other Governors on a matter of common concern to all Americans: the provision to our men and women in the Armed Services, on duty away from home, of effective opportunities voluntarily to vote by State absentee ballot in elections of Federal, State, and local officers.

It is basic to our American freedom and to the paramount importance which Americans attach to the rights of individual citizens that every eligible person who wishes to exercise the right to vote should have a fair, uninfluenced opportunity to do so. In the case of individuals serving their country in the armed forces, the assurance of this opportunity to exercise the free right of suffrage should be a special obligation of the State and Federal Governments.

Under plans approved last December, it is probable that approximately three million men and women may be in the Active Forces of the United States at the time of the 1956 Elections. Of this number, assuming a continuation of circumstances hitherto existing, it is reasonable to estimate that between a half-million and a million who are of voting age and otherwise eligible to vote, will then be overseas, scattered in various parts of the world and at sea.

The Armed Services stand ready to give every assistance, as they did in World War II, in providing a chance for each serviceman and servicewoman voluntarily to vote, if he or she wishes. The experience of World War II, when some 2,700,000 servicemen voted in the 1944 Election, shows that *effective* opportunities for service people to vote overseas by State absentee ballot depends on close working cooperation between the Armed Services and the several States and, especially, on there being generally uniform provisions in State laws as to voting qualifications, regulations, and administrative provisions.

In order for a serviceman overseas to vote by State absentee ballot, he must appropriately apply in writing by air mail for such ballot to his domiciliary voting place, receive the ballot overseas by air mail pursuant to such application, execute the ballot overseas under usual safeguards to insure secrecy, and return the ballot by air mail to his domiciliary voting place in time to be counted. The mobility of troops, the volume of air mail, the problems involved in providing overseas to service personnel accurate voting information relative to 48 States, the hazards of armed service, and other causes contribute toward burdening the ability of the Armed Services to assist. One thing, however, experience in World War II has made certain: the greater the uniformity in State voting laws, the more effective is the opportunity of overseas service people to cast ballots which will arrive home in time to be counted.

I am informed that various uniform provisions which were adopted by many States in their voting laws during World War

II, have lapsed or have been modified in ways departing from the uniform criteria which made servicemen voting then a practical possibility. It was stated last winter that the voting laws of three-quarters of the States fell short of the criteria established in World War II as substantially necessary to assure effective overseas voting by service people.

There was introduced in the Congress on January 26, 1955, H.R. 3121, a Bill "to permit and assist Federal personnel, including members of the Armed Forces, and their families, to exercise their voting franchise, and for other purposes," (a copy of which is attached). This Bill has my support, and I shall ask the leaders of both parties to join on a non-partisan basis in speeding its passage through the Congress.

Part of this Bill concerns only Federal activities and seeks to codify and improve existing Federal law. The rest of the Bill, however, concerns the States, and contains recommendations to them to enact uniform legislative provisions, which are expressed in careful detail in Title II. These uniform provisions have been tested against the experience of World War II voting in order to meet the criteria which were then found necessary to provide effective opportunities to vote.

I hope that you will wish to have introduced and enacted in the 1955 Legislative Session of your State the uniform voting provisions above referred to. If this action is not taken in 1955 by your State Legislature, there may be neither the time nor the occasion for your State Legislature to act effectively in 1956, without a Special Session.

Therefore, I urge you to deal promptly with this matter, which concerns the individual rights, as citizens, of the men and women who are defending our country all over the world.

I am asking the Secretary of Defense to coordinate all activities of the Federal Government in the field of servicemen voting, and in due course he or his designee will directly offer to your State such cooperation and assistance as his office may be able to afford.

Please accept my personal regard and do not hesitate to ask for any help that I can give in furthering this basic American cause.

Sincerely,

DWIGHT D. EISENHOWER

30 ¶ Letter to Chan Gurney, Acting Chairman, Civil Aeronautics Board, on the West Coast-Hawaii Case. *February 7, 1955*

Dear Mr. Gurney:

I desire to amend my letter of February first with reference to the West Coast-Hawaii Case.

As you know, I believe in the strength of competitive enterprise if based upon sound economic considerations but it must not be wasteful duplication at the expense of the Federal Government. Both carriers operating on this Seattle/Portland-Hawaii route have built up substantial business. Moreover, since my original action in this case I have received from you information to the effect that within two years all air line subsidies in the Pacific area will probably have been eliminated or will at least approach that point. Renewing the certificates of both carriers for a limited period would afford them an equal opportunity to demonstrate their capacity to develop adequate traffic to operate without subsidy or to prove definitely that the route cannot economically support two carriers. Accordingly, I request the Board present for my approval a revised order in this case which would certify both Northwest Airlines and Pan American World Airways for operation between Seattle/Portland and Hawaii for a temporary period of three years from now.

Sincerely,

DWIGHT D. EISENHOWER

NOTE: In his letter of February 1, the President returned without approval the Civil Aeronautics Board order in the West Coast-Hawaii case and requested a revision of the order. On February 2, the Board announced that the revised order prepared in accordance with the President's instructions in his February 1 letter would not provide for renewal of Northwest Airlines' service to Hawaii but would authorize the continuation of Pan American World Airways' e x i s t i n g Seattle/Portland-Hawaii route for a period of 5 years. The President's letter of February 1 and the announcement as to the revised order were released by the Board on February 2, 1955.

31 ¶ Special Message to the Congress Concerning Federal Assistance in School Construction. *February 8, 1955*

To the Congress of the United States:

For the consideration of the Congress, I herewith propose a plan of Federal cooperation with the States, designed to give our school children as quickly as possible the classrooms they must have.

Because of the magnitude of the job, but more fundamentally because of the undeniable importance of free education to a free way of life, the means we take to provide our children with proper classrooms must be weighed most carefully. The phrase "free education" is a deliberate choice. For unless education continues to be free—free in its response to local community needs, free from any suggestion of political domination, and free from impediments to the pursuit of knowledge by teachers and students—it will cease to serve the purposes of free men.

STATE AND LOCAL RESPONSIBILITY FOR EDUCATION

A distinguishing characteristic of our Nation—and a great strength—is the development of our institutions within the concept of individual worth and dignity. Our schools are among the

guardians of that principle.   Consequently—and deliberately—
their control and support throughout our history have been—and
are—a State and local responsibility.

The American idea of universal public education was conceived as necessary in a society dedicated to the principles of
individual freedom, equality, and self-government.   A necessary
corollary is that public schools must always reflect the character
and aspirations of the people of the community.

Thus was established a fundamental element of the American
public school system—local direction by boards of education responsible immediately to the parents of children and the other
citizens of the community.   Diffusion of authority among tens of
thousands of school districts is a safeguard against centralized
control and abuse of the educational system that must be maintained.   We believe that to take away the responsibility of communities and States in educating our children is to undermine
not only a basic element of our freedom but a basic right of our
citizens.

The legislative proposals submitted to the last Congress were
offered by the Administration in the earnest conviction that education must always be close to the people; in the belief that a
careful reassessment by the people themselves of the problems
of education is necessary; and with a realization of the growing
financial difficulties that school districts face.   To encourage a
nation-wide examination of our schools, the 83rd Congress
authorized funds for Conferences on Education in the 48 States
and the Territories and for a White House Conference to be
held in November this year.

THE CURRENT PROBLEM

These are the facts of the classroom shortage:

The latest information submitted by the States to the Office of
Education indicates that there is a deficit of more than 300
thousand classrooms, a legacy—in part—of the years of war

and defense mobilization when construction had to be curtailed. In addition, to keep up with mounting enrollments, the Nation must build at least 50 thousand new elementary and high school classrooms yearly. It must also replace the thousands of classrooms which become unsafe or otherwise unusable each year.

During the current school year, about 60 thousand new classrooms are being built. Capital outlays for public school construction will reach an all-time high of 2 billion dollars this year. During the last 5 years, new construction costing over 7 billion dollars has provided new classrooms for 6,750,000 pupils in our public schools. During that time more than 5½ million additional children enrolled in school. Thus the rate of construction has more than kept pace with mounting enrollment. But it has only slightly reduced the total classroom deficit.

As a consequence, millions of children still attend schools which are unsafe or which permit learning only part-time or under conditions of serious over-crowding. To build satisfactory classrooms for all our children, the current rate of school building must be multiplied sharply and this increase must be sustained.

Fundamentally, the remedy lies with the States and their communities. But the present shortage requires immediate and effective action that will produce more rapid results. Unless the Federal Government steps forward to join with the States and communities, this emergency situation will continue.

Therefore—for the purpose of meeting the emergency only and pending the results of the nation-wide conferences—I propose a broad effort to widen the accepted channels of financing school construction and to increase materially the flow of private lending through them—without interference with the responsibility of State and local school systems. Over the next three years, this proposed effort envisages a total of 7 billion dollars put to work building badly needed new schools—in addition to construction expenditures outside these proposals.

THE RECOMMENDATIONS

1. *Bond Purchases by the Federal Government*

The first recommendation is directed at action—effective as rapidly as school districts can offer bonds to the public for sale.

I recommend that legislation be enacted authorizing the Federal Government, cooperating with the several States, to purchase school bonds issued by local communities which are handicapped in selling bonds at a reasonable interest rate. This proposal is sound educationally and economically. It will help build schools.

To carry out this proposal, I recommend that the Congress authorize the appropriation of 750 million dollars for use over the next three years.

2. *State School Building Agencies*

Many school districts cannot borrow to build schools because of restrictive debt limits. They need some other form of financing. Therefore, the second proposal is designed to facilitate immediate construction of schools without local borrowing by the school district.

To expand school construction, several States have already created special State-wide school building agencies. These can borrow advantageously, since they represent the combined credit of many communities. After building schools, the agency rents them to school districts. The local community under its lease gets a new school without borrowing.

I now propose the wider adoption of this tested method of accelerating school construction. Under this proposal, the Federal Government would share with the States in establishing and maintaining for State school building agencies an initial reserve fund equal to one year's payment on principal and interest.

The State school building agency—working in cooperation with the State educational officials—would issue its bonds through the customary investment channels, then build schools for lease to local school districts. Rentals would be sufficient to cover the payments on principal and interest of the bonds outstanding; a payment to a supplemental reserve fund; and a proportionate share of the administrative expenses of the State school building agency. In time, the payments to the reserve fund would permit repayment of the initial Federal and State advances. When all its financial obligations to the agency are met, the local school district takes title to its building.

I recommend that the Congress authorize the necessary Federal participation to put this plan into effect so that State building agencies may be in a position to issue bonds in the next three years which will build six billion dollars worth of new schools.

3. Grants for School Districts with Proved Need and Lack of Local Income

My first Message to the Congress on the State of the Union stated the view that "the firm conditions of Federal aid must be proved need and proved lack of local income." In my judgment, any sound program of grants must adhere to this principle. Some school districts meet the conditions. In them the amount of taxable property and local income is so low as to make it impossible for the district either to repay borrowed money or rent a satisfactory school building.

I now propose a program of grants-in-aid directed clearly and specifically at the urgent situations in which the Federal Government can justifiably share direct construction costs without undermining State and local responsibility. Under this proposal the Federal Government would share with the States part of the cost of building schools in districts where one of the following conditions is met:

(a) The school district, if it has not reached its legal bonding limit, cannot sell its bonds to the Federal Government under Proposal 1 because it cannot pay interest and principal charges on the total construction costs.

(b) The school district, if it has reached its legal bonding limit, is unable to pay the rent needed to obtain a school from a

State agency on a lease-purchase basis, as described in Proposal 2.

The State would certify the school district's inability to finance the total construction cost through borrowing or a rental arrangement. It would also certify that the new school is needed to relieve extreme overcrowding, double shifts, or hazardous or unhealthful conditions.

The Federal and State aid would be in an amount sufficient for a school district to qualify under either Proposal 1 or Proposal 2 for financing the remainder of the building costs. The requirement that Federal funds be matched with State-appropriated funds is an essential safeguard to preservation of the proper spheres of local, State, and Federal responsibility in the field of public education.

By authorizing this program of joint Federal-State aid to supplement the financing plans set forth in Proposals 1 and 2, a workable way will be provided for every community in the Nation to construct classrooms for its children. I recommend that the Congress authorize the appropriation of 200 million dollars for a three-year program.

4. *Grants for Administrative Costs of State Programs*

In addition to immediate school construction, the nation needs to plan sound long-term financing of the public schools free from obsolete restrictions. Our State Conferences on Education will help accomplish this. Out of these meetings of parents, teachers, and public-spirited citizens, can come lasting solutions to such underlying problems as more efficient school districting and the modification of unduly restrictive local debt limits.

The Federal Government, having helped sponsor the State Conferences on Education, should now move to help the States in carrying out such recommendations as may be made. I propose, therefore, that the Federal Government furnish one-half of the Administrative costs of State programs which are designed to overcome obstacles to local financing or to provide additional State aid to local school districts.

For this purpose I recommend a total authorization of 20 million dollars with an appropriation of 5 million dollars for the first year of a three-year period.

————

This program is sound and equitable. It accelerates construction of classrooms within the traditional framework of local responsibility for our schools. It does not preclude other proposals for long-range solutions which undoubtedly will grow out of the State conferences and the White House Conference on Education.

CONCLUSION

The best possible education for all our young people is a fixed objective of the American nation. The four-point program, herein outlined, would help provide proper physical housing for the achievement of this objective. But the finest buildings, of themselves, are no assurance that the pupils who use them are each day better fitted to shoulder the responsibilities, to meet the opportunities, to enjoy the rewards that one day will be their lot as American citizens.

Good teaching and good teachers made even the one-room crossroads schools of the nineteenth century a rich source of the knowledge and enthusiasm and patriotism, joined with spiritual wisdom, that mark a vigorously dynamic people. Today, the professional quality of American teaching is better than ever. But too many teachers are underpaid and overworked and, in consequence, too few young men and women join their ranks. Here is a shortage, less obvious but ultimately more dangerous, than the classroom shortage.

The Conferences now underway and the massive school building program here proposed will, I believe, arouse the American people to a community effort for schools and a community concern for education, unparalleled in our history. Taken together, they will serve to advance the teaching profession to the position it should enjoy.

Federal aid in a form that tends to lead to Federal control of our schools could cripple education for freedom. In no form can it ever approach the mighty effectiveness of an aroused people. But Federal leadership can stir America to national action.

Then the nation's objective of the best possible education for all our young people will be achieved.

DWIGHT D. EISENHOWER

32 ¶ Message to Nationwide Meetings in Support of the Campaign for Radio Free Europe. *February 8, 1955*

[Delivered over closed circuit television from the White House]

I AM happy to be with you tonight for I strongly believe that Radio Free Europe and the Crusade for Freedom are vital to success in the battle for men's minds.

Many of us learned during the war that the most potent force is spiritual; that the appeal to men's minds produces a dedication which surmounts every trial and test until victory is won.

To toughen, strengthen, fortify such dedication to the cause of freedom is the mission of Radio Free Europe.

Substantial progress has already been made. The free world is growing stronger because its peoples are growing in their determination to stand together and in their faith that freedom and justice will triumph.

Radio Free Europe, each day of the year, nourishes this growth.

Here at home, we Americans face the future with confidence. But we must also face up to the dangers that still lurk about us. We must ever work to strengthen our posture of defense and to reinforce our alliances and friendships in the free world.

While we maintain our vigilance at home and abroad, we must help intensify the will for freedom in the satellite countries behind the Iron Curtain. These countries are in the Soviet backyard; and only so long as their people are reminded that the outside world has not forgotten them—only that long do they remain as potential deterrents to Soviet aggression.

The great majority of the 70 million captives in these satellite countries have known liberty in the past. They now need our constant friendship and help if they are to believe in their future.

Therefore, the mission of Radio Free Europe merits greater support than before. It serves our national security and the cause of peace.

I have long given the Crusade for Freedom my strong endorsement. I did that because I am familiar with its purposes, its operations, the people who run it, and, perhaps, most important—its hard-hitting effectiveness as an independent American enterprise.

I know that our country and our friends behind the Iron Curtain can count on you for active participation and leadership in this most critical of all battles—the winning of men's minds. Without this victory, we can have no other victories. By your efforts, backed up by America, we can achieve our great goal—that of enabling us and all the peoples of the world to enjoy in peace the blessings of freedom.

NOTE: This message was broadcast to 35 meetings held under the auspices of the American Heritage Foundation.

33   ¶ The President's News Conference of *February* 9, 1955.

[This is a complete transcript of the news conference of this date. Those portions of the President's replies which were not released for broadcasting or direct quotation at that time are enclosed in brackets.]

THE PRESIDENT. Good morning. Please be seated.

One announcement of little importance to anyone except myself: I hope to get a few hours away from this city starting tomorrow afternoon. I am going down with the Secretary of the Treasury to his farm in Georgia.

I have two announcements of some import, or comments, let us say, first with respect to the foreign situation; the second announcement respecting the domestic.

In the foreign situation we have seen this change taking place in the rulership in the Soviets. We know, of course, when any major change of that kind takes place, that it does express dissatisfaction with what has been going on internally.

Now, what this means to the world is not yet apparent. It won't be apparent for some time. It does not change our basic policies nor the basic methods we employ in pursuit of those policies: a just and lasting peace, to remain strong ourselves while we are doing it, and to help our friends grow strong and confident so that this burden of fear and eventually other and more material-type burdens will be lifted from the backs of men.

We are going steadily ahead, and while we watch every change in the situation, there is no reason for changing our basic attitude.

I want to talk now about something for a moment that affects everybody in America. That is education. Yesterday morning I sent to the Congress a plan which I think is necessary in order that the youth of our Nation will not be robbed of their chance to get the kind of education to which they are entitled; indeed, the kind of education that they need if they are properly to discharge their duties as citizens of the United States.

Education is really bread-and-butter citizenship. It is just necessary to the developing of citizens that can perform their duties properly.

Education very properly in our country has been the duty and responsibility of the locality and the State. That is a very wise provision of our Constitution, reserving as it did all the powers not specifically given to the Federal Government, reserving them to the States. They exercise authority in this field, and they should. However, there are a number of reasons why we are so short of classrooms today. We had a war mobilization that, in more or less degree, affected our country for a long time. We have outmoded laws in many States affecting districts or debts or tax limits, and so on. There have been many obstructions to going ahead in this work.

Now, in spite of that, last year was a banner year in the building of schools. There was more than $2 billion spent. We have to add 50,000 [schoolrooms] a year to keep up with the population. Last year we constructed 60,000, and at that rate we are never going to reach the objective of getting rid of the shortage of 340,000 as of today.

The shortage has not just sprung up overnight. You find a steady growth in it reaching clear back to 1940. It was already, in 1940, something over 160,000, and the estimates show a gradual increase until today, 340,000.

Now, in order to observe the right and responsibility of States and communities in this field and yet for the Federal Government to apply leadership and to give the kind of help it should, compels us to follow a path that is sometimes not as readily discernible as we should like.

The system we have followed is to use the Federal Government to purchase bonds of districts where they are not readily marketable at a reasonable price; to assist the States in forming agencies outside of the State government itself, so that the difficulty of debt and other types of laws can be overcome; and finally in those districts where a clear case of need can be shown, where there is no other way of doing it, a certain amount of grant-in-aid matching with the States.

You will recall that a long time ago—18 months ago, I think, or at least a year—there was appointed with the authority of Congress this White House Conference on Education, which would follow upon the conferences in several States. The idea was that they would meet in the effort to solve this problem, devise a long-range plan. For this reason and in order not to get in the way of the recommendations that will be filed by those conferences, this is an emergency plan so far as construction is concerned, although it does point out certain ways that could be permanently applied to this problem.

The objective is, though, as far as the Federal Government is concerned, to keep the responsibility where it belongs, to apply leadership on a strong basis, to get an emergency program of construction started instantly, and to bring, with Federal help, this problem under control just as rapidly as possible.

Those were the two things I wanted to talk about. We will go to questions.

Q. Marvin Arrowsmith, Associated Press: Mr. President, in the light of Foreign Minister Molotov's tough-talk speech against the United States yesterday, do you think this shakeup in the Soviet Government means a calculated tougher policy towards the United States?

THE PRESIDENT. Well, I think I would not at the moment, Mr. Arrowsmith, speculate on exactly what it is going to mean. It doesn't necessarily mean that, because they would say anything that would suit their purposes at the moment of a great significant change of this kind in their government.

I would say that we must be watchful and alert and pursue our policies as we have been pursuing them.

Q. Merriman Smith, United Press: Mr. President, I don't know whether you are aware of it, because it was announced in Moscow just before the conference started, but one of your old friends and associates was just made Defense Minister by the Russians, General Zhukov. Would you think that, following up Mr. Arrowsmith's question, that General Zhukov's appointment as Minister of Defense would indicate a stronger defense policy on their part, possibly toward this country?

THE PRESIDENT. Well, again, Mr. Smith, I can scarcely interpret that act of theirs in terms of a specific intent on their part.

Now, when I knew Marshal Zhukov, I will say this:

He was a competent soldier. A man could not have conducted the campaigns he did, could not have explained them so lucidly and in terms of his own strength and his own weaknesses and so on, except that he was a well-trained, splendid military leader.

He and I developed personally a practice of getting along and seeing eye to eye on a number of our local problems in Berlin. So far as I was concerned—and I believe he was honest about it—we were trying to set up a pattern, if we could, in Berlin, in our little local place there, to show that even two nations could get along if they would both recognize the folly of not getting along.

What this means today, I don't know. The last time I had a direct letter from him was April 1946, and that was a long time ago.

Q. Robert E. Clark, International News Service: Mr. President, Soviet Foreign Minister Molotov claimed yesterday that Russia's atomic strength is now superior to our own. Do we have any cause to believe this might be true?

THE PRESIDENT. Certainly there is no proof to that effect. I should say that would be rather a remarkable feat, but I believe it is not worthwhile speculating on.

Q. Chalmers M. Roberts, Washington Post and Times Herald: Mr. President, in the Molotov speech yesterday, he said that he did not think in the case of another war that world civilization would be destroyed. This was in some contrast to Malenkov's statement last March in which he said, in a nuclear war both sides would be destroyed.

Could you tell us, aside from the political implications, on a scientific basis, from what you know, something of this as to whether in fact there is a threat in the H-bomb and other nuclear weapons to the whole world?

THE PRESIDENT. Of course, there are, as we know, some threats in the use of nuclear weapons over and beyond the immediately destructive area, where it destroys by shock and the thermal effects, and so on. There are certain radioactive effects that in the immediate vicinity can be very, very bad, indeed, as we well know. There are methods of protection.

Now, when you begin to talk in terms of "Would this destroy

civilization or would it not?" I should say we are talking in comparative terms. What is the destruction of civilization, and, in addition, how many of these things do you use? How near do you approach saturation in any place?

I would say this: the thing is so serious that intelligent people ought to forego a great many lesser ambitions in the effort to achieve an understanding, under a method where the whole world could be assured that that understanding was going to be obeyed by all parties concerned—which means there must be some kind of inspection service where all the world could trust it—that we are not pushing toward that kind of a war. So, whether or not civilization is destroyed, I say it is so serious that we just cannot pretend to be intelligent human beings unless we pursue with all our might, with all our thought, all our soul, you might say, some way of solving this problem. It's that bad at least.

Q. Robert L. Riggs, Louisville Courier-Journal: Returning to your education message, sir, Senator Hill, who is Chairman of the Senate committee on education, and Senator Clements, who is the acting majority leader, criticized your program rather strongly yesterday as being inadequate, and they said it merely loaded more debts on the States and communities which could not afford to pay the debt.

Could you comment on that, sir?

THE PRESIDENT. Did they mention the debt of the United States?

Q. Mr. Riggs: Well, they are—no, sir; they did not.

THE PRESIDENT. There is perhaps some difference in conviction here represented.

I believe that the greatest amount of authority, which means comparable responsibility, must be retained in the localities in our country or we are working steadily away from the system of government that has made this country great. That kind of a system exploits private initiative, local initiative, local care for the expenditures. As quickly as you start spending Federal money in great amounts, it looks like free money. The shibboleth of free money from Washington can certainly damage. So maybe my system is not as extreme as either side would like. I take something that I believe to be effective and good for the United States, and I stand by it.

Q. Garnett D. Horner, Washington Star: Mr. President, to return to the Marshal Zhukov business a moment ago, he was quoted in an interview yesterday as saying that in 1945 you had told him that the United States would never attack the Soviet Union, and he had told you that the Soviet Union would never attack the United States. Also, he said that you had twice invited him to visit here, and he still dreams of doing so.

I wonder if you could tell us your version of that 1945 conversation and your feelings about the prospects of such a visit?

THE PRESIDENT. Well, that is remarkably accurate. Now, when I asked him to visit our country, I was acting as the agent of my government, which directed me to do so; and more than that, arrangements had been made once. My plane had been put at his disposal, and my son was detailed as his aide. I remember he made the remark, "Well, I shall certainly be very safe," with my plane and my son. [*Laughter*]

We were good friends, and we could talk in that fashion.

I explained to him how absolutely impossible it was for a democracy to organize a surprise aggression against anybody. Our processes are open. Every time you get money or you change anything in your military affairs, you go to Congress. It is debated. There is no possibility of a country such as ours producing a completely surprise attack on any other. That is what I was emphasizing to him. Of course, from their standpoint, he felt that Russia was a very peace-loving nation.

Q. Paul Wooton, New Orleans Times Picayune: Mr. President, you have on your desk a report on transportation. Will that be made public soon?

THE PRESIDENT. [Well, it isn't on my desk yet. I don't know whether it is a report; it is a study as I have seen it. It has been going back and forth, and we have been going at it a long time. It isn't ready at this moment, at least, for publication. And its eventual destiny, I have forgotten the details.]

Q. Kenneth M. Scheibel, Gannett News Service: Sir, part of the trouble we are told from Russia is that they are having difficulties with their agriculture and their food supplies. Do you see in that situation any chance for us to do any trading with them, or is that a business of building up our enemy?

THE PRESIDENT. [I think that a question like that comes within the context of so many intertwined questions that you would have to get a whole program laid out in front of you. Now, what does this mean? Everything comes back here, when you really get down to the bottom of things and study them—everything comes back to how much confidence can we develop in the words of people who have not hesitated to break their word in the past? Where do we have deeds and actions to prove what they are trying to do? And I think that every single agreement, engagement, commitment of any kind has always got to have that as its background; because otherwise you are very likely to weaken your position, either psychologically, politically, materially, economically, in some form. So I wouldn't want to comment just on this one facet of such a possibility.]

Q. Joseph C. Harsch, Christian Science Monitor: Mr. President, to refer back to Mr. Horner's question, is that invitation to General Zhukov still open?

THE PRESIDENT. Well, as a matter of fact, this is the first time it has been mentioned to me since I have been in my present responsible post. You can well imagine that I wouldn't stand here and suddenly issue an invitation without consultation with my advisers. So I would say this would be a remarkable thing at the present state of affairs, but I certainly wouldn't hesitate to talk it over with my people if we found it desirable.

Q. Charles S. von Fremd, CBS News: There have been growing reports and speculation, sir, that possibly the Soviet Union does not now hold the political strength that it once did control over Red China. If this is true, it would certainly endanger the present situation in the Formosa Straits. But I wonder, sir, if in telling us whether or not, if you can, you have received such word from your advisers, if you could also let us know whether or not you feel there is a possibility of other satellites breaking away from the Kremlin.

THE PRESIDENT. [I should say this: there is no direct evidence that there has been any weakening of relationships between Moscow and the capitals with which it has been dealing. There is, of course, always hopeful speculation in this line, but no evidence.]

Q. Sarah McClendon, El Paso Times: Sir, the Federal Power Commission and the natural gas industry seem to be waiting to hear this Cabinet committee study on energy supplies and fuel resources. That has been held up for some time. Can you say when that will be ready?

THE PRESIDENT. [Not held up; it is just not ready. I don't know of anything quite so complicated as a study on the energy supplies of the United States in all of its components, because you have imports, you have competition among the various types of energy within our own country, you've got everything from hydroelectric power to power produced by residual oil imported into this country. It is a complicated study that is being worked on all the time.[1] That is all I can say about it at the moment.]

Q. Laurence H. Burd, Chicago Tribune: Mr. President, you mentioned hearing from Marshal Zhukov last in April 1946.

THE PRESIDENT. Directly, I said.

---

[1] On February 26 "The White House Report on Energy Supplies and Resources Policy," prepared by the Advisory Committee on Energy Supplies and Resources Policy, was released by the White House in mimeograph form. The recommendations of the Committee related to (1) natural gas regulation; (2) sales below cost by interstate pipeline companies; (3) eminent domain for natural gas storage; (4) crude oil imports and residual fuel oil imports; (5) petroleum refining capacity; (6) tax incentives; (7) research and development program for coal; (8) unemployment and business distress in the coal industry; (9) coal freight rates; (10) coal exports; (11) mobilization requirements for coke; (12) Government fuel purchasing policy.

Q. Mr. Burd: Could you say what that involved?

THE PRESIDENT. Well, it was—I think I can recall it—it was a letter. You see, I left Berlin in November '45, and he corresponded and he sent me a present. I think it was an enormous bear rug. I still have it, and something else of that kind. That was all.

Q. Clark R. Mollenhoff, Des Moines Register and Tribune: Mr. President, on February 1st the White House overruled the CAB on a decision involving a certificate of Northwest Airlines and Pan American Airlines on flights to Hawaii. That White House action overruled a 5-to-0 decision in the CAB, and last Monday you revised that order after Senator Thye and Representative Judd called on you. I wonder if you could tell us why you revised your decision, and also if you could discuss the general procedure when these independent agency cases, in the CAB, are called to the attention of the White House.

THE PRESIDENT. It is very simple in this case. Information came to my attention that convinced me I had made an error. And so I tried to correct it. The actual facts were these:

I am directed by the Congress to cut down subsidies in this air business, which means that when you have unprofitable competition on lines, you had better look at it very, very closely, because this occasions a greater deficit.

I am also directed to preserve competition so far as this can be done, but always with this other conflicting consideration of cutting down the subsidies.

In this case, it looked like we should get rid of one line on the Hawaiian run; and the line that had the most of the traffic and which had the smallest subsidy last year on that line, at least as far as figures showed, that was the one I was going to go with. I made that decision.

What happened then was that the Chairman of the Board came over to see me and pointed out that all of their calculations showed that within 2 years, they believed, the entire subsidy would be eliminated from the Pacific runs. He showed, therefore, that even if you did happen to have a subsidy, since now you have your computations for subsidies made on the operations of the full line, that here we had a case where we could well afford to go ahead with the competitive system for a while and still believe that we would come out of the subsidy area.

So I said, in that case we will renew this for a short period, which I did for 3 years.

Q. Gould Lincoln, Washington Star: Mr. President, there have been in the newspapers many reports that the Secretary of the Army, Mr. Stevens, is to be replaced. Could you tell us if there is any truth in that?

THE PRESIDENT. There is not a word of it that has come to my ears, Mr. Lincoln, not a word.

Q. Alan S. Emory, Watertown Times: Mr. President, in view of the fact that the education aid message went to the Hill before the highway message, and in view of the substance of your education message, do you think those two factors will silence the critics who have been saying the administration is paying more attention to highways than to schools?

THE PRESIDENT. Well, it is not going to silence critics; of that I am sure. [*Laughter*]

Q. George H. Hall, St. Louis Post-Dispatch: Can you tell us whether the Malenkov resignation was a surprise to this Government or whether we had diplomatic or intelligence reports indicating that it was coming up?

THE PRESIDENT. [Well, I think that our observers and people in Moscow for a long time reported that things weren't exactly as they appeared on the surface, but I never had seen any kind of prediction as to the exact things that happened yesterday, no.]

Q. Lloyd M. Schwartz, Fairchild Publications: Mr. President, the Labor and Commerce Departments reported yesterday that unemployment rose 500,000 in the month to mid-January to a total of 3.3 million, and the factory work force in January was 500,000 lower than a year earlier. Do you find this any cause for concern?

THE PRESIDENT. Well, here is a type of statistic that is examined every week or practically every day by the economic advisers of the Labor and Commerce Departments, in consultation, of course, with myself. Now, there is always a seasonal drop in employment right after Christmas; this year, looking at the comparable curves, it seems that this drop was not as acute as it has been in the recent past.

I don't mean to say that you can be complacent about such things. On the contrary, you watch them with the closest possible concern. However, it is within the bounds, you might say, of historical precedent.

Q. Roscoe Drummond, New York Herald Tribune: Mr. President, how do you appraise the state of affairs in the Formosa Straits with reference to the evacuation of the Tachens and the possibility of a cease-fire?

THE PRESIDENT. I think it would be idle to speculate, Mr. Drummond, on the possibility of a cease-fire. We asked Red China, or the United Nations did, to come in and talk it over. They declined and issued a very bellicose statement. Therefore, on that I couldn't say what may happen.

Now, with regard to the evacuation, it is proceeding exactly according to plan. If nothing happens, it should be completed very soon. There has been no untoward incident. In one case I believe one of our planes got a little lost, wandered in a bad area and got hit, but the crew was saved. There has been no real interference. It looks like it would go ahead for the moment.

Q. Nat S. Finney, Buffalo Evening News: Mr. President, can you tell us whether your freedom of action to order the use of nuclear weapons in connection with the defense of Formosa and the Pescadores is in any way limited by understandings with our allies?

THE PRESIDENT. Well, if the United States, of course, got into trouble alone and were attacked, I don't know of any understanding with any allies that applies. I think understandings with allies applies when you are in any kind of an action in concert with them.   I have not thought of that point in exactly the way you have stated, but I think it would be a United States decision.

Q. Edward T. Folliard, Washington Post and Times Herald: Mr. President, a bill has been introduced which would make former Presidents of the United States members of the Senate.   They would receive pay and quarters, but wouldn't be permitted to vote.   They would be Senators at Large.   It would now affect Mr. Hoover and Mr. Truman, and perhaps ultimately yourself. Do you think the bill has merit?

THE PRESIDENT. [Frankly, I say this, Mr. Folliard: I am not too sure.   Any man who has served in high posts in his government—and this doesn't mean merely the Presidency—has acquired a certain amount of experience where, if his faculties have held together reasonably well, he should be of some value to his country.

[In my own case, I thought I had left the service of my country forever in 1948, I believe in February.   I soon found I was back in, in one form or another.

[I believe those people are always available.   I believe each one of them is proud and feels a sense of satisfaction when his experience and wisdom are called upon.   And if it could be better utilized by giving this rather formal post, I certainly would have no objection.   I would never argue against such a thing.   I am not sure that it would be an exact answer, but it would be all right.]

Q. Robert J. Donovan, New York Herald Tribune: Mr. President, in consideration of the trade program in the House, there has been a move to add import quotas for oil to protect the coal industry.   If this has come to your attention, have you any comment on it?

THE PRESIDENT. [It hasn't come to my attention that specific way.   But we are trying to liberalize trade on a reciprocal basis, particularly in selected commodities.   There has been great progress made in the last 2 years in eliminating quotas from the normal practices of governments with respect to this trade business.

I would very much deplore seeing us going backward and establishing quotas that were at least fixed by law.]

Merriman Smith, United Press: Thank you, Mr. President.

NOTE: President Eisenhower's sixtieth news conference was held in the Executive Office Building from 10:31 to 11:01 o'clock on Wednesday morning, February 9, 1955. In attendance: 230.

34 ¶ Message to Meetings of the Nationwide Clinical Conference on Heart Ailments. *February 9, 1955*

[Delivered over closed circuit television from the White House]

IT IS a privilege to greet you tonight, and to express my gratification at the purpose of your separate but united meetings from coast-to-coast. Your program tonight, as it has been described to me, is another example in our society of the collaboration between free enterprise and pure learning—an instance in which business and the medical profession work together for the common good.

If the annual toll from coronary heart disease were revealed to the American people as a casualty list from the battlefield, the effect would be one of national shock, and a demand that something be done. That something *is* being done, in such programs as the one tonight, is significant, and encouraging.

You, the physicians of America, are linked in this enterprise by a bond far stronger than the cables of a television network. Your bond of union is a common and selfless aim. Your principal motives are first, a concern for the welfare of your patients, and second, that restless curiosity, that hunger for knowledge of better ways, which is the hallmark of the man of science.

Our way of life provides the climate in which the chronic questioner is free to rove, to doubt, to explore, in the endless search for new and fuller answers. Every assistant in a laboratory, every researcher, every medical student, every specialist, every family doctor, is a participant in this search—a search which has added twenty-five years to the American life span within the memory of many of you in this audience.

These new years of expectancy have been a bonus beyond price added to the wealth of our Republic. For them we, your fellow Americans, owe you our grateful thanks.

A nation's strength is directly affected by its people's health. In that light, we must strengthen and support those agencies of Government which are concerned with the problems of national health.

Yet, the role of Government in these matters must always be secondary, and supplementary. The first responsibility lies with the community, determined to foster good health and to provide well for the ailing and the injured; with the scientist, as he works in freedom towards goals of his own choosing; and with the physician, who brings his healing ministry not to the State, or to the mass of people as such, but always to some man, or woman, or child—some individual human being worthy of his dedicated care.

Godspeed you on your mission.

NOTE: This message was broadcast to 32 meetings held under the sponsorship of the American Medical Association.

35 ¶ Remarks at Luncheon Meeting of the Republican National Committee and the Republican National Finance Committee. *February* 17, 1955

YOU CAN well imagine what a great privilege I feel in having this opportunity to visit with you as a friend. Inescapably, as the titular head of the party, you can understand the jealousy with which I regard that party and its success. My most earnest hope is that, when I leave my present post, the party will be healthier, stronger, more vital than it was when I started in that post.

Now we here represent possibly every calling, every phase in life. We have many viewpoints. Yet the first thing I want to point out is this: if we here had a discussion on the philosophy of government—that is, what is Government's role in the life of this Nation, in the life of the individual, what would it do and what would it not do—we would all agree with Lincoln. There would be no real argument among us on the results we would achieve. These different viewpoints we have arise out of our different environments, out of our different backgrounds.

I want to tell you something else that will, I hope, show you my belief. Often, when I see or hear from one of my friends in the party worrying about some particular action, there crosses my mind a sort of useless hope; a hope that that person and I might change places for a week.

I assure you when you take a decent philosophy of government and try to apply it to problems in which there are conflicting pressures and considerations of the utmost moment—whether they be in the foreign field or the economic field or the social field—you will find that this application must reflect a very broad consideration of every opinion about you. The opinion of the Secretary of State, or our leaders in Congress, or of the Secretary of Health, Education, and Welfare—all up and down the line. You strive to achieve in every single decision a further step along the broad highway where all Republicans can with honesty and decency move.

Now I realize that on any particular decision a very great amount of heat can be generated. But I do say this: life is not made up of just one decision here, or another one there. It is the total of the decisions that you make in your daily lives with respect to politics, to your family, to your environment, to the people about you. Government has to do that same thing. It is only in the mass that finally philosophy really emerges.

Now right here let me interrupt myself. I am talking, of course, about the Republican Party, my concept of what it can do to further America. So I just want to say this, so that our balance of values does not get out of order: our great enemy is the Communists. Our great struggle today is a free world against a dictator world. Our greatest enemy is not the Democrats. We certainly know that we can't have better allies when we are fighting anybody from abroad. So let's remember that, and as I talk, let's not build up a picture that the worst enemy anyone can have is a Democrat. Far from it. We just don't think they can do as good a job as we do. As a matter of fact, we know it!

I want to read you something that Lincoln said in 1853. He was discussing the founding of our country. He began by affirming the equal rights of all our citizens, and then he said: "We proposed to give all a chance; and we expected the weak to grow stronger, the ignorant wiser; and all better and happier together. We made the experiment; and the fruit is before us. Look at it—think of it."

Now what I should like to say, as I go ahead in the thoughts I am trying to express to you today is: look at it! Look at the Republican Party's record of the last two years. Think of it! What have we done? Have we done it in the tradition of Lincoln who said that the proper business of government is to do for a community or for a person those things which it or he cannot do at all or so well do for itself or himself; but in all things which the individual or community can do best, government should not interfere.

That is the guiding policy of this administration.

Now, in the thought and hope that Lincoln expressed so well, people came to us from overseas. Some saw here, or thought they saw, streets of gold. Others just saw shoes for their children, or a roof under which they might live securely. But most of them saw a symbol—a symbol of what men believing in themselves could, under God, accomplish, both for themselves, for their children, and for those about them.

Now some liked so much what they saw that they wanted to live in status quo. They wanted to go nowhere. But again most resolved that the principles should be everlastingly applied for the protection of individuals, the strengthening of the Republic, and the inspiration of mankind.

The Republican Party was born in such a resolve. It will remain great and go ahead forever, as long as it lives in that resolve. To take the basic principles of justice and decency, to apply them to the problems of today, and never to desert the effort to push forward in that light.

Think of it! Look at it!

Now, if we are going to do that, let's have a bit of catechism in four simple questions. The first one is: what are the purposes of a political party? Well, one answer is winning elections. But it is certainly not good enough for a thoughtful Republican to win an election and not do something for this country.

I really believe that if we are going to give the purpose of a political party, we would have to say that the first fundamental is to present to all America a political philosophy which should interpret and apply our underlying principles to the current problems of the day.

The second purpose is to convert a multitude of pressures and pleas and special plans and purposes of our people into a composite whole which we call our platform—or our program. Again this program must always be true to the principles of the philosophy under which we live.

Third, the purpose of a political party is to promote individual participation in decisions, those affecting both administration and the conduct and course of the policies of government.

Now I believe any political party that is organized around this thoughtful concept is the greatest asset a country can have. But I believe also if it is banded together solely to seize power, it is nothing but a conspiracy. It must be for the promotion of ideals. The basis of a political party, just like the basis of true free government, is spiritual. Let us not forget it. We must live by ideals.

We could talk for a long time about the second question: how to achieve these purposes I have just outlined. Most of you know more about this than I do. My political experience is short, but I think most of you would agree it has also been quite intense.

I know that underlying every political purpose, every political aspiration and hope, must be work at the precinct level. Our Government means people—of, by, and for the people. We must reach the individual. We must convey to him, and to America, the ideals by which we live, and then convince him. When he is convinced these ideals are great, that the method of application for which we stand is great, we know that he will support us.

Next, on top of that kind of work, we must have good candidates. Here, I think, I could talk to you for the next hour.

As I see the Republican Party, we have such a wealth of brains, of ability combined with personality, that it is a tragedy in any locality for any of us to push into nomination—from alderman up—someone who doesn't represent the ideals and purposes in which we all believe. We must have that kind of candidate. And if we do, it will take an awfully good bunch to beat us.

Now the next question we should answer is: what is the record of Republican purposes? Here of course, one would be tempted to go right back to Lincoln and come on down through our history and talk about anti-trust laws and all the things that our party has done for the progress of man. But just let us take only the last two years in the foreign field.

The Korean War has been stopped. There is no shooting—except in a sporadic way for the moment between Chinese—any place in the world. The Trieste problem has been solved. The Suez problem has been solved. Iran, which only two years ago we thought day by day we were going to see collapse and go to the enemy, has not only been rescued but is orienting itself more and more enthusiastically to the West. In South America, in Central America, great agreements have been made under which one foothold of international communism has been eliminated. We are moving ever steadily toward European unity. In the Pacific we have strengthened the free world by adoption of the Manila Pact and the Defense Treaty with the Republic of China.

So we are strong with our allies. There is less of a critical character in the international situation to keep us tense, giving us greater opportunity to push ahead with reasonable programs to solidify the security of the free world against the communist menace.

I think you are well acquainted with the record of the 83rd Congress. I have tried to find a phrase in which to define what the Republican Party has done at home. I have said we were "progressive moderates." Right at the moment I rather favor the term "dynamic conservatism." I believe we should be conservative. I believe we should conserve on everything that is basic to our system. We should be dynamic in applying it to the problems of the day so that all 163 million Americans will profit from it.

So for the moment I would say the record at home has been dynamic conservatism. You can go into the fields of agriculture, of the freedoms that have been restored to our economy, to the tax system—to everything we have done.

Now the next question: how can our party better achieve its purposes in the future?

First, we must make certain that as we present our philosophy, we apply it to the problems of the times. We must keep it in step. We are not antediluvian, nor are we trying to be men from Mars that will visit us probably in three or four hundred years.

I believe Tennyson said: "Be not the first by which the new is tried, nor yet the last to lay the old aside."

There are many ideas that are tested and true. We must take them and advance them step by step, as we go along with the constantly changing types and kinds of problems with which man is confronted.

Next, I think any party must strive to be national. We must work with all our might to eliminate sectionalism and faction-alism.

And then my favorite subject: let's go after the youth. You know, if you get a 21-year-old to join you, he can probably vote in about fifteen national elections, and you have an accumulative strength. If you recruit each year only men, let us say, of 70, then in three or four years you would have to recruit enough to win another election. But if you get them when they are young and keep adding on and adding on, soon you will be getting the kind of majorities to which the Republican Party is truly entitled.

Now these are some of the thoughts that I wanted to share with you today. Nothing startling, nothing new, in the sense that they represent any great departure from what the Republican Party has been striving to do all the time.

But I think it is worth while to remind ourselves why we are a party, why we work: because then we work with greater enthusiasm, and far more than that: with greater effect.

I really believe that with the cause for which we have to work, with the material we have in this party, with the appeal we can make to youth, and with the kind of candidates that we can produce, we can sweep the country.

NOTE: The President spoke in the Congressional Room, Statler Hotel, Washington, D.C.

36 ¶ Exchange of Messages Between the President and President Chiang Kai-shek of the Republic of China. *February* 18, 1955

I HAVE RECEIVED your kind message of appreciation for the assistance rendered by the armed forces of the United States in the redeployment of the armed forces of the Republic of China from the Tachen Islands.

The manner in which this cooperative endeavor was carried out is a source of real gratification to me and, I am sure, of mutual satisfaction to the officers and men, both Chinese and American, who were responsible for its success. They may justly take pride in having participated in this demonstration of the close and effective cooperation of our two countries in the interests of peace and the defense of freedom.

DWIGHT D. EISENHOWER

NOTE: President Chiang Kai-shek's message of February 14 follows:

On the successful completion of the redeployment of the armed forces from the Tachen Islands, I wish to convey to you my deep appreciation for the assistance and cooperation which you have directed the United States forces to render to the Chinese Government. I also wish to express my admiration for the efficiency and high spirit displayed by the United States officers and men in this operation.

CHIANG KAI-SHEK

37 ¶ Letter to Emil Sandstrom, League of Red Cross Societies, on Completion of the Flood Relief Program in Europe. *February* 19, 1955

[Released February 19, 1955. Dated February 4, 1955]

Dear Justice Sandstrom:

The relief program for the victims of the floods which inundated parts of Central and Eastern Europe last summer is now practically completed. Over $10 million worth of aid has been distributed to these unfortunate people, most of it through the active cooperation of your organization.

The most notable fact about this program has been the strict adherence by everyone to the humanitarian principles of the Red Cross. Relief was given to the needy regardless of race, color, creed or political conviction.   For the first time in many years, it was possible to surmount political boundaries in the administration of relief.   I know that the success of the program is in a large measure due to the untiring efforts of the members of your organization.   Reports received here indicate that Red Cross officials worked long hours, including week ends and holidays, to assure the success of this program.   They can be proud of their work.

I wish to express to you and through you to every member of your organization who participated in the successful accomplishment of this undertaking my sincere appreciation, as well as my congratulations.

Sincerely,

DWIGHT D. EISENHOWER

NOTE: Justice Sandstrom was Chairman of the Board of Governors of the League of Red Cross Societies, with headquarters at Geneva, Switzerland.   At the time the letter was made public the White House announced that 66,551 tons of foodstuffs had been sent in 28 shiploads to areas in Central and Eastern Europe.   The release further stated that the relief program began on November 10, 1954, after the Iron Curtain countries agreed to admit United States ships to their harbors for this purpose.

Justice Sandstrom's reply was released with the President's letter.

38 ¶ Remarks Recorded for the "Back-to-God" Program of the American Legion.
February 20, 1955

THE FOUNDING FATHERS expressed in words for all to read the ideal of Government based upon the dignity of the individual. That ideal previously had existed only in the hearts and minds of men.   They produced the timeless documents upon which the Nation is founded and has grown great.   They, recognizing God as the author of individual rights, declared that the purpose of Government is to secure those rights.

To you and to me this ideal of Government is a self-evident truth. But in many lands the State claims to be the author of human rights. The tragedy of that claim runs through all history and, indeed, dominates our own times. If the State gives rights, it can—and inevitably will—take away those rights.

Without God, there could be no American form of Government, nor an American way of life. Recognition of the Supreme Being is the first—the most basic—expression of Americanism. Thus the Founding Fathers saw it, and thus, with God's help, it will continue to be.

It is significant, I believe, that the American Legion—an organization of war veterans—has seen fit to conduct a "Back to God" movement as part of its Americanism program. Veterans realize, perhaps more clearly than others, the prior place that Almighty God holds in our national life. And they can appreciate, through personal experience, that the really decisive battleground of American freedom is in the hearts and minds of our own people.

Now, if I may make a personal observation—you, my fellow citizens, have bestowed upon my associates and myself, ordinary men, the honor and the duty of serving you in the administration of your Government. More and more we are conscious of the magnitude of that task.

The path we travel is narrow and long, beset with many dangers. Each day we must ask that Almighty God will set and keep His protecting hand over us so that we may pass on to those who come after us the heritage of a free people, secure in their God-given rights and in full control of a Government dedicated to the preservation of those rights. I can ask nothing more of each of you—of all Americans—than that you join with the American Legion in its present campaign.

NOTE: The President's remarks were part of an American Legion program, which was broadcast over radio and television from 8:00 to 8:30 p.m.

39   ¶ Special Message to the Congress Regarding a National Highway Program.   *February* 22, 1955

To the Congress of the United States:

Our unity as a nation is sustained by free communication of thought and by easy transportation of people and goods.   The ceaseless flow of information throughout the Republic is matched by individual and commercial movement over a vast system of interconnected highways criss-crossing the Country and joining at our national borders with friendly neighbors to the north and south.

Together, the uniting forces of our communication and transportation systems are dynamic elements in the very name we bear—United States.   Without them, we would be a mere alliance of many separate parts.

The Nation's highway system is a gigantic enterprise, one of our largest items of capital investment.   Generations have gone into its building.   Three million, three hundred and sixty-six thousand miles of road, travelled by 58 million motor vehicles, comprise it.   The replacement cost of its drainage and bridge and tunnel works is incalculable.   One in every seven Americans gains his livelihood and supports his family out of it.   But, in large part, the network is inadequate for the nation's growing needs.

In recognition of this, the Governors in July of last year at my request began a study of both the problem and methods by which the Federal Government might assist the States in its solution.   I appointed in September the President's Advisory Committee on a National Highway Program, headed by Lucius D. Clay, to work with the Governors and to propose a plan of action for submission to the Congress.   At the same time, a committee representing departments and agencies of the national Government was organized to conduct studies coordinated with the other two groups.

All three were confronted with inescapable evidence that action, comprehensive and quick and forward-looking, is needed.

First: Each year, more than 36 thousand people are killed and more than a million injured on the highways. To the home where the tragic aftermath of an accident on an unsafe road is a gap in the family circle, the monetary worth of preventing that death cannot be reckoned. But reliable estimates place the measurable economic cost of the highway accident toll to the Nation at more than $4.3 billion a year.

Second: The physical condition of the present road net increases the cost of vehicle operation, according to many estimates, by as much as one cent per mile of vehicle travel. At the present rate of travel, this totals more than $5 billion a year. The cost is not borne by the individual vehicle operator alone. It pyramids into higher expense of doing the nation's business. Increased highway transportation costs, passed on through each step in the distribution of goods, are paid ultimately by the individual consumer.

Third: In case of an atomic attack on our key cities, the road net must permit quick evacuation of target areas, mobilization of defense forces and maintenance of every essential economic function. But the present system in critical areas would be the breeder of a deadly congestion within hours of an attack.

Fourth: Our Gross National Product, about $357 billion in 1954, is estimated to reach over $500 billion in 1965 when our population will exceed 180 million and, according to other estimates, will travel in 81 million vehicles 814 billion vehicle miles that year. Unless the present rate of highway improvement and development is increased, existing traffic jams only faintly foreshadow those of ten years hence.

To correct these deficiencies is an obligation of Government at every level. The highway system is a public enterprise. As the owner and operator, the various levels of Government have a responsibility for management that promotes the economy of the nation and properly serves the individual user. In the case of the

Federal Government, moreover, expenditures on a highway program are a return to the highway user of the taxes which he pays in connection with his use of the highways.

Congress has recognized the national interest in the principal roads by authorizing two Federal-aid systems, selected cooperatively by the States, local units and the Bureau of Public Roads.

The Federal-aid primary system as of July 1, 1954, consisted of 234,407 miles, connecting all the principal cities, county seats, ports, manufacturing areas and other traffic generating centers.

In 1944 the Congress approved the Federal-aid secondary system, which on July 1, 1954, totalled 482,972 miles, referred to as farm-to-market roads—important feeders linking farms, factories, distribution outlets and smaller communities with the primary system.

Because some sections of the primary system, from the viewpoint of national interest are more important than others, the Congress in 1944 authorized the selection of a special network, not to exceed 40,000 miles in length, which would connect by routes, as direct as practicable, the principal metropolitan areas, cities and industrial centers, serve the national defense, and connect with routes of continental importance in the Dominion of Canada and the Republic of Mexico.

This National System of Interstate Highways, although it embraces only 1.2 percent of total road mileage, joins 42 State capital cities and 90 percent of all cities over 50,000 population. It carries more than a seventh of all traffic, a fifth of the rural traffic, serves 65 percent of the urban and 45 percent of the rural population. Approximately 37,600 miles have been designated to date. This system and its mileage are presently included within the Federal-aid primary system.

In addition to these systems, the Federal Government has the principal, and in many cases the sole, responsibility for roads that cross or provide access to Federally owned land—more than one-fifth the nation's area.

Of all these, the Interstate System must be given top priority in construction planning. But at the current rate of development, the Interstate network would not reach even a reasonable level of extent and efficiency in half a century. State highway departments cannot effectively meet the need. Adequate right-of-way to assure control of access; grade separation structures; relocation and realignment of present highways; all these, done on the necessary scale within an integrated system, exceed their collective capacity.

If we have a congested and unsafe and inadequate system, how then can we improve it so that ten years from now it will be fitted to the nation's requirements?

A realistic answer must be based on a study of all phases of highway financing, including a study of the costs of completing the several systems of highways, made by the Bureau of Public Roads in cooperation with the State highway departments and local units of government. This study, made at the direction of the 83rd Congress in the 1954 Federal-aid Highway Act, is the most comprehensive of its kind ever undertaken.

Its estimates of need show that a 10-year construction program to modernize all our roads and streets will require expenditure of $101 billion by all levels of Government.

The preliminary 10-year totals of needs by road systems are:

	Billions
Interstate (urban $11, rural $12 billion)	$23
Federal-aid Primary (urban $10, rural $20 billion)	30
Federal-aid Secondary (entirely rural)	15
Sub-total of Federal-aid Systems (urban $21, rural $47 billion)	68
Other roads and streets (urban $16, rural $17 billion)	33
Total of needs (urban $37, rural $64 billion)	$101

The Governors' Conference and the President's Advisory Committee are agreed that the Federal share of the needed construction program should be about 30 percent of the total, leaving to State and local units responsibility to finance the remainder.

The obvious responsibility to be accepted by the Federal Government, in addition to the existing Federal interest in our 3,366,-000-mile network of highways, is the development of the Interstate System with its most essential urban arterial connections.

In its report, the Advisory Committee recommends:

1. That the Federal Government assume principal responsibility for the cost of a modern Interstate Network to be completed by 1964 to include the most essential urban arterial connections; at an annual average cost of $2.5 billion for the ten year period.

2. That Federal contributions to primary and secondary road systems, now at the rate authorized by the 1954 Act of approximately $525 million annually, be continued.

3. That Federal funds for that portion of the Federal-aid systems in urban areas not on the Interstate System, now approximately $75 million annually, be continued.

4. That Federal funds for Forest Highways be continued at the present $22.5 million per year rate.

Under these proposals, the total Federal expenditures through the ten year period would be:

	Billions
Interstate System	$25.000
Federal-aid Primary and Secondary	5.250
Federal-aid Urban	.750
Forest Highways	.225
Total	$31.225

The extension of necessary highways in the Territories and highway maintenance and improvement in National Parks, on Indian lands and on other public lands of the United States will continue to be treated in the budget for these particular subjects.

A sound Federal highway program, I believe, can and should stand on its own feet, with highway users providing the total dollars necessary for improvement and new construction. Financing of interstate and Federal-aid systems should be based on the planned use of increasing revenues from present gas and diesel oil taxes, augmented in limited instances with tolls.

I am inclined to the view that it is sounder to finance this program by special bond issues, to be paid off by the above-mentioned revenues which will be collected during the useful life of the roads and pledged to this purpose, rather than by an increase in general revenue obligations.

At this time, I am forwarding for use by the Congress in its deliberations the Report to the President made by the President's Advisory Committee on a National Highway Program. This study of the entire highway traffic problem and presentation of a detailed solution for its remedy is an analytical review of the major elements in a most complex situation. In addition, the Congress will have available the study made by the Bureau of Public Roads at the direction of the 83rd Congress.

These two documents together constitute a most exhaustive examination of the National highway system, its problems and their remedies. Inescapably, the vastness of the highway enterprise fosters varieties of proposals which must be resolved into a national highway pattern. The two reports, however, should generate recognition of the urgency that presses upon us; approval of a general program that will give us a modern safe highway system; realization of the rewards for prompt and comprehensive action. They provide a solid foundation for a sound program.

DWIGHT D. EISENHOWER

NOTE: The report of the President's Advisory Committee on a National Highway Program, transmitted to the Congress with this message, is entitled "A 10-Year National Highway Program" (H. Doc. 93, 84th Cong., 1st sess.). The study made by the Bureau of Public Roads, referred to by the President, was submitted to the Congress by the Secretary of Commerce in two reports entitled "Needs of the Highway Systems, 1955–84" (H. Doc. 120, 84th Cong., 1st sess.), and "Progress and Feasibility of Toll Roads and Their Relation to the Federal-Aid Program" (H. Doc. 139, 84th Cong., 1st sess.).

40 ¶ Letter Extending Greetings to the Brotherhood Dinner of the National Conference of Christians and Jews. *February* 22, 1955

[Released February 22, 1955. Dated February 19, 1955]

Dear Dr. Clinchy:

My greetings go to those attending the Brotherhood Dinner in Washington on February twenty-second, and to all who join in the observance of Brotherhood Week throughout America.

This observance, during the week of Washington's Birthday, emphasizes once again his words, "to bigotry no sanction, to persecution no assistance."

The ardent belief of our Founding Fathers in human dignity and freedom—enduringly expressed in the Declaration of Independence and the Constitution—has sustained and guided our people toward the greatest possible fulfillment of the American dream—a people at peace, humble before their Creator, tolerant of differences, deriving from their very diversity strength to advance the common good.

Today Americans can be proud of the progress made toward realization of this ideal of brotherhood, proud of the answer thereby given to those who would bind people together in slavery.

Through such efforts as yours this progress will continue toward an America increasingly worthy of those by whose thought and courage and sacred honor our nation was "conceived in liberty and dedicated to the proposition that all men are created equal."

Sincerely,

DWIGHT D. EISENHOWER

NOTE: This letter was addressed to Dr. Everett R. Clinchy, President of the National Conference of Chris- tians and Jews. The Brotherhood Dinner was held at the Mayflower Hotel, Washington, D.C.

41   ¶ The President's News Conference of
February 23, 1955.

[This is a complete transcript of the news conference of this date. All of
the President's replies were released for broadcasting or direct quotation at
that time.]

THE PRESIDENT. Good morning. Please be seated.

I have no general announcements this morning, ladies and
gentlemen. So we will go right to questions.

Q. Robert E. Clark, International News Service: Mr. President, can you tell us how you feel about the Democratic proposal
to cut everybody's taxes by $20?

THE PRESIDENT. The question affects this proposal for cutting
the income taxes of every individual in the United States $20.
You have asked a question, Mr. Clark, that takes some time to
answer, because you asked for my opinion about it.

Now, in the first place, any proposal to reduce taxes is, of
course, popular; and at first glance this is a kind of proposal that
should make an appeal to low income brackets.

Let's take a little closer look at this proposal and start off with
this one observation. Whenever you have inflation, the immediate effect, of course, is to hurt first the people of fixed incomes—
white-collar workers and others who for the moment at least
are on relatively fixed incomes. But in the long run, the person
that is hurt most is the person who lays aside savings in the forms
of pension, insurance plans, and savings bonds for use in his older
age. For example, anybody who paid up all of his share of a
pension by as early as 1939 was getting in 1953 half of the worth
of the pension plan he had bought.

When we talk about decreasing revenues at a time when the
Government, in spite of every saving we have been able to make,
is still spending somewhat more than it takes in, we are reaching
some kind of heights in fiscal irresponsibility. Because this does
have on the surface a popular or appealing appearance, these

people apparently hope it may be passed. They have not had the courage to put it in as a bill on its own merits. They have attached it as an amendment to a bill which is for the continuation of the 52 percent as opposed to the 47 percent taxes on corporations and for the continuation of excise taxes on liquor, tobacco, gasoline, automobiles, transportation, and the like.

From those two continuations of tax programs, we expect and anticipate getting 2,800 million, roughly that kind of money. This $20 exemption would in the first full year of its operation reduce our income by 2,300 million.

We inherited in 1953 a budget that contemplated a 9.9 billion deficit in Federal financing. By hard work—and I assure you it is hard work when you realize that every bureau of Government feels it should have more money—we have reduced that to an expected deficit in 1956 of less than two and a half billion, or in that neighborhood, estimated.

Now we are going back to deficit spending, the most insidious thing that can happen to a free economy, and particularly in its bad effect upon low income groups. I should like to call your attention to a statement by economists of the American Federation of Labor, which said the year 1954 was their finest overall salary year of their history. In spite of the fact that their salary increases were only 5 to 9 cents, or something of that order, in general insignificant or small as compared to salary increases of the past, their purchasing power, due to the stability of the dollar, their overall position in the salary angle was the best of their history.

In the last 2 years, the cost of living has varied less than one-half of 1 percent. From 1939 to 1953 the dollar went from 100 cents to 52 cents. It is that kind of thing that must be stopped if we are to preserve the principles on which this country was established. It is based on a free economy which in turn is based on a stable dollar, which in turn is more important to all low income and fixed income groups than it is to rich people.

Rich people can buy equities, can afford to invest in equities, and as the dollar cheapens, the amount of dollars that they have invested goes up and up. But the fixed income group, the man who is buying an insurance policy, I repeat, or looking forward to living on his pension, is the one that is hurt.

We simply cannot have this kind of thing in responsible government.

Now, I might remark that obviously these people have put this $2,300 million reduction in a tax bill that will keep this 2,800 million for us in the belief that there cannot, then, anything be done about it.

I say if this thing is to be tested in the Congress—and I admit, of course, they have the perfect right to do it—let them do it on its own merits and not attach it to these other bills.

Q. Merriman Smith, United Press: Mr. President, in the light of what you have just said, how, then, do you feel about your goal as you announced in your state of the Union message of achieving a tax reduction in 1956?

THE PRESIDENT. As you know, through the efforts of reducing governmental expenditures, I talked to you awhile ago, we returned last year to the people the greatest tax reduction in history, 7,600 million. With the increased confidence brought about to business, to investors, to purchasers, to everybody else, we have a very healthy upturn in our economy. We hope that will continue. We hope to continue to reduce expenditures. We hope that gross national product will continue to go up, and with no higher taxes we will probably, and believe we can, get to the point that we can return some more in 1956. But it must be done on a thoroughly worked out, analytical basis, so as to achieve the kind of stability in living costs and the proper distribution of taxes that was achieved in the plan of last year which was worked out by so many different groups.

Q. Mrs. May Craig, Maine Papers: Mr. President, would you veto a tax bill with such a rider on it, and require a two-thirds vote?

THE PRESIDENT. Mrs. Craig, I have told this group many

times, I have never yet been able to predict for myself exactly
what I am going to do in such cases until it comes up to me. If
the bill comes up to me in exact form, I might predict, now, what
I could do. But the fact is, it could come up in so many different
forms, with so many different angles, that I think it is best to
wait to see what happens before I make my own predictions to
myself.

Q. Marvin Arrowsmith, Associated Press: Mr. President, is
this Government studying whether to offer surplus wheat to
Russia?

THE PRESIDENT. Well, as you know, this suggestion has been
brought up, and I have directed certain people who have to deal
with this in our Government to look it over.

For myself, I look at it askance. I would not go overboard
on such an idea until everybody who is trained in the whole
business of psychological conflict and all the rest of these things
look at it very coldly and carefully, because I am afraid that
what the United States might mean as a fine gesture of good
will could be twisted and turned to our disadvantage. But in
any event, it will be studied carefully. There will be a recommendation made to me on it.

Q. Laurence H. Burd, Chicago Tribune: Mr. President, can
you say what recent steps have been taken with regard to the
flyers being held by Red China and whether you think the
chances are better or worse for their release than a few weeks
ago?

THE PRESIDENT. Well, there has been no recent development
of note or of great significance. I could not give you an evaluation of chances, whether or not they are now better than they
were. I just believe this: in all of these directions in which we
believe the Chinese Communists have been acting wrongfully
toward us, including these flyers of which you speak, we have
got to insist upon a just and decent settlement and never cease
doing so, never to accept anything as a completion of the problem
until justice has been done.

Q. Mr. Burd: Are we leaving it with the United Nations for quite a lot longer time?

THE PRESIDENT. Well, you say, "leaving it with the United Nations." We use every avenue open to us—through third parties, through the United Nations, everywhere that we can exercise any of our influence, we try to do it, as I say, to get a just solution to these problems.

Q. Chalmers M. Roberts, Washington Post and Times Herald: Mr. President, after the Atomic Energy Commission's report last week on the hydrogen bomb fallout, you commented through Mr. Hagerty that it demonstrated your belief that there should be some agreement on arms, international agreement on armaments. With the U.N. arms meeting about to open in London this week, could you tell us, sir, whether you have anticipated any possibility of agreement, or does the matter appear to still be in deadlock?

THE PRESIDENT. Past history would not give us any great reason for tremendous optimism in this line. However, it is something that I have worked on for years. I know that the war in Europe was scarcely over before I was pleading for some kind of arrangements among the great powers of the earth so that these fears and burdens could be lifted from the backs of men, and particularly once we had found out that the atomic bomb was in existence.

Now, as of today: my views, I must say, have changed very little, if at all, since that time. We must have ways and means of determining that each principal nation party to any kind of agreement is acting in good faith. There must be ways and means of determining that; and once we can determine and make certain, have confidence in the ways and means that this is to be done, then as far as we are concerned we would like to put everything in the pot and go just as far as anybody else would.

Q. Mr. Roberts: Mr. President, may I ask further in that connection, there have been suggestions studied here and elsewhere that there might be a sort of an interim set of agreements to ban further tests of thermonuclear weapons. Has that been brought to your attention, and could you comment on it?

THE PRESIDENT. Well, yes, it has been brought to my attention. We have discussed pro and con. We see nothing of an ad interim nature about this. If this would come about, naturally, if we could get a decent and proper disarmament proposal, I see nothing to be gained by pretending to take little bits of items of that kind and deal with them separately.

Q. Alan S. Emory, Watertown Times: Sir, could you tell us the difference between cutting $1.4 billion in taxes for fiscal '55 and not cutting the taxes for fiscal '56? I believe that the deficit of the current fiscal year minus the tax cut gives approximately $3.2 billion, and the estimated deficit for fiscal '56 plus the tax cut for half of that year under the Democratic plan would also come to $3.2 billion.

THE PRESIDENT. Well, I don't know about '56. I know this, that the actual effect for a full fiscal year under this proposal is something on the order of $2.3 billion. Now, after all, these tax programs and things that are needed to bring confidence to American business and the American consumers are long-term problems, not things that look attractive at the moment because, you say, "we will only go in debt a little bit more next year."

I am talking about a long-term, sound fiscal program for the United States. And remember this: when we talk about these things, as far as I am concerned, I am not talking about any partisan advantage of any kind. I am not talking about a personal attitude. It is not I that may be defeated. What we are talking about here is 163 million people and what is good for them, how they are going to prosper, how they are going to grow constantly stronger and have a better life. That is what we are talking about. The Government owes it to every citizen to live as economically as it can, to cut down expenditures, to keep working on it, and intelligent people ought never to give up on this.

But when we get down to that point, let us by no means live

beyond our income, because if we do, we will damage ourselves irrevocably.

Q. Raymond P. Brandt, St. Louis Post-Dispatch: Mr. President, can we interpret that to mean that there will be no tax reduction until the budget is balanced?

THE PRESIDENT. Well, I don't know that you could make such an interpretation. For example, last year we gave a tax reduction in the belief that that particular tax reduction, worked out carefully, would help in the long run to balance the budget. I believe you can anticipate savings; I believe you can anticipate certain good results from things that you do, administratively and otherwise. Certainly you want to return taxes, because I assure you, every political party likes to cut taxes; there is no question about that. So we will do it as soon as we can, and I would not say by any manner of means that the budget has to be in perfect balance before you can contemplate sincerely another tax cut.

Q. Mr. Brandt: One other question, Mr. President.

THE PRESIDENT. Yes.

Q. Mr. Brandt: Does that mean that a balanced budget is not in sight at this time?

THE PRESIDENT. Well, a balanced budget—I believe I quoted to you from one of my favorite authors, myself, not long ago. [*Laughter*] I read to you a statement I made in '52, I think, that I believed that within 4 years, with careful administrative procedures, with businesslike methods, with examining every expenditure and arranging our tax program, reforming it, we could achieve a balanced budget within 4 years and at a rate of taxation bearable by the American people.

I still believe that, if we do it logically and sensibly.

Q. William Theis, International News Service: Mr. President, do you share the hope expressed by Sir Anthony Eden that there might be at least discussion and possibly settlement of the Formosa problem at the Bangkok Conference?

THE PRESIDENT. I didn't see his statement, but the United States is, and this Government is, on record as seeking every possible means for a cease-fire with justice to everybody in that region.

Q. Mr. Theis: Could you say, sir, whether the Secretary of State went with any special instructions on that matter to Bangkok?

THE PRESIDENT. As you may know, the Secretary of State and I, just before he left, had half a dozen conferences. This subject, of course, was talked at great length, and his plan for having conversations with Mr. Eden and others concerned was very clear and definite. But exactly what could be done, we had no prognostications, you might say, as to outcome.

Q. Charles E. Shutt, Telenews: Would you comment, sir—I know Congress has not been in session too long—as to the harmony in relationship with the Democratic-controlled Congress and your office?

THE PRESIDENT. Well, on a personal basis and meeting with these individuals, it is completely satisfactory. Every time I have asked any individual, any leader of the opposing party to confer with me, or he wanted on his own initiative to institute such a conference, it has been on the most friendly and, as far as I know, profitable basis possible.

Q. Clark R. Mollenhoff, Des Moines Register: Mr. President, in the past you have made it clear that you deplored the fact that certain members of Congress have attacked individuals unjustly on the floor, but you at the same time said that that was a matter for Congress to decide upon for itself.

Now, I wondered what steps you would take if it should come to your attention that someone in the executive agency would call an individual a member of a subversive organization when they had no evidence to sustain that and it was absolutely clear that there was no evidence to sustain it.

THE PRESIDENT. Well, now, I am not a member of the Supreme Court, but I understand they don't answer these very long hypothetical questions. [*Laughter*] When you bring to me facts such as you just now allege, and bring them so that I can study them and not answer them in a press conference where I have nothing of any other side except a statement of accusation, then I will give you my opinion; but not now.

Q. Mr. Mollenhoff: Mr. President, is that an invitation to permit this——

THE PRESIDENT. If you have any information that you believe of wrongdoing in this administration, you are not only at liberty to submit any facts you have, I strongly urge that you do. I assure you they will get the finest kind of consideration.

Q. Frederick Kuh, Chicago Sun-Times: Mr. President, I would like to ask a question in view of our experience with EDC. What alternative have you in mind in the event of an inordinate delay or blockage in ratification and putting into operation of the Paris agreements?

THE PRESIDENT. Well, I must answer the question in this way. As you know, these efforts have been going on now literally for years. At every stage, almost every day, anyone who had official position with respect to these plans—and as you know, I did in Europe before I came back here—had to have alternatives in mind, in part, or sometimes on a whole plan. Always, though, you keep these as a sort of insurance against any catastrophe such as you now again bring up as a possibility.

I strongly hope we won't have to consider any further alternatives. I do not regard this one to be as effective as was the concept of EDC. EDC had the great virtue of bringing about almost involuntarily and, you might say, as one of its corollaries, a greater unification of Western Europe. I must tell you, ladies and gentlemen, today I just cannot overemphasize the importance to the security of the free world of a great economic, industrial, and social connection and indeed finally some greater and better political connection between the nations of Free Europe.

They are a great power if united, 250 million highly educated people, a great productive capacity, great resources; but split up into contesting smaller governments and smaller economies, it is indeed failing to achieve the strength of which it is capable.

So at this moment, this particular plan seems to be the best that can be accomplished, and I am going to put my full strength behind getting this one done. I will take up alternatives afterwards.

Q. Sarah McClendon, El Paso Times: Mr. President, for some reason there seems to be no channel of communications between your office and the office of Speaker Sam Rayburn of the House of Representatives. He says that every time there is a message from the President coming to the Congress that the press get it in advance but he doesn't hear it until it is on the floor; no copy is sent to him and he can't get a copy unless Charlie Halleck or Joe Martin bring him one.

Then recently he has given out three statements publicly aimed at your office, and apparently your office has never received these statements and doesn't know. One was on Dixon-Yates and two were on the Flemming report on oil and gas.

Is there some means—do you know this, and if you didn't know it, will you do something about establishing this channel of communications? [*Laughter*]

THE PRESIDENT. I doubt that the Speaker has to bring to me any complaints about my office through a roundabout course of communication. He and I have been personal friends for years. He is the representative of the district where I was born, indeed, and based on that there has been a sentimental attachment. He has been invited, as has every other Democratic leader, to bring to me anything by reaching for a telephone and calling me up, just exactly as any leader of the Republican Party has. So I cannot believe that he is disappointed or feels any sense of frustration about any lack of communication.

Q. Mrs. McClendon: Well, sir——

THE PRESIDENT. That will be all I have to comment on that.

Q. Robert G. Spivack, New York Post: Mr. President, Senator Knowland said yesterday in a speech that he thought the U.N. could no longer be considered an effective instrument of collective security. I wonder if you could give us your evaluation of the work of the U.N. in recent years.

THE PRESIDENT. Well, of course, ladies and gentlemen, it would take a long time to go back through the entire history of the United Nations. I think I can best sum up my opinion about the need for the United Nations and about its work, about the reasons we should support it, in a very short simple analogy.

We do not cease our efforts in research in cancer, nor do we abolish the laboratories in which this research goes on merely because of lack of success; and we have had a tremendous lack of success.

Here is a laboratory where nations come together and they explore and they talk, and I am not even going to bother this morning to recite to you some of the good things they have done in the Mid-East and elsewhere. They have. But I must say, as long as we have got a forum, regardless of the fact that our opponents do deliberately use it as a propaganda platform, it is a good thing to keep it going. Here is something for which mankind has had a yearning ever since the dawn of history, and I am not going to give up in my time on it.

Q. Edward P. Morgan, American Broadcasting Company: Sir, there seems to have been some confusion in the past about what the administration thought was necessary in terms of aid to Asia, particularly Southeast Asia—military, economic, and in technical assistance. Could you give us now, sir, at this point what you think should be done in that regard?

THE PRESIDENT. You are asking a question that has no final and definite answer. The situation in Asia changes daily, as it does everywhere else in the world. It is human. We have, as far as I know, never had real disagreement in any moment, at least what I call disagreement as to principle, in the whole administration. But there are changing situations. We had a war in Indochina. That war is not going on actively now. We have danger situations developing in a number of these weaker countries. We are constantly working and trying to deal with them on a case by case method, on the merits of each problem, in such a way as to advance the security and progress of the United States of America and her real friends in the free world.

Now, that is what we are trying to do, and there is just no final answer at any one time.

Q. Charles S. von Fremd, CBS News: Mr. President, there has been a considerable amount of talk in the past 2 days over this tax matter, sir, among Republicans on Capitol Hill who accuse the Democrats of making this step as a political gesture rather than one where they are truly trying to help a good many people, and yesterday, after coming out of a conference with you in the White House, Congressman Arends said that it smacked of politics 100 percent. I wonder if that also represents your views or at least to a certain extent.

THE PRESIDENT. I think my record is perfectly clear on one point. I have often criticized here, in front of you people, ideas, plans, and programs. I think I have never challenged anybody's motives. If you are going to talk about motives, you will have to do it on your own responsibility or get someone else to talk.

Q. Louis C. Hiner, Indianapolis News: Mr. President, the Hoover Commission task force this week sent certain recommendations to Congress to cut the volume of Government paperwork. They recommended that you issue an Executive order to support a Government-wide paperwork management program. What are your feelings about their suggestion?

THE PRESIDENT. If they have found a practical way to accomplish something along this line, I am going to design some new type of medal for them—[*laughter*]—because I have been working on it a good many years, particularly in the Defense Department, but even in some other places where I have collaborated on a confidential basis.

It is the hardest thing in the world, and particularly when there are so many growing reasons for every department of Government to get into some new function, to study some new idea, to prepare some new report. With all kinds of needs arising, it seems difficult to cut it down. But if they have found a practical way, they are going to find a very great ally in me. That I assure you.

Q. Garnett D. Horner, Washington Evening Star: Mr. President, could you tell us what you think the effect might be on the work of the Federal Communications Commission of its recent experience of having two witnesses change their testimony in the Edward Lamb case and charge that FCC personnel had coached them into giving false testimony?

THE PRESIDENT. As a matter of fact, that has not come to me officially. I know about it; it has been brought up in conversation in my office. I will have to take a much closer look before I can express any kind of opinion whatsoever.

Q. Roscoe Drummond, New York Herald Tribune: Mr. President, would you give us your reaction to the size of the Republican vote against your trade bill in the House last week?

THE PRESIDENT. Well, Mr. Drummond, I should say this: I was, of course, highly gratified that in the final vote a majority of both parties went for the affirmative side of this bill. This is because I so deeply believe that the welfare of the free world, which so inescapably involves the welfare of the United States, is bound up in a growing volume of trade and trade traffic.

Now, as to the other votes that were not final, there were, of course, times when there was a majority of the Republican Party on the other side. Exactly why these maneuvers were carried out I think puzzled even some of their own leaders. In conversations with them, they did announce themselves as puzzled.

Merriman Smith, United Press: Thank you——

THE PRESIDENT. Well, I just want to say this one thing. [*Laughter*] I have only this one thing left, Mr. Smith, which is not news.

I am grateful to the entire body of the Congress, as I said before, finally for looking at this thing in a statesmanlike way and trying to decide on the basis of what's good for all America.

Thank you very much.

NOTE: President Eisenhower's sixty-first news conference was held in the Executive Office Building from 10:33 to 11:04 o'clock on Wednesday morning, February 23, 1955. In attendance: 227.

42 ¶ Exchange of Messages Between the President and His Imperial Majesty the Shah of Iran. *February* 23, 1955

ON BEHALF of the American people I wish to express my deep appreciation to you for your thoughtful message sent at the conclusion of your recent visit to the United States. It was indeed a pleasure for Mrs. Eisenhower and me to have had Your Majesty and Empress Soraya as our guests.

I am also happy that your visit gave so many Americans an opportunity to become better acquainted with you both. Your sincerity and strength of purpose have increased the bonds of friendship between our countries.

I feel certain that under your able leadership your country will progress and will continue to contribute to the enduring peace which we both so earnestly desire.

DWIGHT D. EISENHOWER

NOTE: The President's message was delivered to the Shah through the United States Embassy in London. The Shah's message of February 11, sent from the SS *Queen Mary*, follows:

On leaving the shores of your great country the Empress and I wish to express our heartfelt gratitude and best thanks to you, Mr. President, and to Mrs. Eisenhower for the generous hospitality and genuine kindness which we have received from you and from officials all over the United States. We are deeply touched by the unobtrusive manner in which everyone has spared no effort to make our stay in America comfortable and enjoyable. I avail myself of this opportunity to send through you, Mr. President, our heartfelt greetings and salutations to the American people. May the torch of freedom so nobly carried by you and your countrymen never be dimmed.

MOHAMMAD REZA PAHLAVI

43   ¶ Remarks at the Annual Breakfast of Masonic Leaders.   *February 24, 1955*

Mr. Chairman, My Friends:

I use that form of address, I hope, with no intimation of egotism in claiming all of you in such capacity.

In the first place, I am unaccustomed to the usages of fraternal orders, and I wouldn't know how to address you properly should I try to follow protocol.   And in the second place, although I notice among this audience certain individuals who to my astonishment—sometimes to my utter amazement—have differed with me on a specific political question, I note also among the audience many that I have classed as my warm personal friends for years. I sincerely trust that all of you feel that we can have differences without breaking a friendship.

But I do feel a very great sense of friendship for individuals of the Americas, because I conceive it to be the first duty of anybody in public office in a free country to sustain freedom wherever it may be alive, or struggling to come alive.   In such a body as this, I feel not only at home, I feel a warm sense of fellowship that I am certain can scarcely be closer were I a member myself of this great organization.

It is for a number of reasons that I feel a distinct sense of pride in coming over here this morning.   First, as you know, I spent a great deal of my life in uniformed service, and I look forward to seeing some uniforms.   To each individual who out in front of the hotel this morning formed part of that colorful guard of honor: my thanks.   I enjoyed it thoroughly.

Then when I came in and the choir greeted us with the Battle Hymn of the Republic, I almost went out to look for a recruiting office.   A little later, when this great band favored us with the "Caissons Go Rolling Along," I started to get up and march around the room.

These things are things that touch the sentiment, the spirit of a man. And it is that, if I may, that I would like to talk to you about for just a little bit this morning: the spirit of the individual—his feeling toward his country, toward the society in which he lives.

And when I mention country, may I say to our South American, our Canadian, and our friends of other nationalities here, I would hope that my words can be felt by you to apply to your country as well.

We hear a lot in our Fourth of July speeches about the great privileges of American citizenship. We are wont to parade them—our rights, our priceless heritage, and our privileges—throughout the world and to ourselves. And they are indeed priceless.

I should like to talk for just a few moments about the responsibilities devolving upon the individual that make possible the maintenance of those rights.

There are great new problems to perform in any society. The care of the sick and the unfortunate, the security of a group in terms of national security and local security, and all the rest. Free government is based on the theory that there will be a certain element of spontaneous cooperation among free people in order to get these jobs done; that they will not all have to be done from a centrally directed authority. The more we allow a centrally directed authority to take these responsibilities and to exercise the necessary authority that goes with responsibility, the more we are deserting the great responsibilities on which rest these great rights and individual liberties.

So one of the prides I feel was the knowledge that I was coming to a group who through its association takes on its own shoulders one of the great civic responsibilities: to help care for the unfortunate, to make certain that they are doing something to discharge that old feeling that we do have a selfish interest, indeed, in the welfare of our brothers. In such a society as ours, unless the whole prospers, the individual cannot prosper; unless the individuals in themselves are prospering, then the whole cannot prosper. We will be serving our own ends of the preservation of our rights and discharging our responsibilities when we do these things.

Government has a function in all of these civic responsibilities, in all these problems. But the genius of our Government has been, of course, its federated principle: a central government of limited powers and authorities, giving to each State, to each community, and above all to each individual, certain things he must do, if this great experiment in government, this great revolutionary movement that is still going on, is to succeed.

The Communists claim it cannot. Those of you who have studied carefully any Communist book will find in it a great dwelling upon inherent contradictions within a free society. They prove to their apparent satisfaction that it cannot succeed.

I believe that you gentlemen, each of you who is participating in the great fraternal work of your organization to help the unfortunate, are setting an example to all of us that we must do our duty, if we are to prove the Communists to be in error.

I could not more express my pride than to say I feel that I am in a group which by its actions recognizes its brotherhood at the feet of the Almighty, and discharges the obligations of brotherhood by doing for others those things that other people deserve merely because they are humans and, like yourselves, children of a common God.

And so in these halting words I hope you can find the real reason for my pride in being invited here this morning before such a body, to express to you a few of the words that lie in my heart. Thank you very much.

NOTE: The President spoke at the Statler Hotel, Washington, D.C. His opening words "Mr. Chairman" referred to Frank S. Land, founder of the Order of DeMolay and Imperial Potentate of A.A.O.N.M.S.

44 ¶ Message to the Inter-American Investment Conference Held in New Orleans.
February 28, 1955

[Recorded on film]

MAY I first express a warm welcome to all of you at the Inter-American Investment Conference in New Orleans. Your conference is the kind of concrete "let's-see-what-we-can-do-to-gether" demonstration that can make a valuable contribution to our hemispheric concept of "the good partner."

I am particularly pleased that this conference has been organized by private businessmen of the Americas for the growth of private business between the Americas.

I do not mean that the Government of the United States can or should be uninterested or refuse to participate in inter-American economic development. Quite the contrary.

There are and will be many opportunities for both direct and indirect Government participation—sometimes in partnership with private initiative; sometimes through the kind of stimulus which may be furnished by the operation of special tax inducements such as Secretary of the Treasury George Humphrey referred to at the Rio Conference; sometimes through a device such as the International Finance Corporation designed to make increased development funds available and also provide for the eventual transfer of the project to private ownership.

But behind all private plans and projects, behind Government help, behind a New Orleans Conference or a Rio Conference, behind the words, the dollars, and the blueprints, there must exist the essential ingredient of faith—North American faith in Latin America, and Latin American faith in North America.

And if today I had to choose only one thought to leave with you, it is the thought of our North American faith in the future of Latin America—economically, culturally, politically, and spiritually.

Each of us in this Western Hemisphere is possessed of many blessings—compared to many other areas of the world. Compared to hundreds of millions of the world's people, our blessings are superabundant.

Should we not, therefore, clasp hands in fraternal friendship, and so conduct ourselves that these blessings shall be multiplied for the good of all?

And so to you conferees of the first Inter-American Investment Conference, I say with all my heart, may good fortune attend your gathering.

45 ¶ Remarks Recorded for the Opening of the Red Cross Campaign. *February* 28, 1955

My Fellow Americans:

Today I should like to talk to you about the campaign for the Red Cross, which we now open.

While I do this, I have asked some of my young girl and boy friends to come in here with me. And this is an important phase of my little talk, because these youngsters are our future leaders. They are our hope for a brighter tomorrow.

Now, many of these lessons of leadership they learn at home, in their churches, in their schools, and in the other organizations to which they belong—like this young Boy Scout. But they learn a lot from the Red Cross in which they are all junior members. They learn that the Red Cross is in fact our big brother. It typifies the spirit of the good neighbor. Now these sentiments—these qualities—are important to a democracy. They mean that we are ready to help one another. These youngsters will learn this as they see the Red Cross rush into disaster areas, to help out the unfortunate, to take care of every kind of disaster that befalls man in peace and in war.

Now for myself I am of course far better acquainted with the Red Cross in war than I am in peace, because I spent so many years of my life in the Army. There they brought to the fighting man in all the Services a touch of home. They made him feel that his sacrifices were worthwhile and appreciated by all of us at home.

The Red Cross is now asking for 30 million members and 85 million dollars.

Personally I think those sights are far too low. Mrs. Eisenhower and I have just renewed our membership in the Red Cross. It is my ambition that by the end of March I can call every single American my fellow member of the American Red Cross.

Thank you, youngsters, for being with me.

NOTE: The President's remarks were recorded at the White House on February 15.

46 ¶ Message to the Pope on the Occasion of His 79th Birthday. *March 2, 1955*

His Holiness, Pius XII
Vatican City

Your championship of the brotherhood of man, your dedication to peace and good will among men, have won this nation's respect and admiration. On your seventy-ninth birthday, I am sure I speak for my fellow Americans in extending to you our country's best wishes for happiness and health.

DWIGHT D. EISENHOWER

47 ¶ The President's News Conference of *March* 2, 1955.

[This is a complete transcript of the news conference of this date. Those portions of the President's replies which were not released for broadcasting or direct quotation at that time are enclosed in brackets.]

THE PRESIDENT. Good morning.

There are two individuals I would like to mention this morning. The first, as to His Holiness, the Pope—his 79th birthday—a man that I have had the honor of visiting personally, admiring him greatly, and particularly because of his unbroken record of opposition to all forms of fascism and communism, I am quite certain that all America would wish this great spiritual leader a very happy day today, and many more of them.

The other man is Ambassador Caffery, just now retiring from the diplomatic service, who holds the American record for length of time as head of a mission. For 29 years he has been head of an American mission in some foreign country, has been responsible for solutions to many serious problems, or at least helpful, and leaves with a brilliant record and the best wishes of the entire Department.

The interesting life he has led, as described by him to me this morning in a short interview, would seem to me to provide some inspiration for able, young Americans to go into that same service, a service that is constantly devoting itself, dedicating itself, to the welfare of the United States all over the world.

Those are the only announcements I have; we will go to questions.

Q. Merriman Smith, United Press: Mr. President, Mr. Churchill said yesterday that Western superiority in the hydrogen bomb will prevent Russia from starting a big war within the next 3 or 4 years. Now, from this, or from your own sources of information, do you get the idea that Russia will pull even with the West in 3 or 4 years?

THE PRESIDENT. Anything dealing with such a subject, any conclusion, is really nothing more than a speculative estimate.

However, we do know that the Western World has had and enjoyed a great lead in this whole field, both in atomic fission and atomic fusion.

Now, exactly how long that lead can be sustained is problematical. And again another factor enters this question: there comes a time, possibly, when a lead is not significant in the defensive arrangements of a country. If you get enough of a particular type of weapon, I doubt that it is particularly important to have a lot more of it. So I think that it would be unwise to attempt any fixed conclusions based on the information available to any of us.

Q. James B. Reston, New York Times: Sir, I wonder if you could straighten us out on your economic foreign policy for Asia.

About 3 months ago, Mr. Stassen and Mr. Dulles sought out the press to develop the thesis that our policy was out of balance, that we had to have a large new economic policy for Asia; then Mr. Humphrey seemed to knock that down; and now yesterday Mr. Stassen seems to have announced in New Delhi that you are sending a new program to the Hill next month.

THE PRESIDENT. Well, Mr. Reston, I think the things that you talk about as being indicative of a struggle within the administration are merely evidences of the long-term intensive study that has been taking place here. This is not an easy subject.

We had a tremendous change in the Far Eastern situation over the past year—the cease-fire in Indochina, where we had been devoting a very great deal of money, as you know.

Now, to take a new look at the situation of what is needed has involved a very long and earnest study, and in the meantime, SEATO has come into existence, so that, as far as I know, there has been no great differences in final conclusions.

There have been different viewpoints presented, and there is evolving a plan soon to be crystallized that will be brought out to the Congress for its approval and for implementation; but that is as far as you can say anything definitely on the thing at this time. It will be one we hope will be helpful to all our friends in that area.

Q. Roland H. Shackford, Scripps-Howard: During the last week there has been published a suggestion, now supported by a resolution in the Senate, that the United States try to get all nations, including Russia, to agree to devote more of their resources to raising living standards, more butter and fewer guns.

Could you give us your thoughts on the general idea by devoting, by giving higher priorities, to living standards, to have a form of economic disarmament?

THE PRESIDENT. I find here recently more and more occasions to refer to my favorite author. I think you might find the same idea in a speech I delivered, I believe, on April 16, 1953: that the United States could not be more devoted to the idea of the products of humans being devoted to human welfare and less to human destruction, than we now are. We believe in it thoroughly.

Now, every one of these plans that is brought forward always has to make this one assumption: that there are ways and means available to us for making certain that everybody is acting in good faith. Good faith is the ingredient that must be implicit in any plan that is finally adopted, and which could gain the confidence of people who don't want to fight.

We know we will never start an aggressive war. We just want to devote ourselves to the prosperity and the security, happiness and safety, greater liberty and development of our own people and of our friends in the world.

I believe there can be a dozen different variations of a plan for disarmament if it is approached in good faith; and now that is the thing that we must seek, we must try to build. When you come down to it, possibly the best way to define American policy abroad in this whole field is how do we develop good faith among the nations so that all peoples can be confident in the words of others.

Q. Joseph C. Harsch, Christian Science Monitor: Mr. President, 2 weeks ago you discussed your early postwar invitation to Marshal Zhukov to visit you, and you said at that time that you would be willing to consider renewing the invitation.

Has there been any consideration of that, and if so, any result?

THE PRESIDENT. Well, I have thought it over personally and, as of this moment, I am not going to issue one. I think there are a lot of things going on in the world. I am going to certainly wait until I discuss again with the Secretary of State conditions that have been developing over the past couple of weeks.

But I repeat that in those days I liked him, I thought he was a very able man. From the personal standpoint, of course, it would be very interesting to see him again. It is something I have not forgotten, Mr. Harsch; I am just not ready to give the final answer on it.

Q. Fletcher Knebel, Cowles Publications: Mr. President, what do you think of the suggestion advanced out in Iowa, and now seconded very heartily by an official Soviet publication called "Soviet Agriculture" that a group of Russians come out to Iowa and see how we grow the tall corn and the hogs? [*Laughter*]

THE PRESIDENT. I think—and I believe I have told this before in front of this body—I think the Russian people, as such, don't want war any more than we do. They want opportunities to advance themselves economically, culturally, and, of course, traditionally Russians are very devoted to all the arts—their aesthetic sense seems to have been highly developed.

Now, I couldn't imagine, if we could relieve this question of all of the inhibitions and the limitations that occur to you because of the situation today in the world, I couldn't imagine anything better than to have some of their agricultural people visit our agricultural people.

I visited once both state farms and collective farms in Russia, and there was no place where I was queried so insistently and in such detail as I was on those farms.

You know, they have a technical expert they call an agronomist for each one of these installations. The agronomist in one case was a woman; came up to me with a shining face, and just as eager to take the opportunity to ask questions, "How do you raise this?" Fortunately, I was raised in a farming area so I could answer some of the questions. [*Laughter*]

"But how much does a person get in the United States for doing this kind of work?" "How do you do these things?" "I am so anxious to go see."

I really believe this would be an area in which some good could come if we didn't have a dozen different difficulties of which we all know, one of which, I believe, is legal.

We would have some difficulty in clearing things under our present laws. There are a number of things to be studied and looked at; but just as a personal opinion as to what good might come out of it, these two peoples, these two representatives of agriculture getting together, I would say it would be good and good only.

Q. Chalmers M. Roberts, Washington Post and Times Herald: Mr. President, I would like to ask a question about Formosa, since it has been about a month since the resolution that you requested was passed by Congress.

Since that time, the Chinese Nationalists have evacuated some islands. Diplomatic negotiations appear publicly, at least, not to have brought any cease-fire.

I wonder if it is a fair conclusion to draw from that, as the situation now is, the question of peace or war in Asia lies entirely with the Chinese Communists, or is anything or can anything more be done from our side?

THE PRESIDENT. I think the first answer to that is you never give up in the pursuit of a legitimate and desirable objective merely because you are defeated the first time and discouraged, and the conditions don't look particularly bright; you don't give up.

Now, as to Formosa and the immediate estimate of the situation there, our Secretary of State is there today. He is visiting with the Generalissimo and, by the time he comes back, certainly will have at least some new ideas or variations of ideas to put into our calculations.

I should say, though, in general, that at least the Western World wants peace in that area; therefore, the only way that we can be embroiled is through some action on the part of the opposing side.

Q. Alan S. Emory, Watertown Times: Mr. President, this spring ground will be broken on a project that was the first new legislative accomplishment of your administration, the Saint Lawrence Seaway. Are there any chances that you will be up there for that ceremony, sir?

THE PRESIDENT. [I have been invited, and I have put it high on what I call my priority list of desirable things to do. But whether I will make it or not, I couldn't say at this time.]

Q. William H. Lawrence, New York Times: There have been reports, especially in South American countries, sir, that the real mission of the Atka in the Antarctic is to seek out some new proving grounds, either for atomic or hydrogen weapons. Can you comment on whether there is any truth in that or not?

THE PRESIDENT. Well, Mr. Lawrence, the report is absolutely without foundation. There is absolutely no intent on the part of the United States to go down into that area to explore for any such reason.

The ship that went down there, this icebreaker, went down to do the preliminary logistic work for a scientific expedition, which will go down to do our part of what is called the world commitment in the development of the geophysical year of 1957–58.

They are going down merely as a preparatory logistic exploration of how we will do our work. It will be done under scientists and for the development and benefit of the world, nothing else.[1]

Q. Robert E. Clark, International News Service: Mr. President, the head of the Senate GOP Campaign Committee said the other day he doesn't think the Republican Party can win in 1956 without you as their candidate. I wonder how you feel about this view that you are indispensable to a party victory, and how it may affect your own plans in 1956?

THE PRESIDENT. Did you ever think of what a fate civilization would suffer if there were such a thing as an indispensable man? When he went the way of all flesh, what would happen? It would be a calamity, wouldn't it?

I don't think we need to fear that.

Q. Sarah McClendon, El Paso Times: Sir, in the Northern District of Texas Court, where many tax cases arise, the Eisenhower Republicans and the Eisenhower Democrats are having quite a squabble over who is going to be the Federal judge.

I wonder if you would support the man, who is Ralph Curry, who is supported by Jack Porter and the Eisenhower Republicans, or Bob Hall, who is supported by Senator Daniel and the Eisenhower Democrats?

THE PRESIDENT. [I am quite certain the Attorney General will bring to me the man he considers best qualified, the man who is, above all, supported by the American Bar Association and given a very high rating; and it wouldn't be anyone who is not qualified. Aside from that, I can't tell you.]

Q. Charles S. von Fremd, CBS News: There has been a bill introduced on Capitol Hill, sir, on the House side, suggesting or

---

[1] On March 28, a White House release stated that an expedition would be sent to the Antarctic in November to begin work on three observation sites in connection with U.S. participation in the program for the International Geophysical Year, July 1957–December 1958. The release further stated that plans for the IGY would lead to the establishment of more than 20 scientific stations on or near the antarctic continent. It also noted that the USS Atka, a Navy icebreaker, had just completed preliminary observations required for the later expedition.

On July 29 the White House announced on behalf of the President that he had approved plans for launching a small unmanned earth-circling satellite as part of the United States participation in the International Geophysical Year.

asking that the electoral college be abolished in determining presidential elections, and in its place the popular vote be substituted. Such bills have been introduced in the past, but they always have been defeated.

However, the people who are for the popular vote point out that the electoral college in their mind is now outdated, and think in some cases a man with the minority of the popular vote could actually be elected President under the electoral college.

Could you give us your views on this matter, sir?

THE PRESIDENT. [I am not so certain that a man couldn't argue both sides of this question; but this has been brought forward in various forms over a great many years, this same proposition.

[I do want to point out one thing about our system: it tends to preserve a two-party system. If you took and made representations in Congress and, I suppose, it would be Congress as well as the President, based upon popular vote, you might begin to get proportionate or splinter parties as you do in other countries—if you made it just a single national thing. That I would deplore.

[But I would say this: while I think our system seems a little awkward and we can smile a little bit at it, it has worked. And while I believe it was at one time claimed that a presidential election was stolen due to the Louisiana vote being thrown out by party manipulation, on the whole it has operated very well. I see no great reason, no great urgency, in changing it.]

Q. Raymond P. Brandt, St. Louis Post-Dispatch: Mr. President, will you comment on the action of the Senate committee yesterday in voting down the $20 tax reduction?

THE PRESIDENT. I was highly gratified. I explained my position on this whole tax proposition last week. I explained what I thought emphatically, even if rather sketchily—and I haven't changed my mind.

Naturally, I am delighted that the Senate has brought out on the floor a bill that does keep on the books the excise and the extra 5 percent corporation taxes and, at the same time, doesn't go in for this reduction.

Q. Mr. Brandt: Did you read Mr. Keyserling's reply to your charges that the bill would bring on inflation?

THE PRESIDENT. [I read only three things someone brought in to my desk that said Mr. Keyserling has a plan for spending a good many more billion dollars, for reducing taxes, and balancing the budget at the same time. That I would doubt was a good economic plan.]

Q. Garnett D. Horner, Washington Star: Mr. President, I understood you to say, in discussing the question about Sir Winston Churchill's speech yesterday on the hydrogen bomb, that the Western World has had the lead in this whole field. Did you mean to put that in the past tense?

THE PRESIDENT. I didn't mean that it doesn't have it now. I mean that it has had, all this time, the lead.

I did merely intimate that in such a thing as this, you couldn't say, looking on into the decades of the future, that this is always to prevail; that is all I meant.

Q. Elie Abel, New York Times: Mr. President, in an interview with Senator Margaret Chase Smith, Generalissimo Chiang Kai-shek has said rather recently that he expects United States moral and logistical support for a reinvasion of the Chinese mainland.

Can you tell us, sir, whether this Government has given the Nationalists any reason to expect such support?

THE PRESIDENT. Well, I thought that this whole thing had been discussed so thoroughly there could be no question of America's attitude in this matter.

The United States is not going to be a party to an aggressive war; that is the best answer I can make.

Q. Benjamin R. Cole, Indianapolis Star: Information has come from the Commission on Intergovernmental Relations that the States are all able to finance their own educational needs; and I was wondering, sir, if that had been brought to your attention, and if it is true, if it would change your views on the needs of the—the requirements of the States for Federal aid?

THE PRESIDENT. Well, I doubt that that is true in detail. I

hadn't heard that before, but I doubt it is true in detail, at least in view of information that comes to me from so many different sources. In any event, I believe the problem to be so serious that the United States Government must take a very positive and definite leadership in this direction.

As you know, I am trying to make that leadership effective in a way that retains to the States and to the localities their traditional responsibility; but I do want to get going.

Q. Edward T. Folliard, Washington Post and Times Herald: This is another political question, Mr. President. We have some information on this, but it came to us secondhand from Chairman Leonard Hall.

Would you, sir, as leader of the Republican Party, tell us how you feel about San Francisco as a convention city, about a late convention, and about a short and merry presidential campaign?

THE PRESIDENT. When they asked me about this selection of cities, I didn't know all of the technical details of television, switching it from one convention to another, or all of the other things that so engaged the attention of the committees.

I said I knew the climate of the areas, and I liked that of San Francisco better than I did Chicago; that was my remark.

Now, I don't know that the timing and the place has any great effect on the succeeding campaign. I doubt that it has.

I rather think it is a good thing to shift around from one city to another. Really that is what I thought: instead of always going back to the same place, switch around in this country. It is a big country, and if the place can accommodate the members of the convention, why, let's go there once in a while.

Q. Marvin L. Arrowsmith, Associated Press: Mr. President, would you like to send any message to Vice President Nixon regarding his statement yesterday that he hopes you will seek reelection? [*Laughter*]

THE PRESIDENT. Did he say that? [*Laughter*]

Q. Mr. Arrowsmith: He did.

THE PRESIDENT. Well, I'll tell you: as you people know, I have always expressed great admiration for Mr. Nixon. I think he is a splendid type of younger man that we want in government.

On the comment he made, I will send him no special message. I probably will have something to say to him when I see him. [*Laughter*]

Q. John Herling, Editors Syndicate: Mr. President, as you know, sir, the A.F. of L. and CIO have signed an agreement to merge their organizations, more than 15 million members.

Would you care, sir, to comment on its possible significance to the country, and its various ramifications; and, too, do you see in such a merger the danger of a labor monopoly?

THE PRESIDENT. Well, quite naturally, I have done a little speculating and thinking of my own on such an important question.

I have asked people in the Government who can devote their whole time to this problem to give me their conclusions, and they will do so.

My own mind will stay open on a lot of the facets of this particular movement and development. But, by and large, I think this: I think the American people, in their individualistic selves are very independent; and I would doubt that any organization can just set itself up and be, in all phases of their political and economic and cultural life, the bosses of any great number of Americans.

I believe that there will be many counterbalancing factors in any attempt to make this just one great, say, political organism, or something of that kind, and these people be the bosses of that many Americans.

Q. Mr. Herling: Mr. President, do you feel there is such a tendency for them to be bosses over American workers who are members of unions?

THE PRESIDENT. Do I what?

Q. Mr. Herling: Do you feel there is any tendency in that direction?

THE PRESIDENT. Well, I didn't comment on that. I merely

said that you were proposing the question in terms of politics. Well, I believe these people are going to be fairly independent politically, as always.

Q. Daniel Schorr, CBS News: Mr. President, referring to your preference to the climate of San Francisco, can it be taken for granted that you will attend the convention?

THE PRESIDENT. No. [*Laughter*]

Q. Merriman Smith, United Press: That is what I was going to ask.

Q. George R. Zielke, Toledo Blade: Mr. President, are you happy that Congress has decided to raise its pay and that of the judges?

THE PRESIDENT. Yes, I am.

In the past, ladies and gentlemen, I have talked to a number of what I thought promising young people, people who are establishing themselves, about the possibility of them getting into government; and I find that, particularly with respect to jobs that bring them to Washington, the economic factor has a very important bearing on their decisions. Frequently they must simply decline; because, they said, "I am a young fellow starting out, and I can't do it."

They must keep a home in their own districts; they must go back often to those districts if they hope to be re-elected, and they have to be re-elected each two years—incidentally which, I think, is a mistake; I would like to see a 4-year term for them. Then they have to set up a new home here; and, as you know, they do have unusual expenses.

Now, they voted themselves this raise, but they also included judges and other parts of the judiciary who have been badly underpaid. This administration has required, for example, that United States attorneys give up their private practices. They were allowed to do that in the past. We require them to give them up.

They should be paid well. And of course, finally, you say they have given themselves a $7,500 raise; we will get half of it back, don't forget that. [*Laughter*]

Q. Lawrence Fernsworth, Concord (New Hampshire) Monitor: Mr. President, last night I heard a very distinguished ex-Senator speak on this subject of pay raises.

He suggested, he thought it would be a good idea to double the pay of a Senator, and he further put forth the suggestion that it would be a good idea for the Government itself to underwrite the campaign expenses of members of Congress.

He thought that would be a great step forward toward eliminating corruption in these expenditures, and he set forth that notwithstanding the Corrupt Practice Act there still is a great deal of that sort of thing going on.

Would the President care to give us his view on that?

THE PRESIDENT. [Well, that is a very broad and very wide question. I don't think I could comment on it usefully. I do applaud what must underlie his reasoning, and that is the effort to get good men to come to Washington, men that are dedicated to this country and will do their best in these places.]

Q. Kenneth M. Scheibel, Gannett Newspapers: Mr. President, getting back to the Russian food situation, has there been any final decision on the proposal that we give them some of our wheat?

THE PRESIDENT. I keep hearing about this proposal we give them some of our wheat, although I don't know where it came from.

I believe there is an Attorney General opinion we may not barter, we may not sell, but we could give.

Now, I want to point out that there has been no report made to us that Russia is really short of grain. On the contrary, within the last, I think, month, or very recently, they shipped three hundred and some thousand tons of grain out of the country.

The United States is never indifferent to human suffering, and in certain areas, as in the Danube area, just recently we put in $10 million worth of wheat, flour, and agricultural products.

There is no purpose and no plan being studied at this time for sending any grain of any kind to Russia.

Q. Jay G. Hayden, Detroit News: Mr. President, in connection with this question of will you or won't you run again, at a press conference some weeks ago you commented that it was a rather large question, and that some time when you had plenty of time at a press conference you would discuss, I believe you said, the pros and cons.

Could we make a date with you, sir, to start in on that at the next press conference? [*Laughter*]

THE PRESIDENT. I would doubt at the next press conference—[*laughter*]—but I'll tell you: if we can have a complete moratorium on it, I might make a date, let's say, a year from today. [*Laughter*]

Merriman Smith, United Press: Thank you, Mr. President.

NOTE: President Eisenhower's sixty-second news conference was held in the Executive Office Building from 10:32 to 11:04 o'clock on Wednesday morning, March 2, 1955. In attendance: 188.

48 ¶ Letter to His Majesty Bao Dai, Chief of State of Viet-Nam.   *March* 3, 1955

[Released March 3, 1955. Dated February 19, 1955]

Your Majesty:

It might be of interest to you to learn firsthand of General Collins' report to me and of our present views and policies concerning Viet-Nam.   General Collins has just left to return to Saigon after a short period of consultations in Washington.   I have discussed developments in Viet-Nam with him at some length.   He has also talked with the Secretary of State and with our Congressional leaders.

It is gratifying to learn from him of the distinct progress that is being made in Viet-Nam by Prime Minister Diem and the Government of Viet-Nam.   General Collins believes that there is a good chance that Viet-Nam can remain free if there is continued effective action on the Government's programs. The Prime Minister's announced programs of land reform and reorganization of the Armed Forces should, when fully carried out, further increase the stability and unity of the Government.

The Government of the United States is vigorously opposed to the forces of world Communism. We continue to support those aspirations of the people of Asia for independence, peace and prosperity. Accordingly, I have concurred in General Collins' recommendation to continue and expand support for Free Viet-Nam.

It is encouraging to me to know that Prime Minister Diem is making substantial progress. The United States Government intends to continue its support of his Government.

Sincerely,

Dwight D. Eisenhower

NOTE: Gen. J. Lawton Collins acted as the President's special representative in Viet-Nam from November 2, 1954, to May 14, 1955.

On May 10 a White House release stated that during General Collins' special mission, which had been extended at the request of Prime Minister Diem, he had assisted the Vietnamese Government in the preparation and implementation of its economic, military, and social programs for the strengthening of Free Viet-Nam. The release added that General Collins had successfully concluded arrangements under which the United States, at the request of the Government of Viet-Nam and with the agreement of the Government of France, had undertaken responsibility for the training of Viet-Nam national armed forces.

49 ¶ Statement by the President Concerning Offer of Food Supplies to Albania. *March 4, 1955*

I HAVE ASKED the League of Red Cross Societies to convey to the appropriate authorities of Albania the desire of the American people to contribute from their food supplies to help alleviate the current food shortage in Albania.

The distribution of this food would be under the supervision of the League of Red Cross Societies which has had broad experience in the administration of relief. Recently it administered a flood relief program to persons in six European countries who were victims of last summer's floods. Feed grain and food were distributed to needy people in these countries regardless of race, color, creed, or political convictions.

It is well known that for some years Albania has not produced enough food to support its population. The resulting shortage of food becomes particularly acute during the late winter and early spring. The present offer is intended to assist in relieving the situation during this critical period.

The friendship between the people of the United States and the people of Albania has been longstanding. Over the years, numerous Albanians have come to this country—many to remain as citizens with bonds of kinship and concern for their fatherland, many others to return and resettle throughout Albania carrying with them warm associations with the United States. Since the early part of this century, American interest in the Albanian people has expressed itself in many public and private actions for their welfare and their relief in times of special stress. I hope that the present offer will be accepted as another manifestation of the interest of the people of the United States in the welfare of the Albanian people.

NOTE: On March 8 a White House release stated that the President regretted that the offer of American food supplies to Albania had been rejected. The release further stated that the administration felt sure that if the Albanian people had been able to express themselves, the offer would have been accepted in the spirit in which it was made.

50 ¶ Special Message to the Congress on the Extension of the Renegotiation Act of 1951.
March 4, 1955

To the Congress of the United States:

I recommend extension of the Renegotiation Act of 1951, as amended, to make its provisions applicable for an additional period of two years. I make this recommendation because I believe the welfare of the country requires it.

In spite of major improvements which we have achieved in our contracting and price redetermination operations, there nevertheless remains an area in which only renegotiation can be effective to assure that the United States gets what it needs for defense at fair prices. In addition, I believe that the entire period of defense expansion and rebuilding which the United States has undertaken since the beginning of the Korean hostilities should be considered as a whole insofar as renegotiation treatment is concerned.

Continuation of the renegotiation authority is necessary for several reasons. Because of the complex nature of modern military equipment, the lack of experience in producing it and the frequent necessity for alterations during the life of a contract, it is impossible for the Government to determine, when the procurement contract is made, what constitutes a fair price and for the supplier to forecast accurately his costs. Moreover, because of limited sources of supply in many cases, there are situations in which the Government is unable to obtain the price benefits that accrue from normal competition.

Furthermore, in the interest of broadening and strengthening the mobilization base, we have encouraged the extensive use of subcontracting. Because the United States has no direct contractual relations with the subcontractors, the only protection against unreasonable prices by them is through the process of renegotiation.

All these factors become particularly important when it is recognized that expenditures by the Government during the next two calendar years will include paying the bills for the completion of the expansion of the Air Force to one-hundred and thirty-seven wings.   The next two years also will see an introduction into the Air Force program of the latest type of supersonic aircraft.   New types of equipment also are being ordered for the Army and Navy and Marine Corps.

As a nation, we recognize that so long as defense expenditures represent more than half of the national budget, we must do everything in our power to see to it that the maximum return is received for each dollar spent.   On the other hand we must also be careful not to interfere unwisely in the traditional commercial relationship between the Government and its suppliers. In extending the Renegotiation Act last year, the Congress instituted new statutory exemptions.   These have lessened the burden imposed on industry by renegotiation and, more important, have concentrated renegotiation in the areas where it is most needed.

I strongly urge that the Congress take action as promptly as possible so that both Government and business will know that this important adjunct to speedy and effective defense contracting will remain available, at least until December 31, 1956.

DWIGHT D. EISENHOWER

NOTE: The act extending the Renegotiation Act of 1951, approved August 3, is Public Law 216, 84th Congress (69 Stat. 447).

51   ¶ Letter to General Omar N. Bradley, Chairman, President's Commission on Veterans' Pensions, Concerning a Study of Veterans' Benefits. *March* 5, 1955

Dear General Bradley:

The Commission on Veterans' Pensions, of which you are the Chairman, has been appointed by me to carry out a comprehensive study of the laws and policies pertaining to pension, compensation, and related nonmedical benefits for our veterans and their dependents. I would like the Commission, on the basis of its studies, to furnish me with a report, including recommendations regarding fundamental principles, which I can use as the basis for making recommendations to the Congress for modernization of these benefits and clarification of their relationship to our broader Government social insurance and family protection programs.

This Nation has always responded generously to the needs of those men and women who have served it so well in times of great danger. Pension and other benefits for veterans have been provided since the Revolutionary War. I am in full accord with this policy.

In recent years, however, rapid and profound changes in our national military, social, economic, and fiscal circumstances have occurred which affect fundamentally our long-standing veterans' pension and compensation programs. In 1940 there were only 4 million veterans. There are now nearly 21 million, and the number is increasing rapidly. The necessity for recruiting large Armed Forces has led to substantial improvements in military pay and other conditions of service. Extensive and timely medical, rehabilitation, and readjustment programs have been established for veterans. Most notable in this respect are the improved medical, prosthetic, and rehabilitation measures for disabled veterans and the readjustment benefits for all new veterans to help them become economically productive and recapture the normal pattern of their lives. To maintain the well-being and strength of our democratic society we have also instituted policies to maintain high and stable employment and developed the broad social security programs to provide economic assistance to the aged and the needy. These developments reflect the growth of the Government's obligations and a more adequate recognition of its responsibilities, and they have also had an important effect on its fiscal situation.

While these fundamental changes were taking place, the traditional pension and compensation programs for veterans and their families were also being further extended and liberalized. Thus under existing laws and regulations many of our veterans will be able to qualify both for nonservice-connected pensions and social security benefits when they reach age 65. In the service connected compensation program the standards for rating disabilities have been modified many times since their development in the years after World War I. Numerous piecemeal legislative changes have also granted legal presumptions of service connection and provided additional specific awards which result in different payments to individuals of the same degree of disability.

These programs are large and very significant. Expenditures for pension and compensation benefits to veterans are almost as large as all benefit payments of the old-age and survivors insurance system and are likely several decades hence to be double their present magnitude. In this situation the need is apparent for a constructive reappraisal of the standards under which such benefits should be provided. It is our duty to arrange our affairs so that future generations will inherit an economic and social structure which is fundamentally sound and in which obligations, including those owed to veterans and their survivors, are distributed equitably and not as an unwelcome burden.

It is in this constructive sense that I have established the Commission on Veterans' Pensions. It is my desire that this Commission systematically assess the structure, scope, philosophy, and administration of pension, compensation, and related nonmedical benefits furnished under Federal legislation to our veterans and their families, together with the relationships between these benefits and others which are provided our citizens without regard to their status as veterans. The objective of this effort should be to bring up to date and correlate these benefits and services so that veterans and their survivors will receive equitable treatment consistent with the orderly development of public policy in this important area.

In this task you will have the full cooperation of the administration, including the facilities of the executive agencies. The White House staff will assist you on administrative housekeeping matters. I should like to keep in touch with your progress, and I ask that your final report with its recommendations be in my hands by November 1, 1955.

Sincerely,

DWIGHT D. EISENHOWER

NOTE: At the time this letter was made public the White House announced the appointment by the President of the Commission as follows: General Bradley, chairman, Clarence G. Adamy, William J. Donovan, Paul R. Hawley, Martin D. Jenkins, Theodore S. Petersen, and John S. Thompson, members.

The Commission was established by Executive Order 10588 of January 14, 1955 (3 CFR, 1955 Supp.).

The report of the Commission is entitled "Veterans' Benefits in the United States" (Government Printing Office, 1956).

52 ¶ Remarks to Distinguished Service Cross Recipients and Commanders Who Participated in the Seizure of the Remagen Bridge. *March 7, 1955*

Gentlemen:

I have asked you to come in here this morning because you know old soldiers' minds are bound to turn back once in a while to dramatic events of war—particularly of the kind that took place at the Remagen bridgehead.

Now, of course, that was not the biggest battle that ever was, but for me it always typified one thing: the dash, the ingenuity, the readiness at the first opportunity that characterizes the American soldier.

You men are only a typical group of the great forces that were in Europe, but it did seem to me that here, on the 10th anniversary of the day you went across the Rhine, you might not mind coming in and saying hello to the man who was responsible for directing this whole overall strategy.

I also brought with me General Spaatz. He typified the unity between the ground-air team on the battlefield that was responsible for victory.

Now I must confess to you that I have done something on my own responsibility. I have organized here the Society of the Remagen Bridgehead. I have prepared for each of you a little certificate which I hope you will keep and retain as of some sentimental value. It is nothing except to say in my little way to you, and through you to all of the 9th Armored Division—and all of the whole Army, Navy, and Air Force behind you that was responsible for this thing—my own personal thanks.

Incidentally, one of these certificates is made out to all the officers and men of the 9th Armored Division, and General Leonard says he is going to send it down to Fort Knox as a memento.

NOTE: The President spoke in the Cabinet Room at 9:30 a.m. Gen. Carl Spaatz and Lt. Gen. John W. Leonard, to whom he referred, participated in the seizure of the bridge, General Spaatz as Commanding General of the U.S. Strategic Air Force in Europe, and General Leonard as Commanding General of the 9th Armored Division.

53 ¶ Remarks to Students Attending the International School of Nuclear Science and Engineering, Argonne National Laboratory. *March* 10, 1955

Admiral Strauss and gentlemen:

It is a very great pleasure to have a part in welcoming you to America and to your entry in the Argonne School.

During World War II, we got into the habit of referring to ventures in terms of operations, Operation "This" and "That." In war, of course, it usually had a martial name.

I can't tell you how pleased I was to hear this project referred to as "Operation Friendship." That is exactly what we mean.

We want you to study in the friendliest of atmospheres, and go back to your country with the certainty that what you are carrying back is not only a new understanding in nuclear science and reactor engineering, but a new understanding of the friendship that all America feels toward each of your countries.

It will be a great personal favor to me if when you do go back, in addition to all of the things that you hope to accomplish in this new field, you will carry my personal greetings of friendship to everyone that you meet in your own countries.

Now, I have been told that Admiral Strauss and I are to have the privilege of shaking hands with each of you. As you go by, I would particularly like to have each of you give me your country's name as well as your own.

Good luck to each of you.

NOTE: The President spoke in the Rose Garden at 9:30 a.m. to students from 19 countries who were members of the first class attending the International School of Nuclear Science and Engineering. The School was inaugurated in March 1955 at the Atomic Energy Commission's Argonne National Laboratory at Lemont, Ill., as part of the atoms-for-peace program.

The President's opening words referred to Lewis L. Strauss, Chairman, Atomic Energy Commission.

54 ¶ Message to the Prime Ministers of the Seven Nations Signatory to the Protocols Establishing the Western European Union. *March 10, 1955*

AT THE TIME when there was under consideration the Treaty to establish a European Defense Community, I made a public announcement of certain principles which would guide United States policies and actions with respect to Western Europe in the event that Treaty should be ratified. Now, in substitution for that Community, a plan has been evolved for a Western European Union. Obviously that Union and related arrangements signed at Paris on October 23, 1954, when brought into force, will serve the vital interests not only of the members of the Union, but of the peoples of the free world, including the United States. The United States has twice been drawn into wars which originated in Europe and today it maintains forces there to help minimize the possibility of another war. It is in the interest of the United States to help reduce such dangers.

To this end the United States committed itself to the North Atlantic Treaty. This Treaty is in accordance with the basic security interests of the United States, and the obligations which the United States has assumed under the Treaty will be honored.

The member nations are seeking to make the Atlantic alliance an enduring association of free peoples within which all members can concert their efforts toward peace, prosperity and freedom. The success of that association will be determined in large measure by the degree of practical cooperation realized among the European nations themselves. The Western European Union and the related arrangements agreed upon in Paris are designed to ensure this cooperation and thereby to provide a durable basis for consolidating the Atlantic relationship as a whole.

It is my belief that the proposed arrangements when effective:

Will promote progress toward unity in Western Europe and draw together those whose past differences have led to recurrent war and gravely depleted Europe's human, material and moral strength;

Will restore sovereignty to the Federal Republic of Germany, a sovereignty which has now been withheld for ten years, during which time the Government and people of that Republic have demonstrated that they are capable of worthily discharging their responsibilities as a self-governing member of the free and peaceful world community;

Will, by controlling armament levels through an appropriate Agency of the Western European Union, assure against militarism;

Will provide a core of unity at the heart of the North Atlantic Treaty Organization, thus permitting adoption of practical defensive measures which offer good hope that any enemy attack could be stopped at the threshold;

Will enable the Federal Republic of Germany to make its appropriately measured contribution to international peace and security, in keeping with the spirit of the North Atlantic Treaty Organization;

Will, through action of the North Atlantic Treaty Council, assure a closer integration of the armed forces in Europe of the member countries, thereby giving assurance that these forces cannot be used for nationalistic aggression or otherwise than for the security purposes envisaged by the North Atlantic Treaty.

At London on September 29, 1954, the United States Secretary of State in order to facilitate efforts to produce an effective collective defense of Western Europe, indicated the conditions under which the United States might be prepared to make a policy declaration similar to that which was announced when the earlier European Defense Community plan was under consideration. I am glad to affirm that when the Paris Agreements have been ratified and have come into force, it will be the policy of the United States:

(1) To continue active in the various organic arrangements established under the North Atlantic Treaty Organization and to consult with other members of NATO on questions of mutual concern, including the level of forces from the respective NATO countries to be placed at the disposal of the Supreme Allied Commander Europe;

(2) To consult, if so desired, with the Agency for the Control of Armaments of the Western European Union with a view to assisting in the achievement of its objective of controlling armament and preventing unjustified military preparations within the members of the Union;

(3) To continue to maintain in Europe, including Germany, such units of its armed forces as may be necessary and appropriate to contribute its fair share of the forces needed for the joint defense of the North Atlantic area while a threat to that area exists, and will continue to deploy such forces in accordance with agreed North Atlantic strategy for the defense of this area;

(4) To cooperate in developing the closest possible integration among the forces assigned to NATO in Western Europe, including those contributed by the German Federal Republic, in accordance with approved plans developed by the military agencies and the Supreme Commanders of the North Atlantic Treaty Organization in accordance with the Resolution adopted by the North Atlantic Council on October 22, 1954;

(5) To continue to cooperate toward Atlantic Security by sharing information authorized by Congress with respect to the military utilization of new weapons and techniques for the improvement of the collective defense;

(6) In consonance with its policy of encouraging maximum

cooperation among the free nations of Europe and in recognition of the contribution which the Brussels Treaty, as amended, will make to peace and stability in Europe, to regard any action from whatever quarter which threatens the integrity or unity of the Western European Union as a threat to the security of the parties to the North Atlantic Treaty calling for consultation in accordance with Article IV of that Treaty.

In accordance with the basic interest of the United States in the North Atlantic Treaty, as expressed at the time of ratification, the Treaty was regarded as of indefinite duration rather than for any definite number of years. The United States calls attention to the fact that for it to cease to be a party to the North Atlantic Treaty would appear quite contrary to our security interests when there is established on the Continent of Europe the solid core of unity which the Paris Agreements will provide.

NOTE: This is the text of identical messages addressed to the Prime Ministers of Belgium, France, the Federal Republic of Germany, Italy, Luxembourg, the Netherlands, and the United Kingdom—the nations signatory to the protocols establishing the Union.

The President's statement on the European Defense Community and the text of the Paris agreements, referred to in the first paragraph of this message, are published in the Department of State Bulletin (vol. 30, p. 619; vol. 31, p. 719, respectively).

55   ¶ Letter to George A. Garrett, President, Federal City Council, Concerning the Redevelopment of Southwest Washington. *March* 10, 1955

[Released March 16, 1955. Dated March 15, 1955]

Dear Mr. Garrett:

The redevelopment and renewal of the blighted areas of Washington is of concern not only to the citizens of the District of

Columbia but to all the American people. All of us want the nation's capital, I am certain, to be the symbol of our country's best efforts to provide decent housing and attractive urban living.

One major redevelopment project is that for Southwest Washington. I understand that it has been under consideration for almost five years and has been the subject of active planning for some three years. The time has come to see it become a reality. It should move forward just as rapidly as a plan can be devised which harmoniously resolves the various problems involved.

It would be a great service to the nation's capital if you would undertake to confer with the appropriate agencies in an effort to bring about agreement on a workable program. As the President of the Federal City Council, and with your broad experiences in civic affairs, I am certain you can render a service of great value. I shall welcome a report of successful progress.

With best wishes,

Sincerely,

DWIGHT D. EISENHOWER

56 ¶ The President's News Conference of March 16, 1955.

[This is a complete transcript of the news conference of this date. Those portions of the President's replies which were not released for broadcasting or direct quotation at that time are enclosed in brackets.]

THE PRESIDENT. I have no announcements, ladies and gentlemen, and we will go right to questions.

Q. Marvin Arrowsmith, Associated Press: Mr. President, are you worried any about the decline in stock market prices and, secondly, do you think the Senate Banking Committee study has contributed in any way to the decline?

THE PRESIDENT. Well, for the second part of your question,

which I will answer first, I have no opinion whatsoever as to the effect of that particular investigation.

What I do believe very thoroughly is this: we are trying to promote an expanding economy in this country, and one of the factors that is necessary in producing an expanded economy is confidence.

So any group or any individual that undertakes to touch upon one of the points of our economy where this confidence is affected, necessarily must proceed with great caution if he doesn't want to do unnecessary damage. I don't know of any particular phase of this investigation that hasn't been conducted in that way; certainly, some of the things that have come out of it have been reassuring. The conduct of our stock markets on the whole looks to be very satisfactory.

I am not only concerned with a drop on the stock market, but any drop in an agricultural price or any other unexplained drop in the prices of parts of our products is of concern to the Government.

Q. Pat Munroe, Albuquerque Journal and Salt Lake City Deseret News: Mr. President, there is a war over water, that is, the Colorado River water, now in progress in the West between southern California and the Rocky Mountain States; and in your state of the Union message you urged Congress to approve a plan to conserve water in the Rocky Mountain States.

Is this still your feeling, sir?

THE PRESIDENT. [Yes. But before I answer the question, let me say this: I don't like the use of that word "war." Let's try to avoid that word.

[Now, of course, it is part of my policy. I believe that water is rapidly becoming, if it is not already, our most precious natural resource. I believe we have got to take measures to save this water at the proper places.

[It is not all done in the same way. I believe the Agriculture Department, in its upstream conservation practices, has just as much responsibility in the matter as does the Interior Department with these great dams in the mountains.

[I might refer you to a book that has recently been printed, one called "Big Dam Foolishness." It is by a man named Peterson, who has apparently put in a life study on this. I have read his book. He undertakes to show that many of our big dams have been constructed under a very false conception.

[However, this whole question of water is important, not only to California and to Arizona and the western slope, but to the whole region, east as well as west.]

Q. Mr. Munroe: Well, sir, southern California has blocked our plan in the Rocky Mountain area with a legal suit before the Supreme Court, and as recently as yesterday, Budget Director Hughes indicated a very firm support for the Upper Colorado plan.

THE PRESIDENT. [Well, I don't know about the Supreme Court; if it is before the Supreme Court, I know I am not going to comment on it.

[But as far as my concept of what is necessary, it has not changed; I still believe the same as I said in my state of the Union message.]

Q. Merriman Smith, United Press: Mr. President, with no effort to violate your desire for a moratorium on the subject, do you agree with Vice President Nixon that the Republican Party is not strong enough to win re-election in 1956 without you? [*Laughter*]

THE PRESIDENT. I thought you were really observing that agreement on a moratorium until you got to your last two words.

I would say this, first of all: as you know, I have been responsible for various kinds of fights in my lifetime. I have never yet gone into any fight with as much strength as I should like to have. The more strength you have, the more certain that you are of victory, then the more certainly you can plan your moves.

Now, I agree that the Republican Party needs strength, needs recruits. I come back to the same old thing I have repeated to you people time and time again: in spite of all the publicity gimmicks, all of the shrewd recruiting systems, there is one thing that will bring Republican Party recruits—fine programs for the benefit of all America and real work in putting them over.

That is the kind of thing that will certainly bring Republican Party strength, and it will be strength enough to win with anybody that is worthy of a place.

Q. Charles S. von Fremd, CBS News: Mr. President, yesterday at his news conference, Secretary of State Dulles indicated that in the event of general war in the Far East, we would probably make use of some tactical small atomic weapons. Would you care to comment on this and, possibly, explain it further?

THE PRESIDENT. I wouldn't comment in the sense that I would pretend to foresee the conditions of any particular conflict in which you might engage; but we have been, as you know, active in producing various types of weapons that feature nuclear fission ever since World War II.

Now, in any combat where these things can be used on strictly military targets and for strictly military purposes, I see no reason why they shouldn't be used just exactly as you would use a bullet or anything else.

I believe the great question about these things comes when you begin to get into those areas where you cannot make sure that you are operating merely against military targets. But with that one qualification, I would say, yes, of course they would be used.

Q. Matthew Warren, Du Mont Television: Mr. President, in view of the devastating effects of our modern thermonuclear weapons and the secrecy surrounding their development, how do you think we can maintain an adequate civilian defense?

THE PRESIDENT. Of course, you are touching one of the most serious problems facing us today, and it is all the more serious because it is one of those facts that human beings just rather recoil from looking squarely in the face, do not like to do it.

Not long ago, the Atomic Energy Commission published a rather long paper giving a considerable amount of information on the effects of thermonuclear weapons and, particularly, the fallout.

The purpose of it was to show that while it is known that down-wind from these things you can get a long area in which there could be very serious consequences, it is also possible for the individual to take care of himself. It was intended, given the proper amount of work the man will do, to be reassuring and not to be terrifying.

The great chore you have here is to give people the facts, show them what they can do, get the Federal leadership, get the participation of the States and the municipalities, without terrifying people.

I have one great belief: nobody in war or anywhere else ever made a good decision if he was frightened to death. You have to look facts in the face, but you have to have the stamina to do it without just going hysterical. That is what you are really trying to do in this business.

Q. Alan S. Emory, Watertown Times: Mr. President, two questions, sir: could you tell us the purpose of Governor Dewey's visit with you after our conference this morning; and, second, the Chief Justice of the United States recently, in a speech in St. Louis, said that he did not think the Bill of Rights, if proposed today, would pass.

I wondered if you cared to comment on that?

THE PRESIDENT. Well, I fail to see much relationship between your two questions. [*Laughter*]

As to the first one, I haven't the slightest idea. Governor Dewey asked to see me, and the date was set up; he is coming in.

Now, the second one, I never heard such a statement made. You say the Chief Justice of the United States said this?

Q. Mr. Emory: Yes, sir.

THE PRESIDENT. Well, I have got a tremendous admiration for him and for his mind, and I am certain that he has thought over well what he had said.

But I would say this: if it were up for passage today, I would be one of those out campaigning for its adoption. That is about all I can say.

Q. John Herling, Editors Syndicate: Mr. President, this has to do with the expanding economy you referred to earlier.

THE PRESIDENT. With the what?

Q. Mr. Herling: The expanding economy—that you are concerned with.

As you know, there is much concern in labor and management circles about the impact of automation on our human and economic relations; and since automation does affect every part of our national life, the question has been raised as to whether a Presidential commission might undertake a study of its impact and ramifications; and would you give us some idea of what your thinking is on the subject of automation.

Second, would you consider the possibility of supporting such a commission to aid the country in facing the problems growing out of automation?

THE PRESIDENT. [Well, let's be quite clear. I would not attempt to give a specific answer to a specific question that you asked; on a spur-of-the-moment attitude or circumstances, it would be foolish for me to do so.

[This matter of automation—another word that has now arisen to plague us some—has been discussed habitually by my economic advisers, by others in the administration, and naturally I have listened and read on the subject.

[The one striking thing you should remember is this: exactly the same thing has been going on for a hundred and fifty years; exactly the same fears have been expressed right along; and one of the great things that seems to happen is that as we find ways of doing work with fewer man-hours devoted to it, then there is more work to do.

[I believe that it would be false to assume that the amount of work we are going to have to do is going to remain static, when we are looking for an expanding economy. It is going to expand.

[The work to do is going to expand not only in, you might say, arithmetic progression, along with the amount your economy expands, but there are other things to do because man will have other needs and other desires and want things to use. So I really believe that my own feeling is that the danger is often exaggerated.

[On the other hand, I certainly will hope and will expect that the proper agencies of Government continue earnestly their investigations on this subject, their watch on the development; and if any danger seems to be appearing upon the horizon that is unforeseen, then it is possible that even a commission would be the right answer. But I couldn't say now.]

Q. Marshall McNeil, Scripps-Howard: Mr. President, I have two questions about an old one. The Dixon-Yates contract is apparently tied up in the courts, and a majority of the TVA Board has lately asked you again for appropriations for the Fulton steam plant.

I wondered whether that would prompt you, sir, to reconsider the problem of power in west Tennessee; and, the second question, would the construction of a plant, generating plant, by Memphis itself not fit into your philosophy, sir?

THE PRESIDENT. Well, I know of no reason—to take your second question first—I know of no reason whatsoever that Memphis hasn't a complete right to manufacture or set up any producing plant it wants to. Certainly I would favor it.

I have nothing at all against local ownership of power. I think in many cases it is not only a good thing; in some cases it has been proved to be very effective.

But there is one thing I always want to point out to you people when I talk about governmental authority, responsibility and operation. Don't forget this: when the Federal Government does this, they can print money to do the job. Nobody else can, and there is a very great difference; because the second that the Federal Government starts to print money to do these things, they are taking one cent, or at least their proportion, out of every dollar that any of you might happen to have in your pockets. That is the effect of cheapening money, and I don't think we ought to go in for that.

Now, as to the review of this case, it has not come up to me in any way in that form, and I don't know whether there is any reason for review or not. But I do say: for anything that falls within the State or city authorities, I have no objection to their doing it, whatsoever.

Q. Raymond P. Brandt, St. Louis Post-Dispatch: Mr. President, there seems to be some confusion about your position about allowing a person to be confronted with his accuser in a governmental case.

The Department of Justice says that when you said a man shall be entitled to be confronted with his accuser, he should know who it was, and so forth.

They said that was only for criminal cases. I got the idea it was for the security cases, also.

THE PRESIDENT. No, I believe there are certain cases, Mr. Brandt, where you couldn't possibly bring out all of your accusers, for the simple reason that you may work for a number of years to get people in places where they can look for these things that, by their very nature, are destructive of the United States system and of the welfare of the United States of America.

Now, those people you cannot destroy.

If in the course of their operations they bring up information, remember this: you are not determining anything about the legal rights or the application of the Bill of Rights to this man's case. What you are trying to determine is, is he fit to work for the United States Government? Should you take the responsibility of saying, in spite of the fact that we cannot put the man, the accuser, up in front of this man and let him cross-examine, should we continue him in a sensitive position?

I do believe this: I do believe that we are going to be able to do more in finding nonsensitive areas in which to place such people.

Q. Mr. Brandt: On that point, sir, some of these accusers have been proved to be doing it for money and for other reasons.

THE PRESIDENT. Yes.

Q. Mr. Brandt: Now, the accused has no way of knowing whether the charges have been made in good faith.

THE PRESIDENT. Mr. Brandt, I know that any honest person charged with the responsibility for protecting the interests of the United States and the Federal Government, would be the last to say that any system you can devise here is going to be perfect.

Indeed, I don't believe that probably any lawyer would say that the judicial and the criminal procedures that we have in our country are perfect. We try to get them as nearly just as we can, and we do apply the Bill of Rights.

Now, in the Federal Government, in putting a man to work for the Federal Government and paid by the Federal Government, there is a slightly different problem, though, than whether you are accused of cheating your neighbor or doing something else. It is, simply, you have got to do the best you can in these conflicting considerations; but, as far as you can, as far as is humanly possible without violating the security of the United States, to obey and to follow the Bill of Rights, that is what must be done.

Q. Mr. Brandt: May I ask one point on that? You said there are some plans now for the nonsensitive positions.

THE PRESIDENT. I say we think we can do better.

Q. Mr. Brandt: On the nonsensitive positions?

THE PRESIDENT. We always have had this; it is simply a question of operating just as well as we can.

Q. Garnett D. Horner, Washington Star: Mr. President, some weeks ago a report was published that the thermonuclear device that was exploded in the Pacific a year ago was a super-H-bomb with a jacket of natural state uranium that gave it greater power at less cost. Could you tell us if that was correct, and anything else about the development of the so-called bargain basement U-bomb?

THE PRESIDENT. [Well, I will tell you, you are asking technical questions about this bomb, and while I possibly could give you a fairly accurate answer, I think it would be unfair to ask me to give you one that you could write about.

[I say this: you go ask Admiral Strauss about it, because he will give you every piece of information that is in the public domain. I don't think I should attempt to answer it.]

Q. Charles E. Shutt, Telenews: Mr. President, two people in your administration have mentioned the possibility of war, impending war, in Asia.

THE PRESIDENT. What is that? Mentioned what?

Q. Mr. Shutt: Admiral Radford said last night in a speech that there was a distinct possibility that war could break out at any time.

Secretary Dulles also said that he came back from his visit with a sense of foreboding.

Could you give us your views about the possibility of a conflict in the Far East, sir?

THE PRESIDENT. Well, of course, you have to answer that one in generalizations.

Why do we keep any kind of security forces? Because there is always a possibility of war.

We are living in a time when it would be foolish to say that it is characterized by normal serenity, the kind of peaceful relations which we hope for among nations of the world. Therefore, the possibility is greater than, we would say, that we were raised with—that is, any of you if, unfortunately, you are as old as I am. We were raised in an atmosphere of complete confidence; there was no thought of war, and our military forces fell away to very, very small numbers.

And if you read a little bit of the history of the Spanish-American War and the opening of World War I, you will see that is true.

So the possibility is greater now than it was in those days; consequently, there is greater vigilance required of us, greater concern, greater diversion of our man-hours and our resources to the making and keeping and sustaining of armed forces than there would be otherwise. That is one of the reasons, of course, that the great policies of any enlightened nation must be the producing of conditions that will be more peaceful.

Q. Mr. Shutt: Would you say, sir, that we would be prepared for any eventuality in that area?

THE PRESIDENT. Well, again, you want specific answers for something that, it seems to me, you yourself should know.

You prepare in the generality, and you can't tell what kind of a surprise might be prepared for you in any part of the world. But you are striving, and again I quote it to you, for what Washington called "that respectable posture of defense that is consonant with the times in which we live," the kind of weapons, the kind of possibilities that we face. That is the best answer I can give you.

Q. Dickson J. Preston, Cleveland Press: Mr. President, the Olympic Committee of the Western Hemisphere Nations have just voted to hold the pan-American games in 1959 in Cleveland. This will be the first time they have been in the United States; and they will bring athletes from all the Americas to this country. I wondered if you would comment on that, sir?

THE PRESIDENT. Well, that is the kind I like to comment on. [*Laughter*]

I am not only highly gratified, but I will tell you, if I am alive and healthy, I would hope to attend.

Q. Mr. Preston: Thank you.

Q. Sarah McClendon, El Paso Times: Mr. President, there seems to be some confusion in the minds of people in the gas industry about a letter written by Mr. Morgan of your staff to Congressman Glenn Davis in which Mr. Morgan implies that the Flemming report on gas is not necessarily your views, but it is the views of your Cabinet advisers.

Would you clear up, would you comment on that?

THE PRESIDENT. Certainly. The Advisory Committee has prepared their views and submitted them to me; there has been no action on my part at all, giving it final approval.

Q. William S. White, New York Times: I wonder if you would care to comment, sir, on the action of the Senate on the tax bill of yesterday?

THE PRESIDENT. Would it be allowable to just say "Hurrah!" [*Laughter*]

Q. Alice F. Johnson, Seattle Times: Mr. President, on September 17, 1950, the Denver Post quoted you as telling a Denver audience that quick admission of Alaska and Hawaii to statehood would show the world that America practices what it preaches, and that you hoped Congress would pass the statehood legislation then before it.

Can you please tell us, one, what has happened in the meantime to change your mind about Alaska and, two, are there any circumstances under which you would favor giving Alaska statehood now?

THE PRESIDENT. When did you say I was quoted that way?

Q. Mrs. Johnson: September 17, 1950, when you were——

THE PRESIDENT. 1950?

Q. Mrs. Johnson: Yes.

THE PRESIDENT. I think I have explained my position with respect to Alaska in front of this group time and again.

I think there are national security considerations which must be amply catered for before I can remove my objections to the statehood of this area.

Now, I have never said anything against statehood for Alaska if those things are taken care of, and I have tried to explain in general what they were. Nothing has occurred to change that.

At the time in 1950 when I said that, I was not responsible at that moment for the national security of the United States. I didn't bear the responsibility I do now.

Now, I don't mean to say that I have changed my mind. I still think that any territory of the United States has got a right to strive to achieve the standards normally accepted for statehood, but we have got a very, very difficult, tough problem up there. As I say, my position has been stated in front of this body several times.

Q. Joseph Chiang, Chinese News Service: Mr. President, under your great and distinguished leadership, does the United States Government have any plan to help 13 million overseas Chinese who are willing to make every sacrifice to go back home in the mainland of China to liberate their loved ones from the Chinese Communist enslavement?

THE PRESIDENT. [Well, I will simply say this: the problem is often spoken of; I have heard of no particular suggestion for solution of it. But I do know that you have all these overseas Chinese. I at this moment wouldn't know the answer, I admit.]

Q. Richard L. Wilson, Cowles Publications: Mr. President, there seems to be some special circumstances coming up in the automobile industry which would justify asking you if you have any position on the guaranteed annual wage.

THE PRESIDENT. As you know, this administration has several times urged the extension of unemployment insurance and tried to lead the States into making this system such that we don't have local distress in these great areas, so often affected by unemployment.

But when you come to talking in the exact terms of the guaranteed annual wage, I don't know in what form it will appear. I don't know what will be demanded; and, therefore, I would prefer not to talk about any specific proposal until it has been presented and gone over by the Secretary of Labor and my advisers. Then I would have something to say about it. But I do believe in the extension of unemployment insurance.

Q. Milton Friedman, Jewish Telegraphic Agency: Sir, will you ask the Attorney General to draft recommendations to activate and implement your request in the state of the Union message to revise the McCarran-Walter Immigration Act?

THE PRESIDENT. [Well, I made the recommendation to Congress. Whether there is any other step that is necessary I will have to look up and see whether I should——

341

Q. Mr. Friedman: Sir——

THE PRESIDENT. [I said I made the recommendation in the state of the Union message.]

Q. Robert Roth, Philadelphia Bulletin: Mr. President, if I may refer for a moment to the civilian defense question that was asked before, at a hearing before the Senate Armed Services sub-committee last week, Mayor Joseph Clark of Philadelphia made this statement, I am quoting:

"Until the President himself takes a far more active part in formulating and carrying into effect a sound national civil defense policy, our major American cities will continue vulnerable to enemy attack."

I wonder if you would comment on that assertion?

THE PRESIDENT. [Well, any city, of course, is always going to be vulnerable; it is the degree of vulnerability that is necessary.

[Now, this is somebody's opinion, apparently, of what I should do; I have got many opinions of what everybody else should do. But I am trying to do my duty. If he sees it differently, why, I would be glad to have his advice.]

Q. Lloyd M. Schwartz, Fairchild Publications: Mr. President, the Attorney General's Special Anti-Trust Study Group has just recommended the repeal of the Federal laws which give these State fair trade laws their antitrust immunity.

I wonder whether you could tell us whether you agree with his finding, and whether you intend to send appropriate repeal legislation up to the Hill?

THE PRESIDENT. [Well, no, I haven't heard of it; but you know, in the Justice Department you have these special sections for all these various functions of the Justice Department. That particular section is headed up by Justice Barnes, who is supposed to have one of the finest legal minds in this whole business.

[Eventually this recommendation will come to me, but I hadn't heard of it before.]

Q. Edward T. Folliard, Washington Post and Times Herald: Mr. President, this question goes back to a news conference on

February 23d. A reporter, Clark Mollenhoff of the Cowles Publications, asked you a question, and the sense of it was this: What would you do if a Government official called an employee a Red, and had no evidence to back it up?

You invited Mollenhoff to submit proof, in fact, you urged him to do it. Mollenhoff then wrote you a letter in which he cited the case of Wolf Ladejinsky.

Have you any comment to make on that case now?

THE PRESIDENT. [Only, so far, this: all the individuals now, I believe, that were involved in the case have come back; and aside from the recommendations of the Attorney General to prevent such cases from arising in the future, which have been published as instructions to the executive department, what's to be done in the particular case is still under investigation. A final report has not been made.]

Merriman Smith, United Press: Thank you, Mr. President.

NOTE: President Eisenhower's sixty-third news conference was held in the Executive Office Building from 10:31 to 11:01 o'clock on Wednesday morning, March 16, 1955. In attendance: 212.

57 ¶ Statement by the President Announcing the Appointment of Harold Stassen as Special Assistant to the President for Disarmament Studies.
March 19, 1955

THE MASSIVE resources required for modern armaments, the huge diversion of materials and of energy, the heavy burdens of taxation, the demands for years of service of vast numbers of men, the unprecedented destructive power of new weapons, and the international tensions which powerful armaments aggravate, have been of deep concern to me for many years.

At the same time the tragic consequences of unilateral disarmament, the reckless moves of Hitler when the United States was weak, the Korean aggression when our armed strength had been rapidly diminished, and the vast extent of the armament now centered around the opposing ideology of communism, have been equally apparent to me.

The recent session of the Disarmament Commission of the United Nations has again resulted in no progress and no clear crystallization of thinking on this subject. It has an inseparable relationship to our constant objective of peace.

I have, therefore, established a position as Special Assistant to the President with responsibility for developing, on behalf of the President and the State Department, the broad studies, investigations and conclusions which, when concurred in by the National Security Council and approved by the President, will become basic policy toward the question of disarmament. The position will be of Cabinet rank. When indicated as desirable or appropriate under our Constitutional processes, concurrences will be secured from the Congress prior to specific action or pronouncement of policy.

I have appointed Harold Stassen as a Special Assistant for discharge of this responsibility. He will be expected to take into account the full implications of new weapons in the possession of other nations as well as the United States, to consider future probabilities of armaments, and to weigh the views of the military, the civilians, and the officials of our government and of other governments.

For the time being, and for the presentation of the Mutual Security Program to the Congress, he will also continue to discharge his responsibility as Director of the Foreign Operations Administration, but he will begin this new task promptly upon this appointment.

58   ¶ Remarks at 11th Annual Washington
Conference of the Advertising Council.
March 22, 1955

I THINK this is about the shortest introduction I have ever had.

One of the continuing problems of government, of course, is how to keep in touch with the grassroots, how to get into the understanding of the last citizen, in the remotest hamlet, the things that he should know about his government, so that he can make intelligent decisions, and how conversely, government is to know what those people are thinking. So, if nothing else, you can detect when there is a misunderstanding of facts or, indeed, maybe just a failure to have the facts that government could provide.

Among all the agencies that have served a useful purpose in this regard, none has been more effective than this agency—the Advertising Council. Your accomplishments are referred to constantly in the circles of the administration, and always in terms of the greatest admiration and respect, and a feeling of obligation for what you are doing.

I want to make this very clear because some of the things I would like to talk about may intimate that I think you have been guilty of some failures. I don't mean it in that sense either. But I do mean that I believe there is a tremendous opportunity for all Americans in certain fields. Of all the people who are capable of taking advantage of those opportunities, this body by its past record would seem to be among the foremost.

I don't think it is necessary to point out that life has become intricate. And here at home, among the intricacies of living, the intricate relationship that each individual has toward his government and toward his community and everything else, has been one of the reasons why we have necessarily had educational bodies of which this is one.

But when we enter the international field we run into complexities that seem almost to dwarf our understanding of what we are doing to ourselves when we accept, let us say, paternalistic gifts of the government, without understanding for that we may be surrendering some of our ancient liberties.

Today there is a great ideological struggle going on in the world. One side upholds what it calls the materialistic dialectic. Denying the existence of spiritual values, it maintains that man responds only to materialistic influences and consequently he is nothing. He is an educated animal and is useful only as he serves the ambitions—desires—of a ruling clique; though they try to make this finer-sounding than that, because they say their dictatorship is that of the proletariat, meaning that they rule in the people's name—for the people.

Now, on our side, we recognize right away that man is not merely an animal, that his life and his ambitions have at the bottom a foundation of spiritual values. Now this—these facts seem to make it very odd that we fear the inroads that communism is making in the capture of the minds and souls of men.

They are, too. They are winning great adherents in many areas of the world. And we wonder why. And then we say, "But we are the ones that glorify the human; our doctrines ought to appear to the man in Burma or in Viet-Nam or Formosa or Mid-Africa, or the Middle East."

Something is happening. And we are not presenting our case very well. Now we do know that, of course, man has his materialistic side, and his physical side, and there has got to be a decent, materialistic basis for the development of his culture, his intellectual capacity, and the attainment of his spiritual aspirations. So we can't neglect that; we neglect it at our peril. It is in that field that we have got to meet our enemy very successfully.

For example, as we try to hold together the free world and try to lead it to cooperate spontaneously in its opposition to communism, we develop methods by which each country—each nation—and each individual, indeed, if we can bring that about—can achieve a continuous rise in his living standards to achieve that physical state of well-being, where these other things can occupy his attention and lead him on to a more solid partnership with a country such as ours.

So we develop a trade plan. Now a trade plan, my friends, is not just an altruistic method to open markets to the access of people all over the globe. Like all other foreign policy, its genesis is the enlightened self-interest of the United States. But it is in recognition of this fact, that if the United States itself is to prosper, it must have means by which it can sell its products and therefore it has to buy others.

But on top of that, it is a means of leading the free world to an understanding that this physical, intellectual, spiritual being, man, can cooperate under this kind of system effectively and to his greater advancement, rather than to surrender to the blandishments of communism.

Now these are complicated subjects. When we talk about these principles, they have a different application in every subject, in every nation, indeed they have a different application in every sector of our own country.

But it would be fatal, in my opinion, here at home to allow the accumulated minor objections of each district or of each industry, because of real or fancied damage, to an enlightened trade policy, to defeat us in this great purpose of the economic union—a legitimate economic union of the free world in order that it may cleave to these great spiritual truths, which in turn make it a unity in opposing communism.

What I am trying without benefit of developed argument, is to express to you what is in my heart and mind, to convince you that, valuable as your work is at home—as much as it must be continued in combating those who are losing confidence and faith in our country—that we must undertake the task of laying before the people of the world the facts of today's life. Those are the facts of today's struggle, and the ways and means by which we may all cooperate to the greater security of all, and to the greater prosperity of all.

To say that the solution of such a problem can be accomplished without acute pain being suffered here and there, or by some locality or by some group, would be completely silly. Of course, there is going to be pain in every cure. There is pain to the operation that restores usefulness to a broken leg, or any other kind of operation. We are not going to do any of these things without a price. But if we understand ourselves what we need to do in the world to advance our own interests, economically and from the standpoint of security, to achieve and maintain the values that we see in private enterprise—understanding how that means communion and trade with other countries—then we can undertake the task of helping others to understand it also.

It is a very subtle job, I should say. The United States cannot be in the position of just preaching to others and say, "See how successful we are. Now you just get on the bandwagon and do the same way and you will have the same results." Everybody has got to take these great principles and interpret them in his own way, applying things in his own way to his own task. Otherwise it would not be freedom, and it would not be the kind of decision in which we believe. We believe that everybody should, so far as possible, decide for themselves.

Now this is what I honestly am convinced of: that unless we make it possible, through enlightened methods, for the free world to trade more freely among the several parts of that free world, we are not going to win the ideological battle. I do not expect us to fail in this process. But I do believe that every American, dedicated to his own country and proceeding from that place, can be helpful if he tries (a) to get his fellow American to understanding what is really going on in the world, and (b) to get others to understand it without necessarily preaching at them.

I am not pleading for any special form or any special detailed method of doing this. Groups such as this have great staffs. You dig out the facts. You put them together. From those facts you draw reasonable conclusions and then you take those conclusions as the basis of a plan that you start out to place before others and get them to accept it.

So I am really pleading for an intelligent look at the great world today. How quickly you will find that every problem in the great world affects us at home. We cannot escape them. We are part of it. We are intertwined. Our future and lives, even our freedoms, may be intertwined with theirs. If we can work that one out, we can help the world forward in this kind of union, one that is based upon our great spiritual belief that man is a dignified individual and is not the slave of the state; that every man has a right to aspire toward intellectual advancement, cultural advancement, and with a decent economic base on which to do these things.

If we get to going forward in that concept and each doing his legitimate and proper part, there is no more chance for communism in the world than there would be for one of us to take off and fly to the moon without the aid of science.

So I came over here this morning, first, to say thank you very much for what you have done, and to say that in my belief what you can do is far greater than all you have accomplished in the past. I think I have met every year with this group. There is no group I would rather meet with. I believe in you. I believe in what you are doing. And I believe that, therefore, because you are so good, you can't put any limit, geographical or otherwise, on your work.

NOTE: The President spoke in the District Red Cross Building at 11:30 a.m.

59   ¶ The President's News Conference of *March* 23, 1955.

[This is a complete transcript of the news conference of this date. All of the President's replies were released for broadcasting or direct quotation at that time except for the last, which is enclosed in brackets.]

THE PRESIDENT. Good morning, ladies and gentlemen, I have one announcement and one comment to make before we go to questions.

The Secretary of Commerce is going to Europe in mid-April in the interests of promoting freer trade among the free nations, and while there, is going to attend at least five great industrial fairs at which will be exhibited, of course, products of American industry and the like.

His detailed schedule can be obtained from the Secretary of Commerce.

The comment I want to make affects a question asked me last week.

Someone asked me a question—I have forgotten whom—quoting the Chief Justice as having made a statement to the effect that if the Bill of Rights were now put before the American people, it would be the judgment of the Chief Justice that that would not be approved.   And I asked this individual whether he was sure as to what the Chief Justice said.

I must assure him he is mistaken.   This so bothered me that although I stated here that I had the greatest confidence in the Chief Justice's judgment, patriotism, and dedication, that still—if that were an issue—I would go out, at least, and do my part to help get this Bill of Rights adopted.

Actually, when we looked up the speech—and a copy is in Mr. Hagerty's office now where you can see it—he said that his faith in the good sense, the soundness of the American people, was such that if this were now put before the American people, he was sure it would be adopted.

So, whoever the questioner was, I would like to assure him he was mistaken in the premise that he proposed.

We will go to questions.

Q. Robert E. Clark, International News Service: Mr. President, Senator George has proposed that the United States take the initiative in arranging a Big Four conference after the Paris accords are ratified, without waiting for a demonstration of good faith by Russia. Can you bring us up to date on how you feel about a Big Four meeting at the chiefs of state level?

THE PRESIDENT. Of course, you open up a subject that is really involved. However, I have said time and again there is no place on this earth to which I would not travel, there is no chore I would not undertake if I had any faintest hope that, by so doing, I would promote the general cause of world peace.

Now, international meetings have a number of purposes, and one of them, let us not forget, is just sheer propaganda.

Nevertheless, we must never abandon the hope that in some new conference some constructive step will be taken and start this weary world at last on the path that could lead hopefully and definitely toward a better agreement.

I have, I believe, noted—and I think the State Department has—that at this time, while the Paris agreements are still unratified in certain countries, that it is best not to muddy the water, not to introduce any new subject.

However, once that is done—and I am not going to speak about the matter of initiative, I do not believe that that in itself is particularly important—but I do believe there have got to be new exploratory talks.

I think they would be taken up at first on a different level from the chief of state.

You must remember that in this country the chief of state has different constitutional and other types of duties than the chiefs of state in most other countries. The head of a government abroad is spared many of the duties and responsibilities that here fall upon the head of the state.

So this meeting at the summit, which we so often hear about, is not so simple for us as it might be for some other countries.

So I believe that that out of the way, now from a position of strength—that is, moral and spiritual strength very greatly enhanced through this exhibition of unity—it probably would be time to begin the kind of exploratory talks that might lead to something constructive.

Now, I have used as examples in the past the kind of thing I would regard as deeds that would show the good faith of Russia.

I have never meant, and never intimated, that those deeds would be limited to the examples I gave.

In a dozen different ways this might be done. And I repeat that this Government, as long as I am the head of it, is never going to be backward in seizing upon any kind of opportunity that will apparently advance this cause.

Q. Charles S. von Fremd, CBS News: At past conferences, sir, you have indicated that such good deeds, or deeds not words, on the part of Russia might be approving an Austrian peace treaty——

THE PRESIDENT. That is right.

Q. Mr. von Fremd: ——or free elections in Germany, and a free and united Korea.

Would you still hold to these deeds before such a Big Four meeting could take place?

THE PRESIDENT. I give them only as examples. There could be a dozen others, as I said just a few minutes ago. It doesn't necessarily have to be those two.

Suppose, well, suppose the proposition that I made on December 9, 1953,[1] before the United Nations, were suddenly accepted, as far as you could see, in complete good faith. Instantly, you would start a conference on a technical and political level between the two countries that would necessarily be directed toward some kind of peaceful pursuits of mankind, and you would—no

---

[1] The President, on December 8, 1953, delivered to the United Nations an address entitled "Atomic Power for Peace."

matter, we don't know how far it would grow. There could be another one.

There would be a deed, not words.

Q. Paul R. Leach, Knight Newspapers: Mr. President, has any thought been given to this Government to the admission or inclusion of Western Germany in such a conference?

THE PRESIDENT. Let me answer that in this way, which, possibly, is just not quite as direct as you would like it.

This subject of what we may do is discussed at least twice a week between the Secretary of State and myself.

Manifestly, we have talked time and again as to the possibility soon of including Western Germany in the conference that might take place.

But, of course, I would assume that the very first ones would possibly be limited to the four, because, as quick as you add one, where is the limit to what you must add. And you don't want to kill the possibility of a constructive conference by putting down details or conditions in advance that, when you add on to them from the other side, would just make it an impossible situation.

You see the logic of that move?

Q. Mr. Leach: Yes.

Q. Merriman Smith, United Press: Mr. President, do you have under consideration an actual conference on, say, the Foreign Minister or Secretary of State level?

THE PRESIDENT. No, no; not exactly—that would be untrue to say that.

We do take this up, constantly discussing it among ourselves, frequently with one of our allies, just to keep the thinking on the same level so that if particular conditions, favorable conditions, arise, we can move ahead.

Q. Richard L. Wilson, Cowles Publications: Mr. President, I wonder if you would clarify one point in this respect: would the initial conference, if successful, be followed by a meeting of the heads of state, or should it be followed by the——

THE PRESIDENT. That depends, I would think, Mr. Wilson, on what was accomplished.

If any significant thing were brought forward where the presence of the heads of state could give it a solemnity, possibly a promise of success not otherwise obtainable, as I say, I would go anywhere.

And let me make one gratuitous remark here: I sincerely hope that this group, at least, will not try to put me, on this subject, in any partisan attitude.

In this subject, I am as sincerely bipartisan and nonpartisan as I know how to be.

I respect the opinions of everybody that comes in honesty to me on it, and I have no thought of building any kind of special viewpoint in this country in support of somebody else's viewpoint.

Q. James B. Reston, New York Times: Sir, in that regard, would you welcome, would you favor, taking Senator George and other representatives of the Congress to such a conference, if it were held?

THE PRESIDENT. Indeed, yes, if they should find it convenient and want to go.

Some of these trips, you must understand, are anything but comfortable and convenient experiences, and it is entirely possible that they would prefer to be present only for some very significant thing.

But I would tell you this: there would be no disposition to keep the thing secret from them.   They would be invited.

Q. Chalmers M. Roberts, Washington Post and Times Herald: Is it correct to infer from what you said, sir, that your thinking is that when you mention starting with a Big Four meeting, that you are thinking essentially of a further meeting regardless of the level only on the German unification and the Austrian treaty question, or is it possible that a general East-West meeting might be on a larger pattern than that?

THE PRESIDENT. I have never inferred in any way that it would be limited to those two things.

Those were simply quoted as evidences of Soviet good will and good faith that would open up the whole subject of all of our differences.   Everything could come before such a conference.

Now, I must tell you this: you will recall in about the summer of 1951, representatives of these four powers met in the Rose Palace in Paris, I think, for 4 months merely trying to agree on an agenda, which they never did; and the conference could not be held.

Maybe you could go to a nonagenda conference; I would have no objection.

What I am saying is, the things you are talking about are merely instances, already agreed upon in large part.   And the Western powers made great concessions in Austria, completely accepted the Soviet viewpoint, but nothing was done on it.

Q. Mr. Roberts: May I ask a second point: Senator George, in his remarks on this matter, raised the possibility or suggested the possibility of meeting with the Chinese Communists as well as with the Soviet Union.

Would you consider any meeting of that type either separately on Asian matters or together on world problems?

THE PRESIDENT. Well, I think at the present moment it is completely academic, because every suggestion that has been made of peace in the Far East to the Red Communists has been accepted only, from their viewpoint, as insults to them.

I think it is completely academic; there is no use speculating on it.

Q. Edward P. Morgan, American Broadcasting Company: Sir, last week, Representative Walter of Pennsylvania severely criticized the Post Office Department for seizing copies of Izvestia and Pravda in the United States mail.

Mr. Walter said that if he had his way about it, he would, on the contrary, have these papers translated into English and distributed to everybody so, as he put it, they could see how nauseating communism could be.

Colleges, too, have protested that this ban has complicated their research.

THE PRESIDENT. Yes.

Q. Mr. Morgan: And it is reported that the CIA has had some difficulty in its own research thereby.

Does this restriction have your approval, sir?

THE PRESIDENT. Well, let's make clear this: I am not going to disapprove it with no more than I know about it in detail at this moment. But I will say this: ever since I found that war records—that is, military records—were hidden away and, apparently, we were going to keep them from the American people forever, I have been against censorship.

I don't like censorship, and I don't know the reason for this one. It hasn't been brought yet to my attention except through the newspapers. And, unfortunately, I haven't had a chance to look into it. I don't know what it is about, really.

Q. Daniel Schorr, CBS News: Mr. President, in view of all you have said this morning about the possibility of a Big Power meeting, I am somewhat confused about the remark of Senator Knowland yesterday, after his visit to you, that Senator George's view was not your view.

Is there, in fact, any great difference?

THE PRESIDENT. Well, as a matter of fact, I don't think there is any great difference between anybody's view here.

This is what I really believe: everybody, in talking about an item such as this, gets a particular detail which he emphasizes in his own mind to a very great degree, and suddenly a quarrel springs out of it.

I think all of the gentlemen to whom you refer are sincerely seeking peace; some believe one thing, some another.

Now, the Secretary of State, under my direction, is responsible for carrying these things forward. I think that his attitude toward it is eminently correct and proper and conciliatory.

We are trying to seek a peace with honor, and we are simply trying to avoid that kind of useless bickering and the using of international conferences merely for propaganda purposes, disappointing people.   That is the futile kind of thing we are trying to avoid, and that is all.   Otherwise we are all for seeing, can we advance the cause of peace?

Q. Joseph C. Harsch, Christian Science Monitor: Sir, I wonder if you can clarify something I am not quite clear on.

In your last press conference, referring to the use of atomic weapons, you said that when it was a question of strictly military targets for strictly military purposes, you saw no reason why they shouldn't be used just exactly as you would use a bullet or anything else.

On January 12, we were talking about atomic weapons in connection with police action as distinct from a major war, and within that context you said you did not think that normally we would use the atomic weapons, because, you thought, you could not conceive of atomic weapons as a police weapon, and there was some further remark there that it was so destructive.

THE PRESIDENT. Well, Mr. Harsch, the difference here, I think, is perfectly simple.   A police action is not war; a police action is restoring order.

Now, you don't send in bombs to restore order when a riot occurs.   You get police people to restore order.   Occasionally there may be a life lost if someone is too tough about it.

But when you get into actual war, you have resorted to force for reaching a decision in a particular area; that is what I call war.

And whether the war is big or not, if you have the kind of a weapon that can be limited to military use, then I know of no reason why a large explosion shouldn't be used as freely as a small explosion.   That is all I was saying last week.

But that is different from trying to restore order.   Incidentally, if you want to follow some of these things off into the realm of great philosophical conjecture, suppose you won a war by the indiscriminate use of atomic weapons; what would you have left?

Now, what would you do for your police action, for your

occupation and restoration of order, and all of the things needed to be done in a great area of the earth?

I repeat, the concept of atomic war is too horrible for man to endure and to practice, and he must find some way out of it. That is all I think about this thing.

Q. Mr. Harsch: Sir, I am a little stupid about this thing.

THE PRESIDENT. Well, I am glad you didn't say *I* was! [*Laughter*]

Q. Mr. Harsch: It would seem to me there is big war at one end, just a local police action in which one person might be killed at the other; and, in between, what the military people would say was limited war. The Korean War, in a sense, was a limited war.

THE PRESIDENT. It became one, anyway.

Q. Mr. Harsch: It became one.

If we got into an issue with the Chinese, say, over Matsu and Quemoy, that we wanted to keep limited, do you conceive of using this specific kind of atomic weapon in that situation or not?

THE PRESIDENT. Well, Mr. Harsch, I must confess I cannot answer that question in advance.

The only thing I know about war are two things: the most changeable factor in war is human nature in its day-by-day manifestation; but the only unchanging factor in war is human nature.

And the next thing is that every war is going to astonish you in the way it occurred, and in the way it is carried out.

So that for a man to predict, particularly if he has the responsibility for making the decision, to predict what he is going to use, how he is going to do it, would I think exhibit his ignorance of war; that is what I believe.

So I think you just have to wait, and that is the kind of prayerful decision that may some day face a President.

We are trying to establish conditions where he doesn't.

Q. Raymond P. Brandt, St. Louis Post-Dispatch: Mr. President, have you any plan to take an active part in saving your foreign trade program in Congress?

THE PRESIDENT. Well, I can't go to the floor and debate, Mr. Brandt.

After all, we all know that, but this is what I think: the foreign trade program, as a notice to all peoples that we recognize their problems, that we are earnestly trying to establish the kind of economic base on which cultural values and spiritual values can be properly developed and bring about a greater union among us, that kind of a program is so essential to the United States today that I would use every bit of influence that I can properly and appropriately bring to bear to have it passed.

I think this is a very critical item now before the United States of America, not merely before Government, but before the whole country.

Q. Walter T. Ridder, Ridder Papers: Mr. President, do you believe that the release of the Yalta documents might cramp styles in future conferences?

THE PRESIDENT. Well, I would hope not.

Among allies, gentlemen, I want to call your attention to this one fact: you make treaties, and good faith is involved.

Now, the one place, if you will read history, is that treaties have always fallen down when it came to actual war, if any one country felt that its vital considerations were going to be damaged through the purposes of its allies.

You can go back through the history of coalitions, and you will find great evidence of this.

As a matter of fact, one soldier said that he always considered Napoleon the greatest soldier that ever lived, until he woke up one day and found that he always fought against coalitions. And then he lost some of his respect.

Now, this is one way of defining the difficulties of coalitions. Good faith is involved; so that while I earnestly believe that all documents should be published, not attempting to pin or assess blame for success and failure, I believe when the good faith with an ally is involved we want to be exceedingly careful. Moreover, I think such documents should be confined, in general, to those things that are of political and military significance. Casual conversation, I think, should not be included.

I would hope that our country would never be legitimately charged with bad faith, and in this particular case I think it wasn't. They had been, I believe, in communication with our ally for a long time about it. However, there was some difference of opinion.

Now, in this matter, let me repeat, there is nothing, as I can see, to be gained by going back 10 years and showing that, in the light of afterevents, that someone may have been wrong, or someone may have been right.

People that are so sure that we could do this, forget one thing: you can never recapture the atmosphere of war. You have the great advantage of events.

I think I have often told you that one of the most severe decisions I had to make in the war was to direct the capture of Pantelleria. Yet that was so easy that most of you don't even know where Pantelleria was. And in the afterevent, it made not a ripple in history. Yet the decision was so difficult that had the predictions of the pessimists been realized, I certainly would have been relieved.

So that you can never tell, at the moment, is history going to say this was right or this was wrong.

If we believe these people acted for what they thought was the best good, of the cause for which they were fighting, of their country, well, then, let us take and lay the thing out dispassionately so that we, in our turn, may profit from their mistakes. But don't let's try to just damage reputations by such means.

Q. Ingrid M. Jewell, Pittsburgh Post-Gazette: Mr. President, Senator Bricker thinks that his proposed amendment——

THE PRESIDENT. I couldn't quite hear you.

Q. Miss Jewell: Senator Bricker believes that his proposed amendment has a good chance of going through this year because he thinks you have changed your mind about it since last year. Have you changed your mind?

THE PRESIDENT. No.

Q. Clark R. Mollenhoff, Des Moines Register: You suffered one of your sharpest defeats in the House on this postal pay bill. I wonder if you would give us some of your own personal views as to why you oppose the 10 percent in favor of the 5 percent?

THE PRESIDENT. Since 1945 the postal clerks and carriers have gone from something of an order of a $1700 wage to a $3200, something of a 92-percent raise. The top scales, I think, of those same grades have gone up about 94 percent. I give you that statistic just to show that these people have not been neglected.

Moreover, when you begin to talk about pay scales you have got to take in not merely the percentage that one group now may receive as opposed to another group; you have got to go back into the whole background and history of the thing.

Exactly the same way in the opposite sense with some of the military. Some of the military grades have been neglected, and we need to raise them or we are not going to have proper people there.

I sent to the Congress a plan, for both civil service people and postal people, that had been studied long and earnestly in a great effort to do the right thing by the individuals themselves, to do it sensibly and in accordance with efficient governmental management of the great processes we have to carry out.

Now, I believe still that that is a correct program for the readjustments and revisions of classification and the scale of increase that it proposes; and any great increase over that would cause me, as I said in a letter, the gravest concern.

Q. Sarah McClendon, El Paso Times: Mr. President, I believe Vice President Nixon has spoken to you about the merit of completing the Inter-American Highway, and he said at the present rate it won't be completed until 15 or 25 years have passed.

Have you and he—have you agreed on a plan for speeding up the financing of this, so it may be completed?

THE PRESIDENT. No.

In his report to the Cabinet he mentioned this, and gave his conclusions as of tremendous importance.

Now, the next thing that will happen will be that State and Commerce will unquestionably make a recommendation to me as to what we should do in the way of getting the necessary appropriations. I believe they are relatively small.

But I will say this: instinctively, I am on his side. I believe that this road should be completed.

Q. Marvin L. Arrowsmith, Associated Press: Mr. President, is any effort being made by either this Government directly or through the British to negotiate a cease-fire in the Formosa Strait, I mean any new efforts as an attempt through the U.N.?

THE PRESIDENT. As of this moment?

Q. Mr. Arrowsmith: Yes.

THE PRESIDENT. No, there is no particular or specific program now in progress, but I should say this: that, of course, the British, with representation in Peking, have always represented our viewpoint, which is that any just, reasonable solution of the difficulty in the Formosa Straits would receive our most earnest and sympathetic attention.

We ourselves supported putting it before the United Nations, but there is no specific plan at the moment.

Q. William H. Lawrence, New York Times: Mr. President, in your concluding remarks about the Yalta papers a moment ago, you said if we believe these people acted for the best good; is it correct to interpret that to say that you believe they acted for the best good as they saw it?

THE PRESIDENT. Well, I meant my remark, Mr. Lawrence, in this way: so far as I know, I have never in public questioned a man's motives, even if I thought he was mistaken; I have criticized military leaders in staff schools in my time very severely. I certainly would not question his motives.

I question the motives of no man when I wasn't there and know nothing about what he was doing.

Q. Mr. Lawrence: May I ask one supplementary question?

THE PRESIDENT. Yes.

Q. Mr. Lawrence: You were a responsible field commander at the time and informed of general strategy. Did you record or do you remember a decision that you reached at that time at your own level as to the rightness or wrongness of Yalta?

THE PRESIDENT. No.

The only faint connection I had was this: the British and American contingents met in Malta before going on to Yalta. I didn't have time to go down. I was engaged in a very heavy battle, and I sent my Chief of Staff down to represent what our operational plans for the spring were, and to tell them. They were all approved.

As a matter of fact, it was sent down for information.

But I did tell two or three of the individuals involved that the Western allied forces were going to get at least as far as the Elbe in this operation—our calculations were that we had now used up all the disposable reserves the Germans had to put on the western front, and that we were going to penetrate deep into Germany—and I would hope, therefore, that these people would have that knowledge before they made any agreement.

However, don't forget this: all during that year of 1944 the European Advisory Commission had been meeting in London, and these plans were worked out by the Advisory Commission. As far as I know, Yalta had only the job of approving them, because all these countries had been represented on that Commission. I believe John Winant was our representative.

I merely said that we were going to go further east into Germany than the line they described to me, and that is the only thing I knew about.

I never was at Yalta; I didn't even go to Malta.

Q. Edward T. Folliard, Washington Post and Times Herald: Mr. President, to go back to the high level conference, Senator George's position, as I understand it, is this: that he would not require the Russians to meet any particular conditions; that is, he would not require that they show their earnestness with deeds rather than with words.

Now, I do not understand that to be your position, Mr. President. I am trying to find out whether there is a real difference.

THE PRESIDENT. Well, there may be. I don't deny that every individual that approaches these problems has his own detailed solution for them.

I merely want to say that I am seeking an honorable peace and trying to create confidence among the peoples of the free world, not just bouncing around to do nothing.

Now, there is this one thing, the argument on the other side: there have been at least two changes within the last couple of years in the personnel of the ruling group in the Kremlin. Consequently, you have at least the element of, let us say, faint hope that new individuals may be different from the old ones; that may make some exploratory talks very valuable. And as long as we are differentiating between a final big so-called meeting at the summit and exploratory talks—well, exploratory talks, I could make a lot of concessions to have that carried out.

Q. Robert G. Spivack, New York Post: Mr. President, if we may return to the Far East for a moment: one of the solutions that has been suggested for ending the Far East crisis has been a U.N. trusteeship for Formosa. I wonder if this Government is receptive to that idea?

THE PRESIDENT. I believe I won't talk about that one this morning. I dislike ever saying "No comment" to you people, but that is one that I have not talked in detail because, for my own part, I had not up to this moment taken it as an acceptable solution to people we are trying to keep on our side.

Q. Frederick Kuh, Chicago Sun-Times: Mr. President, in your consideration of a Four Power conference, is it your premise that the Russians will be willing to participate in such a conference within a matter of some months after ratification of the Paris agreements?

THE PRESIDENT. I don't know. That is one of the subjects we

discuss constantly: what would be their attitude toward an invitation? And maybe it would be even worth while finally to find out what that is.

But I don't know, and I don't think anyone else could really make a good guess.

Q. Nat S. Finney, Buffalo News: Mr. President, did you intend to assign a lower order of priority to the deeds of an Austrian treaty and German elections, and North Korea? Does what you said give them a lower order of priority of importance than they have had heretofore?

THE PRESIDENT. I couldn't imagine what would make you ask such a question. Nothing I have ever said would indicate that.

No. I am merely giving these indications of something that would mean to me, "Look, these people are talking business." They have violated their word so often, they have left us hanging on the limb. As a matter of fact, our great interest in all of these past agreements and papers is why did we trust them so much.

All I want to know is what can I depend on to mean to me this: we are approaching this seriously and earnestly; that is all.

Q. John L. Cutter, United Press: Mr. President, a member of your liaison staff has been up to the Congress to see a member of the Michigan delegation regarding the establishment of a jet airbase near Cadillac, Michigan. Does that mean that the White House has any particular interest in that one particular place?

THE PRESIDENT. [This is the first time I have heard of it; and if anyone has an interest in it, it certainly must be personal. I know nothing about it.]

Merriman Smith, United Press: Thank you, Mr. President.

NOTE: President Eisenhower's sixty-fourth news conference was held in the Executive Office Building from 10:31 to 11:04 o'clock on Wednesday morning, March 23, 1955. In attendance: 211.

60   ¶ Remarks to Representatives of the American Voluntary Societies Cooperating in the United States Escapee Program.   *March* 25, 1955

WELL, ladies and gentlemen, of course, I am not going into a dissertation on statistics. About all I can say is, thank you for the extraordinary understanding that you exhibit by your very participation in this kind of work.

If we are to win this ideological struggle going on in the world, if we are going to stand for freedom and opportunity and the dignity of the human, we have got to be ready to do those things voluntarily that give some other individual the right to be dignified as well, to enjoy opportunity, to live in freedom.

And of course we know from our own history, going way back into the dim past, that freedom is not won easily, nor is it won without sacrifice.

Whenever we allow anybody else's freedom to be cut down, by that much our own is endangered. Consequently, the work that you are doing is not only completely humanitarian, as I see it. It is also in furtherance of the idea that this thing—this concept of freedom—is not going to be kept alive and flourish in the world unless we do those things that are expected of free men, and make sure that everybody else has a similar opportunity.

So it is in that spirit that I say: thank you very much. I assure you that this administration, in its own several jobs spread all over the United States and over the world, is dedicated to the same ideas here that you are doing in the practical, every day work-a-day field. These are things that have to be done, things of the greatest importance.

So, my gratitude for that, and my best wishes for your continued success. I didn't realize you were 3 years old today, but that is good. I hope you continue to grow.

NOTE: The President spoke in his office at the White House following introductory remarks by Harold E. Stassen, Foreign Operations Administrator.

The voluntary organizations, sponsored by various religious, national, and special purpose groups, cooperated with the U.S. Escapee Program in assisting refugees and escapees as they came across the line from the Iron Curtain areas. The U.S. Escapee Program was established early in 1952 to assure that the escapees find an adequate welcome in the free world.

61 ¶ Joint Statement Following Discussions With Prime Minister Scelba of Italy. *March* 28, 1955

THE PRESIDENT received today and had discussions with His Excellency, Mario Scelba, Prime Minister of Italy, who is making an official visit to this country.

The Prime Minister was accompanied to the White House by His Excellency, Gaetano Martino, Foreign Minister of Italy; His Excellency, Manlio Brosio, Italian Ambassador to the United States; Massimo Magistrati, Director of Political Affairs, Italian Ministry of Foreign Affairs; and Paolo Canali, Adviser to the Prime Minister.

The Secretary of State, John Foster Dulles; the American Ambassador to Italy, Mrs. Clare Boothe Luce; and the Assistant Secretary of State for European Affairs, Mr. Livingston Merchant, were in attendance with the President.

The President and the Prime Minister reviewed the general problems of East-West relations as they affect the peace and security of the world today. They also discussed aspects of Western defense pertaining to the partnership of Italy and the United States in the North Atlantic Treaty Organization.

Developments in the creation of the Western European Union were also touched upon and the President expressed to Prime Minister Scelba the gratification of the American people at the important role Italy has been playing in the carrying forward of all measures leading to Western European integration and the solidarity of the North Atlantic community.

After the discussions were concluded, the President and Mrs. Eisenhower entertained at an official luncheon at the White House in honor of the Prime Minister and Signora Scelba and their party.

62 ¶ The President's News Conference of *March 30, 1955.*

[This is a complete transcript of the news conference of this date. Those portions of the President's replies which were not released for broadcasting or direct quotation at that time are enclosed in brackets.]

THE PRESIDENT. My first announcement this morning is to express—and, I think, on behalf of all of you—a deep regret at the death of Harold Beckley, Superintendent of the Senate Press Gallery, who has been on this door ever since I have been holding press conferences in this room. I think all of us would like to join in expressing our regret to those that were close to him.

I want to mention briefly these bipartisan lunches I am having today and tomorrow, merely to assure you that there is no specific or special purpose behind them.

We started talking about them two or three weeks ago. It was some little trouble to find two days in succession that were blank on my luncheon calendar and convenient to the people on the Hill.

We have at least arranged it, and we expect to talk over the world situation in general. There is no agenda, no specific subject to be discussed.

As you know, the French and Italian Parliaments have both ratified the Paris agreements, and I couldn't possibly exaggerate in expressing my satisfaction.

I speak as one who was sent over there some years ago to work on this proposition. I was very strong for EDC. When EDC was rejected, I though this was the next best we could do.

I am delighted that the Parliaments have gone this far with the unification of our security arrangements in that area.

Now, that's all the announcements I have.

We will go to questions.

Q. Merriman Smith, United Press: Mr. President, within the past week Admiral Carney has been quoted as saying that there might be a Red Chinese attack on Matsu, followed in a month or about a month, by an attack on Quemoy.

We understand that you feel otherwise and, furthermore, don't like the expression of this sort of estimate on Admiral Carney's part.

I wonder if you could discuss that situation for us.

THE PRESIDENT. Ladies and gentlemen, I have tried to say it many times: none of us possesses a crystal ball. We cannot pretend to the accuracy of the ancient prophets when we talk about the future.

I have heard the possibility of war discussed many times during my governmental career, and I have seen it occur on two or three occasions.

But to prophesy when a war is going to break out is to assume that we have an accuracy of information that, I think, has never yet been attained by a country that was to be attacked.

What I have tried to say is this: in this poor and distressed world, the danger, the risk of war is always with us, and we have got to be vigilant. We have got to be careful. And while we are doing it we have got to be as fair and as large-minded as we know how, to accommodate and to understand the fears and the ambitions of others that might lead them into a risky venture and such a tragic thing as this; at the same time so conducting ourselves that the world knows we are strong, strong in our principles, in our faith, also strong militarily and economically. I don't believe there is any possible way as of this time of describing the situation any better.

If I can make a comment, it is this: I do not believe that the peace of the world, the tranquillity of the world, is being served at this moment by talking too much in terms of speculation about such things. I think that is all I have to say about it.

Q. Joseph C. Harsch, Christian Science Monitor: Mr. President, a military question: would you tell us whether, in your opinion, the United States can successfully defend Formosa, even if we should give up or refrain from doing anything about the offshore islands of Quemoy and Matsu?

THE PRESIDENT. I think that the attitude and the calculations of this Government were pretty well laid out before the Senate and the House at the time of the passage of the recent resolution asking for authority to act under given situations.

However, I would say this: a terrific burden would depend upon the forces and the people occupying Formosa as to the possibility of its defense.

You have to have forces there who are of high morale, who have something in which to believe if they are going to fight well, as that is the only way men fight. They don't fight just to get out and shoot at each other, so they must believe in something. And we must be careful not to destroy their morale. That is a factor that you must always calculate when you talk about surrendering this place or that place or doing anything else.

Now, as I say again, even for me, I don't think there is much to be gained by speculation in this field. But I do want you to see this one factor that is terrifically important if you are going to make a successful military defense of any area.

Q. Ray Scherer, National Broadcasting Company: Mr. President, could you assess the present possibility for a cease-fire in the Formosa Straits?

THE PRESIDENT. No, I can't. And if you will pardon me, I think we have talked enough about Formosa. I don't believe I have anything more to say about it.

Q. Clark R. Mollenhoff, Des Moines Register: Mr. President, Representative Price of Illinois has said that Allen Whitfield, who you nominated for the Atomic Energy Commission, is a professional politician, and he criticized the administration for what he said "making the Atomic Energy Commission the dumping ground for job-hungry Republicans."

I wonder if you could tell us if you intend to withdraw the nomination, as he demanded; how you happened to select Whitfield, and what particular qualifications you thought he brought to the job.

THE PRESIDENT. [That is like defending yourself against "beating your wife." [*Laughter*]

[I have tried to tell you people, and I assure you I have tried to follow this theory in the appointment of people: I have appointed those people that are close to me and on whom I must depend for advice and counsel in many things, including the selection of subordinates. I have depended on their advice and counsel in the selection of the people they need. These people close to me I trust.

[Then, once they are selected, they have to pass certain tests. There are certain field tests, and all kinds of things that they go through. If they are found to measure up they are appointed.

[In the case of Mr. Whitfield, I think that there is probably no worse being said against him than being said against lots of people. But I know of no one that we have appointed whose standing in his community, whose reputation, whose readiness to serve his government, are not of a very high order.]

Q. Raymond P. Brandt, St. Louis Post-Dispatch: Mr. President, Secretary Dulles has said that it will take months to prepare for a Big Four conference. We have had the conditions laid down for the Russians coming in. Could you tell us some of the subjects that could be discussed at a Big Four conference?

THE PRESIDENT. Well, Mr. Brandt, it is not an easy question, because there are so many different kinds of meetings that have been proposed by different people.

One proposal, coming from a very eminent source, has been that we merely meet without an agenda, and we have a broad talk. Well, now, there are many dangers in such a meeting because it could be considered, let us say, social. If it is a social sort of get-together, trying to be friendly, there are many people in the world that are interpreting actions as well as words, and they are interpreting them in terms of what has happened to them and what does this meeting mean to them? That is one kind of a meeting that you have to watch.

Moreover, if you would have a meeting, certain questions would almost have to be examined; for example, let us say, the unification of Germany or some question affecting Germany. The wheels are now moving to make Germany, West Germany, a completely independent country. How can you talk about Germany unless Germany is present? But if you ask Germany, where do you stop?

There are all sorts of things to be decided in these preparations before you can just meet and have something that is promising for the peace of the world. I would certainly hesitate to be a party to a meeting where people would have a right, merely because you meet, to expect more than you really believe you can deliver.

Now I reiterate, the United States Government is ready to do anything. We will meet on any basis as long as we are not, in so doing, creating an impression we think is damaging.

Q. Mr. Brandt: Isn't it true, sir, that the lower level conference would work out an agenda?

THE PRESIDENT. Well, I don't know whether they would even have to work out an entire agenda, Mr. Brandt.

I quoted to you the other day the example in the Rose Palace in Paris in 1952 when, after meeting for 3 months to decide upon an agenda for another meeting, they abandoned the effort; they could not do it.

But they would have to make a sufficient preparation for this thing so we could try to determine, at least, or we could have some confidence of what we are getting into. It is a very serious question.

Q. Richard L. Wilson, Cowles Publications: Mr. President——

THE PRESIDENT. Could I interrupt just a minute?

Q. Mr. Wilson: Yes, certainly.

THE PRESIDENT. I was asked by a listener whether each person—no, stand up—whether each person asking a question would speak loudly and get as close to a microphone as he could. I forgot it this morning. [*Laughter*]

Q. Mr. Wilson: They will have to raise this for me, sir.

THE PRESIDENT. Well, they always do that on the stage, you know. [*Laughter*]

Q. Mr. Wilson: Perhaps that will put you in a good humor for this question. [*Laughter*] It may fall within your earlier remark that you did not want to discuss Formosa.

However, it has been stated in the newspapers and on the radio that your position is one thing or another with respect to Quemoy and Matsu; but I have not heard, sir, you express your opinion as to these recent discussions or whether or not the recent accounts in the press are true. So I would ask you, do——

THE PRESIDENT. The recent accounts are true?

Q. Mr. Wilson: Yes, sir. Do you disagree with the proposition that there may be an attack on Matsu from April 15th onward?

THE PRESIDENT. Well, certainly, I will go back to that subject long enough to say this: I cannot say that there will not, because I don't know. But I do say that if anyone is predicting it will be that soon, and can give me logical reasons for believing it will be that soon, they have information that I do not have.

Q. Charles E. Shutt, Telenews: There has been a great deal of talk lately, alleged in many quarters to be very partisan; and yesterday on Capitol Hill, Senator Smathers and Senator Carlson said perhaps we were getting into an election year a year earlier and, perhaps, a moratorium should be declared on mudslinging.

Would you comment on that, sir, the partisan talk that has been going on recently?

THE PRESIDENT. In some things I think a man's conscience has got to determine his own actions, but it has apparently very little to do with the actions of others.

If I have been guilty of mudslinging anywhere, I would be glad to account for it and to apologize to my unintended victim.

I don't believe in mudslinging. I don't believe it does any good. As a matter of fact, I think it would be a good moment to just say how much I have respected and admired the attitude that Senator George has taken, for example, in trying to preserve a true bipartisan, unpartisan approach to all our foreign problems.

[I wouldn't even talk, therefore, about a party that contained such a man who is working as hard as he is to make the foreign affairs of the United States go forward successfully.]

Q. Sarah McClendon, El Paso Times: Sir, I seem to recall in World War II that military personnel were warned not to talk. And isn't it very poor military strategy, to say the least, for us to go out here talking about our enemies' war plans?

THE PRESIDENT. As a matter of fact, you have something there. I meant to express something of that kind when I said I didn't believe that we were doing the United States much good by speculating too much into the future on this thing.

There are just certain things in the world—if you are going to live in the confidence that you are right, ready to protect your rights, but you are not going to resort to aggressive force yourself, then you have got to be patient and strong in your patience, not to let anybody run over you, but not to try to say, "They are going to attack me today; therefore, I attacked them yesterday so that I don't get in bad trouble."

Q. Marvin Arrowsmith, Associated Press: Mr. President, not meaning to transgress on your enough-about-Formosa remark, but will Admiral Carney be reprimanded for his remarks of last week?

THE PRESIDENT. Not by me.

Q. Alan S. Emory, Watertown Times: Mr. President, Congressman Walter of Pennsylvania has attacked Mr. Edward Corsi, the new Special Assistant to the Secretary of State on Refugee and Migration Problems, as allegedly having been a member of several Communist-front organizations.

I wondered if you would comment, sir, on your personal acquaintance with Mr. Corsi and whether you think any individual who had been active in a Communist-front organization would have a chance of getting that high a job in the State Department?

THE PRESIDENT. [Well, you have got a lot of "ifs" in there in that question.

[Now, actually, I have met Mr. Corsi. I have talked to him. My appointment of him again was on the recommendations of people I trust. He was put in that position actually, of course, by the Secretary of State. The Secretary of State has reported to me that he has been very valuable in the position.

[I know nothing about these accusations against him, but I am sure that it could be looked up if you go to the Secretary of State.]

Q. Chalmers M. Roberts, Washington Post and Times Herald: A couple of weeks ago you appointed Harold Stassen as a Special Assistant for Disarmament. I wonder if you could give us a little of your thinking behind the creation of that job, and just what the scope of it is.

THE PRESIDENT. Well, the concept is very simple.

Here is something that is a terrific problem in the world. We all know what burdens are created by the maintenance of these sterile, unproductive agencies we call defense units and organizations. We are putting billions and billions into them. We would like to reduce them.

Now, each department of Government, as far as I can see, almost each individual in such a country as ours, has some particular idea of what he thinks might work. On some sides they want purely, let's say, a theoretical approach. On other sides they will go to the extremes of *quid pro quo*: "Don't do a thing, just build more bombs."

What is our thinking? There was nobody in the Government, up until I appointed Governor Stassen to this post, that was responsible for getting together all of the different ideas affecting disarmament and putting them together so the administration can say, "This is our program, and this is what we are trying to do in this field."

State approaches this from one way, Defense approaches it from another, your economic people approach it from still another. You have all sorts of viewpoints; and some think this will work, that will work.

Let us have somebody with a small staff who cannot only do something to bring together, draw together, these views, but to devise a short, easily expressed program, maybe that all of us here could adopt and say, "Yes, that is good."

Now, that is what he is for.

Q. Mr. Roberts: Could I ask, sir, is it your thinking that disarmament is an instrument on the way to what you have called the *modus vivendi* or that you get disarmament agreement after you have created an atmosphere in which——

THE PRESIDENT. Personally, I believe these things have got to go hand in hand. Fear begets fear.

Now, you have armaments. If you are going to say, "Let us be more peaceful, let's make a more peaceful arrangement somewhere, and then we can reduce armaments," they will say, "Well don't you think we had better do this at the same time?"

Then as we make this nice arrangement, there won't be quite so much capacity for one nation to attack another.

I think you have now given a perfect example of the kind of thing that we should like to have some brains giving exclusive attention to: what is a good explanation of the sequential steps that must take place if this is going to have any chance of success?

Q. Laurence H. Burd, Chicago Tribune: Mr. President, has this Government received any recent report from the United Nations on its effort to release the flyers held by Red China, and if not, are we going to ask for one, or take any other steps?

THE PRESIDENT. Only the report, Mr. Burd, that they are still working actively in this field. That is the report.

Q. Robert G. Spivack, New York Post: Mr. President, before, you mentioned some of the obstacles that are in the way, or the difficulties that are in the way of a Big Four conference; I wonder about one that you didn't mention.

Do we know yet whether things have shaken down in Russia and who the top man in the Russian Government is now?

THE PRESIDENT. No, I think we know nothing more than what is apparent on the face of things. That is, if you take the organization at face value, why then, you would say Marshal Bulganin is the head. But I think it would be a bold man to say that they knew he was the true principal influence in the government today.

Q. Francis M. Stephenson, New York Daily News: With all respect, Mr. President, I would like to ask you by whose authority your aides are giving out such information as whether or not we are going to war to ten or twenty men who invite them out to dinner? Don't you think the New York Daily News is entitled to that news?

THE PRESIDENT. [Well, I am not, of course, responsible for the friends that my subordinates have, nor can I be responsible for exactly what they say.

[Now, I am sure someone expressed a personal opinion. Whether or not they have a right to do so, possibly you can say they have to talk to everybody if they talk to one. But, so far as I know, the individual concerned had no idea of the questions that were going to be asked him.

[I want to make clear he does have a right to his personal convictions. But he cannot utter them properly, in my opinion, if he is going to create difficulty for his administration, for his commander in chief, or in violation of any announced policy of an administration, because then he doesn't belong as a member of the team.]

Q. Mr. Stephenson: Well, it has reached a point, Mr. President, where we have to invite your aides to dinner before we can get such very important information, whether we are going to war.

THE PRESIDENT. [My dear sir, why do you suppose I come over here every week? I am not asking you to see anybody else. I come over here every week to subject myself to your questions for a half hour. Now you can ask any question of substance, but don't ask me to criticize somebody else when I don't even know the circumstances of the meeting.]

Q. William M. Blair, New York Times: Mr. President, the bipartisan farm bloc in Congress is making an effort to change the administration's farm program and restore high rigid price supports. Their concern is that the farm economy is going down and endangering the rest of the economy.

Do you share this view, sir, and do you intend to back Mr. Benson in his program?

THE PRESIDENT. Well, I want to make this remark: every—it is true that farm prices have fallen, and it is a development that has caused the gravest concern over a number of years. I think they fell some 19 points in the 2 years just prior to '53, and some 8 or 9 since then.

But I must point this out: every bit of that drop has been under the 90 percent rigid price supports. The flexible price support program has not yet been effective, and it will not become effective until the '55 crops are ready for marketing. So that to say that the flexible price supports or to hint or to imply that they are responsible for this drop is just, in my opinion, not correct.

Of course we are giving attention to it. We are looking at every possible thing there is to do in this field. But the purpose of flexible price supports is to discourage production in those items in which we are constantly building up surpluses, to transfer our agriculture a bit, so that we can really get supply and demand in better balance.

Q. Robert E. Clark, International News Service: Mr. President, this is a question that applies to the long-range defense of Formosa rather than the current crisis.

Brigadier General Frank Howley recently toured Formosa and

the Far East, and has made several proposals for strengthening our position in dealing with the Chinese Communists.

One of these is that we arm the Chinese Nationalist Army with atomic weapons. Another is that we make it clear to Red China that one more aggressive step on their part will mean their complete destruction by our atomic power.

Can you give us your opinion on this?

THE PRESIDENT. You say he recommended that?

Q. Mr. Clark: That is right.

THE PRESIDENT. [I haven't heard it, Mr. Clark, and I have not seen the two points or at least the first point discussed in detail.

[I do not believe that, as I say, the cause of peace is now to be served by making any further commitments about the area at all, I mean commitments in terms of intention.]

Q. Merriman Smith, United Press: Mr. President, what do you think of the position taken by the man you nominated as Comptroller General in opposition to your highway program? He has told Congress that he thinks the financing system is unsound and, possibly, illegal. I refer to Mr. Campbell.

THE PRESIDENT. Well, Mr. Smith, I nominated to the position of Comptroller General the man I thought was best qualified in the United States. Mr. Campbell was my associate and assistant when I was at Columbia University. He was the treasurer of a very large organization. He is a splendid accountant, and he is certainly an honest gentleman.

Now, the last thing I would ever ask any man that I appoint to high office is what are going to be his decisions in specific cases.

If any man would pledge to me that he was going to make a certain decision because I asked him, he would never be appointed.

So I have to concede to him his right to follow his own judgment and convictions. But I do tell you this, I think he is wrong. [*Laughter*]

Q. Lawrence Fernsworth, Concord (New Hampshire) Monitor: I don't wish to break the moratorium, Mr. President. I am merely asking for clarification.

There has been some speculation since your statement that a year hence you would answer the question concerning your candidacy; there has been some speculation that you are awaiting the primaries in New Hampshire, in the first week of—the second Tuesday of March.

Would you comment on that, sir?

THE PRESIDENT. You know, some of these questions, I am going to refer them to this body and see whether they actually do break the moratorium. [*Laughter*] I haven't even thought about the primaries in New Hampshire. And you are informing me now of something that I do recall—that they do come in March. [*Laughter*]

Q. Charles E. Egan, New York Times: Could you tell us when or if that committee you named to study transportation has reported to you yet, the committee headed by Secretary Weeks?

THE PRESIDENT. [I will have to explain my answer to this extent: we have had preliminary discussions on it. Whether the final report came to me I can't say at this moment.]

Mr. Hagerty: Not yet.

THE PRESIDENT. [Not yet. We have had preliminary discussions and, therefore, I couldn't be certain.]

Q. Elie Abel, New York Times: Could you give us your thought, sir, on what arrangements you would like to see made for the future of the Foreign Operations Administration which, I believe, expires June 30?

THE PRESIDENT. Well, I think that theoretically we had a good organization. But there are a number of considerations that apply. I believe that in some ways it is best to get the end item defense portions of those expenditures really included in the Defense budget as separate items—I don't mean to say thereby to reduce the necessary expenditures for our own defense—and then to take over in a separate bureau, possibly in the State Department, something like the Internal Revenue is organized in the Treasury Department. I would visualize something like that.

I want to make clear, if the answer is something different, don't accuse me of bad faith. I am giving you my personal idea of how it could be done well.

Q. Daniel Schorr, CBS News: I understand, sir, we were remiss in journalistic enterprise last week. Mr. President, how about the squirrels? [*Laughter*]

THE PRESIDENT. Well, I'll tell you: I think first you ought to interview the squirrels and find out if anybody is unhappy. [*Laughter*] I don't see any reason for producing another pressure group until we find out they are really unhappy, with a freedom I would personally dearly love. [*Laughter*]

Merriman Smith, United Press: Thank you, Mr. President.

NOTE: President Eisenhower's sixty-fifth news conference was held in the Executive Office Building from 10:34 to 11:03 o'clock on Wednesday morning, March 30, 1955. In attendance: 217.

63 ¶ Statement by the President on the Death of Joseph Pulitzer and Robert R. McCormick.
April 1, 1955

IN THE PASSING of Joseph Pulitzer and Colonel Robert R. McCormick, American journalism has lost the services of two of its outstanding publishers. Although frequently on opposite sides of public issues, both were staunch champions of a free press so essential to our own freedoms.

Mrs. Eisenhower joins me in extending personal sympathy to their families for the great personal loss they have suffered.

64   ¶ Letter to the President of the Senate and to the Speaker of the House of Representatives Concerning the Inter-American Highway.
April 1, 1955

[Released April 1, 1955. Dated March 31, 1955]

Dear —————:

For some time I have had under consideration the desirability of accelerating the completion of the Inter-American Highway which extends from the United States to the Canal Zone via the Central American countries.

The early completion of the Inter-American Highway in close cooperation with the affected countries is a clearly established objective of United States policy.

Although this project has been under construction sporadically since 1934 and the Congress has appropriated funds in the amount of $53,723,000 to date for its completion, the incompleted state of the project prevents realization of maximum benefits.

Recently I have sought the advice of interested agencies of the Government and I am convinced that for economic and political reasons now is the appropriate time to speed completion of the Inter-American Highway.   I believe this would be the most significant single action which the United States can take in Central America and Panama to bring about the most mutually advantageous results.

Among the considerations which make me feel that an accelerated construction program on the highway is essential are these:

1. A completed highway will provide a very important contribution to the economic development of the countries through which it passes.

2. There will be an opportunity for increased trade and improved political relations among these countries and the United States.

3. The resultant increase in tourist traffic would not only improve cultural relations but also serve as a very important element in the development of their economies through earnings of foreign exchange.

4. The existence of such an all-weather highway would be of substantial security importance, both in providing overland contact and communication as far southward as the Panama Canal, and in bringing an important physical link between these countries in our common defense of the Western Hemisphere against aggression from without and subversion from within.

The stabilizing effect of these factors will tend to bar any possible return of communism which was so recently and successfully defeated in this area.

It is estimated that the amount needed to complete the Inter-American Highway in a three-year period is $112,470,000, of which $74,980,000 would be the share of the United States, leaving $37,490,000 as the combined share of the several cooperating countries on the usual 2:1 matching basis.

In the Federal-Aid Highway Acts of 1952 and 1954 Congress authorized the expenditure of $56,000,000 for this project. Funds actually appropriated against these authorizations have totaled $6,750,000, leaving a balance of $49,250,000 yet to be appropriated. Of this amount $5,750,000 is currently included in budget estimates now pending before the Congress. In order to accelerate the highway work sufficiently to permit its completion within the next three years, an additional authorization of $25,730,000 will be needed. It will also be necessary to increase our 1956 appropriation request from $5,750,000 to $74,980,000.

In the near future I shall transmit to the Congress the necessary budget request to carry out this program, and I trust that the Congress will give this proposal for accelerated completion of the Inter-American Highway its most favorable consideration.

Sincerely,

DWIGHT D. EISENHOWER

NOTE: This is the text of identical letters addressed to the Honorable Richard M. Nixon, President of the Senate, and to the Honorable Sam Rayburn, Speaker of the House of Representatives.

On April 12 the President sub-

mitted to Congress a request for a supplemental appropriation for completing the highway (H. Doc. 126, 84th Cong., 1st sess.). H.R. 5923, authorizing the appropriation, was approved July 1, 1955 (69 Stat. 244).

65 ¶ Statement by the President on the Retirement of Sir Winston Churchill, Prime Minister of the United Kingdom. *April* 5, 1955

WE HAVE just had official word that my old and very dear friend, Sir Winston Churchill, has retired from his position as head of Her Majesty's government in the United Kingdom.

Naturally, an event such as this recalls to my mind many stirring incidents both of war and peace. I have greatly respected and valued my associations with a man so great as Winston Churchill.

And now, if I dare, I should like to address a word directly to Sir Winston. All of us in the free world can respect your decision, Sir Winston, to retire from official office, to live now a somewhat more serene life than has been possible in a position of such great responsibility as yours. But we shall never accept the thought that we are to be denied your counsel, your advice. Out of your great experience, your great wisdom, and your great courage, the free world yet has much to gain, and we know that you will never be backward in bringing those qualities forward when we appeal to you for help, as all of us are bound to do.

Good luck to you in retirement. To you and your family all the happiness that it is possible for you to have.

Now for the rest of us, I hope that I have spoken the words you would like to speak, no matter how haltingly or how roughly. Thank you.

NOTE: The President made this impromptu statement to newsmen in the Rose Garden.

66 ¶ Statement by the President on the Appointment of Anthony Eden as Prime Minister of the United Kingdom.   *April 6, 1955*

SIR ANTHONY EDEN, my good and long time friend, has been named the new Prime Minister of Her Majesty's government in the United Kingdom.   He is a great successor to a great Prime Minister.

In war and in peace, Sir Anthony has been an outstanding spokesman of the free world.   I know that he will continue unceasingly to serve the cause of world peace and freedom.

I join with my fellow Americans in felicitating him, a statesman of world stature, as he undertakes his new responsibilities.

67 ¶ Memorandum to the Director of the Office of Defense Mobilization Relating to the Buy American Act.   *April 7, 1955*

[Released April 7, 1955. Dated April 5, 1955]

Memorandum for
The Director
Office of Defense Mobilization

Pursuant to Section 3(d) of Executive Order 10582, December 17, 1954, you are hereby designated to furnish advice to Executive agencies with respect to the rejection of bids or offers to furnish materials of foreign origin upon the ground that such rejection is necessary to protect essential national security interests.

It is my conviction that exceptions under this provision of the Executive Order should be made only upon a clear showing that the payment of a greater differential than the Order provides for is justified by considerations of national security.

DWIGHT D. EISENHOWER

NOTE: This memorandum was addressed to Arthur S. Flemming, Director, Office of Defense Moblization.

The text of Executive Order 10582 is published in title 3 of the Code of Federal Regulations, 1954 Supplement.

68   ¶ Remarks to the Easter Egg Rollers on the South Grounds of the White House. *April* 11, 1955

GOOD MORNING, folks.

I didn't come out here to make you a talk.   I came out to welcome you to the White House grounds, to congratulate you on the weather you are having for the egg-rolling, and to hope that every youngster here has a wonderful time, and nobody gets lost.

Last year there were quite a number lost, but we found out it wasn't the children that were lost at all; it was just the parents.

This time I hope that everything will work out so that you can all stay together and have a wonderful time.

Mrs. Eisenhower is sorry she couldn't be here to say "Welcome," but I assure you that she feels that way.

So have a good time, and I hope it doesn't rain today.

Goodbye.   Thank you very much.

69   ¶ Statement by the President on the Mutual Security Program.   *April* 11, 1955

I SHALL submit to the Congress next week my recommendations for our nations mutual security program, including economic aid to the free nations of South and East Asia.

By tradition and conviction, our nation is committed to the independence and self-determination of all peoples. This determination, rooted in our own revolt against colonial status, is exemplified by our encouragement of Cuba and the Philippines to assume full freedom and control of their own destiny as independent nations.

The United States, moreover, is dedicated to the furtherance of opportunity for free nations to improve their economic well-being. We consistently encourage their efforts to meet the needs and to satisfy the aspirations of their peoples.

Throughout our history, and especially in the post-war years, the American people have made substantial personal sacrifices so that other peoples may enjoy internal stability and hope for the future. Cooperation has been offered by our people not to preserve the status quo but to encourage progress.

In accord with our political and spiritual heritage, the United States is ready to intensify its cooperation with the free nations of South and East Asia in their efforts to achieve economic development and a rising standard of living. This is in harmony with our programs elsewhere.

The motivation behind this cooperation is twofold: Our fixed belief in the worth and dignity of the human individual whatever his race or flag may be; and our dedication to the principle that the fruits of national growth must be widely shared in every society.

As a people, we insist that the dignity of the individual and his manifold rights require for their preservation a constantly expanding economic base. We are convinced that our own continued economic, cultural and spiritual progress are furthered by similar progress everywhere. For this reason we stand ready to work in genuine cooperation and partnership with the free peoples of the world—in a cooperation and partnership which does not exact from them any sacrifice of their independence, in thought or in action, but rather contributes to their progress and freedom as well as our own.

I will submit shortly certain recommendations to the Congress as a basis for our part in this cooperation.

We seek to evolve a consistent and stable economic policy which will assist free nations in their efforts to achieve a sound growth for their economies.

The peoples of the world, dedicated to the preservation of peace, recognize that man must go forward and that the interests of all free people are indivisible. America's foreign economic policy expresses that attitude.

NOTE: For the President's message to the Congress on the mutual security program, see Item 76, below.

70 ¶ Remarks at The Citadel, Charleston, South Carolina. *April* 12, 1955

General Clark, Members of this distinguished audience, and members of the Corps of Cadets of The Citadel:

I would need scarcely search for words in order to express to you something of the great feeling of honor I have in the receipt of this honor through such a distinguished institution and at the hands of one of my oldest friends in the military services. I am sure that you must feel yourselves how moved I am by the circumstances of this meeting.

Quite naturally, with my background, a ceremony such as this carries me back forty and more years. I see myself marching. Incidentally, I see myself again resenting the presence of VIP's that interrupted some vacation or period of my own and who had me out in full dress, marching for the edification of an audience and of that particular VIP.

There was one redeeming feature, occasionally, about such occasions. Sometimes this VIP had the wit and the knowledge to suggest to the Commander that it might be sort of recompense to the Corps if punishments were remitted. But of course that was in the years gone by, and I am not certain what the custom is now. And of course, I am not really familiar any longer with the rank of the individual that has the right to ask such a great favor. But, moreover, since I am now, by vicarious graduation, a sort of member of this body, whether or not he might consider it affrontery on my part to ask, I wouldn't know.

But passing those things, if I could attempt to leave with you young men a message this morning, it would be one truly of congratulation. I am informed that 95 percent of this graduating class is going into some element of the military services, either Reserves or Active. I suppose that that sort of percentage applies throughout the years. Certainly I have met many of your alumni throughout the years that I served with in the Army.

Now, what I want to speak to you for just a minute is of both the opportunities of men who are going into the Armed Services, Active and Inactive, and something about the scope of the responsibilities and problems that you will meet.

First of all, the opportunities. You are given that most priceless of opportunities: to work directly and specifically for the welfare of the United States of America, and there is no greater honor that is achievable by any American.

And secondly, what I want to say to you is the scope of the understanding you must achieve if you are now to do the task far transcends what your illustrious Commandant or Superintendent and I understood when we were waiting on the plain at West Point forty or more years ago receiving our diplomas and entered into the regular service.

Today, a man to do his duty in the military services must study humanity first of all—what makes humans tick. Not only as regards to your own companies, to be for them the leader and the model, but since you must be one of the principal apostles of peace, you must try to understand other people. You must try to understand the heart of America and how to translate that heart to other peoples. You must know something of economics, and of course your profession will make you know something of law and engineering and many of the sciences; but above all, we come back to it: you must try to understand people.

How else, I ask you, are we to achieve peace in this world, unless there be a magnificent growth of understanding? Mere knowledge is not enough. The highest star man in this Corps of Cadets, unless he strives for understanding and achieves understanding, by which to interpret and to relate among themselves all the facts that he may have learned in science and social science and the humanities, cannot be a leader.

And I know that in this institution just as in all others, we have our devoted educators trying to get over to all of their students that thought: let us strive to understand—understand each other, and our Nation to understand others, and help them to an understanding of ourselves.

I do not mean to say for an instant that all of these opportunities, all of these responsibilities—all of these things—are exclusive to the soldier, to the sailor, to the air man, to the Marine. Of course not. But since the man in the services holds up his right hand and swears to uphold the Constitution of the United States and to serve her to the depths of his ability, through life unto death, it comes home, possibly, to him a little more sharply than it does to others.

Now already, my friends, I have violated my promise that I was not going to keep you here long, but if I could just leave with you this thought: America is bound to watch you. They know you are a graduate of The Citadel. You know they know you have the early phases of your preparation for the highest form of citizenship. They are going to watch you. They will expect much of you.

And for my part, now that I know I am one of your alumni, I know you are going to succeed—each of you.

Thanks again for the great compliment of your review, and I think it would be not out of place to say that my eye since early youth has been accustomed to the sight of good soldiers—neat, soldierly-appearing people that show the evidences of training. I have seen no body that excels this one, and I congratulate you and all that are responsible for it. I congratulate the great State that supports you.

Good luck to you, and thanks again for this great honor.

NOTE: The President spoke on the Parade Grounds, immediately after receiving an honorary degree of Doctor of Laws. His opening words "General Clark" referred to General Mark W. Clark, President of The Citadel.

71 ¶ Letter to the Chairman of the Joint Committee on Atomic Energy on the Proposed Agreement for Cooperation with NATO on Atomic Information. *April* 13, 1955

Dear Senator Anderson:

Pursuant to Section 123 of the Atomic Energy Act of 1954, I hereby submit to the Joint Committee on Atomic Energy a proposed agreement for cooperation regarding the communication of atomic information to the North Atlantic Treaty Organization.

Under the terms of the proposed agreement, the United States will communicate to the North Atlantic Treaty Organization, so long as that Organization continues to make substantial and material contributions to the mutual defense effort, atomic information which the United States considers as necessary to

(1) the development of defense plans;

(2) the training of personnel in the employment of and defense against atomic weapons; and

(3) the evaluation of the capabilities of potential enemies in employment of atomic weapons.

Other members of the North Atlantic Treaty Organization agree to make atomic information available to the Organization on a similar basis.

Atomic information made available pursuant to the proposed agreement will not be transferred to unauthorized persons or beyond the jurisdiction of the North Atlantic Treaty Organization, and will be safeguarded by the stringent security regulations in force within the North Atlantic Treaty Organization. Under the terms of the proposed agreement, which will remain in force for the duration of the North Atlantic Treaty, transfers of atomic information by the United States will only be made in accordance with the Atomic Energy Act of 1954.

The North Atlantic Council strongly endorsed the proposed agreement, and I consider it to be a great stride forward in the strengthening of our common defense. It is my firm conviction that the proposed agreement will enable the North Atlantic Treaty Organization, consistent with the security and defense of the United States, to evolve more effective defense plans concerning the use of atomic weapons than have heretofore been achieved. Accordingly, I hereby determine that its performance will promote and will not constitute an unreasonable risk to the common defense and security, and approve the proposed agreement for cooperation. In addition, I hereby authorize, subject to the provisions of the Atomic Energy Act of 1954, the Honorable George W. Perkins, United States Permanent Representative to the North Atlantic Council, to execute the proposed agreement and the Department of Defense, with the assistance of the Atomic Energy Commission, to cooperate with the North Atlantic Treaty Organization and to communicate Restricted Data to that Organization under the agreement.

Sincerely,

DWIGHT D. EISENHOWER

NOTE: This letter to Clinton P. Anderson, Chairman, Joint Committee on Atomic Energy, was released at Augusta, Ga. Released at the same time was a letter to the President from the Secretary of Defense recommending approval of the proposed agreement. Secretary Wilson's letter and the proposed agreement are published in Senate Report 267 (84th Cong., 1st sess.).

72   ¶ Special Message to the Congress on United States Membership in the Proposed Organization for Trade Cooperation.   *April* 14, 1955

To the Congress of the United States:

The United States continuously seeks to strengthen the spiritual, political, military, and economic bonds of the free nations. By cementing these ties, we help preserve our way of life, improve the living standards of free peoples, and make possible the higher levels of production required for the security of the free world. With this objective in view, I recommended to the Congress in my message of January 10, 1955, the enactment of legislation designed to promote a healthy trade expansion and an increased flow of private capital for economic development abroad.

Consistent with that broad purpose, the United States over the past seven years has participated in the multilateral trade agreement known as the General Agreement on Tariffs and Trade. This key element in the nation's foreign economic policy has been carried on under the authority vested in the President by the Congress in the trade agreements legislation. After several months of intensive review of the trade rules in the General Agreement, the United States and 33 other participating countries last month agreed upon certain revisions of those rules. A new instrument was also drafted which would set up a simple international organization, to be known as the Organization for Trade Cooperation, whose purpose is the administration of the General Agreement.

I should like to recall the circumstances that gave rise to the General Agreement and this country's participation in it. I should also like to stress some of its benefits to us which justify the continued existence of the General Agreement and United States membership in the Organization for Trade Cooperation.

The economic and political dislocations produced by World

War II jeopardized, in the postwar years, the re-establishment of healthy, expanding international trade. Many countries had little to export and lacked the means to buy the products of other countries. Widespread resort to restrictions on imports and to discriminatory bilateral trade arrangements threatened a return to economic isolationism and narrow channels of government-directed trade. There was a great need for cooperative efforts to reduce unjustifiable trade restrictions and to establish a set of principles, mutually beneficial to the free nations of the world, for the reconstruction of world trade.

In this state of world affairs, the United States and a group of friendly nations negotiated a series of tariff agreements among themselves. They also negotiated a set of trade principles or rules to protect the tariff concessions. These tariff agreements and trade rules were incorporated in a multilateral trade agreement, the General Agreement on Tariffs and Trade.

The trade rules consist basically of provisions which this nation, since 1934, has incorporated in bilateral trade agreements to protect our interest in the tariff concessions granted to us in such agreements. They provide, for example, that tariff concessions should not be nullified by the imposition of other restrictions; that quantitative restrictions should not be imposed on imports; that trade restrictions, when used, should be nondiscriminatory as between countries; and that concessions granted to one country should be extended to like products of other countries in accordance with the unconditional most-favored-nation principle.

To provide the degree of flexibility required to meet the varying needs of participating countries, the General Agreement provides for specific exceptions to the basic rules. Under certain circumstances waivers may be granted to countries to depart from these basic rules. The United States has obtained such a waiver to restrict imports of agricultural products on which we have government programs.

The General Agreement through the trade rules and the tariff negotiations sponsored under it, has served well the purpose for which it was designed: the orderly expansion of international trade. Thirty-four countries, whose trade accounts for nearly four-fifths of the world's total trade, are now participating in this cooperative effort. World trade has expanded at a rapid rate, and for many countries foreign trade now represents a higher ratio to total output of goods than in the prewar years.

An important benefit to this country results from participation in multilateral trade negotiations under the General Agreement. Doing so makes it possible for us to obtain more tariff concessions on our exports than would be forthcoming from bilateral negotiation. This country, as a party to the multilateral agreement, obtains benefits from concessions which other countries would be unwilling to negotiate except in a multilateral undertaking.

Some measure of the value of these multilateral trade agreement negotiations to the United States is indicated by the fact that we have been able to obtain concessions covering about 50 percent in value of our exports.

Another advantage to this country through our participation in the General Agreement has been manifest during the past two years. Restrictions on the part of other countries against dollar imports are permitted under the trade rules for genuine balance of payments reasons, and as the balance of payments position of other countries has improved, we have been able to persuade them to relax such restrictions. Between 1953 and the beginning of 1955 ten Western European countries had removed quantitative restrictions on dollar imports amounting to about 60 percent of such imports. Since the beginning of this year additional restrictions have been removed. In the absence of the General Agreement it would be more difficult to persuade these countries to relax such controls. We are thus moving toward full realization of the tariff concessions that have been granted our exports since 1948. It is the policy of this Government to utilize the consultative procedures of the General Agreement to press for the discharge of these commitments for the benefit of our foreign trade.

In addition to the general relaxation of restrictions on dollar imports that has been accomplished, we have been successful in persuading other countries to remove discriminatory restrictions against imports of particular dollar goods. This Government has protested the inconsistency between the discriminatory action in those cases and the principles of the General Agreement. Certain discriminatory restrictions have thus been removed on imports from this country of such items as coal, apples, cigarettes, lumber, potatoes, textiles, automobiles, tobacco, petroleum, wool, and motion pictures.

A further important contribution of the General Agreement to the extension of trade is the assurance against wholesale increases in tariff rates in export markets. Our exporters, therefore, can proceed with their plans for sales in markets abroad with a greater degree of certainty as to tariff rates. Participating countries may, of course, consistently with the trade rules, raise tariff rates in individual cases where serious injury to domestic industry is threatened.

The revised General Agreement has been thoroughly reviewed within the Executive Branch of the Government. I believe it has been improved and strengthened. It protects the legitimate interests of this country and provides a firm basis for orderly trade expansion among the free nations of the world. The necessity for the United States to restrict imports of agricultural products with regard to which we have government programs is fully recognized. The right of this country to protect the legitimate interests of its industries and labor is clearly provided for. The rules of trade regarding the imposition of discriminatory import controls have been tightened and should assist in the efforts to remove and to prevent discriminatory restrictions against United States exports. The spirit with which the participating countries cooperated in the task of review and revision of the General Agreement was heartening and augurs well for its future vitality.

The United States and the other participating countries concluded on the basis of seven years' experience that the organizational provisions of the General Agreement should be changed to provide a continuous mechanism for the administration of the trade rules and the discussion of mutual trade problems. Under present arrangements these activities are confined largely to the annual sessions of the parties to the Agreement. The participating countries therefore have proposed to set up an Organization for Trade Cooperation for more effective administration of the trade rules and related activities.

The Organization for Trade Cooperation would be established by a separate agreement among the participating countries. In addition to administering the General Agreement, it would provide a mechanism through which arrangements for trade negotiations could be facilitated. It would also serve as a forum for the discussion of trade matters and for the amicable adjustment of problems involving the trade rules. The Organization would have no supra-national powers. It would conduct no trade negotiations; this would be done by the countries who choose to participate in the negotiations and to whatever extent they choose.

The United States delegation which took part in the revision of the General Agreement was specifically instructed to reject all efforts to expand the functions of the new organization into fields other than trade. One measure of the success of the negotiations from the standpoint of the United States is the fact that the proposed Organization for Trade Cooperation is thus limited in its functions. Its effectiveness, in my judgment, will be enhanced by the fact that it has such specific and limited responsibilities.

I believe the reasons for United States membership in the proposed Organization are overwhelming. We would thus demonstrate to the free world our active interest in the promotion of trade among the free nations. We would demonstrate our desire to deal with matters of trade in the same cooperative way we do with military matters in such regional pacts as the North Atlantic Treaty Organization, and with financial matters in the International Monetary Fund and in the International Bank for Reconstruction and Development. We would thus cooperate further with the free world, in the struggle against Communist domination, to the greater security and the greater prosperity of all.

Such action would serve the enlightened self-interest of the United States. As a member of this Organization we could work more effectively for the removal of discriminatory restrictions against our exports. We could help establish conditions favorable to convertibility of currencies. We could further the expansion of markets abroad for the products of our mines, our farms and our factories. We could assist in the development of conditions conducive to the international flow of investment capital so urgently needed to expand production throughout the free world, especially in its underdeveloped areas.

Failure to assume membership in the Organization for Trade Cooperation would be interpreted throughout the free world as a lack of genuine interest on the part of this country in the efforts to expand trade. It would constitute a serious setback to the momentum which has been generated toward that objective. It would strike a severe blow at the development of cooperative arrangements in defense of the free world. It could lead to the imposition of new trade restrictions on the part of other countries, which would result in a contraction of world trade and constitute a sharp setback to United States exports. It could result in regional re-alignments of nations. Such developments, needless to say, would play directly into the hands of the Communists.

I believe the national interest requires that we join with other countries of the free world in dealing with our trade problems on a cooperative basis.

I herewith transmit copies of the agreement providing for an Organization for Trade Cooperation, and I recommend that the Congress enact legislation authorizing United States membership in that organization.

DWIGHT D. EISENHOWER

NOTE: The President's message of January 10, referred to in the first paragraph, appears as Item 6, above. The text of the agreement providing for an Organization for Trade Cooperation is printed in House Document 140 (84th Cong., 1st sess.).

The message was released at Augusta, Ga.

73 ¶ Telegram to Senator Thurmond Saluting James F. Byrnes as a Great American.
April 16, 1955

The Honorable Strom Thurmond
c/o Aiken Chamber of Commerce
Aiken, South Carolina

Please give my warm greetings to your guest of honor, Jimmy Byrnes. I am fortunate to count him my good friend and with countless others salute him as a great American.

DWIGHT D. EISENHOWER

NOTE: This telegram was sent in connection with a testimonial dinner given Mr. Byrnes by the Aiken Chamber of Commerce. It was released at Augusta, Ga.

74 ¶ Letter to Secretary Dulles Regarding Transfer of the Affairs of the Foreign Operations Administration to the Department of State.
April 17, 1955

[Released April 17, 1955. Dated April 15, 1955]

Dear Mr. Secretary:

The Mutual Security Act of 1954 provides for termination of the Foreign Operations Administration by June 30th of this year. Accordingly, I shall issue within a few days an Executive Order transferring the affairs of the Foreign Operations Administration, except for certain military functions which are charged to the Defense Department, to the Department of State as of June 30,

1955. Any subsequent transfers, modifications or elimination of functions, or other organizational changes, that should be determined advisable or necessary, prior to June 30, under the guide lines given here, will be covered in a supplementary Executive Order.

The Foreign Operations Administration established two years ago, was intended to centralize all governmental operations, as distinguished from policy formulation, that had as their purpose the cooperative development of economic and military strength among the nations of the free world. That function it has performed well, but the Foreign Operations Administration has been regarded by many as merely a temporary unit of government, established solely to meet certain short-term economic and military requirements. It has come to be widely recognized, however, that the functions and the need for cooperative development of economic and military strength among the free nations are continuing and integral parts of the fabric of our international relations. The new organization is intended to reflect this public recognition.

The placing of general responsibility for economic operations as well as for policy in this field within the Department of State offers assurance that, under a permanent government establishment, we are providing a long-range basis for this kind of international cooperation. It is emphatic recognition of the principle that the security and welfare of the United States are directly related to the economic and social advancement of all peoples who share our concern for the freedom, dignity, and well-being of the individual.

In the reorganization of Mutual Security activities two years ago, there was set forth a number of applicable basic considerations. In our discussions of recent weeks we have agreed that those considerations are still valid and should apply to the new organization and to the new administrative arrangements in the Department of State. This letter summarizes our discussions of these matters and of the arrangements which should govern the future operations of the Mutual Security program.

Two years ago I stated that the Secretary of State, under the President, must be the official responsible for the development and control of foreign policy and all relations with foreign governments, to include policies affecting mutual security. The policy authority then fixed in the Secretary of State is now extended to include supervising authority over operations. The Executive Order will provide for this.

It also was stated that related Mutual Security operations should be brought together in a single organization under a single management. Consistent with this approach we should avoid dispersal of operating responsibilities either within the Department or to agencies outside the Department.

A third objective stated in 1953 was the freeing of the Secretary of State from operating responsibilities so that he, assisted by his Under Secretary, could devote a preponderance of attention to foreign policy. These two important considerations are recognized in the Executive Order which will assign maximum responsibilities to a single key official within the Department of State.

In accordance with these organizational guide lines, the following administrative arrangements will obtain within the Department of State:

1. A new semi-autonomous organizational unit, to be known as the International Cooperation Administration, will be established in the Department of State, to carry out the transferred functions.

2. Provision will be made for a Director of the International Cooperation Administration who will be the key official within the State Department referred to above.

3. The Director of the International Cooperation Administration will report directly to the Secretary of State and will, on the Secretary's behalf, give supervision and direction to the Mutual Security operations performed within the State Department.

4. Except for those matters which, because of their nature, require final decision by the President, the Secretary of State will

be responsible for coordinating all Mutual Security programs, which will of course include the establishment of arrangements with the Secretary of Defense for effectively coordinating Mutual Security programs involving the Department of Defense.

5. Since time is pressing, it is essential that the work of reorganization begin without delay. The key to success is the individual selected to head the new Bureau within your Department. He must be a man of such stature and standing and of such operational experience that you can trust him with full responsibility in the field of operations, so as to minimize the demands upon your own time.

If such a man is now known to you and available for the position, please recommend him to me promptly. If you need more time in the selection of a qualified person, then I request that you get in touch immediately with Mr. Joseph M. Dodge, who has been acting for me in working out the general principles of this reorganization, so that with him you may devise and set up temporary machinery fitted and empowered to begin at once the work of reorganization.

6. I am instructing the Director of the Bureau of the Budget and my Advisory Committee on Government Organization, in connection with their general responsibilities for advising me on Executive Branch organization, to give close attention to the new organizational arrangements and to recommend such organizational improvements as will be considered appropriate.

7. Any advisable or necessary changes in organization and personnel should be accomplished in a manner that will ensure equitable treatment to the Government personnel employed in the Administration of the transferred programs.

8. The appropriations for all the Mutual Security programs for the fiscal year 1956 should be made to the President, who will, as in the past, delegate the allocation of funds and other authorities to the appropriate agencies, at the same time setting certain limits on their exercise and reserving certain determinations to himself.

No major reorganization of this character can be accomplished quickly and to attempt to do so could jeopardize the implementation of existing programs which are so important to our relations with other nations. The Foreign Operations Administration has a large staff which operates in many countries and administers a number of different but related programs. It will take a minimum of six months to effectuate the desirable changes without unnecessarily disturbing projects and programs now under way.

It will, therefore, be necessary to obtain as part of the legislation to extend the Mutual Security programs beyond June 30, 1955, authority similar to Section 525 of the existing Act which would give flexibility, for a period of at least six months after the effective date of the transfer of the Foreign Operations Administration.

Sincerely,

DWIGHT D. EISENHOWER

NOTE: On May 9 the President issued Executive Order 10610 (3 CFR, 1955 Supp.), transferring the affairs of the Foreign Operations Administration to the Department of State. On May 25 John B. Hollister was nominated as Director of the newly created International Cooperation Administration.

This letter was released at Augusta, Ga.

75 ¶ Statement by the President on the Death of Albert Einstein. *April* 18, 1955

FOR TWENTY-TWO years, the United States has been the freely-chosen home of Albert Einstein. For fifteen years, he has been a citizen of the United States by his own free and deliberate choice. Americans welcomed him here. Americans were proud, too, that he sought and found here a climate of freedom in his search for knowledge and truth.

No other man contributed so much to the vast expansion of twentieth century knowledge. Yet no other man was more modest in the possession of the power that is knowledge, more sure that power without wisdom is deadly. To all who live in the nuclear age, Albert Einstein exemplified the mighty creative ability of the individual in a free society.

76   ¶ Special Message to the Congress on the Mutual Security Program.   *April* 20, 1955

To the Congress of the United States:

I recommend that the Congress authorize, for the Fiscal Year ending June 30, 1956, the Program for Mutual Security outlined in this message. The program reflects the greatly improved conditions in Europe and provides for the critical needs of Asia. It encourages private overseas investment and private enterprise abroad, fosters an increase in cooperative effort, emphasizes loans rather than grants wherever possible. I consider the program an indispensable part of a realistic and enlightened national policy.

The fixed, unwavering objective of that policy is a just, prosperous, enduring peace. On this fundamental position, we base our broad approach toward our world trade, our military alliances, our exchange of information and of persons, our partnership with free nations through the Mutual Security Program. This partnership is rooted in the facts of economic and defense interdependence and also in the understanding and respect of each partner for the cultural and national aspirations of the other.

The recommendations in this message are an essential complement to the foreign economic program outlined in my message of January 10, 1955. That program is designed to develop the economic strength and the security of the free world through healthy trade expansion among the free nations and through an increased flow of investment capital particularly to underdeveloped areas. The lessening of barriers to trade in the free world is a vital component for the successful implementation of our national policy for security and peace.

We must recognize, however, that certain free world countries, because of the aftermath of war and its continuing threat or because of less developed economies, require assistance which will help them achieve stable national health and essential defensive strength.   The Mutual Security Program is designed to deal with these specific problems in the national interest and in the cause of peace.   The program stands on its demonstrated worth.

Its cumulative success is especially evident in Western Europe today.   The free nations there have attained new levels of production, larger volumes of trade, expanded employment, and rising standards of living.   They have established strong defense forces which, although deficient in some respects, now constitute a significant deterrent to aggression and add substantially to the free world's defensive power.   Their own national efforts and their cooperation with each other are the prime reasons for their success.   However, the United States Mutual Security Program and its predecessor, the European Recovery Program, deserve an important portion of the credit.

The program I now recommend to you for Fiscal Year 1956 proposes no economic aid for the original Marshall Plan countries in Western Europe.   These nations are capable of meeting current defense goals without such support.   Deliveries of arms from previous appropriations will continue under constant review to insure that the latest weapon developments and strategic thinking are taken into account.   Our initial contribution toward the arming of German forces is already funded by previous Congressional action.

In Spain and Yugoslavia, which were not in the Marshall Plan, defense programs can be successful only with further strengthening of their economic base.   New appropriations are needed to continue our cooperation with them.   Likewise the special circumstances of the city of Berlin require continued support for that outpost of freedom.

But the immediate threats to world security and stability are now centered in Asia. The preponderance of funds requested of the Congress will be used to meet the threat there. Within the vast arc of free Asia, which extends from the Republic of Korea and Japan to the Middle East, 770 million people, one-third of the world's population, reside. Most of them are citizens of newly independent states. Some have been engaged in recent war against the Communists. All are threatened. Capital is very scarce. Technical and administrative skill is limited. Within the area, however, abundant resources and fertile lands are ready for development.

Now is the time for accelerated development of the nations along the arc. The major responsibility must necessarily lie with the countries themselves. At best, foreign capital as well as foreign aid can only launch or stimulate the process of creating dynamic economies. In this light, the United States has the capacity, the desire, the concern to take the lead in friendly help for free Asia.

For example, we can assist in providing and mobilizing capital for useful and constructive development. We can encourage our successful private industry to join with the people of free Asia in building their private industry and facilitate the way. We can consult and advise on the means by which a free nation builds upon the initiative of independent farmers to achieve a steady advance toward better standards of living, in contrast to the mounting failures of collectivist agriculture.

It is clear that most of the nations of free Asia prefer to quicken their cooperative march toward these objectives through the Colombo Plan Consultative Group which was established in 1950 to promote mutual economic development. We welcome this initiative. As a member of the Group, we shall continue to work in strengthening its cooperative efforts.

The varied nature of national situations requires that our cooperation be essentially bilateral. Some of the nations are members of the Manila Pact and their treaty obligations give rise to special economic problems. Most are members of the Colombo Plan. Most, except for Japan, have very little industrial capacity.

The requested authorization includes substantial funds to further our mutual objectives in this area. Of these funds I suggest that we can achieve the maximum return if $200 million is set aside for the establishment of a President's Fund for Asian Economic Development, with broad rules enacted by Congress for its use through loans and grants, and with adequate latitude to meet changing circumstances and to take advantage of constructive opportunities.

To help assure the most effective use of these funds, this appropriation should be available for use over a period of years. Wisdom and economy in their use cannot be achieved through speed. A small, firm, annual commitment out of this $200 million may prove in many instances to be the most fruitful method.

Because of the continuing threat of aggression and subversion in Asia, a large part of the amounts requested for military assistance and direct forces support is to build and maintain the defensive forces of our allies there. This includes the substantial costs of maintaining and improving the defenses of the Nationalist Government of China in Formosa and provides for military equipment and supplies for Korea.

The newly achieved stability in Iran has decreased the Communist threat and has opened the way to the use of oil resources. These eventually will bring revenues to the nation for the further development of the land and the opening of new opportunities for its people. Pending resumption of sufficient revenues from oil, however, limited defense and economic support must be provided.

In the Near East, our stalwart North Atlantic Treaty Organization allies, Greece and Turkey, are both making significant progress. But neither of them can alone support the substantial armed forces which they maintain for their own defense and for the NATO force goals in that area. Their initiative in promoting security arrangements in the Balkans, and Turkey's vigorous efforts for Middle East defense, reinforce the need for continued support of their efforts. Iraq's action in joining with Turkey in a defensive security arrangement is another favorable development.

The continuing tension between the Arab States and Israel handicaps the peoples of all Near East nations. We should continue to work with the governments and peoples on both sides to improve their economic status and accelerate their progress toward lasting peace between them. Our cooperation is beginning to bring results, particularly in the development of water resources. Such developments in the Palestine area can go far to remove present causes of tension.

In the vast continent of Africa the long-range effect of our cooperation is extremely significant. This continent and its resources, the progress of its people and their relationship to the free world are of growing importance. Requested appropriations for this area are needed in the effort to promote welfare and growth for the peoples of Africa.

In Latin America, I recommend intensification of our technical cooperation program. In this area, more than a decade ago, technical cooperation was first undertaken in a systematic manner. The programs have proved their high value in many of our sister republics. No international programs have ever had such widespread welcome and support. Indispensable to the economic development of many free nations, they also reflect the deep humanitarian spirit of the American people.

Technical cooperation programs have contributed effectively to the efforts of the other American Republics to strengthen and expand their national economies. These efforts have likewise been aided by our very large inter-American trade, substantial private investment, more extensive lending by the Export-Import Bank, and credits by the International Bank for Reconstruction and Development. As a result, Latin America has achieved a remarkable rate of economic development. In addition to the technical cooperation programs for Latin America, I recommend a continuation of our modest contribution to the Organization of American States and further economic support to meet the critical situations in Guatemala and Bolivia.

Our programs of national action are not in any manner a substitute for United Nations action in similar fields. Every instance of effective measures taken through the United Nations on a human problem improves the ultimate prospect of peace in the world. Therefore, I strongly recommend that the United Nations Technical Assistance Program, in which sixty governments participate and which is carried out by the United Nations and its specialized agencies be supported in a continuing and adequate manner. The United Nations Children's Fund has carried out an especially appealing and significant work. We have done our full share to make this work possible. We should continue to do so.

Persons who have escaped from totalitarian oppression, often at great peril, and refugees uprooted by war and disaster deserve further support in 1956 through programs administered by the United States, the United Nations, and the Intergovernmental Committee for European Migration.

One of the unique, least expensive, and most fruitful aspects of the Mutual Security Program is the participation, largely in humanitarian projects, of forty-seven voluntary organizations representing many millions of our citizens. These organizations do an exceptionally effective work in helping the escapees and refugees become self-supporting. They distribute large quantities of food on a people-to-people basis. But certain costs for transporting food, and for supplies beyond their own voluntary resources, are needed and should be provided.

In total, for Fiscal Year 1956, I recommend that the Congress approve funds totaling $3,530 million for the Mutual Security Program, as proposed in the Budget Message. Of this amount $712.5 million is for economic programs, including $172 million for a continuation of Technical Cooperation programs, $175.5 million for special programs, $165 million for development assistance, $200 million for the special President's Fund. $100 million is for a worldwide contingency fund. I request $1,000.3 million for Defense Support which serves both economic and defense purposes by supplementing the efforts of countries, particularly in Asia, carrying out defensive measures beyond their current financial capacity. $1,717.2 million is for military assistance and direct forces support. Included in this amount is $500 million to cover expected losses to present military assistance programs by operation of the Supplemental Appropriation Act, 1955.

The Foreign Operations Administration has proved to be an effective and efficient instrument for conducting the Mutual Security Program. An able and devoted group of men and women have successfully conducted the program under direct line authority from the President.

The Congress provided in the Mutual Security Act of 1954 for the termination of the Foreign Operations Administration by June 30 of this year. As I indicated in my letter to the Secretary of State of April 15, I shall issue an Executive Order effective June 30, 1955, transferring the affairs of the Foreign Operations Administration to the Department of State, except for certain military aspects which will be transferred to the Department of Defense.

This transfer to permanent Departments of the Government will reflect the significance of this program as an integral part of our foreign policy. In the implementation of the program, the facilities of all agencies of the Executive Branch will be used where appropriate, and to the maximum possible extent on a contract basis. However, it is essential that responsibility for the non-military operations continue unified; to fragment this responsibility among several agencies would seriously detract from their effectiveness. The reorganization will continue the role of the Institute of Inter-American Affairs in carrying out cooperative programs for the advancement of the well-being of the peoples in the other American Republics.

The continuity of operations and the adjustments of internal relationships within the Department of State after June 30, 1955, will require a period of transition. I recommend that the Mutual Security Act of 1955 include broad authority to revise the organization during a period of six months following June 30, 1955.

The International Cooperation Administration will be a new semi-autonomous unit within the Department of State. Its Director will report directly to the Secretary of State and will, on the Secretary's behalf, give supervision and direction to the mutual security operations performed within the Department of State.

This responsibility will require that the International Cooperation Administration have the capacity to make and carry out operating decisions within broad policy guides established by the Secretary of State. It will likewise require that the Director of the International Cooperation Administration have his own complement of supporting staff and program personnel, both in Washington and in the field. It will be his responsibility to assure that appropriate policy guide-lines are secured from the Secretary of State, and within those guide-lines he will issue the necessary instructions to the field to carry out its policy.

Based on the experience of the past two years, three out of every four dollars appropriated for the entire Mutual Security Program will be immediately spent within the United States for commodities, services, machinery, and other items. Insofar as feasible and consistent with the effective meeting of our goals overseas, the commodities will include food, cotton, coal, and other goods for which our capacity or surplus supply most readily matches requirements. Approximately $350 million of agricultural products are expected to be used in the Fiscal Year 1955. This includes a significant export of major surplus crops. Shipments under the Mutual Security Program will be in addition to but coordinated with sales of surplus agricultural commodities for foreign currencies under the Agricultural Trade Development and Assistance Act.

The other twenty-five percent of the dollars will be spent overseas in a manner that will add directly to the accomplishments of the Mutual Security Program.   For example, the offshore procurement contracts assist in establishing a defense production base in key points in the free world.   In addition, these expenditures will indirectly add to the power of other nations subsequently to purchase with these dollars other needed goods from the United States.

I recommend continuance of the authority in the present Mutual Security Act to meet unexpected events by transfer of funds, appropriated for one geographic area or purpose, to another geographic area or purpose.   Experience in recent years has demonstrated that flexible authority is highly desirable to move with dispatch to meet new circumstances, to overcome new dangers, or to capitalize upon favorable developments.

New procedures approved by the Congress last year now make possible maximum integration of domestic procurement of military equipment for our own and allied forces, increased flexibility in the flow of military equipment to our allies and greatly simplified procurement and accounting arrangements.   Under the new procedures, the military departments procure most of the equipment for this program as a part of their regular procurement operations, with military assistance funds reserved to repay the Services at the time the equipment is delivered.   Under present law, military assistance funds which are reserved remain available for obligation and expenditure until June 30, 1957.   To further improve the present arrangements, I recommend that current and proposed military assistance funds be made available until expended, as is now provided in the case of most Department of Defense appropriations for procurement.

In conclusion, I wish again to emphasize the essential role of the Mutual Security Program.   The program for the arc of free Asia has had a thorough review by all the Departments of the Government concerned, and it has been recommended to me by the Council on Foreign Economic Policy and the National Security Council after extensive study.

We are making renewed and intensified efforts to develop a successful basic policy on the question of disarmament and we will persist in this effort. But until success is assured beyond doubt, the best prospects of peace and the grim essentials of security together demand the continuance of both our national and mutual defense programs.

The other free nations need the United States, and we need them, if all are to be secure. Here is a clear case of interwoven self-interest. The necessary expenditures to equip and maintain United States armed forces of air and land and sea at strategic points beyond our borders are never called aid. The necessary expenditures to enable other free nations associated with us to equip and maintain vital armed forces at these same strategic points beyond our borders should not be considered as aid. These, in fact, are defense alliance expenditures clearly safeguarding in the most desirable manner, and at times in the only possible way, the security of the United States and of other free nations.

Our economy cannot be strong and continue to expand without the development of healthy economic conditions in other free nations, and without a continuous expansion of international trade. Neither can we be secure in our freedom unless, elsewhere in the world, we help to build the conditions under which freedom can flourish by destroying the conditions under which totalitarianism grows—poverty, illiteracy, hunger and disease. Nor can we hope for enduring peace until the spiritual aspirations of mankind for liberty and opportunity and growth are recognized as prior to and paramount to the material appetites which Communism exploits.

Apart from any obstacles created by the Communists, this is a long-term process. Patience, resourcefulness and dedication are required as well as the creative application of knowledge, skill and material resources to the solution of fundamental human problems, ancient in their origin. In that spirit, the Mutual Security Program is designed for the benefit of all free nations.

DWIGHT D. EISENHOWER

77 ¶ Citation Presented to Dr. Jonas E. Salk and Accompanying Remarks. *April* 22, 1955

[Citation read by the President]

BECAUSE of a signal and historic contribution to human welfare by Dr. Jonas E. Salk in his development of a vaccine to prevent paralytic poliomyelitis, I, Dwight D. Eisenhower, President of the United States, on behalf of the people of the United States, present to him this citation for his extraordinary achievement.

The work of Dr. Salk is in the highest tradition of selfless and dedicated medical research. He has provided a means for the control of a dread disease. By helping scientists in other countries with technical information; by offering to them the strains of seed virus and professional aid so that the production of vaccine can be started by them everywhere; by welcoming them to his laboratory that they may gain a fuller knowledge, Dr. Salk is a benefactor of mankind.

His achievement, a credit to our entire scientific community, does honor to all the people of the United States.

[Remarks of the President]

Dr. Salk, before I hand you this Citation, I should like to say to you that when I think of the countless thousands of American parents and grandparents who are hereafter to be spared the agonizing fears of the annual epidemic of poliomyelitis, when I think of all the agony that these people will be spared seeing their loved ones suffering in bed, I must say to you I have no words in which adequately to express the thanks of myself and all the people I know—all 164 million Americans, to say nothing

of all the people in the world that will profit from your discovery.
I am very, very happy to hand this to you.

NOTE: The President spoke in the Rose Garden, following the intro- duction of Dr. Salk by Secretary Hobby.

78 ¶ Citation Presented to the National Foundation for Infantile Paralysis and Accompanying Remarks. *April* 22, 1955

[Citation read by the President]

I, DWIGHT D. EISENHOWER, President of the United States, present this special citation to the National Foundation for Infantile Paralysis for its unswerving devotion to the eradication of poliomyelitis.

The American people recognize a debt of gratitude to the Foundation and to its founder, the late President Franklin D. Roosevelt, whose personal courage in overcoming the handicap of poliomyelitis stands as a symbol of the fight against this disease.

Without the support and encouragement of the Foundation, the work of Dr. Jonas E. Salk and of many others who contributed to the development of a preventive vaccine could not have gone forward so rapidly. The Foundation displayed remarkable faith in sponsoring and determination in fostering their valiant effort for the health of all mankind.

The generous voluntary support of the Foundation by the American people has been dramatically justified. In their name, I am privileged to make this award to the National Foundation for Infantile Paralysis.

[Remarks of the President following the presentation of the citation to Basil O'Connor, President of the Foundation]

And there, of course, remains the great problem of rapid production, distribution on the fairest possible basis, and to that problem as Secretary Hobby has said, you and many others are working and contributing to carry the thing forward until there is no more poliomyelitis remaining in the United States. And I thank you and all of the Foundation of which you are President.

NOTE: The President spoke in the Rose Garden. Mr. O'Connor was introduced by Secretary Hobby.

79 ¶ Address at the Annual Luncheon of the Associated Press, New York City. *April* 25, 1955

Mr. McLean, Mrs. Secretary Hobby, and ladies and gentlemen:

Always, I feel it is a special privilege when I can meet with men and women of the newspaper profession. Our newspapers have traditionally been a guarantee that truth will reach every part of our own country and all the free peoples of the world. I have heard you referred to as a one-party press. If this is true, I do trust that the slogan, the purpose, the aim of your party is to spread the truth. If that is so, I apply for membership. Never was it more important than it is today that the people of the entire world have free access to the truth.

Recently I read a story about one particular segment of the newspaper community of America and how it helped spread the truth even beyond the barriers devised against its communication—into the homes of the Communist-dominated lands.

Some twenty thousand newspaper boys voluntarily conducted a fund-raising campaign for the Crusade for Freedom. That Crusade brings truth to those behind the Iron Curtain, to people who otherwise could not have it. Of course, the boys' campaign is not one of the normal functions of the American newspapers— but the incident gives heartening evidence of newspaper people's unflagging interest in the maintenance of freedom and of human hope for peace.

Certainly, I am inspired by the knowledge that boys of this nation will freely give of their time and their energy—and more important, their hearts—to help bring information of today's world to those whose masters provide them nothing but propaganda.

In this day, every resource of free men must be mustered if we are to remain free; every bit of our wit, our courage and our dedication must be mobilized if we are to achieve genuine peace. There is no age nor group nor race that cannot somehow help.

Just over two years ago I had an opportunity to appear before the American Society of Newspaper Editors. I then pledged your Government to an untiring search for a just peace as a fixed and abiding objective. In our search for peace we are not bound by slavish adherence to precedent or halted by the lack of it. The spirit of this search influences every action of your Administration; it affects every solution to problems of the moment.

It prompted my proposal before the General Assembly of the United Nations that governments make joint contributions of fissionable materials to an International Atomic Energy Agency for peaceful research—so that the miraculous inventiveness of man may be consecrated to his fuller life.

It inspired last week's offer of polio information, research facilities and seed virus—so that Dr. Salk's historic accomplishment may free all mankind from a physical scourge.

It provides the reason for a plan that, after lengthy study, I am able now to announce. We have added to the United States Program for Peaceful Uses of Atomic Energy an atomic-powered merchant ship. The Atomic Energy Commission and the Maritime Administration are now developing specifications. I shall shortly submit to the Congress a request for the necessary funds, together with a description of the vessel.

The new ship, powered with an atomic reactor, will not require refueling for scores of thousands of miles of operation. Visiting the ports of the world, it will demonstrate to people everywhere this peacetime use of atomic energy, harnessed for the improvement of human living. In part, also, the ship will be an atomic exhibit; carrying to all people practical knowledge of the usefulness of this new science in such fields as medicine, agriculture and power production.

The search for peace likewise underlies the plan developed for expanding foreign trade embodied in H.R. No. 1 now before the Congress.

In every possible way, in word and in deed, we shall strive to bring to all men the truth of our assertion that we seek only a just and a lasting peace.

There is no precedent for the nature of the struggle of our time.

Every day, in our newspapers, we are confronted with what is probably the greatest paradox of history.

Out of an instinctive realization of the horror of nuclear war the hunger of virtually every human being on this planet is for tranquil security, for an opportunity to live and to let live, for freedom, for peace. And yet, defying this universal hunger, certain dictatorships have engaged in a deliberately conceived drive which periodically creates alarms and fears of war.

In our uneasy postwar world, crises are a recurrent international diet; their climaxes come and go. But so they have—in some degree—since the beginning of organized society. By their effect on human action, the peril within them is either magnified or diminished.

A crisis may be fatal when, by it, unstable men are stampeded into headlong panic. Then—bereft of common sense and wise judgment—they too hastily resort to armed force in the hope of crushing a threatening foe, although thereby they impoverish the world and may forfeit the hope for enduring peace.

But a crisis may likewise be deadly when inert men—unsure of themselves and their cause—are smothered in despair. Then, grasping at any straw of appeasement, they sell a thousand tomorrows for the pottage of a brief escape from reality.

But a crisis is also the sharpest goad to the creative energies of men, particularly when they recognize it as a challenge to their very resource, and move to meet it in faith, in thought, in courage.

Then, greatly aroused—yet realizing that beyond the immediate danger lie vast horizons—they can act for today in the light of generations still to come.

The American people, one hundred sixty-four million of us, must recognize that the unprecedented crises of these days— packed with danger though they may be—are in fullest truth challenges that can be met and will be met to the lasting good of our country and to the world.

Two great American objectives are mountain peaks that tower above the foothills of lesser goals. One is global peace based on justice, mutual respect and cooperative partnership among the nations. The other is an expanding American economy whose benefits, widely shared among all our citizens, will make us even better able to cooperate with other friendly nations in their economic advancement and our common prosperity.

The fundamental hazard to the achievement of both objectives is the implacable enmity of godless communism. That hazard becomes the more fearsome as we are guilty of failure among ourselves; failure to seek out and face facts courageously; failure to make required sacrifices for the common good; failure to look beyond our selfish interests of the moment; failure to seek long-term betterment for all our citizens.

Recognizing the ruthless purposes of international communism, we must assure, above all else, our own national safety. At the same time we must continue to appeal to the sense of logic and decency of all peoples to work with us in the development of some kind of sane arrangement for peace.

But when a nation speaks alone, its appeal may fall on deaf ears. Many nations must combine their voices to penetrate walls of fear and prejudice, and selfishness and ignorance.

The principal objective of our foreign policy, therefore, as we search for peace, is the construction of the strongest possible coalition among free nations. The coalition must possess spiritual, intellectual, material strength.

In things spiritual, the common effort must be inspired by fairness and justice, by national pride and self-respect. It must be based on the inalienable rights of the individual who—made in the image of his Creator—is endowed with a dignity and destiny immeasurable by the materialistic yardstick of communism.

In things intellectual, the coalition must manifest such common sense and evident logic that all nations may see in it an opportunity to benefit themselves. Certainly, it must proclaim the right of all men to strive for their own betterment—and it must foster their exercise of that right.

In things material, the friendly partnership must be sinewed by expanded economies within all its member nations, mutually benefiting by a growing trade volume that must be joined in realization that their security interdependence is paralleled by their economic interdependence.

By sound economic thinking and action, we Americans can hasten the achievement of both our great goals—peace among the nations; a widely shared prosperity at home.

We have an unmatched production system. But even our economy will not thrive if confined to our own land. So to sustain our own prosperity and economic growth we must strengthen the economic bonds between us and others of the free world. Thus we confront the communist with a vast and voluntary partnership of vigorous, expanding national economies whose aggregate power and productivity, always increasing, can never be successfully challenged by the communist world.

The issue is clean-cut. Either we foster flourishing trade between the free nations or we weaken the free world and our own economy. Unless trade links these nations together, our foreign policy will be encased in a sterile vacuum; our domestic economy will shrink within its continental fences. The enlargement of mutually beneficial trade in the free world is an objective to which all of us should be fully dedicated.

Ours is the most dynamic economy yet devised by man, a progress-sharing economy whose advance benefits every man, woman and child living within it.

Last year, our Gross National Product exceeded 357 billion dollars. Twenty years ago few would have believed such an achievement even a remote possibility.

Nevertheless, continuation of current rates of increase will bring us by 1965 to 500 billion dollars or more as our Gross National Product. This will mean a tremendous advance in the living standards of the American people.

But a 500 billion dollar economy by 1965 can be achieved only within the framework of a healthy and expanding free world economy.

Trade expands markets for the increased output of our mines, our farms and our factories. In return we obtain essential raw materials and needed products of the farms and factories of others. Likewise, the markets provided here for the products of other free world countries enable them to acquire from us capital equipment and consumer goods essential to their economic development and higher living standards.

American agriculture sells abroad from one-fourth to one-third of major crops such as wheat, cotton and tobacco. Without these export markets there can be, under current conditions, no enduring prosperity for the American farmer.

American factories and labor likewise have an important stake in foreign trade. Last year this country sold over 9 billion dollars of industrial products abroad. Over 3 million workers—American workers—are directly dependent on exports for their jobs. Jungles the world round are being tamed today by American bulldozers; new mines are being opened by our drills and equipment; fields that have been cultivated by hand for centuries are yielding new harvests to our agricultural machines; our automobiles, trucks and buses are found wherever there are roads; and new industries to employ the teeming millions within the underdeveloped nations are being equipped with our machine tools.

The expansion of our foreign trade should proceed on an orderly basis. Reductions in tariffs and other trade barriers, both here and abroad, must be gradual, selective and reciprocal. Changes which would result in the threat of serious injury to industry or general reduction in employment would not strengthen the economy of this country or the free world. The trade measures that I have recommended to the Congress were prepared in recognition of these facts.

Now, to abandon our program for the gradual reduction of unjustifiable trade barriers—to vitiate the Administration proposals by crippling amendments—would strike a severe blow at the cooperative efforts of the free nations to build up their economic and military defenses. It could result in increasing discrimination against our exports. It could lead to widespread trade restrictions and a sharp contraction in world trade. This would mean lowered production and employment at home. It could mean a retreat to economic nationalism and isolationism. It would constitute a serious setback to our hopes for global peace.

Two-way trade, I believe, is a broad avenue by which all men and all nations of good will can travel toward a golden age of peace and plenty. Your Administration is committed to help building it. I personally believe it is to the common good of all 164 million of our people and I shall not relax my personal effort towards its achievement.

We shall succeed, given the support of all who—unaffrighted by crises—are prepared to act on today's problems while they work for tomorrow's better and happier life. The accomplishment of this goal is worthy of the best effort of all Americans. Through you—you who gather here—and all your associates dedicated to the mission of spreading the truth, a more rapid progress can be made.

As we build a richer material world, we must always remember that there are spiritual truths which endure forever. They are the universal inspiration of all mankind. In them, men of both the free world and the communist world could well find guidance. Do we remember those words of our faith—"All things whatsoever ye would that men should do to you, do ye even so to them"?

Do we remind ourselves that a similar thread of peaceful and lofty exhortation reveals itself in the words of every one of the world's historic religious leaders? Every one of them—their followers today people great nations.

The Far East, the Middle East, the Near East, the West—Asia and Africa and Europe and the American hemisphere—all alike possess in their heritage the same universal ideal. Why then should we permit pessimism to slow our efforts; despair to darken our spirits?

Cannot we convince ourselves and others that in cooperation there is strength?

Cannot you, men and women of the pen, propagate knowledge of economic truth just as your professional forebears spread the truths that inspired our forefathers to achieve a national independence? For when all people, everywhere, understand that international trade—peaceful trade—is a fertile soil for the growth of a shared prosperity, of all kinds of cooperative strength, and of understanding and tolerance, the fruits thereof will be another historic step on the road to universal peace.

I thank you, President McLean and ladies and gentlemen, for the honor you have accorded me by allowing me to appear before you.

NOTE: The President spoke at the Waldorf-Astoria Hotel, New York City, at 2:00 p.m. His opening words referred to Robert McLean, publisher of the Philadelphia Evening and Sunday Bulletin and President of the Associated Press, and Mrs. Oveta Culp Hobby, Secretary of Health, Education, and Welfare.

80 ¶ Letter to Harvey S. Firestone, Jr., Upon Accepting Honorary Chairmanship of the United Service Organizations. *April 26, 1955*

Dear Mr. Firestone:

I have accepted the honorary chairmanship of the USO because I know what a great contribution it has made, and is still making, to the well-being of the men and women who serve in our Armed Forces.

More than just a Camp Show or a chance for an hour's diversion, more than just relaxation or warm hospitality, the USO means to the men and women in the Armed Services that they have a host of friends in the homes of America. No matter what part of the country a serviceman comes from, no matter what his race or religion, he wants to feel confident that what he is doing is important to other human beings, and that they are grateful for it.

Such assurance fortifies spirit and morale, strengthens the ties in heart and mind which unite the individual serviceman with his fellow citizens, which make him feel that he is part of America! He must have such assurance, if he is willingly and ably to perform the vitally important duties which our times and our nation's good demand of him.

For these reasons the work of the USO must go forward. The continued support of our people through united community campaigns will assure that it will go forward.

Sincerely,

DWIGHT D. EISENHOWER

NOTE: Following his acceptance of the honorary chairmanship from a delegation from the United Service Organizations, the President handed this letter to Mr. Firestone, Chairman of the Board. The group met with the President in his office at 11:30 a.m.

81 ¶ The President's News Conference of *April 27, 1955.*

[This is a complete transcript of the news conference of this date. All of the President's replies were released for broadcasting or direct quotation at that time.]

THE PRESIDENT. Good morning, ladies and gentlemen. I have no announcements, so we will go right to questions.

Q. Marvin L. Arrowsmith, Associated Press: Mr. President, between last Saturday and yesterday this Government seems to have changed its mind some about insisting that Nationalist China participate in any discussions between the United States and Red China concerning the Formosa area, at least with respect to a cease-fire. Can you tell us why the change, if you regard it as a change?

THE PRESIDENT. Well, I think the change is far more apparent than real.

Last Saturday it was stated we were not going to talk about the affairs of Nationalist China except with them present. I believe that Mr. Dulles made this point clear also at his own press conference, saying we would not discuss the affairs of the Chinese Nationalists behind their back; but that as a test of good intent, if the Chi-Com wanted to talk merely about cease-fire, we would be glad to meet with them and talk with them, but there would be no conferring about the affairs of the Chinese Nationalists.

So I think that the one statement may have erred in not being as complete as it should have been, but I don't believe it was a reversal of attitude.

Q. Robert E. Clark, International News Service: Mr. President, there have been reports that you have been in private communication with Marshal Zhukov and have asked him, among other things, to use his good offices to help obtain the release of American flyers imprisoned by Red China; is that correct?

THE PRESIDENT. Well, it is correct that I had some personal

correspondence, but it was because of the nature of our two positions and based upon old friendship. It was absolutely personal.

I am not at liberty to say what was in it until he releases it.

I assure you there is nothing in it that was of such a great significance that it ought to disturb anybody, but it was personal.

Q. David P. Sentner, Hearst Newspapers: Mr. President, do your remarks in the previous question on Red China mean that any discussion with Communist China will be limited to cease-fire discussions, or possibly the release of the American prisoners?

THE PRESIDENT. Well, you are correct in making the observation. Anything that doesn't affect the Chinese Nationalists, and there seems to be an opportunity for us to further the easing of tensions, the advancement of world peace, and certainly getting back our prisoners, of course we would talk about it.

I merely meant to say that when it comes to talking about the affairs that involve our ally bound to us by treaty we are not going to talk behind their backs. That was the one caveat I put on the answer.

Q. Laurence H. Burd, Chicago Tribune: Mr. President, do we have any assurance or any indication that Nationalist China would agree to a cease-fire if Red China did; and was that one of the topics of the Admiral Radford-Robertson mission in Formosa?

THE PRESIDENT. You open up a subject that every time a man tries to make an answer he runs the risk of one word giving a false impression.

But so far as I know, the Chinese Nationalists are not firing now except in defense of the territories they are now occupying. They are not attacking the mainland, so far as I know, except in retaliation. Consequently, I believe that a cease-fire on their side would be purely academic.

They are firing only in defense, as I understand. But that was not any special item that had come up, so I can't give you any more accurate answer than that one.

Q. Kenneth M. Scheibel, Gannett Newspapers: Mr. President,

would you care to comment on the work of the Congress so far?

THE PRESIDENT. I talked about the matter with some of my friends on the Hill within the last two days, and they said it was too early.

They said you never know how a Congress is going to—what is going to be its schedule and its rate of performance, and they said you just can't really talk about it yet.

Q. Mrs. May Craig, Maine Papers: Mr. President, are you saying that a cease-fire is not of interest to the Nationalist Chinese or that you will talk with them separately about a cease-fire?

THE PRESIDENT. Well, Mrs. Craig, I didn't say that it was of no interest to them. I did say they are not fighting at this moment. Therefore, a cease-fire is purely on the Chi-Com's part.

Therefore we can talk to the Chi-Coms about their own firing without damaging the interests of the Chinese Nationalists; that is all.

Q. Raymond P. Brandt, St. Louis Post-Dispatch: Mr. President, does the postponement of the administration's testimony on the Bricker amendment mean that you are thinking in terms of a substitute or a compromise?

THE PRESIDENT. Well, when you say "compromise," Mr. Brandt, of course, you can mean anything, and it could mean anything to anybody else.

I think I have made my position perfectly clear on this subject before this group. I have not changed my mind one iota.

The Constitution had as one of its principal reasons for coming into being the conduct of the foreign affairs of the United States as a single unit, not as 48 States.

I believe I quoted something of one of the treaties, 1783 treaty, I believe it was, by which the British were going to evacuate certain of our forts on the Northwest Frontier.

Then some of the Colonies decided, because we were then under the Confederation you will remember, that they just would not obey those treaties. So the British didn't evacuate the forts, and we were almost at war again.

In foreign affairs the United States is a single nation meeting with others. It is not 48 meeting with others, and we must not forget it.

So we must never agree to any kind of arrangement that would weaken this position vis-a-vis the other nations of the world, which means weakening the provisions now in the Constitution for conducting foreign affairs.

Now, on the other hand, I have equally said the United States has gotten a great fear that treaties can be written that are in violation of the Constitution. And if it would reassure the people of the United States to have an amendment saying that any treaty or executive agreement in conflict with this Constitution shall have no force or effect, I am perfectly willing to say it. But I will go no further.

Now, that is my opinion about the amendment.

Q. James B. Reston, New York Times: In the statement that was issued, sir, on Saturday, the State Department said: "In the Formosa region we have an ally in the free Republic of China, and of course the United States would insist on Free China participating as an equal in any discussions concerning the area."

THE PRESIDENT. That might be a touch of an overstatement because I have agreed with what Mr. Dulles said. I agreed with it before he said it.

I believe it is perfectly legitimate for us to talk to the Chi-Coms about stopping firing.

Now, if we overstated the case Saturday, well, that was to that extent an error in terminology.

Q. Clark R. Mollenhoff, Des Moines Register: Your information policies in the Defense Department have been under some rather severe criticism by editors in the last few weeks.

I wondered if you would like to comment on that and what part you had, if any, in formulating those policies.

THE PRESIDENT. Well, I haven't formulated policies that are administrative within any department. But I have insisted on this—I believe we have mentioned this before: anything that is a technical military secret of the United States shouldn't be put out before us, before any of us, that do not need to know, merely because of a desire of one section of the department or another to be first to make such an announcement.

A trained intelligence system can get a terrific source of information out of the combined documents that can be procured on the newsstands and the libraries of the United States.

Now, that is as it should be because to inform ourselves, we have to be ready to inform others. But we do not need to turn out such things as an airplane able to fly straight up or to do some other thing that seems to be a strange new principle. It is that to which I object, and that only.

Q. Mr. Mollenhoff: Mr. President, there seems to be some order that states that what information comes out must be to the benefit of the armed services, and this creates some confusion as to what information is to the benefit.

THE PRESIDENT. Of that I never heard. You will have to go back to Mr. Wilson and question him.

Q. Joseph R. Slevin, New York Journal of Commerce: In view of fears that declines in automobile production and home building may cause a dip in business activity after midyear, could you give us the administration's views of economic prospects for the balance of 1955?

THE PRESIDENT. Of course, I meet with economists and others of the administration on these subjects all the time.

The economist—his expert advice would be that you should seek the highest rate of production and prosperity that can be sustained, but don't get into a false rush and then fall back; that unjustified rises are to be followed by immediate drops is not true prosperity and doesn't bring about the feeling of confidence we want.

So they watch them. All I can say is no one has uttered to me the fears you express in terms of earnest warnings. They have said: "These are facts and it looks like we have got to be very watchful and careful."

As you know, the Federal Reserve Board the other day, so far as the stock market is concerned, raised the margin requirements another 10 percent, I think more as a red flag to the business community and others than as any thought that it would have a direct effect.

Q. Sarah McClendon, El Paso Times: Sir, are we correct in assuming that you did approve this Millikin-Byrd substitute to the Neely amendment which the Senate Finance Committee approved last night?

THE PRESIDENT. Yes. The one about the general authority of the President in case—yes.

As a matter of fact, I think it was a very fine one.

Q. Mrs. McClendon: Yes, sir.

Well, now, Senator Lyndon Johnson interprets that to mean for the first time in history we will have full authority in the President to decide if imports of foreign crude are interfering with national defense and hurting the domestic oil industry. Is that the way you would interpret it, not only to apply it to oil but to all commodities?

THE PRESIDENT. I doubt whether I would answer it as a hypothetical case.

I would say this: in everything that the President does in this field he must take into consideration the standing of all America, 164 million people. One of the greatest functions of all that 164 millions is their own protection.

There is never any one of these cases that comes up in any way where the question of national security doesn't enter.

Now, here they have merely mentioned specifically the question of national security, but it is a matter that is almost inherent in the function itself.

Q. Ray L. Scherer, National Broadcasting Company: Mr. President, the broad picture. Do you see any signs, any tangible signs, of a general abatement of tension between East and West, and if so, could you enumerate them?

THE PRESIDENT. George Patton used to say that no man is a soldier unless he has a sixth sense, and then he would describe that sixth sense. It was, I must say—for him it seemed to work—it was suddenly to make your decisions on your own guess, and throw all of the G–2 people out the window.

Now, I will confess I have the feeling that things are on the upswing. But I can take every single favorable point and balance it by something that doesn't look too favorable. But I do believe this: more of the world is beginning finally to have confidence that the United States is not trying to establish a new form of colonialism, doing it just through purchases, money, and economic penetration.

I believe that they are beginning to understand the United States is genuinely devoted to peace, that we are a peaceful people who want full opportunity to develop ourselves, and that in going along they are beginning to see that our efforts to help others have had not only our own enlightened self-interest as an inspiration, but also the knowledge that others must advance if we are to continue to do so.

This you see coming out in a number of ways. Suddenly Russia says: "We are ready to conclude this Austrian Treaty now."

Or, the tension seems to die down in some other area. But, at the same time, you will see a build-up of airplanes around the Formosa area, on the Chinese mainland. You will see your trouble in South Viet-Nam. So, as you sit and live with these things you have a very difficult time proving anything either way. But I do say, I still have my feelings.

Q. Charles S. von Fremd, CBS News: Mr. President, you just mentioned, sir, the Russian move in Austria.

A few weeks ago you mentioned that as one of a series of possibilities that might be a sign of Russian good faith of deeds not words, which might, in turn, be a factor in a decisive meeting at the summit, or an eventual Big Four meeting. Do you feel that way now, sir?

THE PRESIDENT. I don't know whether it will lead to the Big Four meeting in terms of the heads of states, or heads, at least, of governments.

I do mean this: it is a step. Already there has been agreed that the ambassadors will meet in Vienna. Assuming that meeting will be successful, we will know then the Big Four will meet then in terms of their foreign ministers. And if that leads to something that might demand higher concurrence, it is possible. But I say at this moment I see no reason for that summit meeting. But, as I say, anything might grow out of it.

Q. Edward T. Folliard, Washington Post and Times Herald: Mr. President, the 10th anniversary of V–E Day is coming up. Do you have any reflections on that event?

THE PRESIDENT. Well, yes.

Of course, I think we knew 6 weeks before that that victory was certain and was coming very quickly. It merely became a question of the day. But I think May 8th [9th] represented for a great many people in Europe at that time practically the realization of all their dreams and, you might say, their ambitions. Certainly I thought it marked for me, you might say, the end of an active career. I saw a nice farm over the other side of the ocean—and it still is a long ways away, isn't it? [*Laughter*]

After all, when you are my age, 21 months is still a long time. [*Laughter*]

I do believe this: I believe that there was in the hearts of all the fighting men, all of the people that were in uniform in Europe on that day, I believe there was a genuine desire for peace and the hope that there would be no more war.

That hope has not been realized. It has encountered its defeats, but I still believe it is a mighty force in the world, and I favor it. I don't hesitate to write or communicate with old friends that I knew in those days in an effort to get them to try to help us advance one step along the road. To refer again to my old friend Marshal Zhukov, I believe he was intently devoted to the idea of promoting good relations between the United States and the Soviet Union at that time. As I say, I haven't seen him since November of 1945. But in other instances, the Frenchmen and the Britishers and the others that I knew, I still am in close contact with them.

But I must say this: I wish that in this cold war we could now get some victory that would make us feel as good as we did that day of May 1945.

Q. Andrew F. Tully, Jr., Scripps-Howard: Mr. President, are you going to attend the U.N. meeting in San Francisco?

THE PRESIDENT. The answer has not been finally and completely developed, but I would say the chances for me going are very, very poor.

Q. Mr. Tully: Poor, did you say?

THE PRESIDENT. Very poor; because I have got other engagements that are very pressing at that time.

Q. Roscoe Drummond, New York Herald Tribune: Mr. President, in a broadcast for use behind the Iron Curtain for radio liberation, the Vice President expressed a view this week that the greatest barrier to peace was the fact that the Soviet people are still held in tyranny by their own government.

I wondered if you would say whether you share that view, or would like to elaborate on it?

THE PRESIDENT. Well, I think it is a little speculative.

After men's minds have become persuaded of the truth of something, though it be wrong, they can support that idea if they believe it to be true.

Now, we don't know how far the Soviet leaders have succeeded in persuading their people that communism is, in fact, an ideal existence. And I should say that if you had tried to establish in this country communism as of 1917, there would still be such a seething unrest in this country, such a determination, that it would long ago have disappeared.

So just how violent may be any mass resentment to this domination we really don't know, and I think that it would be idle to speculate.

Q. Robert J. Donovan, New York Herald Tribune: Sir, without going into the substance of your letter to Marshal Zhukov, could you tell us when it was sent and how and about, whether it was very long or not?

THE PRESIDENT. You sound to me like you ought to turn into being a Sherlock Holmes. [*Laughter*]

Well, it was, I would say, recently. As a matter of fact, I don't remember the exact date, but within the last three weeks.

Q. John Kenton, New York Journal of Commerce: Mr. President, while we are waiting for the details of your atomic ship proposal to be worked out in detail, I wonder if you could tell us a little bit about the background of how the plan came to be worked out and, specifically, whether the idea originated with a Government official or in a suggestion from private industry.

THE PRESIDENT. Well, now, I have warned you people plenty of times that when you go to begin a search for the initiation of an idea, the memory can play you very, very sad tricks.

I think that as far as bringing this thing forward as a proposal to do something about it, I think it was mine. And any of you people check me differently.

Mr. Hagerty: That is right.

THE PRESIDENT. But I really can't say that. I think it makes little difference.

The administration learned, through its technical experts, not only that it was possible—we knew it was possible the second that the test model for the Nautilus was successfully tested—but there came the idea: now, suppose we had a merchant ship? And then we made some studies what it would cost, and admitted it was going to cost more than another kind.

But what value would this have, particularly in the effort to get the whole world to understanding that the peaceful uses of atomic energy could, under favorable circumstances, far overshadow its destructive force? Then it began to loom up as possibly one of the finest ways, because when you think of the great cities and the millions that live on the seacoast, this ship could start out and visit almost every port in the world before it came back.

Well, that sounded like a very good idea. And so we adopted the idea one day at a meeting—I forget what meeting it was—and they are going after the specifications. The plan will go before the Congress as soon as it can be worked out in sufficient detail.

Q. John L. Cutter, United Press: Mr. President, in connection with this matter of Government information there have been some complaints about the press not being permitted to cover a conference at the Department of Health, Education, and Welfare.

THE PRESIDENT. I asked about it, and they are covering one this morning.

Q. Milton B. Freudenheim, Akron Beacon Journal: Mr. President, last week the Defense Department abolished the requirement that key workers in defense industries be required to name friends and relatives who are members of Communist fronts; and recently also Attorney General Brownell announced that the witnesses, former Communist witnesses, would no longer stay on the payroll as consultants.

This looks like it might be a change in emphasis in the internal security field. Would you comment?

THE PRESIDENT. Well, I will have to defer the question. You will have to hunt up the facts. I haven't heard of that, and it is brand new to me.

Q. John Herling, Editors Syndicate: This has to do, Mr. President, with the minimum wages.

Since the administration bill for 90-cent minimum was introduced several months ago, all bills introduced since by Republicans and Democrats—there have been about nearly 50 on the same subject—call for at least a dollar minimum.

In view of this development, do you see any possibility of the administration changing its position, or do you think it will remain inflexible on the subject?

THE PRESIDENT. The subject was studied a long time, brought up before the Cabinet, of course, by the Secretary of Labor, and with all of the charts showing the reasons for changes.

Since the minimum wage was fixed at 75 cents, the cost of living has gone up sufficiently to justify a rise in the minimum wage to, I believe it was, 86.4. Now, I am not going to take my oath on that, but it was close to that.

So we decided that 90 cents was a good round figure, would be over and above that.

We said it should go higher, but we wanted to put our emphasis, if this were possible, on the spreading of this minimum wage rather than raising it, because the minimum wage today in any covered industry affects very, very few people. But there are many, many thousands working who are not covered by the minimum wage field at all.

We would like to see a spread rather than just the rise, because we don't think the rise is so meaningful.

Q. Edward P. Morgan, American Broadcasting Company: Mr. President, what can you tell us, sir, of this Government's views now towards the sticky situation in Viet-Nam and, particularly, whether the Government thinks there may be the necessity to change the policy of recognition of Premier Diem?

THE PRESIDENT. I can't give you any final answer because, as you know, it is still under discussion.

We have called General Collins back here, a man in whom we have the greatest of confidence and who has been right in the thick of things out there, and who has been supporting, of course, Premier Diem.

Now, there have occurred lots of difficulties. People have left the Cabinet, and so on. You know what most of those difficulties are. It is a strange and it is almost an inexplicable situation, at least from our viewpoint. But he has come back because we have up not only the need to clarify ideas as to future policy, but there is the question of aid for Asia. His testimony, of course, would be valuable not only to us, but he will testify before committees on the Hill. What the exact terms of our future policy will be, I can't say.

Q. Elie Abel, New York Times: Could you give us your reaction, sir, to the recent statement of former President Truman that the press is treating you with special tenderness and granting to you an immunity which some of your predecessors——

THE PRESIDENT. I can only say if you are, thank you. [*Laughter*]

Listen, I am not above saying that I often need friendly treatment.

Q. Benjamin R. Cole, Indianapolis Star: Mr. President, could you tell us what role you believe the Federal Government should play in the polio vaccine program?

THE PRESIDENT. Well, I think that they have tackled it correctly. I believe very greatly in the power that can be developed by the humanitarian agencies of this country when they work together in cooperation. And if they have the direction which is to be given them through the Advisory Committee set up in Mrs. Hobby's Department, I believe that we will get the most rapid possible distribution of this vaccine.

Now, the reason I opposed—originally at least—any compulsory role for the Federal Government, I believe it would slow it up. By the time you established more bureaus and all of the rest of the stuff, I believe you would be in trouble.

I believe it is going just as fast as it can. I get the reports—I think by August first, as I recall, they believe a hundred percent of the children from 1 to 9 will be vaccinated. And by November first, I think, a hundred percent of those up to 19. There will be six companies producing this. They will put it into a pool, and this Advisory Committee will lay out the priorities in which it is to go out, and I suppose with a careful eye—I know with a careful eye for any threatened emergency or anything of that sort. We will certainly do the best we can.

I would not hesitate to use any power of government, if necessary. I just believe that others can do it better.

Q. Cabell Phillips, New York Times: Mr. President, I have two questions on the refugee program.

THE PRESIDENT. Yes.

Q. Mr. Phillips: First, sir, would you express whether or not you are satisfied with the way the refugee program is now operating? And, second, whether or not you will support proposed revisions of the Refugee Act which have now been introduced in the Senate—I am not sure of the House.

THE PRESIDENT. The answer to the first question is no. The next one is yes.

Q. Joseph Chiang, Chinese News Service: Do you think Chinese Communists now realize America sincerely believes in peace so that she humbly came to America for help to seek peace?

THE PRESIDENT. Well, you are asking me to interpret people who are a very long ways away and with whom I am not too well acquainted.

I would say this: I take their words with reservations, but with hope. Does that answer your question?

Q. John M. Hightower, Associated Press: Mr. President, can you tell us whether you initiated your correspondence with Marshal Zhukov and whether you had an answer from him?

THE PRESIDENT. I believe I shall say no more about that at the moment, and for a very definite reason.

Ladies and gentlemen, if someone abroad writes to me on a personal basis he expects to have that confidence observed. Now, I think every person in this room would want that correspondence, if it were humanly possible, to lead to some betterment of the world situation.

I don't know whether it ever can, but it is a slim hope. It is one of those points we must preserve. I am not going to violate his confidence in saying who initiated this correspondence.

Q. Lloyd M. Schwartz, Fairchild Publications: Mr. President, in regard to the trade bill, as approved by the Finance Committee,

I wondered whether you found anything objectionable in the revision of the escape clause provision.

THE PRESIDENT. I haven't read it. But I did have time this morning for one brief conversation with one of my staff who said there were a couple of amendments put on that will take a little bit of study to see whether we can accept them entirely.

Now, I didn't even have time to find out what they were, I am sorry.

Q. Roscoe Drummond, New York Herald Tribune: Mr. President, may I ask a brief question about this matter of making military information easy or too easy for an enemy to get?

May I ask whether you feel entirely relaxed about the pamphlet issued by the Republican Policy Committee of the Senate detailing information about new weapons and related military information?

THE PRESIDENT. I heard about this pamphlet just before I came over. They gave me some idea that made me think that there had been a blunder that occurred. Now, for the past 2 years—I say "a blunder"; somebody, I think, gave out information that I wouldn't have given out, at least.

For some 2 years and 3 months I have been plagued by inexplicable, undiscovered leaks in this Government. But we mustn't be too astonished when we recognize the great numbers of people in this town who necessarily know details of one kind or another.

I just don't believe that it is justifiable for any governmental official to release anything that applies to the secret war plans, war policies, war purposes and war equipment of this Government. That is the kind of thing that foreign intelligence systems spend thousands and thousands of dollars to get, unless we give it to them for nothing. And since we don't get it for nothing, I just don't believe in that kind of a trade.

Now, this is what I believe in giving away: I think today to hold secret any document of the World War, including my own mistakes, except only when they are held there by some past agreement with a foreign nation that has not yet been abrogated, it is foolish.

Everything ought to be given out that helps the public of the United States to profit from past mistakes, to make decisions of the moment; that is current information. But this is one thing. I say it doesn't help any of us to make a decision merely to know that a plane can fly 802 miles instead of 208. That is a secret we should not be giving out. That is the kind of thing I am talking about, and that only, I assure you.

John L. Cutter, United Press: Thank you, Mr. President.

NOTE: President Eisenhower's sixty-sixth news conference was held in the Executive Office Building from 10:31 to 11:06 o'clock on Wednesday morning, April 27, 1955. In attendance: 189.

82   ¶ Special Message to the Congress Concerning a Program for Low Income Farmers.
April 27, 1955

To the Congress of the United States:

In this wealthiest of nations where per capita income is the highest in the world, more than one-fourth of the families who live on American farms still have cash incomes of less than one thousand dollars a year. They neither share fully in our economic and social progress nor contribute as much as they would like and can contribute to the Nation's production of goods and services.

This human problem is inadequately pictured by charts and figures. Curtailed opportunity begets an economic and social chain reaction which creates unjustified disparity in individual reward. Participation diminishes in community, religious and civic affairs. Enterprise and hope give way to inertia and apathy. Through this process all of us suffer. This problem calls for understanding and for action.

We must open wider the doors of opportunity to our million and a half farm families with extremely low incomes—for their own well-being and for the good of our country and all our people.

Recommendations to achieve this end have been made to me by the Secretary of Agriculture. I transmit them to you, with my general approval, for your consideration.

The Secretary's recommendations for starting the program are based on the accompanying Report prepared for him by the Department of Agriculture, entitled "DEVELOPMENT OF AGRICULTURE'S HUMAN RESOURCES, a Report on Problems of Low Income Farmers." This report, more than a year in preparation, emphasizes the long-range nature of the low-income problem in agriculture and will serve to stimulate continuing study and action. Nevertheless, an immediate start is extremely important.

The essential cooperative nature of the undertaking is clear. The recommended program is cooperative as regards individual and group action, as regards private and public agencies, and as regards agencies at local, State and Federal levels.

The Secretary's fifteen point program recognizes that this is not exclusively an agricultural problem but that opportunities for off-farm employment are a part of the solution. Recommendations emphasize the voluntary approach, the importance of working with young people, and the desirability of broadening the program as experience is gained. In all matters, the urgency of the problem is recognized. The proposed program, however, is one of prudence as well as zeal.

A many-sided attack is essential. We need an integrated program in which each part contributes to the whole. Each will be more effective if the others are adopted. Together, they will help toward a solution within the framework of freedom for the individual, respect for his rights as an American citizen, and opportunity to participate more fully in the economic life of our Nation.

Proposals for enabling legislation and the necessary appropriations shortly will be presented to the Congress for consideration.

DWIGHT D. EISENHOWER

NOTE: Secretary Benson's recommendations, in the form of a letter dated April 26, were released with this message. The letter and the report, entitled "Development of Agriculture's Human Resources," are printed in House Document 149 (84th Cong., 1st sess.).

83 ¶ Remarks to the Committee for a National Trade Policy Following Congressional Action on the Proposed Trade Agreements Extension Act. *April 28, 1955*

SINCE you people already know what I think about this, I see very little reason in saying anything except "Thank you," saying that in every language that I know, using every word and every expression, because I am truly grateful. There, of course, have been encouraging developments. The bill having just passed the House, and, after long study and examination in Senate Committee to have come out 13 to 2—at least in its general features—I thought was a tremendous victory. And I know how much you people have had to do with it.

Whatever we do in this regard, though, we must always remember that in projects affecting human affairs, victories are never really won because life is an unending fight, and everything that applies to the welfare of humans is something that goes on and progresses. We never wholly conquer disease. We never wholly conquer ignorance. We will never have perfection. So that there will always be a struggle going on to balance against the hope of immediate and sometimes selfish gain the long-term good of a great nation and of a whole world. That is the kind of thing in which you have engaged yourselves and along which you have come so far already.

But it will continue. I merely beg of you not to look at any one skirmish as a victory in a campaign or in a war. As you know, the administration is dedicated in many ways not only through H.R. 1 but through other plans and methods to breaking down barriers—tiresome and burdensome customs procedures and all the rest of it—around the world. The administration is dedicated not only to promote trade between ourselves and another country, but between those countries as among themselves, so as to increase our prosperity and make them better customers of ours.

I really believe that in this whole field of international trade, we must think of it as the greatest instrument or weapon in the hands of the diplomat as he strives to promote peace. We must think of it also as the connecting link, really, between a prosperous economy here at home, widely shared, and a growing and stronger free world capable of marching without fear of attack, fear of any kind of interference on the part of potential enemies, toward a better and a brighter future for all of us.

So, believing those things so deeply in my heart, you can understand that I don't really have the words in which to say "thank you" adequately. But I do assure you I mean it.

Good luck to all of you.

NOTE: The President spoke in the Rose Garden at 3:00 p.m.

84 ¶ Remarks at the Cornerstone-Laying Ceremony for the American Federation of Labor Building. *April 30, 1955*

President Meany, ladies and gentlemen:

I take it as right neighborly that you, President Meany, and your associates should ask me to come across from the other side of Lafayette Square, where I have a temporary leasehold, to visit you on this historic occasion at the place which we hope will be your permanent home for many, many years to come.

I came for a number of reasons, among which were an opportunity again to salute that great and vast army of Americans who with their hands produce our material wealth; to return friendly calls that have been made to my office by leaders of the labor movement; and likewise because I read this in the letter of President Meany asking me to be here.

He said, "We have constantly observed the principle of placing our responsibilities as American citizens above our obligations and duties as members of labor unions."

So far as I am concerned that is the philosophy that should guide the American of every calling, no matter what it is—to place the long-term good of America, all America, above any immediate and selfish reason. And in that spirit, I salute this group of leaders and every single individual that belongs to the labor movement, and indeed all labor in America.

President Meany, in his address, adverted to the previous occasion of the laying of a cornerstone for the American Federation of Labor, and he spoke of President Wilson being here. President Wilson said, among other things, on that occasion: "If you come at me with your fist doubled up, you will find that I will double mine no less swiftly than you do yours. But if you come to me in the spirit of friendliness and negotiation, you will find that I will say, 'Come let us sit down together and there, I assure you, we shall find that our differences are far more imaginary than real.'"

Now again I believe that on that occasion, Mr. Wilson spoke something that all Americans should well heed. Because we shall never be rid of strife in this world—international and, in some degree among ourselves, so long as humans are human and the millenium has not arrived. But the character of men and the character of nations will be determined by the method in which they meet to solve their differences. If we acknowledge that the difference is honestly agreed, then let us meet in what we like to term the Christian spirit and reach an answer that is for the good of all. It seems to me that Mr. Wilson spoke something that was worthy then of the great man, Samuel Gompers, who as your President, was worthy of the entire movement that we call the American labor movement.

For myself, I should like to tell you again, I am no stranger to work. Mr. Meany referred to a terrible 60-hour week. I reminded him several times that when I finally was fortunate enough to enter the Army, my workweek just before that was 84 hours, and it was 52 weeks a year. I certainly can appreciate what the labor movement has done for the men and women of America and what we must continue to do to make certain that this growing and advancing prosperity is widely shared so that all may participate in it.

Finally, President Meany made a pledge. And he used the words of Samuel Gompers in a great pledge to President Wilson.

In return, I can say only this: so far as the Almighty will give to this administration and to me personally the ability to discern the proper tasks, we shall do nothing but devote our efforts to try to lead this world—this Nation of ours—toward enduring peace, toward a better prosperity and equal justice for all here at home.

Now in conclusion, may I say I am not only pleased, I am very proud that this great assembly—this great association—soon to become greater by its junction with another great organization, will by that measure have still greater responsibilities in carrying out the kind of pledges that have been made by your leaders of the past, and I am sure are earnestly followed by your leaders at this moment.

I am proud to be here, and to participate in this ceremony. Thank you all very much.

NOTE: The President's opening words "President Meany" referred to George Meany, President of the American Federation of Labor.

The pledge made by Samuel Gompers, first President of the AFL, at the dedication of the headquarters on July 4, 1916, and repeated by Mr. Meany, follows:

"Let us do all that we can to help the man at the head of the affairs of our country, the President of the

United States, to see to it that we are kept out of actual war with any Nation. Be true to yourselves, true to each other, true to the organized labor movement, true to the institu-tions and the flag of our country, which we shall uphold at all times and against all obstacles no matter from which quarter they may come."

85 ¶ Remarks at the Annual Meeting of the United States Chamber of Commerce. *May 2, 1955*

Mr. President, ladies and gentlemen:

It is indeed a great honor to welcome you here to the Capital City and to have the privilege of spending with you these few minutes.

The very word "commerce" is filled with connotations characteristic of our problems of the day. Commerce based upon the productivity, the energies, and the brains of men like-wise provides that material base to satisfy the material and physi-cal wants of man and on which are built those opportunities for cultural and spiritual advancement so necessary to his well being, his progress, and his happiness.

Commerce here at home has made us what we are. As I was driving over here a few minutes ago, there crossed my mind a speculation. A hundred years ago today, Franklin Pierce was President. Had he been invited to a body with similar functions, aspirations, and purposes as yours, what would he have talked about?

Well, railroads were beginning to come in. We knew some-thing of steamships, but largely even our farms and certainly our communities were self-supporting. Commerce as such had not attained for people the tremendous significance that it has in this modern day, when almost every man and every community are specialists. The man is a machinist, the city is a steel city such as Gary or Pittsburgh, or an automobile city such at Detroit, or an agricultural town such as Abilene, Kansas. But everybody does something and produces something in the way of services that must go to someone else, or they have no value and bring no profit to the producer.

Commerce, its free propagation and progress in this country, has brought today the great organism—this great institution that we call modern America.

Now it has done that without the desertion of the basic principles that were applicable 100 years ago—as well as 177 years ago when our documents—our founding document was written. We still believe that, in the aggregate, the initiative of the individual, his aspirations and his hope of bettering himself and his family—his ambitions—if directed equally toward the common good as toward his own betterment, will produce the greatest good for all of us.

And though today we talk about a greater need for governmental relationships with the private individual, and with business, and with our various localities, yet we forget that basic principle at our peril, and we must not—ever—no matter what we hope for in the way of advantage from governmental regulation or direction, or any kind of regimentation, we must never accept it if it means the surrender of this vital principle: of living by our own initiative and our individual freedoms to develop ourselves physically, intellectually, and spiritually.

Now the point I should like to make is this. We have proved these things here at home. We understand them thoroughly. The point I want to make, then, is they are just as vital internationally as they are nationally.

It is true we do not accept and need not accept any overall governmental structure that will take the place in international life that our Federal Government takes in our own living. But think of the things you do by cooperation and by working together. That is the kind of thing we want in the international world, where the central fact of our existence is that we and our system are challenged.

We are challenged by a doctrine that holds us to appeal to and act under all of those things most selfish in man. The Communists say: "You people boast that you say what you please, you think what you please, you worship as you please, you earn as you please." And they say they appeal to all that is idealistic in man; appeal to him and say: "Forget yourself, build up the state."

But to do that, the Communists have to make the state not only the ruler; they have to substitute for our convictions as to an Almighty—as to religious faith—they have to substitute likewise that state organism. That we flatly reject.

In any event, that communistic international dictatorship is seeking to destroy our way of life. If we then will apply among our friends in the world—the independent nations—the same principles in thinking, in cooperation, respect for common values, and in trade, in commerce, that we have among ourselves, we are as certain of defeating communism as we are that we are all in this hall this moment.

My friends, an enlightened trade policy in the international world for the United States means only this: we are trying to build a bridge, a permanent bridge, that will connect a growing and widely-shared prosperity at home with international peace. And that's all there is to it.

We hope to do this intelligently and wisely. But here and there we are going to uncover some dislocations in our economic development and in the economic developments of others, and we must make some concessions. And some of them—for people here and there—will be a bit painful. But if we keep in sight that underlying aspiration of all America—to continue to grow under the blessings of Almighty God with the tremendous opportunities that have been ours because of individual liberty—as long as we cooperate together for the common good, we cannot lose; we simply cannot lose. And we will soon adjust all local or painful experiences of the moment into a greater benefit for all, including those temporarily inconvenienced.

So I say: as this country was born in the self-sacrifice of its patriots, in their determination to work together, in their respect for one another—if we apply those principles today to ourselves at home, and to our tackling of our relationships with our friends abroad, we can dispel fear from our minds, and we can, as we achieve success, lead happy and full lives in perfect serenity and security.

I feel that the aspiration for global peace based on justice and on decency and respect for others means that we must continue to prosper at home, and those two goals are worthy of the best efforts of any American.

I thank you again for the honor of your asking me here. It has been a great pleasure to see you all. Good morning.

NOTE: The President spoke at Constitution Hall at 11:30 a.m. His opening words "Mr. President" referred to Clement D. Johnston, President of the U.S. Chamber of Commerce.

86 ¶ Special Message to the Congress on United States Participation in the International Finance Corporation. *May 2, 1955*

To the Congress of the United States:

The establishment of the International Finance Corporation and our participation in it will strengthen the partnership of the free nations. In my message to the Congress, January 10, 1955, on the foreign economic policy of the United States and in my annual Economic Report transmitted to you January 20, 1955, I stated that I would recommend at the appropriate time legislation to permit United States participation in the Corporation as part of our effort to increase the flow of United States private investment funds abroad.

I now forward to you the Articles of Agreement of the International Finance Corporation and an Explanatory Memorandum approved by the Executive Directors of the International Bank for Reconstruction and Development. I recommend that the Congress enact legislation authorizing me to accept membership in the Corporation for the United States and providing for the payment of our subscription of $35,168,000 to the $100 million capital stock of the Corporation as set forth in the Articles of Agreement. The subscription was included in the Budget.

The entire free world needs capital to provide a sound basis for economic growth which will support rising standards of living and will fortify free social and political institutions. Action to that end by cooperating nations is essential.

In its own enlightened self-interest, the United States is vitally concerned that capital should move into productive activities in free countries unable to finance development needs out of their own resources.

Government funds cannot, and should not, be regarded as the basic sources of capital for international investment. The best means is investment by private individuals and enterprises. The major purpose of the new institution, consequently, will be to help channel private capital and experienced and competent private management into productive investment opportunities that would not otherwise be developed. Through the Corporation, we can cooperate more effectively with other people for mutual prosperity and expanding international trade, thus contributing to the peace and the solidarity of the free world.

Economic recovery, notably in Western Europe, enables nations other than the United States to participate substantially in furnishing capital to the less developed areas. The International Finance Corporation is an undertaking in which all nations, as members of the International Bank for Reconstruction and Development, will be able to pool some of their resources to spur such investment. All subscriptions to the Corporation will be paid in gold or dollars.

The Corporation, as an affiliate of the International Bank, will serve as an international agency, which will provide, in association with local and foreign private investors, risk capital for financing the establishment, improvement, and expansion of productive private enterprises in member countries when other sources of funds are not available on reasonable terms. This type of risk or venture capital is most urgently needed.

By providing the margin of capital needed to attract other funds, the Corporation will help expand private investment abroad. It will make its investments without guarantee of repayment by the member governments concerned. Accordingly, it will complement the activities of existing international investment institutions.

The Corporation will not duplicate the operations of the International Bank for Reconstruction and Development, for the investments of the International Bank are guaranteed by its member governments and are of fixed-interest nature in projects not usually attractive to risk capital.

Since the Executive Directors of the International Bank would serve *ex-officio* as Directors of the Corporation, and the President of the Bank would serve as Chairman of the Corporation's Board, effective collaboration between the two agencies and operating economy is assured.

Nor will the Corporation's operations duplicate the work of the Export-Import Bank. That Bank, an agency of the United States Government, is an instrumentality of our foreign and trade policy. It is not designed to provide venture capital; its loans are at definite interest rates with fixed schedules of repayment.

The Corporation will not hold capital stock nor participate in operating control but will rely on private management. It will not be a holding company retaining its investments on a long-term basis, but will dispose of its holdings to private investors as opportunity offers so that it can reinvest its funds in new activities. Since its main mission is to supply risk capital where it is needed, its investments will be highly flexible.

In some cases the Corporation may take fixed interest obligations, in others it may receive obligations bearing a return related to the earnings of the enterprises, and in others its holdings may be obligations convertible into stock when sold by it to private investors. Thus, the Corporation will supplement private investment, and will operate only in association with private interests which are willing to carry a large share of the total investment in each enterprise. In no event will it supply capital for an enterprise which could reasonably be expected to obtain the funds from private sources.

United States participation in the International Finance Corporation will be a step forward in our foreign economic policy in cooperation with the other free nations. It is, however, only one step among several which we must take. In my message to the Congress on January 10, 1955, I outlined other important steps.

These actions—such as extension of the Trade Agreements Act, United States membership in the Organization for Trade Cooperation, simplification and improvement of customs valuation procedures, increased tourist allowances, changes in the law concerning the taxation of income from foreign sources and further developments in tax treaties designed to encourage private investment abroad, continued technical cooperation with other countries, and necessary programs of foreign assistance—are essential to a sound and foresighted foreign economic policy for the United States.

I urge the Congress to enact promptly the legislation permitting the United States to join with the other free nations in organizing the International Finance Corporation—an important part of our foreign economic program which will foster more rapid advance by free people everywhere as they strive to improve their material well-being.

Dwight D. Eisenhower

NOTE: The Articles of Agreement and the explanatory memorandum referred to in the second paragraph are printed in House Document 152 (84th Cong., 1st sess.).

The International Finance Corporation Act authorizing United States membership in the International Finance Corporation was approved August 11, 1955 (69 Stat. 669).

87 ¶ Citation and Remarks at Presentation to
Field Marshal Pibulsonggram of Thailand of the
Legion of Merit, Degree of Chief Commander.
May 2, 1955

CITATION TO ACCOMPANY THE AWARD OF
THE LEGION OF MERIT
(DEGREE OF CHIEF COMMANDER)
TO
FIELD MARSHAL P. PIBULSONGGRAM
ROYAL THAI ARMY

For exceptionally meritorious conduct in the performance of
outstanding services to the United Nations and to the cause of
freedom as Prime Minister and Minister of Defense, Kingdom of
Thailand. Following the outbreak of hostilities in Korea on 26
June 1950, military forces from the Kingdom of Thailand were
among the first to respond to the call of the United Nations to
meet the challenge of enemy aggressor forces with armed resistance. With the approval of his Council of Ministers, Field
Marshal Pibulsonggram directed the organization, training and
equipping of a regimental combat team in Thailand, establishing
a forward headquarters in Korea. Immediately upon their attainment of operational readiness he placed an infantry battalion,
two frigates, an air force transportation detachment, and a Red
Cross medical unit at the disposal of the Commander in Chief,
United Nations Command, to support active military operations.
Throughout the uncertain months which followed, he worked
untiringly to further the spirit of cooperation within the United
Nations' first great international fighting force. A resourceful
and inspiring leader, he was instrumental in expanding the activities of the Joint United States Military Advisory Group to Thailand to include continuing training programs, thereby insuring
the maximum mobility and combat effectiveness of the Royal

Thai Armed Forces. By his outstanding professional skill, sound judgment and keen foresight, Field Marshal Pibulsonggram contributed significantly to the missions and objectives of the United Nations Command, reflecting the highest credit upon himself and the Royal Thai Armed Forces.

DWIGHT D. EISENHOWER

[Remarks of the President]

Your Excellency, it is a great privilege for me to present to you the highest award that this Government can give to anyone not a citizen of this country.

It is a special privilege, because in this way we can take note, we hope, of the cooperation of one who has done so much to stand by our side as all of us attempt to defend human freedom, dignity, and liberty in the world.

My earnest compliments to you, sir.

NOTE: The President spoke in the Rose Garden. Field Marshal Pibulsonggram's response follows:

I am very grateful to you, sir, that when I arrived in your great country, everywhere I received a very cordial welcome—a treasured welcome. And this morning I had the occasion to have an audience with you, Mr. President, and now I receive this decoration from Your Excellency. I feel very honored. I try as forcibly as I can to lead my country to secure peace in the world. They will be always at your side—in any way—to create the peace of the world.

88 ¶ Remarks at the Governors' Conference Dinner. *May* 2, 1955

Governor Kennon, ladies and gentlemen:

It scarcely seems a year since at least a number of you and I were privileged to meet over at the White House. I assure you that I truly appreciate the invitation that Governor Kennon tells me is a return engagement of that party.

Washington is a great city of precedents, and you do something or you don't do something because Abraham Lincoln did it, or McKinley, or Grover Cleveland, or somebody else. I was very anxious to meet the Governors back in 1953 and they looked up the record, and I believe somewhere around 1908 and another time in 1925 all the Governors had been invited in.

Well, I wanted to see them, so I asked them in. The next year it seemed more necessary than ever to ask them back, and they came back. And then I was certainly astonished but still highly honored they should come back again.

I hope we have started a precedent, because there are a number of things wrong with Washington. One of them is, I think, almost everybody here has been too long away from home. But the duties of an official here being what they are, it is very difficult indeed for him to keep in touch with the people who bear comparable responsibilities back home. And so it is probably a very salutary experience for the people in Washington for the Governors to come in; they being so perfectly aware of the affairs in their own States they report what is going on, talk and think over and tell us something of their convictions, their opinions, the facts as they know them, in any State from Maine to California.

Now Governor Kennon said that you people came in to be oriented. As far as I am concerned, that is a very secondary purpose—possibly even less. This meeting is to bring us back closer to the people of your States.

I cannot imagine a body of greater dignity anywhere than the assembled body of Governors. Our forefathers readily understood the need for diffusing power, and they diffused it not only functionally but geographically. And if ever we lose that part of the system they set up, we will lose the United States as we know it.

The assembled body of Governors is, without official power, still one of the most important bodies that I could possibly imagine. And certainly I am honored to meet with them, and I hope that you, like myself, can say "I have profited" by each of your meetings here.

Now, it doesn't particularly bother me whether or not all of you agree with me. In fact, I have heard something more than rumors, I should say, that two or three of you, at least, disagree violently with most of the things in which I believe. And I should say this: they are just as welcome as anybody else, because America is a place of differing convictions, and if anyone wants to sit in an ivory tower and hear only from those people who believe with him, again, America will not be what he would hope it would be.

Honest sharpening of our wits in dealing with honest men, differing with them, and thrashing out of troubles is the best assurance that our country will stay in the pattern that was laid out for us 178 years ago.

And I should say that the only requisite other than that we be honest is that we try to be informed, and that is not always easy. We know the world is complex. We know that our own daily, local lives become more complex in everything from distributing of a vaccine to the handling of problems dealing with Iran or Formosa or China, or anything else.

All along the line, different factors come to bear, the problems become very complex and no clean-cut simple answer is obtainable. But as we do meet with as much energy as each of us can marshal and we meet in all honesty, we are certain that the great composite opinions and convictions of this country, as represented unofficially in a body of Governors, will be a decision that will see America through any crisis.

So that you can understand how proud I am that the Governors have for three straight years met here in executive, off-the-record sessions, doing their best to give us the facts from their own particular areas—their convictions—their opinions.

I am not going to take up any of your time, or burden you this evening with any of the problems now bothering me. This is scarcely an occasion to turn into one of your executive or business sessions. I do want to assure you that I am honored to be your guest. I want to present to you Mrs. Eisenhower's deep regret that she couldn't come, but she does have a doctor who has ordered her to take it easy for a while. She asked me especially to say to all of the ladies of this group that she is deeply sorry that she couldn't be with you. Among you, of course, are many of her old friends as well as mine. She would love to have greeted you.

When I got here I was told I didn't have to talk at all. When I said, well, if I did, what shall I talk about, he said about a minute. I have exceeded my time. Ladies and gentlemen, good night, good luck, and I hope to see you again.

NOTE: The President spoke at the Mayflower Hotel, Washington, D.C. His opening words "Governor Ken- non" referred to Robert F. Kennon, Governor of Louisiana.

89 ¶ Statement by the President on Approving a Proposed Agreement With Turkey for Cooperation in the Peaceful Uses of Atomic Energy.
May 3, 1955

ON THE recommendation of the Atomic Energy Commission I am glad to approve this proposed agreement between the Republic of Turkey and the United States for cooperation in the unclassified scientific study of atomic energy and development of its peaceful uses.

This historic occasion signalizes the completion of negotiations for the first agreement for cooperation in the peaceful uses of atomic energy under the new Atomic Energy Act. It is another example of the vision of the Congress in enacting this law to meet the needs for peaceful atomic development at home and abroad. This occasion also marks another among the many instances of friendly exchange and mutual cooperation between our two nations.

Over a year ago, President Bayar of Turkey when visiting the

United States made specific reference to the atoms-for-peace program and stated that "we who are dedicated to the security of the free world have no choice but to give this plan our total endorsement". The initialing of this proposed agreement marks the first major step in a new field of United States-Turkish cooperation which gives promise of wide benefits to mankind.

It augments the many evidences of mutual trust and teamwork in scientific and technical development such as the educational and other training programs we have carried on with Turkey for several years.

The proposed agreement will promptly be sent to the Joint Committee on Atomic Energy of the Congress as required by the Atomic Energy Act of 1954.

NOTE: A White House release of the same day stated that the President gave his formal approval to the proposed agreement in a letter to Dr. Willard F. Libby, Acting Chairman of the Atomic Energy Commission, signed at the conclusion of ceremonies at which the agreement was initialed and notes were exchanged.

The release further stated that under the proposed agreement the AEC would lease to Turkey up to 6 kilograms of uranium 235. It added that this fissionable material would be drawn from the 100 kilograms of U-235 approved by the President for use in construction of small scale research reactors and for other research purposes in foreign countries as a part of the United States atoms-for-peace program.

The text of the agreement and of the President's letter to Dr. Libby are published in Senate Report 572 (84th Cong., 1st sess.).

90 ¶ The President's News Conference of *May* 4, 1955.

[This is a complete transcript of the news conference of this date. All of the President's replies were released for broadcasting or direct quotation at that time.]

THE PRESIDENT. Please be seated.

Good morning. Ladies and gentlemen, before we start the questioning this morning, I want to talk a little bit about a subject close to all our hearts; that is Dr. Salk's vaccine.

It is a very emotional subject because we are dealing with human lives, the lives of children of tender age; therefore, I think it is very incumbent upon all of us to proceed very carefully.

We should neither make the problem look too easy, and we shouldn't try to do anything here except to get out the facts and give people the very finest understanding that it is possible to give.

First of all, it has been assumed, I think, too often, that the entire problem is one of distribution; this is not true.

I have talked in one or two instances directly to scientists themselves—the question of safety—we must be absolutely sure that we are doing something that is safe and good.

One of the questions that comes up is the methods of actual testing of this vaccine. If you may test it in one way it can be done in a relatively short time. As quickly as you go to a system that may be more accurate, you run into a group of new technical problems that might delay the production of this vaccine for a good many weeks.

There has been suspected on the part of the scientists a reaction or a development that you might call the provocative effect of this vaccine.

You or I or a little child, which would be important, might have latent polio virus in his system, and in normal cases might pass through this period with no serious effects. He would have a few slight symptoms, but it would amount to nothing more.

Now, the actual puncture of the skin to give this shot might— they have not proved this, but it is just possible that it might cause some trouble.

All of these things are being studied by our scientists daily, almost on a 24-hour basis, and with all of the scientists we can mobilize to it to make certain as we proceed that the one thing that we must be careful of is that saving lives on a wholesale basis is achieved.

Now, the first great quantities of this material to come out of our laboratories have been purchased in advance by the national poliomyelitis society, and that is being distributed free to our children of the first and second grades.

They contracted for this material before it was known that it could really be produced. But in order to encourage the laboratories, the scientists, to go ahead with this system so that we would have it available this summer, the Foundation did so, and is making it available free. It is being distributed according to the plan that they laid out, a plan approved by the national advisory commission that Mrs. Hobby has collected.

Now, one thing has been the determination of the Government from the start, as far as its part of it is concerned, there will never be a child in the United States denied this emergency protection for want of ability to pay. Of that we are absolutely certain, and no difficulty along that line is anticipated.

In the distribution of this material, you have to deal with the amounts that are to become available as quick as the amounts taken off by the national society have been supplied.

There have been constant meetings, and the plan or the organization procedure is something of this sort: first, the national advisory committee decides upon the allocation, and the allocation, in general, is to each State according to its number of youngsters from 5 to 9. That is the basis for distributing these amounts until that day comes when it is plentiful and anybody can have it anywhere, as long as there is a priority to be observed.

Then, they also get the agreement and have gotten the agreement of each of our producing companies that this will be shipped to the States in exact accordance with the ratio thus decided upon.

The State then informs the Secretary of Health, Education, and Welfare as to the places they want this shipped in order to get this vaccine used. And they name the hospitals or the schools or whatever are the public facilities they have for getting the injections accomplished.

These are sent to the producing companies who make the shipments. The reports then again come back to the Secretary, so that we know that the actual amounts allocated by this whole system have been shipped out, and are available in the State. And there is where the State picks up the authority for the actual giving of the vaccine to the children of the State.

Now, that is a rough approximation. Let me see if I have looked over any—the matter has already been discussed with the Governors of the States by the Secretary of Health, Education, and Welfare. And the Secretary is giving me a report which I may get this week covering every single detail, factual and planning detail, of the whole matter. As quickly as I get it, I will make it available to the public. You people will have it as soon as I can get hold of it.

Now, I think that covers the situation. I want to emphasize again that the matter of inability to pay is never going to have the slightest thing to do with this, and that it is going to be distributed equitably to every State in the Union, according to the standards set up by this advisory committee.

Q. Robert E. Clark, International News Service: Mr. President, are you giving any active consideration at this time to compulsory Federal controls on distribution?

THE PRESIDENT. Well, yes. I have given all sorts of consideration to it. As a matter of fact, I can't tell you the number of conferences.

We believe that the system we have just laid out is the very best plan for getting this to the children in the quickest possible time and on the most equitable basis, because, in the long run, the

States must enter this problem in some way or other. There is no other way to devise the machinery.

Q. Kenneth M. Scheibel, Gannett Newspapers: Mr. President, do you have any evidence that there is racketeering going on in the distribution of this vaccine?

THE PRESIDENT. No. There was a—it is a rather laborious explanation.

At one time apparently our producing companies thought that methods for producing and testing were all in hand; it was all ready. Over and above what they were preparing for their original contract with the society, they were preparing a small amount for commercial distribution.

Some of that, and a very small amount apparently, got out. There was no black marketing about it at all. It was a legitimate transaction, and here and there a few people, not of the groups I have described, the youngsters I have described, got it; but that was apparently something of a very transitory character.

Q. Walter Kerr, New York Herald Tribune: Mr. President, granted that it is a legitimate operation, do you care to comment on the propriety of that distribution while the vaccine is in short supply?

THE PRESIDENT. Well, I don't want to comment without knowing somewhat more of the facts than I do. But I do say this: apparently they thought they had the problem all solved. This was going along swimmingly, everybody was going to have all they wanted, and they were getting into the commercial field.

I am not going to comment on it at the moment because that is all I know. The report of Mrs. Hobby may bring up that particular point.

Q. Martin S. Hayden, Detroit News: Mr. President, in describing this process you mentioned it goes to the States for hospitals, schools, and so forth.

Is there anywhere in this process a point at which a private doctor can get it for distribution to children in this level?

THE PRESIDENT. I am certain the States will have to do it

through private doctors. If we don't use all of the 100,000-and-some private doctors in this country, I don't see how this could be done. But I mean the States themselves will have to establish the systems under which the private doctors do this service for the children.

Q. Mr. Hayden: In other words, sir, you would assume that in addition to the children who get it free under planned programs, that other children in that age group whose parents are willing and able to pay will be able to?

THE PRESIDENT. Well, now, let's don't go too fast. This is one of these cases where you had better be safe than sorry.

All of the vaccine now coming out has already been contracted for. We are talking about the vaccine that is going to come out as long as there is a shortage. People within these critical age groups need, I believe it is, the first two shots, because I believe the booster shot doesn't come along until 7 months later.

Now we are talking about that time. If the States want to handle it entirely, let us say, through a medical association, it would sound to me all right. But the State will have the responsibility that the amount allocated to it under this formula is used properly to serve the interests of that State.

Q. Martin Agronsky, American Broadcasting Company: Mr. President, I don't want to get you into an area, sir, in which you may not be expert. But I would like to go into some of the medical points that you made.

You said that if this injection were given, and the person who got it had latent poliomyelitis germs, that there was a possibility, according to the doctors, that they might develop a case of poliomyelitis.

Now, under those circumstances, sir, considering the experiences out in California, out West, is it still considered wise by the doctors to go ahead on a national scale?

THE PRESIDENT. You mean now?

Q. Mr. Agronsky: Yes, sir.

THE PRESIDENT. In a general case, yes.

Now, they are checking up on a number of things. For example, in the time of highest incidence, when apparently these germs are everywhere, each of us may have some of them. It may be that they will decide there is a certain period of this year when they shouldn't give this at all. Remember this: never has there been such a rush job as this done, and scientists are watching it day and night.

I think I can comment no further on the strictly medical possibilities. But they are going ahead with the distribution under the present system.

Q. Mr. Agronsky: They consider it safe and wise still to do it?

THE PRESIDENT. That is right. Under those amounts and, I think there is one company that has not yet been cleared.

Q. Frank van der Linden, Nashville Banner: Mr. President, just to change the subject a little bit, the Governors of Tennessee and Kentucky spoke for about an hour yesterday with your general counsel and with Labor Secretary Mitchell, asking for some help to settle these telephone and railroad strikes. I wonder what the administration is doing to settle those two strikes?

THE PRESIDENT. Of course, we have set up a Mediation and Conciliation Service for settling of strikes. The law does not intend that the executive department, as such, intervene except only in the case where national emergencies occur.

Now, from the beginning of this strike I have been kept in almost daily touch with the Secretary of Agriculture [Labor]. He has kept in touch with the Mediation Service, and in some cases with the principals.

I understand that these parties in this strike have come very, very close together, and the prospects for settlement are bright indeed. And I know these two Governors talked yesterday with the Secretary; I had a report on it this morning.

I am told I said "Secretary of Agriculture." I meant Secretary of Labor, I am sorry.

Q. Robert W. Richards, The Copley Press: The Governors of Illinois and Wisconsin said that an overwhelming majority of the

Governors attending the conference in the last 2 days favor your highway program over the Gore bill. Can you comment on that, sir?

THE PRESIDENT. As you will recall, last year I couldn't attend the Governors' Conference up in New York. Vice President Nixon delivered my message, in which I asked the Governors' Conference to establish a transportation road committee and to work with the committee I would set up, and we would devise a program.

Now, the program that that committee of Governors set up for building the highways of this country is almost identical with the plan brought up by the Clay committee. And so it is what I stand behind. So far as I know, there never has been any rescission of the Governors' action, of their approval at that time.

Q. Nat S. Finney, Buffalo News: Mr. President, some new agricultural legislation is pending on the Hill, and I wonder if you could refresh us as to your views on that farm problem generally, and the legislation.

THE PRESIDENT. I am delighted to do so. [*Laughter*]

Last year we finally had passed a farm bill. It is good legislation. But it has not yet had an opportunity to be in effect. It will not go into effect until the crops of the 1955 year begin to come to market. So all of the farm squeeze which has taken place, and it has taken place, has been under the old law, the 90-percent rigid parity price supports.

Now, the law that we have is designed to bring production and consumption as nearly into line as we possibly can.

It was passed with bipartisan support. And right now Senator Eastland, I noticed—I think it was yesterday or the day before— made a talk in which he said one of the contributory causes, the difficulties, in the cotton industry is the old price law, 90 percent rigid. Senator Ellender so much feels this way that he says he is not even going to hold hearings in the Senate on this new proposal.

This plan that was devised last year should have its full opportunity to work and see whether we can't bring about a better prosperity in the farm area that will really be permanent and sound economically.

Q. Irene Albert, Clearwater Sun: Mr. President, I wanted to ask one more thing about the Salk vaccine.

In Florida we have a high polio incidence, and the parents there are much disturbed for fear there will not be sufficient polio vaccine to inoculate the children in the 5-to-9 age group.

THE PRESIDENT. I have been assured that even with this one company out, there is still enough to reach all the 5-to-9 group before August first.

Q. Miss Albert: Before the heavy polio season sets in for the summer?

THE PRESIDENT. That is right.

Q. Miss Albert: Thank you, sir.

Q. Donald H. Shannon, Los Angeles Times: Secretary of the Air Force Talbott last week told reporters that you knew about his opposition to further expansion of the aircraft industry in southern California, and that you were all for it, were the words he used.

Mr. Talbott's policy has caused alarm in California and in Congress here, and it is on the ground that the aircraft industry is being singled out for dispersal, although no such policy is being applied to other industries. Would you comment on it, sir?

THE PRESIDENT. Well, this is the first time I have heard this charge, because for the past 2½ years, I think, almost every time the subject of dispersal has come up, it has been dealt with on a generalized basis. Everybody that I know of in the administration, and particularly the head of the office of ODM who is principally concerned, is in favor of dispersal of industry of all kinds.

This is the first time I have heard that the Air Forces would be particularly singled out.

Q. Lloyd M. Schwartz, Fairchild Publications: Mr. President, there seems to be some confusion in the Senate Labor Committee as to whether you agree with Secretary of Labor Mitchell that the Fair Labor Standards Act ought to be extended to cover employees of interstate retail chains. I wonder whether you could say whether you share this opinion?

THE PRESIDENT. Of what law?

Q. Mr. Schwartz: It is the wage-hour law. He suggested that it cover interstate retail chain employees.

THE PRESIDENT. I am not going to try to answer that in the detail in which you have asked it, because I don't know that much about it.

I do believe, and I have been through study and through conferences with Secretary Mitchell, that there are areas to which a minimum wage should be extended, where the people are not covered now and they should be.

Now, I am not going to try to pin it down as you did.

Q. Garnett D. Horner, Washington Star: Mr. President, Senate and House conferees have agreed on a compromise postal pay raise bill which calls for an average raise of 8.8 percent. There have been predictions that you would veto such a bill. Can you tell us what your reaction is?

THE PRESIDENT. Well, there may have been predictions, but you remember I have never predicted it. In just a few days I will have to study that very carefully, and my answer will be apparent at that time.

Q. Charles S. von Fremd, CBS News: I hesitate to ask this question, sir, because it is a very personal one, and I hope it will not offend you, and that you realize I ask it only because of the nature of the position you hold in the world today.

It was brought up some weeks ago by the Chairman of the Democratic National Committee, who said he did not think you would seek reelection, and gave as one of the primary reasons the health of your wife. And over the weekend Dr. Snyder indicated that, unfortunately, Mrs. Eisenhower has not completely recovered from her recent illness. And I wonder, sir, at the risk of intruding into your private personal life, if you could comment on this to enlighten us a bit in this matter.

THE PRESIDENT. Well, I think it is a legitimate question.

With respect to anybody else's comment about such things, I haven't a word to say.

With respect to Mrs. Eisenhower's health, I would say that her general health for the past 2 years has probably been better than normal, if we go back for a period of the last 10 years.

She did have a very serious virus infection a good many weeks ago, and it seemed impossible for her to throw it off.

She also has an allergy to some of these drugs that some of the rest of us can take without any great difficulty, and it has been a real problem for the doctors to bring her back to her accustomed state of health.

Now, that is the situation.   She is, of course, not as robust and strong as some people, but she is a good healthy person, I think, in the general meaning of that word.

She has had—this spring—difficulty which, unfortunately, a number of my other friends have had, too.

Q. Alan S. Emory, Watertown Times: Sir, the Republican National Committee late last week put out a publication and a covering press release which said that corollary evidence showed that Governor Harriman of New York, who, at the time, was our Ambassador to Moscow, was the real architect of the Yalta agreement.

Does the information that has reached you through military, public, and private channels tend to substantiate that remark?

THE PRESIDENT. I never heard of that remark. Of course, I knew nothing about the Yalta agreements; it would be futile for me to attempt to comment.

I was never asked during the war to give my opinion on a single postwar prospect of a political character, never; so I know nothing at all about this matter.

Q. Sarah McClendon, El Paso Times: Sir, of course you know that many farmers, small farmers, are having a very hard time now because of their limiting cotton acreage allotments——

THE PRESIDENT. Yes.

Q. Mrs. McClendon:——and there is some concern been expressed by civic leaders and even ministers in some parts of Texas that these small farmers are being urged now by some subordinate officials of the Department of Agriculture to sell out to large landowners.

What do you think about Government officials urging hard-pressed small farmers to sell out to big dealers?

THE PRESIDENT. Well again, of course, I have never heard of such a thing. Frankly, I don't believe it. I don't believe that governmental officials—unless someone who thought they were on a friendly basis might say, "Well, you are not doing too well here, why don't you sell out?" And you might say that to me or I might say that to you—[*laughter*]—but I wouldn't——

Q. Mrs. McClendon: Sir, I wouldn't dare.

THE PRESIDENT. ——I wouldn't necessarily assume that is the official position of your newspaper because you said it. [*Laughter*]

Q. Marvin L. Arrowsmith, Associated Press: Mr. President, has there been any progress toward arranging any kind of negotiations with the Chinese Communists on a cease-fire since we talked to you last week?

THE PRESIDENT. No. As a matter of fact, as far as this country is concerned, we are sort of in a wait-and-see attitude.

There are, as you know, a number of countries that are interesting themselves in this, and conducting explorations. But there is really nothing new to report.

Q. Joseph R. Slevin, New York Journal of Commerce: Mr. President, with respect to the farm legislation, do you anticipate that the decline in farm prices and farm income will stop as the administration's flexible support program is allowed to become effective?

THE PRESIDENT. Well, I think it will eventually.

As I have insisted from the beginning, the farm program is like so many other things. You get into a great trend in this country—we piled up these billions of dollars' worth of surpluses—you can't cure that in a minute.

There are all sorts of laws and pieces of laws that will help to reduce these surpluses and get things back on a better balance between supply and demand. But as of now, you couldn't pass any law that just suddenly would turn this around.

Q. John M. Hightower, Associated Press: Have you considered, sir, setting up a United States military base on Formosa?

THE PRESIDENT. Well, you know we have a MAAG and things of that kind there now. There are small elements of American forces there. But there has been no suggestion made that we would put in a big major base on Formosa.

Q. Robert J. Donovan, New York Herald Tribune: Sir, coming back to the Salk polio for a moment, under this system that you have outlined for distribution allocation to the States, how can you be sure, sir, that the polio in that system—that the vaccine will reach the schoolchildren as it is intended? And what will be done if it did not?

THE PRESIDENT. Of course, I am going to assume that States are responsive to the needs of their people. I am going to assume that they will follow the technical advice just exactly as this administration would.

If they are going to give it to others, I would think that the people of that State would make short shrift of that kind of a decision.

Now, as quickly as you say the Federal Government will pass a law, and that down in a certain State such and such a person will do so-and-so, or do such-and-such to another person, you get into constitutional questions of the gravest kind.

What we are assuming that this country does want is to eliminate polio as rapidly as possible among its children. And I think we have got a right to assume that.

Q. Laurence H. Burd, Chicago Tribune: Mr. President, have you had any additional communication with Marshal Zhukov since our last meeting?

THE PRESIDENT. No.

Q. Mr. Burd: Is there anything more you can tell us since our last meeting?

THE PRESIDENT. No, none.

Q. William H. Lawrence, New York Times: Mr. President, the military manpower reserve program is coming up in the House either today or tomorrow, and I was wondering, sir, whether events in the last few months have caused you to increase or lessen your own desire for such a program?

THE PRESIDENT. Mr. Lawrence, I have been working for a proper reserve program for the United States certainly since 1929, and I am not going to stop now.

Now we are making progress at last. There seems to be a widening understanding of the need for this kind of thing. And it looks to me like the bill that is now coming out shows that we are really making progress. I applaud it.

Q. Edward P. Morgan, American Broadcasting Company: Mr. President, you have issued an order rather strictly restricting conditions under which congressional committees can get income tax returns. Can you tell us why this was done and whether it was to cover some specific situation?

THE PRESIDENT. No. It is a matter of the most delicate character. But the orders that I issued were completely coordinated with the chairmen of the committees that were affected by the order.[1] And so far as I know, they are completely satisfied with them.

Q. Donald J. Gonzales, United Press: Mr. President, has consideration been given to the placing of some additional ground forces, as such, on Formosa, even though we aren't going to put in a big base?

---

[1] The White House indicated after the news conference was completed that the coordination had been effected specifically with Senator Lyndon B. Johnson, Senate Majority Leader, Senator Harry F. Byrd, Chairman of the Senate Finance Committee, Representative Sam Rayburn, Speaker of the House, and Representative Jere Cooper, Chairman of the House Ways and Means Committee.

THE PRESIDENT. Well, I have thought of everything out there that might be needed. But to make it a permanent station for American ground forces, I have not had such a recommendation from anybody yet.

Q. Charles E. Shutt, Telenews: Mr. President, Western Germany is about to become a member of the free nations, sovereign nations, once again. Would you comment on that, sir?

THE PRESIDENT. Well, of course, it is something for which this Government has been working for a long, long time. We are delighted, and we hope that it goes forward smoothly and without a hitch.

Above all, we do hope that this development will bring about an elimination at long last of some of the principal causes of one of the most tragic things that has afflicted Europe for a long time; that is, that apparently implacable mutual hostility between the French and the Germans.

I believe that with removal of some of the causes for that friction, Europe will be on a new era of prosperity and security.

Q. Elie Abel, New York Times: We have been told time and again, sir, that in the event of an attack on the coastal islands of Quemoy and the Matsus, that you would make the decision about whether we resisted—the United States, that is.

Now, could you tell us, sir, could you discuss, rather, the criteria that could be applied to distinguish a local attack on those islands from one that appeared to be a preliminary to an attack on Formosa?

THE PRESIDENT. Really you are asking for a staff study. But if there were accumulated in that area, and the attack were started with, material that would seem to be far in excess in its types and kind of what was needed to take the islands, why, you would be justified, I think, in assuming it had a broader purpose.

Moreover, I should like to point out that in all of the statements made by the Red Chinese never have they talked about their purpose of capturing the offshore islands. They have said, "We are going to capture Formosa."

Q. Chalmers M. Roberts, Washington Post and Times Herald: Mr. President, last week you startled some of us with your precision reference to 21 more months. Are we to infer, sir, that you have a calendar on the White House wall that you are checking off? [*Laughter*]

THE PRESIDENT. Well, I am aware of what month it is, at least; I am still aware of that. [*Laughter*]

Q. Samuel S. Wilson, Cincinnati Times-Star: Mr. President, my question concerns your nomination of John Hollister as your new foreign aid chief.

THE PRESIDENT. Yes.

Q. Mr. Wilson: Could you tell us whether you have had any assurances from Mr. Hollister that he favors the administration's foreign aid program?

THE PRESIDENT. Did I have what?

Q. Mr. Wilson: Did you have any assurances from Mr. Hollister that he favors the administration's foreign aid program?

THE PRESIDENT. No—that is personally, no.

Q. William M. Blair, New York Times: Mr. President, aside from the economics involved in the farm debate on the Hill at the present time, the supporters of the administration program are charging that this is a political maneuver.

Do you agree that it is a political rather than an economic maneuver?

THE PRESIDENT. I think that you people probably know those individuals and some of that maneuvering as well as I do. I will let you make your own deductions.

Q. A. E. Salpeter, Haaretz (Tel Aviv): There have been reports that the administration this year intends to ask Congress for a global sum of military aid instead of undertaking in advance the specific sums to be allocated to each country.

Is this report correct? And if, yes, could you explain the reason for it?

THE PRESIDENT. The program itself will be before the Congress in—I thought it was before there now—soon, anyway, and that will explain it.

Never do you ask merely for a global sum. Of course you have to explain to Congress what you are doing it for.

Now, there has always been retained also in these programs a certain flexibility, left to the discretion of the President in order to meet emergencies. But, in general, the sums for each country are laid out in the bill.

Q. Francis M. Stephenson, New York Daily News: Mr. President, I would like to ask two questions. One is on your plans on dealing with the Hoover Commission reports and recommendations, and I also would like to ask the status of the transportation report.

THE PRESIDENT. Yes.

On the Hoover Commission report, it comes to our attention, you see, in segments. And as each segment comes up, why, it is studied and either something is done about it at the moment or it may be referred to Congress, because it has to go to Congress, as you know.

There is no set procedure where a special committee is set up to handle that. It affects the several departments, and they make their recommendations to me.

The transportation report is a brilliant piece of work in its analysis of our difficulties and in the purposes it announces that it wants to achieve.

It was seven, I believe, seven Cabinet officers before whom appeared the transportation experts of the United States.

The purpose, of course, is to make competitive influences more governing in our whole transportation system. It looks forward to that kind of a result.

The person to remember, of course, here, is the general consuming public. They are the people who use the transportation, both the personnel transportation and the freight.

There are details of that report [1] that will be most argumentative, and will give rise to, I think, a very lot of discussion, probably heated discussion. And it should be so. But I think the basic principles are commendable; certainly I approve of them and the purposes they announce.

John L. Cutter, United Press: Thank you, Mr. President.

NOTE: President Eisenhower's sixty-seventh news conference was held in the Executive Office Building from 10:58 to 11:32 o'clock on Wednesday morning, May 4, 1955. In attendance: 188.

91 ¶ Letter to the President of the Senate and to the Speaker of the House of Representatives on Revision of the Philippine Trade Agreement. *May 5, 1955*

Dear—————:

The President of the Republic of the Philippines, in a letter to me dated March 7, 1953, requested examination and adjustment of the 1946 Trade Agreement between the United States and the Republic of the Philippines as being vital to the economic stability of his country and to its permanent trade relations with the United States. Discussions on specific Philippine proposals for revision began last September between a United States Delegation and a Philippine Mission designated for the purpose, and

---

[1] On April 18, the report prepared by the Presidential Advisory Committee on Transport Policy and Organization (15 pages, mimeographed) was released by the White House. The report includes recommendations on (1) a national transportation policy; (2) increased reliance on competitive forces in rate making; (3) the maintenance of a modernized and financially strong system of common carrier transportation. In addition the Committee made recommendations concerning the special problem of Government rates.

Members of the Advisory Committee included the Secretary of Commerce, Chairman; the Secretary of Defense, and the Director of the Office of Defense Mobilization. Ad hoc participating members were: the Secretary of the Treasury, the Postmaster General, the Secretary of Agriculture, and the Director of the Bureau of the Budget.

culminated in the signing on December 15, 1954, of a Final Act of Negotiations in which each agreed to recommend to its Government the revisions contained therein.

A copy of the Final Act, with corrections agreed to in an exchange of letters between the Chairmen of the United States and Philippine Delegations, and a copy of a memorandum from the Secretary of State on this subject, are transmitted herewith.

Revision of the 1946 Agreement cannot be effected without the authorization of the Congress. I believe that the revision, as proposed in the Final Act of Negotiations, would be beneficial to both the United States and the Philippines and would contribute materially to the improvement of the already friendly political and economic relations between them. I earnestly urge, therefore, that appropriate legislation be enacted at this session of the Congress to permit revision of the 1946 Agreement in accordance with the recommendations contained in the Final Act.

Sincerely,

DWIGHT D. EISENHOWER

NOTE: This is the text of identical letters addressed to the Honorable Richard M. Nixon, President of the Senate, and to the Honorable Sam Rayburn, Speaker of the House of Representatives.

The documents transmitted with the letters are published in House Document 155 (84th Cong., 1st sess.).

92 ¶ Remarks at the Dedication of the Washington Hebrew Congregation Temple. *May 6, 1955*

Ladies and gentlemen:

A few moments ago, before this service began, I was privileged to meet some of the distinguished members of this congregation in the library. Several of them voiced a word of amazement that the President of the United States should attend a service of a faith not his own and, in spite of other preoccupations, come both to the religious service and to the dedication of this great Temple.

I personally think that this is natural. There is nothing unique or particularly extraordinary about it. This country is a spiritual organism. Let us go back for a moment to its founding. The men who led the revolution against England well understood that they were fighting for spiritual values.

Do you recall such words as "Taxation without representation is tyranny"? They did not say taxation was wrong. Indeed, they knew its need—possibly as well as we do. But without representation, without being a part of the authority that levies those taxes, it became tyranny. "I know not what others may do," said Patrick Henry, "but as for me, give me liberty or give me death."

Liberty—a spiritual value. They claimed these. They fought for them. They died for them. And they gave us this nation.

Now, wherein was their claim for these rights, these spiritual rights of man? You find them in the Declaration of Independence. "We hold that all men are endowed by their Creator with certain inalienable rights," said they.

These rights, then, come not because we have emigrated to this great and glorious land, crowded with God's resources, not because we have been more fortunate than our brethren elsewhere, but because each is a child of God. And any true American must recognize in another American those rights endowed by God, because if we don't, we are not true to the concepts of the men who wrote the Declaration of Independence.

Consequently, today the President of the United States, the official head of the country, is after all the official head of a great nation that is religious in its background and has a spiritual foundation on which to stand. Therefore, it is entirely fitting and in keeping with his Office that he should come to such a great and significant event in the lives of one part of the great faiths that have made this country what it is, to pay his respects to that faith, and to this event and to the people who have made it possible.

This building—a house of worship—will bring to many thousands in the future and through the years a renewed appreciation of the fact that they do have the rights that this country confers upon them, because that country was born and has existed in the knowledge that God is the source of all power.

If this great Temple continues to serve in that way, if its officials—its rabbis—continue to bring home to the hearts of all people who here come to worship that we owe all in the end to the Almighty and not merely to the good fortune of our birth, then it will indeed have served a noble purpose and one that we may all salute with great joy—with great satisfaction.

One more word about the rights that we enjoy. It is not enough to know that God gave those rights to you and to your neighbor. It is well to remember this also: you may not protect those rights only for yourself. You must protect them for all, or your own will be lost.

The Boston Tea Party took place, of course, in the Boston Harbor, and Massachusetts was the scene of the first outbreak of our Revolutionary War. But had not the other Colonies recognized that if Massachusetts went under, they also went under; that if the rights of Massachusetts and her citizens could be destroyed and trampled under foot, theirs also would suffer a like fate, then there would have been no successful war and no eventual United States.

And so I say I come here in great pride in the capacity of official head—temporarily—of this country, to pay my respects to all who have built it, to all the good that shall come out of it, and to offer my felicitations to each member of this congregation who will have such an inspiring place hereafter to come for their worship.

So my little part in the dedication of this Temple is merely to say it is a most gratifying thing to me, both personally and officially, that it is a completed building.

Thank you.

NOTE: The Washington Hebrew Congregation is the oldest institution for Hebrew worship in the Nation's Capital. Its charter was signed by President Franklin Pierce.

93 ¶ Remarks to Delegates to the General Assembly of the Organization of World Touring and Automobile Clubs. *May* 10, 1955

IT IS indeed a pleasure, ladies and gentlemen, to invite you here to the White House grounds and give me an opportunity to say a word to you. If there is one enthusiastic booster for international travel in the world, I would certainly be numbered among those who come close to the top. Having traveled a bit myself, I am quite certain that it is a very, very useful thing, in bringing to each of us an understanding of those things we need to know in the world, if we are going to achieve any progress whatsoever toward this great goal of peace.

In this country, for one reason or another, we have, possibly, been more backward in the building of roads we need than we should have been. We have a plan that is now before our legislative body to develop the kind of roads that will make it most convenient for you people to come over and visit all parts of this great country very easily, and we would hope with a great deal of increased convenience over what you would now experience.

But on top of that, we are interested in getting the entire Pan American Highway completed so that travel north and south is easier. We like to see roads springing up everywhere because we are certain that as you people from all countries come to visit us, and we come to meet you, there is going to be nothing but good come out of it.

Just as people are afraid of the dark, they are afraid of people they don't know—they think they must be strange creatures. But as they get to know each other, we see that they respond to the same kind of impulses, the same kind of needs and admiration, and respect the same kind of values. So that is the sort of thing that must underlie this search for peace.

I think you people are doing not only a useful but an indispensable part of the task in bringing it about. I realize that these representatives here really represent some 20 million people, and I am told there are 31 countries here represented, which makes it a truly significant body, one that is certain to carry back when you go back to your own homes much of value from your associations here together, in the exchange of ideas. For my part I wish you every kind of good luck and success in the work you are doing. I can't tell you how I would really like to walk up and down Pennsylvania Avenue carrying a banner and cheering for you because I think you are on a job that needs to be done, and I know you will do it well. I thank you a lot for letting me have a chance to talk to you.

NOTE: The President spoke in the Rose Garden at 11:00 a.m.

94 ¶ Remarks at the Republican Women's National Conference. *May* 10, 1955

Miss Adkins and ladies:

I realize there have been a number of speakers in front of you this morning, and there possibly may be some question in your minds as to what I could add to the information already given you.

Not long ago I was at one of Miss Adkins' breakfasts for ladies. It is her custom to have each one of these Republican ladies present whatever ideas are in their minds. Finally it happened that before it got around to the very last lady and my turn, that the last lady on deck was a Negro lady. She felt a little bit in the position that I do now: most of the things had been said. But she looked these people in the eye, and she said, "Well, since each of the prior speakers have referred to this most auspicious and enjoyable occasion, you must admit that I add to this most auspicious occasion, a touch of color!" Well, I tell you, she took over the meeting—but I don't have her advantage.

But these people who have spoken this morning to you have given you a series of facts, plans, convictions that are the basis of the confidence and optimism that we feel today.

There is one generalization to make as we proceed in our thinking about the Republican Party as an agency for serving this great country and that is that the public must be an informed public, if a republic or a democracy is to be a success.

There are certain decisions that people—the people as a whole must make. If they are not informed, they cannot make those decisions intelligently. They will be hit and miss, and therefore only accident will make a decision a correct decision.

We must be informed. Consequently, these people, in trying to present to you the facts, are doing a service but no greater service than you yourselves are doing by gathering together and in meeting with these people of your government, informing yourselves, so that in turn you can carry these facts—these truths— back to the localities from which you came.

The twin objectives of this Administration are a widely shared increasing prosperity at home, and peace abroad.

I think you have heard much on both these subjects this morning. With prosperity at home we must not forget that prosperity can never be the product of a static organism. There must be a growth: there must be an expansion that keeps up with and even exceeds the expansion of our population as we achieve a new number of two-and-a-half to two-and-three-quarters of a million more people a year.

Among other things we need are road programs, health programs, all of those things give to our people the right to enjoy every kind of spiritual growth to which they aspire, to achieve new intellectual heights and to have a greater material standard of living.

If each of our citizens has a right and an opportunity to work for those three things—and to achieve them in some measure each year—then we are getting what we call a growing prosperity widely shared. And that means roads and schools and hospitals and factories, wide employment and an increasing income for agriculture and the industrial worker—everybody. There is no class, no group, no individual that may be omitted and still have this objective achieved.

Now, peace abroad.

The central fact of our time, of course, is the implacable hostility of a doctrine which heads up into the group in the Kremlin which has announced its intention of conquering the world, believing in the overthrow of other forms of government by force, and substituting its own dictatorship of the proletariat for representative and free forms of government.

I shall not bore you with all of their claims about the weaknesses of capitalism and free democracies and free republics. We know that to be a fact.

In this struggle, they have one thing that is important. They have unity. It is the unity that is achieved by force—a knife in the back. People must conform or they are eliminated.

That is not the kind of unity we have, nor which we seek. But we do know we must have a unity among those nations that do not want to fall prey to this kind of existence—to fall prey to the spreading threat of communism. So we must have a community of interest that brings about the spontaneous unity that we want. That is, if we are to present a unified strength in the free world against a unified strength of the Communist world, there must be a great spiritual basis, an intellectual basis, a material basis, that leads people and nations to want to hold together and to oppose this evil.

That, my friends, is really the basis toward which we work in order to gain the strength that will oppose communism so firmly at every critical point in the world. Its progress will be stopped gradually as people everywhere become informed and understand the appeal that freedom has for the human soul as opposed to slavery. Then it will begin to atrophy—to dry up—and finally go the way of all dictatorships.

But to achieve that material, intellectual, and spiritual community of interests among the free world—the peoples of the free world—is a difficult task. It is one that engages your government, both branches—legislative and executive—all the time, every day.

We must make certain that people can make a living; that they can satisfy natural human wants; that they understand what they are working for; that they are to see a brighter day by working spontaneously with the free nations of the world as against this great communistic threat. That is the basis for all the things you hear called foreign aid—mutual security. Everything we do is to achieve the solidarity of partnership with our neighbors, recognizing their rights, recognizing their right to express their opinions and convictions and influence decisions as we move ahead. That will make that solidity of communion and partnership that can achieve success from a position of strength.

I think it entirely possible that Secretary Hoover has spoken to you some of the events of the past two years—those things that give reason to believe that we are somewhat on the upswing in this great, age-old effort of man.

Here I might pause just to say that always the United States has been a peace-loving nation. We have never wanted to fight wars. And in recognition of this fact, I thought it well, sometime back, to appoint a man of national stature to a specific position, to look into all questions of disarmament—which means also the promotion of peace. There can be no true disarmament without peace, and there can be no real peace without very material disarmament.

And so Governor Stassen's position, to study and devise plans and ways of implementing them in this great field of disarmament, is in fact a sort of secretarial position for peace. We give one man in the Administration the job of thinking of this and doing nothing else. I believe that nothing else is symbolizing in this form the effort and purpose of the United States—it can be nothing but beneficial both at home and abroad.

As for myself and for the Secretary of State and others involved, including those in the Legislature, we stand ready to do anything, to meet with anyone, anywhere, as long as we may do so in self-respect, demanding the respect due this Nation, and there is any slightest idea or chance of furthering this great cause of peace. We will not stand on minor questions of protocol or any other inconsequential question, if that opportunity of advancing the cause of peace is presented and there is the slightest chance that it may bring for our children and those that come after us a better world in this respect.

So it is, then, that these facts have been presented before you this morning, before the backdrop of two great purposes—a widespread prosperity at home and peace abroad. We are pursuing them tirelessly and energetically. It is the methods and the implementation of these purposes that constitute the governmental facts that must be carried back to our people.

Personally, in such a problem, in such a purpose, I believe that women are better apostles than men. Men are engrossed in many kinds of activities. They earn the living. They are engaged in business all day, and they are very apt, at times, to lose that great rounded concept of man that women almost always have before them: that he is a spiritual, and intellectual, and a physical being. He is not merely someone trying to get a higher wage. He wants a higher wage for a purpose, to give greater opportunity in all three of these fields to his family. Because women think of these things in their process of homemaking, think of them in terms of children and the family, I believe that their influence in spreading the basic doctrines of this kind is more profound than that of men.

Consequently, it is always an honor to come before you and urge a group like this really to get at it and let us go.

Now certainly I would be remiss if I left this platform without talking for a moment about the word "Republican." I read in the papers that the Republicans are a minority party. Now I will venture one thing, that the people who believe as we do, who will follow along in the paths marked out by the two great objectives, in the programs of implementation that have been described to you by certain Cabinet officers and will be furthered in large measure later in your meetings—these people that want to do as we do are the vast majority of the American people. This means, my friends, that real evangelical work in the business of educating, of informing, will make the Republican Party the majority party, and keep it that way.

A very great early President of the United States said that if he was forced to choose government without schools or schools without government, he would unhesitatingly choose schools. He meant, of course, that if he had to have a government over an ignorant people, or an informed people who would later find the necessity of having a government, he would of course take the informed people.

That is what we need to do now. We do not need to go out merely to exhort. We merely need to go out and show what the facts of this day and time are—what it is that the United States wants, what it is that the people of the world want. The people of the world want exactly what we do. They want opportunity and peace. They want security.

All right: let us go out and show that is exactly what the Republicans are bringing to the people, offering it in full measure richly and with everybody entitled to his share. No one can ask more than to do his share in bringing about such a great objective, such a great purpose.

Ladies and gentlemen, there are some gentlemen here—I thought I made a mistake there, for a moment—if I could make one simple request of you, it would be this: that as you go back, each to your own purposes and efforts in your own localities, it is not that we try to teach and preach Republicanism just because we worship the word.   Let us go back to Republicanism and find the great purposes for which it stands, the great programs that have been brought forward by the consultation of people throughout this land—advisory bodies of citizens, governmental officials, professionals, everybody that could help.   That great program is there to help achieve the purposes that we state. Then we can talk "Republicans" because almost everybody will be Republicans.

Thank you a lot.

NOTE: The President spoke at the Mayflower Hotel, Washington, D.C., at 12:00 noon.   His opening words "Miss Adkins" referred to Bertha Adkins, Assistant to the Chairman of the Republican National Committee.

95   ¶ The President's News Conference of *May* 11, 1955.

[This is a complete transcript of the news conference of this date.   Those portions of the President's replies which were not released for broadcasting or direct quotation at that time are enclosed in brackets.]

THE PRESIDENT.   Please sit down.

Only one short announcement this morning, ladies and gentlemen.

This morning I am going to have the opportunity to see Mr. McElroy, who is chairman of the White House Conference on Education that will meet this year.   It is a conference to which I attach the greatest hopes.

For the first time in history, as preliminary to that conference, every one of the 48 States and our Territories are having State or Territorial conferences on education.   We will bring together their experiences, their ideas, and plans; and certainly the whole field of education should get a tremendous boost from the work of these people.   The reason I mention it is because a little later in the morning I may have a formal statement to make after I meet with him.

All right.

Q. Merriman Smith, United Press: Mr. President, could you tell us, sir, your preferences for time and place for a Big Four meeting? I ask this question against the background of rumors,——

THE PRESIDENT. Yes.

Q. Mr. Smith:——or reports from Europe that this country favors a meeting in July in Switzerland.

THE PRESIDENT. Actually I have no preference except to the extent that I should like to see the meeting held, if held at all, in one of the so-called neutral countries.

You must understand this whole idea is still in the exploratory stage. We have issued an invitation because of reasons that finally seemed to us to be cogent, and such a meeting would probably result in at least some clarification of the air.

But our foreign ministers will now meet in Vienna in connection with the Austrian Treaty, presumably. They will decide whether the invitation is acceptable in its terms, its ideas, and then they will discuss such things as place and timing.

As I have said often, I will go anywhere anytime if any good is to be done, and this earlier meeting ought to determine whether it seems useful.

Q. William H. Lawrence, New York Times: Could you tell us, sir, some of the reasons why you did change your mind about the feasibility and desirability of a summit conference now and in advance, so to speak, of a protracted foreign ministers' meeting?

THE PRESIDENT. Well, of course, this business of foreign affairs, things change from day to day.

The mere fact that it appeared that the Austrian Treaty was to be signed did not in itself seem to me, as I think I told you in April some time, a reason for a meeting at the summit. But I said of course that situation can change rapidly.

Now, there has been a growing sentiment discernible throughout the world that from a meeting like this something might come. There has been clear evidence presented through the press, through correspondence, through our contacts through diplomatic sources, that there is a vague feeling some good might come out of such a conference.

When, then, to hold such a conference: just to put a stamp of approval on something that may have been done by foreign ministers? Or to try to stimulate thought, and possibly even to define the areas in which you would expect your foreign ministers to work so that something might be accomplished?

Finally, I felt this: this business of trying to reach a clarification of issues, if such a thing is possible, is so important that you can't stand on any other principle except do your utmost as you preserve your own strength of position, as long as you are not sacrificing it, as long as you are not expecting too much. Don't be just stubborn in your refusal to expect anything, but go ahead and see what you can find about it.

Now, it does also do this: it gives a personal opportunity to sense an atmosphere in that circle. However, I think those vague, rather generalized reasons are really lying behind this.

There is no expectation on my part that in a few hours, a few days, or a few weeks this world is going to be turned around. By no means, and I am not going, if I do go, under any such thought.

But I would hope that my own mind will be clarified a little bit. Maybe the platform from which we may later work will be a little clearer even to ourselves.

Q. Charles E. Shutt, Telenews: There has been much speculation, sir, as to what might be discussed at this meeting. Would it be proper for you to tell us what you feel would be the most important topic that could be discussed?

THE PRESIDENT. I would think the most important thing that could possibly be done at such a meeting would be to define the lines or directions in which we commonly would want our foreign ministers to work to see whether there is any opportunity to relieve the tensions in the world. Beyond that, I don't even possibly say what the subject would be. Certainly there would be no agenda except in the most generalized form, to talk about a general group of subjects; no agenda in the sense that foreign ministers would normally meet.

Q. Chalmers M. Roberts, Washington Post and Times Herald: Mr. President, to follow that question, do you have in mind the idea of working on specific matters, such as the German unification problem, or are you thinking now that it may be possible to have a larger framework of discussion, such as some general East-West settlement in Europe?

THE PRESIDENT. I don't think that either of your assumptions is quite correct as I now visualize it. I think that we merely, I repeat, could define the areas in which people would start to work.

Now, when they start to work in any area, you find it affects every other area. I think there could be no limitation, and at the same time you couldn't possibly give an exact description of what you are going to do. You are going to meet, try to discover whether you believe the other people are sincerely hoping to relieve tensions. If so, what are the areas of greatest tension and what can these people do?

Q. Mr. Roberts: Sir, may I ask a further point. You spoke yesterday to the Republican Women about disarmament, for example.

THE PRESIDENT. Yes.

Q. Mr. Roberts: Would that be included in this type of discussion?

THE PRESIDENT. I wouldn't see any possibility, if you are going to relieve tensions, that you didn't have to discuss disarmament. But what I say is you would neither limit it, you wouldn't exclude it, nor would you necessarily put it down as a particular agenda.

I don't believe that such a conference could design a specific agenda for your foreign ministers. You could only describe lines that they would take, the attitudes we have, and the general areas they would explore.

Q. Raymond P. Brandt, St. Louis Post-Dispatch: Mr. President, can you give us any idea of how long the meeting at the summit would take?

THE PRESIDENT. I can only tell you what it is I've been guessing. I would think that, oh, if you met a matter of 3 days, I think it would completely cover the issues, as far as I am concerned. All the issues could be raised.

Q. Mr. Brandt: How long would the foreign ministers meet, can you guess on that?

THE PRESIDENT. Oh, I wouldn't guess—I wouldn't guess.

Q. Mr. Brandt: Would that be a matter of weeks or months?

THE PRESIDENT. Could be; I wouldn't guess. And of course, after the foreign ministers meet, then you can establish if any progress was made at all. What you would probably establish would be numbers of meetings of experts in particular fields. There is no use really of speculating as to what the outcome of a chain of events can be. This is certainly experimental.

Q. Mr. Brandt: Would you go back to your old plan after the foreign ministers had come to some agreement, the Big Four would then meet again to formalize it?

THE PRESIDENT. I wouldn't know, I wouldn't know. It would certainly in that case have to be a—we would have to have developed sufficient confidence in what had been done, and it would have to have sufficient significance to us and to the world that it would be worthwhile to make a formal signing to be—something, let us say, historical.

Q. John Herling, Editors Syndicate: Down from the summit for a moment, sir, this has to do with a domestic problem. As you predicted last week, the Louisville and Nashville Railroad strike was settled through the appointment of an arbitrator, and I wonder whether you would care to comment on the role of arbitration in labor-management disputes generally, sir.

THE PRESIDENT. Oh, I don't think it would be profitable to launch into a discussion of my ideas about it, except I would express the greatest gratification that both sides here finally accepted arbitration, that the Mediation and Conciliation Board was successful in bringing them together, and the strike has been settled. It is a very great boon to the South, and I am very gratified.

Q. Mr. Herling: Sir, there is a strike still going on, the telephone strike.

THE PRESIDENT. Yes. I will be just as happy when that is settled.

Q. Mr. Herling: Through arbitration, sir?

THE PRESIDENT. Well, they are working, the Mediation Service is still in contact.

Q. Mr. Herling: And therefore the pattern of arbitration will be just as useful?

THE PRESIDENT. In my opinion, yes.

Q. Elie Abel, New York Times: Sir, could you give us your views on whether you would favor a congressional delegation or a small group of congressional leaders going to this meeting at the summit with your party?

THE PRESIDENT. Well, I wouldn't know yet. You must remember that there was an invitation issued, and we sort of described in our note what we thought would be a good procedure. We don't know whether that is going to be accepted.

I would say this: when it comes down to anything definitive that is going, possibly, to result in any kind of formal agreement or treaty, then I would say it is always profitable to have a congressional committee with them.

Q. Mrs. May Craig, Maine Papers: Mr. President, I had understood you to say that you would require deeds from the Communists before you would meet with them, to show their specific attitude. Have you had any deeds of that description?

THE PRESIDENT. One of them I described was the signing of the Austrian Treaty. Now, it is true I talked about others, but if this one indicates what they are apparently trying to make it appear to indicate, well, then, I am going to try to find out whether it is absolutely sincere.

Q. Laurence H. Burd, Chicago Tribune: Mr. President, would

you regard it as possible or likely that the Far Eastern situation might come up at such a conference, that is, that there wouldn't be any geographic limits?

THE PRESIDENT. It might be an agreement to limit it, in order to look for success, to limit it to certain areas. I would say at this top one, if you had the heads of government at the one conference, I would think the general conversations would tend to go around the world, be global in character.

Q. Lucian C. Warren, Buffalo Courier-Express: Speaker Rayburn on Monday raised the question about the way you make appointments, and it was in connection with your nomination of William Kern, an Indiana Democrat, to replace Jim Mead, a New York State Democrat, on the Federal Trade Commission; and Speaker Rayburn said on Monday that he thought it was cruelly handled, and a cruel thing to do. He also said he had not been consulted about any appointments for minority jobs, that is Democrats in Government, and also Majority Leader McCormack said that he had not been consulted.

I wonder if you have any comment on that?

THE PRESIDENT. [No, I have no comment on that.]

Q. Andrew F. Tully, Jr., Scripps-Howard: Mr. President, the Hoover Commission has reported a number of wasteful shopping practices on the part of the military; for instance, the 60-year supply of hamburger, and up on the Hill they are complaining that they can't seem to find anybody in the military to take responsibility for these things. I was wondering, sir, if you have any plans to hold anybody's feet to the fire about this? [*Laughter*]

THE PRESIDENT. Am I getting a bad reputation around here?

Q. Mr. Tulley: As commander in chief.

THE PRESIDENT. I do know that Secretary Wilson and Mr. Hoover themselves have been in conference. I believe they exchanged letters and are getting together so that they can together study these things in detail, and see where difficulties are.

I think there can be a lot of misunderstanding arise about just a bare fact.   You may have a lot of hamburger.   I understand this is for emergency purposes, used by the Navy and the Marines. I am told that if you actually fed it out to all the messes, that you could consume it in 5 days.   But you don't do that.   It is held for emergency purposes; and therefore, at the amount that you consume it, I don't know how many years it would last.

Q. Mr. Tully: Do you think that is not too much, sir?

THE PRESIDENT.   Well, I haven't examined what they have, but I will tell you this: if you kept in your emergency ammunition supplies only the amounts that you use yearly for practice, you would be in an awful defensive fix.   Now I don't know, I haven't looked up the details.   I don't intend to, because Secretary Wilson ought to be capable of doing that, and I think you can get an answer from him.

Q. Marvin L. Arrowsmith, Associated Press: Mr. President, Senator Margaret Chase Smith is telling the Republican Women's Conference today that she hopes with all her heart that you will run again, but that her present impression is that you will not do so.   Do you have any idea where she got such an impression?

THE PRESIDENT.   Well, of course I would like to thank her for her complimentary opinion of me; but as for the rest of it, I haven't the slightest idea where she got that impression.

Q. James B. Reston, New York Times: Mr. President, in view of the confusion over the polio vaccine, sir——

THE PRESIDENT.   Yes.

Q. Mr. Reston: ——would you give us your view as to where the responsibility lies in this situation?   Is there a Government responsibility here?

THE PRESIDENT.   There is certainly a Government responsibility to take leadership in this thing and see the thing goes ahead as fast as it possibly can.   Now, every conference I have had has been that the firms have cooperated perfectly—the firms making this.   They have no complaint whatsoever.

The entire amount of this product is contracted for by the Foundation.   There will be no other orders filled of any kind until that contract is completely fulfilled. I believe it is either until all children from 5 to 9 are vaccinated, or until a given date some time in the future, whichever is earlier, I think.

I would say this: during the week, I will have the final report of all the agreements, all the recommendations of the advisory board and the Secretary of HEW. By Monday or Tuesday I ought to be in shape to determine if there is any more action of any kind that I am expected to take.

Q. Mr. Reston: The question that is being asked, certainly the question that our mail reflects, is why many of these things that are now being done were not done before all the hoop-la about the original announcements in April.

THE PRESIDENT. I think it was merely because of two things: the great pressure to bring this out as quickly as they had any reason to believe it was a useful and effective product; and therefore, some of the exhaustive tests through which such a product normally goes, probably they tried to shortcut a little bit. I don't know; the report will have to show. I am not a scientist, as you well know.

Q. Edward P. Morgan, American Broadcasting Company: On that same subject, sir, during the last week of June 1949 the Cutter Laboratories of Berkeley, California, was convicted in Federal court in San Francisco on a 12-count indictment, alleging violation of the pure food and drug laws.

In your opinion, sir—two questions—in your opinion, is that a matter that should have been taken into consideration by the Government in licensing Cutter for the production of Salk vaccine; and if so, would a situation of this kind be more easily handled by a situation such as Canada seems to be doing so successfully with government controls?

THE PRESIDENT. [Well, I never heard of the incident that you bring up, and certainly I wouldn't be in position at this moment to comment as to whether that has any possible effect on the current situation.

[It would seem to me that the people in it, the experts and

doctors in HEW and the advisory commission brought in, would certainly be aware of all pertinent facts that you bring up; and if that had any influence, they would have taken it into consideration. I don't know.]

Q. Merriman Smith, United Press: Mr. President, you used a phrase two questions back on that, "they probably tried to shortcut a little bit." To whom are you referring, sir?

THE PRESIDENT. I meant that the scientists in putting this out probably thought that they had used all of the regular methods, but probably didn't use some of the more exhaustive ones that they may think now should be doublechecked.

Look, I am speculating on that particular point. I say I haven't got my report, and I am not making any statement that is to be taken as authoritative on that point, but they have stopped the vaccinations while they take a doublecheck on something. Now, what that is, I am not sure.

Q. Sarah McClendon, El Paso Times: Sir, I believe you received a letter from Congressman Bell the other day, setting forth the great social as well as economic effects of the drought on people in small towns, as well as farms and ranches. The Agriculture Department has set June 15th, I believe, as the end of much of the temporary relief to people in the drought area—in the hay program and other forms.

I wonder if you had given any thought to a long-range program that would take into consideration the economic and social effects of the drought in the Southwest?

THE PRESIDENT. I don't know of any time that the matter isn't under discussion. Certainly for the 2 years and more that I have been here there has always been some area that is in drought. We have taken up this matter with Congress. We have done what we can, and I don't know how you can take up really long-range plans of such kinds, because you hope that the drought doesn't last forever. A drought is supposed to be an emergency.

Q. Mrs. McClendon: Sir, I believe Mr. Bell set forth that

these people are going to need some works projects plans in a long-range way as well as temporary relief.

THE PRESIDENT. Well, I am not prepared to talk about it this morning.

Q. Martin Agronsky, American Broadcasting Company: Mr. President, considerable misgivings seem to have arisen as to the efficacy of the Salk polio vaccine in a medical sense. Could you, from your knowledge and your conversations with the experts on this, tell us whether the U.S. Government still regards the Salk polio vaccine as able to do what everyone originally thought it would do; that is, prevent polio with 80 to 90 percent of those who are injected with the vaccine?

THE PRESIDENT. I believe it absolutely. I can't say what the Government—that's a lot of people. I know what I believe, I believe these experts. They are very competent and I believe it can do it.

Now there have been, I think, something like 52 cases of polio out of more than five million injections. Now, they want to find out merely whether these 52 cases had any relationship at all to the fact that they were injected. They are trying to be doubly safe, and I applaud their caution in this matter. But I believe it just implicitly that this will, within a measurable time, really eliminate polio in this country.

Q. Mr. Agronsky: Mr. President, it is not the medical theory that is in question here at all, it is merely the manner that the vaccine is being manufactured.

THE PRESIDENT. Well, that is what I think.

Q. James A. Reynolds, Congressional Quarterly: Mr. President, what kind of progress would you say your legislative program has been making in Congress so far this year, and what kind of support would you say Republican Congressmen have been giving this program?

THE PRESIDENT. The question is too generic, too broad, for me to discuss this morning.

I'd say this: anyone that would attempt to predict or to comment very much on progress of Congress at this time has forgotten the Congress is capable of doing an awful lot, sometimes in a week, and then seems to have a period of inaction almost for a month. It is rather erratic in its output. [*Laughter*] I mean, erratic in the rate of output. I would say this: as far as I am concerned, things are coming along pretty well.

Q. Richard L. Wilson, Cowles Publications: Mr. President, has a decision been reached to allow Russian agricultural specialists to come to this country and study agriculture here?

THE PRESIDENT. I would like to answer definitively, but I am not certain. We have discussed it, and, generally speaking, I think it has. But I am a little bit uncertain whether I am talking about something that has yet been finally crystallized; that is my difficulty. Actually, I think it has been straightened out.

Q. Mr. Wilson: Do you still favor it?

THE PRESIDENT. Yes.

Q. Matthew Warren, DuMont Television: Mr. President, yesterday the House apparently killed the hopes for Hawaii and Alaska for statehood, for some time to come. I wonder if you would comment on that, sir.

THE PRESIDENT. I have always favored, as you know, the separation of these two bills and handling each one on its merits.

Now, if you put them together you instantly accumulate for your bill the opposition that applies to either one and to both. You take the aggregate and apply it to each one.

I would like to see the bills separated, and always have stood for that. And I would still like to see it.

Q. Clark R. Mollenhoff, Des Moines Register: Mr. President, I wonder if you would have any comment on Zhukov's statement over the last weekend, in the light of your letters to him.

THE PRESIDENT. No, none. They have no connection whatsoever, the two incidents.

Q. Walter Kerr, New York Herald Tribune: Mr. President, I wonder if you have had an opportunity to see a report on the latest Soviet disarmament plan.

THE PRESIDENT. On what?

Q. Mr. Kerr: On what has been described as the recent Soviet disarmament plan submitted to the summit.

THE PRESIDENT. You mean the one submitted through the Disarmament Commission in London?

Q. Mr. Kerr: Yes, sir.

THE PRESIDENT. Well, I have just had a chance to glance at it.

Q. Mr. Kerr: Do you care to comment on it, sir?

THE PRESIDENT. No, not at the moment. The whole question is so confused. It has still some of the elements they have always had in it. They want to get rid of one kind; we would like to get rid of everything. It is something that has to be studied before you can really comment on it.

Q. Charles S. von Fremd, CBS News: Over the weekend, sir, photographs of the May Day celebrations in Moscow indicated that ex-Premier Malenkov has now risen somewhat within his party again, and now ranks third, directly behind Bulganin and Khrushchev. I wonder, sir, on whatever indications you may have received through our intelligence people, whether this does indicate that there is still an unsettled thing going along in Moscow as to who actually is the supreme ruler.

THE PRESIDENT. Well, I don't know whether this has any significance about it, but it certainly seems to be the case that the situation is not what it was when Stalin was alive. He seemed to have the situation in personal control every minute of the day. In other words, he was a true dictator. This is a somewhat different system.

Q. Ray L. Scherer, National Broadcasting Company: Have you had a chance to examine General Sarnoff's recommendations on cold war strategy?

THE PRESIDENT. He came to see me about it. We had a long talk.

Q. Mr. Scherer: I was wondering if you looked at the report.

THE PRESIDENT. Well, he discussed some of the things that he was going to put in it, and he went around and talked to various members of the Government.

I believe thoroughly in General Sarnoff's general proposition, that when you are spending all the money we are for direct defense through security establishments, it is just unthinkable to limit ourselves too much in this whole field of information service that is necessary to a cold war.

Q. Mrs. May Craig, Maine Papers: Mr. President, I didn't know I could ask two questions. In reference to your reply on Austria, do you regard that as a satisfactory treaty or are we agreeing to it because we cannot get better?

THE PRESIDENT. Oh, we agreed to this treaty way back in 1949. Section 16 has been eliminated completely, which had to do with repatriation, and there are still some details to be ironed out. But as far as we are concerned, this Government has agreed to that treaty for many, many months.

Q. Robert G. Spivack, New York Post: Last week you told us that no child would be denied the vaccine because of inability to pay, and afterwards there seemed to be a little confusion about just what sort of plan of operation you had in mind.

As I understood, the Federal Government, if necessary, would buy up all the Salk vaccine, but could you tell us how indigence would be determined, and also whether it would be administered free of charge.

THE PRESIDENT. Well, of course I can't tell you all the details of how we would do it, but I will tell you this: the second I find out that any child in the United States is denied this by reason of lack of money to pay for it, I am going to move as hard as I can, and I will certainly make someone listen to me very earnestly before there is any defeat on that one.

Q. William M. Blair, New York Times: Mr. President, over the weekend the Surgeon General of the United States changed his position on going ahead with the Salk vaccine. Was that purely a medical decision, or was that a decision of policy within the administration?

THE PRESIDENT. Well, I don't understand any such question. I have discussed that two or three times this morning.

That was the doctor's opinion and his decision. The Government would know no more about the factors in this than this body would. What would you know what to do with such technical things? I wouldn't.

The doctors have to decide what to do in such a case. They decided it wasn't fair to go ahead until they checked more. That's all there was to it.

Merriman Smith, United Press: Thank you, Mr. President.

NOTE: President Eisenhower's sixty-eighth news conference was held in the Executive Office Building from 10:33 to 11:02 o'clock on Wednesday morning, May 11, 1955. In attendance: 211.

96 ¶ Statement by the President Concerning Community and State Conferences on Education. *May 11, 1955*

MR. NEIL H. McELROY, Chairman of the Committee for the White House Conference on Education, and I discussed with the Secretary of Health, Education and Welfare, the Commissioner of Education, and Mr. Roy Larsen the State Conferences to be held in the forty-eight states, the four Territories, and the District of Columbia prior to the White House Conference to be held this November in Washington.

Tens of thousands of our citizens will participate in these State Conferences. They seek to develop improved measures for the provision of adequate classrooms and teachers, the effective and economical organization of our school systems, and the increase of public interest in education.

These conferences will, I know, make a vital contribution to the welfare of all our people by developing programs of action to improve education.

I am particularly glad to hear that the National School Boards Association and the National Citizens Commission for the Public Schools, both of them private, nongovernmental organizations, have been encouraging additional community conferences on education. Both of these groups, as well as the Advertising Council, which is assisting them, are to be congratulated on this important effort.

I hope that every community will hold such a conference. The community, State, and White House conferences—taken together—will strengthen the continuing public interest in education which is the cornerstone of our free society.

97 ¶ Message Recorded for Use in Conjunction With Observance of Armed Forces Day.
May 12, 1955

My friends here at home and overseas:

We Americans have constantly pledged that we will never permit aggression. But we must always be prepared to defeat it. On May 21st the Armed Forces of the United States will hold "open house" to give our own and other peace-loving people the best possible opportunity to see how ready we are, in military terms, for any threat to our security or to the peace of the free world. As Commander-in-Chief of the Armed Forces of the United States I earnestly hope that all who can will accept this invitation to become better acquainted with the armed components of our National power for peace.

98 ¶ Message to President Koerner of Austria on the Signing of the Treaty Restoring Austrian Independence. *May* 15, 1955

[Released May 15, 1955. Dated May 13, 1955]

THE AMERICAN people join me in rejoicing with you and the Austrian people on the historic occasion of the signing of the treaty restoring Austrian independence. This moment of supreme satisfaction to Austria, for which we Americans have worked so diligently, would not have been possible without the staunch determination of the Austrian Government and its citizens and their devotion to democratic principles.

The conduct of the Austrian people during the ten long years they have labored under the heavy burden of foreign occupation has commanded the profound respect of all the American people. I am confident that the many ties which bind our two peoples together will continue to constitute the basis for ever friendly relations between Austria and the United States.

As a country dedicated to the fundamental principles of freedom and liberty, the United States will ever maintain an interest in the independence of Austria. The American people are proud and happy at the prospect of Austria being able to play her full part in world affairs with dignity, self-respect, and freedom.

NOTE: The President's message was presented to President Theodor Koerner by Secretary of State John Foster Dulles on May 15 in Vienna.

99 ¶ Remarks of the President During Secretary Dulles' Television Report on His European Visit. *May* 17, 1955

[Broadcast from the President's Office at 7:00 p.m.]

FOSTER, it is good to have you here to tell us something of the significant events that took place during your recent visit to Europe. You realize that through the cameras in this room your report will go to the entire nation. And so I hope that in addition to the details of that trip, you will tell us something about the developing scene in the international field as you see it, and something of the prospects for real progress in our incessant search for peace.

[*At this point Secretary Dulles stated that the week was so crowded with events he hardly knew how to start. The President then resumed speaking.*]

Well, I will tell you, Foster, I think that it might be well to go clear back to 2 years ago. Then you will remember with our colleagues in the legislative branch in both parties the administration was developing the policies intended to produce, and basic to that policy was the belief—the conviction—that only through cooperative strength developed in the free world could we really face up to this threat that the communist dictatorship posed to all free men. We believed, as you know, that until Western Europe had been united, until there were some German forces joining the NATO organization, and until we had some confidence in the Russian word through deeds rather than mere protestation, that it would do little good to have talks with them. And you will realize that you and I finally decided that I should make some pronouncement along this line, and did so, on April 16 of 1953.

Now we agreed at that time that if we could through the kind of steps I have just mentioned, arrive at the point where we had a real basis for going ahead, even if only with faint hope of real

38023

progress, that we might finally develop between ourselves and with the Soviets a new relationship that would at least allow some hope of progress toward this great goal of peace that is of course the great dream of every American.

So, against that kind of backdrop, I think you could relate the events of recent times and on your—just your recent trip to Europe, to tell us about the story as you see it.

[*At this point Secretary Dulles discussed Germany's member-ship in NATO, his talks with NATO Council members regarding Asian problems, and the signing of the Austrian State Treaty. He also discussed the proposed 4-power talks and the dangers as well as the opportunities in such a meeting, in particular the danger that hope would be raised so high that it couldn't be realized. The President then resumed speaking.*]

Foster, I don't believe that danger is quite so great as it was once, because my mail shows this: that the American people are really pretty well aware of what is going on. They realize this is merely a beginning and not an end. I have taken tremendous hope and confidence from the tenor of the remarks I have seen in our newspapers, and commentators, and everybody else—I am sure that there is greater maturity than we would have expected several years ago.

[*At this point Secretary Dulles discussed the implications of the Soviet policy shift, and spoke again of the proposed summit meeting. He stressed the need for adhering to established policies having bipartisan support in undertaking the solution of problems at the meeting. The President then resumed speaking.*]

In a word, we want to stay strong and will stay vigilant, but we are not going to extinguish the hope that a new dawn may be coming, even if it rises—the sun rises very, very slowly.

Thank you very much, Foster. It has been a real privilege to hear such a brilliant report on a very significant two weeks.

NOTE: The full text of the broadcast was published in the Congressional Record (vol. 101, p. 6605).

The address of April 16, 1953, to the American Society of Newspaper Editors, referred to by the President, is published in the Department of State Bulletin (vol. 28, p. 599).

100 ¶ The President's News Conference of
May 18, 1955.

[This is a complete transcript of the news conference of this date. All of
the President's replies were released for broadcasting or direct quotation at
that time.]

THE PRESIDENT. I have no statement, ladies and gentlemen. We
will proceed to questions.

Q. Marvin L. Arrowsmith, Associated Press: Mr. President,
Senator Morse yesterday accused Mrs. Hobby of gross incom-
petency and said she should be removed from office. That was
criticism in connection with the handling of the Salk vaccine
program.

Do you have any comment on those remarks or do you care
to say how you feel Mrs. Hobby has been handling the program?

THE PRESIDENT. I will take the second part of your suggestion
and talk about that. I don't think I would waste my time on the
first part.

Mrs. Hobby, in my opinion, has proved in her office that all
of the good opinion built up about her in her work during the
war as head of the WAC corps was fully justified. She has been
highly efficient. Her counsel in the places of Government has
been eagerly sought—a person of great character.

In this whole Salk vaccine business, I think America is forgetting one thing: the thanks we owe to tremendous groups of
scientists, devoted doctors, people that have worked night and
day, including the people in the Public Health Service, 20 hours
a day, to bring to us this great boon for the protection of our
children and grandchildren.

Now, she herself has been, when you come down to it, merely
the agent of these great scientists and doctors, to work out the
plans through which they thought that their findings, and this
vaccine, could be brought to our people in the earliest possible

point of time, and so directed that those people who need it most, the children, would get it first.

In this great anxiety to do the thing rapidly and broadly, there were certain scientific facts that weren't quite, let's say, wholly satisfactory to these scientists themselves. They were not sure that their test methods were as accurate as they should like. When they found certain evidence appearing, they went back to the job of testing again, and temporarily held up the distribution and administering of this vaccine.

Now, the vaccine, I believe, of two companies—Parke, Davis and Lilly, I believe, are the names—have been released; and they are going ahead with this process so as to get it in full flow again.

Mrs. Hobby has been at the center of this whole business of agreeing with the advisory committee how was the way to do it, how we can speed it up. But they always have held up this stand-ard, safety, making certain that they are not doing something that would work against the life of the child, but to protect the life of that child.

So I think that we really ought to remember at times the debt we owe all of those people for the devoted work they have put into this thing.

Q. Merriman Smith, United Press: Mr. President, Senator Symington wants to know whether this country has lost control of the air to Russia. Do you think so, sir?

THE PRESIDENT. Well, that is a very generalized statement "lost control of the air."

As anybody who is experienced in warfare knows, control of the air is a relative thing, and anybody with a certain amount of air force in action can gain control over a place where he chooses to concentrate his air, for a temporary space of time, even in the face of quite great general superiority on the other side.

The Germans did it to us as late as January 1, 1945. Those of you who were in the European theater on that day will remember what a drenching our airfields got even though we later destroyed a great deal of that attacking force.

Now, as of today, most of you people are rather familiar with the character of our Air Force, including its scientific character.

Back in about 1948–49, we began to build heavily these B–36, well knowing it was a transition aircraft. It was an aircraft that did give us a big intercontinental bomber at the same time that we knew that the day of the big jet bomber was coming along.

But you have to standardize at different periods on particular types. Now, those B–36 planes were good planes for their day, and they are now being phased out as others will come along.

So in the very new ones, since with this possession of this intermediate bomber we had a chance to work for a really fine type in the B–52 and its successors which will certainly come along, we may not have as many B–52's as we should like at this moment. I don't know the exact number, but to say that we have lost in a twinkling all of this great technical development and technical excellence as well as the numbers in our total aircraft is just not true.

Q. Charles E. Shutt, Telenews: Mr. President, in his report to the Nation last night, Secretary Dulles favored a cautious approach on the Big Four meeting. Some observers on Capitol Hill feel that that might be too timid an approach. Would you comment, sir?

THE PRESIDENT. Well, no, because I can't—I don't quite understand the—I can't understand the question, really.

Of course you are going to be cautious. "Cautious" means to proceed at something no matter how hopefully, with caution for your own, let's say, safety, security, or other interests.

Now, as I say, and, as Secretary Dulles said, we are approaching this thing now from a greater position of strength than we ever had before.

We have the unity of Western Europe more nearly assured than before. We are now, by treaty, going to have German forces. We have the Austrian Treaty completed. We are in a better position than ever before. We are stronger. But that does not mean we will be less vigilant.

Now, I don't mean to say that the search for evidences of good faith and the chances to, let's say, lower the burden of armaments and to bring about some progress in peace, they won't be any the less intensive. Of course, they will. But it does not mean, caution, that you are not going to hunt for peace, it means you are going to look out for yourself.

Q. Martin S. Hayden, Detroit News: Mr. President, going back to this airpower question, apparently Senator Symington was aroused because of a report that in Moscow they had seen a flight of new intercontinental bombers or something of the sort.

I would like to ask you, sir, has there been any Russian air development reported that has thrown off your previous planning as to Russian air strength? In other words, have you been greatly startled by any of this.

THE PRESIDENT. I believe this: that from time to time, in several lines of scientific endeavor, aircraft and others, there has come in evidence that exceeded predictions of where they would be at any particular moment.

I remember approving the statement that was issued on that aircraft. I have forgotten the details of it, so I want to be a little bit guarded in my speech. But we do know that they flew past— they didn't fly past on May Day, you know, it was bad weather— but in practice for the May Day they flew past several times, a number of airplanes, among which were a few items which, by the size of their engines, the size of the airframe, would certainly be capable of long-distance flight, carrying heavy loads.

Now, what their condition is inside, what their readiness of technical perfection and all the things that we know go into one of these things, nobody knows.

Q. James B. Reston, New York Times: Sir, you told us 2 weeks ago, I believe, that you were proceeding, or the Government was proceeding, with direct conversations with Communist China about the situation in the Formosa Straits.

Where do we stand on that now?

THE PRESIDENT. Proceeding, did you say?

Q. Mr. Reston: Well, I thought, I got the impression that the Government was looking into the possibility of direct negotiations.

THE PRESIDENT. I think the Secretary of State announced shortly after he came back from Asia, as I recall, that if there seemed to be profitable chances for talking on the one subject that he said, the cease-fire in the Straits, he would be quite ready to do it.

I think there is nothing additional to add since then. I know of nothing that has occurred that would change his readiness or his receptiveness to that idea for that one purpose only. But I do not know of anything else on this day.

Q. Robert E. Clark, International News Service: Mr. President, this is a double Big Four question: do you think you might visit any other European city, as London or Paris, en route to or from a Big Four conference; and if it were possible, would you like to have Marshal Zhukov present at the Big Four conference?

THE PRESIDENT. Well, I hadn't given any thought, Mr. Clark, to either question.

As you know, I have a tremendous number of friends in both those cities, and on a friendly basis I would like to drop in. But there might be a lot of protocol questions that would make such a visit a very difficult affair.

I couldn't say, to answer your second question, who the Soviets should choose as the personnel of their delegation. But if Marshal Zhukov were there, he and I at least would have a chance to talk personally and, I think, to talk over events since 1945 among ourselves. We might just get some item of value out of it; I am not sure.

Q. Pat Munroe, Salt Lake City Deseret News: Mr. President, we hear reports on Capitol Hill that both Russia and Great Britain will steal the show from American businessmen at the United Nations Atoms for Peace Conference in Geneva in August.

Some say that our Atomic Energy Commission is actually

discouraging industry in this country from putting its best foot forward.

I wonder if you have any comment, sir?

THE PRESIDENT. Well, I should say someone is very badly mistaken in two ways.

First, as to our purpose in going to this meeting, we are not going to this meeting to conduct a contest. As long ago as December 9, 1953, I asked publicly other nations of the globe to cooperate with us in placing before the entire world the knowledge concerning the possible peaceful uses of atomic energy.

If anybody comes there ready to follow up along that line, and to show concretely and constructively that they are ready to devote the atomic science to the betterment of man and not to his destruction, I will applaud just as loudly as I know how, and particularly if that is an effective thing.

Now, when it comes down to the discouragement by the AEC, the AEC then must be doing two things, because they are the ones that come to me and hold out in front of me the great opportunity we have here.

The reactor that we are to put there—while it is a simple one, and one of the relatively less expensive—it is an actual operating reactor that we are putting in there, in cooperation with the Swiss Government and the Secretary General of the United Nations.

We asked, I believe, 1100 scientists to prepare papers on this— no, we asked American scientists, I believe 1100 American scientists responded with papers that could be presented there on this business of peaceful uses.

I forget the number of American industries that are cooperating. I expect it really to be a very splendid exhibition of what America, an aroused America, in this line can do.

And, therefore, I can say this: I sincerely hope that others put their best foot forward because ours is going to be something that no one can laugh off. [*Confers with Mr. Hagerty*]

Seventy-five industrial firms, I am given to understand.

Q. William H. Lawrence, New York Times: I wonder, sir, as a military man yourself, and as Commander in Chief, if you could give us your opinion as to the effect on both morale and the re-enlistment rate in the military forces, if all the commissaries and PX's were to be shut down as the Hoover Commission now suggests?

THE PRESIDENT. Well, I am sorry you added the last two or three words, because——

Q. Mr. Lawrence: I will withdraw them, sir. [*Laughter*]

THE PRESIDENT. The reason being this, Mr. Lawrence: I have not read that report, and they may put in some qualifications.

I have never believed in the uncontrolled spread of the Post Exchanges of the United States Army. But I believe that to take away the commissary privileges and the Post Exchange privileges from military, uniformed personnel, wherever they may be, when those are really needful things in order to give them the normal business of living, and give it to them at a decent price, I believe it would be a terrible injustice to those people.

On the other hand, it is one of those things in which just judgment must come in, in order that a privilege is not abused and becomes something that is intolerable.

Q. Edward J. Milne, Providence Journal: Mr. President, in connection with the NATO Council visit—some of us were at Norfolk the other day—Admiral Wright was not himself doing any griping, but there was some suggestion that, perhaps, the forces assigned to SACLANT are not adequate for the mission.

I wonder if you, in connection with the visit, would care to comment on your views on the adequacy of this strength.

THE PRESIDENT. Well, no, I can't because I have not heard the complaint, and the Navy Department has not brought up to me lately detailed reports of the strength of SACLANT.

Q. Mr. Milne: Would you feel from what you do know, sir, in general, that we are relatively better off in terms of a new battle of the Atlantic than we were during the opening of World War II?

THE PRESIDENT. I think so, by all odds.

Q. Robert J. Donovan, New York Herald Tribune: Mr. President, I wonder if I could ask these two questions: it was reported last week that Mrs. Hobby, for purely personal reasons and not because of the Salk controversy, would leave the Government in a few months. One, I wondered if you had heard of that and, two, I wondered, sir, if you could comment on the supply of this vaccine. It seems to be shorter than we had expected; and I wondered if you had had any report and knew how much was available or whether you are going to ask for——

THE PRESIDENT. Mr. Donovan, I will do my best to answer both questions. But you must realize that as much as I do my homework to keep up with the business of this Government, there are details that really could be best answered in some of the departments rather than to come to me.

First, Mrs. Hobby placed me on notice some many months ago that conditions might arise that would compel her to leave Government.

Now, the only thing I will say about it is this: if she has to go, I will be very, very disappointed. I think she has not only proved her own worth, but I think she is a symbol of something in which I very deeply believe: that properly trained women of this country are just as capable of carrying heavy executive jobs as are the men. And I think she has done a mighty magnificent job.

Now, as to supply, the report I had this morning was that— what time was it? [*Confers with Mr. Hagerty*]

Yes. They have enough in their hands for the first go-around, that is, the first shot of all the people that they had calculated on, that is, the first and second grades.

If some of those shots are not given by the time that school is out, particularly in the South, their plan is to set up days for meeting either at the schoolhouses or other places where these shots will be given. So the only estimate I was given this morning on amounts was that they had enough on hand and in sight to do that.

Q. Ray L. Scherer, National Broadcasting Company: Mr. President, can you shed any light on the report that there is a plan for Mr. Nixon to make a good will trip to Europe, including a possible stopoff in Moscow?

THE PRESIDENT. No such plan has been mentioned to me.

Q. Andrew F. Tully, Jr., Scripps-Howard: Mr. President, have you had any correspondence lately with Marshal Zhukov?

THE PRESIDENT. No.

Q. Mr. Tully: Do you plan it, sir?

THE PRESIDENT. What?

Q. Mr. Tully: Do you plan to?

THE PRESIDENT. Not at the moment.

Q. Sarah McClendon, El Paso Times: Sir, the military reserve manpower bill was changed somewhat, as you know, by the House Armed Services Committee, and there was quite a talk yesterday in the House by Congressman Brooks of Louisiana about the buildup of the Red Forces, in addition to other reports on the airpower we have been getting.

I wonder if you still think, in view of these changes, that this bill will be sufficient to give this country, if passed, the protection it needs?

THE PRESIDENT. Well, this bill, of course, I would not claim is perfection in the sense of getting our military manpower trained and prepared as I should like to see it, but it represents a very great step forward. Consequently, I support it not only passively, I support it very actively, and urgently hope that it will be passed; although later, unquestionably, we will find features in which we will want to improve it even more.

Q. Garnett D. Horner, Washington Star: Mr. President, can you tell us yet your views about the postal pay raise bill which Republican leaders in Congress predict you will veto?

THE PRESIDENT. Well, I haven't been studying more earnestly for a long time than I am studying on that bill. As a matter of fact, I have studied a couple of hours this morning. I am still studying that bill.

Q. Alan S. Emory, Watertown Times: Mr. President, on Monday Secretary Hobby told the Senate Labor Committee that no one could have foreseen the public demand for the anti-polio vaccine.

What do you think was the difficulty in foreseeing the great public demand for the vaccine?

THE PRESIDENT. I don't know to what she is referring. You have to go and ask her the question.

Q. Lawrence Fernsworth, Concord (New Hampshire) Monitor: Mr. President, the plight of the American Indians has recently been discussed in a certain sector of the press, *Look* magazine, and a church publication. One of these articles talks of the Indians from South Dakota as being obliged to haul water in rusty barrels from 30 to 100 miles; talks of disease, poverty, and high infant mortality. It describes the plight of the average American Indian as being little better than was the plight of the refugees in Korea.

One of the proposals suggested in one of these articles is a 4-point program for the American Indian. Another is a relocation program.

Now, it has been noted that one of the pledges during the Republican campaign was that this matter, the welfare of the American Indians, would receive attention. Could the President tell us whether any progress has been made in that direction?

THE PRESIDENT. I note that there has been progress made with the Indians in the progressive granting of citizenship, where this has been applicable, and so on.

The particular case you bring up, I don't know about. I will look it up, because I agree with your implicit criticism, if such conditions exist, it is high time they were stopped. I think it can be stopped.

Q. Walter Kerr, New York Herald Tribune: Mr. President, in its recent note——

THE PRESIDENT. Would you identify yourself?

Q. Mr. Kerr: I beg your pardon, sir, Walter Kerr of the Herald Tribune.

THE PRESIDENT. Thank you.

Q. Mr. Kerr: In its recent note to the Soviet Government proposing Four Power talks, the United States, like Britain and France, has suggested an exchange of views on the great problems of the day.

I wonder if you would care, either today or perhaps at an early conference to come, if you would care to discuss what you regard as what great problems you had in mind when you approved the text of that note.

THE PRESIDENT. I think that Mr. Dulles pointed out last evening that the purpose of this one conference would be to try to discover directions or paths for searching for solutions to these great problems. I think he enumerated some of them, such as the problem of the satellite states, the unification of Germany, the—I forget the adjective he used, but at least the penetration of so many nations supported by the Cominform, the international communistic organization. He named a few of that kind, and that is the kind of thing, I think, that would probably be mentioned as you search for ways that these should be approached.

Would you set up special groups? Would you turn it over to ordinary diplomatic exchanges, or what could you do? That is the kind of thing I think would be talked about.

Q. Chalmers M. Roberts, Washington Post and Times Herald: Mr. President, last night you used the phrase that you felt there was a greater maturity among the American people now than some time ago when you were discussing the possible——

THE PRESIDENT. If I used the word "maturity," I probably meant knowledge or understanding, in that sense.

Some years back, I was struck by the fact that we were probably going to extremes in this thing. It was either black or white. You either had a war right now, or peace that was wonderful, and you would get it.

I believe that people have learned through a dozen attempts, through rebuffs, through the reading in the newspapers and hearing on the television and the radio about the process and progress of these conferences, that you don't expect too much.

But, on the other hand, you don't ignore any chance to reach some agreement that may represent one tiny step toward this great aspiration of men.

Now, I should possibly not have used the word "maturity," but I do mean knowledge and understanding of these facts.

Q. Mr. Roberts: I was wondering, sir, whether that phrase or thought covered this aspect: there have been some people in Congress, including members of your own party, who appear to take the position that even to go to such a conference is an act of appeasement. And I wondered if you felt that that attitude was really not expressive of the American people today.

THE PRESIDENT. I don't believe it for a minute. May I be personal? I have met with these people through months, and there is no appeasement in my heart that I know about.

As I understand, appeasement is selling out rights or other people to gain some fancied immediate end of your own. I just can't believe that America in general either wants it or that they suspect their government in general is apt to fall into that trap.

Q. Edward P. Morgan, American Broadcasting Company: Following up Mr. Roberts' question, and referring somewhat to both your and Mr. Dulles' observations last night about maturity and sophistication of American thinking, as reflected in your mail, and so forth, do you think, sir, that we may have to make a rather deep adjustment in our thinking under the light of present developments abroad on such things as East-West trade, and what neutrality for Germany means in both Russian and other terms?

THE PRESIDENT. Well, I think this: certain sectors of our population unquestionably will have to make adjustments, because they have not thought these things through.

You can say one thing: trade is the greatest weapon in the hands of the diplomat.

Now, how he uses it, whether it is in negative fashion or in positive fashion, to gain the legitimate ends of his government, that is great statesmanship and, particularly, international statesmanship.

So, just to adopt a policy and say, "We won't trade," and think that only good will come out of that is, I think, false.

We have to say "When does trade in what things benefit us most and our friends."

Remember, we have got friends in this world; this business of trade is a very complicated business. So I would say as long as we are not helping the war-making powers directly of other people, we should study the question objectively and what it means to us, and not just go by preconception.

Q. Mr. Morgan: Could you just——

THE PRESIDENT. I am trying to get around as far as I can.

Q. George H. Hall, St. Louis Post-Dispatch: There have been some suggestions that the Hoover Commission wants to make some changes or rather the Hoover Commission task force wants to make some changes in the setup of the TVA. Would you like to see any change whatever in the setup as it is now constituted?

THE PRESIDENT. Well now, that is a question I couldn't say, because as much as I have been in this TVA in question-and-answer periods, I certainly don't know all the details of its organization.

I think that the Hoover Commission has served a very great purpose for this country. And this time, you remember, the second time, it not only had strictly organizational problems, it had organizational and functional problems to take up.

In other words, was the Government in business it shouldn't be in, or should it get into something that it wasn't in, or was it doing it in the right way or in the right places? It has had a very broad charter under which to operate.

As its subcommittee reports come up to the committee itself, they will be studied by the combined brains of some very great Americans. Finally, they come to the executive department and to the Congress simultaneously. Some answers are reached.

Now, just exactly what they proposed here, I don't know. But I would say this: as you will recall, we will never wreck the TVA. It is a going historical concern. It's served a useful purpose. It was put up for particular purposes and, actually, if you go back to the original bill, I don't think many people can quarrel about the purposes for which it was originally set up.

Q. Henri Pierre, LeMonde (Paris): Mr. President, would you care to comment about the next visit of the Soviet leaders in Yugoslavia and, generally speaking, about the idea of a neutrality belt of states between the two worlds?

THE PRESIDENT. Well, no, I cannot even say what is behind this visit, except, obviously, there is hope of *rapprochement* of some kind, that we don't know the details about at all.

And I do say this: that there seems to be developing the thought that there might be built up a series of neutralized states from north to south through Europe.

Now, remember this: in the agreement of the neutralization of Austria, it does not mean a disarmed Austria. It is not a blank, it is not a military blank. It is on the order of Switzerland.

Switzerland is committed to the sustaining of its own neutrality and, I believe, would fight to the death for it.

All right. That kind of a neutrality is a far different thing from just a military vacuum.

Merriman Smith, United Press: Thank you, Mr. President.

NOTE: President Eisenhower's sixty-ninth news conference was held in the Executive Office Building from 10:32 to 11:02 o'clock on Wednesday morning, May 18, 1955. In attendance: 202.

101 ¶ Memorandum to Federal Agencies Directing Participation in a National Civil Defense Exercise. *May* 18, 1955

[Released May 18, 1955. Dated May 16, 1955]

To the Heads of All Departments and Agencies:

On June 15 and 16, 1955, a national Civil Defense test exercise will be held. The forty-eight States, the District of Columbia, and the United States Territories and Possessions will participate.

Vigilance and preparedness under all circumstances all of the time is essential to the civil defense of our country. Every community and every citizen must be ready to act swiftly and with confident knowledge of what they are about. Not only will such vigilance and preparedness minimize the effects of any disaster, it can powerfully deter aggression itself.

Therefore, I hereby direct each department and agency of the Executive Branch of the Government, both at the national and field level: To cooperate fully with Federal, State and local civil defense authorities; to take part in this civil defense exercise; and to the extent feasible under the terms of Executive Order No. 10529, dated April 22, 1954, to authorize the release of Federal Employees who are enrolled in local civil defense organizations to perform such civil defense duties as are assigned during this exercise.

Dwight D. Eisenhower

102 ¶ Veto of Postal Field Service Compensation Bill.   *May* 19, 1955

To the United States Senate:

I return herewith, without my approval, S. 1 "To increase the rates of basic compensation of officers and employees in the field service of the Post Office Department." I take this action for three reasons. First, the bill creates new discriminations or inequities which would affect many thousands of postal employees. Second, the bill creates grave administrative problems such as the establishment of thousands of individual pay rates. It forces awkward and unfair administrative practices in a government department whose operations affect every person, every enterprise, every community in the country. Third, the bill imposes a heavier burden upon the taxpayer than is necessary to establish salary rates throughout the department, which will compare favorably with rates for similar work elsewhere in government and in private industry.

At the outset of this Administration, the Postmaster General began a comprehensive study of the entire postal system.

The principal purpose was to discover effective ways and means by which the American people could be assured more speedy, certain, economical and efficient handling of their mail. Obviously, this purpose can be achieved only if *first,* postal employees are dedicated and satisfied in career service because of fair compensation, good working conditions, adequate benefits in vacations, insurance, sick leave and old-age security; and *second,* the Department's administrative structure, incorporating the best management practices, is so designed that merit and responsibility are recognized and rewarded.

In accordance with the findings of the comprehensive study, on January 11, 1955, by special message to the Congress, I recommended an increase in the salaries of postal employees which would be composed of two elements—a general increase in postal pay and a reclassification of postal positions that would eliminate inequities. To accomplish these purposes I recommended a 5 percent pay raise and adjustments in classification to bring about proper wage relationships among the various jobs in postal service. The cost of the reclassification proposals would have brought the total increase to 6½ percent, with an aggregate annual cost of $129 million.

Those recommendations, if adopted, would have placed the salaries of postal employees in proper relationship to the salaries paid for similar work in nearly all the larger cities. The pay raises recommended were substantially greater than the increase in the cost of living since the last adjustment in postal wages.

Subsequently, the House Post Office and Civil Service Committee, by a substantial bi-partisan majority, reported a bill— H.R. 4644—which, although approximately $30 million a year more costly than my recommendations, embodied the essential elements of a reclassification system. In the matter of reclassification, that bill, as reported by the Committee, could have been, and still can be, with certain corrections, the basis for legislation which would establish fair relationships between the salaries of various positions in the postal service on the sound principle of equal pay for equal work and more pay for more difficult and responsible work.

It has always been recognized that in the consideration of pay legislation, there can be a reasonable difference of opinion as to what constitutes an appropriate increase. But there can be no compromise with the principle of fairness, and any pay legislation must be fair to *all* to whom it applies. It must be workable administratively and not be excessive in cost.

The bill before me fails to meet these criteria. Specifically:

(1) It discriminates against large groups of postal employees such as rural letter carriers, special delivery messengers, and many supervisors and postmasters. These total tens of thousands.

(2) Aside from creating new and serious administrative problems, the total cost of the bill, approximately $180 million a year,

is substantially greater than is necessary to adjust postal salaries to a fair level, either from the standpoint of pay for comparable work or from the standpoint of increase in the cost of living.

I regret the necessity of the action which I am taking. It is my earnest hope and recommendation that the Congress will quickly consider and enact postal pay legislation that will be in the public interest and fair to all of the half million employees who man the Postal Service. To meet this test, such legislation should provide a reasonable increase in pay for all postal field service employees. It should provide for reclassification of postal positions to bring about proper wage relationships so as to eliminate inequities. It should not discriminate against some groups in favor of others, and it should be administratively workable.

Because the enactment of such legislation will substantially increase the postal deficit, I wish again to emphasize the imperative need for postal rates that will make the Postal Service self-supporting and be based on service rendered to the user. We can no longer afford to continue a costly deficit operation paid for by millions of taxpayers in amounts out of all proportion to the postal services that they as individuals receive.

DWIGHT D. EISENHOWER

103 ¶ Remarks to the President's Committee on the Employment of the Physically Handicapped. *May 23, 1955*

General Maas, Judge Cathey, Prizewinners in the Essay Contest, and Ladies and Gentlemen:

It is a great privilege to meet again with this Committee, even though my meeting with you is for a few brief moments only.

We have a country dedicated to equality of opportunity. We make much in many Fourth of July speeches that this equality of opportunity goes to all, regardless of race, color, religion, and so on. It seems to me that we might extend it, at least within our own hearts and minds, to include: "Or to any who may be somewhat physically different or handicapped so long as that person can be made a useful member of society."

No one wants to be a ward of charity. Indeed, this word "opportunity" seems to me to contain much that means happiness for the human—opportunity to expand and to be useful, to know that he is contributing his share to the advancement of that great society of which he is a part.

I think it even goes this far: we can differentiate between a government that is based upon individual opportunity, and one that is based upon regimentation, in this way: opportunity brings that richness of productivity in which all may share. Individual initiative, harnessed together for the good of the whole, is the most productive inspiration and impulse we have.

Regimentation does nothing but distribute deficits—deficits that occur when we don't take advantage of these great impulses in the human heart and mind to produce what he can for himself and for his society.

I repeat I believe, therefore, that opportunity—individual opportunity and freedom—enriches a whole society, and regimentation merely distributes the losses that have occurred.

So it seems to me we cannot afford for one moment to neglect placing opportunity in front of all that are capable of doing anything whatsoever with it. And the mere fact that a person may be minus a limb or one of his senses, or anything else, has nothing to do with it, any more than do the other differences among humans that we conclude should not be allowed to sway us in the government that is applied to all.

I could think of no greater service that this Committee over the years has contributed to the United States than to bring to each—not only the handicapped people themselves, but to all of us—the fact that opportunity does truly belong to all. We are not going to be satisfied until it is brought to them, and they are allowed to take full advantage for their own betterment and that of our glorious country.

Thank you so much for the opportunity to be with you once again. It is truly a great privilege. Good morning.

NOTE: The President spoke at the annual meeting of the Committee in the Departmental Auditorium at 10:00 a.m. His opening words "General Maas, Judge Cathey" referred to Melvin J. Maas, Chairman of the Committee, and Sam M. Cathey, Judge of the Police Court of Asheville, N.C., who was chosen as the "Handicapped American of the Year."

104 ¶ Remarks at a Dinner Sponsored by the District of Columbia Republican Women's Finance Committee. *May* 23, 1955

Mr. Vice President, ladies and gentlemen:

Had there been any doubt in my mind as to where I was coming this evening, it would have been removed when I heard the cheers and the yelling. I thank you from the bottom of my heart.

Anybody attempting a serious task cannot fail to have a very heart-warming experience when he realizes that friends watching him approve of the general course of action he takes and the decisions he makes. So I simply could not overemphasize the feeling of gratitude that I have for you here.

Now, permit me to talk for a moment about the Republican Party and why I am so proud of being a member of the Republican Party. I believe that the greatest honor, the greatest distinction, that can come to any American is to feel that in his own niche he has been of service to the United States of America. I firmly believe that the Republican Party is today the finest political organism we have through which the electorate can do its part in preserving for the future the kind of America we have inherited, and, at the same time, make of the American government a dynamic sort of organism to make certain that every man, woman, and child can remain proud, always, that he is an American.

This country was founded on the theory that man has his origin through a divine power. Our forefathers said "We hold that all men are endowed by their Creator with certain unalienable rights." That was the explanation our forefathers gave to the world, whose good opinion they understood was necessary at that moment for the existence of this nation.

As we maintain and follow up that kind of thinking, we realize that any party that purports to be useful in the support of America must recognize that moral basis on which we are founded, and support it in every possible way. Which means, in simple language, that every individual among us has been created in the image of his Maker. He has equal rights, equal opportunities. He is not to be regimented or controlled unnecessarily, but to be given every opportunity to live according to his concepts of justice, decency, and right. That is America.

Now this kind of concept does not mean that we forget the unfortunate, that we neglect the poor. On the contrary, it asserts that we are in a very definite sense our brother's keeper. When in this modern world the incidents and the circumstances of industrial production and mass production in our factories have brought about conditions that were unknown to our forefathers, we will never let those individuals, those free Americans—we will never let them down.

We follow the great concepts of our forebears: that every individual must remain free, that he must have his rights, that government must be divided not only functionally but geographically, that our control of others is limited to that necessary for the good of the whole. That is the kind of doctrine that the Republican Party presents to America for its approval and is the kind of thing that has been going on for the last two years and more, and which you people have been so kind as to approve. And I believe it is because the administration has tried to carry on in these basic concepts in accordance with your thinking.

Now we have been told that the Republican Party is a minority party. And I suppose by statistical records that is true. But it is not true that the doctrine I have been so roughly expounding as belonging to you and to me and the administration is minority thinking in this country—not by any means. That is majority thinking.

We are not trying to go back to the horse cars; we are not trying to fly to Mars. We believe that America is advancing to many expanding eras of prosperity, a prosperity widely shared among all our citizens. And in going to that place, we take the principles of the past and apply them to the problems of the moment. That's all there is to it. It is a very simple sort of idea.

And we are not doing it for the glorification of the Republican Party, but for the benefit of 160 million Americans.

Now it is, to my mind, a rather appealing and inspiring party this evening which has been brought together merely by women. I believe that women are more apt than are we men to live by strong convictions and spiritual values. They have the family to keep together, the children to raise, and they recognize that all our values are not material. And so, when they believe in something, they put their hearts into it. And I should like to express my particular appreciation to the women who make such a party as this possible—who have worked so hard to bring it about.

I would not want to say that we have not great leaders among the men. We do. You have one on the platform—the Vice President. And we have dozens of others of his age in the Republican Party who bring inspiration to all of us by their dedicated service to the United States of America. But to these women who have made this party possible, my humble appreciation, my deepest thanks, and the thought that by doing this kind of thing all over the Nation they will inspire thousands and millions of others who think as we do to join us, and finally to adopt our label—Republicans.

Thank you very much.

NOTE: The President spoke at the Sheraton-Park Hotel, Washington, D.C.

105 ¶ Remarks to the National Association of Radio and Television Broadcasters.
May 24, 1955

President Fellows, ladies and gentlemen:

It is a great honor to appear before this distinguished body. In my mind there is some doubt as to the exact capacity in which I do appear. I see some of my friends of the press here. They know that I have been on Presidential press conferences where there has been television present. So it raises a question—Do I come as a co-worker or as a sponsor?

I understand that this is the first time in the history of your organization that a President has appeared before you. Governments notoriously move slowly, and sometimes this is a virtue. But I think that after this length of time, it is safe to make a tentative conclusion that radio and television are here to stay, and a President, therefore, can afford to take them quite seriously. Actually, not only here to stay but a mighty force in our civilization, one that is certain to grow. And because it will grow and be more powerful in its influence upon all of us, conventions such as this have very deep social and professional problems to consider, on which they must reach proper conclusions.

Nothing has been so important to us as an informed public. As long ago as Jefferson's time he said were he forced to choose between a government without schools or schools without government, he would unhesitatingly take a civilization in which he had schools without government, well knowing that an informed public would soon discover the need for government and establish a proper one among themselves. And in the reverse case, he apparently did not know what might happen, because government with an uninformed public can be, as we know, very vicious.

One of the things that has made us an informed public is the fact that we have had a free press, and now these great institutions, the radio and the television, have moved in to take their place alongside the older media of mass communications. And this means, if we are to draw any lessons from the past, that they in turn must be free.

It behooves you, then, I think, to discover the formulae and to evolve them among yourselves and to announce them and to follow them so that they will keep these great media free in the truest sense of the word.

We must not wait for governmental regulation, or compulsory governmental intervention in the form of suits and anti-trust actions and all the rest. We must grow up with this great force, assuring the freedom of people to express their proper opinions, with the whole industry governed by the same rules that govern newspapers, the normal rules of decency and good taste. As long as those are observed, any proper opinion—any opinion—can be expressed before the public.

There is a tremendous responsibility here—in some ways, I think, transcending that that is placed before the publisher. The publisher puts in your home a piece of print. It is essentially cold—although, of course, we admit that some writers have an ability to dress it up and make even disagreeable facts at times look fairly pleasant. But with the television or with the radio, you put an appealing voice or an engaging personality in the living room of the home, where there are impressionable people from the ages of understanding on up.

In many ways therefore the effect of your industry in swaying public opinion, and I think, particularly about burning questions of the moment, may be even greater than the press, although I am sure that my friends here of the press will have plenty to criticize in that statement. Nevertheless, it is something different, and you do introduce personality as well as cold fact. I think, again, that places added responsibility to see that the news, in those areas of the radio and television field that have to do with the dissemination of facts, is truthfully told, with the integrity of the entire industry behind it.

I once heard an expression with respect to newspaper standards: the newspaper columns belong to the public and the editorial page belongs to the paper. And, for myself, I find that an easy standard to follow and to apply as I examine a newspaper. I should think that some such standard could be developed among you. Of course you want to entertain. Of course you want people to look at it, and I am all for it. And I think everybody else is. But when we come to something that we call news—and I am certain that I am not speaking of anything you haven't discussed earnestly among yourselves—let us simply be sure it is news. Let all of the rest of the time be given to entertainment or the telling of stories or the fanciful fairy tales that we sometimes find in other portions of publications.

Now, to remain free, the government does have to interfere or to intervene, possibly, in your industry more than it does in those that deal with the printed word. After all, there seems to be only one canopy of air over the United States and in the rest of the world, and so there must be some means of deciding who is to use the various channels available. We shall always hope, of course, that that is done fairly and without any relationship of partisan politics or any other inconsequential factor so far as this great medium and problem is concerned. But beyond that one necessary intervention and the enforcement, as I said, of the rules of decency, my only plea is this: that you people take thought and counsel among yourselves to insure that this medium—these two great media—remain free—completely free of domination of any unfair kind and they belong to the people. Thus, as I see it, you will do a great and growing part in informing the public.

Now, just a moment on my favorite subject. I quoted Jefferson to you but I think if Jefferson were alive today he would state the proposition in language so much more emphatic than he then used that you would scarcely recognize the similarity. Never was it so important as it is today that the American public is informed. We have burning questions abroad that stretch from a four-power conference around the world to the Indonesian crisis—the Indo China crisis. It is absolutely essential that the Americans know the actual facts of these problems. Moreover, that they be helped to gain an understanding of the relationship between these facts, because knowledge alone, necessarily—always remember—is not sufficient. We must understand.

We must understand the relationship between the farmer working in Kansas in a wheat field, and the need for wheat in far off Pakistan or some other country. We must understand these things if we are to know why we have to promote trade, why we have to promote truth about our country abroad, why we are so anxious to take America in picture and in word and in printed form, and indeed in our arts, in our entertainment of troops, to other countries, to let them see, insofar as we may: What is America? Why are we so proud of it? Why has it brought the greatest standard of living and given the greatest opportunity for intellectual and spiritual development? This is the way that we must win the so called cold war. This is the way that we must win our way to peace.

I think everybody in the television and radio professions has a right to think of himself as a man bearing a great responsibility as a crusader and help to do this job of education, of ourselves and of others about us, and to bring home here an understanding of what goes on in the rest of the world.

I think today Jefferson's statement might be paraphrased to say: If I had to have international free communications or some kind of world government that could enforce the peace, I would unhesitatingly choose complete, free, international communications. And then we would be sure that we would find ways for sovereign nations to achieve man's age-old aspiration: peace among men with prosperity fairly shared by all.

I repeat, my friends, it has been a great honor to appear before you. If I have started a precedent, I am very proud of it, and I do trust that future Presidents will find it not only convenient but practically necessary to appear before you and tell you, in their turn, what is on their hearts at the moment.

Thank you, and good morning.

NOTE: The President spoke at the Sheraton-Park Hotel, Washington, D.C., at 11:30 a.m. His opening words "President Fellows" referred to Harold E. Fellows, President of the Association.

106　¶ Letter to Ross Rizley, Chairman, Civil Aeronautics Board, Regarding the States-Alaska Case.　*May* 25, 1955

Dear Mr. Rizley:

I am returning herewith the decision and proposed order of the Civil Aeronautics Board in the States-Alaska Case (Docket No. 5756, et al.).

I am in general agreement with the major aspects of the Board's proposed action in this case and I approve of the Board's proposed order except as it relates to the duration of the certificates for Alaska Airlines and Pacific Northern Airlines. I am in full agreement with the Board's view that a merger between Alaska Airlines and Pacific Northern would be an important step forward in strengthening air transportation between the States and Alaska and at the same time reduce the need for Federal subsidy support. While three-year certificates might well encourage and facilitate such a merger, such certificates would create serious problems for both carriers in the matter of financing new equipment. I am convinced that there are other steps that the Board can take within its authority to encourage and facilitate such a merger, and I trust that the Board will take all such steps as are reasonable and appropriate.

In view of the great importance of air transportation with up-to-date equipment to the people of Alaska and the future development of the Territory, the certificates of Alaska Airlines and Pacific Northern should be extended for five years. You have advised me, through the Director of the Bureau of the Budget, that in the opinion of the Board a five-year extension will enable the carriers to finance the purchase of new equipment on a sound basis with consequent benefit to the people of the Territory in better service and more effective competition.

Accordingly, I request that the Board present for my approval a revised order in this case that is consistent with the above comments.

Sincerely,

DWIGHT D. EISENHOWER

NOTE: On May 27 the President approved the revised order providing for renewal of the certificates for the Pacific Northern and Alaska Airlines for a period of 5 years rather than 3 years. The proposed order, referred to in the first paragraph of this letter, and the revised order dated May 25 were made public by the Civil Aeronautics Board.

107 ¶ Special Message to the Congress Transmitting Conventions and Recommendations Adopted at Geneva by the International Labor Conference. *May 26, 1955*

To the Congress of the United States:

In accordance with the obligations of the United States of America as a member of the International Labor Organization I transmit herewith authentic texts of four Conventions and eight Recommendations adopted at Geneva by the International Labor Conference, as follows:

Convention (No. 99) concerning minimum wage fixing machinery in agriculture, adopted June 28, 1951;

Recommendation (No. 89) concerning minimum wage fixing machinery in agriculture, adopted June 28, 1951;

Convention (No. 100) concerning equal remuneration for men and women workers for work of equal value, adopted June 29, 1951;

Recommendation (No. 90) concerning equal remuneration for men and women workers for work of equal value, adopted June 29, 1951;

Convention (No. 101) concerning holidays with pay in agriculture, adopted June 26, 1952;

Recommendation (No. 93) concerning holidays with pay in agriculture, adopted June 26, 1952;

Recommendation (No. 94) concerning consultation and co-operation between employers and workers at the level of the undertaking, adopted June 26, 1952;

Convention (No. 103) concerning maternity protection (revised 1952), adopted June 28, 1952;

Recommendation (No. 95) concerning maternity protection, adopted June 28, 1952;

Recommendation (No. 96) concerning the minimum age of admission to work underground in coal mines, adopted June 19, 1953;

Recommendation (No. 97) concerning the protection of the health of workers in places of employment, adopted June 25, 1953;

Recommendation (No. 98) concerning holidays with pay, adopted June 23, 1954.

I transmit also the report of the Secretary of State with regard to the several Conventions and Recommendations, together with copies of letters from the Secretary of Labor to the Secretary of State setting forth the coordinated view of the interested departments and agencies of the executive branch of the Government with respect to the various instruments.

It is the opinion of those departments and agencies that the Conventions and Recommendations cited above fall within the purview of Article 19, paragraph 7(b), of the constitution of the International Labor Organization, which provides in the case of a federal state that Conventions and Recommendations which the federal government regards as appropriate under its constitutional system, in whole or in part, for action by the constituent states, provinces, or cantons rather than for federal action shall be referred to the appropriate federal and state authorities for their consideration. It is in accordance with the foregoing provisions that ratification of the Conventions by the United States is not deemed appropriate and that I submit the Conventions and Recommendations to the Congress for such consideration as it may wish to give.

I do not favor the enactment of Federal legislation with respect to the subject matter of the Convention (No. 101) and corresponding Recommendation (No. 93) concerning holidays with pay in agriculture, the Recommendation (No. 94) concerning consultation and cooperation between employers and workers at the level of the undertaking, and the Recommendation (No. 98) concerning holidays with pay, so far as it relates to private employment.

Existing Federal legislation adequately covers the substance of the Recommendation (No. 96) concerning the minimum age of admission to work underground in coal mines and the Recommendation (No. 98) concerning holidays with pay, as it relates to employees of the Federal Government. Accordingly, I do not advise the enactment of additional legislation by the Congress with respect to those subjects.

I am sending texts of the Conventions and Recommendations to the Secretary of the Interior in order that they may be transmitted to the Governments of Alaska, Guam, Hawaii, and the Virgin Islands for such action as may be deemed suitable. I am also transmitting the texts of the Conventions and Recommendations to the Secretary of the Interior for appropriate action and advice with regard to American Samoa, and, with the exception of the Recommendation (No. 96) concerning the minimum age of admission to work underground in coal mines, to the Secretary of the Interior and the Secretary of the Navy for appropriate action and advice with regard to those areas of the Trust Territory of the Pacific Islands under their respective jurisdictions.

DWIGHT D. EISENHOWER

NOTE: The text of the conventions and recommendations, the report of the Secretary of State, and the copies of letters from the Secretary of La-bor, transmitted with the message, are printed in House Document 172 (84th Cong., 1st sess.).

108   ¶ Remarks at Dedication of the Armed Forces Institute of Pathology, Walter Reed Medical Center.   *May* 26, 1955

Mr. Secretary, General DeCoursey, distinguished guests, my old friends of the Service, and ladies and gentlemen:

For the enlightenment of this audience, it is indeed fortunate that Dr. DeCoursey saw fit to tell us about pathology. Because for myself, I assure you, I have learned more in the last five minutes than I knew in my entire life before.

But I did not come here to talk scientifically and that is my excuse for not being better briefed in that particular subject. We are here today to dedicate a great building of stone and concrete and other materials. This in itself is an important event, because I am told that this building is arranged better and more efficiently for the conduct of the work here to be done than any other that this country has erected.

A good workman deserves good surroundings, and a good place in which to work, and so if we had nothing more here to dedicate than the building itself, it would still be an occasion worthy of note.

But the true dedication is probably more to the impulses which led to the erection of this building. Concern for human life, and not merely to lengthen out the span of our years, although to some of us here present this in itself is getting important, but to ease man of sufferings and difficulties and the lengthening of life's span so that he may yield to the common good more from the God-given talents that are his, so that he can contribute more to the spiritual and intellectual and cultural and economic development of our time.

Another impulse is that of cooperative effort. The Secretary spoke of an example of unification. I think some years ago those of us who were advocating unification of the Services saw something of this kind in the offing, even though we were ignorant of the exact form these developments would take. For that reason, I couldn't be happier that all of the Services are combined in this effort.

And then I think it gives us an example of how government should operate in providing and doing its part in advancing the welfare of our nation and our people. Lincoln said, you know, "The function of government is to do for people those things which they cannot do at all or so well do for themselves, but in those things which people can do better, the government ought not to interfere." Here is one of those typical partnership efforts that bring government and science and individuals all together to do a great job for humanity.

If we review only some of the accomplishments of the medical services of the united services, we would have a very long list. Following our armed units into the far corners of the globe, they have brought back to us a knowledge of diseases, or they have practically prevented them from ever reaching our shores. But I remember very well in the days of my youth when the term "yellow jack" was one of terror in the West and Southwest. People would not even venture into some of our coastal cities in the South because of the fear of yellow fever. Yet Service personnel, through their dedication, and their training, their devotion, brought about a knowledge of that disease and began to stamp it out, and finally practically eliminated it.

So in the same fashion, other diseases coming under control have each had as one of the contributing factors these great dedicated officers, doctors and technicians, nurses and others of the Armed Services' Medical Corps.

So here we see people working in the conviction that man—man himself—is important, his health, his ability to contribute. We see also the conviction that man, under God, can conquer his physical surroundings and make this place—this world—a better place in which to live. All of these thoughts, all of these impulses come together, as we think of the erection of this building and the services it is going to perform; and indeed it inspires us.

And so I should first like to pay my tribute to the men who thought of this building, the men whose work brought about here a proper home for the people working in this pathology for the united services. I want to pay tribute to all people who in any way have had a part in the development of the whole institution from the time of the Civil War, and to the accumulation here on this spot of the combined assets that will do so much for us.

So we can hope that this will make men more productive, their lives more rewarding, and in so doing, perhaps we will have a more secure country, a more peaceful world.

And so I dedicate this building to the conquest of disease so that mankind, more safe and secure in body, may more surely advance to a widely shared prosperity and an enduring and just peace.

Thank you very much.

NOTE: The President's opening words "Mr. Secretary, General DeCoursey" referred to Charles E. Wilson, Secretary of Defense, and Brig. Gen. Elbert DeCoursey, Director of the Armed Forces Institute of Pathology.

109   ¶ Special Message to the Congress
Recommending Amendments to the Refugee Relief
Act.   *May 27, 1955*

To the Congress of the United States:

The Refugee Relief Act of 1953 has now been in effect for almost two years.

It was enacted to enable the United States to participate with other nations in a great humanitarian effort for the relief of tragic victims of the postwar world, and for the reduction, in a measure, of over-population stresses in friendly nations.   Thus we would promote friendly relations with the nations of the world. Beyond this, it was our purpose to further the interests of the United States by bringing to our shores an eminently desirable immigration within the absorptive capacity of this country.   The immigrant has brought greatness to our land and a tremendous love for his adopted country.   The foreign-born and their descendants—which include all of us—have given devoted allegiance to the United States, in war and in peace, and have helped give to America a unique position of leadership among the nations.

During the last year and a half, substantial progress has been made in setting up the complex organization required to administer the technical requirements of the Act.   The necessary cooperation of the various governmental agencies, including those related to medical and security matters, has been enlisted. Over 30,000 visas have actually been issued.   Nearly 85,000 applicants are in various stages of processing.

Nevertheless, the purposes of the Act are not being achieved as swiftly as we had all hoped.   As a result of the experience gained in administering the Act to date, important administrative instructions designed to expedite the procedures under it have already been issued.   The men and women handling the program are fully aware of the urgency of their mission.   I am assured by the Secretary of State that further administrative improvements can and will be made.

Experience has demonstrated, however, that administrative improvements are not enough. A number of the provisions of the Act require amendment if the Act's objectives are to be fully achieved. I urge upon the Congress the following:

(1) The Act, at present, contains specific categories of eligibility with specific numbers allotted to each category. It now appears that because of some of the technical requirements of the Act and the growing prosperity in Western Europe, there may not be enough applicants to fill the quotas in some categories. I recommend that there be a provision for the use of unused numbers. Such unused numbers might well be used, for example, for orphans on a worldwide basis.

(2) The Act limits the term "refugee" to those who have not been "firmly resettled." Experience has shown that this provision tends to exclude the hard-working and the adjustable, the very people we want most as new citizens. Moreover, it appears that "resettlement" is such a vague term as to create conflicts in interpretation and delays in clearing applications.

I recommend that this limitation be withdrawn so that, where the refugee otherwise qualifies on a selective basis, he will not be barred because he is diligent and competent.

(3) A similar difficulty is presented by the terms of the Act which require that an "escapee" or "expellee" also be a "refugee." Under the Act this unduly limits the escapees and expellees who may be admitted. This, again, serves to exclude some of the most desirable people who have, at great sacrifice, at least temporarily resettled themselves. I am sure it is enough that a person be a qualified "escapee" or "expellee" to meet the standards on which we all agree. They should not also be required to be "refugees" within the narrow definition of the Act.

(4) The requirement that a "refugee" be living away from his traditional home has excluded many tragic victims of disaster whom I am sure the Congress intended to admit. This includes

Netherlands' farmers whose land has been ruined by floods of salt water, Greek mountain people whose herds have been despoiled by Communist invaders and many similar victims of catastrophe. The restriction should be relaxed.

(5) The Act contains a salutary provision enacted by the Congress for the benefit of aliens who are here in the United States and who fear persecution if required to return abroad. There is a limitation, however, within this section which has caused undue hardship in some cases. It requires that the person show "lawful entry as a bona fide non-immigrant", before he is eligible for this humanitarian relief.

I recommend to the Congress that the section be amended to permit the Attorney General to waive this requirement in meritorious cases where the person is otherwise qualified under the Act. It is estimated that this would not involve more than a few hundred cases, but in the case of each individual human being such an amendment would satisfy the beneficent purposes of the Congress.

(6) Obviously people who have risked their lives to escape from totalitarian nations often have no passports. The Refugee Relief Act, however, requires passports and in many cases this has served to defeat the very purpose of the Congress. I recommend amendment to permit waiver of the need for passports and similar documents in the discretion of the Secretary of State and the Attorney General as is already provided in the basic immigration and nationality laws.

(7) Under the Act, no escapee or refugee is entitled to a visa unless there is available complete information regarding his history for two years past, except on waiver by the Secretaries of State and Defense, if it is determined to be in the national interest.

No such requirement is applicable in the case of regular immigrants under the Immigration and Nationality Act of 1952.

This two year history, in the case of recent escapees, is often impossible to obtain. Yet these are the very people who have been actively stimulated to risk the perils of escape by our own information program broadcast through the Iron Curtain.

I have faith in the competence of our security personnel, and I recommend that this inflexible requirement be eliminated from the law, leaving it to the sound discretion of the security officer to make his recommendation on the basis of all the facts available. If he is in doubt, he will not certify the refugee or escapee as a proper security risk.

(8) Another obstacle to the achievement of the purposes of the Act is the requirement of individual sponsorship and guarantees of each application for admission. Where responsible, voluntary welfare organizations are prepared to give assurances with respect to applicants by name, it is unnecessary to add the burdensome requirement that individual sponsorship of each such applicant also be provided. I recommend that where such agency assurances are given, individual assurances not be required in addition.

(9) At present, special visas may not be issued to wives, husbands or children of persons admitted under the Act unless they all come to the United States together. If the members of the person's family are following at a later time and are otherwise admissible, then the special visas should be equally available to them.

(10) There are many refugee families in Western Europe whose members would make useful and productive citizens of the United States, but who would face separation if they should avail themselves of the provisions of the Refugee Relief Act. This they are unwilling to do. They would face separation because of the fact that one of their members is ineligible for admission to the United States under the health standards of our general immigration laws, particularly as respects tuberculosis.

We in the United States no longer regard tuberculosis with dread. Our treatment standards are high and modern treatment is increasingly effective. The United States, to its own benefit, could permit many of these families, within the existing numerical limitations, to enter under safeguards provided by the Attorney

General and the Surgeon General of the United States assuring protection of the public health and adequate treatment of the afflicted individual and also assuring that such individual will not become a public charge. I urge that the Congress give consideration to amendments that would enable this to be done.

It is my earnest hope that the changes in the Refugee Relief Act that I have above outlined can be accomplished during the present session of the Congress.

The enactment of these changes will permit effective administration of the Act by the Executive branch of the Government and greatly aid the success of the program. The persons permitted to enter the country under the program will make a fine contribution to the body of our citizens. And we shall again reaffirm that the great tradition of sanctuary lives on in America.

DWIGHT D. EISENHOWER

110 ¶ Citation and Remarks at Presentation of the National Security Medal to J. Edgar Hoover. *May* 27, 1955

CITATION TO ACCOMPANY THE AWARD OF
THE NATIONAL SECURITY MEDAL
TO
JOHN EDGAR HOOVER

The President of the United States takes pride in presenting the National Security Medal to

JOHN EDGAR HOOVER

for service as set forth in the following

CITATION:

As Director of the Federal Bureau of Investigation for 31 years, he has made an outstanding contribution to the national security of the United States. Exercising exceptional tact, perceptiveness, judgment, and brilliant leadership in a position of great responsibility, he has established the highest ideals of federal law enforcement and has directed them to realization. His tireless efforts have brought to a new height of effectiveness the law enforcement machinery of the United States Government. Through his well-grounded and clearly defined concept of investigative procedures, reinforced by his recognized integrity and high personal prestige, he has won international recognition for the federal law enforcement system of the United States.

DWIGHT D. EISENHOWER

[Remarks of the President]

Mr. Hoover, your dedication and devotion to public service are so long and so well known, your accomplishments in that service are so great and so well known, that it seems idle for me to try to say anything that could add to the dignity of this ceremony.

Perhaps it is just best for me to say I am proud to be an agent for our people in conferring upon you this highest award that the Government has, and to say that your real reward—as all of us here know—is in the hearts, the thanks and the gratitude of our entire nation.

NOTE: The President spoke in the Rose Garden. Mr. Hoover's response follows:

Thank you, Mr. President. I am deeply grateful for this honor which you have accorded me. I realize that it has been brought about through the dedicated accomplishments of the personnel and my associates in the Federal Bureau of Investigation, as well as by the magnificent support which you as President and which the Attorney General has afforded us over the years.

It is a pleasure, indeed, to serve as one of your subordinates.

111 ¶ Statement by the President on Safe Driving.   *May 27, 1955*

I URGE every American to take maximum care for safe driving on this Memorial Day weekend and during the following period of heavy summer traffic. I am joined in this request by Harlow Curtice, Chairman, and the members of the President's Committee for Traffic Safety as well as—I am sure—every motorist in our nation.

Throughout the nation there is now beginning an exceptional effort to "Slow Down and Live" on our highways. I know that this program will have the full attention and complete support of all our citizens so that we may accomplish a great and continuing reduction in the number of deaths and injuries on our roads.

There can be no matter of greater urgency for all of us than insuring the safety of our families and fellow citizens.

112 ¶ The President's News Conference of *May 31, 1955.*

THE PRESIDENT. Good morning, please sit down.

I have several little announcements. First, as to personal activities, the month of June looms up as a very busy one for me. I am going to West Point on the 5th, I believe; Penn State on the 11th; I am going then to participate in this relocation exercise in the middle of the month.

Then on the 20th I am going out to extend the greetings of the American people on the opening of the United Nations. That will be on the 20th.

And then, from the 22d to the 27th, I am in New England.

It is possible that some of those absences will catch a Wednesday, I am not sure.

This is an odd day, too; this is Tuesday, isn't it? [*Laughter*]

About the four fliers: we have been in, of course, some communication about these things now for some days.

The four fliers arrived in Hong Kong, I believe, at 2:30 our time this morning, left there at 4:30, are on their way now to Honolulu.

The families of these four people have been contacted by the Secretary of the Air. He is picking up close members of the families, and is going to take them to Honolulu to meet them. That should take place, I guess, some time tomorrow evening, something of that kind.

Now, I want to talk a little bit about polio; the polio program seems to be losing some of its difficulties and inescapable snarls.

Of course, there has been delay. The delay has been brought about by two things: the care that was necessary in giving the tests, repeating the tests, to make certain that children and youngsters were not unduly exposed due to preventable cause; and, second, the new problems discovered by the producers in the mass production of this kind of a product.

I should like myself to give two words of caution to everybody.

No vaccine is perfect protection against disease. You will remember that Dr. Francis found this one effective in, I believe it was a range of 60 to 90 percent, depending upon the range.

But I believe also it was found that any child having taken this vaccine had acquired an immunity that was three times as great as one who had not taken it. And then we must remember that it does take time for these great factories, when they are working on a mass production basis, to retool, get their machinery and everything in order, so that they both meet the tests and produce the volumes that are needed.

Now, as to distribution, remember I told you that the first priorities went to children, the first and the second grade. They were the ones that had been specified by the polio foundation— supported, of course, by all our doctors and scientists.

Within the next 30 days all the vaccine will be produced to

carry out that program. Certainly within the next 60 days it will be complete.

After that, the Federal Government will be responsible for the allocation of the vaccine as it comes out in volume to the States to meet the needs of the 5 to 9 group first; and the States will be responsible after they have their properly allocated amounts to make certain that the methods and distribution have taken place in accordance with the regulations.

The Government, of course, to make certain that no child is denied this vaccine because of money, has asked for $28 million; I most earnestly hope that legislation will soon be enacted.

A very favorable development, one point that has been questioned by some, has been the assurance that doctors will observe the priorities established by the Government in cooperation with the scientists who have been working on the problem. We have the pledge of the American Medical Association that doctors will observe these priorities and will themselves keep complete records of every child who is vaccinated, so that we can get the exact results of this whole great process as the year rolls on.

I think that covers all the—I said I was going to the United Nations—yes.

I have no further statements. We will go to questions.

Q. Robert E. Clark, International News Service: Mr. President, do you have any word about prospects for obtaining release of the other 52 Americans still held by Red China, including the other American flyers?

THE PRESIDENT. No, not at this moment.

Q. Merriman Smith, United Press: Mr. President, could you clarify that 30- to 60-day reference you made? You said——

THE PRESIDENT. Well, General Scheele assures me that within 30 days we will have, tested and on the shelves, the vaccine to carry out this entire program of the polio association, and that certainly within 30 days after that it will have been completed, actually administered.

Q. Mr. Smith: You mean administered?

THE PRESIDENT. Actually administered.

Q. Ray L. Scherer, National Broadcasting Company: Do you think the release of the flyers by the Chinese Communists represents a sincere effort on the part of the Chinese Communists to relieve tensions?

THE PRESIDENT. Our messages from various sources imply that that is their stated thought; that it was a token on their part to do something in helping release tensions. But I must say that everything that happens in the world these days has to be studied, examined, and, I would say, more carefully watched than would be implied in just a hit-or-miss guess as to what it means at this moment.

Q. Charles S. von Fremd, CBS News: Mr. President, at this very moment on Capitol Hill the Senate Labor Committee is holding a closed door meeting, and the indications are that they will recommend that you be given sweeping standby powers to handle the many problems of the Salk anti-polio vaccine.

Do you desire such powers, and could you discuss this?

THE PRESIDENT. Well, this is what I believe: I believe the American people are doing this in pretty good fashion.

I believe the polio program is coming along better than we could have expected, unless we would have counted on a degree of luck that was almost a phenomenon.

I think the voluntary program is working. I don't know that we need anything extra. I have not seen the bill in its details. But if they vote standby powers of some kind, why, of course, I shall carry out whatever is expected of me.

Q. Kenneth M. Scheibel, Gannett Newspapers: Mr. President, there are reports that you have selected Mr. Folsom of the Treasury Department to replace Mrs. Hobby in your Cabinet. Would you comment on that, please?

THE PRESIDENT. Why, that is a very simple one: Mrs. Hobby has not resigned.

Q. Mr. Scheibel: Do you expect her to resign, sir?

THE PRESIDENT. I am not expecting anything. We all know

that she has a very difficult domestic problem. Now she is carrying on as well as she can under those conditions, and I don't know what is going to happen.

Q. Charles E. Egan, New York Times: Mr. President, there have been frequent reports that your advisers, including Secretary of the Treasury Humphrey, have told you that you can balance the budget next year and cut taxes. Would you care to comment on that, please?

THE PRESIDENT. Could balance the budget and cut taxes?

Q. Mr. Egan: Both.

THE PRESIDENT. Well, of course, that would be a wonderful thing.

I think no one has said it to me in those emphatic terms. It would be a wonderful thing to have both. But I am sure that the first thing we must do is balance the budget.

Q. Robert J. Donovan, New York Herald Tribune: Four weeks ago we reached an agreement with Turkey, sir, on the bill authorizing Turkey to build atomic research reactors in Turkey. At the time there were indications that there might be further agreements along this line.

Could you tell us whether any of those have come about?

THE PRESIDENT. Well, I think within the week there will be four to five or something of that kind, maybe even as many as six, new agreements signed and announced.[1]

Q. Robert G. Spivack, New York Post: Mr. President, in connection with the vaccine, there is one question that seems to be bothering some parents. You will recall that when the vaccine was first given out, when children were first immunized or first inoculated, they were told that the second shot had to be given 4 or 5 weeks later. Now, in some cases that 4- or 5-week period has passed, and some people wonder if the shot wears off, or the effect wears off.

---

[1] Later in the day the White House announced the signing of proposed agreements with Brazil and Colombia. Similar agreements with the United Kingdom, Canada, and Belgium were signed on June 15; see Item 123, below.

I wonder if Dr. Scheele or anyone else has discussed that with you?

THE PRESIDENT. They have told me about a succession of two shots to be followed, I believe, 7 months or more later by a booster. But now the point that it may not be available for the second shot and they are worrying as to whether they are going to get it soon, I have not heard it discussed at all.

Q. Mr. Spivack: You don't know if they would have to get another shot, you mean?

THE PRESIDENT. No. I don't know, but I do know we are publishing about noon a rather lengthy statement on the thing. And I will have that question looked up and included, if it is possible.
[*Addresses Mr. Hagerty*] Will you do that?

Q. Mrs. May Craig, Maine Papers: Mr. President, in relation to budget and tax cuts, does the revelation of progress in Soviet aircraft mean that you might have to increase your budget for our air defense?

THE PRESIDENT. I haven't had any such recommendations yet from the Air. There has been, of course, a greater number of these planes exposed to view, as I remarked at another press conference, than we had anticipated they would have at that moment.

But there are many, many factors, as I tried to explain that morning. One of them is that we have an interim plane, the B–36, which is still a very good plane. We have had the others coming off, and we did authorize the factories that are producing 52's to step up their actual production. But whether or not that will require any change in the budget, I am not yet sure.

Q. Lloyd M. Schwartz, Fairchild Publications: Mr. President, the Defense Production Act is due to expire on June 30, and the administration reportedly has been considering whether to ask Congress to amend it to include emergency price and wage control authority for use in case of an emergency.

I wonder if you could clarify just what the administration's position is on this proposal?

THE PRESIDENT. I have discussed that question so often in this group it seems to me, at least, to be almost a waste of time to repeat my views. They have not changed.

I have always believed that on balance it would be a good thing to have certain controls if they could be strictly limited and quiet people's fears in times of peace.

But the fears do exist on the part of a great portion of our people that these controls, if there, would be improperly exercised.

The psychological situation, therefore, has always seemed to me to make it unwise to ask for them, and on the theory that the Congress would probably be in session or could be quickly called into session if an emergency arose.

Q. Sarah McClendon, El Paso Times: Sir, you nominated a Mr. John Brown of Houston for a place on the Fifth Circuit Court, and Mr. Brown allegedly at one time was an attorney for a shipping company that was involved in the Texas City disaster. The Government was on one side represented by the Justice Department.

Now there has come forward a report that some paper was allegedly changed by this gentleman, and the Justice Department though, although they were on the opposite side with him, apparently later gave a recommendation for him to be a judge of the Fifth Circuit Court, which is the same court that had jurisdiction over this Texas City case.

I wonder if you knew of these facts and took this under consideration when you nominated him?

THE PRESIDENT. Well, assuming that they are facts, I knew nothing about them.

Now, I go over the record of every single man that is appointed a judge. I go over it carefully, and wherever possible I bring him in, to meet him. I have attempted to appoint to the Federal judiciary only the finest people in the locality, people that are recommended by the American Bar Association, who have the recommendations of the people of standing in the community as to character and ability, quality, and so on.

I never heard such a word about Mr. Brown.

Q. Martin S. Hayden, Detroit News: Sir, I would like to ask two related questions, if I could.

In Detroit there is apparently increasing danger of an automobile strike in one or two of the big companies. Does the administration feel that the economic results of such a strike would be such as to require immediate Government intervention, if it comes?

THE PRESIDENT. Well, this Government has gone on this theory: that the executive department, as such, will not project itself into the details of private negotiations between employer and employee.

We do have a mediation service. When troubles arise they are called upon to assist in settling those things. But for the Government to step in and take a side, we feel is unjustifiable, and only in the case of a national emergency, I mean such a strike creating a real emergency, would the Government be justified in intervening.

Q. Mr. Hayden: The second question, sir: have your economic advisers given you any information which would give you any opinion on this issue of a guaranteed annual wage; is it a good thing, bad thing?

THE PRESIDENT. One thing that I believe I have put in one or two state of the Union messages is that I believe that the States should be encouraged and even urged to extend unemployment insurance in terms of time. I believe the maximum was 26 weeks up until a few weeks ago when, I believe, one or two States have broken through to 30 weeks. But many, many States don't have even the 26 weeks.

So I have always maintained that any process that helped to support this would be good, although I would prefer to see it through the States.

But aside from that, I would express no opinion at this moment when this particular point is one of such bitter argument between two opposing groups.

Q. John Herling, Editors Syndicate: Mr. President, several weeks ago you referred to the administration's proposal on the minimum wage law, and you explained that the first part, the 90-cent minimum recommended by the administration, was not as meaningful to you as the expansion of coverage for more workers who were not at all affected by a minimum wage law.

Now, may I ask, sir, does this mean that the administration specifically recommends legislation to broaden such coverage?

THE PRESIDENT. Well, didn't I say that in my state of the Union speech? I think, if I recall, in January of this year I asked the Congress to consider all of those classes that are not covered and to determine those that could profitably and properly be covered. That is the kind of extension I was talking about.

I have not specifically recommended any class or group, that is, agriculture groups, retail groups, or anything else. I have not said a word about that.

Q. Mr. Herling: The confusion, I think, sir, in some minds is that the administration is specific on the 90 cents but not specific on the inclusion of those to be brought under coverage; and, therefore, there was some doubt expressed, sir, as to the interest of the administration in having such coverage made this year.

Now, may I ask, sir, whether the administration specifically wants coverage this year?

THE PRESIDENT. Why, indeed, yes, so long as I—I already recommended it.

Now, the 90 cents is specific because we gave the facts and figures on which we developed that level.

As I recall, since the last raise in minimum wage to 75 cents, there had been a total rise in that time in the cost of living to justify a minimum wage of something on the order of 85.6 or 86.5, and we took the 90 cents as a good leveling-off figure. That was the way we arrived at it.

Now, as to the others, we said this is something which must be studied by Congress, because every single one of these groups, there are pros and cons about it, and it's going to be a very difficult business. I want the coverage extended to every area where it is feasible and a practicable thing to do.

Q. Marvin L. Arrowsmith, Associated Press: Mr. President, it was just 3 years ago tomorrow, I think, that you returned from Europe and got into politics. [*Laughter*]

This is a rather broad question, but I wondered if you cared to say how you like the game of politics after 3 years?

THE PRESIDENT. Well, Mr. Arrowsmith, the term "politics" as such seems to be one of those words that means many things to many people.

We so often use it in a derogatory sense; and I think in the general derogatory sense you can say, of course, that I do not like politics.

Now, on the other hand, any man who finds himself in a position of authority where he has a very great influence in the efforts of people to work toward a peaceful world, toward international relationships that will eliminate or minimize the chances of war, all that sort of thing, of course it is a fascinating business. It is a kind of thing that would engage the interest, intense interest, of any man alive.

There are in this office thousands of unique opportunities to meet especially interesting people, because the Government up here in Washington has become the center of so many things that, again, you have a very fascinating experience in meeting scientists, leaders in culture, in health, in governmental action, from all over the world.

There are many things about the office and the work, the work with your associates, that are, well, let's say, at least intriguing, even if at times they are very fatiguing. But it is a wonderful experience.

But the word "politics" as you use it, I think the answer to that one, would be, no, I have no great liking for that.

Q. David P. Sentner, Hearst Newspapers: Mr. President, now that the official request for an appropriation for the so-called atomic peace ship has been made to Congress, could you tell us some further details about the plan, such as how long you might expect it to be built, whether there would be any American exhibit of culture and industrial know-how outside of the atomic field, and whether you might be expected to participate in some part of its voyage.

THE PRESIDENT. I get some new ideas over here once in a while, anyway. [*Laughter*]   I hadn't thought of that one.

Now, as to its details of construction and what it will do, there are still discussions going on because, manifestly, as a thing like this develops, new ideas such as yours come along.

I think we can find probably someone more entertaining to put on that ship than a man my age and background.   [*Laughter*]

It is true, as I visualize it, it will be a peaceful ship with many an exhibition really of American culture, of the arts and industry. On top of that, I would hope that it would actually carry cargo as it went around the world on unscheduled runs, be ready to pick up such cargoes it could, so that everybody could see it performing a useful service in the world, but nevertheless have all the things that you just have mentioned.

Q. Edward T. Folliard, Washington Post and Times Herald: Mr. President, Representative Joe Evins of Tennessee says he has written you a letter to this effect, that if you go to a Big Four conference that you take Senator George of Georgia along as a special assistant.

He says this would be an example of unity in the American people.

THE PRESIDENT. Well, no one could have greater admiration for Senator George than I.   He and I have had talks about this very subject, and I think we are in complete agreement on what should be done.

I think I have explained a number of times that our conception of a Big Four conference will be, let us say, a testing of temperaments or atmosphere, a discussion of problems in general, and an attempt to determine methods and procedures that might work in the attempt to solve specific problems in the world.   It will not in itself be a conference to attempt the solution of these specific problems.

Therefore, it would seem to me that the time for Senators and members of the Legislature to be with you is when you come to the actual working out of the detailed problems that might result conceivably in some kind of an agreement.

Therefore, you want people there that are ready to explain this to their committee members, every phase of it, all of the background and what you might call the legislative history of the agreement.

When we are in this general talk, I assume that the meeting is to be very small, as small as is possible under the circumstances of the number of interpreters and just experts you have to have with you.

Q. Nat S. Finney, Buffalo Evening News: Mr. President, has the fact that these aircraft appeared over Moscow earlier than was anticipated caused any speedup in civil defense and related programs?

THE PRESIDENT. Whether or not there will be any increase in terms of budget this year, I don't know. It hasn't been brought up to me in those terms.

But I do believe this: I would be hopeful that it would bring about and inspire a speedup in the enthusiasm of the average citizen to do his part in this, because I must reiterate that civil defense is largely a job that falls on each of us ourselves. We cannot be assured civil defense by any bureau or any amount of money doing the work for us because we have to do it ourselves.

It's a matter of discipline, it's training, it is local work largely; and the Federal Government, at best, can get into the thing with leadership, with models, with examples, and of course in certain instances with storages of supplies and all the rest of it.

Q. Herman A Lowe, Manchester (New Hampshire) Union Leader: Mr. President, the paper took a poll among a number of top military leaders such as General Van Fleet, Admiral Denfeld, General Stratemeyer, on the question of Quemoy and Matsu, and they were almost unanimously agreed that this would not solve any problems or ease any tensions in the Far East. I wondered if you would comment on it?

THE PRESIDENT. What would not ease it, those two islands?

Q. Mr. Lowe: The surrender of those two islands to the Communists.

THE PRESIDENT. Well, I don't want to join in any guessing game here; and of course, these people, I think, are indulging in a little bit of a guessing game. But I personally don't see how the abandonment of those islands would help our situation any in the Far East.

Now, there are people in the world, of course, that believe it would make a great difference. I don't believe it would make a great difference there.

Q. Laurence H. Burd, Chicago Tribune: Mr. President, can you tell us anything more definite about the decision of the Western Powers on the time and place of a Big Four conference? Lausanne, Switzerland, has been mentioned as one possible——

THE PRESIDENT. Well, there has been no decision reached, and I don't suppose that there can be for some time.

It is a laborious business of transferring these things back and forth between the several governments concerned. So I think place and time of meeting is yet to be determined. We have no fixed convictions, although I think we would like to have it at a reasonably early date.

Q. James B. Reston, New York Times: Going back to Mr. Arrowsmith's question about your 3 years in politics, could you recall for us, sir, what your role was in the selection of Mr. Nixon for Vice President——

THE PRESIDENT. Oh, yes.

Q. Mr. Reston: ——in Chicago?

THE PRESIDENT. Surely.

Q. Mr. Reston: Was he selected as your personal selection, or was he one of a number of different persons whom you approved of, or what?

THE PRESIDENT. I would be glad to give it to you.

As I have reminded you people before, my experience in politics has been a little intensive, even if short. And the first thing I knew about the President or any presidential nominee having any great influence in the vice-presidential selection was, I think, about the moment that I was nominated. I said I would not do it, I didn't know enough about the things that had been going on in the United States. I had been gone 2 years. And so I wrote down the names of five, or maybe it was six, men, younger men, that I admired, that seemed to me to have made a name for themselves. And I said, "Any one of these will be acceptable to me."

And he was on the list.

Q. Mr. Reston: Mr. President, could I pursue that? Could you recall who were the five men—[*laughter*]—and, secondly, what I was trying to get at was what is your philosophy about the role of the nominee in the selection of the Vice President? Is it your view that the convention is sovereign, it can pick anybody it likes, or should it, in your judgment, follow the recommendation of the presidential nominee?

THE PRESIDENT. Well, I would say this, Mr. Reston: it seems obvious to me that unless the man as chosen were acceptable to the presidential nominee, the presidential nominee should immediately step aside, because we have a Government in this day and time when teamwork is so important, where abrupt changes could make so much difference. If a President later is suddenly disabled or killed or dies, it would be fatal, in my opinion, if you had a tense period on, not only to introduce now a man of an entirely different philosophy of government, but he, in turn, would necessarily then get an entirely new Cabinet. I think you would have chaos for a while.

So I believe if there isn't some kind of general closeness of feeling between these two, it is an impossible situation, at least the way I believe it should be run.

I personally believe the Vice President of the United States should never be a nonentity. I believe he should be used. I believe he should have a very useful job. And I think that ours has. Ours has worked as hard as any man I know in this whole executive department.

Q. Edward P. Morgan, American Broadcasting Company: I may be mistaken about this, sir, but I had the impression earlier that you might not be able to go to San Francisco, and I wondered if that were a fact, what might have changed your decision, and whether it had anything to do with preparations, your preparations, for the so-called summit meeting?

THE PRESIDENT. Well, as a matter of fact, when the invitation was first issued, I didn't know when this summit meeting might take place, and so I just returned a rather noncommittal answer, told them I would answer later.

Also, the date specified first that they wanted me conflicted with another engagement I had. And then they asked me for the 18th, and it cleared up everything, and so I am going. I mean the 20th—pardon me.

I should like very much to extend to this group a welcome on behalf of the people of the United States, [on] the 10th anniversary. I think that it is well that the whole country review the record of accomplishment and failure, and we kind of fix in our own minds again what are our hopes and our expectations for such a body. So I would hope to do my little part by going out there to bring us all to thinking about it a little more seriously.

Q. Walter Kerr, New York Herald Tribune: Mr. President, may we take it from your answer to a previous question that at a summit meeting you would not consider it advisable to raise specific questions such as the unification of Germany or Eastern Europe?

THE PRESIDENT. Well, I don't mean to say, Mr. Kerr, they won't be raised. Of course they will. But what I mean is that I don't believe that at such a meeting you can thrash out every detail that would finally have to be worked out if you are going to have an agreed-upon plan or scheme for doing this, a plan to which our great ally, Western Germany, could agree, and all others concerned. As you know, we expect Western Germany to be one of our finest allies, and we are not going to ignore their wishes in any thing.

Merriman Smith, United Press: Thank you, Mr. President.

NOTE: President Eisenhower's seven-tieth news conference was held in the Executive Office Building from 10:32 to 11:05 o'clock on Tuesday morning, May 31, 1955. In attendance: 165.

113   ¶ Statement by the President on the Polio Vaccine Situation.   *May* 31, 1955

I WOULD LIKE to issue the following statement about the polio vaccine situation. The last week has been both eventful and encouraging.

A committee of scientists is now screening polio vaccine before it is released for public use. The Surgeon General of the Public Health Service tells me that it is hoped to release some vaccine within a few days. Batches of vaccine must pass the most careful tests that scientists can devise and be as safe and effective as man can make the vaccine.

According to Dr. Francis' report on last year's field tests, the child who was vaccinated had a three times better chance of avoiding polio than the child who was not vaccinated.

There has been delay in the vaccination program. But remember—we are dealing in this field with the lives of our children and our grandchildren. Because of scientific work that was done during that delay science has learned new things about the way viruses behave in large scale manufacture and about the way we should make vaccine. Scientists have been able to design testing techniques of greater sensitivity and production techniques which build in a greater factor of safety and additional checks on the final product. So from that delay science has gained new knowledge, new safeguards.

I want to caution the people of our nation about two things:

First: No vaccination program can prevent all cases of the disease against which it is directed. Let us not forget that Dr. Francis reported the polio vaccine as used in the 1954 field trial was found to be 60 to 90 percent—not 100 percent—effective in the field trials last year.

Second: Although the manufacturers are now moving toward full scale production and distribution of this vaccine, it will take them varying periods of time to "retool" to meet the revised production standards. During the months immediately ahead we must be patient while our limited supply of vaccine is used first to help protect those who need it most.

Every parent and every child should be grateful to those scientists who have been working without rest and without relief during recent weeks to find answers to the problems that caused the delay. They have found these answers and another battle in the continuing fight against polio has been won.

DISTRIBUTION

Since April 12 the National Foundation for Infantile Paralysis has been furnishing free vaccine for children in the first and second grades, and for children in the third grade who participated in the field tests of vaccine last year. More than 5½ million children have been vaccinated—including one of my grandchildren, a first grader. This free vaccination program is the initial method for getting the vaccine to our children. No vaccine is now being distributed in any other way.

Sufficient vaccine to complete the Foundation's program should be released within 60 days. Until it is finished all vaccine produced will go to the Foundation.

The fact that some children do not get their second injection promptly will not reduce the effectiveness of the first injection. Dr. Salk, himself, stated last week that the level of immunity developed by the first injection would last many months.

DISTRIBUTION WHEN THE FOUNDATION PROGRAM IS COMPLETED

As soon as the Foundation program is completed, distribution must continue to proceed in a fair and orderly manner.   The Secretary of Health, Education and Welfare presented to me two weeks ago a sound plan for the distribution of the vaccine.   I promptly endorsed that plan and made it public.

Briefly the voluntary control plan for distribution will work as follows:

1. *Priorities.* The vaccine must be used first for those most susceptible to polio.   Not only is this just, but also by reducing the incidence of the disease among those most likely to get it we increase the protection for all of us.   The National Advisory Committee on Poliomyelitis Vaccine and the Secretary of Health, Education and Welfare have recommended that the vaccine be administered first to children of the ages of 5 to 9, inclusive.

I strongly endorse this recommendation and call upon our people to adhere strictly to the age 5 to 9 priority during the months ahead.   No person not in the 5 to 9 age group should be vaccinated until the children of these age groups have received two vaccinations.   The doctors of the country, through the American Medical Association, have pledged their support of these priorities.

The age group of second priority will be established and announced in due course.

2. *Output of the Manufacturers.* Each of the manufacturers of the vaccine has individually agreed to distribute his entire output of vaccine in accordance with this overall plan adopted by the Secretary of Health, Education and Welfare on the recommendation of the National Advisory Committee.

3. *Allocation to States.* The Secretary of Health, Education and Welfare will compile reports on the total output of the manufacturers and allocate the vaccine to each State on the basis of its population of unvaccinated children within the 5 through 9 age group, and subsequently, for other age groups.

4. *State Responsibility.* The States will advise the Secretary of Health, Education and Welfare as to their general plans for distribution of the vaccine and, specifically, their shipping instructions for manufacturers. This information then will be transmitted to the manufacturers.

5. *Vaccination Programs.* To assure that no child is denied vaccination by reason of its cost, some states and localities may operate mass free public vaccination programs for all children.

Other states may provide free vaccination only for children whose parents are unable to pay, through clinics, schools and preschool programs, or by furnishing free vaccine to private physicians. In those States, a portion of the State allocation of vaccine will flow into normal drug distribution channels for the exclusive use of children in the priority age brackets—to be administered by family doctors.

To assist the States in providing free vaccinations, I have recommended that the Congress enact legislation making $28 million available to the States for the purchase of vaccine. This legislation is now being considered by the appropriate Committees of the Congress and I urge its immediate adoption.

6. *Keeping of Records.* Doctors, as well as all manufacturers and distributors of the vaccine, will keep records of the vaccine they handle. Cooperation to this end has been pledged by the doctors, the manufacturers and the distributors.

This plan for distribution of the vaccine can go into effect as soon as the free vaccination program of the National Foundation for Infantile Paralysis is completed. Under it, the Federal Government will assume responsibility for the equitable allocation of the vaccine among the States, and the States will assume responsibility for the direction of distribution within their borders.

The program will operate in a sure and orderly way, given the full cooperation of the State officials, the manufacturers, the distributors, the medical profession, and the people of the Nation. I am confident that the program will receive that support.

For these reasons I do not believe that regulatory legislation in this field is necessary.

We all hope that the dread disease of poliomyelitis can be eradicated from our society. With the combined efforts of all, the Salk vaccine will be made available for our children in a manner in keeping with our highest traditions of cooperative national action.

NOTE: The report referred to early in this message was prepared by Dr. Thomas F. Francis, Director, Poliomyelitis Vaccine Evaluation Center, University of Michigan. Entitled "An Evaluation of the 1954 Poliomyelitis Vaccine Trials," the report, dated April 12, 1955, was published by the Center.

Later in the statement the President referred to a plan of distribution which he had received from the Secretary of Health, Education, and Welfare and had made public. This plan was in the form of a report to the President dated May 16, 1955. Mimeographed copies of this report (34 pages with appendixes) were made available by the White House.

114　¶ Message to the Senate Transmitting the Austrian State Treaty.　*June* 1, 1955

To the Senate of the United States:

With a view to receiving the advice and consent of the Senate to ratification, I transmit herewith the State Treaty for the Re-Establishment of an Independent and Democratic Austria, signed at Vienna on May 15, 1955.

There is further transmitted for the information of the Senate the report made to me by the Secretary of State regarding the aforesaid Treaty.

The Austrian State Treaty represents the culmination of an effort by the Western Powers extending over a period of more than eight years to bring about Soviet agreement to grant Austria its freedom. The restoration of Austria's freedom and independence has been a major objective of United States policy since the pledge of Austrian liberation made by the Governments of the United States, the United Kingdom, the Union of Soviet Socialist Republics and France in the Moscow Declaration of November 1, 1943. Until last April, the Soviet Union, while professing a desire for Austrian independence, by its actions and policies blocked the redemption of that pledge. The reversal in policy by the Soviet Government following its failure to prevent ratification of the Paris Pacts has now permitted the conclusion of an Austrian treaty and has won for freedom another important triumph. Moreover, it has emphasized clearly the significance of Western unity to the future of free men in every part of the world.

The Treaty provides for the termination of the occupation and the reestablishment of Austria, within the borders as they existed on January 1, 1938, as a sovereign, independent and democratic state. All occupation forces will be withdrawn within ninety days of the coming into force of the Treaty, and so far as possible not later than December 31, 1955.

After seventeen years of occupation, the Austrian Government and people are naturally anxious that ratification of the Treaty may be effected as quickly as possible. The pledge of the Moscow Declaration will have been fulfilled only upon entry into force of the Treaty and the consequent withdrawal of foreign occupation troops from Austria. I urge, therefore, that the Senate take early and favorable action with respect to the Austrian State Treaty.

DWIGHT D. EISENHOWER

NOTE: The text of the treaty and the report of the Secretary of State are published in Senate Executive G (84th Cong., 1st sess.).

115 ¶ Remarks on Acceptance of a Palestinian "Lamp of Freedom" From the United Jewish Appeal. *June* 3, 1955

I AM DELIGHTED, on behalf of the Allied Forces who, advancing from the west, did so much to crush Nazi tyranny, to accept this beautiful and ancient relic of Jewish civilization.

I am certain that those Forces—the American forces and their Allies—were representing only what we would call the heart of freedom, the belief that all people are entitled to life, liberty, and the pursuit of happiness—that where these are denied one man, they are threatened for all.

And so I am sure those Forces felt that in uncovering these camps, relieving the disasters and correcting the terrible conditions under which those people were living, they were not doing it fundamentally and merely because they were Jews, or anybody else. They were unfortunate human beings, and I think the heart of America and the heart of Britain and of France and the other Western Allies responded to that kind of inspiration and were delighted to do it.

It was a tremendous privilege and a great change from the killing of war to turn your armies to saving human lives and human dignity.

I sincerely trust that all those people are now living in health and happiness, or at least under conditions that are those of self-respect and decency.

Thank you very much for this treasure, which is unique and I have nothing like it, I assure you.

NOTE: The President spoke at a ceremony in the Rose Garden following the presentation of the lamp by William Rosenwald, General Chairman of the United Jewish Appeal.

Mr. Rosenwald's remarks follow:

As Supreme Commander, Allied Expeditionary Forces, Europe, in World War II, you led the Allied Forces to victory, threw down the gates of the concentration camps and helped to save from extermination the remnant of the once-great Jewish populations of Europe.

By your sympathetic understanding of the problems involved, and by your effective action, you set a pattern of humane and helpful treatment. Your example prevailed in the American zones of occupation and served to revive and restore the newly liberated Jews of Central Europe and those who sought haven there.

As an instance of your friendly concern, on September 17, 1945, you paid a special visit to Camp Feldafing on the Day of Atonement, the first to be observed by liberated Displaced Persons. You raised the morale of the DP's when you said to them, "You are here only temporarily and you must be patient until the day comes—and it will come—when you will leave here for the places you wish to go."

By your memorable prophecy you sounded the keynote for the lifesaving program of the United Jewish Appeal in the decade that followed.

It is an honor therefore, to present to you, as a mark of our esteem and of our profound appreciation, this ancient lamp from the Land of the Bible bearing the following inscription:

TO DWIGHT D. EISENHOWER

President of the United States of America

who has kept the Lamp of Freedom burning

Presented in deepest gratitude by the

UNITED JEWISH APPEAL

for his distinguished humanitarian service
to victims of Nazi tyranny

This antique lamp from the Land of the Bible, dating from approximately 50 C.E., symbolizes twenty centuries of Jewish history in which each generation renewed its devotion to freedom's ideals.

116 ¶ Veto of Bill for Relief of Kurt Glaser.
June 3, 1955

To the United States Senate:

I return herewith, without my approval, S. 143, "For the relief of Kurt Glaser."

The bill would accord permanent residence immigration status to a native of Czechoslovakia who entered this country in July 1951 from Austria as an exchange visitor under one of the programs authorized by the United States Information and Educational Exchange Act of 1948.

All of the exchange programs are founded upon good faith. We can maintain them as effective instruments for promoting international understanding and good will only if we insist that the participants honor their commitments to observe the conditions of the exchange in the same way that they expect the United States to honor its obligations to them. On the one hand, exchange aliens must return to the country from which they came. On the other hand, the United States must not permit either immediate reentry or other evasion of the return rule. Otherwise, the countries from which our exchange visitors come will realize little or no benefit from the training and experience received in the United States, and we shall fail to promote good will toward and better understanding of our way of life.

Unfortunately, the United States Information and Educational Exchange Act does not specifically obligate exchange personnel to return to the country from which admitted and to remain there for a minimum period before being eligible to regain admission to the United States. Administrative requirements have been imposed to compensate for this lack of a specific statutory requirement. Within the last year, however, a number of cases have arisen in which humanitarian and equitable considerations have argued so persuasively against imposing such a requirement that the Congress has been willing to consider and to enact a number of private bills to adjust the status of exchange personnel. By permitting them to remain in the United States for permanent residence, these bills have granted them immigration status without regard to the normal procedures under our immigration laws.

Up to the present time, most of the circumstances which have led to the enactment of each bill have been exceptional. Even though I have recognized that the principle underlying each bill was at variance with the basic concept and philosophy of the exchange programs, I have not been willing to require deportation at the possible risk of creating undue hardship and, in several cases, of jeopardizing the safety of the individual concerned.

Such considerations are not present in the case of Mr. Glaser. I am satisfied that both he and his sponsor understood their obligations to terminate his stay. In fact, the State Department's records indicate that a basic purpose of the sponsoring company in seeking exchange visitors was to train foreign engineers in the company's specialty in cooperation with the International Center of the University of Louisville. Furthermore, certification was signed by the Vice President of the company in which the following appears: "An attempt will be made to insure, insofar as possible, that any exchange visitor coming under the program of the sponsoring agency will adhere to the conditions under which he was admitted to the United States and will depart from the United States on completion of the purpose of the visit." Finally, there is no evidence that a return to Austria will work any hardship on either the company or Mr. Glaser beyond that of disrupting an association which has proved productive, useful, friendly, and profitable.

Under the circumstances, therefore, I feel it is my duty to disapprove this bill and at the same time to recommend enactment by the Congress of a clear statutory requirement that exchange personnel return home and remain there for a minimum period before being eligible to reenter the United States for permanent residence. Such provisions of law will protect the purposes of the exchange program, will prevent unjustifiable evasion of immigration procedures, and will establish legislative policy to guide the Committees of Congress in taking action on future private bills which would set aside the general law. Legislation for this purpose has been forwarded to the Congress by the Department of State this week. I urge its prompt consideration.

DWIGHT D. EISENHOWER

117   ¶ Remarks at the United States Military
Academy Alumni Luncheon, West Point,
New York.   *June* 6, 1955

*General Bryan, my classmates, and all the sons of West Point
here assembled:*

I am indeed highly privileged to have these few moments to
say a word to you. The hall is packed with my personal friends.
My life does not have the freedom that it did once that would
allow me to search each out and exchange a word as I would like
to do. So, by according me this privilege, I can say God bless
each one of you, I should like very much to see you and talk to
you alone.

I am very mindful of the admonition we have, that we are to
clear this hall early, and I am not going to be guilty of consuming
too much of your time. Morcover, my next engagement is to
pay my respects to the distinguished president of this association,
and I hope I may conduct your good wishes to him, at the same
time—General Fenton.

I think any man in this spot would search his heart in the
effort to find some new way in which he could pay a special
tribute to our alma mater. I am not going to pretend that I
know enough about this institution to be here in the position of
a preceptor. There are people here who have devoted their
lives—I heard General Bryan say he personally was on his fourth
tour here—have devoted their lives to bettering this institution.
And I, for one, think they have done it.

Last evening I was reading an advance copy of a book written
by Colonel Reeder—I hope he will take it as a plug, too. It is a
book about plebes in West Point. An old grad came to West
Point on the day before the graduation parade, and three plebes
were standing in their rooms, bracing as hard as they could. And
the old grad said, "Don't they haze plebes around here any

more?" And these plebes looked at him with some amazement considering their positions. And he said, "I do hope, when you get to be yearlings, you will really restore the plebe system."

As we all know, the place isn't what it used to be, and never was. I think that is lucky for all of us.

The special tribute I would like to pay would be more about methodology, I think, than anything else. As some of you may know, my experience in my new life is short but it has been rather intensive; and I have had a very great deal of opportunity to compare standards and methods and practices—in the life I now find—with the standards and methods and practices that I knew through 40 years of service with my associates from this Academy, and others that make up the Armed Services.

We are trained to deal in facts. To be truthful. To present our case as forcefully, as eloquently, as our talents may permit. To accept the judgment handed down by our commander and to perform our duty to the very best of our ability.

We learned long ago from the examples of those leaders we admire, that bad deportment is never to be confused with strength of character. If a man is sure of himself and the integrity of the processes he has used to reach his decisions he can be strong but he can be mild.

In the life that we find outside the Armed Services there seems to be a prevalent notion that if you call enough names, if you hammer enough desks, that you are a great leader. Happily, this Academy has never subscribed to any such false belief.

Now the reason I mention this is because I find throughout this country an ever-growing respect for West Point. A few years back, I was a member of a board called by Secretary Forrestal to determine whether or not the Air Force should have their own Academy, and I declined to serve as chairman because my mind was made up—but I was perfectly willing to serve and cast my vote the way I thought it should be.

On that board was an eminent group of educators, presidents of colleges, deans of great schools, professors. Without exception they testified to the excellence of the education in West Point and in Annapolis. Both institutions they searched very carefully through the medium of task forces. And they were struck by this one fact. They said there seems to be a spirit prevalent in these places that makes the truth and integrity the first thing—the first standard that all students must observe. The breadth of the education here impressed them. Because there was, of course, a sort of prevalent notion in our country that if you were trained for the military, you were necessarily narrow. They commented at great length upon the type of education here, the methods used so as to produce leaders who did deal in truth, in fact, and in sound conclusion.

I think their opinions of West Point are fully borne out by a record that was communicated to me yesterday by the Superintendent, that this institution provided more Rhodes scholarships in the next class than any other in the country. I believe there are four to go from the Academy, and there would have been more except that cadets had to compete against cadets in the final competition.

Moreover, I think it is perfectly fitting and quite wonderful that the First Captain, the man who in the military tactics is concerned for military discipline and procedures, won the highest awards from the tactical staff, and is one of those men showing not only the breadth of his own comprehension but of the education he has here received.

So I say again, if with the great spirit—the purposes—of this Academy, if we can show and continue to show through this spreading knowledge of our Academies throughout the country, we may finally convince people that leadership is something of the heart and of the head. It is not merely of a fluent and wicked tongue. I could cite examples all through our history. And I do say this: I believe that if we have found a man who has had to resort to desk-pounding, if he were a great leader, he was in spite of that habit and not because of it.

To each of you my very best wishes. I hope that in the few

571

hours remaining before graduation, I will get to see some more of you that I have not seen.   Thank you for your attention.

NOTE: The President spoke in Washington Hall at 1:22 p.m. His opening words "General Bryan" referred to Maj. Gen. Blackshear M. Bryan, Superintendent of the Academy.

Later the President referred to Brig. Gen. Chauncey L. Fenton, USA (Retired), who was President of the West Point Association of Graduates and of the West Point Alumni Foundation.

118   ¶ Address at the Graduation Ceremonies, United States Military Academy, West Point, New York.   *June* 7, 1955

General Bryan, members of this graduating class, West Point Alumni, ladies and gentlemen:

In the year 1915 I was one of a hundred sixty-four cadets who through four West Point years had eagerly looked forward—just as you of this class have done—to the moment of graduation. Actually we thought of it as liberation; but forty busy years have somewhat changed that youthful viewpoint.

During our Academy careers, we had, to the best of our ability, or at least to the maximum of our inclination, prepared ourselves in the lessons and the experiences of the past for a future that, we complacently felt, was predictable in pattern and design.

None among us could have realized that the world in which our fathers and we had lived was, at that moment, disappearing.

True, in Europe there was a war! But this tragic fact did not alarm us as it should have, for the Nation itself was not awake to the great threat thereby imposed on it.   Wars—bloody and prolonged or one-sided and quick in their outcome—were in some countries still considered almost normal instruments for the achievement of a nation's objectives.   The First World War erased all grounds for such smugness.   Even our own country finally became a participant.   Great European empires were de-

stroyed. The world was confronted with human losses of staggering and unprecedented proportions.

By that war's end, over three years after our graduation, mankind had come to understand that any war is a human disaster—
and in any major war the extent of the disaster is global. None
escapes its effects.

Most of my class lived to see this lesson driven home with stun-
ning emphasis more than two decades later. A second global
conflict closed, just ten years ago, with a weapon that could make
of war a catastrophe approaching almost the extermination of
mankind.

By the calendar, exactly forty years separates my class from
this one of 1955. Yet by the changes mine has seen—in the weapons of combat and the tools of peace, in the balance of international power, in the thinking of men—there might as easily be
forty as four decades separating us.

Obviously, change is inescapable in human society. Since the
beginning of history, the quality of a nation has been measured
by its capacity to meet and to master evolving circumstances; the
capacity of a man has been gauged, in part, by his flexible adjustment to the new and novel without sacrifice of principle or abandonment of standards. But change, in the leisurely days of the
past, was gradual and evolutionary; the armies of Napoleon
moved across Western Europe with no more speed than those of
Caesar, his predecessor by eighteen centuries.

Now, within a single generation, a natural process has become a
cataclysmic rush. This should generate neither a despairing belief
that the tide of events is beyond human control nor an apathetic
acceptance that human ability is not equal to the immense problems newly arisen. It does mean that we must think better and
faster and more wisely than ever before.

When gas warfare was first introduced in combat in World
War I, the techniques necessary to adjust for use the crude protec-
tive equipment of the time were both laborious and exacting.
Because of this there grew up a saying in the Army that when a

gas attack was met there were only two kinds of soldiers on the battlefront—"the quick and the dead."

Of the nations of today the future will say that there were two kinds: those that were intelligent, courageous, decisive, and tireless in their support of high principle—and those that disappeared from the earth.

The true patriots of today are those who are giving their best to assure that our own country will always be found in the first of these categories.

You, who graduate today, will be servants of the civil power, committed to quick obedience. But you may someday be responsible for the lives of men—possibly the fate of a campaign. No signal from headquarters will then communicate to you the proper action. The moment will not wait on the completion of a staff study. The arena of decision will be your own mind and conscience, naked of others' counsel. To be ready for that crisis is one mission of the American soldier.

The other is vastly different. Although you are to be leaders in the profession of arms, trained for the winning of battle, you are members of a vast team, the American Nation. Its historic objectives have always been human dignity, human peace, human prosperity. These, as a public servant, you must help attain. In this, no mastery of command can substitute for an intelligent comprehension of the economic goals, the political impulses, the spiritual aspirations that move tens of millions of people. But your greatest opportunity for enduring contribution to America may well come at a council table, far removed from war.

This country now approaches a Big Four Conference.

The populations of the countries to be represented at this Conference constitute only a fraction of mankind. And free nations do not claim any right to speak for others.

Therefore, this prospective meeting of the Four Powers can at best be only a beginning in a renewed effort that may last a generation. It is a task that may result in a long series of conferences. In them, this Government, meeting with others, will further extend its search for ways in which the peaceful aspirations of mankind may be advanced.

Though only a few individuals will be at those conferences to speak for America, yet in a definite sense we shall all be there—all of you, all the citizens of this great land. For the American words spoken in a world council will be of moment only if they conform to the spirit that is the true strength of our country.

Militarily and materially we are strong. More important, we are strong in the partnership of many allies. But above all, our Nation is strong in its support of principle: we espouse the cause of freedom and justice and peace for all peoples, regardless of race or flag or political ideology. Though in this strength we have reason for confidence, we likewise have need for wisdom, and the caution that wisdom enforces—at the conference table itself, in the halls of government, in every place of business and in every home in America.

By caution, I mean: a prudent guard against fatuous expectations that a world, sick with ignorance, mutual fears and hates, can be miraculously cured by a single meeting. I mean a stern determination that we shall not be reckless and witless, relaxing our posture merely because a persistent foe may assume a smiling face and a soft voice.

By wisdom, I mean: a calm awareness that strength at home, strength in allies, strength in moral position, arm us in impregnable fashion to meet every wile and stratagem that may be used against us. But I mean also a persevering resolution to explore every decent avenue toward a lasting and just peace, no matter how many and bitter our disappointments. I mean an inspired faith that men's determination and capacity to better their world will in time override their ability to destroy it; and that humanity's hunger for peace and justice is a mightier force than a few men's lust for power.

By the Preamble to the Constitution, the common defense—the first mission of the soldier—is elevated to a like rank with the loftiest objectives of men and women united in a free society. Its execution, therefore, deserves and demands the best that's in you.

Nevertheless, your entire lives may and should be as seriously devoted to leading toward peace as in preparing yourselves for the tasks of war. Almost certainly, some of you will sit at future council tables as principals or as staff advisers. Your second mission, then, will be to represent accurately the heart and purposes of America.

These purposes are rooted in spiritual values.

Thus:

We are determined to preserve intact the traditions and principles which constitute what we call the American Heritage— the political, intellectual, moral truths that animate America. In this sense we must forever remember that the liberty and rights of the individual, limited only by the restriction that he infringe not upon the equal liberty and rights of others, are the cornerstone of our national existence. Unless we remain true to all that this means in worship, in thought, in speech, in work, and in the products of our individual toil, then all else will be for naught.

We shall protect our system against all enemies, foreign and domestic, and conserve the basic methods, practices, attitudes, and governmental organisms that time has proved most profitable for the solution of our problems. For example, individual initiative, competitive enterprise, the maximum local control of government are rooted in our belief that the human individual is the basis of society and the key to growth and progress. They work! To ignore them in the solution of problems is to water down the American formula for achievement.

We strive to correct the faulty and deficient in such manner that haste for change will not waste resources and effort; that constructive evolution will not degenerate into destructive revolution.

We know we must expand aggressively the application of new scientific knowledge and new techniques to every field of human endeavor for the improvement of man's existence. War necessity made nuclear fission initially a science of destruction, but we aspire to be foremost in harnessing its mighty power for peaceful use and the betterment of human living. Finally, we seek constantly to enrich the cultural content of our daily living. We hope to fortify the spirit of all of us in a wise understanding of our country's role in this time of quick and vast change and to prepare her better to lead toward peace.

As soldiers you will live by the traditions of the Service—built in the halls and on the campus of this greatest of all academies of its kind, and on many battlefields from Bunker Hill to the Korean mountains. They are a spiritual heritage whose intact preservation must be a first concern. All the wit and knowledge you may achieve can count for little in a desperate clutch unless there burns within you the inspiration springing from great traditions.

But—you must be ruthless in a self-imposed command never to rest in the pursuit of new knowledge, in your application of it to your own duties. You will be pioneers in the search for new ways to strengthen the common defense from the platoon to the General Staff. Many times you will feel that your mistakes outnumber your triumphs. But without the yeast of pioneers, the United States Army or any other organization of men cannot escape degeneration into a ritualistic worship of the status quo.

All of us gratefully acknowledge, as our fathers before us, our dependence on the guidance of Divine Providence. But this dependence must not tempt us to evade our personal responsibility to use every one of our individual and collective talents for the better discharge of our lifetime missions.

Working and living in this spirit, you as soldiers will make yourselves and the Army a professional counterpart of the American Way—jealously conserving principle; forceful in practice; courageous and calm in present crises; steadfast and patient in the long campaign for a secure and peaceful world; stout of faith in yourselves, your Alma Mater, your country and your God.

NOTE: The President's opening words "General Bryan" referred to Maj. Gen. Blackshear M. Bryan, Superintendent of the Academy.

119   ¶ The President's News Conference of *June* 8, 1955.

THE PRESIDENT. Ladies and gentlemen, there is one item each in the foreign and domestic fields that I would like to call attention to. One is the invitation of the Soviet Government to Chancellor Adenauer to talk over some of their mutual problems. I think it is only a natural consequence of the developments that are taking place in Western Europe that the Soviets should issue such an invitation.

As you know, the consequence of those developments has been the establishment of the Western Republic of Germany as an independent nation, and therefore it seems to be a logical gesture on the part of the Soviets to invite them in for a talk.

Now, of course, the decision of what's to be done about the invitation is exclusively that of the Federal Government of Western Germany, Chancellor Adenauer himself. The only point I want to make is that we know Chancellor Adenauer. We have the utmost faith and confidence in him, and we know one thing, that he will stand by his allies and friends.

The item in the local scene I wanted to mention was just a report that I saw yesterday on employment. The May employment apparently hit an alltime record, although it is not the highest peak that we have ever had, the '53 peak, I believe, of 63 million. This figure was 62,700,000. But employment for May was up a million over April and unemployment was down a half a million, figures which certainly are cause for gratification.

Those two items are the ones I wanted to mention.

We will go to the questions.

Q. Merriman Smith, United Press: Mr. President, have you received any reply from the Russian Government on our invitation to meet in Geneva on the 18th?

THE PRESIDENT. No, we have not.

Q. Chalmers M. Roberts, Washington Post and Times Herald: Mr. President, if I understand correctly, one of the premises of your trimming the manpower in the Army has been the idea of a ready, trained reserve. The reserve bill was sidetracked in the House recently because of a segregation rider affecting the National Guard in the States, and also an amendment which would appear to rule out the sending of such reserves to countries where we have these Status of Forces agreements.

I wonder if you could tell us what plans the administration has to get this bill out, if my assumption is correct that you feel that it is vital.

THE PRESIDENT. Well, of course, I feel the reserve bill is vital, and if the House situation has gotten so difficult that they can do nothing there now, why, then, I will most urgently hope that the Senate can do something about it.

I want to bring out again, I suppose it is only natural that I should speak very feelingly on anything that affects the Armed Forces of the United States. I certainly lived among them many years.

This reserve bill is more essential than ever before to the security of the United States. We need trained men in every single section of this country. We acknowledge, as we look at the probable face of future warfare, if ever we must face that tragedy, we acknowledge that every hamlet and important city of the United States is likely to be on the front lines.

If that is true, why do we not want someone in those front lines that is trained and ready to do something sensible and logical instead of giving way, as most of us would, undoubtedly, to the hysteria of the moment and just light running? We have to have discipline. We have to have people that are trained as to what to expect, and respond logically.

So, from the standpoint of the United States and the character of warfare, I am merely showing that over and above the old need of reinforcing active units to carry on conventional types of warfare, you need somebody every place, where each State—over and above its National Guard contingents—can have somebody there who is disciplined and ready to act and support all the police and fire prevention action that must take place locally.

Then our own National Guard units need people who have been thoroughly grounded in military training.

Next, we must carry on our conflicts if we have to wage them, or our mobilizations if we have to order one, with people who haven't been off to war already one or two or three times and now are raising families. It certainly is unjust to depend for training only on the people who have already done their stint in defending our country.

Finally, entirely aside from the whole question of fairness, the whole question of national security, comes the individual himself. It is these individuals who must defend the United States, and why should they not have the advantage of some prior training?

Now these are the reasons for a reserve bill.

Now, I am just as anxious to get this thing done as I can possibly be. In some details, the bill as was finally brought out on the floor before it was amended had changed some of the items in which I believed. But the bill, on the whole, as it came out of the committee represented a tremendous advance over anything we had ever had. I believe that we just must have it, that is what I believe. I believe it is terrifically important.

You mention the question of relationship between that and the size of active forces. Of course, there is a relationship, but I say, and I assure you that in my opinion no increase in the Armed Forces, active forces, of a logical size could possibly compensate for not having a reserve. We must have it. That is the way I feel about it.

Q. Mr. Roberts: Could I ask on the specific point of the segregation amendment how you stand on that?

THE PRESIDENT. I think the record of this administration on carrying out its pledges in this whole field of segregation is a good one. We have worked hard to take the Federal responsibility in this regard, and to carry it forward so as to get real advancement.

I believe, on the other hand, that it is entirely erroneous to try to get legislation of this character through tacking it on to something that is so vital to the security of the United States as the security program. The mere fact that we can't all have our ways about particular things in social progress—does that mean we don't want to defend our country?

Why do we make the defense of our country dependent upon all of us getting our own ways here?

Now, as I say, I think the administration's record here stands up very, very well indeed, compared with any other administration I know of. But I just don't believe that it is the place to have any kind of extraneous legislation, I care not what it is.

Q. Lloyd M. Schwartz, Fairchild Publications: Mr. President, the Senate Labor Committee yesterday voted a $1 minimum wage bill, which is 10 cents more than you recommended. Now, as I understand it, Governor Adams reportedly has told the legislative leaders on the Hill that the dollar is acceptable to the administration. I wonder if you could tell us whether you would——

THE PRESIDENT. He said what? I didn't——

Q. Mr. Schwartz: He reportedly has told legislative leaders that the 1-dollar wage bill is acceptable, and that you would sign it.

THE PRESIDENT. Well, I don't know who gave you that information, because I am sure the Governor didn't tell me that. [*Laughter*] I think I would be interested. [*Laughter*]

Now, actually, my recommendations and the reasons for them were given in my annual message, and I have seen nothing to change them. I did advocate a 90-cent minimum wage with extensions in the fields where Congress could find it applicable and logical.

I should like to point out again that one of the reasons given for the 90-cent was recognizing certain increases in the cost of living since the last minimum wage, the 75-cent one, was enacted.

I want to point out again that since January of '53, the cost of living index has varied within 1 percent. It has been a record of stability in these last months.

That stability, let me say, is not any particular favor to rich and wealthy people and to great corporations. What it is important to is the person who has to meet a monthly budget and who has to look forward to his old age, living on pensions and insurance policies. Stability of the dollar is one of the things that makes this economy continue to expand and grow and give to all of our people the confidence to which they are entitled.

I do believe that the reasons given there in that state of the Union speech are still sound.

Q. James B. Reston, New York Times: Mr. President, since Chancellor Adenauer is going to be in this country, I believe, next week, are you planning to see him at that time before you go to the Big Four meeting?

THE PRESIDENT. Oh, yes. He is coming to lunch with me. I thought I had—haven't we announced that?

Mr. Hagerty: Yes, June 14th.

THE PRESIDENT. He is coming to lunch on June 14th.

Q. Charles S. von Fremd, CBS News: Mr. President, I would like to go back to the Big Four again, sir.

THE PRESIDENT. Yes.

Q. Mr. von Fremd: At West Point yesterday you said that we must have prudent caution to keep any hopes of great expectations for accomplishments from growing too large, and your Secretary of State and other leading officials in and out of the administration have voiced the same warning.

The Russians for some time have indicated they didn't think that very much could be accomplished at a meeting, and I wonder, sir, if you do think there is a real chance for having accomplishments of note at the meeting at the summit.

THE PRESIDENT. I also said in that talk that we would never cease searching out any new method or avenue that might lead toward peace, and I told you people, a couple of weeks ago, that there is a great faith in the world that a talk at the summit might open up one of these new paths that we could follow logically and properly.

All I have tried to say is this: let's not expect too much from the first one, but let us do hope that we have opened up a new way, a new thought, a new feeling or atmosphere in the whole business, and maybe then our work will be fruitful instead of constantly frustrating.

Now, I also tried to point out, let's not expect it all at once. If we do get an encouraging feeling about this thing, then let us pursue it courageously, sincerely, and thoroughly, no matter how many years it takes. That is all I am trying to say.

Q. William H. Lawrence, New York Times: Mr. President, in connection with that last answer you gave, in seeking and searching——

THE PRESIDENT. Yes.

Q. Mr. Lawrence: ——I wonder, sir, why is it necessary to limit in advance the deliberations of the heads of state to only 3 days instead of, say, a week? Or would you extend it if you found that the opportunities were good?

THE PRESIDENT. I think some of you people know, you might say, the constitutional limitations that are on the President in this country from going away and staying as long as he pleases. Sometimes with Congress in session, you can get the necessary bill before you that required pretty instant action, because it has taken a long time to staff it.

There are numbers of reasons why the President is not as free as is a Prime Minister to go some place and stay a long time. The only thing that we tried to do when we issued the invitation was to give intimation that there was some limitation on the time the President could be absent.

Now, if it takes 4 or 5 days or any other period that is reasonable and will allow me to do my work, that is still acceptable. But we don't want just to make this another propaganda mill, where, if I should leave by compulsion of my duties, then it would look like I was trying to wreck the conference.

That mustn't be, don't you see?

Q. Mr. Lawrence: Yes.

THE PRESIDENT. And you must guard against it.

So therefore, for the heads of state, the Big Four, so called, conference, there must be understood to be a definite time limit.

Q. Douglass Cater, Reporter Magazine: Mr. President, I wonder if you could expand your thinking on this use of the anti-segregation amendments on legislation. As I understand it, the aid-to-the-schools bill is bottled up in a Senate committee because of that same conflict, that there is an attempt to add an amendment that would prevent aid to States which permitted a continuation of segregation.

Would that apply the same way you think as on national defense legislation?

THE PRESIDENT. My own feeling about legislation is a simple one. If you get an idea of real importance, a substantive subject, and you want to get it enacted into law, then I believe the Congress and I believe our people should have a right to decide upon that issue by itself, and not be clouding it with amendments that are extraneous.

I am not talking about the school bill now or the reserve bill or any other. I am saying as a general proposition, why not put these things up on their own and decide them? That is my feeling and my conviction about it.

Q. John Herling, Editors Syndicate: Before Labor Secretary Mitchell left for Geneva, I believe he consulted you in regard to the Conference of the International Labor Organization which he is now attending.

Yesterday the U.S. delegation split at Geneva, split on their attitude toward the subject of seating delegates from Soviet and other Communist countries in the various bodies, various sections of the International Labor Organization. And Mr. W. L. McGrath, who is the U.S. employer delegate, has sharply criticized the U.S. Government and the U.S. labor delegates for being soft on communism.

Would you care to comment on the administration policy in regard to our participation in the ILO?

THE PRESIDENT. Well, I can't answer your question in detail this morning. I can say that ILO is one of those organizations which we believe have been beneficial, and in which we intend, of course, to continue our membership and presence.

The particular argument of which you speak has not been brought to my attention. I couldn't possibly attempt to answer it. I don't know what the criticism was. I don't know what the decisions were on, but I will try to be ready to answer it at a later date.

Q. Milton B. Freudenheim, Detroit Free Press: Mr. President, will you comment on the Ford settlement, the guaranteed wage in Detroit, as to whether it is in line with your recommendations to Governors on State unemployment compensation.

THE PRESIDENT. Of course, my recommendations to States stand for themselves. They have been made and have been made public. I would not comment on the terms of contracts as between employers and employees. I have not allowed those things to come into the White House, and refuse to do so, except when there is definitely the national good or a national emergency in question. And on top of that, similar contracts are still under negotiation. So I have nothing to say.

Q. Robert Roth, Philadelphia Bulletin: Mr. President, it was said today in a piece by the Alsop brothers that their purely social relationships with old personal friends——

THE PRESIDENT. I didn't understand. That what?

Q. Mr. Roth:——that their purely social relationships with old personal friends who are employees of the National Security Council are being interfered with by orders from above. They see in this an indirect imposition of censorship.

Would you comment, sir, on whether you regard this as a Government intrusion into the private affairs and the proper functioning of reporters?

THE PRESIDENT. I have a press secretary, some of you may

know—[*laughter*]—and if there are any complaints, I think they should be lodged there first, so I can find out something about it.

Q. Sarah McClendon, El Paso Times: Mr. President, Mr. Seaborn Collins, the National Commander of the American Legion, was criticized by Mountbatten, the British Lord of the Admiralty, for speaking against communism to the British Empire Service League, and he said he was setting forth what the American Legion believed should be done to defeat communism and not what the U.S. Government thought, and he said he was not presuming to tell any other government what to do, but it seems that Mountbatten said that this was talking about politics at a veterans meeting.

I wonder if you would say what you think about the fitness of veterans everywhere considering communism as an issue of aggression.

THE PRESIDENT. Well, I think we could talk a very long time on that, Mrs. McClendon. But I did notice in that same account that after that little difference of opinion publicly, that both Mr. Collins and Dickie Mountbatten sat down together and had a good time, and apparently there wasn't anything rancorous about the argument.

Q. William Graves, Salt Lake City Deseret News: Mr. President, at this session a bill has been introduced by Senator Bennett of Utah which would provide an 18-man commission to study dispersal of U.S. industry against possible atomic attack, and Dr. Flemming of the Office of Defense Mobilization and, I believe, Secretary Talbott of the Air Force and several others have indicated support for this type of proposal.

I wonder if you would tell us your feeling on that type of plan.

THE PRESIDENT. I haven't talked to any of my advisers on this particular point, but I would say this: we have been trying to get the interests of the United States—national industries, and so on—into the real study and concern for this matter of dispersion. So therefore, if the organization of a committee would create a greater interest, determination to do something about it, I believe we would be very glad to see it done.

Let me make just one observation as we go past—the thinking on this subject. By "dispersion," you don't mean picking up a great enormous Willow Run factory or some great shoe factory and moving it out in the desert. What you do mean is this: American industry is constantly expanding; so, as it expands, do you want to continue this process of concentration at particular and critical areas which increases your vulnerability, or isn't it the part of wisdom to attempt dispersion?

That is really what you mean by a dispersal of industry. Moreover, if a new plant of any kind is built making some new product, why do you crowd it in where they are possibly making engines or gears or any other thing of that kind? I think it is just a matter of the future and to get decent, proper policies to govern them.

Q. Walter Kerr, New York Herald Tribune: Mr. President, did I understand you correctly to say that it is all right with you if a summit meeting should last 3, 4, or 5 days, provided that you knew in advance when it would end?

THE PRESIDENT. Well, look. Do you suppose for one minute that if I am ready to pick up and go from any place to Timbuktu to the North Pole to do something about this question of peace, that I am going to stand on a matter of 24 hours? I am trying merely to say it must be a meeting of limited length, an agreed upon, limited length, not that rigidly done. They can say from 3 days to 5 days or 3 days to 6 days, I don't care. But I just must have, if I am to attend, must have a limited time understood.

Q. Edward J. Milne, Providence Journal: Mr. President, are you concerned about, or have you made any inquiries about the long delay in the Senate committee's action on Allen Whitfield as your appointee to the Atomic Energy Commission? That has been hanging fire now for several months.

THE PRESIDENT. As a matter of fact, I haven't looked it up lately, and I couldn't give you any answer on it this morning.

Q. Richard L. Wilson, Cowles Publications: Mr. President, what are the precise areas which might be discussed, or which might be the subject of agreement at the Big Four conference?

THE PRESIDENT. I don't think you can state them precisely. I think there are problems in the world today that have created differences on which there are different convictions expressed which are obvious to us all.

We have made no great progress on most of these in late years. I think the great hope would be, what is a method, what kind of an approach can we make to these problems that might give promise of real progress?

Disarmament? After all, we know this: there is something that is different in the world. After all, the Russians are inviting in Mr. Nehru to try to win over the neutralist countries. They have made an unprecedented type of visit to Yugoslavia. They have invited in Chancellor Adenauer.

There is a change going on.

Now, in such a changing sort of atmosphere, we may discover some way that an accommodation can be made in which we can have full confidence, which would possibly give all of us some lightening of the burdens we are carrying.

Q. Mr. Wilson: Leaving Germany out of the question for the moment, is there anything in the neutrality idea which might offer the basis for agreement?

THE PRESIDENT. You mean the neutrality for others not including West Germany?

Q. Mr. Wilson: Yes, sir.

THE PRESIDENT. Well, that one I hadn't thought of, but I see that Tito rejected it. At least, that is what I read. I don't believe I have seen an official account of it; I believe I saw in the paper that he had rejected any idea of neutrality for his country. But I would say this: I personally don't believe America is ever going to be happy as long as any people with a historical record of independence are kept enslaved by someone else, by foreign domination, specifically meaning the Eastern satellites.

Now, if those people of themselves chose a neutral position instead of the position they now occupy and it were an honest neutrality, it would be a tremendous advance for them.

Q. Mr. Wilson: Sir, under those conditions, could there be any modification of our position in Germany which would match a modification of the Russian position and the satellite states?

THE PRESIDENT. Now, Mr. Wilson, make no mistake. The position of Western Germany is going to be determined by Western Germany. We have recognized them as a sovereign nation, and just as we wouldn't expect some other country to determine our policy toward neutrality, we must give to Western Germany the complete right to solve their own problems.

As I have already stated, I have the utmost confidence in the belief that these people are going to act in full concord with their friends and allies.

Q. Mr. Wilson: What I was pursuing, sir, was the fact that we have forces in Germany just as the Russians have forces in the Balkan countries.

I wanted to ask if there was any adjustment or modification of the disposition of those forces which might provide the basis for an agreement.

THE PRESIDENT. Well, you are bringing up now one of the substantive problems that are certain to arise: what are going to be the forces and the stations of forces all through central and western Europe? I couldn't possibly hazard a question on that in advance.

Q. William Theis, International News Service: Mr. President, we have heard on the Hill that during the preliminary discussions of the Big Four meeting, you have taken a rather strong position that you would go to any neutral country, but you did not want to go to Geneva. I wonder, for the record, if you could clear up the background on that for us, and perhaps highlight it.

THE PRESIDENT. The only thing I have heard against Geneva was, you know, it is a tremendous tourist center; and if you are

589

going to have a meeting in the summertime, I think it gets quite difficult for the Swiss people themselves.

Now, I think we should go to a country known as a neutral, like Sweden, Switzerland; and Switzerland being central and convenient, is the one that seems to be indicated.

I think we did prefer Lausanne. As a matter of fact, I did, at least. But I never made this a question of "either this or else," never.

Q. Mr. Theis: I think the implication in this report was that you did not particularly want to be associated with what happened at Geneva about a year ago in the Indochina situation.

THE PRESIDENT. Actually, we were no party to that particular one, but I wouldn't—maybe you've got a—say it's a good thought there. [*Laughter*]

Q. William M. Blair, New York Times: Dr. Scheele, the Surgeon General, reported yesterday that the original concept of testing the Salk polio vaccine, when transferred to the commercial laboratories, failed to stand up.

Now, they didn't find this out until a team of scientists made their plant-by-plant inspection.

My question, sir: does the Public Health Service have an obligation to make sure that the requirements that they lay down are carried out?

THE PRESIDENT. Well, now, I guess I had better be careful, because I am not so certain about the law in the matter. But I do know that they have all agreed to meet the specifications, and therefore I think they could withdraw their license for manufacture; I don't want to be too severely criticized if I misunderstand the law in this case.

What has happened here is this: the scientists met and gave their very best conclusions with respect to a certain matter. The events have proved that there was a little bit of something lacking in this, and they had to be corrected.

I think that the Secretary of HEW was very wise in saying safety, caution are the words that we should think of here rather than mere haste, because mere haste could have had a lot of disastrous effects.

I think the scientists themselves are all agreed as to what now must be done and they are pushing it to do it.

Q. Roscoe Drummond, New York Herald Tribune: Mr. President, in connection with Mr. Adenauer's visit to Moscow, could I ask whether from our standpoint we either object in principle or feel any special anxiety about the normalization of diplomatic relations between the West German Republic and the Soviet Union.

THE PRESIDENT. Well, yesterday in my conference with the Secretary of State this matter didn't come up. As far as I am concerned, not a bit. I think that Chancellor Adenauer is one of the great statesmen of the world, and I believe he is a perfectly sound, solid citizen, and I trust him to take care of the interests of Western Germany.

Q. Ray L. Scherer, National Broadcasting Company: Mr. President, you mentioned the Yugoslav visit of the Russians.

THE PRESIDENT. Yes.

Q. Mr. Scherer: Do you share the belief of some that this country should reappraise its military aid to Yugoslavia in view of that country's new relation to the Soviet Union?

THE PRESIDENT. As I pointed up before, this is a world of change. Everything changes, and you reappraise policies monthly, weekly, daily. Just exactly what details of these programs might now need looking at, I am not sure; but I do believe this: merely because a country is striving to be somewhat neutral from their viewpoint as they look at this struggle in the world does not lessen particularly our interest in them.

Our opponents seem to show more interest, almost, in the neutrals than anybody else. Of course, they don't have to worry about the peoples allied with them. They have different methods. But they are very, very greatly concerned in these neutrals; and, of course, we should be.

We do want to win them to a great conviction that the freedom of action, the national independence, the right of people to determine their own fates, that we believe in, is the one for them to adopt.

Merriman Smith, United Press: Thank you, Mr. President.

NOTE: President Eisenhower's seventy-first news conference was held in the Executive Office Building from 11:02 to 11:34 o'clock on Wednesday morning, June 8, 1955. In attendance: 208.

120 ¶ Statement by the President Upon Signing the Postal Field Service Compensation Act. *June* 10, 1955

I HAVE today approved the Postal Field Service Compensation Act of 1955. This Act represents the greatest forward step for our postal employees in more than a century.

The new law will bring about the elimination of inequities in the Postal Field Service which for years have violated the principal of equal pay for equal work and discouraged employees from seeking advancement. The salary plan which the measure provides for firmly establishes that principle. It will at last place the wages for postal service positions in proper relationship to each other. Incentives for advancement are finally a reality. A fair pay increase is granted to each and every employee.

The Act represents a major step in the Administration's personnel program of providing Federal employees with a salary structure and employment benefits comparable to those available in the more progressive companies of private industry.

NOTE: As enacted, the Postal Field Service Compensation Act of 1955 is Public Law 68, 84th Congress (69 Stat. 88).

121   ❡ Address at the Centennial Commencement of Pennsylvania State University.   *June* 11, 1955

COMMENCEMENT speakers, by tradition, scan the future. They strive to predict, in general terms at least, the sort of success that awaits the graduates who properly apply themselves to their jobs and professions—and, of course, follow the advice of the speaker!

But the man who spoke at my commencement did not hint that I should be the first in a half century to receive an honorary degree here. Certainly I could not foresee, by the widest stretch of imagination, that one day the faculty and trustees of this University should consider me worthy of honorary membership in the Class of 1955 at Pennsylvania State—the Centennial Class of this most distinguished school. I am grateful for this honor and delighted by my association with this class. I am particularly grateful that my youngest brother—younger brothers being confirmed skeptics about their elders—raised no objection and in person made the presentation.

Earlier this week I joined in reunion with my own Class of 1915 at West Point. Most of us had grown gray and some of us more than a little bald; but these changes were slightly compensated, I thought, by an appearance of wisdom that we did not possess forty years ago. I am sure we all felt privileged, greatly privileged, to have lived in a day of marvels and of tremendous growth in America's stature. Although we were silent about it, I am certain that every one of us envied the men in the Class of 1955 as much for the opportunities and discoveries ahead of them as for their youth, their boundless energy, and their idealism. And in this feeling I am doubtless joined by thousands of alumni here as they applaud and congratulate you of this Class of 1955.

Of course, you men and women venture forth into a world where human nature differs little, if at all, from human nature in 1915 or in the Age of Pericles. Human relations—the art of getting along with the people who work beside you and with those who live thousands of miles away—does not change in its essence with the centuries. But the age of nuclear energy, in its industrial and economic aspects, will likely bear no more resemblance to the age of steam than a jet-powered plane to an old-fashioned box kite. Indeed, the social pattern of living may be transformed beyond recognition, for I think it can be stated almost as an axiom, demonstrated by the history of mankind that:

Out of the use of a new and great energy source, along with boundless opportunities, come new and great human problems that require new and great solutions produced by broadly informed, wisely sympathetic, spiritually inspired minds.

On this campus this morning, I had the privilege of inspecting the first atomic reactor of its kind established under university auspices. This research facility was made possible by the foresight of the trustees of this University who financed the structure and its operation. The Atomic Energy Commission provides only the fuel. In consequence, within several weeks, the atom will be at productive work here at Penn State. Here also the economic and human problems created by this new energy will be simultaneously studied by the distinguished faculties of this institution of learning.

Nuclear energy is too new for any man to chart its limits or predict its course with accuracy. But in ten short years the curtain has been pushed aside sufficiently to afford glimpses that have aroused atomic hopes commensurate with the awful dimension of atomic fears.

The extent of the economic and industrial changes that we can anticipate is indicated by estimates that world sources of uranium potentially available contain as high as twenty times the energy of the known world reserves of coal, petroleum, and natural gas combined. But power is only one of the results of nuclear fission. Many engineers and scientists believe that radiation and radioactive isotopes may provide even greater peacetime benefit.

They are already opening new horizons in medicine, agriculture, and industrial processes.

Our Nation has no desire for a monopoly on the knowledge and practice of these possibilities. We want the world to share—as we always have.

Moreover, we know that the human talents essential to the advancement of science are not restricted to this country. Throughout the free countries there are men and women of great ability who, given the opportunity, can help further to advance the frontiers of knowledge and contribute to the peace and progress of the peoples of all nations.

Progress to date in nuclear science is not, of course, exclusively an American achievement. An international cooperative effort broke the barriers and made possible man's use of atomic energy. For maximum progress in the future, we must work for a continued partnership between the world's best minds—in science, engineering, education, business, and the professions.

In recognition of these facts, I proposed before the General Assembly of the United Nations on December 8, 1953, that Governments begin then and continue to make joint contributions from their stockpiles of fissionable materials to an International Atomic Agency. Although a year later, the United Nations adopted the resolution recommending the formation of such an international agency, the Soviet Union has indicated no willingness to share any part of its nuclear stockpile with such an agency. Our offer still stands.

But we cannot wait on Soviet decisions.

Already we have made substantial progress under Congressional authority toward agreements with friendly foreign governments for participation with us in the task of forwarding peaceful atomic progress. Agreements with Turkey, Lebanon, Israel, Italy, Spain, Switzerland, Denmark, Colombia, Brazil, and the Argentine Republic have been initialed. Others are being negotiated. Now we move in further action.

We have developed two new programs that I shall submit to

the Congress in the conviction that they reflect the spirit and intent of law and of the American people.

First: we propose to offer research reactors to the people of free nations who can use them effectively for the acquisition of the skills and understanding essential to peaceful atomic progress. The United States, in the spirit of partnership that moves us, will contribute half the cost. We will also furnish the acquiring nation the nuclear material needed to fuel the reactor.

Second: within prudent security considerations, we propose to make available to the peoples of such friendly nations as are prepared to invest their own funds in power reactors, access to and training in the technological processes of construction and operation for peaceful purposes.

If the technical and material resources of a single nation should not appear adequate to make effective use of a research reactor, we would support a voluntary grouping of the resources of several nations within a single region to acquire and operate it together.

Our purpose is to spark the creative and inventive skills latent in the free world, to pool them and to put them to work for the betterment of the conditions under which men must live.

The research reactors acquired under this program will be fertile seeds for progress sown in the receptive soil of the free nations. The cost to the people of the United States will be small indeed when measured against the certain returns, tangible and intangible.

The second proposal will be of immediate interest mainly to the power-short areas of the world where atomic power may be economically feasible even today. Some of the countries, however, lack the knowledge and experience needed to construct and operate a commercial power reactor. This we can share for constructive purposes with friendly countries without real risk to our national security. Such sharing is expressly contemplated by the new Atomic Energy Act.

Together, these two provisions are designed, within the limits of prudence, to clear away some of the obstacles that have impeded progress in nuclear science and to permit its peaceful application by all who propose to make it serve mankind. Here is an invitation—to scientists and engineers, to industries and governments—to pool their energies and creative talents that this great achievement of the human mind may bear the fruit of its infinite promise.

The people of the United States instinctively reject any thought that their greatest scientific achievement can be used only as a weapon. Our increasing progress in its peaceful applications is evidence of that fact.

While we build atomic-powered ships for war—because we must—we have the desire, the determination to build atomic-powered ships for peace. And build them we shall! The first atomic-powered merchant ship, at its ports of call, will be a laboratory demonstration that man can harness this unlimited energy for normal, peaceful, prosperous life.

While we design bombs that can obliterate great military objectives—because we must—we are also designing generators, channels and reservoirs of atomic energy so that man may profit from this gift which the Creator of all things has put into his hands. And build them we shall!

The two proposals I have outlined here are the gateway to a broad avenue of world progress in the peaceful uses of atomic energy.

Surely those of the Russian people—who, despite their Communist overlords, still think for themselves and who still retain respect for human dignity—are moved by the same feelings as we.

I still hope earnestly that the Soviet Union may join in an international effort to harness the atom for man's good. But I have such unlimited confidence in the creativeness of free minds and in the capacity of free men that I know we will, with or without the Soviets, achieve a more abundant life for those who join together in this historic venture.

As for the social and political problems that will accompany this development, their outlines can be foreseen but dimly. Their solution will be a task in which you men and women who graduate today will be engaged intensively, probably throughout your lives. Some questions immediately suggest themselves.

Will there prevail the deep desires shared by the vast majority of all people on the earth who want peaceful use of this and all other technical advancements? Can they defeat the designs of those few evil men who would use command of this energy for their control of human destiny? In this question are involved such vital alternatives as war and peace, armament and disarmament, death and life.

Another group of questions is of a somewhat different character. As nuclear and other technological achievements continue to mount, the normal life span will continue to climb. The hourly productivity of the worker will increase. How is the increase in leisure time and the extension in life expectancy to be spent? Will it be for the achievement of man's better aspirations or his degradation to the level of a well-fed, well-kept slave of an all-powerful state?

Indeed, merely to state that question sharply reminds us that in these days and in the years ahead the need for philosophers and theologians parallels the need for scientists and engineers.

These two questions merely hint at the enormous problems and possibilities that will confront your generation. Scores of others will present themselves in the changing picture in agriculture, industry, and the arts. The answers can be found only by broadly informed, wisely sympathetic, spiritually inspired minds, the product of general education that properly blends the practical and technical with the liberal and cultural.

In this country we emphasize both liberal and practical education. But too often it is a liberal education for one and a practical education for another. What we desperately need is an integrated liberal, practical education for the same person—for every American youth who can possibly obtain its blessings. Hand and head and heart were made to work together. They must work together. They should be educated together.

In colonial Philadelphia, there was a printer who was likewise a scientist and who was hailed the wisest man of his day—a builder of international understanding and friendship. In nineteenth century Illinois, there was a rail-splitter who was likewise a lawyer and who was hailed a champion of humanity—a builder of freedom for all men. Despite their lack of formal schooling, they were educated men. Education today can nurture for us the possibility of a thousand Franklins and a thousand Lincolns in a generation, where before we were fortunate to have one.

To gain proficiency, sometimes even world acclaim in a specialized skill or profession, knowledge and training are the principal requisites. But to understand how one skill fits into another, how one profession complements and depends on another, how all human enterprises constitute an immense, interdependent society—only education can develop that understanding.

In our modern higher education, we have, I believe, three principle difficulties. First, in its practical aspect, we simply are not providing it to sufficient numbers of young men and women.

Second, we are not as proficient as we should be in providing a broad citizenship education to those who specialize in the many technical fields.

And third, even in liberal education, we have permitted it to become too much a specialization, rather than a broad, liberating influence on the mind, the attitude, the character of all students.

What we need is general education, combining the liberal and the practical, which helps a student achieve the solid foundation of understanding—understanding of man's social institutions, of man's art and culture, and of the physical and biological and spiritual world in which he lives. It is an education which helps each individual learn how to relate one relevant fact to another; to get the total of relevant facts affecting a given situation in perspective; and to reason critically and with objectivity and moral conscience toward solutions to those situations or problems.

I repeat: this kind of education is sorely needed in this country—and throughout the world.

The peoples of this earth share today a great aspiration. They all have a common dream of lasting peace with freedom and justice. But the realization of the dream calls for many types of cooperation based upon sympathetic and thorough mutual understanding. In turn, such understanding is dependent on education that produces disciplined thinking.

Throughout the world, mutual suspicions flourish in ignorance and misunderstanding. They can be dispelled only with knowledge and wisdom.

If we are to have partners for peace, then we must first be partners in sympathetic recognition that all mankind possesses in common like aspirations and hungers, like ideals and appetites, like purposes and frailties, a like demand for economic advancement. The divisions between us are artificial and transient. Our common humanity is God-made and enduring.

I know that you who today complete your education at this great university in its centennial year recognize that truth. As you apply it to the problems you meet—as productive leaders, as American citizens, as members of the free world community— you will grow in personal stature and in your contribution to human peace, human independence, human advancement.

122 ¶ Joint Statement Following Discussions With Chancellor Adenauer of Germany.
June 14, 1955

THE PRESIDENT, the Chancellor, the Secretary of State and their advisors met this morning and discussed the problems of concern to their two nations. They reviewed the political developments which have taken place since the Chancellor's last visit and noted with satisfaction that the bonds of friendship between their nations have become very close. They are of the opinion that the recent favorable developments in Europe are the result of the consistent, sound policies followed by the United States, the Federal Republic and their allies.

A large part of their discussion was devoted to the relationship between the nations of the free world and the Soviet Union and particularly the recent developments such as the willingness of the Soviet Union to participate in the Four Power conference and the invitation of the Soviet Government to the Chancellor. They agreed that one of the objectives of the forthcoming four-power meeting will be to pave the way for early German re-unification. It was confirmed that in their combined opinion the concept of neutrality is in no way applicable to Germany and that only in collective security arrangements can Germany assure its independence.

As a result of their discussions, they are reassured that there is a very broad field of understanding between them. They are convinced that the achievement of the policies upon which Germany and the United States are embarked will continue to require closest cooperation in the future. These policies are based on a common adherence to the furtherance of a just and enduring peace among the nations of the world.

123 ¶ Statement by the President on Proposed Agreements With Belgium, Canada, and the United Kingdom for Cooperation on the Civil Uses of Atomic Energy. *June* 15, 1955

I AM HAPPY to accept the recommendation of the Atomic Energy Commission that approval be given the proposed bilateral agreements for cooperation concerning the civil uses of atomic energy signed today on behalf of the Government of this nation and the Governments of Belgium, Canada and the United Kingdom.

These proposed agreements are a logical extension of the previous active partnership between these nations and the United States for the development of atomic energy. The United Kingdom and Canada supplied knowledge and skill and manpower to play a full and fruitful part in the wartime joint effort which culminated in the first release of atomic energy. Belgium and Canada have provided uranium, the basic raw material for the wartime and the postwar atomic energy programs. All three have freely cooperated to further our common defense and security, strengthen the bulwarks of the free world, and help to open the way into the development of peaceful uses of the atom which holds forth so much promise and hope for betterment of human living and easing of international tensions.

Now, acting under the authorizations of the Atomic Energy Act of 1954, we are privileged to enter into bilateral agreements which enlarge that promise and brighten that hope. The wisdom of the Congress in making this possible is exemplified by these proposed agreements. They lengthen the reach of cooperation among us looking toward the civil uses of atomic energy.

The pace of progress toward the goal of the atoms-for-peace program is accelerating. Important events are just ahead, such as the International Conference on Peaceful Uses of Atomic Energy at Geneva in August.

Again on this occasion, as many times earlier, I pledge the unremitting cooperation of this nation to realize the benefits of atomic energy as a measure to promote lasting peace.

NOTE: At the time this statement was released the White House announced that the proposed agreements had been signed by representatives of the four governments at a White House ceremony that morning.

The text of the agreements and related papers are published in the Congressional Record (vol. 101, pp. 8661 ff., 8757 ff.).

124 ¶ Letter to William Randolph Hearst, Jr., Regarding His Appointment to the President's Committee for Traffic Safety and Its Advisory Council. *June* 18, 1955

[Released June 18, 1955. Dated June 17, 1955]

Dear Bill:

I have learned from Harlow Curtice of your willingness to serve as Chairman of the Advisory Council to the Committee for Traffic Safety.   It is gratifying to know that you will be turning your interest and broad experience in traffic problems to the urgent traffic safety program.

In extension of this, I should like to ask you, as Chairman of the Advisory Council, to serve also as an *ex officio* member of the Committee.   By doing so, you can contribute significantly to strengthened Committee liaison with the national highway safety organizations represented on the Advisory Council.   I need not emphasize to you the importance of a close tie between the two groups.

I sincerely hope that you will be able to undertake this direct liaison responsibility.

With warm regard,

Sincerely,

DWIGHT D. EISENHOWER

Mr. William R. Hearst, Jr.
President
Hearst Consolidated Publications, Inc.
New York City 19, New York

125   ¶ Letter to T. S. Petersen Requesting Him To Serve on the President's Committee for Traffic Safety.   *June* 18, 1955

[Released June 18, 1955. Dated June 17, 1955]

Dear Ted:

This note is to request that you accept appointment to the Committee for Traffic Safety as the representative of businessmen.

As you know, Harlow Curtice has been serving in the dual capacity of Chairman and business representative. He now believes that the functioning of the Committee will be improved by having an individual other than the Chairman to represent each of the seven fields of interest covered by the Committee membership.

In view of your demonstrated interest in traffic accident prevention in California, I am certain that your participation in the work of the Committee will be of great benefit. I sincerely hope that you will be able to undertake this responsibility.

With warm regard,

Sincerely,

DWIGHT D. EISENHOWER

Mr. T. S. Petersen
President
Standard Oil Company of California
San Francisco 20, California

126 ¶ Address at the Tenth Anniversary Meeting of the United Nations, San Francisco, California. *June* 20, 1955

[Broadcast over radio and television at 3:00 p.m.]

President Van Kleffens, distinguished representatives of the member nations of this great organization, ladies and gentlemen:

This, my second appearance before the United Nations, gives me, as Chief Executive of the United States, the great privilege of joining with you in commemoration of an historic date—significant, momentous, for all mankind.

I am privileged to bring you a special message from the Congress of the United States. Last week the Congress unanimously adopted a resolution requesting me to express to all of you here, on behalf of the people of the United States, our deep desire for peace and our hope that all nations will join with us in a renewed effort for peace.

Later this week my close friend and associate, Secretary John Foster Dulles, speaking with my full confidence and concurrence, will address you on appropriate elements in the foreign policy of the United States. Because of this circumstance, it seems fitting that I, today, speak principally in terms of my country's unswerving loyalty to the United Nations and of the reasons for our tireless support of it.

A decade ago, in this city, in this building, the Charter of the United Nations was signed by its fifty founding members. Into a world, shattered and still at war but hopeful and eager for a new dawn, was born an international organization, fashioned to be the supreme instrument of world peace.

For this nation, I pay respectful tribute to you whose faith, and patience, and courage, and wisdom have brought it through ten tumultuous, frequently discouraging, sometimes terrifying—but often rewarding years. That there have been failures in attempts to solve international difficulties by the principles of the Charter, none can deny. That there have been victories, only the willfully blind can fail to see. But clear it is that without the United Nations the failures would still have been written as failures into history. And, certainly, without this organization the victories could not have been achieved; instead, they might well have been recorded as human disasters. These, the world has been spared.

So, with the birthday congratulations I bring, I reaffirm to you the support of the Government of the United States in the purposes and aims of the United Nations, and in the hopes that inspired its founders.

Today, together, we face a second decade. We face it with the accumulated experience of the first ten years, as well as with the awful knowledge of nuclear weapons and the realization that a certain and enduring peace still eludes our persistent search.

But the summer of 1955, like that one of 1945, is another season of high hope for the world. There again stirs in the hearts of men a renewed devotion to the work for the elimination of war. Each of us here is witness that never in ten years has the will of many nations seemed so resolved to wage an honest and sustained campaign for a just and lasting peace. True, none of us can produce incontestable evidence to support this feeling. Nevertheless, all of us, I think, will testify that the heartfelt longings of countless millions for abundance and justice and peace seem to be commanding, everywhere, a response from their governments. These longings have strengthened the weak, encouraged the doubtful, heartened the tired, confirmed the believing. Almost it seems that men, with souls restored, are, with faith and courage, resuming the march toward the greatest human goal.

Within a month there will be a Four Power Conference of Heads of Government. Whether or not we shall then reach the initial decisions that will start dismantling the terrible apparatus of fear and mistrust and weapons erected since the end of World War II, I do not know.

The basis for success is simply put: it is that every individual at that meeting be loyal to the spirit of the United Nations and dedicated to the principles of its Charter.

I can solemnly pledge to you here—and to all the men and women of the world who may hear or read my words—that those who represent the United States will strive to be thus loyal, thus dedicated. For us of the United States, there is no alternative, because our devotion to the United Nations Charter is the outgrowth of a faith deeply rooted in our cultural, political, spiritual traditions.

Woven into the Charter is the belief of its authors:

That man—a physical, intellectual and spiritual being—has individual rights, divinely bestowed, limited only by the obligation to avoid infringement upon the equal rights of others;

That justice, decency and liberty, in an orderly society, are concepts which have raised men above the beasts of the field: to deny any person the opportunity to live under their shelter is a crime against all humanity.

Our Republic was born, grew, stands firm today in a similar belief!

The Charter assumes:

That every people has the inherent right to the kind of government under which it chooses to live and the right to select in full freedom the individuals who conduct that government.

Hence the Charter declares:

That on every nation in possession of foreign territories, there rests the responsibility to assist the peoples of those areas in the progressive development of free political institutions so that ultimately they can validly choose for themselves their permanent political status.

Our long history as a republic manifests a self-imposed compulsion to practice these same principles.

The Charter recognizes that only those who enjoy free access to historical and current facts and information, and through objective education learn to comprehend their meanings, can successfully maintain and operate a system of self-government. Our Republic, likewise, maintains that access to knowledge and education is the right of all its citizens—and of all mankind.

Written under the shadow of war, the Charter is strong in the conviction that no nation has a right to employ force aggressively against any other. To do so, or to threaten to do so, is to defy every moral law that has guided man in his long journey from darkness toward the light. Those who wrote it clearly realized that global war has come to pose for civilization a threat of shattering destruction and a sodden existence by the survivors in a dark and broken world.

Likewise they recognized that the first responsibility of every nation is to provide for its own defense; and, in pursuance of this responsibility, it has the clear right to associate itself with other like-minded peoples for the promotion of their common security.

But they who wrote the Charter emphasized that in the formation of such associations, within the framework of the United Nations, it is incumbent upon the contracting parties to inform the world by solemn assurance, always supported by deeds, that the sole purpose is defense, devoid of aggressive aims.

We as a nation believe these truths that are expressed in the Charter. We strive to live by them. So:

We shall always maintain a government at home that recognizes and constantly seeks to sustain for the individual those rich economic, intellectual, and spiritual opportunities to which his human rights entitle him.

In our relations with all other nations, our attitude will reflect full recognition of their sovereign and equal status. We shall deal with common problems in a spirit of partnership.

Insofar as our technical, material, and intellectual capacities permit and wherever our aid, including the peaceful use of atomic energy, may be needed and desired, we shall continue to help others achieve constantly rising economic levels. Thereby, we trust that they will have increased opportunity to attain their own cultural and spiritual aspirations.

We shall work with all others—especially through this great organization, the United Nations—so that peaceful and reasonable negotiations may replace the clash of the battlefield. In this way we can in time make unnecessary the vast armaments that—even when maintained only for security—still terrify the world with their devastating potentiality and tax unbearably the creative energies of men.

As some success in disarmament is achieved, we hope that each of the so-called great powers will contribute to the United Nations, for promoting the technical and economic progress of the less productive areas, a portion of the resultant savings in military expenditures.

An abiding faith inspired the men and women who devised the great Charter under which you work. We of the United States share that faith. We hold fast to the hope that all nations in their intercourse with others will observe those amenities of deportment, customs and treatment of other nationals as are sanctioned by tradition, by logic, and by friendly purposes.

We and a majority of all nations, I believe, are united in another hope: that every government will abstain from itself attempting, or aiding others to attempt, the coercion, infiltration, or destruction of other governments in order to gain any political or material advantage or because of differences in philosophies, religions, or ideologies.

We, with the rest of the world, know that a nation's vision of peace cannot be attained through any race in armaments. The munitions of peace are justice, honesty, mutual understanding, and respect for others.

So believing and so motivated, the United States will leave no stone unturned to work for peace. We shall reject no method however novel, that holds out any hope however faint, for a just and lasting peace.

May I recall to you the words of a great citizen of this country, Abraham Lincoln, which, though uttered in a different context, apply to the problem which the world now seeks to solve.

He said: ". . . The dogmas of the quiet past are inadequate to the stormy present. The occasion is piled high with difficulty, and we must rise with the occasion. As our case is new, so we must think anew and act anew. We must disenthrall ourselves, and then we shall save our country."

In such a body as this, it seems fitting that we should add to Lincoln's words: "Each for himself, our country and humanity."

The object of our second decade is still peace—but a peace of such new kind that all the world will think anew and act anew.

It cannot be a mere stilling of the guns—it must be a glorious way of life. In that life the atom, dedicated once as man's slayer, will become his most productive servant. It will be a peace to inspire confidence and faith so that all peoples will be released from the fear of war. Scientists will be liberated to work always for men, never against them. Who can doubt that in the next ten years world science can so beat down the ravages of disease and the pangs of poverty that humankind will experience a new expansion of living standards and of cultural and spiritual horizons. In this new kind of peace the artist, teacher and philosopher, workman, farmer, producer, and scientist will truly work together for the common welfare.

These hopes are not new. They are as old as history. But now as we meet on this tenth anniversary in the city where was born the United Nations, we must realize that at last they are steadily and surely attainable. This is new. Our part is to rededicate ourselves to the ideals of the United Nations Charter. May we here and now renew our determination to fulfill man's ancient dream, the dream which so inspired the founders of this organization.

Thus our duty will be nobly done, and future generations will behold the United Nations and stand up to call it blessed.

May I please express to your President my grateful thanks for his invitation to address this distinguished body. To each of you my gratitude for your courteous attention.

Thank you very much.

NOTE: The President spoke at the San Francisco Opera House. His opening words "President Van Klef- fens" referred to Eelco N. van Kleffens, President of the United Nations General Assembly.

127 ¶ Remarks to the National Association of Television and Radio Farm Directors.
June 21, 1955

Mr. Atwood, Mr. Secretary, ladies and gentlemen:

It is a fact, of course, that I am interested in farm programs from two angles: one as a farmer and one as a governmental official. And I find my ideas don't always agree when I take the two viewpoints.

I couldn't tell you how necessary I feel it is that the whole country be accurately informed on farm problems. They are basic. It is a basic industry. The prosperity of the agricultural community is absolutely necessary to the prosperity of the nation; and vice versa we can state the same truth—that the prosperity of the nation is necessary for the prosperity of the agricultural community.

I have been very much interested, since I came here, to find the interest that there sometimes is in promoting an idea that is not exactly true. For example, we know that there has been a falling farm income over some years. There have been always the steady rising of costs, although we have succeeded for the last couple of years in keeping living costs rather stable. But there has been a squeeze on the farmer.

Now I suddenly find that many people blame the flexible price support law passed last year. And only people like you can inform the public that it has not yet gone into effect, that the 1955 crops are not yet in. So I don't see how it could have much effect on the price situation as it existed up to this moment.

As an individual farmer, I might say that I am completely dis- interested. Until I get out of this job, I don't get any interest in the income and the debts of my farm.   That is something that purely belongs to the fellow who is leasing it.

I do, though, believe that in such items as farm prices, and in all other items that you can learn about as you come to this Capital City, you are doing a great service when you inform the American public.   There is no question about the commonsense—the logic of the decisions that will be reached by the American public when they are informed.   But they must be informed, and accurately. When you have the mission of getting hold of the information, not only about the farm programs, but the things that will interest the whole farm community, you are doing a tremendously great service.

The Secretary and I and this administration approach this farm problem basically from this viewpoint: the farmer is not just a farmer, he is a citizen of the United States, first and always. He is interested in his country.   His boy has to go into the Services when he is called.   He has to pay his taxes for all of the roads and the schools and everything else that is done if there is Federal money involved.   He has to participate in his government in every possible way.

Therefore, he must know about these things so that he can fit into his concept of the whole his own particular problem, not merely viewing it in its isolated sense: that I am getting a little squeezed this year, or there is a drought or something, so let's have something done.   He must see it in the fabric or with the background, the backdrop, of the entire picture in which his government and Nation's economy is concerned.

So I think that if we are truly going to interpret the farm problem and farm programs to the farmer, we have got to raise our sights a long way and interpret, with that particular phase of the picture, the background that is such an essential part.

I am told by the Secretary of Agriculture that this group has done a yeoman's job in this regard.   For it I hope you will accept my thanks, my gratitude, and more than that my utter conviction that you are doing a truly great service to farmers and to the United States of America.

NOTE: The President spoke in the Rose Garden. His opening words referred to Frank Atwood, President of the Association, and Ezra T. Benson, Secretary of Agriculture.

128 ¶ Remarks to the National 4–H Conference. *June* 21, 1955

I COULD USE a lot of you up on my farm right now, as you know that we are trying to get it into order and shape.

We talk about farm problems. We talk about farm products. And you have heard often of the importance of the farm economy to the entire national economy. You have heard about the importance of this crop and that crop and what it means in national income.

As I see so many young people, I am tempted to talk for just a moment about the most important crop of all in this country: yourselves.

You produce the future producers of our agricultural supplies of all kinds, and you send to the city annually some one-half of your entire personnel. These cities get their infusion of new blood from our agricultural regions. The point that I should like to make is that I believe you have more than an ordinarily good opportunity to prepare yourselves well for leadership in the future activities of our country.

As a farm individual, you are first close to the soil and from the soil must come all the things by which we live. You are a business person. You have to be a professional person if you are going to farm correctly—at least the scientists are scaring me to death about the things I don't know about my farm. And you must be a working man, you must be able to take care of the things that you do in order to produce a good cow, or calf, or a crop of corn, or wheat, or cotton—whatever. So you are gaining, in the practical way, an all-round experience of the problems of the various classifications of our citizenship, as you are gaining like- wise an understanding of our whole economy and where the agri- cultural economy fits into it.   In this whole effort I think that membership of the 4–H Clubs with their stress upon citizenship— becoming good citizens, good leaders—is probably one of the greatest products that our agricultural regions are giving us to- day—I am sure of it.

I wish that I could have a few minutes with each of you, to try to tell you what I believe is in front of you, not in terms of the commencement speaker, who labors in very measured, solemn tones to paint the horrible side of the future and the challenges in front of you, but just to talk a little bit about some of the things I believe maybe I have learned, and how much I envy you what is in front of you—to stop and think of the things you are going to see.   It is so fascinating that we could stand here for the rest of the day talking about them.   In this great and fast-changing world, you are not only going to participate, you are going to be leaders—on the farms and in the cities.   You are going to in- fluence others, and you are learning today in the best possible way through these 4–H endeavors and these 4–H Clubs how to do it well.

I think the only real thought I want to leave with you is this: I congratulate you heartily both on when you were born, what you have done, and what you are going to do.

Thank you a lot, and goodby.

NOTE: The President spoke in the Rose Garden at 12:30 p.m.

129 ¶ Statement by the President Upon Signing the Trade Agreements Extension Act.
June 21, 1955

ENACTMENT of the Trade Agreements Extension Act of 1955 is an important milestone in the development of our country's foreign economic policy. Supplemented by early approval of United States membership and participation in the proposed Organization for Trade Cooperation, the Act can contribute significantly to economic growth and economic well-being throughout the free world. In this way it will materially strengthen the defense capabilities of our friends abroad, and advance the mutual security of us all.

I am particularly gratified that this measure was supported by overwhelming majorities in both political parties. This bipartisanship demonstrates anew our unity in dealing with matters affecting our relations with other countries.

NOTE: As enacted, the Trade Agreements Extension Act of 1955 is Public Law 86, 84th Congress (69 Stat. 162).

130 ¶ Memorandum to Federal Agencies on the Community Chest Campaign.   *June 22, 1955*

[Released June 22, 1955. Dated June 21, 1955]

To the Heads of Executive Departments and Agencies:

In the National Capital Area the Community Chest Federation unites six Community Chests and more than one hundred Red Feather agencies or services in one federated campaign to provide local health, welfare and recreational programs vital to the building of a healthy, strong and safer community in which to live, work and play.

To act as Chairman of the Government Unit in this important appeal, I appoint the Honorable Harvey V. Higley, Administrator of Veterans' Affairs.

I ask that you give Mr. Higley your fullest measure of support and assistance and that all persons in authority in the Federal and District Government take a personal interest and extend their complete cooperation to this important charitable appeal. Such cooperation should logically include the assumption of equitable unit goals, the effective solicitation of all employees, and the setting up of an adequate collection method for the convenience of those who wish to make contributions on an installment basis.

To avoid a separate financial appeal the USO–USO Camp Shows will again be included in the Red Feather Campaign. This national and international program continues to be essential to the morale and happiness of our men and women of the Armed Forces both at home and overseas.

It is my hope that all officials and employees will be given the opportunity to contribute voluntarily, and that they will want to do so generously, mindful of the fact that this is one appeal for the yearly support of over one hundred Red Feather agency programs and the USO. Each individual's giving should reflect a fair share towards the support of these worthwhile services for a full year of effective operation.

Dwight D. Eisenhower

131 ¶ Remarks at the Vermont State Dairy Festival, Rutland, Vermont. *June 22, 1955*

Governor Johnson, Senator Aiken, Senator Flanders, distinguished guests—fellow members of the Brown Swiss Dairy Cattle Association—my fellow Americans:

Much has been said by former speakers of the honor I have done this State by coming here. Let me make one thing clear— very clear: no greater honor can come to any individual and citizen of this country than to be received in friendly fashion by a cross-section of his fellow citizens.

You have honored me.

I think, first, I should like to remember my manners and thank you—each of you—as representatives of my host State for the warm reception I have had, for the beautiful presents given me. As a matter of fact, for the prestige I shall have in Pennsylvania when I can show a cow that has no other like it around there. They will come to see that farm if for no other reason than that cow.

Now I had a number of reasons for coming here. I think they can all be summed up in one word: self-education.

I don't think I know enough—ever—about the people of the United States, with whom I am privileged to meet and mingle when I go on a trip like this. Particularly, I have been denied too many opportunities to go to the northern three States of the New England group. I have long wanted to come here, and for two years I have carried it as a determination. And finally, I got the permission of Governor Adams to come—and here I am!

Now one of the first things I want to learn is where Calvin Coolidge got a certain skill that I have not acquired. He held the same position I now hold. He had a distinguished record, and held it for a long time, and he spoke so rarely that he got the nickname "Silent Cal."

My own experience in this regard is exemplified by the fact that the day before yesterday I spoke in San Francisco, and here again I am today, still talking. I find that my tongue is clattering in my ears a great deal, and I would like to know what Vermont secret he had that allowed him to avoid this particular responsibility.

There is another thing I want to learn; old as I am, there is a lesson in romance I have heard attached to Vermont—told me by that now distinguished citizen, Sherman Adams of New Hampshire.

He said there was a Vermont couple that were going to get married, but Mary thought that John ought to save a thousand dollars before they really were married.   And they agreed, they thought it was a good thing.   And he worked all winter long, and when June again approached, Mary thought it was a nice time to think of marriage, and she said, "How much have you saved?" Well, John looked a little bit sheepish and didn't want to confess, but after a while he said, "Thirty-five dollars."   She said, "That's near enough, John."   [*Laughter*]

Ladies and gentlemen, that is a confidence—the emotion—the idealism—that we normally associate with Vermont when we say the word "Ethan Allen."

By the way, I hear my cow came from Ethan Allen's farm. And am I glad!—I think I shall call her "Mrs. Ethan Allen."

Actually, I came here just to see you—to see people.   I want to know you better.   There are certain things I do know about you. I know that Americans everywhere are the same, in their longing for peace, a peace that is characterized by justice, by consideration for others, by decency above all, by its insistence on respect for the individual human being as a child of his God.

All of us want that.   All of us want the institutions of America preserved.   It makes no difference what party label you attach to an American, we have equal veneration for our Constitution, for the basic principles that have been so beautifully upheld in this State, so well described in that tribute to the people of this State by Calvin Coolidge, just read to you a little while ago. Those are the things America wants.

But what we must find out is: what are the methods by which we approach all of these things?   What are the traits we must ourselves display and hold on to?

We know we must be determined.   We know we must not sacrifice principle for mere expediency.   But do we know also that the responsibility is on us to attempt to understand others as we think they should understand us?   Do we even make the mistake of assuming that the rest of the world knows us, knows our peaceful intentions, knows that we want nobody else's land, nobody else's rights, that we covet nothing?

We merely want to live in peace with all the world, to trade with them, to commune with them, to learn from their cultures, as they may learn from ours. I assure you, my friends, they do not know it. Even nations we know enlightened still have much to learn about America. Indeed, every single citizen of every other State has something to learn about you.

It is probably a pity that every citizen of each State cannot visit all the others, to see the differences, to learn what we have in common, and to come back with a richer, fuller understanding of America in all its beauty, in all its dignity, in all its strength, in support of moral principle.

I think as we think on these things, in lieu of travel, we do become stronger. As we think of our neighbors, as we try to apply with him or with her the spirit of the Golden Rule, we are doing the same in a very definite sense in our relationships with all the world.

That, ladies and gentlemen, is what will strengthen America and in the long run, thoroughly practiced, will help bring peace. We will remain strong always, but always in one hand will be the olive branch held out to all who will take it in honesty and in integrity.

That is what I feel about America, in its principles, its basic hopes and aspirations.

I come to you, not only to understand you better, but to ask you only to support, always, those principles, to think of them and to expand them in your own mind into method, as to how we shall do it; and then you will always make your own contribution to the peace of the world, so that our sons may stay at home, the products of our toil may be used for our schools and our roads and our churches, and not for guns and planes and tanks and ships of war.

And now as I say goodby and go for my first chance to use that beautiful fishing rod—a product of Vermont that was given me a few moments ago—I want to say only this, in terms of the greatest sincerity and honesty: if you do think on these things and devise for yourself your ideas of what should be done, if you will communicate those ideas to others, hammer out a common solution on the anvil of debate and argument and discussion, you will be doing your full part in bringing about this age-old dream of mankind: peace on earth, goodwill toward men.

Thank you.

NOTE: The President spoke at the Rutland Fairgrounds at 3:05 p.m.

132 ¶ Remarks at a Breakfast for Vermont Women Representatives of Dairy and Agricultural Organizations, Chittenden, Vermont. *June 23, 1955*

OF COURSE, Mrs. Proctor and ladies, there is really nothing for me to say except thank you.

I thank you, of course, for this present. But far more for the cordial friendliness you have exhibited to me here. I count this breakfast a great opportunity to be a little closer to you people, to meet you, to exchange a hand-clasp and to go away believing that I have made some new friends among a people with whom I am going to leave a big portion of my heart.

Thank you.

NOTE: The President spoke at Mountain Top Inn at 8:58 a.m.

In his opening remarks the President referred to Mrs. Mortimer R. Proctor, of Proctor, Vt., in charge of women's activities for the Vermont State Dairy Festival, who presented a corsage of red clover, the State flower of Vermont.

133 ¶ Remarks at the State Capitol, Concord, New Hampshire. *June 23, 1955*

Governor Dwinell, Mr. Speaker, distinguished guests and my fellow Americans:

I wonder whether your imaginations could picture yourself the recipient of such a glowing commendation as has been heaped upon me by your Governor and by the people of this State for whom he spoke?

If your imaginations are equal to that task, then you must know something of how I feel, you must know how inadequate are words in any effort to reply effectively and truly feelingly.

I can only say I am overwhelmed by your kindness.

Now, I had many reasons for coming on this trip. The simplest one of all, the one that explains it best, is merely a matter of self-education.

No man in responsible office can ever know enough about this country. He must seize opportunities to go and learn. And he finds there arc spots that he has visited less than, possibly, some others. One of the great gaps in my education is that I have not visited this northern tier of the New England group as much as I should have liked.

And so I am seizing the opportunity between a speech out in California and possibly even more prolonged talking in Europe to come here to mingle with you, to learn something of what you are thinking, to gain strength from you.

There are among you many of my old comrades of the Armed Services, people who served with me in war and peace. And they will know from their courses in staff colleges, and listening to lectures, that the commander often visits his troops, and the purpose is supposed to be to inspire them to do their duty better, to carry on in better fashion, to do the work that they are sent into the field to do.

I found early in war that this whole process was reversed in my case. I went out to visit the troops so that I could come back and do my job better.

My admiration for the young American on the battlefield is unexcelled. And I have found in later times that my admiration for his counterpart in every hamlet, every city, every farm of America is exactly the same.

When I feel that I have gotten a grip on what Americans are thinking, then I am perfectly certain that I am right.

In these feeble words, I am trying to tell you the serious reason for my visit among you. There are some reasons not quite so serious in character.

In my White House staff we have a lecture every morning. The chief of the staff has one subject: New Hampshire. Most of us have had a bit of education—we have unquestionably learned something—but above all things we have had our curiosity excited. We want to find out whether the golf greens are greener, the fish are bigger, more plentiful and more cooperative, whether the hills are really as beautiful as he says, whether all of the people are as healthy and strong and completely independent and virile—well!—all of the good words that we apply to people.

I expect to find every one of them here.

People often ask me what my ideas are on how long I would like a residence in 1600 Pennsylvania Avenue. My own thought is: they should ask how long it is going to take Governor Adams to finish up his series of lectures on New Hampshire, because he doesn't seem to be a third of the way through them yet.

In any event, just to know you is a great honor. To have heard the words I have heard is a greater one.

I hope in the next day or two to see as much of each of you, perhaps have the great privilege of greeting some of you individually, or shaking you by the hand, talking to you, if even for a brief moment. If I do have that privilege, I assure you that it is one I shall treasure.

If I do not, I would ask you to remember that I wanted to do so.

This is one of the great days of my life, marred only by the fact that Mrs. Eisenhower could not be with me, because she would have enjoyed it just as much as I.

Thank you very much.

NOTE: The President spoke at 4:15 p.m. His opening words referred to Governor Lane Dwinell, and Charles Griffin, Speaker of the House of Representatives, New Hampshire State Legislature.

134   ¶ Remarks at the Belknap Lodge Picnic Grounds, Laconia, New Hampshire.
June 23, 1955

Senator Bridges, distinguished guests, my fellow Americans:

Until I heard Senator Bridges talk just now, I had thought that there was no promoter of New Hampshire in the world to equal Sherman Adams.

I now think that we should stage a contest and have it done in front of a crowd like this, and by the degree of applause we can find out who can win. But it is going to be a close race, that I assure you.

I noticed that when Senator Bridges was speaking, there were certain interruptions—[*laughter*]—well, you people seem to find that ridiculous, but I am a farmer now and that was a very sweet sound to me. Now that I find that beautiful calf mine, she is sweeter than ever, and she is going to make some nice noises around Gettysburg, I hope.

I am not only grateful for what I have learned of New Hampshire this evening. I am certainly grateful for the New Hampshires, because they will be the first chickens on my farm. I expect to get all of the benefits that he talked about, of early feathers, and early eggs, and big eggs, and all the rest of it.

I am delighted to be here this evening. I am delighted to see you. To each of you, my thanks for the warmth of your welcome. Indeed, I might say now, that as I have traveled through your

State this afternoon, I have seen many people along the road, in the villages, and in the towns and in the country.   To you and to them, to every one who has given me a smile, or a "Hi Ike"— [*mooing calf*]—my grateful thanks.   [*Laughter*]

Now, you see!—I think that's fine!   [*More laughter*]

After all, it's a New Hampshire talking!

Good luck to each of you.   Thanks for a wonderful evening, which I have enjoyed to the full.

Goodnight.

NOTE: The President spoke at 8:30 p.m.

135   ¶ Remarks at the Lincoln High School, Lincoln, New Hampshire.   *June* 24, 1955

Governor Dwinell, the New Hampshire Congressional Delegation, Governor Adams, distinguished guests, my fellow Americans:

Of course I am not going to make a speech.   But I am in New Hampshire and it seems fitting that I should try to express one or two thoughts as to what New Hampshire has come to mean to me.

For a long time, New Hampshire has been a source of strength and aid.   We have a sturdy Congressional delegation from New Hampshire in the Congress.   At the head of that delegation is a very Senior Senator whose knowledge of public life has been long dedicated to the public good.   Today he, with other forward-looking Americans in Washington, is trying to hammer out through the anvil of debate and legislative processes a program which will conform to the deepseated desire of America for peace—for peace abroad and a widely shared prosperity here at home.

Americans covet no other country's land.   We covet no additional power.   We need no additional prestige.   We want—in a land where each man is the king of his own castle—we want mere opportunity to expand, to continue to grow, and opportunity to attain our deepest spiritual and intellectual aspirations.   That is what we want.   That is what a forward-looking program means. That is what your delegation, under the leadership of Senator Bridges, is seeking.

Now New Hampshire has come to mean some other things to me, because I have had Sherman Adams by my side.

Once, in the war, General Marshall and General Bradley and I happened to be talking together and the conversation turned to the qualities that we were constantly seeking in the generals that served in the Army, in order that the job of the war would be most quickly and effectively accomplished.

Now all such qualities as courage, and decisiveness, and consideration for men—everything that you would think of as a necessary quality in a general, were discussed—his tactical skill, his vast experience, his reputation, and so on.

But finally we came down to this one thing—the first quality you must seek in a general is exactly the same quality that you must seek in any man who serves the public: selflessness.

I think that Sherman Adams in the last two years—and I must say I have long sought for an opportunity to express a little bit more accurately my feeling of indebtedness to Sherman—here, it seems to me, is the proper place to do it—for these past two years, I think that he has exhibited this quality of selflessness as much as any man I have known.

He has not sought honor for himself.   He has sought, in his position, almost an anonymity, to serve his country by working with the legislators, by working with the staff that is set up in the White House, by advising me and trying to keep me from stumbling too often.   He has found that last, possibly, one of his toughest problems.

In any event, I think that I could express my feelings this morning by thanking New Hampshire and the town of Lincoln for sending to me Sherman Adams, to serve as the head of the staff that, without publicity, with no credit other than that which goes with that of a conscience that recognizes duty well done, is working day by day to further all of those programs that we believe will actually promote peace in the world and prosperity—a widely shared prosperity at home.

It has been a great honor for me to come to New Hampshire. It is a greater honor for me to come to this one little spot that is so dear to the heart of my good friend, my chief of staff Sherman Adams.

Thank you all. It has been fine to meet you.

NOTE: The President spoke at 10:42 a.m.

136   ¶ Remarks at Ceremonies Commemorating the Discovery of the Old Man of the Mountain, Franconia Notch, New Hampshire.   *June* 24, 1955

Governor Dwinell, Members of the New Hampshire Congressional delegation, distinguished guests and my fellow Americans:

Only a few moments ago, I had the first opportunity of my life to look at the Old Man of the Mountain. The natural question asked me was, "What did you think of it, Mr. President?" I answered, as anyone would in polite conversation, and said: "Remarkable. Wonderful. Interesting."

The real thought that crossed my mind was: what does the Old Man of the Mountain think of us?

He has been there through time. In his lonely vigil up at the top of that mountain—let us not try to go back to what he may have been thinking through those ages before our civilization first discovered him—150 years ago he saw great ox carts going through these roads where now we travel in an instant. He saw the fastest means of transportation—the horse. Finally he saw stage coaches. He saw only here and there a habitation, a sparsely settled wilderness.

He has seen mankind go from the sailing ship and from the horse and buggy to the jet airplane and the ability to cross the ocean in a few hours. He has seen the great sciences of radio and television come to us. He has seen every American have, with his morning breakfast, the day's news of the world. He has seen the great electronics industry—electric lights, telephones and telegraphy, and all the things by which we live today. All of these changes have come about.

But can you believe, as he stands up there, almost in infinite majesty, that he thinks it is of great concern that we travel at a rate that multiplies the speed of our forefathers?

I believe he thinks of something deeper than that. Possibly he recalls the words with which our Forefathers started the greatest of all human documents: "When in the course of human events it becomes necessary for one people to dissolve the political bands which have connected them with another, and assume among the powers of the earth that separate and equal status to which both the laws of nature and nature's God intended them, a decent respect for the opinions of mankind impel them to declare the reasons which have led to their separation. We hold these truths to be self-evident, that all men are created equal, that they are endowed by their Creator with certain unalienable rights. Among these are life, liberty and the pursuit of happiness."

These immortal words must mean a great deal to the Old Man of the Mountain. He must contemplate them from time to time. I think we—with him—understand life. We know the instinct of self-preservation, and we know what living means to us, in our separate capacities, in our separate areas. We know what liberty is: the individual right to do as we please as long as we do not infringe upon similar rights of others.

But the pursuit of happiness—he must have noted that those writers did not create this government to give us happiness. Far better they knew than to try to define happiness for any one of us—the pursuit of happiness in liberty each according to his own desires, to the deepest aspirations of his own soul.

Now, what have we done about it? Where do we find happiness?

Possibly that is what he is wondering today.

We know certain things. We know we would like to be at peace. We do not want to send our boys off into the Armed Services to serve in foreign lands. We do not want to dwell in fear. We do not want to contemplate the horrible things that could happen to us in a new war.

At home we want to live comfortably. We want to be well-informed. We want to have neighbors around us that we like.

But as we pursue happiness, are we thinking only of these material things? Then how do we attain it?

If we attain money to do certain things, then we want more money. If we attain a high office, we want a higher one. If there is no higher one we would like to invent it. We always want something more.

Now, what is there more? Maybe the "more" is to try to discover what others around us find as their idea of the pursuit of happiness, what is it that mankind wants, instead of each of us separately? Can we integrate the desires, the aspirations, the hopes of our community, and then do our part to achieve that?

In so doing, I wonder whether the Old Man wouldn't approve of us more than he may at present? Because he well knows, if he has watched us, that each individual is made up of two sets of qualities. One we call the noble: courage, readiness to sacrifice, love for our families, respect for others.

And he knows also those other qualities, of selfishness and greed and ambition, and things that set men one against the other, and nations one against the other. He recognizes the right of a group, whether it be community, or whether it be nation, to protect itself, to make certain of its own security. But certainly he must applaud every effort we make to understand others, whether it be individuals, or cities, or States or nations, to understand others as we understand ourselves, and in this way bring somewhat closer, each by his own efforts, that great dream of mankind: a peaceful world in which each of us may continue to develop.

Whether we do it through church, or through our schools, through any kind of community enterprise, through the family, through our own reading, we do not seek knowledge for itself. We do not seek acquaintanceship with the classics merely that we may quote a line from it.

We seek the knowledge and the thinking of the past that we may bring it together—here today—and help forward, each in his own little fashion, that great progress that I am certain the Old Man of the Mountain yet hopes that mankind will achieve: that objective of peace on earth, goodwill to men.

I would not for a moment leave this stand with the thought that we may have these things merely by thinking, or hoping, or wishing. But behind every effort there must be an aspiration, there must be a devotion to a cause.

If we are sufficiently devoted to the cause of peace, to the kind of progress of which I speak, we will be strong, and then we will be able to cooperate with others, because only strength can cooperate—weakness cannot cooperate, it can only beg; we will be able to cooperate and to help lead the world toward that promised goal.

So I would say our best birthday present to the Old Man of the Mountain is that we make up our minds, each in his own fashion, to do his part in bringing about that hope for mankind that the Old Man must have.

Thank you a lot. It has been a great pleasure to meet you all. Goodbye.

NOTE: The President spoke at 11:30 a.m.

137 ¶ Remarks at Lancaster, New Hampshire. *June 25, 1955*

Ladies and gentlemen:

Thank you all for this lovely present.

When I heard the list of dignitaries that your chairman just listed, it reminded me of the war—a great group of soldiers standing out here would have thought there was an awful lot of brass coming around the corner. This is sort of the political brass.

We are having a good time in New Hampshire for the past day and a half. We started way down south and have been all around—played golf—got rained out—doing all right up until this moment—everything has been lovely. Spent the night with Secretary Weeks and will be in New Hampshire up until noon today when we leave at Berlin.

As I was coming in, someone told me that there was only one speech you could make in this town, which was quite long ago, that the good Lord could have made a better place than Lancaster, but he didn't. Which does seem sort of a nice way of saying this place is beautiful.

I am grateful to the band for playing Hail to the Chief as I came up here. I am astonished at the crowd out here this morning, but I would be a liar if I didn't say I was highly pleased that you did turn out.

It is good to see you all. Maybe I can come back again.

Thank you a lot.

NOTE: The President spoke at 9:10 a.m. The chairman of the welcoming committee, Wilbur M. Schurman, presented a leather wallet to the President.

138 ¶ Remarks at Jefferson, New Hampshire.
June 25, 1955

NOT LONG AGO General Summerfield learned that I was leaving Washington and was going to come to New England, and he told me about this gathering of Postmasters, and among other things asked me to bring his greetings to you and sort of served notice that if I didn't stop here and visit with you a minute, I had better not come back.

Entirely aside, my friends here, from my pleasure in meeting with each of you this morning, I am looking out a little bit for my own skin and standing all right with my Postmaster when I get back there.

I think this gives me just an appropriate chance to say something about the appreciation I have of the services of the good public servant, the individual who takes a job in the government and does it with his full heart and soul so that the kind of service that we are supposed to render our people is actually received by them.

General Summerfield tells me that the Postmasters of the United States, all through the United States, are doing just that kind of job. He is very proud of them, and nothing could give me greater pleasure than to come here and—through you to the rest of them—say thanks a lot, because that is the kind of thing that the Federal government ought to be giving to our people everywhere.

I see up at the end there are some Boy Scouts that I hope to get a chance to stop and say Hello, because of my admiration and affection; and at the other end I see a choir, so I think I am promised a song; and just behind me are practically all the political brass of New Hampshire and part of Washington. So that just sort of brings the whole crowd together, and if I can hear the song and see the boys, the last word I will say is: a very hearty good morning, it is very wonderful to be with you.

NOTE: The President spoke at the Hotel Waumbak at 9:25 a.m. to a meeting of the New Hampshire Chapter of the National Association of Postmasters.

139 ¶ Remarks at the Hansen Ski Jump Area, Berlin, New Hampshire. *June 25, 1955*

Chairman Halvorson, distinguished guests, ladies and gentlemen:

I am sure you realize that a loudspeaker system and a position on this platform to speak into the microphone is a poor substitute for what I should really like to do: to go through this throng and to meet each of you, to tell you something of how I feel about this visit to New Hampshire.

I have been traveling through this lovely State for two days. Everywhere I have encountered an obvious hospitality and a cordial welcome that have touched my heart.

I have seen your beautiful skies, your lofty mountains, your great dairy herds, and many of your other industries. It has been, for me, a tour of real education.

I have been accompanied by your State officials, and everywhere local committees have participated in ceremonies and arrangements that have made my trip all the more enjoyable.

Particularly am I indebted to Governor Dwinell and his family, to Senator Bridges, to Senator Cotton, to Congressman Merrow and Congressman Bass and their lovely wives. All of them have been giving of their time to make my visit the more instructive, the more interesting and the more enjoyable.

In fact, they are busy men, you know, and I am quite sure that they are rather glad that this meeting marks the sort of official termination of my visit in New Hampshire; because out of their sense of friendship and loyalty they are staying with me, and possibly they realize their desks are piling high with work back in Washington and back in Concord.

This particular visit this morning has been sort of a climax for all of us.   I have accumulated so many gifts that I am moved to remind the chairman there is a very important one he forgot. He should have provided a truck to carry them away.   But there seem to be enough cars in this cavalcade that I think we can tuck them in here and there and nothing will be left behind, I assure you.

Now, my friends, I just want to say this: never have I had a more pleasant time than I have had on these two days.   It has been a unique experience to come up in these northern sections of your State, to see you people, to learn something of the country-side, and to have the chance to greet some of you face to face.

And I would like, as I leave this State, to transmit a message through you to every citizen that I can reach who has greeted me along the roadside, who has been in one of the crowds that has extended to me such a cordial welcome: I am grateful—deeply grateful.

And I tell you this: I am going to accept that invitation to come back, just as soon as possible—which means certainly as soon as I have another kind of livelihood than I now enjoy.

And I want to warn the Democratic Mayor of Berlin that the next time I come I am not going to be kept out of the city.   I am going right down the middle of it; and the only way he can stop it will be to turn out the police force, because at that time I will not be accompanied by so many police of my own.

Thank you, ladies and gentlemen—each of you—for coming out this morning, to give me a chance to say to you "thank you," and to greet you in this fashion.   It has been a wonderful morning for me.

Thank you again.

NOTE: The President spoke at 10:50 a.m. His opening words "Chairman Halvorson" referred to Alf Halvorson, Executive Secretary of the Chamber of Commerce of Berlin, N.H.   Later in his remarks he referred to Mayor Aime A. Tondreau of Berlin.

140 ¶ Letter to Helen Keller on the Occasion of Her 75th Birthday.   *June 26, 1955*

[Released June 26, 1955. Dated June 17, 1955]

Dear Miss Keller:

Please accept my warm congratulations on your forthcoming seventy-fifth birthday. The story of your accomplishments is not only a monument to your own great gifts of mind and heart. It is also an enduring inspiration—in many lands—to those who suffer physical handicaps and to those who seek to help the disabled toward richer lives. With all who honor you, I am glad to join in best wishes and in the hope that future years will bring you happiness.

Sincerely,

DWIGHT D. EISENHOWER

Miss Helen Keller
American Foundation for the Blind, Inc.
New York, N.Y.

NOTE: This letter was released at Parmachenee Lake, Maine.

141 ¶ Remarks at the Fawn Presentation Ceremonies, Rangeley, Maine.   *June 27, 1955*

WELL, Candy, I thank you very much, and I am sure that the children of Washington will enjoy the deer.

Now I hope the deer likes its new home, too. But it may be like a lot of other folks that go to Washington, they find out they have left a lot behind.

I am sure if I were going away from these woods, along these lovely lakes and rivers, and had to go live in Washington, I would think twice, wouldn't you?

But I will take it down.

Good luck to you, and thank you very much.

NOTE: The President spoke at 2:05 p.m. Candy Tibbetts, the 12-year-old daughter of Mr. and Mrs. Verde Tibbetts of Rangeley, Maine, presented the month-old fawn as a gift from the children of that area to the children of Washington, D.C. It was placed in the National Zoological Park in Washington.

142 ¶ Remarks at the Skowhegan Fairgrounds, Skowhegan, Maine. *June 27, 1955*

Governor Muskie, Senator Smith, Senator Payne, members of Maine's Congressional delegation here present—and my fellow Americans:

No man can receive greater acclaim than to be received in friendly fashion by a gathering of real Americans. So, from the bottom of my heart, I thank you—the Governor for his official welcome, Senator Smith for all that she has so extravagantly said about my accomplishments, and each of you for the courtesy you have paid me by coming out here today that I might say hello.

There are no thanks due me for coming to this section of the United States, for long have I felt that my education was sadly lacking, in that I did not have an intimate acquaintanceship with this region. I have satisfied a long-felt desire to come here. And incidentally, I should like to point out one thing: the Office that I hold being what it is, I did not come alone. Now there must be millions of Americans as ignorant as I was of the beauties of this region. And think of all the newspaper people, photographers, and others that now should be educating those people and possibly they will come and get the same firsthand knowledge that I had.

Now, if this does not happen, either the power of the press is not what we thought it was, or these newspaper people that travel with me haven't the proper sensibilities to appreciate beauty when they see it.

I am grateful for the warmth of the welcome I have received

all along the line, from young and old, from men and women, from workers and people who seem to be on vacation. And I might say, the most touching welcome that I received was from what the guides call "midges" and I call plain black flies. I am certain that during all these years when I did not come, they have been waiting on me, because they swarmed around me with their cannibalistic tendencies, and I am sure they will probably starve until I get back here.

My friends, as much as I have found here different, in the way of your scenery and your glorious lakes and streams and woodlands and piles of timber along the road, such as I have never seen, I find the basic fact is this: Americans are Americans everywhere. In our basic beliefs, in our basic aspirations, in our hopes for the future and for our children, we are one.

We want peace in the world. We want prosperity at home, a prosperity that is widely shared, with everybody happy in his job. We have come to realize these two aspirations are related. We cannot have prosperity without peace. And there can be no peace unless we are prosperous.

We are the world's leader—economically, productively; and because we are this, we must also take the lead in many other ways, morally and politically, in leading the free world to bind itself together in a common appreciation of these basic values: the dignity of man, his right to be free, his right to exercise all of his privileges of worship and of thought and of speech, of action and of earning. In fact, to exercise every personal privilege as long as he does not violate similar rights of others.

Now, if we are going to be bound together in these things, we must realize that we can't do that, we can't attain them all, without sacrifice. As your forefathers came into this region and built their homes, their cabins, and began to conquer the wilderness, they had to sacrifice something, they had to sacrifice the safety of the lands from which they came, they had to part from loved ones, they had to make sacrifices to give to us what we have today.

If the world is going to be bound together in a system of mutual advancement—international trade—international security—with all of us sharing in that security and in that trade, here and there we must make sacrifices.

Let us make them courageously, as our forefathers did, so that we may enjoy real and secure and permanent peace, and not merely an uneasy cessation of the firing of the guns.

We want permanent peace based upon confidence, based upon justice and decency, wherever the American government is represented. That is what we are struggling for—in every chancellery in every capital of the world, those who are our friends and those who may be hostile to us.

We are coveting nobody's property. We want to assume power and rule over no one else. We want to live a life that gives to each of us the utmost opportunity for spiritual, intellectual and material and economic development, for ourselves and for our children.

I find in my few days that I have been privileged to travel across this northern tier of the New England States, those sentiments are as widely shared and deeply felt as they are anywhere in the United States.

Indeed, may I say to you that because of this, though I come among you as a stranger, I have felt no more at home in any other town or city that I have visited in this country.

And so my real word of thanks is this: that you have let me feel that you do stand with one another shoulder to shoulder, and shoulder to shoulder with all of the other localities and States and regions of the United States—that all of us, together, may march along to that fuller life, strong, secure, but tolerant and ready to help the other fellow, as we expect him to do his part in this great venture.

Now before I leave I would like to say thanks in a little bit more intimate way. Everywhere across this State today I have encountered smiles and shouts and "Hi Ikes" and waves of the hand—as I have met them here on this fairground.

I can't reach each of you personally with a shake of the hand. I cannot even speak to all of the citizens I saw today. But if to you, and through you, I could let each of you know how sincerely I do appreciate the warmth of your friendliness, how earnestly I want to come back—as your Governor said, no matter what my job may be—then indeed I shall be content.

And now one final word.   In every audience such as this, there are literally hundreds of people who have served in the Armed Services during the period I was there—men and women. Some of them have served actively in the same theater, on the same battleground as I have.

To them I just want to say this one thing: during all those years that you were abroad, while your loved ones were suffering their fears for you, and you were encountering the dangers that finally won the war, we were upheld by a belief that we were fighting for freedom, for the rights of men as individuals, and for peace.

I believe that those aspirations—slowly and tortuously it is true, but still steadily—are marching on toward achievement; and I believe that is the thought that all of us can take with us to our beds each night and thank our God that it is true.

Goodnight—goodbye—and thanks.

NOTE: The President spoke at 4:35 p.m.

143   ¶ Remarks at the Dow Air Force Base, Bangor, Maine.   *June* 27, 1955

Governor Muskie, members of the Maine delegation in Congress, the Secretary of State, Mr. Dulles, other distinguished visitors— and my fellow Americans:

I have been on a fine two-day visit in your State, and I am delighted that someone arranged so that as my last act in this State on this trip I could say goodbye and thank you to so many of you.

I have made a lot of new friends and had a lot of fun.   I have met people old and young, men and women, all of them warmly hospitable to me.   I have met a lot of your trout and one or two of your salmon. I have met midges that are the only things, so far as I know, that completely whipped me. Of course, I just call them black flies, but the guides call them "midges."

I have learned a lot. I have learned a lot about the beauty of your State, about your warmheartedness. I wish that I could have stopped and spoken to every single individual that did me the great honor of coming out on the street and waiting for my cavalcade to pass, or who has—like you here—come out to a locality, to a grandstand or a fairground or to an airfield, and allowed me to say "It's so good to see you—another American."

It has been a bit of a vacation. Now I go back to work. The Secretary of State—to insure that my vacation is at an end as I get into the air—is going to give me a lecture on the way down to Washington.

I think I had better be about it, without more ado. Let me again say to each of you that all of this work is for one thing: peace on this earth, for which we all aspire.

Goodbye—good luck—it has been an inspiration to be among you. I hope that some day I can come back when, as a speaker said today, when I have another job and am not in such a hurry.

Thank you. Goodnight.

NOTE: The President spoke at 8:33 p.m.

144 ¶ Remarks on Presentation of the Distinguished Service Medal to General Ridgway, and Accompanying Citation. *June* 28, 1955

MATT, for some forty-three years, I guess, you and I have been associates and friends in war and peace. At every stage of your career and our association together, that kind of close communion with you has been a source of real satisfaction to me.

I remember the days of war where you performed so gallantly

and effectively. And I remember the days of peace and the great contributions you have made.

Now, as the last act of our official association together, it is a great honor to pin this on you. But I hope it means no lessening either of our friendship or of my ability to call on you when I want to talk to you about things.

CITATION TO ACCOMPANY THE AWARD OF
THE DISTINGUISHED SERVICE MEDAL
(THIRD OAK LEAF CLUSTER)
TO
GENERAL MATTHEW B. RIDGWAY

The President of the United States of America, authorized by Act of Congress July 9, 1918, has awarded the Distinguished Service Medal (Third Oak Leaf Cluster) to

GENERAL MATTHEW B. RIDGWAY, UNITED STATES ARMY

for exceptionally meritorious service in positions of great responsibility from 30 May 1952, to 30 June 1955:

As Supreme Allied Commander, Europe, General Ridgway was charged with the responsibility of welding an effective military structure for the defense of Western Europe. Through dynamic leadership, he furthered the development of the elements of the North Atlantic Treaty Organization into an alert, efficient, fighting team. He advanced the prestige of the Allied Forces and strengthened the bonds of friendship and cooperation among the many nations serving together in the common defense of democratic principles. In discharging this grave responsibility, he displayed indomitable spirit, inspirational application of military skills, and a sincere concern for the furtherance of the causes of freedom. As Chief of Staff of the United States Army he continually demonstrated the highest order of leadership, professional competence, astute judgment, and devotion to duty. Under his brilliant direction, the Army was maintained in a state of combat readiness, and fulfilled its world-wide commitments in a manner which contributed significantly to the advancement of the foreign policies of the United States. Ever mindful of the well-being and dignity of the individual soldier, he constantly worked to improve the welfare of the men entrusted to his care. His keen professional ability and great strength of character, displayed in his every action, have been an inspiration to the entire Army. His selfless dedication to the service of his country represents the highest form of patriotism, and merits the gratitude of not only the American people but of free peoples everywhere.

DWIGHT D. EISENHOWER

NOTE: The President made the presentation in the Rose Garden at 11:00 a.m. General Ridgway's response follows:

Mr. President, for you to take time from your multiple heavy duties to make this award in the presence of my superiors, and Mrs. Ridgway and Matty, touches me very deeply.

I look back over those years, sir, with profound affection and respect of the highest order.

It seems to me, Mr. President, that in this particular time that all of history points to the harsh fact that until we are much nearer this goal of a peaceful world to which you inspiringly lead, that we must maintain this Army in which you have such an abiding faith as a strong element in the defense of this Nation.

As I turn over my duties to the splendid officer who succeeds me, I have absolute confidence, Mr. President, that if ever our security or our liberty are threatened, that this magnificent Army of ours will valiantly play its ultimately decisive role in those defenses.

I thank you from the bottom of my heart, sir.

145 ¶ Message to the Congress Transmitting Final Report of the Commission on Intergovernmental Relations. *June 28, 1955*

To the Congress of the United States:

Pursuant to the provisions of Public Law 109, 83rd Congress, as amended, I hereby transmit to the Congress of the United

States the final report of the Commission on Intergovernmental Relations.

One hundred sixty-eight years ago the Founding Fathers designed our federal form of government in response to the baffling and eminently practical problem of creating unity among the thirteen States where union seemed impossible. The framers of our Constitution reached a solution now recognized as one of the most significant advances in the history of representative government.

Since their day, our federal structure has been adapted successfully to such phenomenal changes as a forty-fold increase in our population, the industrialization of our economy, and the rapid urbanization of our society. No other federal system, since established, has so effectively blended the capacity for energetic and responsible national action and the spirit of local initiative and autonomy.

In our time, however, a decade of economic crisis followed by a decade of war and international crises vastly altered federal relationships. Consequently, it is highly desirable to examine in comprehensive fashion the present-day requirements of a workable federalism.

The interests and activities of the different levels of government now impinge on each other at innumerable points, even where they may appear to be quite separable. The National Government's defense policies and programs, for example, have important repercussions on virtually every phase of State and local activity. Conversely, the effectiveness of our national defense policies depends on a myriad of State and local activities affecting the health, safety, and social and economic welfare of our people.

Because of this increasingly intricate interrelationship of national, state, and local governments, it is important that we review the existing allocation of responsibilities, with a view to making the most effective utilization of our total governmental resources.

To this undertaking the Commission on Intergovernmental Relations has made a notable contribution. Its report includes numerous specific recommendations. Insofar as these would entail action by the Executive Branch, I shall see that they are given the most careful consideration. I commend to the attention of the Congress, as well as of State and local executives and legislatures, the recommendations pertaining to them.

The Commission on Intergovernmental Relations is the first official body appointed to study and report on the general relationship of the National Government to the States and their local units. Consequently, the Commission wisely devoted much of its time to an examination of the general nature of our federal system, and of the means whereby it can be made to work more effectively. I am confident that its report will result in increased and sustained interest in this vitally important problem of government.

DWIGHT D. EISENHOWER

NOTE: The final report of the Commission is published in House Document 198 (84th Cong., 1st sess.).

146　¶ The President's News Conference of *June* 29, 1955.

THE PRESIDENT. Ladies and gentlemen, I have only one announcement this morning. The Premier of Burma, U Nu, is visiting us in the United States, and I shall have him for lunch, following an official visit in my office.

I merely want to express great gratification that he came over. The returning travelers and observers in that area have spoken of him in the most glowing terms as to ability and his leadership qualities. So I am very anxious to meet him, and we expect to have a very pleasant time this noon.

Q. Merriman Smith, United Press: Mr. President, could you

tell us something of the physical arrangements for the Big Four meeting? some of the people who are going with you and, if possible, when you will leave here?

THE PRESIDENT. Well, I should say I shall leave either Friday evening or possibly about Saturday noon. I do want to be in Geneva on Sunday morning at a reasonable hour, and I may, just for convenience, start on Friday night rather than Saturday noon.

Now, it's been agreed that there will be a limited number of people at the conference; and except for myself and two or three, what you might call, stenographic and secretarial help from my own office, the delegation will be largely the State Department—the Secretary of State and his principal assistants.[1]

I think that is about all I know about it at the moment.

Q. Pat Munroe, Salt Lake City Deseret News: Mr. President, we had a recent editorial which suggested that, perhaps, this Geneva Conference was a meeting at the semi-summit; and I wondered if you feel that Premier Bulganin, as head of the Soviet delegation, will be able to speak for the collective heads of the Soviet Union or if you hope that Mr. Khrushchev, Marshal Zhukov and, perhaps, some others will come along with the delegation, sir?

THE PRESIDENT. Well, of course, you raise one of the, you might say, questions that constitutes an existing puzzle. No one really knows who carries the dominating influence in that group. But let's remember this: there are different forms of government everywhere. Ours is one of those in which the head of the state is also head of a political party and head of a government. Now,

---

[1] On July 1 the United States delegation to the Geneva Conference was announced by the White House as follows: the President; the Secretary of State; Dillon Anderson, Special Assistant to the President; Charles E. Bohlen, U.S. Ambassador to the Soviet Union; Robert R. Bowie, Director, Policy Planning Staff, Department of State; James C. Hagerty, Press Secretary to the President; Douglas MacArthur II, Counselor of the Department of State; Livingston T. Merchant, Assistant Secretary of State for European Affairs; Herman Phleger, The Legal Adviser, Department of State; and Llewellyn E. Thompson, U.S. Ambassador to Austria.

in Britain, for example, you have a parliamentary form of government, and the head of the government is not the head of the state whatsoever. So in no case can you have, as I see it, exact counterparts from each state to be represented in a conference such as this kind, because governmental forms differ. So you would have to hope merely that the people who do have some powers of decision in their own governments will be the ones that are there.

Maybe the speculation of your editorial is just as good as anybody else's on this point.

Q. Robert E. Clark, International News Service: Mr. President, you dropped several teasers in New England this last week which sounded both as if you might and might not be a candidate in 1956. Since you appear to have relaxed your own moratorium on the subject, I wonder if you can shed any fresh light on it for us.

THE PRESIDENT. Well, I think you are making an assumption not necessarily true. A man going off where he is trying to have a good time—if people kid him a little bit, he has got to answer in kind. [*Laughter*]

Q. Charles L. Bartlett, Chattanooga Times: Mr. President, one of the justifications for the Dixon-Yates contract was that the Memphis area needed the power, needed the 600,000 kilowatts. Last week, as you probably know, the Memphis City Council voted to build a steam plant of their own of about 600,000 kilowatts. I wonder if, in your opinion, the Government should now proceed with the Dixon-Yates contract or cancel it at the cheapest possible terms.

THE PRESIDENT. I haven't had this matter brought up to my attention by any of my responsible associates since I saw that suggestion in the paper. But I do know this: that when I was first visited by a delegation from Tennessee and I suggested that the city of Memphis go ahead and build their own plant, they said it was an impossibility under the whole TVA system and the

TVA contract; it was an impossibility.[1] That's all I know about it.

Q. Edward T. Folliard, Washington Post and Times Herald: Mr. President, this is related to——

THE PRESIDENT. Could you speak a little louder, Mr. Folliard?

Q. Mr. Folliard: Yes.

This is related to Mr. Clark's question.

I wondered if Sherman Adams was going to be able to finish those ecstatic lectures on New Hampshire for the White House staff?

THE PRESIDENT. Well, he seems to be generating a very great capacity for doing it in a hurry. [*Laughter*]

Q. Ray L. Scherer, NBC News: Along the same line, you said several times during the tour that the purpose of the trip was a matter of self-education.

THE PRESIDENT. Yes.

Q. Mr. Scherer: It was sort of a matter of education for newsmen, too, and some of us got educated into the notion that the people up there would like to see you stand for re-election.

I was wondering what general impressions you brought back from your tour.

THE PRESIDENT. Of course, you possibly saw my friends along the roads, and we don't know who was behind in the alleys. [*Laughter*]

Q. Charles E. Shutt, Telenews: Mr. President, I wonder if you could tell us at this time how optimistic you are toward any positive results coming from the Geneva Conference, sir?

THE PRESIDENT. Well, I have tried to explain that. I think that the world, including ourselves, deserves a renewed opportu-

---

[1] On June 30, at the direction of the President, the White House made public a letter of the same date from the Chairman of the Tennessee Valley Authority to the Director of the Bureau of the Budget, regarding the decision of the city of Memphis to construct its own power plant. Also released was a formal resolution adopted by the TVA Board on June 30 regarding this matter. The White House statement noted that the President had requested the Director of the Bureau of the Budget to confer promptly with the Atomic Energy Commission and the Tennessee Valley Authority to determine whether it was in the interest of the people of the area to continue or to cancel the Dixon-Yates contract.

nity now through such a meeting to attempt to discover what are the general intentions of all of us. We, trying to explain ours eloquently and intimately as we can to those who oppose us, trying to get the same impression of their intentions and purposes, through this method we may find ways of putting problems in new channels or in places and under particular studies where some real progress toward an easing of tensions, and so on, may be made.

Q. Charles von Fremd, CBS News: Mr. President, the mutual security program of the administration is running into some difficulty in the House where critics apparently believe that now that Russia is on the run, so to speak, on the defensive, that we can cut back somewhat on our foreign aid spending.

Do you have any comment?

THE PRESIDENT. Well, of course, we have cut way back from the level that we once maintained.

The finest statement on this whole proposition that has been made, almost, was in the report of the House Committee, the House Committee on Foreign Affairs. On about page 3 or 4, as I remember, you will find a couple of paragraphs that tell about the things that have been accomplished through this program.

They even went on to say that at last, finally, they have come to the place where they no longer have to ask for an explanation of what is being accomplished or what is desired, that the results are proving themselves. And then they go ahead to name, I think a half a dozen countries where great benefits to the United States have sprung from this program. And they reached the conclusion that with things going so well, with even an apparent change in the general Soviet attitude toward the world and toward us, this is no time to abandon the theory of a strong America binding to herself strong allies and helping them to be strong both internally and externally, that we should not now abandon that policy.

It is a very splendid statement, and I would commend it to all of you for reading.

Q. William Theis, International News Service: Mr. President, there have been indications on the Hill that there would be introduced before this session ended some resolution expressing this Government's endorsement and hope in the future of the satellite peoples. Will you encourage or support such a move at this time?

THE PRESIDENT. Well, I don't know in what words such a resolution would be couched. In fact, I haven't heard of any such purpose.

I have constantly, over the past years, stated my general attitude toward this proposition, that until such states as these have a right themselves, by their own free will, to determine their own forms of government and destiny, that there could be no real peace in the world. I am sure that is true.

Q. Robert G. Spivack, New York Post: Mr. President, do you believe that if this were a Republican-controlled Congress, that the desegregation amendment to the Reserve manpower bill would be passed?

THE PRESIDENT. Well, I wouldn't even speculate on that. I don't know anything about it.

All I have ever said on that is that I would like to see one bill, which is so terrifically important to the United States, be handled specifically on its own merits and without the introduction of any other kind of matter, no matter how desirable any such legislation might be in anything.

Q. Chalmers M. Roberts, Washington Post and Times Herald: Mr. President, at the UN meeting at San Francisco last week after you spoke, most of the other speakers stressed their feeling for the need of some sort of worldwide agreement on disarmament, especially in the nuclear field.

You have had Harold Stassen working on this problem for some time, and I wondered if you expect that he will have for you before Geneva, or by the time you go, any formalized program that you can present there or discuss there or make public at that time?

THE PRESIDENT. Well, I would say not a formalized program, Mr. Roberts.

What I do believe is that through his efforts our Government and all its parts, I mean legislative leaders and the executive departments, can come together on a general type of approach to this problem, that we can then inform the American people of the general approach, and then try to make progress under that plan.

In each case it would have to be a specific, probably, conference to take each item; I mean a specific step—might be the same conference—but it is going to be a very long and tortuous road to follow.

Q. Mr. Roberts: Do you expect, sir, to make public what proposals he comes up with before you begin to negotiate them at the conference?

THE PRESIDENT. I don't expect to make public anything before we have got our own minds crystallized and know that we have searched out all of the pitfalls in such discussions and such programs, and are ready to stand back of something. To do otherwise merely raises a speculation and doubt. Again, I don't know of any two people in the world that agree on this subject in its details. I have personally been studying it for, I know, 40 years, so I think we have got a pretty tough one. And the reason I have put one man and given him the sole responsibility to find the areas of agreement—out of that will come a basic principle, a basic method, that we will follow, and it will constitute the real foundation of the whole structure that we will try to build.

Q. Mrs. May Craig, Maine Papers: Mr. President, in relation to Mr. Theis' question, the House passed last week 367 to nothing a resolution of Democratic Mr. McCormack of Massachusetts, expressing sympathy with the satellites, condemning colonialism of all kinds, and asking that the United Nations and any organization in which we participated do what they could to release them.

Did you favor that resolution? Did you know about that?

THE PRESIDENT. As a matter of fact, I didn't know about that. Maybe I was fishing that day, I don't know.

Q. Mrs. Craig: 367 to nothing.

THE PRESIDENT. Well, I still say that there are all kinds of nuances in any such statement, possible complications, that make you very careful in uttering an official statement.

For example, if you believe that, how far are you going? You are certainly not going to declare war, are you? So there instantly you fix for yourself limitations on how far we, as a people, will go in accomplishing this thing. That means, therefore, that we use peaceful means and means that are not provocative. We use moral suasion, we use refusal to be drawn into any seeming approval of such a situation; but we do place limits on ourselves instantly when we think about the thing. And so that means that there is a problem. It is not just as simple as just saying something and forgetting it.

Q. William H. Lawrence, New York Times: Is there an agreed termination date on this Big Four meeting? I rather gathered from the San Francisco dispatches that Mr. Molotov and Mr. Dulles did not agree on that point.

THE PRESIDENT. I don't know whether there has been a complete agreement. What there is, as an examination of my own duties will, I think, show to anyone, any reasonable person, is that there is some limitation on the time I may spend as far away as Geneva at a time when Congress is in session and approaching the end of the session.

So we have simply stated that such-and-such a time is as long as I personally can stay in Geneva.

Q. Mr. Lawrence: And you feel, sir, that having stated that in advance, you do not run the propaganda risk of which you spoke earlier?

THE PRESIDENT. I think I don't run any risk with reasonable-minded people; I am sure of that.

Q. Sarah McClendon, El Paso Times: Sir, I believe I am right in this, that you have always taken a stand consistently against price controls, and that was in your '52 campaign and what you have done since.

Now, I wonder if you feel there should be any exception in the price of gas at the wellhead?

THE PRESIDENT. Of course, you bring up a question that has been one of the most argumentative in all this field of Federal control over the natural resources of America.

There is a bill in Congress now, progress is certainly being made, and here is the problem: how do you defend adequately and properly a consuming public, and how do you encourage at the same time the utmost in exploration and exploitation of the natural resources, in this case gas?

One way you could kill off all exploration and raise the price of gas unconscionably would be just to stop exploring for it. So just a simple answer of saying, "We are going to control gas at 8 cents a thousand," or something like that just won't do it. So this is a complicated problem, and my feeling is this: Congress is actually making progress because they are trying to devise a bill which, at one and the same time, protects the consumer but which, at the same time, will encourage exploration.

All the details of this bill I am not completely certain about because, after all, I have not had time to study it. But it seems to me that progress is being made in this complex problem.

Q. Hazel Markel, National Broadcasting Company: Mr. President, I would like to ask you, in returning to the U.N. Conference, that either by your own presence there or by the subsequent report of your Secretary of State, if you feel more or less happy and confident about the summit meetings.

THE PRESIDENT. About the——

Q. Miss Markel: About the summit meeting at Geneva.

THE PRESIDENT. Oh. You mean what I have picked up——

Q. Miss Markel: Yes. Are you confident that it is going to be successful?

THE PRESIDENT. I think this—I am trying not to expect too much, Miss Markel, but I do say this: there is obviously some change that has come about in the Soviet attitude. If that change is one that makes it easier to live with them, easier to negotiate with them, easier to solve problems that arise from day to day, then that cannot help having eventually a fine effect on the entire situation, the general situation.

Now, no one believes that the great Marxian doctrine of world revolution has been abandoned by its advocates. No one believes that, and we have got, therefore, to be careful. But if we can find ways that will take some of the burdens of fear and tension off of people, we ought to explore them to the maximum.

I personally believe, from what I learned in San Francisco and through my talks, that the chances for that were better than I thought they were 2 months ago.

Q. Miss Markel: Thank you, sir.

Q. Frank van der Linden, Nashville Banner: Senator Kefauver charged on the Senate floor yesterday that the Budget Bureau was trying to conceal what he called a scandal in the Dixon-Yates contract negotiations regarding the employment of Mr. Adolphe Wenzell of the First Boston Corporation.

Senator Knowland says there is no corruption in it, and that he thinks you were just trying to help the Tennessee Valley get some power.

I wondered if Mr. Hughes of the Budget Bureau had cleared with you his refusal to give Mr. Kefauver the information he was asking down there?

THE PRESIDENT. Mr. Hughes came to see me, went over the situation, and I repeated to him the general instructions, I think, that I expressed once publicly in front of this body: that every single pertinent paper on the Yates-Dixon contract from its inception until the final writing of the contract would be made available, I think I said at that time, to the press, to any committee.

Now, I do stand on this: nobody has a right to go in, wrecking the processes of government by taking every single file—some of you have seen our file rooms and know their size—wrecking the entire filing system and paralyzing the processes of government while they are going through them.

These files are filled with every kind of personal note; I guess my own files are filled with personal notes from my own staff all through, they are honeycombed with them. To drag those things out where a man says to me, "I think so-and-so is a bad person to appoint to so-and-so, and you shouldn't have him," all he had was his own opinion. You can't drag those things out and put them before the public with justice to anybody, and we are not going to do it. But at the time that I gave those instructions, Mr. Hughes, Mr. Strauss, whoever else was involved, got together every single document that was pertinent to this thing and put it out.

Now, as far as the Wenzell report, Mr. Wenzell was never called in or asked a single thing about the Yates-Dixon contract. He was brought in as a technical adviser in the very early days when none of us here knew about the bookkeeping methods of the TVA or anything else.

He was brought in as a technical adviser and nothing else, and before this contract was ever even proposed.

Q. Allan W. Cromley, Daily Oklahoman: Mr. President, you said progress——

THE PRESIDENT. I said what?

Q. Mr. Cromley: A while ago you said that progress was being made in regards to gas legislation.

THE PRESIDENT. Yes.

Q. Mr. Cromley: Recently, Mr. Rayburn, after the House approval of the bill, I mean the House committee approval, said, "I think it is going to take the endorsement and power of the administration to get this bill passed and, of course, that means the President of the United States."

I just wondered if that means you will endorse and support the bill, sir?

THE PRESIDENT. Well, I get many advisers, but it has not been brought up to me yet.

Q. Alan S. Emory, Watertown Times: Mr. President, on Friday the Senate passed a bill authorizing the Civil Aeronautics Administration to obligate 4 years in advance $63 million a year for Federal aid to airports.

The Commission on Intergovernmental Relations, which reported to you yesterday afternoon, advocated that the CAA authorize such aid at least 2 years in advance.

Does this proposal for advance obligation of aid to the airports run in the face of administration fiscal policy or does this meet with your approval, sir?

THE PRESIDENT. I haven't had any study; as a matter of fact, I haven't heard of this particular proposal you bring up. I can't answer it, sorry.

Q. James B. Reston, New York Times: As I understand it, sir, there are no decisions to be taken at the Geneva meeting, and the conversation is to be fairly general.

Now, I wondered, in the light of that, what your approach is to publicity at that meeting? Is it your view that the views of the various sides should be widely publicized or not?

THE PRESIDENT. Well, now, in the first place, I don't mean to say that necessarily there will be no decisions. I would not expect solutions to any problem that bothers the world to come up, but there could be decisions on how we would approach them. I would hope some of those would come about.

As to publicity, I must say that that is one element—it is always, of course, a necessary element of these things—that has not yet come up for study. But I personally would hope that more than just the stereotyped, what do they call them, final communiques which, I think, probably annoy writers as much as they do me— there would be something more than that come out.

Q. Martin S. Hayden, Detroit News: Mr. President, some of us over in this corner, sir, think that maybe you said something you didn't mean to. A minute ago you said no one doubts the axiom that the Marxian revolution has been abandoned by its advocates.

THE PRESIDENT. No, I didn't say that at all.

Q. Mr. Hayden: You mean nobody thinks it?

THE PRESIDENT. I said no one thinks for a minute that the Marxian doctrine has been abandoned by its advocates. I believe that—was that correct?

[*Chorus of "Yes, yes"*]

Q. Paul A. Shinkman, King Features Syndicate: Mr. President, it has been suggested that you might take the occasion of your visit to Geneva to make one or two other stops before returning home. Is that a possibility?

THE PRESIDENT. Well, there have been a number of invitations; but because of their very number it makes it, I think, almost an impossibility.

Whatever time I have got over there I think I should devote to business. As you know, Europe is covered with my good friends. Nothing would give me greater satisfaction than to go into two or three of these cities. But I don't think I can do it.

Q. Milton B. Freudenheim, Akron Beacon Journal: Mr. President, Democrats in the House have been proposing and pushing a plan to finance long-range highway building by drastic increases in taxes on tires and also gasoline. Have you any comment on that, sir?

THE PRESIDENT. Yes, to this extent: first of all, I think everybody agrees that America needs roads, needs them badly, and needs them now, and they ought to be built on a coordinated, comprehensive basis, and that building ought to start.

Now, the question of financing raises problems. Either you must find some way to finance these things out of current revenues as you go along, which means very greatly increased taxes, and in this case that would be on related products, gasoline, tires, and so on, or you must find some method of having a bond issue.

If you had the bond issue, then you have the problem: do you want to add it to the national debt or do you want to put it under a special organization in which liquidation is provided for, and which will get this whole sum of debt off our books as rapidly as possible.

The Governors of the United States, and the Clay committee which I had appointed, in cooperation developed a plan that made road building, plus a bond issue which would be liquidating, under a U.S. corporation.

Now, here is one of the reasons against just raising taxes and trying to do it in that way, getting in a lot of revenue and building that much each year: where are the States going to get the money to do their part of this thing?

It seems to me that we have got to recognize occasionally the very great responsibility, authority, and power that should reside in our States, allowing them to have decent sources of revenue. If we put the maximum amount that the traffic will bear on all of these things, I don't know where the States' revenue is going to come from.

So we devised a plan that we thought met the needs of the situation in the best possible fashion, and I am for it now just as strongly as I was when it was devised by the Governors and by the Clay committee and put before the public.

Q. Richard Harkness, National Broadcasting Company: Mr. President, the Senate has passed a resolution, the House is scheduled to follow suit, sir, creating a bipartisan commission of 12 members to study and report on the Government's loyalty-security program. Do you see any constructive accomplishment in the report of such a committee?

THE PRESIDENT. Well, you say constructive accomplishment. I wouldn't want to answer in those terms.

I say this: I have no objection. This administration has nothing to hide.

It is a difficult problem. I have always maintained that I am ready to cooperate in any legitimate properly organized investigation of the Congress. Anything they do in this line, we will cooperate and do the best we can to bring to light all of the pertinent facts.

Q. Clark R. Mollenhoff, Des Moines Register and Tribune: Mr. President, a little while ago you stated that Mr. Wenzell was never called in about the Yates-Dixon contract, and there seemed to be some testimony before the SEC and before a committee that he had served as a consultant. I wondered if you were——

THE PRESIDENT. He did serve as a consultant at one time.

Q. Mr. Mollenhoff: On the Dixon-Yates?

THE PRESIDENT. No, I think—now, I will check this up. My understanding is that quickly as the Dixon-Yates thing came up he resigned, and we got as our consultant a man named Adams from the Power Commission here itself to come over and be the consultant so as to have him, because he [Wenzell] was connected with a great Boston financial company.

Q. Mr. Mollenhoff: Mr. President, had you been informed that he had no connection at all with the Dixon-Yates?

THE PRESIDENT. My understanding of it—that part of it—there may have been an overlap of a week or two; there I am not sure.

Q. Mr. Mollenhoff: Would there be any change in your position on that if there was material that he had served as a consultant on that?

THE PRESIDENT. If he had served as a consultant on that and brought in a definite recommendation to us, I would be very delighted to make that public. But I just don't believe there is a thing in it about it. However, I will have it checked again. [*Addresses Mr. Hagerty*] Will you take that up? [1]

---

[1] A White House release, issued later in the day, stated that at no time did Adolphe Wenzell take part in any policy decisions either with regard to the inception of the proposals which led to the Dixon-Yates contract or the development of Government policy with regard to that contract.

In 1953, long before any proposal concerning the Dixon-Yates contract had been made, the release stated, Mr. Wenzell at the request of the Director of the Budget, prepared an analysis of the records and accounting systems of the Tennessee Valley Authority, particularly as to comparison of its annual report of earnings with those of similar private industry which have different requirements as to taxes, interest rates, and the like.

However, the release stated, one exception should be noted to keep the public record exactly straight. The one exception referred to was that from January 14 to April

Q. Gould Lincoln, Washington Star: Mr. President, Senator Lyndon Johnson of Texas yesterday made a statement praising what the Senate had done in a legislative way, and he also said that a certain party leader made a speech last fall saying that a cold war of partisan politics would follow the election of a Democratic Congress. He inferred that possibly that certain party later might have something to say about it. *[Laughter]*

THE PRESIDENT. Well, ladies and gentlemen, I said in the campaign—and I assume that his allusion to me is not so hazy that we can't take that as a—*[laughter]*—I said this: if you do this, how are you going to fix responsibility either for failure or success? So the very fact that he gets up and makes this statement would indicate to me that someone is confused as to where credit lies, or blame.

Now, you have just given me a big chance to read a little list of legislation I want, not been passed yet. *[Laughter]*

So if we are to get this fine cooperation now, let me read you something that I think the American people would be interested in; because I can conceive of nothing that is more important to them than to get this list:

    Highway construction

    Military reserves—for once in my life I even asked for an opportunity to go on the radio after the conclusion of that last exercise so I could tell the American people what I

3, 1954, Mr. Wenzell did serve as technical consultant to the Bureau of the Budget and in that capacity he did give advice to the Bureau of the Budget on such matters as the form of securities that might be marketable, the rate of interest that might be used, and the necessity for various protective clauses and relative costs that entered into preliminary, exploratory discussions that the Atomic Energy Commission and the Bureau of the Budget were conducting at that time.

The release added that prior to the time that the definite proposal of April 10, 1954, was made—which later developed into the Dixon-Yates contract—Francis L. Adams, Chief, Bureau of Power, Federal Power Commission, had been called in and was serving as Bureau of the Budget consultant; that Mr. Wenzell did not serve as consultant from April 10, 1954, and had no connection with any subsequent discussion; and that he was presently serving as Assistant to the Director of Technical Operations of the International Bank for Reconstruction and Development.

thought about this thing of reserves. This is vital to all of us. Why are we fooling around about it?

Military survivor benefits

Housing legislation

Health program

School construction

Mutual security authorization and appropriation—I believe that is up today, and if anything should go through in a hurry that should.

Refugee Act amendments—and you all know about the needs for them.

Water resources—the Upper Colorado and the Frying Pan and the Cougar Dam up in the Northwest, all trying to get started and all waiting because they are not done.

Customs simplification—something that is just vital to us; well maybe that is too strong a word, it is terribly important.

Minimum wage and other labor bills

The atomic ship

Hawaiian statehood

Now, I am just delighted, and I am glad to give credit for everything that has been done.

I will thank everybody, personally if I can get a hold of him, that has voted for the necessary legislation. Now I want some more.

Q. John E. Kenton, *New York Journal of Commerce:* On the question of the atomic ship, sir, you are surely aware of some criticism that has been raised in Congress by members of both parties——

THE PRESIDENT. Yes.

Q. Mr. Kenton: ——against your conception of the plan on the ground that it——

THE PRESIDENT. That is right.

Q. Mr. Kenton: ——it would not contribute much to real progress of the American merchant marine.

In the light of the Senate vote last night, not to proceed with your conception of the atomic ship but rather with the longer-range program, wouldn't you comment on that and tell us whether you still intend to continue to fight for your version?

THE PRESIDENT. I have no doubt there are among you here people who have been serving, or have had your duties, in South American countries, Asian countries, and different European countries recently.

You will find, as you were serving on those tours, that the mass of the world thinks of the atomic science as of great importance to two great power centers, Washington and the Kremlin; that it is a science that has specialized in the destruction of men, the destroying of civilization. They really shudder to think about it.

What I am trying to do as one of the peace moves in this world is to convince the world, not just Russia and ourselves, but to convince the world that here is a science that can mean practically the doubling, let us say, of living standards within a reasonable space of time. Here is a great science opening up opportunities in every way.

Now, one of the ways I would like to bring this about is to have a ship going into every important port of the world, inviting people aboard; they would come by the thousands. I remember the days when the *Empress of Britain* used to go around advertising British goods, and I was one of the crowd that went on to see what they had.

Think of the crowds that would come to see an atomic ship! And they would get the understanding that here, a ship powered by atomic energy, everything on it operating that way, with all the exhibits of what this can do in agriculture and medicine, all of the other sciences, to improve the lot of man. They would soon begin to develop and generate a moral force in this world: "Let's get this uranium turned into peaceful channels and not just in destroying men." I will tell you any way you can do it is cheap.

Now, these people may differ with me as to whether it is

beneficial or not. But some of them haven't differed, because one committee said "Build two ships, not one, build two."

Maybe there is a difference of opinion. But I will tell you if we are going to win this war for peace, let's stop talking about cold war. We are trying to wage a war for peace; if we are going to win it, we have got to inform the world. And one of the ways to inform the world is to let them see these things that can happen with this great science.

I am just sure we have got a hold of something here that can mean more to us in terms of untold billions, we will say, in terms of the lessening of tensions; and then we say, "Oh, this is a waste of money!"

If we are trying to use any money through interchange of students and the Information Services, all of which I stand for and believe in implicitly, to take this and send it around as a physical demonstration of what might happen—I think we are missing a great opportunity if we don't do it.

And thank you.

Q. Merriman Smith, United Press: One more.

THE PRESIDENT. I saw him on his toes.

Q. Robert E. Clark, International News Service: Mr. President, can you tell us how you feel about the Bering Sea plane incident, and whether you agree with the Secretary of State that it was probably due to a trigger-happy Soviet pilot rather than a policy?

THE PRESIDENT. Well, I am sure it was a local occurrence and not something that was directed as a matter of policy.

Now, weather conditions were not good. There was a cloud cover, and there were other things in it that made it look like it was at least local, and part of it misunderstanding.

It was, I think, very encouraging to note that in this incident, at least, there was a different attitude taken by the Soviets than they ever had in a similar one before.

Merriman Smith, United Press: Thank you, Mr. President.

THE PRESIDENT. OK.

NOTE: President Eisenhower's seventy-second news conference was held in the Executive Office Building from 10:31 to 11:06 o'clock on Wednesday morning, June 29, 1955. In attendance: 186.

147 ¶ Veto of Bill To Prohibit Publication by the Government of the United States of Predictions as to Apple Prices. *July 1, 1955*

To the United States House of Representatives:

I return herewith, without my approval, H. R. 5188, "To prohibit publication by the Government of the United States of any prediction with respect to apple prices." This bill would amend section 15(d) of the Agricultural Marketing Act (12 U.S.C. 1141 (j)(d)), as amended, by inserting after the word "cotton" the words "or apples". The effect of this would be to extend to apples the existing prohibitions with respect to the publication of price prospects that now apply only to cotton.

The provision of the Act to which apples would be added is very broad. It applies to any officer or employee of the United States, in either the legislative or executive branches of the Government, except to the Governor of the Farm Credit Administration. It should not be extended to other farm products. In particular, the addition of apples to this provision would further restrict the agricultural-outlook service of the Department of Agriculture since it would prohibit the publication and, on occasion, the formal discussion of future price prospects for apples by any employees of the Department, including cooperative employees of the Federal-State Extension Service.

I believe that it is a vital responsibility of the Federal Government to gather and disseminate accurate, timely, comprehensive, and useful economic information, so that producers and consumers, buyers and sellers may have available to them the maximum amount of economic knowledge. This is especially true of farmers, who generally are not in a position to acquire for them-

662

selves all the necessary facts concerning supply and demand conditions affecting their commodities. Because of the great instability of their prices and incomes, they stand in particular need of accurate, timely, and comprehensive economic information to assist them in the development of their plans for production and marketing. Denial to farmers of this type of information in the case of another major commodity would represent a backward step tending to undermine the foundations of the entire agricultural-outlook service.

It is difficult to see how the cutting off of analysis of price trends and dissemination of price prospects by the Department of Agriculture can in any way assist the farmer. Interpretations of the price situation will still be made by others. At times, these may come from sources whose interests run contrary to those of the apple producers. This legislation would reduce or seriously limit the ability of field workers to counteract price rumors detrimental to the farmers' interests.

For these reasons I have felt obliged to withhold my approval from this measure.

DWIGHT D. EISENHOWER

148   ¶ Joint Statement Following Discussions With Prime Minister U Nu of Burma.   *July* 3, 1955

THE PRIME MINISTER of Burma, His Excellency U Nu, has visited Washington for three days at the invitation of President Eisenhower. The President and the Prime Minister discussed many matters of common concern and exchanged views on current international problems.

The Prime Minister, the President and the Secretary of State reviewed problems of peace and security in Asia. They had a frank discussion of the complex economic problems arising from the existence of substantial surpluses of exportable rice both in

Burma—one of the world's leading rice exporting countries—and in the United States.

Note was taken of the salutary influence of religion as exemplified by the Sixth Buddhist Synod presently being held in Rangoon and attended by leading Buddhist scholars from many nations.

The problem of imprisoned American fliers in Communist China was reviewed.

These talks have been of special value in increasing mutual understanding between Burma and the United States. There is a wide area of agreement and a traditional friendship between Burma and the United States resting firmly upon certain noble concepts to which both countries subscribe. Our two peoples, those of the United States and the Union of Burma, share two fundamental goals, a peaceful world and a democratic way of life.

They reaffirmed their dedication to the ideal of peace and friendly cooperation amongst nations founded on international justice and morality. Both countries are deeply concerned with a subject that is predominant in the minds of all responsible world leaders today—the problem of achieving peace with justice, a peace based upon the liberty of human beings and the security of nations.

Such a peace can best be achieved by loyal steadfast support for the Charter of the United Nations. That is the surest and most practical avenue along which to seek peace with justice in this world. A patient striving to uphold the fundamental moral and religious beliefs underlying the Charter provides the best hope for the fulfillment of mankind's aspirations.

The Prime Minister, the President and the Secretary of State deplored the conditions which force the peoples of the world to divert their energies and talents from a single-minded effort to improve and expand those cultural and economic opportunities by which men can raise the levels of their existence. They renewed their own determination to uphold the principles of the

United Nations in its unceasing effort to save mankind from the scourge of future war.

149 ¶ The President's News Conference of *July* 6, 1955.

THE PRESIDENT. Good morning, ladies and gentlemen. I have no announcements; we will go right to questions.

Q. Merriman Smith, United Press: Mr. President, some of your friends in the Senate don't quite share your feelings about a moratorium on discussing your plans for 1956.

Senator Flanders, in a Fourth of July speech in Illinois, said that you cannot refuse to run in 1956.

My question is, can you? [*Laughter*]

THE PRESIDENT. Well, for myself I don't believe that I can recall that I ever said what anyone else could or could not do; and I think that is a decision I have to reach for myself some time.

Q. Edward H. Sims, Columbia State: I have two questions, sir. Forty-nine Senators in the Senate have introduced a resolution which would direct the Tariff Commission to investigate recent textile cuts made at Geneva; and I believe you have been asked by one of those Senators, Senator Thurmond, if you would join in that agreement.

I wonder if you would comment on that.

The textile industry claims these cuts allow foreign producers to sell some goods below costs that they could be made in this country.

THE PRESIDENT. No, that has not been brought to me yet.

[*Chorus of "Mr. President"*]

Just a minute. I believe the man announced he has two questions; I am sorry.

Q. Mr. Sims: The other question is—thank you, sir—in the Fourth Circuit Court of Appeals there is a vacancy, a judgeship vacancy, and I believe Judge Soper retired as of June 30.

By custom and tradition, these judgeships have been given to the States in that circuit, I believe, for some decades. This time it is South Carolina's turn if that custom is followed.

I wonder if you would say whether you intend to follow that custom.

THE PRESIDENT. That particular one hasn't been brought to me, but I will say this: in the past, we have tried in all the circuit court appointments to give the widespread representation that has been the custom in the past.

Now, whether or not the facts are as stated, whether they are governing in this case, I should say I am not sure, because it has not been discussed with me.

Q. Laurence H. Burd, Chicago Tribune: Mr. President, at the summit conference does this country plan to have a stenographic record kept of the talks of the chiefs of state? And, if so, would you expect that record to be made public at some time?

THE PRESIDENT. I can't answer it. I hadn't thought of it.

I would say that, for the most of these conferences, there would be stenographic reports on any official presentation by any individual. Now, if it did become just general roundtable discussion, there may not; but any formal presentation by any of the governments, I should think there would be a record kept. Now, I am guessing, and I would prefer you ask that of the Secretary of State.

Q. Charles E. Egan, New York Times: Mr. President, there is concern in some quarters that amendments and riders being added to bills up on Capitol Hill are undermining your foreign trade program as represented by the reciprocal trade. I wondered if you have any comments on that?

THE PRESIDENT. Well, any attempt, I think, to fix specific tariffs on specific items by legislation is bound to create a lot of confusion and create great difficulties both for the legislative and executive departments.

Now, as far as the general practice of putting riders or extraneous matter on substantive legislation, I think my views are well known.

I think every item that comes up for legislation should be handled on its own merits and not tied in with something that is irrelevant.

Q. Charles S. von Fremd, CBS News: Mr. President, many Democrats on Capitol Hill are now claiming that your decision to reopen or to restudy the Dixon-Yates matter is a political victory for their side, and claim that it represents a backing down on your part on this whole matter. Could you discuss that with us, sir?

THE PRESIDENT. I hadn't heard this particular point.

The first group that ever came to my office to urge upon me the building with Federal funds of a new steam plant in the TVA were very insistent that this be done. It was the only way they could get a plant; and they said, "The city of Memphis is going to be without power in that whole region."

I recommended to them that the city of Memphis build its plant just like New York City or Abilene, Kansas, would, if they had to have a plant. And they showed to me, or attempted to show to me, that this was impossible in their area because of the type of contract that TVA had made with all its customers. It is an exclusive sort of contract. If you take any power from TVA then you may not, under your contract, get any power anywhere else. That was the situation at that moment.

Actually, I am delighted that the city of Memphis or any other local community, when it comes to the simple building of a power station through steamplant methods, and with no flood control or navigation or other factors in it, do it themselves. I believe we should do it ourselves. So I am not really concerned as to who is claiming political victories. This is in accordance with the philosophy in which I believe.

Q. John Herling, Editors Syndicate: Mr. President, according to yesterday's report, the administration does not now include the minimum wage in its top measures for passage this year. Would you explain, sir, why this change in signals on the part of the administration?

THE PRESIDENT. No one has changed anything that I know of.

Q. Mr. Herling: Sir, they weren't listed in the first five top measures that were indicated as required or "must" bills by the administration.

THE PRESIDENT. There were two gentlemen that I had a conference with yesterday morning, and I understand they met with the press. They named a few bills and said "and others."

Now, this bill was in the "and others," I assure you.

Q. Mr. Herling: Sir, a related question.

[*The President confers with Mr. Hagerty.*]

THE PRESIDENT. I am also told that they announced it specifically when they met the press at 9:30 this morning after the meeting of the legislative leaders.

Q. Mr. Herling: Sir, this is a related question. I was not at the 9:30 meeting.

THE PRESIDENT. Oh.

Q. Mr. Herling: May I ask, sir, in view of the fact that the dollar minimum wage seems to be riding the crest now in the Senate, with both Republican and Democratic support, and in view of the changed wage pattern situation, would you be willing, would you be amenable, to the idea of signing a dollar minimum wage if it came to you?

THE PRESIDENT. Well, I don't know. I never predicted, I think, that I would or would not sign a bill.

I believe, as of today, that the 90-cent program is the correct one gauged by the practices and the record of the past.

Now, if we make the assumption that the 75-cent minimum wage bill was passed, that that was approximately correct, then the 90 cent by all odds is now generous.

I have not yet had any economic advice that I should change my position. So, as of now, I would like to see that get a fair trial in the Congress, will they approve the 90-cent wage, and I won't predict what I will do with the other bills.

Q. William H. Lawrence, New York Times: Mr. President, returning to the Dixon-Yates question, which was raised a moment ago, have you had a report from Mr. Hughes as yet so that you could tell us whether you will or will not cancel that private agreement?

THE PRESIDENT. I had a report just a few minutes ago from Mr. Hughes. But the investigation by the Attorney General and by the Budget Bureau is still going on because there must be determined the complete feasibility of the city building its own powerplant; otherwise, we might proceed quite a ways on that proposition, and find that it was an impossible thing due to some kind of legal or other limitations.

The TVA has reported to me that there will be no need for this power in TVA and, of course, in that event, if that is substantiated, then there would be no need for building this plant.

Q. Mr. Lawrence: Then you would cancel under such circumstances?

THE PRESIDENT. If all of these circumstances meet the standards that we have set up, yes.

Q. Mr. Lawrence: You spoke, sir, of the continuing investigation of the feasibility of the city of Memphis——

THE PRESIDENT. Yes, and that will be——

Q. Mr. Lawrence: Is that likely to take some time, a week or 10 days?

THE PRESIDENT. Well, I didn't ask them. But my impression of this was that it might be finished up in a couple of weeks.[1]

Q. Edward T. Folliard, Washington Post and Times Herald: Mr. President, I have some questions to ask here about the strike here, the streetcar and bus strike here.

Has the strike here been brought to your attention officially?

---

[1] A White House release of July 12 stated that the President invited Edgar Dixon, President of the Middle South Utilities Company and the Mississippi Valley Generating Company, to meet with him that morning. The release further stated that the President expressed his appreciation to Mr. Dixon and his associates for the fine spirit and cooperation demonstrated throughout the proceedings, and praised the good will with which the company officials accepted the Government decision to terminate the so-called Dixon-Yates contract—a decision predicated on Memphis' announced plan to build its own steam generating plant and meet its own power needs.

Is there any suggestion that it is interfering with the operation of the Government, and have you any plans to try and bring about a settlement?

THE PRESIDENT. As you know, all of you, it is my belief that the Federal Government, as such—the Executive portion of the Federal Government—should stay out of industrial disputes as long as it is possible, and to violate that rule only when a national emergency of some kind is obviously occurring.

Now, I have got two or three remarks I would like to make. Of course, I have been kept in touch with this from the beginning. Any important strike is always discussed with me, certainly, daily.

One group that hasn't received any credit, and I think we all owe them a vote of thanks, is the police force of Washington. I have never seen any group move into an emergency, handle a strange situation, with such efficiency and unfailing good humor as they have. And I think that we owe them a vote of thanks.

Now, in respect to the quarrel itself, I believe this thoroughly, particularly in public utilities: both unions and operators have a very great responsibility to the public that they serve. That public is the source of their income, and they should think about them and their convenience. When the governmental workers cannot get to work except by starting an hour early to walk, or because of traffic jams can't get down here, of course it is interfering to that extent with public business.

I believe both sides really ought to stay in practically continuous negotiations seeking an honest answer that will be just to the public and to both sides.

Q. Charles E. Shutt, Telenews: Mr. President, Soviet Party boss Khrushchev made a couple of interesting remarks at our Embassy in Moscow on July 4th.

One was that he made a point of saying the Soviets were approaching the summit conference with considerable strength, and that if we dealt honestly with them, they thought something would come out of it.

The other remark he made was that if there ever was another

war, he hoped that the Soviets and the Americans would be on the same side.

Would you comment on that, sir?

THE PRESIDENT. Well, with the first one, so far as I know, there is no individual in this Government that has ever said that the Russians, the Soviets, are coming to any conference weak. Of course we recognize their great military strength in the world. So that would seemingly be just thrown in for some reason of his own.

So far as approaching it in good faith, we would go there with very hopeful attitudes, but that hope has got to have greater food on which to nourish itself before it can become anything like expectation.

But we are going there honestly to present our case in a conciliatory, in a friendly, attitude, and we don't intend to reject anything from mere prejudice or truculence or any other lesser motive of that kind.

Q. David P. Sentner, Hearst Newspapers: Mr. President, have you received any information as to the makeup of the Russian delegation to the Big Four conference?

THE PRESIDENT. I have received none whatsoever.

Q. Sarah McClendon, El Paso Times: Sir, in the Vinson Reserve bill, he increases the amount of people who can be in the Reserve, but the bill is based on the extension, of course, of the draft, and the present Reserve bills.

Several times it was mentioned there that you could increase the pool of trained people in the Reserve by merely cutting down on the time the draftees have to serve, and by increasing the take of draftees. I wonder if you have any plans to do that?

THE PRESIDENT. Not as of now, no. I am hoping for a bill somewhat on the lines of the one proposed.

Q. Anthony H. Leviero, New York Times: Mr. President, in "Operation Alert" you issued a test proclamation of martial law on a national scale.

I wonder if you would discuss the application of it and where the Governors and other civil authorities would fit into the picture.

THE PRESIDENT. Well, Mr. Leviero, remember, this was an answer to a specific instance.

The problem I was confronted with when I left my office and which I hadn't known before—I refused to let them tell me the conditions under which this problem was to be operated, because I conceive the played (hypothetical) decisions should be made in the proper atmosphere of emergency—I was suddenly told that 53 of the major cities of the United States had either been destroyed or so badly damaged that the populations were fleeing; there were uncounted dead; there was great fallout over the country. Here there was, as I saw it, no recourse except to take charge instantly; because even Congress, dispersed from Washington because of a bomb, would take some hours to meet, to get together, to organize themselves.

It was a terrible situation, one which you would hope would be terminated very quickly as soon as you get Congress together.

Now, because of this unexpected development they handed me, I have asked the Attorney General to look through our entire record of precedents from the beginning of our Government to see what would be the thing that would do the least violence to our form of Government, which would protect the population, protect the national decision. Let's say that particular incident did at least have this benefit: to cause us to study more deeply and in a more analytical fashion our whole history to see what would be the best thing to do under such circumstances.[1]

Q. Clark R. Mollenhoff, Des Moines Register and Tribune: Mr. President, there has been some little controversy that has

---

[1] A 4-page statement was released by the White House on July 7 concerning a report made to the President on that date by the Director of the Office of Defense Mobilization on the Federal agency relocation activities, which were part of a nationwide civil defense test held June 15, 16, and 17.

The release included a statement concerning Director Flemming's report on the draft proclamation providing for limited martial law, which was prepared during the exercises for future study.

arisen between Budget Director Hughes and Senator Kefauver relative to the questioning of five witnesses from the Budget Bureau in the Dixon-Yates controversy, and I wondered if you would care to discuss for us——

THE PRESIDENT. Five witnesses, you say?

Q. Mr. Mollenhoff: Five witnesses in the Dixon-Yates controversy relative to the part that Mr. Wenzell played in the Dixon-Yates case.

THE PRESIDENT. Well, Mr. Wenzell was the only one I heard about.

Q. Mr. Mollenhoff: The thing I wanted to find out was where you thought—how much discretion Mr. Hughes had?

THE PRESIDENT. I think Mr. Wenzell is entitled to tell the investigating committee exactly what he did.

You will remember he was called in to investigate certain accounting and financing systems of power establishments and their tax situation. That was early in this administration, and he, I believe, submitted on that a fairly formal written report. I have no doubt he will show that written report to the committee if they want to see it, although it has no bearing on the thing they are now talking about.

Later he was—for a period, I believe, of 60 days in early '54 was it?

Mr. Hagerty: A little longer.

THE PRESIDENT. Sometime, early spring of '54, he was here as a technical adviser as they were trying to devise some form of contract that would befit the situation.

He, I have no doubt in all matters of fact, will testify freely before this investigating committee.

Q. Mr. Mollenhoff: Mr. President, I had in mind more the discretion that you felt your agency had had, not necessarily Mr. Wenzell, but with regard to other witnesses. There were five other witnesses in the Budget Bureau that the committee had asked to come down; and Mr. Hughes had informed the committee that they should not——

THE PRESIDENT. Mr. Hughes has not talked to me, as I recall it. Now, maybe Mr. Hughes talked to me about it, and it slipped my mind. I have explained my attitude here time and again.

If anybody in an official position of this Government does anything which is an official act, and submits it either in the form of recommendation or anything else, that is properly a matter for investigation if Congress so chooses, provided the national security is not involved.

But when it comes to the conversations that take place between any responsible official and his advisers or exchange of little, mere little slips of this or that, expressing personal opinions on the most confidential basis, those are not subject to investigation by anybody; and if they are, will wreck the Government.

There is no business that could be run if there would be exposed every single thought that an adviser might have, because in the process of reaching an agreed position, there are many, many conflicting opinions to be brought together. And if any commander is going to get the free, unprejudiced opinions of his subordinates, he had better protect what they have to say to him on a confidential basis.

It is exactly, as I see it, like a lawyer and his client or any other confidential thing of that character.

Q. Joseph A. Dear, Capital Times: Mr. President, what is your opinion of the civil defense recommendations contained in the Report of the Commission on Intergovernmental Relations?

THE PRESIDENT. I don't recall what the item was.

Q. Mr. Dear: I mention specifically the recommendation that civil defense should be the primary responsibility of the National Government rather than the States.

THE PRESIDENT. Well, I will tell you this: the problem, of course, divides itself into many phases, those of (a) detecting the intentions of some foreign government; (b) detecting as quickly as possible any evidence of an impending attack against you.

Now, those two things are obviously more the business of the

Federal Government than anybody else or, let's say, the exclusive business.

But, let's go to the other end now for a moment. How are you going to evacuate a city? It has got to be not only municipal responsibility, it has got to be personal responsibility. You can't in this country, by edict from the Federal Government, evacuate any city, because we don't move in that way.

This has got to be an informed and relatively trained citizenry doing this for themselves. So it has got to be a local responsibility and a very active participation by every individual and by every responsible official in the locality, before there can be any usefulness.

Now, this is true, whether it is a mere matter of evacuation or taking shelter or rescuing the wounded or protecting yourself against fallout or anything else that could happen, and it must be a very positive local participation and responsibility.

Q. Nat S. Finney, Buffalo News: Mr. President, there are two conferences at Geneva, and I don't believe you have expressed your feeling for some time about the Atoms for Peace meeting. And I wonder if you could give us your reflections as to the degree of importance you attach to that session.

THE PRESIDENT. I think it is very important. And I do think I told you how gratified I was that so many American scientists and American firms are participating in helping to make this demonstration of the United States very comprehensive, covering the whole field as far as we know it and as far as we are exploring it.

I think that it should be a very beneficial thing. As you know, we are actually erecting there one of these little swimming pool reactors.

Q. Mr. Finney: Sir, do you expect to see that during your visit? I understand that it will be ready to take a look at it.

THE PRESIDENT. I don't know whether I will get—you mean the reactor?

Q. Mr. Finney: Yes.

THE PRESIDENT. I don't know.   But at Penn State I went to see an identical one because I was afraid I wouldn't get to see it any other time.

Q. Edward P. Morgan, American Broadcasting Company: I realize, sir, that this is a delicate matter coming just at this juncture before Geneva, but could you give us the benefit of your thoughts, your own personal thoughts, now on the subject of disarmament?   For instance, do you feel that we, the American people, are going to have to move away somewhat from the concept of total drastic disarmament toward a sort of a standoff?

THE PRESIDENT. I wouldn't want to have anything I now say taken as authoritative, for the simple reason that the more one studies intensively this problem of disarmament, the more he finds himself in sort of a squirrel's cage.   He is running around pretty rapidly, and at times he has a feeling that he is merely chasing himself.

Now, when we come down to it, every kind of scheme of, let us say, leveling off, as I understand your meaning—standby, where you are now—or actually reducing, everything comes back, as I see it, to acceptable methods of enforcement.

How do you enforce such things?   This brings us instantly to the question of examinations, of inspections.

Now, one way to approach this problem is what would we, in the United States, suppose we took a vote of this body today or we started as a committee of the whole to study it, what kind of inspection are we ready to accept?   Are we ready to open up every one of our factories, every place where something might be going on that could be inimical to the interests of somebody else?

When you tackle that problem you really get into the heart of the difficulties involved, entirely aside from the political contention that there can be no easing of arguments until you ease the political tension.

But the other side will say, "But that political tension is never going to ease until you take away some of the threat of these armaments."

All of that is something, I believe, that could finally be resolved.

This question of inspection, what we will accept and what, therefore, we would expect others to accept, is a very serious one; consequently, there is just nothing today that I could say that is positive beyond this point.

We earnestly want to find some answer to this complicated question because, to my mind, it is perfectly stupid for the world to continue to put so much in these agencies and instrumentalities that cost us so much and, if we don't have this war, do us so little good.

Q. Edward J. Milne, Providence Journal-Bulletin: Mr. President, getting back to martial law for a moment, do you suppose that when it is available, when you receive it, that you could let us have the Attorney General's report on this historical analysis?

THE PRESIDENT. I think so, because it would be something, I think, all America could understand.

Now, in what form he is going to prepare his initial recommendations, I don't know; but I certainly think something could be done. This is one that should trouble us all, every one of us should think about it. It is not something merely that the Federal Government does and says: "We are right."

This is a national problem.

Q. Chalmers M. Roberts, Washington Post and Times Herald: Mr. President, is the question of control that you just mentioned in relation to disarmament the type of problem that you expect to discuss at the Big Four meeting?

THE PRESIDENT. No, not any more than this: we don't intend to discuss, you know, substantive problems. But this question might come up: where would we find the best group, the best channel, or the best method in which to place this problem?

That might come up, but we would not attempt to state there what kind of inspection we would be ready to accept or what kind the other side would be ready to accept. But we might say which is the best group that has a chance to come up with an answer that at least we can start studying.

Q. Mrs. May Craig, Maine Papers: Mr. President, the Republican leaders included school construction in your top priority list of measures you wanted. Would you oppose and consider as extraneous an anti-segregation amendment to that bill?

THE PRESIDENT. I would think it was extraneous, yes, for the simple reason that we need the schools. I think that the other ought to be handled on its own merits.

Besides, we do have this: there apparently is plenty of law, because the Supreme Court found it to be illegal, and they have issued, as I understand it, procedural orders that will have to be carried out in due course through the district courts.

Now, why do we go muddying the water? At the moment I do not quarrel with the right of Congress to pass laws on this thing; but I think they ought to do it on their own.

Q. Charles L. Bartlett, Chattanooga Times: Mr. President, on the basis of what you have been told about the role of Adolphe Wenzell in this Dixon-Yates contract, do you regard that role as proper?

THE PRESIDENT. Indeed, yes.

Q. James B. Reston, New York Times: On this disarmament question, sir, are you satisfied that it is possible, through unlimited inspection, to detect the manufacture of these weapons under modern circumstances?

THE PRESIDENT. Well, no. I think, Mr. Reston, that no one can say that through any type of inspection you could find items that have been already manufactured and concealed. Indeed, if there was peacetime work going ahead, as reactors working with even a lower grade, I think there would be no assurance that you could not convert them rapidly into war use; nor, possibly, could you be sure that they weren't actually producing a little bit of, you might say, extra, auxiliary, that was going into weapons.

But I do believe this: there are lots of ways in which this thing can be approached other than just that. For example, let us take the delivery schemes. We know that when you get to long-range bombing you need very large machines and very large fields from which they take off. Now, those can be detected, and there are other ways of approaching it.

We mustn't admit defeat merely because of that one fact to which you call attention.

Q. Mr. Reston: Mr. President, are the weapons themselves not getting considerably smaller so that the second point is not decisive either?

THE PRESIDENT. Well, you mean that they could be introduced into a country, other than by transport after the war starts?

I think there would be some danger of that. But, on the other hand, there is also danger to both sides because the instant one would be found, it would be practically a declaration of war against you, wouldn't it? And so there is a great risk there also.

Q. Martin Agronsky, American Broadcasting Company: Mr. President, on the second point you made of detection of long-range bombers and things like that, you responded that you thought, you were thinking about the introduction of atom weapons into another country——

THE PRESIDENT. Yes.

Q. Mr. Agronsky:——and, possibly, detecting that.

I think what we have in mind is the guided missile where you just need a launching platform.

THE PRESIDENT. Well, a guided missile, though, is not made in a very small factory, and when it is made I think its character can be determined instantly.

You see, the trouble in this other field is you don't know what this material is being made for and it could be hidden away in very small spaces.

But, I don't believe that you could take an extensive guided missile program and conceal it from any decent or effective system of inspection.

Q. Mr. Agronsky: Mr. President, would I be correct in understanding then from what you have said so far on this whole disarmament thing, and on inspection, what you come down to is the question of good faith, that you have to believe that you have arrived at a point where you can trust those because it is impossible to get adequate inspection and control?

THE PRESIDENT. Mr. Agronsky, this is just as true as you are standing there.   In the long run, the kind of peace for which we are seeking, the kind of peace that will allow people to be really tranquil and confident in their daily pursuits, that will be achieved only when nations have achieved that mutual trust of which you speak.

What we are up against now is an interim phase.   We are trying to take a step toward that and to reduce burdens at the same time.

So I should say that, knowing that none of us has that trust in the opposite side, we must search diligently for some means to lessen this danger and proceed a little ways toward the creation of that trust which must, in the long run, be the foundation of any real peace.

Q. Kenneth M. Scheibel, Gannett Newspapers: Mr. President, in view of your desire for more legislation by the Congress, do you think Congress should give up its plans to adjourn within a few weeks?

THE PRESIDENT. No.   [*Laughter*]   I just think that Congress, when it wants to, can do an awful lot in a very short time, and I am hopeful that they will do so.

Q. James B. Reston, New York Times: Mr. President, what ever happened to that air-conditioned press room that you were thinking about?   [*Laughter*]

THE PRESIDENT. Well, you know, I must confess when I came in this morning I was shocked.   I thought we had some kind of chilling arrangements in here, and I agree we are not handling this fairly.

I would be glad to ask you in my office if there were not so many of you; but I can't crowd you in there, and I have no place where I can do it.

Merriman Smith, United Press: Thank you, Mr. President.

NOTE: President Eisenhower's sev- 10:30 a.m. to 12:02 p.m. on Wednes-
enty-third news conference was held day, July 6, 1955. In attendance:
in the Executive Office Building from 180.

150 ¶ Message to the Congress Transmitting the Second Semiannual Report Under the Agricultural Trade Development and Assistance Act. *July* 12, 1955

To the Congress of the United States:

I transmit herewith the second semi-annual report of the President on the activities carried on under Public Law 480, 83rd Congress, as required by that law.

This report contains the details of the programs carried out under the Act through June 30, 1955, including the volume and dollar value of commodities agreed on as well as of those already shipped, together with the planned uses of the foreign currencies generated by sales.

With experience under the Act now running to some ten months, a study is being initiated to analyze the whole problem of disposal of our agricultural surpluses. It will be the intent of this study to try to appraise objectively what the potentialities are for disposals of such surpluses within the framework of the legislative and executive policies that are applicable to legislation such as Public Law 480.

DWIGHT D. EISENHOWER

NOTE: The report is printed in House Document 216 (84th Cong., 1st sess.).

151 ¶ Remarks to American Field Service Students. *July* 12, 1955

WELL, youngsters, it is really good to see you. Years ago I saw some of your predecessors on the steps at Columbia, I remember. We had a big morning at that time. You have just completed your year in the United States, and I am sure that you have learned a lot here, as we have learned a lot from you, because that has been the history of these expeditions.

I understand that now six hundred of our own young Americans are in your countries, sort of repaying a return call. We are delighted.

It seems a bit of fortunate coincidence that I should have an opportunity to see all of you just as I am about to depart for Geneva where, with others, we will try to explore the reasons why this world does not seem to get closer to peace, and to try to find roads that, if the world follows, all of you may live a little bit more tranquilly than have the people of my generation.

History, of course, has left us a rather tangled network of prejudices and hatreds and suspicions that are not easy to eradicate, and these are intensified by differences in ideologies— doctrinaire positions that seem to set men one against another, and make it difficult for us to live like we should like to live.

Now people don't want conflict—people in general. It is only, I think, mistaken leaders that grow too belligerent and believe that people really want to fight.

I hope that you have learned in your year here that this country does have certain basic principles—beliefs—that though not often expressed in the home and in the schools is nevertheless a very basic part of our existence.

We believe in the individual. We believe that every individual is endowed with certain rights—to worship as he pleases, to think as he pleases, to speak as he pleases, to work at the kind of profession that he himself wants.

So, if we live true to these principles, we are bound to have a government—country—that does not want to fight. Because it is one truly of the people and for the people.

And so, as we go to Geneva, trying to interpret this belief and this conviction, we are hopeful that there may be some way in which all of you can live out your lives tranquilly, helping over the years to promote the kind of understanding that you have gathered in the past year, that you will help to spread in your own countries when you go home, helping to spread the understanding that will lead to the peacefulness of your own lives and those that come after you. It is easily possible that the kind of conventions that you people have been having among yourselves, with those you have visited, and that our young Americans are having in your countries, may be far more important in the long run than the kind to which I am going.

Never forget, you have got a long time to live in this world, and so you want to make certain that you do your part with a full comprehension of the facts and with an open-minded, conciliatory attitude toward the other fellow's viewpoint. But, never sacrifice the basic principle that the human being is the important thing on this planet.

I am not sure, youngsters, why I got so serious just as I came out here to see you all, but possibly it is because I have spent so much of my life with young people—young soldiers—young people. I like them, and trust them. And honestly, my confidence in what you—this group—those like you—those that come after you—can do in this world is unbounded.

Don't ever let anyone tell you you are licked.

Good luck to each of you.

NOTE: The President spoke in the Rose Garden at 12:00 noon.

152   ¶ Letter Accepting the Resignation of Mrs. Oveta Culp Hobby, Secretary of Health, Education, and Welfare.   *July* 13, 1955

Dear Oveta:

This is one of the hardest letters I have ever had to write.

For months, since you first discussed them with me, I have recognized that personal obligations and responsibilities might make your resignation as Secretary an inescapable decision. I now have no alternative than to accept it, effective August first. But I and all who know you as a dedicated, inspired American leader will miss your voice and counsel in Government.

Twice, in little more than a decade, you have earned the thanks and respect of your fellow-citizens. Few—men or women—have brought to heavy tasks and critical challenges such great spirit, integrity and vision or such readiness to spend energy and high talent in the country's service.

Under your command in the Second World War, the Women's Army Corps opened a new field of service for American women. From the very outset of its organization, they demonstrated their value and capacity in the most trying circumstances. More than a hundred thousand women, led by you, proved themselves—in their devotion to duty and in their contribution to victory—worthy comrades of our fighting men.

In this Administration, as the first Secretary of the newly created Department of Health, Education and Welfare, you organized into an integrated program many units and agencies of Government. Great qualities of leadership were essential. You brought them to your mission along with a perseverance, a wise patience, a deep understanding of the personal problems of our people, and a dedication that difficulties could not shake. You made the heart in Government a visible fact and an effective influence.

We are still too close to the beginnings of the new Department to see fully and in a wide perspective all that you have accomplished. But I know that history will hail you in this field, too, as a courageous pioneer in the service of your country.

In official Washington, many thousands as well as I will miss you. On the personal side, none will miss you more than Mrs. Eisenhower and myself. But all of us know that wherever you go, whatever you do, every talent you have will be at work for the good of America.

With affectionate regard to you and Governor Hobby,

Sincerely,

DWIGHT D. EISENHOWER

NOTE: Mrs. Hobby served as the first Secretary of Health, Education, and Welfare from April 11, 1953, to August 1, 1955. Her letter was made public with the President's reply at a ceremony held in the Conference Room at the White House. During World War II Mrs. Hobby was head of the Women's Army Corps with the rank of Colonel.

For remarks by the President and Mrs. Hobby following the acceptance of the resignation, see Item 153, below.

153 ¶ Remarks Following the Acceptance of the Resignation of Secretary Hobby. *July* 13, 1955

WELL, OVETA, this is a sad day for the administration. My mind goes back to the day I first met you in London—in 1942 I suppose it was—when you came over there as head of the WAC Corps, something entirely new in my experience. But you were the first one that sold it to me, and I must say it proved itself, under your leadership, to be one of the finest organizations that the Army has ever had.

In these last two years—two years and a half—your talents have again been devoted to the service of your country, and most effectively. And I would think I could best express the feeling of the Cabinet toward you by quoting the Secretary of the Treasury—I am sure he wouldn't mind. The other day in my office, shortly after you had told me that you would have to go, I said to him that we were going to lose you. And his eyes popped open and he said, "What?—the best man in the Cabinet!"

That is the feeling that the whole Cabinet has towards you. I assure you that none of us will forget your wise counsel, your calm confidence in the face of every kind of difficulty, your concern for people everywhere, the warm heart you brought to your job as well as your talents. We are just distressed to lose you, but the best wishes of the entire executive department—indeed, I think of the Congress and all Washington that knows you—will go with you as you go back, and we will be very hopeful that you will have many fine, happy years there from here on.

[*Following Mrs. Hobby's response, the President resumed speaking.*]

Oveta, if I had known that you felt like that, I never would have accepted your letter of resignation.

Mrs. Secretary—I can still say that—thank you very much.

NOTE: The President's letter accepting Mrs. Hobby's resignation appears as Item 152, above.

Mrs. Hobby's response to the President's remarks follows:

Thank you very much, Mr. President.

Mr. President, during the past 31 months, I have had the most singular opportunity. I have had an opportunity to serve with you, to serve a man whose entire life has been devoted to the people of the United States. I have had the most unfailing support and leadership from you in trying to develop sound programs for the American people in the field of health, education, and welfare. And as I look back over the 31 months, Mr. President, when you came to this Office, and realize what has transpired in those 31 months, I am a very, very happy citizen.

In those 31 months we have moved away from the shadow of war; we have moved into the greatest prosperity this country has ever known, with more people working, greater wages, and being able to buy more of the good things of life.

And now perhaps we stand in the area of widest peace, and perhaps on the threshold of a universal peace. When I think of what has been accomplished in your 31 months, I feel humble and grateful to have had a part in it. When I think of the people of the United States who have had their pensions and their social security protected by a stable dollar, Mr. President—the smallest variation in the purchasing power of the dollar in 42 years—the time we have kept records; when I think of the millions of people that have been given an opportunity under social security and the hundreds of thousands that will be given an opportunity under vocational rehabilitation, and when I think of the millions of people that will benefit from your wise policies in education—in letting the people of this country think through their own education prob-

lems and bringing them up here—I feel particularly blessed.

Now, Mr. President, as you go to Geneva for all of us, I believe that every one of us will be praying that there, in that meeting, the first step will be taken toward a truly universal peace. And I for one, Mr. President, have never had such a privilege. I know this country would have been blessed at any time to have had your leadership, but in these crucial years in world affairs, I truly feel that God has had His hand on the United States in the kind of leadership you have given us.

154 ¶ Letter to Secretary Wilson Marking the Third Anniversary of Operation Skywatch. *July* 13, 1955

[Released July 13, 1955. Dated June 21, 1955]

Dear Mr. Secretary:

The third anniversary of Operation Skywatch on July fourteenth affords me an opportunity to express once again my respect and admiration for those citizens who continue to give unselfishly of their time and effort in the Ground Observer Corps.

Through their steadfastness they help to do, in the only way it can be done, a job of vital importance to all Americans. To all in the Ground Observer Corps I should like to say again that I cannot over-emphasize the importance of the role they, volunteers, play in national defense. As you have pointed out, they have undoubtedly strengthened the capabilities of our continental defense system, and in so doing they have helped to deter aggression.

As you mark the third anniversary of Skywatch, please convey to all Ground Observers past and present my personal word of appreciation and congratulations. I hope the effort to seek additional volunteers for the expanded program will meet with the greatest success.

Sincerely,

DWIGHT D. EISENHOWER

155 ¶ Special Message to the Congress Upon Signing the Department of Defense Appropriation Act. *July* 13, 1955

To the Congress of the United States:

I have today approved H.R. 6042, making appropriations for the Department of Defense for the fiscal year ending June 30, 1956, and for other purposes. I have done so because the funds which the bill makes available are urgently needed by the Department of Defense. Except for this imperative need, I would have withheld my approval of the bill, for I am advised by the Attorney General that one of its provisions, section 638, constitutes an unconstitutional invasion of the province of the Executive.

Section 638 deals with the authority of the Department of Defense to rid itself of many of the manifold activities that it has been performing with its civilian personnel, and that can be adequately and economically performed by private industry without danger to the national security. That section states that funds appropriated in the bill cannot be used to enable the Secretary of Defense to exercise this authority if, in the case of any activity of the Department proposed to be terminated, the Appropriations Committee of the Senate or the Appropriations Committee of the House of Representatives disapproves such proposed termination.

The Constitution of the United States divides the functions of the Government into three departments—the legislative, the executive, and the judicial—and establishes the principle that they shall be kept separate. Neither may exercise functions belonging to the others. Section 638 violates this constitutional principle.

I believe it to be my duty to oppose such a violation. The Congress has the power and the right to grant or to deny an appropriation. But once an appropriation is made the appropriation must, under the Constitution, be administered by the executive branch of the Government alone, and the Congress has no right to confer upon its committees the power to veto Executive action or to prevent Executive action from becoming effective.

Since the organization of our Government, the President has felt bound to insist that Executive functions be maintained unimpaired by legislative encroachment, just as the legislative branch has felt bound to resist interference with its power by the Executive. To acquiesce in a provision that seeks to encroach upon the proper authority of the Executive establishes a dangerous precedent. I do not, by my approval of H.R. 6042, acquiesce in the provisions of section 638, and to the extent that this section seeks to give to the Appropriations Committees of the Senate and House of Representatives authority to veto or prevent Executive action, such section will be regarded as invalid by the executive branch of the Government in the administration of H.R. 6042, unless otherwise determined by a court of competent jurisdiction.

One other rider added to the bill is most unfortunate. This rider—contained in section 630—virtually precludes the services from considering the purchase of foreign-made spun silk yarn for cartridge cloth.

This rider—attached to the bill without adequate opportunity for reasons against it to be presented—runs directly counter to the steps which have been taken by the administration in the field of Government procurement policy. No reason appears why foreign-made spun silk yarn, or indeed any other article or commodity of foreign origin, should be singled out for special exemption from the general provisions of the "Buy American" legislation.   By making it virtually impossible for our friends abroad to sell us goods when such goods are materially less expensive to our taxpayers than those that can be procured domestically, such provisions could effect a deadly attrition of our whole international trade policy and bring about impairment of our relations with other nations.

It is my earnest hope that as soon as possible the Congress will repeal section 630 of the bill in its entirety.

DWIGHT D. EISENHOWER

NOTE: As enacted, H.R. 6042 is Public Law 157, 84th Congress (69 Stat. 301).

In response to the President's request, the Attorney General wrote an opinion as to the validity of certain provisions in section 638 of the act. In his letter of July 13, made public July 14, the Attorney General stated that "the proviso which purports to vest disapproval authority in either of the two Appropriations Committees is separable from the remainder of the Act and, if viewed as imposing an invalid condition, does not affect the validity of the remaining provisions."

156 ¶ Message to the Congress Transmitting the Ninth Annual Report on United States Participation in the United Nations.
July 15, 1955

To the Congress of the United States:

I transmit herewith, pursuant to the United Nations Participation Act, the ninth annual report on United States participation in the United Nations, covering the year 1954.

In a decade of trying years, the United Nations has developed from a blueprint for peace into a living, functioning organization. It was fitting that an impressive commemoration of the signing of the United Nations Charter ten years ago should have recently taken place in San Francisco to focus attention on the accomplishments and principles of the United Nations.

I was privileged to bring to this gathering a special message from the Congress expressing, on behalf of the people of the United States, our deep desire for peace and our hope that all nations will join with us in a renewed effort for peace.

Out of the United Nations' many actions in 1954, the following are of special interest to the United States, for they worked to the benefit of American foreign policy.

1. Atomic Energy for Peace:

The atom has unlocked untold opportunities in the world of peaceful progress. I know of no better way to improve the lot of mankind and raise its hopes than by pushing ahead vigorously in the development of the atom for the purpose of peace. That is why I went before the General Assembly in 1953 to ask that all nations apply their ingenuity and resourcefulness in a program of international cooperation in this field.

The faith of the American people in the world's readiness for this challenge have not been disappointed. The progress in a short space of time has been dramatic.

I authorized Ambassador Henry Cabot Lodge, Jr., to announce to the General Assembly in the fall of 1954 the intention of the United States to make available 100 kg. of fissionable material to assist nations in their own programs.

On December 4, 1954, the General Assembly adopted a resolution entitled "International Cooperation in Developing the Peaceful Uses of Atomic Energy." This was done with historic unanimity, after the rejection of Soviet amendments, 60 to 0.

By this resolution the Assembly endorse the establishment of an International Atomic Energy Agency to organize the pooling of atomic knowledge and materials for peaceful ends, and decreed the holding of an international technical conference under United Nations auspices to explore the promise of the atom and develop methods for its practical use. That conference—which may well be the broadest exchange of scientific and technical information in history—is to begin August 8 in Geneva.

United Nations' action in this field made the atoms-for-peace project into an instrument for constructive international progress. It reminded people the world over that the United States is their partner in their search for peace and plenty. It renewed also the hope for real participation by the Soviet Union—a hope which was central to the original proposal. We will welcome the participation of all interested nations in these activities. But we will not slow the wheels of progress if some do not choose to join with us.

2. *Prisoners in Communist China:*

Of all the important matters before the United Nations in 1954, none so strongly engaged the emotions of the American people as the case of the fighting men detained by the Chinese Communists. A historic 47–5 vote by the General Assembly condemned their detention and directed Secretary-General Hammarskjold to leave no stone unturned to seek their release.

The limited success reached thus far proves: the potency of the United Nations in focusing world opinion; the diplomatic skill and irrepressible perseverance of Mr. Hammarskjold in a most difficult task; the steady helpfulness of friendly nations whom divisive propaganda could not frighten away from us; and, by no means least important, the patience and wise self-restraint of our own people. May these qualities serve to convince Communist China that it should end the wrongful detention of all surviving United Nations prisoners, whatever their nationality. The prolonged anguish of these men and their nearest kin arouses the sympathies of the civilized world.

3. *Guatemala:*

The conflict in Guatemala was closer to our homeland than any other which the Security Council has ever faced. In June 1954 Guatemalan patriots began an armed revolt to eject a government whose Communist sponsorship was becoming ever more obvious and to restore a free government.

Immediately the pro-Communist government invoked its right to be heard by the United Nations Security Council. The Council met forthwith. The Guatemalan representative demanded, with conspicuous Soviet backing, that the United Nations intervene to stop the revolt.

The United States Representative, Henry Cabot Lodge, Jr., insisted that the Soviet Union "stay out of this Hemisphere"—a restatement of the Monroe Doctrine in contemporary terms. Further, he urged the Council to let the proper regional body—the Organization of American States—deal with the situation in Guatemala and neighboring countries. He pointed out that if the United Nations were to intervene in local disputes over the heads of responsible regional organizations, the entire system of regional security sanctioned by the United Nations Charter would be in jeopardy.

Today Guatemala is again securely restored to the community of free nations. A challenge by world communism within our hemisphere has been met and overcome.

4. *Disarmament and Security:*

Neither lasting peace nor the real reduction of international tensions can be realized until progress in disarmament becomes a fact. As nuclear capabilities have increased to staggering proportions, disarmament has become, literally, a problem of survival for all mankind.

In 1954, a subcommittee of Canada, France, the United Kingdom, the United States, and the Soviet Union held its first round of private discussions. In five weeks of meetings newly detailed proposals were laid before the Soviet representative, but with no result.

But, in the General Assembly in September, the Soviets gave the appearance of reversing their adamant position and stated their acceptance of at least some principles of a sound program. We are carefully weighing this Soviet step, and the subsequent Soviet proposal in May 1955, in the broad restudy of United States disarmament policy which is now in progress.

By this continuing exploration in the disarmament field, as well as by recommendations for strengthening collective action against any future aggression, and by watchful influence over the dangerous areas of the world, the United Nations in 1954 continued to serve the cause of peace.

5. *Economic and Social Actions:*

The spectacular potentialities of the atom for peaceful purposes must not be allowed to overshadow the slow but sound progress of the United Nations in the economic and social field.

The most far-reaching new step in 1954 was the approval by the General Assembly of the establishment of an International Finance Corporation to stimulate the setting up and expansion of productive private enterprises in underdeveloped countries. The Corporation will be set up as an affiliate of the International Bank for Reconstruction and Development and will provide capital in private enterprises without requirement of government guarantees.

The work of the United Nations on behalf of refugees also received new impetus in a General Assembly decision authorizing the United Nations High Commissioner for Refugees to raise funds and undertake a four-year program designed to achieve permanent solutions for certain refugees in Europe, most of them still unsettled since World War II, who are not eligible for other aid programs. The United States strongly supported this decisive step to solve a distressing human problem.

We are able, in 1954, through the power of the United Nations in shaping world opinion, to further expose the repressive system of forced labor in Communist countries. The outstanding report of the United Nations Ad Hoc Committee on Forced Labor was officially considered for the first time by the Economic and Social Council, which subsequently condemned the use of forced labor for political and economic purposes. The United States Representative, Mrs. Oswald B. Lord, was also able to expose before the General Assembly newly discovered facts and recent regulations which demonstrated that the system of forced labor had been extended with Soviet help to Communist China.

Other economic and social programs of the United Nations and the Specialized Agencies—including technical assistance, Korean reconstruction, aid to Palestine refugees, the Children's Fund, food and agricultural assistance, labor, health, and education—continued to help in making the United Nations known to millions of people around the globe as a living, constructive force. The United Nations Specialized Agencies, specifically the International Labor Organization and the United Nations Educational, Scientific and Cultural Organization, received the tribute of sudden participation by the U.S.S.R.

Whatever the reason for its changed attitude, we welcome it as further proof of the importance and world reputation of the Specialized Agencies; and also as an extension of points at which the Soviet rulers may—if they wish—broaden fruitful cooperation with the rest of the world. This development challenges the United States to maintain its watchfulness and constructive activity in all these fields in which the Soviet Union has at length shown an interest.

The United States representatives have actively used the United Nations' forum to expound our ideas and ideals and reveal the fallacies of communism.

All these things have happened after reduction in the previous year of our American share of United Nations costs and while we worked out a program in which all Americans holding important office at the United Nations were screened in accordance with FBI procedures.

These are highlights from one year's activity in the United Nations' search for peace among nations. That year is chronicled in more detail in the attached report.

The vitality of the United Nations and American support for the United Nations were never more needed than now. We are in a period of great flux in international affairs. There are signs that the world may be entering a new phase in international relationships. For the first time since the United Nations Charter came into force, the Heads of the Governments of the United States, the United Kingdom, France, and the U.S.S.R. will be meeting. They will, I hope, be able to identify the outstanding divisive issues and develop methods to try to solve them. I for one will enter these discussions with a full awareness of the opportunities offered by the United Nations to contribute to the peace of the world. If these meetings reach useful areas of agreement in the handling of international problems, then they will open new vistas looking toward further agreement. This can only mean that the United Nations will have new and wider opportunities to build upon the foundations thus laid.

DWIGHT D. EISENHOWER

NOTE: The report is published in House Document 166 (84th Cong., 1st sess.).

In the third paragraph of the message the President referred to House Concurrent Resolution 157 (84th Cong., 1st sess., 69 Stat. B9).

157 ¶ Statement by the President Upon Signing the Public Works Appropriation Act.
July 15, 1955

I HAVE TODAY approved H.R. 6766, "Making appropriations for the Atomic Energy Commission, the Tennessee Valley Authority, certain agencies of the Department of the Interior, and civil functions administered by the Department of the Army for the fiscal year ending June 30, 1956, and for other purposes." I have approved this bill with great reluctance. There are two matters which are of deep concern to me.

The first is the reduction made in the funds available to the Atomic Energy Commission. The amount provided in the bill, together with the estimated amount carried over from 1955, would provide the Commission with total obligational authority of $1,380,847,000 for operating expenses in 1956. This amount is $144,404,000 less than was requested. A reduction of this magnitude could seriously interfere with the Commission's plans to produce atomic weapons, to develop propulsion reactors for the Navy and the Air Force, and to develop peaceful applications of atomic energy, including the production of electric power.

These are most crucial programs in maintaining a strong national defense and in maintaining this Nation's leadership in bringing the benefits of atomic energy to the service of mankind both here and abroad.

For these reasons, I would hope that the Congress would reconsider its action and make supplementary amounts available so as to avoid serious disruptions in this most vital program.

The second matter which concerns me is the large increase in the number of new construction starts for the Corps of Engineers and the Bureau of Reclamation. Many of these projects which have been added by the Congress have not had detailed engineering studies completed. As a result, we have no basis for determining their financial soundness and their ultimate cost to the Federal Government.

In all, one hundred and seven unbudgeted projects were added by Congress. We can only guess what their total cost to the taxpayers will ultimately be because of this lack of detailed engineering studies on many of them. The best guess that can be made at the present time is upwards of $1.5 billion, but when planning is completed, this guess, in the light of past experience, may well prove to be far too low. While the first-year appropriations made in this bill amount to only about $47 million, the appropriations and expenditures in future years will increase sharply and quickly reach a half-billion-dollar level.

As a consequence of these considerations, initiation of the added projects cannot be undertaken until the detailed engineering plans have been completed and we have a sound basis for cost estimates. In the case of projects involving reimbursable items, such as electric power and water supply, we must be assured that satisfactory financial arrangements have been completed for return of the Federal investment.

The public is entitled to this measure of protection to the tax dollars that go into the construction of these projects.

NOTE: As enacted, H.R. 6766 is Public Law 163, 84th Congress (69 Stat. 354).

158 ¶ Statement by the President Upon Signing the Act Providing for a Highway Bridge Across Lake Texoma.   *July* 15, 1955

I HAVE TODAY signed S. 1318, "To modify the project for the Denison Reservoir on Red River in Texas and Oklahoma in order to provide for a highway bridge across Lake Texoma."

Although the United States is under no legal obligation to build this bridge, there is some equity in having the United States assume part of the costs. The war-caused denial of materials to the States of Oklahoma and Texas made it impossible for the two States to construct the bridge prior to the flooding of the lake by the United States. With the lake now flooded, extra costs of construction will have to be incurred.

However, the war-caused denial of materials, which prevented the building of the bridge before the flooding of the reservoir, was not a factor in 1946 and the years following, and I am at a loss to understand why action on the bridge has been so long delayed. During this period construction costs were increasing rapidly, and under the bill all of these increased costs are assigned to the United States. It seems to me that at the very most, the United States should not have to bear more than the extra costs resulting from flooding. I therefore recommend that the Congress reassess the relative shares assigned by the bill and increase the requirement for local contributions before Federal appropriations are made available.

NOTE: As enacted, S. 1318 is Public Law 164, 84th Congress (69 Stat. 365).

159   ¶ Statement by the President Upon Signing Bill for the Relief of the Highway Construction Company.   *July* 15, 1955

I HAVE TODAY approved H.R. 4182 for the relief of Highway Company of Ohio, Incorporated, although a proviso inserted in the bill gave me some concern because its meaning is not made clear.   That proviso reads as follows:

"*Provided,* That in making such determination of the excessive profits of the Highway Construction Company, the Tax Court of the United States may take into consideration the affiliation of that company with any other company, but the findings of such court shall be limited to determining only the amount, if any, of the excessive profits of the Highway Construction Company and such court shall have no authority under this Act to determine the amount, if any, of the excessive profits of any company affiliated with such Highway Construction Company."

After inquiries concerning the intended effect of this proviso, I am assured that it was designed for the sole purpose of protecting the interests of the United States.

NOTE: As enacted, H.R. 4182 is Public Law 208, 84th Congress (69 Stat. A72).

160   ¶ Letter to the Chairman, House Committee
on Ways and Means, Concerning United States
Membership in the Organization for Trade
Cooperation.   *July* 15, 1955

Dear Mr. Chairman:

I appreciate your July fourteenth letter and readily understand
your problem of arranging adequate Committee consideration of
H.R. 5550 which would authorize U.S. membership in the
Organization for Trade Cooperation.

The Committee on Ways and Means has borne a heavy burden
of difficult and constructive legislation in this session of Congress.
Much of that constructive effort has been concerned with legislation implementing various parts of the Administration's program
in the field of foreign economic policy.

More remains to be done in this field. As your letter indicates,
and as we recently discussed in my office, the passage of H.R. 5550
is especially important. This legislation will do much to vouch-
safe to the American people and the free world the gains which
will accrue from continuation of the enlightened trade policy
provided for in H.R. 1. To assure orderly consideration of trade
problems arising between nations is vital to our own interests as
a great trading nation and to the interests of those joined with us
in the cause of freedom. This great purpose will be powerfully
advanced by Congressional approval of the proposed Organization for Trade Cooperation.

I share your view that it would be ill-advised to launch consideration of H.R. 5550 in your Committee when so little time remains in this session. A matter of this vital importance should
have thorough hearings, discussion and debate.

The wise course of action, therefore, it seems to me, is the one
you suggest in your letter. I am pleased indeed to have your as-

surance that H.R. 5550 will be among the very first measures to be considered by your Committee next year.

　With kind regard,

　　　　　　　　Sincerely,

　　　　　　　　　DWIGHT D. EISENHOWER

NOTE: Chairman Jere Cooper's letter of July 14 was released with the President's reply.

161　¶ Radio and Television Address to the American People Prior to Departure for the Big Four Conference at Geneva.　*July* 15, 1955

[Delivered from the broadcast room at the White House at 8:15 p.m.]

Good evening friends:

　Within a matter of minutes I shall leave the United States on a trip that in some respects is unprecedented for a President of the United States.　Other Presidents have left the continental limits of our country for the purpose of discharging their duties as Commander in Chief in time of war, or to participate in conference at the end of a war to provide for the measures that would bring about a peace.　But now, for the first time, a President goes to engage in a conference with the heads of other governments in order to prevent wars, in order to see whether in this time of stress and strain we cannot devise measures that will keep from us this terrible scourge that afflicts mankind.

　Now, manifestly, there are many difficulties in the way of a President going abroad for a period, particularly while Congress is in session.　He has many constitutional duties; he must be here to perform them.　I am able to go on this trip only because of the generous cooperation of the political leaders in Congress of both political parties who have arranged their work so that my absence for a period will not interfere with the business of the Government.　On my part I promised them that by a week from

Sunday, on July 24th, I shall be back here ready to carry on my accustomed duties.

Now it is manifest that in such a period as I am able to spend abroad, we cannot settle the details of the many problems that afflict the world. But of course I go for a very serious purpose. This purpose is to attempt with my colleagues to change the spirit that has characterized the intergovernmental relationships of the world within the past ten years. Now—let us think for a moment about this purpose. Let us just enumerate a few of the problems that plague the world; the problem of armaments and the burdens that people are forced to carry because of the necessity for these armaments; the problem of the captive states, once proud people that are not allowed their own form of government—freely chosen by themselves and under individuals freely elected by themselves; the problem of divided countries, people who are related to each other by blood, kinship and who are divided by force of arms into two camps that are indeed expected to be hostile to each other.

Then we have the problem of international interference in the internal affairs of free governments, bringing about a situation that leads to subversion, difficulties and recriminations within countries—sometimes even revolutions.

These problems are made all the more serious by complications between governments. These problems of which I speak often have arisen as an aftermath of wars and conflicts. But governments are divided also by differing ambitions, by differing ideologies, by mutual distrust and the alarm that each creates. Because of these alarms, nations build up armaments and place their trust for peace and protection in those armaments. These armaments create greater alarms, and so we have a spiral of growing uneasiness and suspicion and distrust. That is the kind of thing that the world faces today. For these things there is no easy settlement. In the brief time that this conference can exist it is impossible to pursue all of the long and tedious negotiations that must take place before the details of these problems can be settled.

Our many postwar conferences have been characterized too much by attention to details, by an effort apparently to work on specific problems, rather than to establish a spirit and attitude in which to approach them. Success, therefore, has been meager. Too often, indeed, these conferences have been mere opportunities for exploitation of nationalistic ambitions, or, indeed, only sounding boards for the propaganda that the participants wanted to spread to the world.

If we look at this record we would say, "Why another conference? What hope is there for success?" Now, the first thing that I ask you is, "Do we want to do nothing; do we want to sit and drift along to the inevitable end of such a contest—new tensions and then to war or at least to continuing tensions?"

We want peace. We cannot look at this whole situation without realizing, first, that pessimism never won any battles, whether in peace or in war. Next, we will understand that one ingredient has been missing from all these conferences. I mean an intention to conciliate, to understand, to be tolerant, to try to see the other fellow's viewpoint as well as we see our own. I say to you, if we can change the spirit in which these conferences are conducted we will have taken the greatest step toward peace, toward future prosperity and tranquility that has ever been taken in the history of mankind.

I want to give you a few reasons for hope in this project: first, the people of all the world desire peace—that is, peace for people everywhere. I distinguish between people and governments here for the moment, for we know that the great hordes of men and women who make up the world do not want to go to the battlefield. They want to live in peace—not a peace that is a mere stilling of the guns, but a peace in which they can live happily, and in confidence that they can raise their children in a world of which they will be proud.

That common desire for peace is something that is a terrific force in this world and to which I believe all political leaders in the world are beginning to respond. They must recognize it.

Another item. Did you note this morning the speech made by Premier Bulganin in Moscow? Every word he said was along the lines that I am speaking. He talked of conciliation and tolerance and understanding. I say to you, I say to all the world, if the words that he expressed are as truly reflective of the hearts and minds of all the people in Russia, and the hearts and minds of all the people in all the world everywhere, there will be no trouble between the Russian delegation and our own at this coming conference.

Now I want to mention another item that is important in this conference. The free world is divided from the Communist world by an iron curtain. The free world has one great factor in common. We are not held together by force but we are held together by this great factor.

It is this. The free world lives under one religion or another. It believes in a divine power. It believes in a supreme being. Now this, my friends, is a very great factor for conciliation and peace at this time. Each of these religions has as one of its basic commandments words that are similar to our Golden Rule—"Do unto others as you would have them do unto you." This means that the thinking of those people is based upon ideas of right, and justice, and mutual self-respect and consideration for the other man. This means peace, because only in peace can such conceptions as these prevail. This means that the free people of the world hate war; they want peace and are fully dedicated to it.

Now, this country, as other free countries, maintains arms. We maintain formations of war and all the modern weapons. Why? Because we must. As long as this spirit that has prevailed up to now continues to prevail in the world, we cannot expose our rights, our privileges, our homes, our wives, our children to risk which would come to an unarmed country. But we want to make it perfectly clear that these armaments do not reflect the way we want to live. They merely reflect the way, under present conditions, we have to live. Now it is natural for a people steeped in a religious civilization, when they come to moments of great importance—maybe even crises such as now we face—to turn to the divine power that each has in his own heart, for guidance, for wisdom, for some help in doing the thing that is honorable, that is right.

I have no doubt that tonight throughout this country and indeed throughout the free world, that such prayers are ascending. This is a mighty force, and it brings to me the thought that through prayer we could also achieve a very definite and practical result at this very moment.

Suppose on the next sabbath day observed by each of our religions, Americans, 165 million of us, went to our accustomed places of worship, and, crowding those places, asked for help, and by so doing demonstrated to all the world the sincerity and depth of our aspirations for peace. This would be a mighty force. None could then say that we preserve armament because we want to. We preserve it because we must.

My friends, Secretary Dulles and I go to this conference in earnest hope that we may accurately represent your convictions, your beliefs, your aspirations. We shall be conciliatory because our country seeks no conquest, no property of others. We shall be tolerant because this nation does not seek to impose our way of life upon others. We shall be firm in the consciousness of your material and spiritual strength and your defense of your rights. But we shall extend the hand of friendship to all who will grasp it honestly and concede to us the same rights, the same understanding, the same freedom that we accord to them.

We, the Secretary and I, shall do our best with others there to start the world on the beginning of a new road, a road that may be long and difficult, but which, if faithfully followed, will lead us on to a better and fuller life.

Thank you and goodnight.

162 ¶ Remarks at the Keflavik Airport, Iceland. *July* 16, 1955

Mr. President, ladies and gentlemen:

I think it a fortunate circumstance for me that this mission to Europe brought me again to your country which has such a long history of friendship with my own. This is a much more pleasant day than when I last visited you—that was in mid-January.

This trip takes me to Europe in a search for peace. With my colleagues at the Geneva Conference, I shall hope that the cause of peace can be advanced for all the world—that people like yours—like ours—like the thirteen nations that are with us in NATO—all the others can achieve a more tranquil life with freedom and with justice.

I think it a very great privilege that I have a chance here for a very brief period to talk with you about the problems that lie before us and which are common to our two countries.

Thank you very much.

NOTE: The President spoke at 10:50 a.m. His opening words "Mr. President" referred to President Asgeir Asgeirsson of Iceland. President Asgeirsson's remarks follow:

Mr. President, we are very pleased to welcome you to our country. This is a short stop, and we know how pressing your time is and how important your mission.

We wish you well and also success in your important work at the meeting in Geneva. We also wish you success in the work for peace and security.

163 ¶ Remarks Upon Arrival at the Airport in Geneva. *July* 16, 1955

Mr. President:

My wife and I—the party with us—are deeply touched by the honor you have paid us by coming here to the airport to greet us as we land in this wonderful nation of Switzerland.

We are honored that the Governor of the Republic and Canton of Geneva should come out—and the Mayor of the city.

Some eleven years ago, Mr. President, I came to Europe with an army, a navy, an air force, with a single purpose: to destroy Nazism. I came with the formations of war and all of the circumstances of war surrounded that journey at that time.

This time I come armed with something far more powerful: the good will of America—the great hopes of America—the aspirations of America for peace. That is why I have come here, in this beautiful country of yours, to meet with my colleagues from other countries to see whether it is not possible to find some road that will lead all mankind into a more tranquil, better, fuller way of life.

I thank you very much.

NOTE: The President's opening words referred to President Max Petitpierre of Switzerland.

164 ¶ Opening Statement at the Geneva Conference. *July* 18, 1955

WE MEET HERE for a simple purpose. We have come to find a basis for accommodation which will make life safer and happier not only for the nations we represent but for people elsewhere. We are here in response to a universal urge, recognized by Premier Bulganin in his speech of July 15, that the political leaders of our great countries find a path to peace.

We cannot expect here, in the few hours of a few days, to solve all the problems of all the world that need to be solved. Indeed, the four of us meeting here have no authority from others that could justify us even in attempting that. The roots of many of these problems are buried deep in wars, conflicts and history. They are made even more difficult by the differences in governmental ideologies and ambitions. Manifestly it is out of the question in the short time available to the heads of government meeting here to trace out the causes and origins of these problems and to devise agreements that could with complete fairness to all eliminate them.

Nevertheless, we can, perhaps, create a new spirit that will make possible future solutions of problems which are within our responsibilities. And equally important we can try to take here and now at Geneva the first steps on a new road to a just and durable peace.

The problems that concern us are not inherently insoluble. Of course, they are difficult; but their solution is not beyond the wisdom of man. They seem insoluble under conditions of fear, distrust, and even hostility, where every move is weighed in terms of whether it will help or weaken a potential enemy. If those conditions can be changed, then much can be done. Under such circumstances, I am confident that at a later stage our Foreign Ministers will be able to carry on from where we leave off to find, either by themselves or with others, solutions to our problems.

No doubt there are among our nations philosophical convictions which are in many respects irreconcilable. Nothing that we can say or do here will change that fact. However, it is not always necessary that people should think alike and believe alike before they can work together. The essential thing is that none should attempt by force or trickery to make his beliefs prevail and thus to impose his system on the unwilling.

The new approach we of this conference should seek cannot be found merely by talking in terms of abstractions and generalities. It is necessary that we talk frankly about the concrete problems which create tension between us and about the way to begin in solving them.

As a preface, may I indicate some of the issues I think we should discuss.

First is the problem of unifying Germany and forming an all-German government based on free elections. Ten years have passed since the German armistice—and Germany is still divided. That division does a grievous wrong to a people which is entitled, like any other, to pursue together a common destiny. While that division continues, it creates a basic source of instability in Europe. Our talk of peace has little meaning if at the same time we perpetuate conditions endangering the peace. Toward Germany, the four of us bear special responsibilities. While any conclusions we reach would be invalid unless supported by majority opinion in Germany, this problem should be a central topic for our meeting here. Must we not consider ways to solve it promptly and justly.

In the interest of enduring peace, our solution should take account of the legitimate security interests of all concerned. That is why we insist a united Germany is entitled at its choice, to exercise its inherent right of collective self-defense. By the same token, we are ready to take account of legitimate security interests of the Soviet Union. The Paris agreements contain many provisions which serve this purpose. But we are quite ready to consider further reciprocal safeguards which are reasonable and practical and compatible with the security of all concerned.

On a broader plane, there is the problem of respecting the right of peoples to choose the form of government under which they will live; and of restoring sovereign rights and self-government to those who have been deprived of them. The American people feel strongly that certain peoples of Eastern Europe, many with a long and proud record of national existence, have not yet been given the benefit of this pledge of our United Nations wartime declaration, reinforced by other wartime agreements.

There is the problem of communication and human contacts as among our peoples. We frankly fear the consequences of a situation where whole peoples are isolated from the outside world. The American people want to be friends with the Soviet peoples. There are no natural differences between our peoples or our nations. There are no territorial conflicts or commercial rivalries. Historically, our two countries have always been at peace. But friendly understanding between peoples does not readily develop when there are artificial barriers such as now interfere with communication. It is time that all curtains whether of guns or laws or regulations should begin to come down. But this can only be done in an atmosphere of mutual respect and confidence.

There is the problem of international communism. For 38 years now, its activities have disturbed relations between other nations and the Soviet Union. Its activities are not confined to efforts to persuade. It seeks throughout the world to subvert lawful governments and to subject nations to an alien domination. We cannot ignore the distrust created by the support of such activities. In my nation and elsewhere it adds to distrust and therefore to international tension.

Finally, there is the overriding problem of armament. This is at once a result and a cause of existing tension and distrust. Contrary to a basic purpose of the United Nations Charter, armaments now divert much of men's effort from creative to nonproductive uses. We would all like to end that. But apparently none dares to do so because of fear of attack.

Surprise attack has a capacity for destruction far beyond anything which man has yet known. So each of us deems it vital that there should be means to deter such attack. Perhaps, therefore, we should consider whether the problem of limitation of armament may not best be approached by seeking—as a first step—dependable ways to supervise and inspect military establishments, so that there can be no frightful surprises, whether by sudden attack or by secret violation of agreed restrictions. In this field nothing is more important than that we explore together the challenging and central problem of effective mutual inspection. Such a system is the foundation for real disarmament.

As we think of this problem of armament, we need to remember that the present burden of costly armaments not only deprives our own people of higher living standards, but it also denies the peoples of underdeveloped areas of resources which would improve their lot. These areas contain much of the world's population and many nations now emerging for the first time into political independence. They are grappling with the urgent problem of economic growth. Normally they would receive assistance particularly for capital development from the more developed nations of the world. However, that normal process is gravely retarded by the fact that the more developed industrial countries are dedicating so much of their productive effort to armament. Armament reduction would and should insure that part of the savings would flow into the less developed areas of the world to assist their economic development.

In addition, we must press forward in developing the use of atomic energy for constructive purposes. We regret that the Soviet Union has never accepted our proposal of December 1953 that nations possessing stockpiles of fissionable material should join to contribute to a "world bank" so as, in steadily increasing measure, to substitute cooperation in human welfare for competition in means of human destruction. We still believe that if the Soviet Union would according to its ability contribute to this great project, that act would improve the international climate.

In this first statement of the Conference, I have indicated very briefly some of the problems that weigh upon my mind and upon the people of the United States and where solution is largely within the competence of the four of us. As our work here progresses I hope that all of us will have suggestions as to how we might promote the search for the solution of these problems.

Perhaps it would be well if each of us would in turn give a similar indication of his country's views. Then we can quickly see the scope of the matters which it might be useful to discuss here and arrange our time accordingly.

Let me repeat. I trust that we are not here merely to catalogue our differences. We are not here to repeat the same dreary exercises that have characterized most of our negotiations of the past ten years. We are here in response to the peaceful aspirations of mankind to start the kind of discussions which will inject a new spirit into our diplomacy; and to launch fresh negotiations under conditions of good augury.

In that way, and perhaps only in that way, can our meeting, necessarily brief, serve to generate and put in motion the new forces needed to set us truly on the path to peace. For this I am sure all humanity will devoutly pray.

165   ¶ Remarks at the Research Reactor Building, Palais des Nations, Geneva. *July* 20, 1955

I AM very grateful to the experts in charge of this building for conducting me through the reactor building and showing me so many of the working controls and operations.

Of course, I am very pleased that our country is able here to establish this reactor to help the scientists of the world to make progress along the lines of peaceful use of the atomic energy science, for the welfare of mankind.

In the United States we have so far made agreements with 24 different nations for the use of this same type of research reactor. There are students from 19 different countries going to school in the United States, learning about the technology that applies here—and you can see how necessary that is, just by looking around.

There are students from 32 countries undertaking to learn about the use of radio isotopes, and so on. So all in all this business is proceeding, and we are very pleased to have a part in it. We have set aside 200 kilograms of fissionable material so far to assist in the effort.

I am very hopeful that more than governments will get interested in this project. I hope that private business and professional men throughout the world will take an interest, and provide an incentive in finding new ways that this new science can be used.

In the meantime, I hope that everybody who gets a chance to see this one, will learn that there are really many, many ways in which atomic science can be used for the benefit of mankind and not destruction.

Thank you very much.

NOTE: The President spoke at 3:20 p.m.

166 ¶ Statement on Disarmament Presented at the Geneva Conference. *July* 21, 1955

Mr. Chairman, Gentlemen:

Disarmament is one of the most important subjects on our agenda. It is also extremely difficult. In recent years the scientists have discovered methods of making weapons many, many times more destructive of opposing armed forces—but also of homes, and industries and lives—than ever known or even imagined before. These same scientific discoveries have made much more complex the problems of limitation and control and reduction of armament.

After our victory as Allies in World War II, my country rapidly disarmed. Within a few years our armament was at a very low level. Then events occurred beyond our borders which caused us to realize that we had disarmed too much. For our own security and to safeguard peace we needed greater strength. Therefore we proceeded to rearm and to associate with others in a partnership for peace and for mutual security.

The American people are determined to maintain and if necessary increase this armed strength for as long a period as is necessary to safeguard peace and to maintain our security.

But we know that a mutually dependable system for less armament on the part of all nations would be a better way to safeguard peace and to maintain our security.

It would ease the fears of war in the anxious hearts of people everywhere. It would lighten the burdens upon the backs of the people. It would make it possible for every nation, great and small, developed and less developed, to advance the standards of living of its people, to attain better food, and clothing, and shelter, more of education and larger enjoyment of life.

Therefore the United States government is prepared to enter into a sound and reliable agreement making possible the reduction of armament. I have directed that an intensive and thorough study of this subject be made within our own government. From these studies, which are continuing, a very important principle is emerging to which I referred in my opening statement on Monday.

No sound and reliable agreement can be made unless it is completely covered by an inspection and reporting system adequate to support every portion of the agreement.

The lessons of history teach us that disarmament agreements without adequate reciprocal inspection increase the dangers of war and do not brighten the prospects of peace.

Thus it is my view that the priority attention of our combined study of disarmament should be upon the subject of inspection and reporting.

Questions suggest themselves.

How effective an inspection system can be designed which would be mutually and reciprocally acceptable within our countries and the other nations of the world? How would such a system operate? What could it accomplish?

Is certainty against surprise aggression attainable by inspection? Could violations be discovered promptly and effectively counteracted?

We have not as yet been able to discover any scientific or other inspection method which would make certain of the elimination of nuclear weapons. So far as we are aware no other nation has made such a discovery.   Our study of this problem is continuing. We have not as yet been able to discover any accounting or other inspection method of being certain of the true budgetary facts of total expenditures for armament.   Our study of this problem is continuing.   We by no means exclude the possibility of finding useful checks in these fields.

As you can see from these statements, it is our impression that many past proposals of disarmament are more sweeping than can be insured by effective inspection.

Gentlemen, since I have been working on this memorandum to present to this Conference, I have been searching my heart and mind for something that I could say here that could convince everyone of the great sincerity of the United States in approaching this problem of disarmament.

I should address myself for a moment principally to the Delegates from the Soviet Union, because our two great countries admittedly possess new and terrible weapons in quantities which do give rise in other parts of the world, or reciprocally, to the fears and dangers of surprise attack.

I propose, therefore, that we take a practical step, that we begin an arrangement, very quickly, as between ourselves—immediately.   These steps would include:

To give to each other a complete blueprint of our military establishments, from beginning to end, from one end of our countries to the other; lay out the establishments and provide the blueprints to each other.

Next, to provide within our countries facilities for aerial photography to the other country—we to provide you the facilities within our country, ample facilities for aerial reconnaissance, where you can make all the pictures you choose and take them to your own country to study, you to provide exactly the same facilities for us and we to make these examinations, and by this step to convince the world that we are providing as between ourselves against the possibility of great surprise attack, thus lessening danger and relaxing tension.   Likewise we will make more easily attainable a comprehensive and effective system of inspection and disarmament, because what I propose, I assure you, would be but a beginning.

Now from my statements I believe you will anticipate my suggestion.   It is that we instruct our representatives in the Subcommittee on Disarmament in discharge of their mandate from the United Nations to give priority effort to the study of inspection and reporting.   Such a study could well include a step by step testing of inspection and reporting methods.

The United States is ready to proceed in the study and testing of a reliable system of inspections and reporting, and when that system is proved, then to reduce armaments with all others to the extent that the system will provide assured results.

The successful working out of such a system would do much to develop the mutual confidence which will open wide the avenues of progress for all our peoples.

The quest for peace is the statesman's most exacting duty. Security of the nation entrusted to his care is his greatest responsibility.   Practical progress to lasting peace is his fondest hope. Yet in pursuit of his hope he must not betray the trust placed in him as guardian of the people's security.   A sound peace—with security, justice, wellbeing, and freedom for the people of the world—*can* be achieved, but only by patiently and thoughtfully following a hard and sure and tested road.

NOTE: The President's opening words "Mr. Chairman" referred to Nikolai Bulganin, Chairman, Coun- cil of Ministers, U.S.S.R., who served as chairman at this meeting.

167   ¶ Statement on East-West Contacts Delivered at the Geneva Conference.
July 22, 1955

ACCORDING to the adopted agenda, today we meet to discuss methods of normalizing and increasing the contacts between our nations in many fields. I am heartened by the deep interest in this question, which interest implies a common purpose to understand each other better. Unfortunately there exist unnecessary restrictions on the flow between us of ideas, of things and of people.

Like other questions we have considered during the past four days, this one cannot be considered independently or in isolation. All are related by their direct importance to the general objective of lessening world fears and tensions.

To help achieve the goal of peace based on justice and right and mutual understanding, there are certain concrete steps that could be taken:

(1) To lower the barriers which now impede the interchange of information and ideas between our peoples.

(2) To lower the barriers which now impede the opportunities of people to travel anywhere in the world for peaceful, friendly purposes, so that all will have a chance to know each other face-to-face.

(3) To create conditions which will encourage nations to increase the exchange of peaceful goods throughout the world.

Success in these endeavors should improve the conditions of life for all our citizens and elsewhere in the world. By helping eliminate poverty and ignorance, we can take another step in progress toward peace.

Restrictions on communications of all kinds, including radio and travel, existing in extreme form in some places, have operated as causes of mutual distrust. In America, the fervent belief in freedom of thought, of expression, and of movement is a vital part of our heritage. Yet during these past ten years even we have felt compelled, in the protection of our own interests, to place some restrictions upon the movement of persons and communications across our national frontiers.

This conference has the opportunity, I believe, to initiate concrete steps to permit the breaking down of both mild and severe barriers to mutual understanding and trust.

Now I should like to turn to the question of trade. I assume that each of us here is dedicated to the improvement of the conditions of life of our own citizens. Trade in peaceful goods is an important factor in achieving this goal. If trade is to reach its maximum capability in this regard, it must be both voluminous and world-wide.

The United Nations has properly been concerned in making available to the people of the under-developed areas modern technology and managerial abilities, as well as capital and credit. My country not only supports these efforts, but has undertaken parallel projects outside the United Nations.

In this connection the new atomic science possesses a tremendous potential for helping raise the standards of living and providing greater opportunity for all the world. World-wide interest in overcoming poverty and ignorance is growing by leaps and bounds, and each of the great nations should do its utmost to assist in this development. As a result new desires, new requirements, new aspirations are emerging almost everywhere as man climbs the upward path of his destiny. Most encouraging of all is the evidence that after centuries of fatalism and resignation, the hopeless of the world are beginning to hope.

But regardless of the results achieved through the United Nations effort or the individual efforts of helpful nations, trade remains the indispensable arterial system of a flourishing world prosperity.

If we could create conditions in which unnecessary restrictions on trade would be progressively eliminated and under which there would be free and friendly exchange of ideas and of people, we should have done much to chart the paths toward the objectives we commonly seek.

By working together toward all these goals, we can do much to transform this century of recurring conflict into a century of enduring and invigorating peace. This, I assure you, the United States of America devoutly desires—as I know all of us do.

168 ¶ Memorandum to Federal Agencies on the United Fund and Community Chest Campaigns. *July* 22, 1955

Memorandum for the Heads of Executive Departments and Agencies:

This fall over 21,000 health, welfare and recreation organizations will combine their appeals in a United Fund or Community Chest campaign in each of 1900 communities across the country. Many campaigns will include the needs of such national agencies as the Red Cross, USO, and those fighting heart disease, cancer, polio, tuberculosis, cerebral palsy and other health problems. Such campaigns will seek substantially more than the $302,500,-000 raised last year.

The total will be considerably more than will be raised by all the other health and welfare appeals in the country combined. Clearly then, this fund raising effort is the most important in which any of us will be asked to participate during the ensuing year.

The campaigns will be carried on during the period from Labor Day to Thanksgiving. I am asking all branches of the Federal Government, as well as all citizens and organizations, to concentrate their effort and support on the cause during that period.

To assure the leaders of United Community Campaigns of America, representing local Community Chests and United Funds, of the cooperation of the Federal Government, I have approved the appointment of the Honorable George M. Humphrey, Secretary of the Treasury, as Vice Chairman for the Federal Government of United Community Campaigns.

I am confident that you will extend the full cooperation of your Department in each community throughout the United States and its territories and possessions where it conducts its operations. Such cooperation should include the effective solicitation of all employees, the acceptance of equitable unit goals, and the setting up of an adequate collection method for the convenience of those who wish to make contributions on an installment basis.

It is my hope that all employees will give generously—not because they must, but because they may—keeping in mind the wide variety and large number of organizations they will be supporting through their gifts to this single appeal.

Dwight D. Eisenhower

NOTE: This memorandum was released at Geneva.

169   ¶ Letter to Prime Minister Maung Nu Concerning the Gift of the Burmese People. *July 22, 1955*

Dear Mr. Prime Minister:

I know that you will be personally interested in the arrangements I have made for the use of the generous gift from the people and Government of the Union of Burma which you entrusted to me during your recent visit.

As you requested, the money will be used for the benefit of the children of those members of the United States armed forces who lost their lives or were incapacitated in the Burma campaign.   To that end, I have directed that the fund be assigned in three equal portions to the American Legion, the Veterans of Foreign Wars, and AMVETS.   Each of these three prominent veterans organizations has been carrying on worthy programs of assistance to the children of veterans of the armed services of the United States. Each of them, under the terms of its charter, will be able to establish a separate fund to achieve the purpose you indicated. The gift of the Union of Burma will thus strengthen and help to perpetuate the beneficial activities of those organizations.

I wish again to express my appreciation and that of the people of the United States for this heart-warming expression of the close friendship and community of interests that exist between our two countries.

Sincerely,

DWIGHT D. EISENHOWER

NOTE: This letter was released at Geneva. The text of the Prime Minister's letter of June 29, 1955, which accompanied the gift, follows:

My dear Mr. President,

The people and Government of the Union of Burma remember with gratitude the valuable contribution made by the United States towards the liberation of their country from the Japanese militarist yoke. In particular they recall the heroic sacrifices made by the gallant members of the United States Armed Forces who took part in the liberation campaign.

As a token of our appreciation of the sacrifices made by these gallant men, I would ask you to accept this cheque for five thousand dollars ($5,000.00), the money to be used in some appropriate manner for the benefit of the children of those who lost their lives or were incapacitated in the Burma campaign.

Yours sincerely,

MAUNG NU

170 ¶ Closing Statement at the Final Meeting of the Heads of Government Conference at Geneva. *July 23, 1955*

Mr. Chairman, Gentlemen:

I welcome and warmly reciprocate the spirit of friendliness and good intent that have characterized the statements of the two preceding speakers. But I do hope that my silence respecting certain of the statements made by the immediately preceding speaker will not by any means be interpreted as acquiescence on my part—far from it.

But it has seemed to me that in the closing minutes of this conference there is no necessity for me to announce to this conference and to the world the United States position on the important questions we have discussed. These I hope and believe have already been made clear. Therefore it has not seemed particularly fitting once more to recite them in detail. Rather I content myself with some reflections on our work of the past week and an expression of some hopes for the future.

This has been an historic meeting. It has been on the whole a good week. But only history will tell the true worth and real values of our session together. The follow-through from this beginning by our respective Governments will be decisive in the measure of this Conference.

We have talked over plainly a number of the most difficult and perplexing questions affecting our several peoples and indeed the peoples of the entire world.

We did not come here to reach final solutions. We came to see if we might together find the path that would lead to solutions and would brighten the prospects of world peace.

In this final hour of our assembly, it is my judgment that the prospects of a lasting peace with justice, well-being, and broader freedom, are brighter. The dangers of the overwhelming tragedy of modern war are less.

The work of our Foreign Ministers as they strive to implement our directives will be of great importance, perhaps of even more than what we have done here. Theirs is the task, reflecting the substantive policies of their Governments, to reach agreement on courses of action which we here could discuss only in broad terms. I know we all wish them well.

I trust we will all support the necessary adjustments which they may find our Governments must make if we are to resolve our differences in these matters.

If our peoples, in the months and years ahead, broaden their knowledge and their understanding of each other, as we, during this week, have broadened our knowledge of each other, further agreement between our Governments may be facilitated. May this occur in a spirit of justice. May it result in improved well-being, greater freedom, and less of fear or suffering or distress for mankind. May it be marked by more of good will among men. These days will then indeed be ever remembered.

I came to Geneva because I believe mankind longs for freedom from war and rumors of war. I came here because of my lasting faith in the decent instincts and good sense of the people who populate this world of ours. I shall return home tonight with these convictions unshaken, and with the prayer that the hope of mankind will one day be realized.

NOTE: The President's opening words "Mr. Chairman" referred to Premier Edgar Faure of France who served as chairman at this meeting.

171 ¶ Remarks on Leaving Geneva. *July 23, 1955*

Ladies and gentlemen:

As I leave Geneva, I want most of all, in saying goodbye, to thank the Mayor of this City, and each of its citizens who have been so cordial in the welcome they have extended to the American delegation.

My thanks of course include also the government—its President, all its officials, and of course to include the Governor of this Canton.

It has been a very great privilege to be among you and we will carry away many happy memories of your beautiful scenery and your very warm spirit of welcome and hospitality towards us.

I hope, indeed, that maybe some day I shall come back here again, when I am less busy and when I can see more of the people and less of the inner side of council chambers.

Goodbye and good luck to each of you.

NOTE: The president spoke at the airport just before boarding the Columbine to return to Washington.

172 ¶ Statement by the President Upon Signing Bill Concerning Mineral Claims Filed on Public Lands. *July 23, 1955*

I HAVE TODAY approved H.R. 5891. This legislation strongly endorsed by both Secretary of the Interior McKay and Secretary of Agriculture Benson, is one of the most important conservation measures affecting public lands that has been enacted in many years.

In recent years thousands of mining claims have been filed on public lands every year, not for bona fide mining purposes but for the purpose of obtaining claim or title to valuable timber, summer home sites, or grazing land and water. H.R. 5891 will put a stop to such practices. In doing so it will make possible sound management of the timber resources of our public lands. At the same time the legislation will greatly improve the position of the bona fide miner by enabling him to increase his valuable contribution to the development of the Nation's mineral resources.

The legislation represents a great forward step in our conservation program.

NOTE: As enacted, H.R. 5891 is Public Law 167, 84th Congress (69 Stat. 367).

173 ¶ Remarks at Washington National Airport on Returning From Geneva. *July 24, 1955*

Ladies and Gentlemen:

After the hard week that I have been through it's very heartwarming to have such a reception as this as I come back to our Capital City.

Just what will be the result of this conference, of course, no one knows but the coming months will tell much. But in the meantime, we do know that new contacts have been established and there is evidence of a new friendliness in the world. For my part, if there is one man I would single out as deserving the thanks of the American people, it would be Foster Dulles, a man who represents us in every kind of conference with the greatest of dignity and the greatest of skill. I am sorry he is not here this morning— his plane seems to be a little slower than mine and so he is not here at this moment.

Again thanks to all of you for coming out, distinguished citizens and everybody else. It's really great to be home. Thank you.

174 ¶ White House Statement Following Bipartisan Meeting on the Geneva Conference. *July* 25, 1955

THE PRESIDENT and the Secretary of State in their meeting today with the Legislative Leaders of both parties outlined the discussions at the Geneva Conference.

The President assured the leaders that no secret agreements had been made nor had any private papers been initialled during the Conference.

The President expressed the belief that the outstanding feature of the meeting was the apparently sincere desire expressed by the Soviet Delegation to discuss world problems in the future in an atmosphere of friendliness and a willingness to sit down together to work out differences. The President added that this, of course, is a hopeful development but quite naturally, does not, of itself, warrant any relaxation of the mutual security measures we and our allies of the free world are now pursuing.

The Secretary of State then gave a detailed presentation of the day-to-day discussions at the Geneva Conference and an analysis of the final agreed directive.

175   ¶ Radio and Television Address to the
American People on the Geneva Conference.
July 25, 1955

[Delivered from the President's Office at 10:30 p.m.]

Good evening friends:

Secretary Dulles and I, with our associates, went to the Big
Four Conference at Geneva resolved to represent as accurately as
we could the aspirations of the American people for peace and
the principles upon which this country believes that peace should
be based.

In this task we had the bi-partisan, indeed almost the unanimous, support of the Congress.   This fact greatly strengthened
our hand throughout the negotiations.   Our grateful thanks go
out to all your Senators and your Congressmen in the United
States Congress.   Aside from this, we had, during the past week,
thousands of telegrams of encouragement and support from you
as individuals.   Along with these came similar telegrams from
great organizations, church organizations, business and great
labor organizations.

All of these combined served to make us feel that possibly we
were faithfully representing the views that you would have us
represent.   Now peace—the pursuit of peace—involves many
perplexing questions.   For example:

Justice to all nations, great and small;

Freedom and security for all these nations;

The prosperity of their several economies and a rising standard
of living in the world;

Finally, opportunity for all of us to live in peace and in security.

Now, naturally, in the study of such questions as these, we don't
proceed recklessly.   We must go prudently and cautiously—both
in reaching conclusions and in subsequent action.   We cannot
afford to be negligent or complacent.   But, we must be hopeful.

We must have faith in ourselves and in the justice of our cause. If we don't do this, we will allow our own pessimism and our own lack of faith to defeat the noblest purposes that we can pursue.

Now, because of the vital significance of all these subjects, they will be exhaustively surveyed by our government over a period of many weeks. Tonight the most that I can give to you are a few personal impressions and opinions that may have some interest for you and certainly have some bearing on the outcome and on the progress of those negotiations.

Of course, an interesting subject that could be taken up, had I the time, would be the personalities of the several delegations, the relationship or apparent relationships of one to the other— the principal considerations that seem to motivate them. These would all have a bearing on this problem. But I forego them and take up instead just two general opinions in which I am sure every American shares:

The first of these, that we must never be deluded into believing that one week of friendly, even fruitful, negotiation can wholly eliminate a problem arising out of the wide gulf that separates, so far, East and West. A gulf as wide and deep as the difference between individual liberty and regimentation, as wide and deep as the gulf that lies between the concept of man made in the image of his God and the concept of man as a mere instrument of the State. Now, if we think of those things we are apt to be possibly discouraged.

But I was also profoundly impressed with the need for all of us to avoid discouragement merely because our own proposals, our own approaches, and our own beliefs are not always immediately accepted by the other side.

On the night I left for Geneva, I appeared before the television to explain to you what we were seeking. I told you that we were going primarily to attempt to change the spirit in which these great negotiations and conferences were held. A transcript was made of that talk, and I should like now to read you one paragraph from it.

This is what I said with respect to our purpose: "We realize that one ingredient has been missing from all past conferences. This is an honest intent to conciliate, to understand, to be tolerant, to try to see the other fellow's viewpoint as well as we see our own. I say to you if we can change the spirit in which these conferences are conducted, we will have taken the greatest step toward peace, toward future prosperity and tranquility that has ever been taken in all the history of mankind."

During last week in formal conferences, and in personal visits, these purposes have been pursued. So now there exists a better understanding, a closer unity among the nations of NATO.

There seems to be a growing realization by all that nuclear warfare, pursued to the ultimate, could be practically race suicide.

There is a realization that negotiations can be conducted without propaganda and threats and invective.

Finally, there is a sharp realization by the world that the United States will go to any length consistent with our concepts of decency and justice and right to attain peace. For this purpose, we will work cooperatively with the Soviets and any other people as long as there is sincerity of purpose and a genuine desire to go ahead.

In the course of carrying on these discussions there were a number of specific proposals, some of which were items on the official agenda. That agenda contained German reunification and European security, disarmament and increased contacts of all kinds between the East and the West.

Most of these conference meetings were given wide publicity and even some of the specific suggestions made in those conferences likewise were publicized. In any event, I can assure you of one thing:

There were no secret agreements made, either understood agreements or written ones. Everything is put before you on the record.

Outside of these conference meetings there were numerous unofficial meetings—conversations with important members of the other delegations and, of course, very specifically with the Soviet delegation.

In these conversations a number of subjects were discussed and among them the Secretary of State and I specifically brought up, more than once, American convictions and American beliefs and American concern about such questions as the satellites of Eastern Europe and the activities of international Communism. We made crystal clear what were American beliefs about such matters as these.

Now to take up for a moment the items on the official agenda.

Probably no question caused us as much trouble as that of German reunification and European security. At first we thought that these could be dealt with separately, but the American delegation concluded that they had to be dealt with as one subject. We held that Germany should be reunited under a government freely chosen by themselves, and under conditions that would provide security both for nations of the East and for nations of the West—in fact in a framework that provided European security.

In the matter of disarmament, the American government believes that an effective disarmament system can be reached only if at its base there is an effective reciprocal inspection and overall supervision system, one in which we can have confidence and each side can know that the other side is carrying out his commitments. Now because of this belief, we joined with the French and the British in making several proposals. Some were global, some were local, some were sort of budgetary in character. But all were in furtherance of this one single objective, that is, to make inspection the basis of disarmament proposals.

One proposal suggested aerial photography, as between the Soviets and ourselves by unarmed peaceful planes, and to make this inspection just as thorough as this kind of reconnaissance can do. The principal purpose, of course, is to convince every one of Western sincerity in seeking peace. But another idea was this:

if we could go ahead and establish this kind of an inspection as initiation of an inspection system we could possibly develop it into a broader one, and eventually build on it an effective and durable disarmament system.

In the matter of increasing contacts, many items were discussed. We talked about a freer flow of news across the curtains of all kinds. We talked about the circulation of books and particularly we talked about peaceful trade. But the subject that took most of our attention in this regard was the possibility of increased visits by the citizens of one country into the territory of another, doing this in such a way as to give each the fullest possible opportunity to learn about the people of the other nation. In this particular subject there was the greatest possible degree of agreement. As a matter of fact, it was agreement often repeated and enthusiastically supported by the words of the members of each side.

As a matter of fact, each side assured the other earnestly and— often that it intended to pursue a new spirit of conciliation and cooperation in its contacts with the other. Now, of course, we are profoundly hopeful that these assurances will be faithfully carried out.

One evidence as to these assurances will, of course, be available soon in the language and the terminology in which we will find speeches and diplomatic exchanges couched. But the acid test should begin next October because then the next meeting occurs. It will be a meeting of the Foreign Ministers. Its principal purpose will be to take the conclusions of this conference as to the subjects to be discussed there and the general proceedings to be observed in translating those generalities that we talked about into actual, specific agreements. Then is when real conciliation and some giving on each side will be definitely necessary.

Now, for myself, I do not belittle the obstacles lying ahead on the road to a secure and just peace. By no means do I underestimate the long and exhausting work that will be necessary before real results are achieved. I do not blink the fact that all of us must continue to sacrifice for what we believe to be best for the safety of ourselves and for the preservation of the things in which we believe.

But I do know that the people of the world want peace. Moreover, every other individual who was at Geneva likewise felt this longing of mankind. So, there is great pressure to advance constructively, not merely to reenact the dreary performances, the negative performances of the past.

We, all of us, individually and as a people now have possibly the most difficult assignment of our nation's history. Likewise, we have the most shining opportunity ever possessed by Americans. May these truths inspire, never dismay us.

I believe that only with prayerful patience, intelligence, courage and tolerance, never forgetting vigilance and prudence, can we keep alive the spark ignited at Geneva. But if we are successful in this, then we will make constantly brighter the lamp that will one day guide us to our goal—a just and lasting peace.

Thank you. Good night to each of you.

176 ¶ The President's News Conference of *July* 27, 1955.

THE PRESIDENT. Good morning. Please sit down.

I see you haven't got the air conditioning machinery yet. [*Laughter*]

I think that it is needless for me to take too much time in the attempt to emphasize the importance I attach to the week through which we have just passed.

Some of you, of course, were in Geneva. You made your own conclusions as to the personalities that we met, the relationships between them, the degree of sincerity you attach to their words.

But one thing is indisputable. For one week of argument and debate that sometimes was, to say the least, intense, never once did we have a recurrence of the old method of merely talking to constituencies in terms of invective and personal abuse and nationalistic abuse. That in itself is a great gain and one that I hope we shall never lose; because certainly we are going to progress in things of the mind, in things involving policy, only if we discuss differences in objective terms, not in the terms that cause additional antagonism before you get down at all to the heart of the subject that is under discussion.

I don't mean to say that the week was one of such glowing promise that it offers almost a certainty of a new era starting now. I do say there was a beginning of this kind made, and if we are wise enough to do our part, it is just possible that something to the great benefit of man may eventuate.

Now, if I can go from great nationalistic subjects, public subjects, to something that concerns only me and my family: this may not be news, but I got home to be greeted by my daughter-in-law with the statement that if all goes well, I will be a grandfather for the fourth time next Christmas—[*applause*]—which, of course, was a happy ending to the week.

We will go to questions.

Q. Merriman Smith, United Press: Mr. President, in connection with you disarmament proposal, would you extend the privilege of aerial reconnaissance to atomic energy installations?

THE PRESIDENT. Well, I wouldn't want now to go into the complete details that would have to be worked out by professionals and technicians meeting to form the plan that would give effect to the general proposal I made.

I would say this: that everything, the blueprint of which I spoke, the layout of your military establishments, in my opinion, should be complete.

This would not necessarily involve your manufacturing and production plants; but I would certainly, under the scheme I was thinking of, place a minimum of prohibited areas. I think that I would allow these planes, properly inspected, peaceful planes, to fly over any particular area of either country that they wanted to, because only in this way could you convince them that there wasn't something over there that maybe was, by surprise, ready to attack them, you see.

Q. Robert E. Clark, International News Service: Mr. President, can you tell us if you see anything improper in Secretary Talbott's business activities and how you feel about his remaining on as Secretary of the Air Force?

[*Chorus of "Couldn't hear it"*]

THE PRESIDENT. This was a question about Secretary Talbott and the investigation that he is undergoing before the committee of Congress.

I have no objection to answering this at this moment as far as I am able. But I do warn you that it will take me a little bit of time.

First, I do not believe that any man can properly hold public office merely because he is not guilty of any illegal act; and, of course, in this case there is no charge of any illegal act.

But I believe it was in or somewhere about the end of October, early November, of 1952, I tried to explain my conception of what a public servant owed to the Government, to the people— that his actions had to be impeccable, both from the standpoint of law and from the standpoint of ethics.

So what is now involved is, was a proper standard of ethics violated?

This comes, I assume, to this particular point: was an office used improperly or was a man in an office merely trying to use his own personal influence completely divorced from his office? I assume that is the issue that the committee of Congress is now looking into.

Now, I should like to make one thing clear: those parts of Secretary Talbott's official duties with which I have come in contact have been almost brilliantly performed.

He has done, by and large, and so far as I know of these activities, exactly what I believe a Secretary of one of the armed services should do.

I suppose the world knows that for some years he has been a personal friend.

Nevertheless, my feeling at this moment, in a way, is of a bit of suspended animation. I am going to read the complete record of everything that I can find on this myself, and I will have to make final decision on the basis of the ethics involved.

Now, I would not take any action while this investigation is going on because, first of all, the investigation should be conducted while he is a public servant, and he has a perfect right to be heard in every bit of defense he can bring forward.

As far as I am concerned then, the matter is temporarily in abeyance, but it is going to be handled by myself personally.

I do want to make clear again that when I came back and heard about this, no one has intimated any suggestion of fraud or of wrongdoing in the sense of law. That is clearly out of the question.

Q. Edward Milne, Providence Journal-Bulletin: Mr. President, as a matter of principle, and not specifically in Mr. Talbott's case, because we don't yet have all the facts, how do you distinguish the office from the man in the office? What is that fine line? How do you distinguish?

THE PRESIDENT. As a matter of fact, I really am not prepared to talk about that in any length. It is a difficult one. For myself, I think the only way for a public servant is to avoid any indiscretion that even leans in that way or even gives the appearance that an office might be used. But I do want in this case to be completely just and see the whole record.

Q. Frank van der Linden, Charlotte Observer: Mr. President, the Senate Judiciary Committee yesterday indefinitely deferred a vote on the confirmation of Simon Sobeloff, your Solicitor General, to the Fourth Circuit Court of Appeals.

I would like to ask whether you are displeased with that delay, and if that should go through the recess of Congress, do you plan to send up a recess appointment?

THE PRESIDENT. Well, you give me news; I didn't know this.

Now, as you know, Mr. Sobeloff was appointed from a judge-ship to the office of Solicitor General.

In that office, I have had a number of contacts with him, and have been impressed with what I thought was his judicial type of mind. I thought he was an excellent appointment to the court.

Now, I am not going to challenge, by implication or indirection or any other way, the right of the Senate to make its thorough investigation through its committees of any nominee I send up there for any office.

I don't know what it is about, so I can't comment any further except to say I thought it was an excellent appointment.

Q. Sarah McClendon, El Paso Times: Sir, there is a law on the books that says Brigadier General W. W. White, who is Staff Director for Petroleum Logistics, can keep on active duty in his job and, at the same time, draw a salary as former vice president of Esso Export Corporation from his old corporation.

I wondered what you think about the administration of this law that permits a high-ranking officer to be recalled to active duty and serve over a subject that is the same as his former corporation.

THE PRESIDENT. I can't possibly comment on that one until I see the case. This is the first time I ever knew there was a special law applying to a special person. I would like to look that up. [*Addresses Mr. Hagerty*] Will you remember?

Q. William S. White, New York Times: Mr. President, would you care to make any forecast to us of the possibility of a ministerial level meeting with the Chinese in light of what the Secretary of State said yesterday?

THE PRESIDENT. Well, I couldn't guess at this moment as to a meeting at the ministerial level.

I think you know the record of this whole project up to this moment. I read this morning Secretary Dulles' statement, so to my knowledge it is exactly accurate all the way through, what has come about, why we did raise this level of meeting, and sent Mr. Johnson to Geneva to carry it out.

Now, what will come from there, what the next step will be, I am not quite sure.

Q. Clark R. Mollenhoff, Des Moines Register and Tribune: Mr. President, there has been testimony of the SEC Chairman that Sherman Adams intervened before the SEC, which was a quasi-judicial body. Testimony was given by the Chairman on that score. The Democrats are contending that there was something improper in intervening with any quasi-judicial body.

I wondered if you looked into that and you have any comment you would like to make about it.

THE PRESIDENT. I looked into it only to this extent: I am sure that the head of the Commission has given the entire story. I understand he is back before the committee, and certainly if he has omitted any details, he should give them now.

I believe that Governor Adams has informed the Senate committee that he hasn't a single detail to add; that the story has been told and that is all there is to it.

Q. Garnett D. Horner, Washington Evening Star: In connection with the Dixon-Yates matter, and in view of the fact that the Senate Investigation Subcommittee recently brought out for the first time the part played in initiating the Dixon-Yates contract by Adolphe Wenzell of the First Boston Corporation, which corporation later became the financing agent for Dixon-Yates, in view of all of that, do you believe your directions last summer for disclosure of the complete record in the case were carried out by the agencies concerned?

THE PRESIDENT. Well, I didn't know that anyone had alleged that he was the initiator because no such statement has ever been made to me.

But what I have done is this: I have gotten back Mr. Dodge who was Director of the Budget when all this was done, when the 1954, I believe, policy on this whole proposition was made, and he is going down before one of the committees. Isn't that correct?

Mr. Hagerty: Yes, sir.

THE PRESIDENT. He is going down before one of the committees with instructions to do this: to tell every possible item that has anything whatsoever to bear on Dixon-Yates, and see whether we can get the whole list of information properly coordinated and placed before the people that are investigating it.

Q. Edward P. Morgan, American Broadcasting Company: Mr. President, may we go back to the summit for a moment? Now that one of our main objectives at Geneva seems to be in the process of being achieved, namely the lessening of tensions, is there a danger that they may sag so far that they may trip our defenses, so to speak, and if so, do you have some specific proposals by which we might avoid them?

THE PRESIDENT. Well, there may be some little fear of that, but I would think that as long as the United States has such people as Secretaries Dulles and Wilson, people like Admiral Radford and our current Chiefs of Staff, people to keep us alert to all these things, I would doubt that, in fact, we would as a Government sag too far in the direction that you indicate.

Now, your question therefore must be directed towards peoples' thinking, just, "Well, we say we had a nice meeting," and so you forget that item to turn your mind to something else.

I would say scarcely so. I have a number of responses to the talk I made the other evening, and it is astonishing how many agree that what we have to do is to steer the course between never being negative but never being complacent. They agree to that.

It is a difficult thing. And you have to be watchful. But I don't believe that as long as we have people that are so ready to call our attention to those things and things of that nature we need fear much.

Q. Mrs. May Craig, Maine Papers: Mr. President, in relation to the talks with the Red Chinese in Geneva next week, Mr. Dulles said yesterday that in the talks we would make no arrangements which would prejudice the rights of the Nationalist Chinese.

My question is, how can we make any arrangements in the absence of the Nationalist Chinese?

THE PRESIDENT. Well, one of the biggest causes for this meeting is our prisoners and civilians illegally held in China. Certainly we claim that all of our prisoners captured in uniform were illegally held and only four of those have been released. There were fifteen.

The first arrangement we are concerned about is how to get them back. That doesn't involve in any respect the Nationalist Chinese.

Q. Mrs. Craig: However, sir, Mr. Dulles left the door open for almost any other kind of a discussion.

THE PRESIDENT. Well, we will have to learn what it is they want to discuss, just exactly as we learned at Geneva many, many things that others wanted to discuss there, but we said only those things which we, as the representatives of four governments are competent to discuss.

We couldn't determine the fate of an Arab nation or an African nation or a South American or anything else. We weren't there for that purpose.

We must find out, though, what they want to talk about. Then there would have to be a next advance; and it might be, as someone else suggested, eventually you have to go to a ministerial level of meeting to get these straightened out.

I wouldn't know.

Q. Mrs. Craig: Sir, the context of his statement on arrangements was in relation to the Formosa area and not in relation to the airmen.

THE PRESIDENT. Mrs. Craig, I just will have to refer you back to the statement. You were apparently trying to interpret exactly what he meant, and you had better ask him.

Q. Lloyd M. Schwartz, Fairchild Publications: Mr. President, I believe you had a request from the copper industry to invoke the Taft-Hartley cooling-off injunction to put an end to the strike. I wondered if you were considering such action?

THE PRESIDENT. Certain telegrams on this subject came in, and they were immediately referred to the Secretary of Labor.

Of course, the right to bring that up involves, of course, always the existence or threatened existence of a national emergency, though it will take real study to determine what the situation is.

Q. Donald J. Gonzales, United Press: Did you discuss at Geneva with Soviet leaders the possibility of your visiting Russia or their coming to the United States, either socially or at an official level?

THE PRESIDENT. Well, as you know, on the agenda was the subject of liberalizing contacts. We talked a very great deal, not only about officials visiting back and forth, but increasing opportunities for citizens of each country to go more freely within the other to learn for themselves what their opposite numbers in the other country looked like, how they felt and how they lived.

In the very many personal conversations I had with these people, of course, these things never were made in forms of proposals. But opportunities were discussed in a general way—in arranging, let us say—throughout the whole echelons of Government and everything else. But they were never placed in the forms of proposals or definite suggestions.

Q. John Herling, Editors Syndicate: Mr. President, Secretary of Labor Mitchell says that he is recommending to you that you sign the dollar minimum wage which has been passed by both House and Senate.

Do you plan to accept his recommendations, sir?

THE PRESIDENT. I can't say for the moment, because he hasn't been in yet to see me. When he comes in to see me, why, I will make up my mind what to do; but he hasn't been in yet.

Q. Fletcher Knebel, Cowles Publications: Mr. President, you were quoted by congressional sources as having told the Monday meeting that Premier Bulganin jokingly said he hoped you would run again; is that correct? [*Laughter*]

THE PRESIDENT. I don't think I said Premier Bulganin. I said one of my Russian associates. [*Laughter*]

Q. Alan S. Emory, Watertown Times: Sir, there are two interpretations in Congress being placed on your recommendation for 35,000 additional public housing units to be constructed in the law now before the House. One is that these would be entirely new public housing starts. The other is that these would be, as Congress approved last year, replacement units for families made homeless as a result of urban redevelopment or slum clearance projects.

Could you tell us which one is correct, sir?

THE PRESIDENT. Always, one of the special definite purposes of public housing programs was to provide places for those people who were dispossessed by reason of urban redevelopment and slum clearance. I believe, and I say this with some trepidation because my memory is not always correct, I believe that it was in last year's bill that they limited it to that use.

To my mind, the limitation is unnecessary; but I don't know what is the status of the thing before Congress at this moment.

Q. Edward T. Folliard, Washington Post and Times Herald: Mr. President, while you have been away, the bus and trolley strike here has continued.

As I remember it, at the last press conference you suggested that both sides get around a table and try to thrash this thing out and reach a settlement. They haven't done so, and the prospect is that this strike will be on by the time you leave for Denver.

I wonder if you had any further suggestions?

THE PRESIDENT. I really haven't at this moment, Mr. Folliard, for the simple reason I hadn't thought about it since I came back, and no one has made any reports on it.

But I do hold to this: in the long run, the managerial and labor elements in our economy must find means of resolving their own differences or our form of economy and government becomes endangered.

You can have the services of mediators, you can have all sorts of things to protect yourself in the event of grave national emergency, but by and large we must depend upon the good sense of America to meet this type of problem, and I mean the good sense of the people engaged, or we are going to have much more difficulty than we have now.

Q. John Kenton, New York Journal of Commerce: Mr. President, if we may look ahead for the moment to the next Geneva conference beginning next month on atoms for peace, there was a press conference over at the Atomic Energy Commission about 2 weeks ago at which there seemed to be a little bit of confusion over two statements that you, Mr. President, had made at two different times.

One, that our attitude toward this conference was not that we were going into a contest, and the other that we were going to put our best foot forward.

Now, the point was made that the American manufacturing concerns that are going over there to exhibit in the trade fair at Geneva are certainly going over there with the intention of trying to outsell their competitors from other countries, and we never got the point completely cleared as to whether there were any wraps other than the Atomic Energy Law of 1954 on American commercial participation in the conference.

THE PRESIDENT. Well, it is a little difficult to address myself to a question I don't quite understand. [*Laughter*]

But I do say this: we are not going over there just to show that we are better than anyone else in the world in a certain line of scientific advancement.

We are going over there to help incite the interest of all the world in this new science and how it can be helpful to mankind.

I personally went to see this part of the exhibition that we have put over there.

I said we were going to put our best foot forward. If we are going to try to help people in this regard, we are certainly not going to keep two-thirds of our scientists and our industrialists and people working on it at home, and show only one-third of what we have done and what we believe are the opening vistas in this direction.

So I say we are going to do our very best.

But we didn't enter, didn't propose or go to this thing just with the idea of contesting or putting our affairs in comparison with somebody else's.

Q. Ray L. Scherer, National Broadcasting Company: Mr. President, how did you get along with Marshal Zhukov?

THE PRESIDENT. Well, excellently, of course, because—I must reinforce what I have said before.

In the personal contacts of this meeting I saw nothing that violated the strictest rules of good manners and deportment. Quite naturally, Marshal Zhukov and I had the common recollections of 6 months' cooperative work in Berlin, to say nothing of a common reminiscence of the final campaigns of World War II in Europe.

Now, on top of that, he wanted to tell me things about Russia, in general, or about the Soviet Union in general, about his own life, about what is happening there. He came to the first meeting—I believe we had two hours and a half together—and I told him I would regard it quite confidentially; it would never become a part of the official records, because he visited me personally. After all, he is a Marshal, and I happen to be head of a state.

He said, "You are perfectly free to tell any part of it." He didn't come to talk in deep secrecy.

But, in general, it was to impress upon me the deep desire of the Soviets for peace.

He went into many subjects. For example, their new concept of collective leadership; it was a very interesting thing, but it was, also, an hour's conversation. And you can see some evidence of its practice—you don't have just one figure coming to an international conference, you have three or four of them constantly conferring, and apparently producing a viewpoint for the world.

But there was nothing in it except, you might say, a personal and friendly exposition of the same things that we heard in the conference, but on a larger scale.

Q. Clark R. Mollenhoff, Des Moines Register and Tribune: I hate to go back to Dixon-Yates again, but there was one thing

I don't think was completely clear. There were some AEC officials, Mr. Fields and Mr. Cook, who testified that Mr. Wenzell's name was knowingly eliminated from the Dixon-Yates chronology; and, of course, they stated this was on the recommendation of the Bureau of the Budget.

I wondered if you knew anything of this, and if you did know of it, if you would like to comment on whether you thought it was important.

THE PRESIDENT. I don't intend to comment on it any more at all. I think I have given to this conference, time and again, the basic elements of this whole development, and everything that I could possibly be expected to know about it. I said Mr. Dodge, who initiated this whole thing, is going down before the committee to again begin the process of taking this thing from its inception and following it through until he turned over to Mr. Hughes; and I believe that Mr. Hughes is to be there if they want him again.

Now, they can tell the entire story, and I don't know exactly such details as that. How could I be expected to know? I never heard of it.

Q. William M. Blair, New York Times: Are you satisfied, sir, with the Reserve bill that Congress has sent to you?

THE PRESIDENT. No. At least there are one or two items that strike me as being rather thoughtlessly handled. But I haven't studied it in detail yet. I will have to look at it and I could comment on that maybe next week. I haven't studied it in detail, but I have heard of one item of differences in pay that seem incomprehensible to me.

Q. Joseph Chiang, Chinese News Service: Mr. President, do the United States Government agree to have two Chinas if they are sure there would be a peace in the world for a good while?

THE PRESIDENT. Did you say who agreed to that?

Q. Mr. Chiang: Do your Government agree to have a two Chinas——

THE PRESIDENT. The subject in that form has never been discussed that I know of, certainly I have never discussed the subject in that form with Secretary Dulles; but I don't see how it could be under present conditions.

Merriman Smith, United Press: Thank you, Mr. President.

NOTE: President Eisenhower's seventy-fourth news conference was held in the Executive Office Building from 10:31 to 11:03 o'clock on Wednesday morning, July 27, 1955. In attendance: 184.

177 ¶ Remarks at the Ceremony Marking the Issuance of the Atoms for Peace Stamp. *July* 28, 1955

Mr. Postmaster General, distinguished members of the diplomatic corps, my friends:

As the Postmaster General has said, we have here a stamp that looks to the future, and its design has followed that conception. Yet, it tends also to pose to us a question that is as old as history: Shall the inventiveness of man be used for good or for evil?

Every discovery we have made, even the use of fire to warm our bodies, to cook our food, has also been used as one of the devastating weapons of war to bring destruction to enemies. Every single thing that man has discovered can be used for good or for evil depending upon the purpose of man. This would seem to imply that man indeed has to look within himself before he can predict with any certainty, with any possibility of accuracy whatsoever, before he can determine what will be the final results of a great invention such as the discovery of nuclear fission and nuclear fusion.

The United States, as you well know, has been attempting to do its part in promoting the peaceful, the good uses of this new science. The Chairman of the Atomic Energy Commission has outlined some of them to you. And, I should like to go further and leave no stone unturned in order to discover new ways in which all of us nations that love peace can, without threat to anybody else, without fear for our own security, move forward in this field.

Now, because of this belief, because of this feeling, because of this hope, I call your attention to what I think is a fortunate feature in the design of this stamp. We have the world bound together by new forces, bound together by the natural forces of science, and of nature, not split by them.

I hope, I devoutly pray that this is an augury of what will occur in the future—that through these great benefits there will become so deeply impressed upon our minds the benefits that can come from this new science, that finally men will look within themselves and find the courage to reject the impulses of their own avarice, their own selfishness, their own greed, be it individual or national, and attempt at least in this kind of work to proceed toward the good of us all.

Thank you very much for coming.

NOTE: The ceremony was held on the White House lawn. The President spoke following remarks by the Postmaster General and the Chairman of the Atomic Energy Commission, which were also released.

The Postmaster General noted that the stamp carried a quotation from the President's address before the United Nations General Assembly of December 8, 1953: "To find the way by which the inventiveness of man shall be consecrated to his life." Chairman Strauss called attention to the fact that the stamp was dedicated only a few days before the opening in Geneva of the first International Conference on the Peaceful Uses of Atomic Energy.

178 ¶ Statement by the President on Congressional Action Regarding a Nationwide System of Highways.   *July* 28, 1955

I AM deeply disappointed by the rejection by the House of Representatives of legislation to authorize a nationwide system of highways.

The nation badly needs new highways. The good of our people, of our economy and of our defense, requires that construction of these highways be undertaken at once.

There is difference of conviction, I realize, over means of financing this construction. I have proposed one plan of financing which I consider to be sound. Others have proposed other methods. Adequate financing there must be, but contention over the method should not be permitted to deny our people these critically needed roads.

I would devoutly hope that the Congress would reconsider this entire matter before terminating this session.

179 ¶ Statement by the President Regarding Release of United States Airmen by Communist China.   *August* 1, 1955

THE ENTIRE country will feel a sense of relief and hail with joy the announcement that the eleven United States airmen held in Communist China since 1953 are at last to be released.

Our first thoughts go to the men and their families who have been separated for so long. The Government will use every appropriate facility to assure the speedy reunion of these families.

The United States extends thanks to all who have contributed to this humanitarian result, particularly the United Nations and its Secretary General who actively sought this result on behalf of the United Nations Command in which these eleven flyers served.

180 ¶ Special Message to the Congress Recommending Changes in Act Relating to Construction of Irrigation Systems on Federal Projects by Local Agencies. *August 1, 1955*

To the Congress of the United States:

Because of the great importance of Western irrigation to the Nation as a whole, on July 4, 1955 I approved H.R. 103 "To provide for the construction of distribution systems on authorized Federal reclamation projects by irrigation districts and other public agencies." That approval, however, was given with reluctance because of serious defects in the act.

Although it contains desirable features for cooperation between the Federal Government and local agencies, the Act falls short of according to the United States the protection which it requires. Important in that connection is the proviso that title shall at all times reside in the contracting water users. With that proviso in the law the United States lacks the means of assuring that the loans will be repaid, that the systems will be constructed in accordance with the plans, specifications and other engineering requirements of the Secretary of the Interior, and that they will be operated in conformity with the reclamation laws. Accordingly, I recommend that the Act be amended so as to require, prior to the consummation of any loan, the transfer to the United States of the titles to the systems and rights of way held or acquired by the borrowers. Titles to those properties should remain in the United States until the loan is repaid.

In keeping with such recommendation, it is desirable that only revokable permits be granted across any of the lands of the United States. That limitation necessarily follows in view of the fact that the United States will probably advance virtually all of the funds which will be expended in the development of the distribution systems. Moreover, those funds are to be advanced for the specific purpose of effectuating the objectives of the reclamation laws. Thus, as stated, retention of title in the United States will assure to it adequate means of enforcing those laws. For that reason, easements for the rights of way should not be granted by the United States.

As a consequence, the Act should be revised to eliminate those provisions which authorize the Secretary of the Interior or the head of any other executive department to sell and convey necessary rights of way. In lieu of that clause, it is suggested that all rights of way which are granted to borrowers pursuant to the act be brought within the provisions of those Congressional enactments relating to the granting of permits for rights of way across the lands of the United States. The safeguards contained in those Acts are necessary for the protection of the United States.

Because of the fact that large sums of money will be advanced pursuant to the Act, it should contain measures precluding "windfalls" to the borrowers. An amendment explicitly requiring them to account in full to the Secretary of the Interior in regard to all disbursements of borrowed funds and to return at once for application towards amortization of the loans all funds which are not expended in the construction of the distribution systems would suffice as a safeguard against possible "windfalls."

Because of the need for having the corrective measures, that I have outlined applicable to all loans made under the Act, I hope that such measures will be adopted as promptly as possible after the convening of the next session of the Congress.

DWIGHT D. EISENHOWER

181 ¶ Remarks to Members of the Bull Elephants Club. *August 2, 1955*

THANK YOU, Mr. Wolfson, members of the Committee.

My name is Dwight D. Eisenhower. I live in the house to your left front and work in the office to your left. I was told to come out here to meet Bull Elephants, and I must say every day in Washington you learn something.

Of course I am complimented by the sentiments of the resolution you have just heard read. When any American believes that another is qualified for holding public office, high or low, he is paying to that other person a very deep compliment because standards for public service should be, and I think in the main are, such that anyone who holds Federal office, or State or municipal office, is really set apart somewhat in the consciousness of America. So, I am truly grateful to those people for the confidence they express.

Now, if I can say anything that would be worth your while after coming all the distance from the other end of Pennsylvania Avenue through this heat to give me a chance to greet you, it certainly will not be, and should not be, about me, my person, or my future decisions. It should be about the country and the Government for which you work, the Nation that you serve, and the party through which you perform that service. I think it would also be unnecessary for me to go back into what we hope for this country.

We hope, of course, in general terms for peace—peace with honor and security, for a fine flourishing and expanding economy and for the opportunity for all to participate in the productivity that that economy should have.

We hope for growing opportunities for ourselves and for our younger friends, and those coming after us, and our own children. But, when we talk about our party as an instrument to bring those things about, then we get a little closer I think to what we call legislative programs, things to implement the Government's part in achieving these great goals and aspirations.

I assure you that I for one know something of the great part you play in bringing about those programs. I have on my staff a few people who, had they stayed down there, would probably be eligible for membership in the Bull Elephants; Jack Martin and

Gerry Morgan and others and Max Rabb, who have served down on the Hill with you.

They never let me forget what the principal secretaries and the filing clerks and all the others that answer the phones do, what they mean to legislation, what they mean to good will, what they mean to oiling the machinery that will allow a political party to achieve its own will on the Senate and House floors. But, I would like to talk a little bit more, go a little deeper into this matter of a party than just the mechanisms, the oiling of the machinery, the preventing of friction. We want, of course, honor and integrity in Government. We cannot only work for it, we cannot only preach it, we can exemplify it, and by that amount strengthen our party. We can also help to represent to all people in our own districts, in our own municipalities, and here in Washington, the desire of the Republican Party that this Nation go forward as it was conceived—where individual opportunity for every man should be equally shared, where opportunity should be limitless so far as his capacities, his own ability, will enable him to take advantage of it.

We want no regimented state. We want no direction from the Federal Government where that is not necessary. We want, in our individual sense, the maximum of freedom so long as we do not trespass on the freedom of others.

But, when we come to the problem of determining where does the Federal Government's responsibility begin and end in all this—now we are really attacking the problem that each political party must solve for itself, in specific terms, before I think it can stand up and say: this is the party through which you can achieve the kind of ambitions of which I am talking, or this is the party that has another doctrine.

It is idle to say that the Federal Government can be as stand-offish with respect to the affairs of Detroit, Michigan; or Abilene, Kansas; or San Antonio, Texas; as it was let us say 100 years ago. Life has gotten more complicated.

Our whole international situation affects each of us more closely than it did then, and the Federal Government is solely in charge of foreign relations. So, we have to determine: where do we want the Federal Government to go into this business and where do we want it to draw the line that they shall not go past. That is the kind of problem we have.

For myself I believe this—I believe that it is stated better by Lincoln than any other man—he said the function of Government is to do for the individual all of those things which he cannot do at all or which he cannot so well do for himself; but in all those things where the community or the individual can take care of his own affairs, the Federal Government ought not to interfere. That isn't quite an exact quotation, but it is almost exact. Now that is the kind of rule I think we should set up for ourselves.

We must never be a party that is indifferent to the sufferings of a great community where, through some unusual cause, people are out of work, where people can't educate their own children, where through any kind of disaster, natural or economic, people are suffering.

We must not only be alive to the requirements of that situation, but we must be alive to preventing it. But we must not put the Federal Government into this thing to the extent that we kill individual initiative, that we destroy the local responsibility for as far as it should reach in these matters. If we do, then we are starting to thread the way to regimentation, to Federal control.

I believe that if we stand for what I would call the great middle way in determining this line between Federal control and proper functions of the Federal Government, that if we stand irrevocably, inevitably, for decency and honor in Government, if we stand for peace abroad, for strength by which we protect ourselves while we are bringing about more peaceful relations, then in general we are doing what the Republican Party stands for. I believe if successful in carrying out this kind of a program, the Republican Party will continue to stay in power. That is because it will have proved itself worthy of the confidence of the United States, will have proved that it is in the hands of competent, devoted, loyal people who are extremists neither in the terms of being a reactionary or of believing in complete Federal control and responsibility, whether it be power, or whether it be anything else. It will have proved that we are the kind of people who can be trusted with the running of Federal, State, and local government.

Now, if we are going to achieve the kind of organization that I so roughly pictured, if we are to be successful in that, it is not enough merely to have fine presidential, vice presidential, senatorial, gubernatorial, and congressional candidates—all the way down the line.

We must also have loyal workers, workers that provide the staffs as you do for the leaders of such a group, who are devoted to a cause, because you believe in something. You believe in something that, because of the vastness of this Nation, is sometimes difficult to explain, but which you have in your heart very clearly written there. You believe in something, and you are carrying it out, in order for our Nation to have the benefit of that kind of a policy and program, and not primarily because you want to work in Washington. And I say that especially on a day like this!

Your efforts are above selfish ambition, no matter how ambitious one may be, and of course ambition is necessary. Someone told me the other day: ambition is like tempering steel—too little and the steel is no good; too much and it is brittle and breaks. Something to think about. Little bit like salt in your food. Of course you must have it, but your ambition, your burning ambition, must always be for the country—and for yourself as it fits into doing the very best you can for that country.

Now, I suppose that a person here could take up a lot of the special bills before Congress that I am interested in, plead for help, and probably do a better job than I do when I sometimes address some of your bosses. I am not going to do that. It is not my function here this morning, but rather to thank you. For all of the work you have done, for the work you are doing, thank you very much, very much indeed, and I hope that again one of these days I will get a chance to see you. Thank you for the compliment of coming out in this heat to see me. Goodbye.

NOTE: The President spoke on the South Lawn of the White House. His opening words referred to Norman Wolfson, President of the Club, which consists of administrative and secretarial assistants to the Republican Members of Congress. Mr. Wolfson read the following statement:

Dear Mr. President:

It would be superfluous to tell you of the pleasure it is for us to meet with you today. We are not going to petition you to accept the Republican nomination again in 1956 for we know the constant efforts, so much more persuasive than ours could be, toward that end. But, we of the Bull Elephants Club, male assistants to the Republican Members of the House, would like to impart two thoughts at this time. It is with profound respect that we look on you as the leader of the people of the United States and of our Republican Party. We also state without a dissenter among our ranks that if you do accept the Republican nomination next year, we, who in many instances are a direct liaison to the grass roots of the voting forces throughout the United States, will devote our unceasing efforts, our whole-hearted support, our very all to easing the burden of your campaign.

Most sincerely yours,
GIB DARRISON
(Miller, N.Y.)
MONTY MONROE
(Betts of Ohio)
PAUL SQUIRES
(Harden of Indiana)
NORMAN WOLFSON
(Kean of N.J.)
Chairman, Bull
Elephants Club, Ike Committee

182 ¶ Statement by the President Upon Signing the Mutual Security Appropriation Act.

August 2, 1955

I HAVE TODAY approved H.R. 7224, the Mutual Security Appropriation Act, 1956, which appropriates $2,765,875,000 for further carrying out the Mutual Security Act of 1954.

There are several provisions in the Act relating to Direct forces support and Defense support where particular countries are named as eligible recipients of assistance in specified amounts. I regard these provisions as authorizations, and also as limitations on the availability of the amounts specified, rather than as directives.   To construe them otherwise would raise substantial Constitutional questions.

NOTE: As enacted, H.R. 7224 is Public Law 208, 84th Congress (69 Stat. 435).

183   ¶ Citation and Remarks at Presentation of the Medal of Freedom to Robert B. Anderson. *August 3, 1955*

[Text read by Commander Edward L. Beach, Naval Aide to the President]

CITATION TO ACCOMPANY THE AWARD
OF THE MEDAL OF FREEDOM TO
ROBERT B. ANDERSON

TO ROBERT B. ANDERSON, for exceptionally meritorious service in furtherance of the security of the United States.

As Secretary of the Navy Mr. Anderson rendered a brilliant performance in the administration of that service.   As Deputy Secretary of Defense he continued to apply in superb fashion sound judgment and keen foresight in formulating and resolving programs of interest to this nation and its allies.

Through his work in international affairs—in particular, his service as Defense Member of the Operations Coordinating Board and his participation in meetings of the North Atlantic Council and in the development of the St. Lawrence Seaway program— he has contributed to the sound advancement of our national security.

In these activities and in many other ways Mr. Anderson has rendered great service to his country.   It is my pleasure to award him the Medal of Freedom.

DWIGHT D. EISENHOWER

[Remarks of the President]

I must say that if you give these only to persons going away, I really am fairly disappointed to be giving you this. It has been a wonderful experience to have you here. I am sorry you are leaving us so early—next Friday, I believe—but we will look forward to your coming back sometime to the service of your country because the kind of performance you have rendered is one that we would like to see repeated often here.

NOTE: The President spoke in the Rose Garden. Mr. Anderson replied:

"Thank you, sir.

"Mr. President, I would say that there has never been a more rewarding experience of my life, and I have never had a greater privilege nor a greater honor than to serve under your administration and to serve with Mr. Wilson. All I can say now is that I will always be obedient to any wishes that you may have, and God bless you in your work."

Mr. Anderson served as Secretary of the Navy from February 4, 1953, through May 3, 1954, and then as Deputy Secretary of Defense through August 4, 1955.

184 ¶ Statement by the President Upon Signing Bill Relating to the Red River Flood Control Project. *August* 3, 1955

ALTHOUGH H.R. 4362, relating to the construction of Cooper Dam and Reservoir on South Sulphur River, Texas, and to the construction of certain other improvements on various of its tributaries, contains features which I believe violate good governmental fiscal practice, I have approved the bill because of its generally worthwhile purpose.

The act will modify the authorized flood control project for the Red River below Denison Dam to provide for construction of Cooper Dam and Reservoir on South Sulphur River, Texas, and for construction of channel improvements, levees, and drainage works along various tributaries in Texas, Oklahoma, Arkansas, and Louisiana. Construction is authorized substantially in accordance with the recommendations contained in a report of the Chief of Engineers and is subject to the conditions that local interests contribute toward the cost of construction of Cooper Dam the amounts allocated to water supply and, with respect to other works, (a) provide lands, easements and rights-of-way, (b) hold and save the United States free from damages, and (c) maintain and operate the works.

The act requires local interests to contribute toward the cost of construction, maintenance and operation of Cooper Reservoir the amounts allocated to water supply, but it makes no provision for a local contribution in consideration of the benefits from enhancement of land values attributable to the flood protection anticipated from the improvements which are authorized. Failure of the act to require adequate sharing of costs in consideration of these benefits is a serious departure from a well established policy under which those who receive the benefits from an increase in property values due to higher land use made possible by a project are expected to share in the cost of the project improvements.

The specific effect of the non-incorporation in the bill of the existing general policy will be to increase the Federal cost of the project by more than $900,000. Not only does it seem inequitable to relieve the beneficiaries of the enhancement of land values from this project from the standard requirement for cost sharing which has been imposed on the beneficiaries of other similar projects, but equally important, it will almost certainly be cited as a precedent for similar waivers of local participation in many other projects unless corrective action is taken.

For these reasons I earnestly hope that the Congress will reassess the sharing of costs authorized by the act and increase the requirement for local contributions before Federal appropriations are made available.

NOTE: As enacted, H.R. 4362 is Public Law 218, 84th Congress (69 Stat. 449).

185 ¶ The President's News Conference of
August 4, 1955.

THE PRESIDENT. Good afternoon, ladies and gentlemen.

With Congress over, I suppose it is time for a brief roundup of successes and failures.

We talked about a great deal during this session and now we will apparently have a recess for a while.

In the field of foreign affairs I think this Congress, like the one before it, has shown a complete appreciation of the need for bipartisan approach, and I think that any advances that the Government has been able to make in the whole field of foreign affairs must be credited likewise to the action of Congress as well as to the skill of our Secretary of State and many other negotiators.

I think that the whole record of both the 83d and 84th Congresses in this respect—and I am talking about the mass votes and support—has been commendable, and certainly I for one am deeply grateful.

Now, in the field of domestic legislation, we have first of all to look at the background of the actual situation. America is today enjoying almost unprecedented prosperity. I think last month our employment was an alltime high, with unemployment well below 4 percent.

The incomes are up, purchasing is up; and above all, America has had over this period of the last 2½ years a sound stabilized dollar which has, of course, preserved the values of pensions and insurance policies and the like.

Now, if we are going to keep that kind of thing moving, it means that there must forever be action, not only in the economic and industrial field on the part of the individuals in our system of free enterprise, but Government as well; where its actions in the whole field of credit and taxation and other kinds of economic legislation touch upon our economy, it must look forward to the future. It cannot rest on any record, no matter how good.

757

I think, about the end of June, I was asked here about the record of Congress and the legislation I thought I needed; and besides referring back to my opening state of the Union speech last January, I reached in my pocket and pulled out a little list, which I still have.   [*Laughter*]

Now, you will remember there were 13 items on it: highway construction, military reserves, military survivors' benefits, housing legislation, health program, school construction, mutual security appropriation, Refugee Act amendments, water resources, customs simplification, minimum wage, the atomic ship, and Hawaiian statehood.

Of those 13, only 4 have been enacted into law, although it is true that before June there were others that did affect this whole economic situation and our domestic circumstances.

But of these 13, only military reserves, housing legislation, mutual security appropriation, and minimum wage were enacted into law, and some of those, in my opinion, with provisions that were not wise.

There are four of the remaining nine that I think are absolutely vital to our future, and some that must be handled as soon as Congress comes back.   They are: school construction for our children, the health program, the highway program, and the water resources.

You will remember in the water resources program, when I mentioned that before, I brought up especially such projects as the Upper Colorado River, the Frying Pan, and the Cougar, and others.   I still believe that we must attack these things intelligently on a broad base or we cannot expect to continue the kind of prosperity, the kind of full employment, that we are now enjoying.   And so it would be completely futile on my part to say that in this field, in this domestic field, that I believe we have been as successful in this past Congress as we should have been.

We must make progress, and it will be my earnest effort as quickly as the next Congress opens, to bring these things very emphatically to the attention of both the House and the Senate.

I think that is all I have to say. We will go to questions.

Q. Robert E. Clark, International News Service: Mr. President, Premier Bulganin appears to have rejected your aerial inspection and military blueprint plans on the grounds that they are unrealistic. Can you tell us how you feel about this, sir?

THE PRESIDENT. I believe his exact language was that he thought his proposal of May 10th with its provisions for inspection were more realistic than were the suggestions I made. Speaking informally at Geneva, I said if they trusted that kind of an inspection system, it was all right with us; we would adopt both. And I proposed—I said, let's take them both.

Now, we are engaged here in the beginning of developing methods by which we can tell, we can have great confidence that the other fellow is doing exactly what he said he would do; and secondly, we would hope that this would be an approach toward real disarmament.

Now, these are matters that take long examination by experts. I don't understand that the Premier closed the door, and I merely say we are ready to accept and examine any kind of system that looks fair to us and to both sides.

Q. Charles S. von Fremd, CBS News: The Atomic Energy Commission announced today, sir, that from what they, from their own explorations, that the Russians had exploded some type of thermonuclear bomb. I wonder if you could tell us what significance this means to you, and if it represents possibly something that might not be as optimistic as you felt at the summit.

THE PRESIDENT. I believe you made one error in your premise. I do not believe they said "thermonuclear." I believe they merely said an explosion of atomic character.

I am not going to attempt at this moment to interpret this incident in terms of Soviet intent. I would say that if in their scientific development, if they found that they had come to the place where they could go no further without tests, they just made tests as a matter of course.

You know, there have been several series since 1949 when the first one, I believe, was detected.   This could mean anything, but not necessarily, as I see it, not necessarily a change in their, let us say, more conciliatory attitude that they have shown in the past weeks and months.

Q. Edward T. Folliard, Washington Post and Times Herald: Mr. President, it seems as if something is always happening to puncture that moratorium you talked about in the spring. Yesterday some Ohio Republicans called on you to urge you to run again, and they represented you as saying this: that if you could foresee what the situation will be a year from now, presumably the world situation, if you could foresee that, then you could say what your plans for 1956 would be.

They also quoted you as remarking on the strong sense of duty one gets in a long service, long career in the armed services.

Could you say, Mr. President, whether Geneva has made it more or less likely that you will run in 1956?   [*Laughter*]

THE PRESIDENT. Eddie, I can say this: this now pushes my year that I don't have to answer this far forward.   I said a year from the last question would be the moratorium.

Q. Mr. Folliard: I might withdraw that question. [*Laughter*]

THE PRESIDENT. I was talking to a group of very staunch Republicans, I assure you, and naturally questions such as you bring up now normally arise when there is such a gathering of that kind.

What I intended to imply, that if I now were such an infallible prophet that I could understand all about the world situation, the domestic situation, and my own situation, including the way I felt, and possibly with the health and everything else, as of that moment, then there would be no great excuse for deferring the decision.

I have not that gift of prophecy.

Q. Frank van der Linden, Nashville Banner: Mr. President, Senator George led a delegation of Congressmen and Senators from the cotton and textile States into your office Monday for discussion of a proposal to move some of this surplus cotton overseas, and also to levy import quotas on textiles. I wonder what your policy is going to be on that, sir.

THE PRESIDENT. I think that very soon the Secretary of Agriculture will be able to come up with something that, if it does not wholly meet the views of everybody in the administration, that we shall have to say, what we intend to do in the immediate future.

Now, just one word about that delegation. Senator George suggested a meeting. I invited him up, and I think it was the first idea that two or three were to come with him. It ended up, I believe, with 60 or about that.

But I want to make this clear. I found that for a moment, at least, my office was a place for a debating society. There were views expressed that were as bitterly antagonistic to this 2-price system and quota system as you can well imagine. So it is one of those questions for which there is no easy answer, and I am not going to try to forestall the completion of studies within the Cabinet so that it can be announced at the proper time.

Q. Chalmers M. Roberts, Washington Post and Times Herald: Mr. President, to return to the disarmament matter a minute, I take it from what you said about Bulganin's statement, you are not discouraged about the prospects of some progress in this field as a whole. Is that correct, sir?

THE PRESIDENT. Well, Mr. Roberts, here is the situation: our foreign ministers are going to meet in October, there was opened up at Geneva a more or less broad road of approach to these several problems which were agreed that the foreign ministers should study, and among them was disarmament. So I think that the statements that Mr. Bulganin has made should not be taken as at all foreclosing his readiness or the readiness of the Soviet representatives to discuss the matter.

Q. Mr. Roberts: Could I ask this also, sir? Is it your intention that when the U.N. Disarmament Subcommittee meets later this month, that the United States will have a new and complete program to offer, or will it be pretty much what you made public at Geneva?

THE PRESIDENT. I can't answer in complete detail. As you know, Governor Stassen is working on this constantly and is trying to coordinate the views of the several departments of Government, and there will unquestionably be new ideas of more specific type than I expressed at Geneva.

At Geneva I expressed a readiness on the part of the United States to pursue a course of mutual reciprocal disarmament in any, almost any type where we could be sure that everybody was acting in good faith. My inspection proposal was just a mere beginning that I wanted to propose of a type of inspection system that would ensure that confidence.

I think, therefore, that you can expect some new proposals, but naturally none of them will be in a final, fixed and rigid position. Otherwise there would be no room for negotiations.

Q. Sarah McClendon, El Paso Times: Sir, Senator Matthew Neely said it would be a conflict of principle as well as a conflict of interests for the Defense Department to continue to have as its petroleum logistics director General W. W. White, who is also on the payroll of Esso Export Corporation.

You said last time you would inquire into this situation. I wonder if you have had time to do so.

THE PRESIDENT. I understand that my press secretary had given you the answer.

Q. Mrs. McClendon: No, sir.

THE PRESIDENT. The answer is that there was no special legislation passed for General White. It was legislation that dates from 1941, and I believe renewed in 1948, which does not apply to reserve officers, which General White is. He is not a regular officer at all; he has the title of General, though in the reserves. It authorizes the Government to employ such people without requiring them to go through the same divesting of interests that you do regulars.

That is the situation under which General White was employed and, of course, it would be idle to employ as a consultant anyone who didn't know something about the petroleum business. He is bound to come from the petroleum industry.

Now, I believe beyond that, the Defense Department has issued a very complete statement; and beyond what I have said, I should say, "Go to see Secretary Wilson."

Q. Milton B. Freudenheim, Chicago Daily News: Mr. President, I have been asked to ask you whether you will be able to go to Chicago for the Governors' Conference.

THE PRESIDENT. Well, I don't think there are any plans. I don't even think I have had any negotiations with them on that subject at all for this particular meeting.

Q. Mr. Freudenheim: Another question that they asked me to ask you——

THE PRESIDENT. That they asked? Who is "they"?

Q. Mr. Freudenheim: The Chicago Daily News.

THE PRESIDENT. Oh, I see. All right. [*Laughter*]

Q. Mr. Freudenheim: I think you may have indicated as to your plans for calling a special session on highway legislation. Were you telling us a moment ago that you would wait until Congress came back?

THE PRESIDENT. No, I didn't say I would wait. As of this moment, after all, a special session is a rather critical and serious thing, an expensive thing. I have not by any manner of means dismissed the possibility that that might be needful, but as of now, I have made no such decision whatever.

Q. Mr. Freudenheim: Thank you, sir.

Q. William Theis, International News Service: Mr. President, could you tell us now as to what your intentions are as to signing the housing bill?

THE PRESIDENT. Well, I have just gotten the preliminary studies on it, and actually I was talking about it within the half hour. I couldn't say exactly, because it does have some features that I am not certain yet whether they are permissive or directive, and I must take a look at that part of it.

Q. Richard L. Wilson, Cowles Publications: Mr. President,

recently in Congress and in the newspapers, the suggestions have been made that some sort of a new negotiation is under way with the Red Chinese which might involve the status of Quemoy, Matsu, and Formosa. Is any such negotiation under way, and if not, what is the nature of the present negotiations?

THE PRESIDENT. The present negotiations were called to discuss the question of nationals of one country retained within the territory of the other.

Now, it was admitted that the discussions might find other subjects which could be discussed, but both the Secretary and I have frequently stated we are not going to discuss the affairs of our friends when our friends are absent. We count the Nationalists on Formosa as our friends. We are not going to discuss their future or their destiny or anything about them until they are there.

Q. Charles E. Shutt, Telenews: Along that same line, sir, it has been suggested in some quarters that further negotiations be planned with the Red Chinese as a result of the Geneva talks that are going on now. If after suitable preliminary conferences were held, would you at all favor a summit meeting with all parties concerned to settle Asian tensions?

THE PRESIDENT. I think not at this time. I think it would be far too much in advance to talk about the possibility of a summit meeting. They have implications that do not follow upon meetings at a somewhat lower level.

Now, I believe the Secretary has said that it is within the realm of possibility that these meetings will lead to negotiations possibly on ministerial level, but I think nothing further has been hinted at.

Q. David P. Sentner, Hearst Newspapers: Is there any possibility that you might call a special session of Congress to deal with the highway legislation?

THE PRESIDENT. Well, I tried to answer that question a minute ago. There is always the possibility, but as of this moment, I have no decision. I have made no decision of that kind.

Q. Mr. Sentner: And if the next Congress takes it up without a special session, do you plan to make a new proposal for financing the method of construction?

THE PRESIDENT. I did say in my original recommendations that I recognized there could be more than one method of financing, but at a time when we wanted definitely to allocate certain user type of money to the paying of those roads, we needed the roads now, and when Congress very definitely and I think maybe a lot more people do not want to raise the public debt, there remained one method: the corporation or the authority method. And that is the one I proposed.

I might accept some modification, of course I would. But what I want first of all is roads, and then a way to pay for it that will be acceptable and fair to the taxpayers.

Q. Clark R. Mollenhoff, Des Moines Register: Mr. President, I wonder if you could tell us how you feel Air Secretary Talbott's activities measured up to the standards that you wish to maintain in your administration?

THE PRESIDENT. I think the record speaks for itself. I have nothing more to add to that.

Q. Martin Agronsky, American Broadcasting Company: Mr. President, it has been remarked that in the negotiations at Geneva, that we have been referring to the representatives of the Chinese Communist Government as the People's Republic of China. In return, the Chinese Communists are referring to us as the United States instead of apparently the usual title, which is a capitalistic aggressor. And generally the atmosphere seems to be one in which people now think there has been a change in the attitude of our Government toward the possible recognition of the legitimacy of the Chinese Government, that is, the Chinese Communist Government.

Has there been any development along those lines, sir, and does this difference in nomenclature that we are now officially using have any significance?

THE PRESIDENT. Well, I would say this: the change of nomenclature is without significance, because possibly—I wasn't even personally aware of any change. When you are sitting in conference and your conferees may refer to a particular group under a certain name, you naturally are in the habit of referring to it the same way. So this question of nomenclature is without significance whatsoever.

Now, several times I have stated that as long as Red China is branded as a dictator by the United Nations, which it still is, due to the fact that its armies are in North Korea, we have no choice of our own, and I don't know how the United Nations has a choice of its own. There are other outstanding complaints which I have outlined time and again, and I have no idea that under existing circumstances there would be a change of the kind you indicated in our policy.

Q. Robert J. Donovan, New York Herald Tribune: Did you say "branded a dictator" or "branded an aggressor?"

THE PRESIDENT. Well, I mean "branded an aggressor." If I said "dictator," I was wrong. Branded an aggressor by the United Nations for going into Northern Korea, you will recall.

Q. Joseph R. Slevin, New York Herald Tribune: Mr. President, do you believe there is a serious threat of inflation?

THE PRESIDENT. What is that?

Q. Mr. Slevin: Do you believe that there is a serious threat of inflation at this time?

THE PRESIDENT. I wouldn't say "serious threat," but let us remember that any free economy is always in a situation of balance, even though it is going forward in its expansion and in its productivity. There are always present the two, twin dangers of deflation and inflation, and the function of Government so far as it affects this matter at all is to be watchful, to be vigilant and alert, and to take measures from time to time that tend to move in one direction if the signs are we are moving in the other. But as of this moment we have, I repeat, an activity, a productivity, that is almost beyond calculation, measured by former standards. So the time is here to be watchful; but I wouldn't say there was serious danger, no.

Robert E. Clark, International News Service: Thank you, Mr. President.

NOTE: President Eisenhower's seventy-fifth news conference was held in the Executive Office Building from   2:32 to 2:55 o'clock on Thursday afternoon, August 4, 1955. In attendance: 201.

186   ¶ Letter to the Treasurer of the United States Appointing Her Chairman of the Interdepartmental Savings Bond Committee. *August 4, 1955*

Dear Mrs. Priest:

I have today issued an executive order establishing the Interdepartmental Committee for the Voluntary Payroll Savings Plan for the Purchase of United States Savings Bonds. This Committee will have the function of promoting the purchase of United States Savings Bonds by employees in the Executive Branch of the Government through regular voluntary pay allotments on the Payroll Savings Plan.

The maintenance of stability in the economic life of the individual, the community and the Nation is well served by the widespread distribution of the national debt through the purchase of United States Savings Bonds by the people. It is important to the welfare of our country that this support of the national debt-management function be continued and fostered to the greatest extent possible. Federal employees should be encouraged to maintain their leadership in the purchase of Savings Bonds through the Payroll Savings Plan and thus by example give impetus to the movement throughout the business and industrial community.

I hereby appoint you as Chairman of the new Interdepartmental Committee.

Sincerely,

DWIGHT D. EISENHOWER

187 ¶ Memorandum to Federal Agencies Concerning the Voluntary Payroll Savings Plan for the Purchase of U.S. Savings Bonds.
August 4, 1955

Memorandum to the Heads of Departments and Agencies:

I have this day issued an executive order establishing the Interdepartmental Committee for the Voluntary Payroll Savings Plan for the Purchase of United States Savings Bonds.

This Committee provides a vehicle for the effective promotion of the Payroll Savings Plan. The maintenance of stability in the economic life of the individual, the community and the Nation, is well served by the widespread distribution of the national debt through the purchase of United States Savings Bonds by the people. It is important to the welfare of our country that this support of the national debt-management function be continued and fostered to the greatest extent possible. Federal employees should be encouraged to maintain their leadership in the purchase of Savings Bonds through the Payroll Savings Plan and thus by example give impetus to the movement throughout the business and industrial structure.

The functions of the said Committee are, in general, the same as those performed by the Interdepartmental Committee for the Peacetime Voluntary Payroll Savings Plan for the Purchase of United States Savings Bonds established by Executive Order No. 9953 of April 23, 1948. That order, which is superseded by the order issued today, designated Edward F. Bartelt, Fiscal Assistant Secretary of the Treasury, as Chairman of the committee established by it. Mr. Bartelt served as Chairman of the Committee until his recent retirement from the Government service.

The new order provides that the Chairman of the committee established thereby shall be appointed by the President. I have appointed Mrs. Ivy Baker Priest, Treasurer of the United States, as Chairman of the Interdepartmental Committee for the Voluntary Payroll Savings Plan for the Purchase of United States Savings Bonds. I urge that each of you give Mrs. Priest your full support and cooperation in carrying on the work of the Committee.

DWIGHT D. EISENHOWER

188 ¶ Citation Accompanying the Distinguished Service Medal Presented to Admiral Robert B. Carney. *August 4,* 1955

[Text read by Comdr. Edward L. Beach, Naval Aide to the President]

THE PRESIDENT of the United States takes pleasure in awarding the Distinguished Service Medal (Gold Star in lieu of Fourth Award) to

ADMIRAL ROBERT B. CARNEY, UNITED STATES NAVY

for service as set forth in the following

CITATION:

For exceptionally meritorious service to the Government of the United States in a duty of great responsibility as Chief of Naval Operations and Member of the Joint Chiefs of Staff for a period of two years commencing 17 August 1953. Exercising the highest quality of command leadership during this period of international tension, Admiral Carney displayed foresight and keen understanding in directing the unified commands for which he was executive agent. He greatly furthered combat readiness of Naval operating forces by insisting upon incorporating the latest scientific developments into naval construction programs. As a Member of the Joint Chiefs of Staff he participated in the formulation of strategic plans for the defense of the United States and the establishment of policy dedicated to maintaining peace and freedom throughout the world.   In this capacity he fostered and promoted the most harmonious relationships among the Services.   Admiral Carney's contribution to the aspirations of mankind and to the Government of the United States will always reflect the highest credit upon himself and the United States Naval Service.

DWIGHT D. EISENHOWER

NOTE: The President made the presentation in the Rose Garden.

189 ¶ Memorandum of Disapproval of Bill Concerning Term of Office of Subversive Activities Control Board Members.   *August 6, 1955*

I AM withholding approval of S. 2171, an Act "To amend the Subversive Activities Control Act so as to provide that upon the expiration of his term of office a member of the Board shall continue to serve until his successor shall have been appointed and shall have qualified."

The language of this bill is incorporated in identical terms in S. 2375 which I have approved today.   Under the circumstances, approval of S. 2171 is unnecessary and would result in a nullity and possible confusion.

DWIGHT D. EISENHOWER

190 ¶ Exchange of Letters Between the President and Chancellor Adenauer of Germany on the Geneva Conference. *August 6, 1955*

[Released August 6, 1955. Dated August 1, 1955]

Dear Mr. Chancellor:

I was most happy to receive your letter of July twenty-fifth, expressing satisfaction with the results of the recent Geneva Conference. I particularly appreciate what you said about my contribution to those results. At the same time, I am fully aware that progress at Geneva would not have been possible without that unity of peaceful purpose among the Western Allies which you, Mr. Chancellor, have done so much to establish.

We must now look forward to a period of arduous and continuing negotiation in the effort to achieve the aims of peace and justice for all men in an atmosphere which will permit the growth of freedom. As you know, I consider that the reunification of your country is of first importance in the process of establishing foundations for a lasting peace. I agree fully with your view that the maintenance of Western unity is vital to the ultimate achievement of these objectives and welcome your assurances of cooperation toward this end on the part of the German Federal Government.

With assurances of my high esteem and personal regard,

Sincerely,

DWIGHT D. EISENHOWER

NOTE: Chancellor Adenauer's letter, dated July 25, follows:

Dear Mr. President:

On this day I should like particularly to tell you how strongly I am impressed by the united bearing of the western powers during the negotiations of the past week. I know, dear Mr. President, what a great part you played in this, for which I should like to express to you my sincere thanks.

I believe that you can look back on the results of the four power conference of the past week with much satisfaction. The discussions have without doubt clarified the positions of both sides. The door is opened to further negotiations. The west can approach these negotiations with closed ranks. It is especially valuable that agreement with the Soviets was successfully reached upon a common agenda, which provides a useful basis, in the western interests, for the future negotiations.

I feel that we should be quite clear that only by maintaining the united attitude of the west will we succeed in bringing the Soviets to a reasonable solution of the large problems which affect us all in equal manner. On the way to this end, which will be long, wearisome, and full of risks, close cooperation is required on the part of everyone of good will.

I may say to you that you can fully rely in this matter upon the attitude of the German Federal Government.

With friendly greetings and best wishes,

Sincerely yours,

ADENAUER

191 ¶ Message to the United Nations Conference on the Peaceful Uses of Atomic Energy at Geneva. *August 8, 1955*

[Read by Lewis L. Strauss, Chairman, Atomic Energy Commission]

Members of the Conference:

Please accept my warmest greetings and sincere good wishes, on behalf of the people of the United States, for the success of this first international conference on the peaceful uses of atomic energy, held under the auspices of the United Nations.

You—the world's foremost nuclear scientists and engineers, who are penetrating the mysteries of atomic energy—most surely know how the atom stands ready to become man's obedient, tireless servant, if man will only allow it.

The knowledge and vision which you possess carries with it a great opportunity—and a great challenge. Your lives are dedicated to the search for knowledge and truth. You hold the respect of your peoples because they look to you for words of calm, unadorned scientific fact.

You can best unfold to the peoples of the world the bright promise of the benign atom.

You meet in Geneva under conditions favorable to this great purpose.

No other scientific gathering of such scope and importance, or of such widespread interest, has ever taken place. The peoples of the world are represented. At hand is a rich opportunity to restore old lines of free scientific communication which have been disrupted for so many years. The knowledge and skills which each of you has acquired in his own country to put the atom to work for peaceful purposes will be circulated and shared in the friendly atmosphere of hospitable Switzerland with its age-old tradition of freedom.

This atmosphere is encouraged also by the fact that the United Nations Resolution of last December 4, which created your Conference, limited its concern to scientific and technical matters. It is expressly nonpolitical.

You meet, therefore, as free men of science, interested only in enriching man's store of knowledge about this wonderful discovery.

Science speaks in many tongues. The advancement of the nuclear arts has been the work of men of many nations. That is so because the atom itself is nonpolitical. It wears no nationality and recognizes no frontiers. It is neither moral nor immoral. Only man's choice can make it good or evil. The phenomenon of nuclear fission having been revealed to man, it is still left to him to determine the use to which it shall be put.

On December 8, 1953, I had the privilege of addressing the General Assembly of the United Nations on the subject which occupies this conference—world cooperation for the peaceful uses of atomic energy.

I stated then, and I reaffirm now, that the United States pledges its determination to help find ways by which the miraculous inventiveness of man shall not be dedicated to his death, but consecrated to his life.

This pledge which we gave twenty months ago has become the law of our land, written into our statutes by the American Congress in the new Atomic Energy Act of 1954. The new act states in forthright language that we recognize our responsibilities to share with others, in a spirit of cooperation, what we know of the peaceful atomic art. To further encourage such cooperation with other nations, the new act relaxed the previously existing restrictions on independent atomic research and development by private industry, thereby further clearing the way for cooperation with others.

Since our new Atomic Energy Act became law a year ago, we have striven in many ways and ever in a spirit of good will to translate its words and its purpose into concrete action.

That is the way we interpret our responsibility and the responsibility of all nations of good will.

We appeal not alone to governments to join with us in this cooperative endeavor. We are hopeful also that business and professional groups throughout the world will become interested and will provide incentives in finding new ways that this science can be used.

All of the enlightened nations of the world are spending large sums every year on programs of health, education, and economic development. They do so because they know that disease, ignorance, and the lack of economic opportunity are the dark breeding places of disorders and wars.

Every scientific tool available has been brought to bear in this effort.

Atomic science is the newest and the most promising tool of all.

In your capable hands, I am confident it can be made to perform greatly for the betterment of human living.

Dwight D. Eisenhower

NOTE: The conference was held at Geneva, August 8–20. On July 1 the White House announced that the U.S. delegation would consist of Lewis L. Strauss, Chairman, Dr. Willard F. Libby, Vice Chairman, and Dr. I. I. Rabi, Dr. Detlev W. Bronk, and Dr. Shields Warren, members.

192 ¶ Statement by the President Upon Signing the Reserve Forces Act of 1955. *August 9, 1955*

I HAVE TODAY approved the Reserve Forces Act of 1955. Although the bill falls short of the program which I sent to the Congress by my special message on January 13, 1955, and which the Department of Defense urged the Congress to adopt, nevertheless the bill does contain provisions that will definitely strengthen the Reserve structure.

(1) It provides a statutory means of assuring that our Federal Reserves will be composed of prior-trained men on a planned basis.

(2) It will permit an increase in the Ready Reserve manpower ceiling from 1,500,000 to 2,900,000.

(3) It clearly establishes the obligation to participate in reserve training and provides for effective and reasonable enforcement measures to achieve this participation.

(4) It authorizes the President to order up 1,000,000 Ready Reservists in an emergency proclaimed by him.

I am, however, concerned by the failure of the bill to afford the same guarantees of prior training for the National Guard as it has done for the Reserves. The bill is also deficient in failing to grant authority to induct into the Reserve if sufficient numbers to meet military requirements are not obtained voluntarily.

The securing of sufficient numbers in the Reserve on a voluntary basis will undoubtedly be hampered by the unwarranted disparity under the bill between the $78 per month offered to members of the National Guard who volunteer to undergo initial active duty for training, and the $50 per month provided for members of the Reserve who undergo identical, initial training.

In my special message of January thirteenth and in recommendations of the Department of Defense, it was urged that provisions be included to insure a hard core of prior-service personnel to the National Guard. Not only did the Congress fail to include such provisions, but it also excluded the National Guard from the provisions for interim incentives to secure participation of prior-service personnel in the various reserve training programs.

I have serious doubts that in the absence of further statutory authority, the National Guard can fully attain its planned size, and the standards of military proficiency and readiness, that are essential in our mobilization planning. I am, therefore, instructing the Secretary of Defense and the Joint Chiefs of Staff to conduct a continuing review of National Guard programs and standards to determine whether they meet the imperative requirements of our first line defenses.

The bill reduces the present eight-year military obligation to six years. The effect of this reduction will not manifest itself to any great degree in the immediate future. Such reduction is, however, a matter that merits careful study to determine whether, at some future period, it will be necessary to request restoration of the eight-year obligation.

Taking into consideration all factors and the essential need to build strong reserves, I am instructing the Secretary of Defense to take immediate and effective action to utilize the means that the bill provides to augment and strengthen the Reserve Forces throughout the country and to prepare for presentation to the next session of the Congress amendments necessary to correct the deficiencies in this legislation.

NOTE: The Reserve Forces Act of 1955 is Public Law 305, 84th Congress (69 Stat. 598). For the President's message of January 13, see Item 12, above.

On August 13 the President issued Executive Order 10629 (3 CFR, 1955 Supp.) authorizing enlistments in the Ready Reserve of the Army Reserve and Marine Corps Reserve.

A White House release of that date quoted the President as saying: "No time should be lost in moving toward the goal of stronger Reserves as rapidly as the new law permits. It is my sincere hope that young Americans will respond to this volunteer program in such measure as to insure its success."

193 ¶ Statement by the President Upon Signing H.R. 7684 Authorizing Salary Payment to an Interim Appointee to the Atomic Energy Commission. *August* 10, 1955

I SIGN this measure because of the necessity of its first section which permits payment of salary to an interim appointee to fill the existing vacancy on the Atomic Energy Commission.

The second section is an unnecessary piece of legislation and irrelevant to the first section. I have previously expressed my views on this method of legislating and will not repeat them here. The purpose of the second section is stated to be to give all Commissioners equal access to information necessary in the performance of their duties as Commissioners. Existing law fully accomplishes this with its provisions for equal responsibility and equal authority for each member of the Commission. Most Commissioners have previously indicated their belief that the existing law is adequate and clear. The Chairman of the Commission has nevertheless recommended that I sign the bill and I accordingly do so.

NOTE: As enacted, H.R. 7684 is Public Law 337, 84th Congress (69 Stat. 630).

194 ¶ Statement by the President Upon Signing the Housing Amendments of 1955. *August* 11, 1955

I HAVE TODAY signed S. 2126, the Housing Amendments of 1955. This Act contains important provisions which were recommended by the Administration and which are needed so that the Federal Government may help private enterprise and our local communities to eliminate and prevent slums and urban blight and to provide good housing for all of our people.

The Act provides additional authority and funds for the broadened program of slum clearance and urban renewal authorized by law last year. It also continues the Federal Housing Administration's loan insurance aids, thereby enabling families of moderate income to acquire or improve their own homes. Our people benefit doubly from these measures, because they result in more and better housing and because they help to maintain a high level of employment in the construction industry and in the many other industries which supply it with materials and equipment.

The Act carries out my recommendations for enlarging and improving the present temporary program under which funds are advanced to local public agencies for the planning of their public works. Such advance planning will make it possible to begin construction as necessary. In addition, the Act provides new aid for meeting the very urgent housing needs of military personnel and their families.

Because of these very important and desirable provisions of the Act, I have given it my approval despite several other provisions about which I have serious objections.

I had recommended to the Congress a two-year program of Federal aid to local communities for the construction of 70,000 new low-rent public housing units. Instead, the Act provides for 45,000 new units on a one-year basis. The full program which I recommended is needed, and it can be carried out by our local communities and the Federal Government in a more orderly and efficient manner over a two-year period. It is also important for the low-rent housing aids to be coordinated with the slum clearance and urban renewal aids, and for each of these types of aids to be made available by the Federal Government only to communities which have adopted workable programs for dealing with the problem of slums and urban blight in their own midst. The Act fails to make adequate provision for carrying out these objectives.

I also have serious objections to the provisions of the bill which would create still another independent agency in the executive branch by detaching the Home Loan Bank Board, including the Federal Savings and Loan Insurance Corporation, from the Housing and Home Finance Agency. The primary purpose of the Home Loan Bank Board and the Insurance Corporation is to assist savings and loan associations and building and loan associations in providing funds for the purchase of homes. Such associations are now making almost 40 percent of all home loans and constitute our largest single lender group in the field of home financing. The Housing and Home Finance Agency was established to enable one accountable official, under the supervision of the President, to coordinate Federal programs designed to encourage private financing of homes with other housing and community development activities of the Government. The grant of independence for the Home Loan Bank Board is a backward step which will seriously impair such coordination and thrust an unnecessary supervisory burden on the President.

In addition, the Act makes several other changes in basic housing laws which, at best are of questionable necessity. New lending authority totaling many hundreds of millions of dollars is provided which was not recommended by the Administration and is not made subject to the normal appropriation review process. For example, the bill authorizes a greatly enlarged direct-lending program for construction of purely local public works. I believe that there was inadequate study of the appropriateness or extent of the need for this type of aid. In the matter of the college housing program, while this program has been a desirable one and its expansion was justified, the reduction made by the bill in the interest rate to an artificially low level will curtail, if not completely eliminate, the availability of private investment funds which have begun to flow toward college housing. The result will be that instead of more capital being available for this type of loan, there will be substantially less capital in the aggregate.

It is my hope that the defects in the Act will be corrected by the

Congress at the earliest opportunity in the light of further study and of actual experience in its administration.

NOTE: As enacted, S. 2126 is Public Law 345, 84th Congress (69 Stat. 635).

195 ¶ Statement by the President on the Death of Ambassador John E. Peurifoy and His Son.
August 12, 1955

I HAVE just been informed of the tragic death of Ambassador John E. Peurifoy and his son. A brilliant career diplomat, Ambassador Peurifoy served his country exceptionally well for many years. The United States and the free world has lost an outstanding champion of freedom and peace.

On the personal side, Mrs. Eisenhower and I have lost a valued friend. We extend our deepest sympathy to Mrs. Peurifoy in the great loss she has sustained.

NOTE: Mr. Peurifoy was serving as Ambassador to Thailand at the time of his death in an automobile accident.

196 ¶ Memorandum of Disapproval of Bill for the Relief of the E. J. Albrecht Company.
August 12, 1955

I HAVE WITHHELD my approval from the bill (H.R. 1393) "For the relief of the E. J. Albrecht Company."

The bill directs the Secretary of the Treasury to pay $142,-007.75 to the E. J. Albrecht Company as reimbursement for actual losses sustained by it in performing its contract with the United States for the construction of the outlet works for Sardis Dam on the Little Tallahatchie River, near Sardis, Mississippi.

After an exhaustive review, the Court of Claims dismissed this claim as being without merit. While this decision was based on legal grounds, the opinion issued by the Court in connection with its decision shows, particularly when taken in conjunction with the rest of the record, that there is no basis for affording relief to the contractor on equitable grounds. From these sources it is clear that the overriding causes of the losses which the contractor sustained were its own acts or omissions and the weather conditions it encountered in the performance of the work. I see nothing in these circumstances giving rise to equitable liability on the part of the government.

The continued success of the policy of awarding public contracts by competitive bids depends, of course, on the knowledge that successful bidders will be held to their bids with the same strictness as if they were dealing with private contractors. Relieving bidders of losses occasioned by the submission of bids that were successfully low because of over-optimism or failure to account for risks would not only strike a serious blow at the integrity of the competitive bidding system but would be unfair to more provident bidders who might otherwise have received the awards. It would deprive the government of benefits resulting from favorable circumstances occurring during the performance of a contract while requiring compensation for losses encountered as a result of unfavorable circumstances.

There are no circumstances in this case that would serve to distinguish it from others wherein contractors with the United States have suffered losses for which the government was not responsible. In view of this fact and in the absence of any equitable considerations in favor of the contractor, I perceive no merit in the claim for special treatment in this case.

Accordingly, I am constrained to withhold my approval from the bill.

DWIGHT D. EISENHOWER

197   ¶ Memorandum of Disapproval of Bill To Change the Military Record of Stephen Swan Ogletree.   *August* 12, 1955

I HAVE WITHHELD my approval of enrolled enactment H.R. 6232, Eighty-fourth Congress, "To include as Spanish-American War service under laws administered by the Veterans' Administration certain service rendered by Stephen Swan Ogletree during the Spanish-American War."

The effect of this legislation would be to determine by legislative decree, contrary to the facts, that, for the purpose of laws administered by the Veterans' Administration, Stephen Swan Ogletree rendered at least seventy days' active military service as a member of Company G, 2d Regiment, Alabama Volunteer Infantry, and was honorably discharged therefrom. No benefits would accrue by reason thereof prior to the date of receipt of an application to be filed subsequent to the date of its enactment.

There have been a number of affidavits submitted in support of Mr. Ogletree's contention that he served on active duty during the Spanish-American War. These affidavits are all dated some twenty-nine or more years after the occurrence of the events to which they relate. In some, the affiant could "almost" swear that Mr. Ogletree served with Company G, 2d Regiment, Alabama Volunteer Infantry. In others, the affiant states that Mr. Ogletree did serve with that organization. However, most of these affidavits are entirely consistent with the official records of the organization which show that any service of Mr. Ogletree with that organization was prior to the time that it entered into active federal service. In addition, the statement of one individual, who was of the opinion that Mr. Ogletree did serve in active federal service, indicates that during such period the commanding officer of the company was J. H. Brazila. The records of the company show that Brazila did not command the company while it was in federal service. Therefore, it is apparent that the passage of time has dimmed the recollection of the individuals who made these affidavits and that they have become confused as to the actual period of time during which the company was in federal service or when Mr. Ogletree was a member thereof.

Military records pertaining to Mr. Ogletree show quite clearly that he was not a member of Company G, 2d Regiment, Alabama Volunteer Infantry, while that organization was in federal service. The frequent muster rolls submitted on behalf of that organization, certified by the commanding officer and by the individual who acted as mustering officer, not only show the men who were present with the organization but also all men who were members of the organization during the period and who were absent for any reason whatsoever. The name of Stephen Swan Ogletree does not appear on any of these muster rolls.

Company G, 2d Regiment, Alabama Volunteer Infantry, was mustered into federal service on May 31, 1898. During the Spanish-American War, regulations provided that before volunteer organizations were mustered into the service of the United States, the members thereof should be medically examined to determine whether or not they were physically qualified for active military service. Retained records of the 2d Regiment, Alabama Volunteer Infantry, clearly show that Mr. Ogletree was medically examined in accordance with such regulations, that he was rejected for service because of physical disqualification at least 12 days prior to the time that this organization was mustered into the service of the United States, and that he was returned to his home at Eufaula, Alabama, through issuance of a "request for transportation", which provided as follows:

M. No.: *28570* Request for Transportation
Good for: *One* days from date. Date: *Mobile, Ala., May 19, 1898*
To: *The L & N RR Co.*
For: *John H. Nowlund and 26 men; no* pounds extra baggage
Co. & Regt.: *Co. "G," 2d Regt. Ala. Vols.*
From: *Mobile, Ala.* To: *Eufaula, Ala.*
Via: *The L & N and Central of Ga.*
En route from: *Mobile, Ala.* To: *Eufaula, Ala.*

Remarks: *Recruit, Co. G, 2d Regt., Ala. Vol., rejected by Medical Board; issued on authority of telegram dated May 3, 1898, H. C. Corbin, AG,* [*Adjutant General*].   See other side.
[Other side]   *   *   *   *Stephen S. Ogletree*   *   *   *

Section 131 of the Legislative Reorganization Act, approved August 2, 1946 (60 Stat. 812), provides, pertinently, as follows:

No private bill or resolution (including pension bills), * * * authorizing or directing * * * the correction of a military or naval record, shall be received or considered in either the Senate or the House of Representatives.

H.R. 6232 would change the military records of Stephen Swan Ogletree.

Section 207 of the Legislative Reorganization Act, supra, established the Army Board for the Correction of Military Records.   That Board was established for the purpose of reviewing military records and recommending to the Secretary of the Army the correction of any such records, where, in the judgment of the Board, such action might be necessary to correct an error or remove an injustice.   Upon the recommendation of the Board, the Act authorized the Secretary to take corrective action.   No application for the correction of the military records of Stephen Swan Ogletree has been received by that Board.

The Congress, by general legislation, has determined that cases of this character should be considered by the Army Board for the Correction of Military Records rather than by the legislature itself.   The affidavits which have been presented in Mr. Ogletree's behalf are entirely consistent with the fact that any service which he may have rendered was prior to the time that the organization was mustered into federal service.   Official records pertaining to the matter show quite clearly that Mr. Ogletree was not at any time during the Spanish-American War in the service of the United States.   Under such circumstances, to determine by legislative decree that he rendered any active military service during such war and was honorably discharged therefrom would be entirely discriminatory.   There is nothing in law or equity which would justify approval of this bill. To do so would confer upon Mr. Ogletree benefits provided for Spanish-American War veterans to which he is no more entitled than are other individuals who may have been members of local volunteer units prior to the time the unit was mustered into the federal service, but who were physically disqualified for federal service and were rejected prior to the mustering-in of the unit. I cannot, in justice, approve this enrolled enactment.

DWIGHT D. EISENHOWER

198 ¶ Memorandum of Disapproval of Bill Amending the Internal Revenue Code of 1954.
August 12, 1955

I HAVE WITHHELD my approval from the bill H.R. 6887, "To extend for one year the application of section 108(b) and to amend section 2053 of the Internal Revenue Code of 1954." This bill would extend for one year a section of the Revenue Code designed to facilitate certain railroad reorganizations. In addition, it would safeguard certain bequests to charity from the pyramiding effect of State and Federal inheritance and estate taxes.

Federal law properly exempts bequests to charity from estate taxation. In some situations, however, the intent of the Federal law is negated by the imposition of State taxes on charitable bequests. As a result of a provision of Federal law designed to prevent tax avoidance, such State taxes in turn give rise to increased Federal tax liabilities. H.R. 6887 is intended to relieve charitable bequests in these situations to the extent that Federal legislation can do so.

I am sympathetic with the objectives of both portions of the bill. However, I am informed that there are three defects in the part of the bill dealing with the estate tax, which are sufficiently serious to require my disapproval.

First, this legislation would often increase Federal tax liabilities on estates containing bequests to charity.

Second, the legislation would, in certain situations, accrue not to the benefit of charity but to other heirs.

Third, it would disturb existing well established relationships between Federal and State inheritance and estate tax liabilities based on the credit against Federal tax liability allowed for taxes paid to States since 1926. Since the State tax on the charitable bequest is deductible under the bill, it would no longer be counted in determining the amount which may be claimed by the estate as a credit for State taxes paid against the Federal tax liability. However, the tax imposed under the so-called State pick-up laws, which are designed to absorb the full credit allowable against the Federal estate tax, is based upon the total State tax otherwise levied (including the tax on the charitable bequest). Consequently, many State pick-up laws would not pick up the full amount allowable as a credit. Enactment of this bill would probably stimulate State legislation to enlarge the credit for taxes paid to States.

In view of these defects in the legislation, I must reluctantly withhold my approval from the bill, H.R. 6887.

My reluctance would be greater, however, had I not been advised that the defects in section 2 of the bill can be remedied and that section 1 and section 2, appropriately remedied, can be enacted so as to apply retroactively without any serious difficulty.

DWIGHT D. EISENHOWER

199 ¶ Memorandum of Disapproval of Bill To Reconvey to Former Owners Certain Lands Acquired for Reservoir Projects in Texas.
August 12, 1955

I HAVE WITHHELD my approval from H.R. 7195, "To provide for adjustments in the lands or interests therein acquired for reservoir projects in Texas, by the reconveyance of certain lands or interests therein to the former owners thereof."

The bill would authorize the Secretary of the Army to make adjustments in the land holdings of the United States acquired for five Texas reservoir projects (Belton, Benbrook, Garza-Little Elm, Grapevine, and Whitney Reservoirs) by reconveyance of certain lands to former owners, or the grantee, devisee, or successor in title of a former owner of contiguous property.

The Secretary has no authority to adjust land holdings where title has been acquired by purchase. The bill would provide the Secretary with authority to make such adjustments through reconveyance of lands or interests in lands to former owners at what the Secretary determines to be the original purchase price, adjusted to take into account improvements, damages, or interests retained by the United States.

However, H.R. 7195 goes further and requires the Secretary to determine whether the rights of a grantee, devisee, or successor in title of a former owner of contiguous property are equitably superior to the rights of the former owner himself. The law reports are replete with decisions which disclose the problems with which courts have been confronted in giving just recognition to asserted equitable interests in title to a tract of land. Moreover, in such cases the courts have enjoyed the historic cautionary benefits of the judicial process, such as notice and hearing, rights of intervention, the rules of evidence, and judicial precedents in a particular jurisdiction with respect to the application of equitable principles.   The bill does not provide, and the Secretary of the Army does not have, comparable cautionary benefits for an administrative proceeding in which he would be required to engage in the subtle problems involved in weighing justly the equitable superiority or inferiority of the rights, on the one hand of a former owner of a tract, and, on the other hand, of those of the grantee or successor in title to a contiguous tract of property.

This provision would unjustly expose the Secretary to a series of burdensome and time-consuming administrative proceedings which are entirely alien to his statutory responsibilities.   It would inevitably subject him to criticism from unsuccessful contestants. These unnecessary burdens and the attendant criticism can, and should, be avoided.

It is my firm opinion that, except for the return of lands or interests directly to the former owners or their heirs in cases of this kind, lands no longer required for project purposes should, if determined to be excess to the needs of the Department, be reported to the General Services Administration for disposal in accordance with general legislation providing for the disposition of excess and surplus Government-owned property.   I see no reason for establishing a new and special category of priority holders based on a chain of title from a former owner of contiguous property.

I have approved legislation authorizing similar adjustments by reconveyance of lands to former owners (or their heirs) upon application by them at Demopolis Lock and Dam, Alabama, and at Jim Woodruff Lock and Dam, Florida and Georgia, because I am convinced of the soundness of the principle behind the revised reservoir land acquisition policy of the Departments of the Army and the Interior.

I recommend that the Congress reconsider H.R. 7195 and enact a bill along those lines for the five reservoir projects in Texas to which the bill is applicable.

DWIGHT D. EISENHOWER

200 ¶ Memorandum of Disapproval of Bill for the Relief of Fred P. Hines. *August* 12, 1955

I HAVE WITHHELD my approval of S. 204, 84th Congress, "An Act For the relief of Fred P. Hines".

The bill would direct the Administrator of Veterans' Affairs to pay to Mr. Fred P. Hines the sum of $778.78, which sum represents the amount claimed as the cost of private hospital and medical expenses incurred in connection with the treatment of a disability not connected with his active military service in the Spanish-American War.

On July 20, 1953, I submitted a message to the Senate (S. Doc. No. 62, 83d Cong.) returning without my approval S. 152, 83d Congress, a bill identical to this bill except that S. 204 eliminates the payment of attorney fees in connection with the claim. No new evidence has been submitted in the interim, and the legislative history of the current bill contains no information which would justify a change in my position in the matter.

Under the circumstances and for the reasons set forth in my earlier message, I could take no other action than to withhold approval of S. 204.

Dwight D. Eisenhower

201 ¶ Memorandum of Disapproval of Bill To Amend the Civil Service Retirement Act. *August* 12, 1955

I AM WITHHOLDING approval of S. 1041, a bill "To amend the Civil Service Retirement Act of May 29, 1930, as amended, to provide for the inclusion in the computation of accredited service of certain periods of service rendered States or instrumentalities of States, and for other purposes."

This bill would provide additional retirement benefits to those Federal and District of Columbia employees who also have been, are now, or in the future may become employees of the States or of State instrumentalities on Federal-State programs financed either wholly or in part by Federal funds, in 5 types of agricultural programs and in programs of vocational education.

The bill is not approved because it would (1) make improper use of Federal funds to pay for services never received by it, (2) result in an unsound shifting of fiscal responsibility from State to Federal Government, (3) set an undesirable precedent, and (4) constitute an unsound approach to a desirable goal of increased employee mobility.

First, and most important, these additional retirement benefits would not be based upon Federal employment but on State employment.   States and State instrumentalities are responsible for paying for services rendered to them, and there is no assertion that such obligations are not met.   Federal retired pay is a basic element in the compensation system provided by the Federal Government in exchange for work performed by its employees.   To provide additional compensation payable out of the Federal Civil Service Retirement Fund on the basis of work performed for another employer appears to be an unnecessary and improper use of Federal funds.

Second, the financing principle followed in this bill is unsound. The Federal Civil Service Retirement Fund has been built up by contributions from Federal employees and from the Federal Government as an employer.   Under the bill the affected employees would now pay retirement contributions for their State service as if it had been Federal service but since the ultimate annuity payments would average several times such contributions, the major portion of the cost of this bill would be borne by Federal taxpayers. This shift of fiscal responsibility from the actual employer, the State or State instrumentalities, to the Federal Government would be accomplished with no corresponding transfer of funds.   This unsound fiscal policy could become an even more serious matter if the program were to be extended to all employee groups having similar claims.

Third, the bill appears to establish an undesirable precedent for making similar payments on the basis of employment in many other Federal-State cooperative programs. The record on the bill indicates that over 80 such programs have already been identified. Extension of similar benefits to employees of all such programs would lead far afield.

Fourth, although the bill seems to have the sound objective of encouraging transfers of employees between State and Federal employment, I do not believe that it moves toward this objective in a proper manner. A firmer, more acceptable step would be to extend the Federal old age and survivors system to include Federal employees. With employees of an increasing number of States also covered under that system, both Federal and State retirement systems would share a common base and all OASI benefits would be preserved in moving from one employer to another. Recommendations to the Congress will be made on this matter early in the next session.

DWIGHT D. EISENHOWER

202 ¶ Statement by the President Upon Signing Bill Amending the Agricultural Trade Development and Assistance Act. *August* 12, 1955

I HAVE TODAY approved S. 2253 "To reemphasize trade development as the primary purpose of title I of the Agricultural Trade Development and Assistance Act of 1954." When I signed the Agricultural Trade Development and Assistance Act of 1954 a year ago I expected that constructive benefits would result from the disposal of agricultural surplus commodities abroad under the provisions and safeguards of that legislation. The experience of the past year, during which agreements providing for the sale of surplus commodities valued at $469 million have been reached with 17 nations, has proved that hope to have been well founded. The agreements have been negotiated so as to safeguard usual marketings of the United States and to avoid undue disruption of world prices and world markets. The foreign currencies accruing from the sales are programmed for economic developmental loans, market development, educational exchange, and various United States expenditures abroad, with substantial benefit to both the recipient countries and ourselves. This program should lay the basis for a permanent expansion of our agricultural exports on a normal commercial basis.

This amendment to Public Law 480 will permit the expanded future operation of this program within the same safeguards existing in the basic law. I take pride in the cooperative and constructive manner in which this program has operated during the past year. I feel sure that a continuation of the same spirit will make possible an expanded effort of greater mutual benefit during the coming year and an eventual replacement of this program by expanded commercial sales.

NOTE: As enacted, S. 2253 is Public Law 387, 84th Congress (69 Stat. 721).

203 ¶ Letter to Maj. Gen. John S. Bragdon Appointing Him as Special Assistant to the President To Coordinate Public Works Planning. *August* 12, 1955

Dear General Bragdon:

Realizing the vital role of public works in the nation's economy, the Council of Economic Advisers last year established a small unit to devote itself to coordinating the planning of public works. The work of this unit has confirmed the need for continued systematic attention to this function. In order to make this work more effective and to broaden its scope and responsibility, I hereby appoint you as Special Assistant to the President to serve as coordinator of public works planning.

In the performance of these duties, one of your responsibilities will be to keep me informed with regard to:

(a) The various types and amount of the public facilities required by an expanding economy to meet human needs at the national, state, and local levels.

(b) The current long-range plans and programs for the accomplishment of such works by agencies of the Federal Government and by similar agencies of the States and of local governments, and the interrelationships of these programs.

(c) The possibilities for the acceleration of public works construction in the event that economic conditions make such acceleration desirable.

You also will advise and assist the Federal Government agencies responsible for public works to the end of strengthening their forward planning activities. In these and your other activities you will cooperate with the Council of Economic Advisers and with the Bureau of the Budget. For the above purposes and such other activities as may be necessary in the effective planning of the nation's public works, you are authorized to call upon the Secretaries of Defense; Interior; Agriculture; Commerce; Health, Education, and Welfare; the Administrator of the General Services Administration; the Administrator of the Housing and Home Finance Agency; and other departments and agencies responsible either for direct public construction or for assistance to States and to local governments, to assist you in the coordination of long-range plans and programs for such public works construction activities. You are also authorized to establish an Advisory Committee on Public Works to include persons designated by the Secretaries of Defense; Interior; Agriculture; Commerce; Health, Education, and Welfare; the Administrator of the General Services Administration; the Administrator of the Housing and Home Finance Agency; the Director of the Bureau of the Budget; and by the heads of such other Federal agencies responsible for public works as may be necessary.

You are also authorized and directed (a) to establish close working relationships with the executives and public works agencies of the several States and local government bodies, and (b) to invite them to inform you with regard to their public works planning functions. You also may invite representatives of State, city and local governments to constitute an Advisory Committee on the public works problems at these levels of government.

You may provide yourself with such staff as is necessary to assist you in the performance of these duties. You are authorized to organize temporary task forces made up of personnel from the various Federal departments and agencies. You may employ consultants as experts for specific purposes related to your duties. You are requested to attend the meetings of Federal Government committees or interdepartmental groups which may deal with public works problems.

It is my desire that the coordination of Federal Government public works planning and cooperation with the States and with local government bodies be advanced as rapidly as possible. As this activity progresses, you are requested to make recommendations to me for its further strengthening and improvement.

Sincerely,

DWIGHT D. EISENHOWER

204 ¶ Exchange of Messages Between the President and Chancellor Adenauer on the Air Force Disaster in Germany. *August* 13, 1955

[Released August 13, 1955. Dated August 12, 1955]

I HAVE RECEIVED your expression of regret concerning the Air Force disaster in Germany. I am most grateful for your sympathy and have made your kind message known to the American people.

DWIGHT D. EISENHOWER

NOTE: Chancellor Adenauer's message, received by the Secretary of State, follows:

On the occasion of the serious disaster which occurred to the United States Air Force by the crashing of the troop transport near Edelweiler, I would like you to transmit to the President of the United States my deepest sympathy. I express my sincere condolences to the relatives of the soldiers who met with the fatal accident.

205 ¶ Memorandum of Disapproval of Bill Extending the Domestic Minerals Purchase Programs. *August* 14, 1955

I HAVE WITHHELD my approval of H.R. 6373, an act "To amend the Domestic Minerals Program Extension Act of 1953 in order to extend the programs to encourage the discovery, development, and production of certain domestic minerals".

This bill, by Congressional action, would direct the continuation of the existing domestic minerals purchase programs under the Defense Production Act for certain minerals after defense needs have been met. Moreover, it would continue such purchases at prices considerably in excess of market price. It would direct the establishment of two new manganese buying depots and the reopening of a third. It would commit an additional 150 million dollars for the purchase of double the original program quantities of these minerals.

Pursuant to the Defense Production Act of 1950, as amended, certain purchase programs were established for these minerals during the Korean hostilities. Public Law 206 of the 83d Congress extended for two years the termination dates of these programs. H.R. 6373, in effect, would direct the expansion of these programs so as to require the Government to buy far greater quantities of these minerals than are necessary for defense purposes. As a result, Government assistance to the producers of several minerals will be continued under the guise of defense needs when such needs do not exist.

Furthermore, the fiscal arrangements that are provided for in H.R. 6373 are unsound. The bill would by-pass the usual budgetary processes and the customary review by Congressional committees. It would direct the use of the defense borrowing authority conferred by the Defense Production Act.

Finally, the provisions of H.R. 6373 would apply to only a small segment of the domestic minerals industry and would not reach the fundamentals of the problem. Indeed this bill would make solution of the overall problems of the industry more difficult.

I am conscious of the desirability of developing a long-range minerals program for the United States to assure an adequate mobilization base and to preserve a sound minerals economy. The Advisory Committee on Minerals Policy so advised, and the Office of Minerals Mobilization has been established in the Department of the Interior to determine and recommend such a program. The funds to make the necessary studies have just become available, and work toward the development of a long-range program has begun.

The interests of the domestic minerals industry will be better served by proceeding with the careful development of a long-range minerals program than by approving a stopgap measure extending substantial Government aid to only a segment of the industry. Meanwhile, with the exception of a single manganese depot, the existing domestic minerals procurement program remains uncompleted, and sales by domestic miners to the Government will continue under the provisions of the regulations now in effect.

DWIGHT D. EISENHOWER

206 ¶ Statement by the President Upon Signing
Bill Concerning Public Transit Services in the
District of Columbia.   *August* 14, 1955

DUE TO a labor management dispute and resultant strike, the
people of the City of Washington have been without transit services for 45 days.   Neither party to the dispute that gave rise to
this stoppage of service has discharged its obligation to the public.

I am opposed to any attempt to settle labor disputes through
legislation of the character of S. 2576.   My approval of this bill
is for an entirely different, but it seems to me, a cogent reason.
The law creating the Capital Transit Company more than 20
years ago established a direct relationship between the Company
and the Congress in that the Congress reserved to itself the power
of determining the termination date of the Company's franchise.
This Congress has done in S. 2576.   Moreover, both the Congress
and the Commissioners of the District of Columbia have concluded that Capital Transit Company, beginning several years
ago and continuing up to the present time, has failed to measure
up to its responsibilities as a public utility in the District of
Columbia.   The effective date of cancellation of the Company's
charter and franchises has been fixed by Congress as one year
after the date of the bill's enactment, and the bill authorizes the
District Commissioners to contract with that Company or others
for transit services in the intervening period.

I urge that the Commissioners act with wisdom in protecting
the best interests of the public.

NOTE: As enacted, S. 2576 is Public Law 389, 84th Congress (69 Stat. 724).

207 ¶ Presidential Statement Upon Signing Order Prescribing a Code of Conduct for Members of the Armed Forces While in Combat or Captivity. *August 17, 1955*

NO AMERICAN prisoner of war will be forgotten by the United States. Every available means will be employed by our government to establish contact with, to support and to obtain the release of all our prisoners of war. Furthermore, the laws of the United States provide for the support and care of dependents of members of the armed forces including those who become prisoners of war. I assure dependents of such prisoners that these laws will continue to provide for their welfare.

NOTE: The Code of Conduct was issued as part of Executive Order 10631 (3 CFR, 1955 Supp.). The White House release containing the President's statement noted that the order initiated a positive program to fortify military personnel against techniques and devices used on United States prisoners of war.

The release also stated that the President expressed gratification concerning studies and recommendations made by the Secretary of Defense's Advisory Committee on Prisoners of War. The Committee's report, entitled "POW" (Government Printing Office, 1955), was released by the Department of Defense.

This statement was released at Lowry Air Force Base, Denver, Colo.

208 ¶ Remarks on the Hurricane-Flood Disaster in the Northeastern States. *August 22, 1955*

ALL OF US know, of course, that there has been a very disastrous flood and hurricane in the East. There is much suffering in that region. I received last evening a telegram from E. Roland Harriman, Chairman of the Red Cross. He addressed me both as President and as Honorary President of the Red Cross. He said—and these are excerpts only:

"In this period of catastrophe among the citizens of the six

States affected by floods, I want to assure you that the entire resources of this organization in people, supplies, and money are being fully utilized to bring assistance to all those who are in need. Reports from our chapter in the flood area convince me that the cost of adequately caring for the thousands of families affected will cost many millions of dollars. So that relief work could proceed rapidly I have already made an allotment of $2 million from Red Cross funds and I have appealed to the American people to contribute to a Red Cross disaster fund which will be earmarked entirely for flood sufferers. Since Federal funds released by you are by law primarily for reconstruction of public works rather than direct assistance to individual sufferers, sincerely hope you will urge support of Red Cross appeal which funds will be used entirely to meet human needs.

"At this hour the American Red Cross is operating 107 shelters, housing and feeding 12,000 homeless, and providing clothing to everyone who needs it. We have established headquarters operating around the clock in disaster areas, have more than 400 nurses and 150 physicians who have volunteered for service. Thousands of other volunteers are helping. We estimate over 8000 families will require Red Cross assistance after the emergency is over."

My reaction is, of course, we will pitch in and help. I sincerely hope that before tomorrow night has been reached that Mr. Harriman, Chairman of the Red Cross, will be assured of all the funds he needs to carry out this work with all the help he is getting from the Federal service and from the States affected. The heart of America is not going to stand still while other Americans are in distress and in need of help.

As some of you may know, ever since the beginning of this disaster the Federal Government has been cooperating with the Red Cross in the States affected so as to relieve suffering and to carry on the work of rescue. The Defense Department in particular has been busily engaged in this work and from all States I have had reports of the marvelous work they have done. To assure myself that the Red Cross and Federal Government and the States are cooperating effectively in this regard, leaving no opportunity amiss in order that we may be helpful, I am going to meet Mr. Harriman about eight tomorrow morning in Hartford, Connecticut. To that meeting I have invited the other Governors of the States affected to send representatives or to come in person if their work will allow them to do so just that we may have a little coordinating talk to make sure that everything possible is being done. From there I will proceed to Washington before returning here to Denver Wednesday night.

NOTE: The President spoke in his office at Lowry Air Force Base, Denver, Colo. His remarks were recorded for broadcasting over radio and television.

On August 23, the White House released the text of messages concerning the disaster exchanged between the President and Her Majesty Queen Elizabeth II. The text of similar messages between the President and Prime Minister Eden of the United Kingdom, King Baudouin I of Belgium, Franz Bluecher, Acting Chancellor of Germany, and President Gronchi and Prime Minister Segni of Italy, were released on August 24.

On October 15, the White House announced interim procedures to assure the Small Business Administration of funds to meet disaster loan requirements in the northeastern States.

The messages and the White House announcement were made public at Lowry Air Force Base.

209 ¶ Remarks Following a Meeting With the Governors of Flood-Stricken States at Bradley Field, Hartford, Connecticut. *August 23, 1955*

[Broadcast over radio]

My Fellow Americans:

I have met here with the Governors and Federal officials that you have heard mentioned in this broadcast. Like the rest of you, I read in the papers, saw on the television, and heard on the radio about this great disaster. You can have no conception of what has happened until you come here and listen to these Governors, what has happened in each State—industries flattened, cities practically paralyzed, communications halted, people out of work, suffering—in certain instances missing members of their families, not knowing where they are.   This is a case where the Federal Government, the State government, the county government, the city government will do every possible thing they can. But they operate under laws—laws made by your representatives. And those laws are necessarily limited in the scope of authority they delegate.

Governor Peterson has mentioned how meager are the funds now available to the Federal Government for this specific purpose. I am going to consult immediately with the leaders of Congress. If necessary, I shall call a special session.   But what I want to talk about now just for a moment is this: the great value of Red Cross money.   Red Cross money is not limited.   It goes to people who are in need—to human beings, not just to cleaning roads and rebuilding schools but to people that are hungry, or cold and have no place to go.   In my opinion everybody in America within the sound of my voice will sleep better tonight if he turns in everything that he can spare to meet this great disaster that has happened to our fellow Americans.   This is a chance where each of us can rise to an emergency and prove that the American people regardless of governments, regardless of the limitations on them can meet an emergency and do it well.   I hope you will do it instantly so that by tomorrow night Mr. Roland Harriman here, the Chairman of the Red Cross, will know that he doesn't have to be meager or stingy in the allocations he makes to these areas.

In the meantime, I pledge again the Federal Government—and I pledge on the part of all these Governors who made the pledge to me that State governments are going to do everything that is possible to alleviate this situation.   We're going into the business of seeing whether we can prevent these floods in the future on a long-range basis, whether we can get insurance through some cooperation between insurance companies and State and Federal governments to prevent the kind of losses that have been suffered by our industries. We're going to try to get work in here to employ these people usefully. We're going to do everything that's possible and won't you do your part right away—quickly? Thank you very much.

NOTE: In the second paragraph the President referred to Val Peterson, Administrator, Federal Civil Defense Administration.

210 ¶ Address at the Annual Convention of the American Bar Association, Philadelphia. *August 24, 1955*

President Wright, Mr. Chief Justice, Senator Pepper, other distinguished guests, and my friends:

Before I begin the expression of the thoughts I deem appropriate to this occasion, I should like to advert briefly to the tragic incident of our national life that I know is now uppermost in the hearts and minds of all America. I refer, of course, to the tragic disaster on the eastern coast of our country.

We stand in the shadow of the hall in which was written the Constitution of the United States. Implicit in that document is the conviction, the belief, the faith, that Americans would perform by voluntary cooperation those deeds which in other governments, up to that time, had to be performed by direction, by regimentation, by order of Government. Some of those group problems that they thought would be thus solved are those great humanitarian problems that occur when one section of our country suffers the kind of catastrophe that has just been visited upon portions of our eastern coast. Woodrow Wilson said the highest form of democracy is the spontaneous cooperation of a free people. It seems to me now we have one of those most unusual opportunities to exhibit that spontaneous cooperation.

Frankly I feel we should not wait for the National Red Cross, our agent in such affairs, to appeal to us for help. I believe we should seize the opportunity to give to them—to force upon them—more than they can use, to make certain that disaster is alleviated, that all of those people in those destroyed villages and towns, will understand that America's heart has not forsaken them, that we are proud to help.

———

Naturally I am honored that once again I am invited to speak before this great representation of the American Bar Association; particularly in this summer of 1955.

This is the first of a series of meetings celebrating the John Marshall Bicentennial. John Marshall was a soldier in the War for Independence, a Congressman, a diplomat of outstanding ability, a Secretary of State.

But his reputation for greatness most firmly rests on his service as Chief Justice of the United States. It was in that office that he established himself, in character, in wisdom, and in his clear insight into the requirements of free government, as a shining example for all later members of his profession.

In his day, the truth about the nature of the Union and the purposes that joined widely separated states into one Republic—about the Constitution and the application of its principles to the problems of the times—was obscured by the fog of sectionalism, selfish interests, and narrow loyalties. Through a generation, he expounded these matters and formulated decisions of such clarity and vigor that we now recognize him as a foremost leader in developing and maintaining the liberties of the people of the United States.

He made of the Constitution a vital, dynamic, deathless charter for free and orderly living in the United States.

Thus his influence has been felt far beyond the confines of the legal fraternity. One result of his work was to create among Americans a deep feeling of trust and respect for the Judiciary.

Rarely indeed has that respect been damaged or that trust betrayed by a member of the Judicial branch of our three-sided government.

Americans realize that the independence and integrity and capacity of the Judiciary are vital to our nation's continued existence. For myself, this realization is understandably with me most sharply when it becomes my duty to make a nomination to the Federal Bench.

To the officers and members of the American Bar Association, I express my grateful acknowledgment of the assistance they have rendered, as a public service, in aiding me and my trusted advisers in the review of professional qualifications of individuals under consideration for Federal judicial positions. You have helped secure judges who, I believe, will serve in the tradition of John Marshall.

No other kind will be appointed.

Obviously, a rough equality between the two great political parties should be maintained on the bench. Thus we help assure that the Judiciary will realistically appraise and apply precedent and principles in the light of current American thinking, and will never become a repository of unbalanced partisan attitudes.

As we turn our minds to the global rather than the primarily national circumstances of our time, I feel that John Marshall's life and his works have even a more profound significance than is to be found in our veneration for the American courts and for his memorable services during the formative years of the Republic.

The central fact of today's life is the existence in the world of two great philosophies of man and of government. They are in contest for the friendship, loyalty, and support of the world's peoples.

On the one side, our nation is ranged with those who seek attainment of human goals through a government of laws administered by men. Those laws are rooted in moral law reflecting a religious faith that man is created in the image of God and that the energy of the free individual is the most dynamic force in human affairs.

On the other side are those who believe—and many of them with evident sincerity—that human goals can be most surely reached by a government of men who rule by decree. Their decrees are rooted in an ideology which ignores the faith that man is a spiritual being; which establishes the all-powerful state as the principal source of advancement and progress.

The case of the several leading nations on both sides is on trial before the bar of world opinion. Each of them claims that it seeks, above all else, an enduring peace in the world. In that claim, all identify themselves with a deep-seated hunger of mankind. But the final judgment on them—and it may be many years in coming—will depend as much on the march of human progress within their own borders, and on their proved capacity to help others advance, as on the tranquillity of their relations with foreign countries.

Mankind wants peace because the fruits of peace are manifold and rich, particularly in this Atomic Age; because war could be the extinction of man's deepest hopes; because atomic war could be race suicide.

The world is astir today with newly awakened peoples. By the hundreds of millions, they march toward opportunity to work and grow and prosper, to demonstrate their self-reliance, to satisfy their aspirations of mind and spirit. Their advance must not and cannot be stopped.

These hundreds of millions help make up the jury which must decide the case between the competing powers of the world.

The system, or group of systems, which most effectively musters its strength in support of peace and demonstrates its ability to advance the well-being, the happiness of the individual, will win their verdict and their loyal friendship.

You of the American Bar Association will play a critical part in the presentation of freedom's case.

The many thousands of men and women you represent are, by

their professional careers, committed to the search for truth that justice may prevail and human rights may be secured. Thereby, they promote the free world's cause before the bar of world opinion. But let us be clear that, in the global scene, our responsibility as Americans is to present our case as tellingly to the world as John Marshall presented the case for the Constitution to the American public more than a hundred years ago. In this, your aptitude as lawyers has special application.

In his written works and innumerable decisions, John Marshall proved the adequacy and adaptability of the Constitution to the Nation's needs. He was patient, tireless, understanding, logical, persistent. He was—no matter how trite the expression—a Crusader; his cause, the interpretation of the Constitution to achieve ordered liberty and justice under law.

Now America needs to exercise, in the Crusade for peace, the qualities of John Marshall. Peace and security for all can be established—for the fearful, for the oppressed, for the weak, for the strong. But this can be done only if we stand uncompromisingly for principle, for great issues, with the fervor of Marshall— with the zeal of the Crusader.

We must not think of peace as a static condition in world affairs. That is not true peace, nor in fact can any kind of a peace be preserved that way. Change is the law of life, and unless there is peaceful change, there is bound to be violent change.

Our nation has had domestic tranquillity largely through its capacity to change peacefully. The lone exception was when change, to meet new human concepts, was unduly resisted.

Our Founders would scarcely recognize the nation of today as that which they designed; it has been so greatly changed. But the change has been peaceful and selective; and always conforming to the principles of our founding documents. That has made it possible to conserve the good inherited from the past while adjusting to meet constantly rising goals. In that way we have kept in the front ranks of those who respect human dignity, who produce increasingly and who share fairly the fruits of their labors.

This is the kind of peace that we seek. Our program must be as dynamic, as forward looking, as applicable to the international problems of our times as the Constitution, under John Marshall's interpretations, was made flexible and effective in the promotion of freedom, justice and national strength in America.

That is the spirit in which the American delegation went to Geneva. We asserted then—and we shall always hold—that there can be no true peace which involves acceptance of a status quo in which we find injustice to many nations, repressions of human beings on a gigantic scale, and with constructive effort paralyzed in many areas by fear.

The spirit of Geneva, if it is to provide a healthy atmosphere for the pursuit of peace, if it is to be genuine and not spurious, must inspire all to a correction of injustices, an observance of human rights and an end to subversion organized on a worldwide scale. Whether or not such a spirit as this will thrive through the combined intelligence and understanding of men, or will shrivel in the greed and ruthlessness of some, is for the future to tell. But one thing is certain. This spirit and the goals we seek could never have been achieved by violence or when men and nations confronted each other with hearts filled with fear and hatred.

At Geneva we strove to help establish this spirit.

Geneva spells for America, not stagnation, then, but opportunity—opportunity for our own people and for people everywhere to realize their just aspirations.

Eagerness to avoid war—if we think no deeper than this single desire—can produce outright or implicit agreement that injustices and wrongs of the present shall be perpetuated in the future. We must not participate in any such false agreement. Thereby, we would outrage our own conscience. In the eyes of those who suffer injustice, we would become partners with their oppressors. In the judgment of history, we would have sold out the freedom of men for the pottage of a false peace.   Moreover, we would assure future conflict!

The division of Germany cannot be supported by any argument based on boundaries or language or racial origin.

The domination of captive countries cannot longer be justified by any claim that this is needed for purposes of security.

An international political machine, operating within the borders of sovereign nations for their political and ideological subversion, cannot be explained away as a cultural movement.

Very probably, the reason for these and other violations of the rights of men and of nations is a compound of suspicions and fear. That explains.   It cannot excuse.   In justice to others and to ourselves, we can never accept those wrongs as a part of the peace that we desire and seek.

We must be firm but friendly.   We must be tolerant but not complacent.   We must be quick to understand another's viewpoint, honestly assumed.   But we must never agree to injustice for the weak, for the unfortunate, for the underprivileged, well knowing that if we accept destruction of the principle of justice for all, we cannot longer claim justice for ourselves as a matter of right.

The peace we want—the product of understanding and agreement and law among nations—is an enduring international environment, based on justice and security.   It will reflect enlightened self-interest.   It will foster the concentration of human energy—individual and organized—for the advancement of human standards in all the areas of mankind's material, intellectual and spiritual life.

Can we achieve that sort of peace?   I think we can.   At times it may seem hopeless, far beyond human capacity to reach.   But has any great accomplishment in history begun with assurance of its success?   Our own Republic is a case in point.   Through a long generation there was almost a unanimous world conviction that the United States of America was an artificial contrivance that could not long endure.

And the Republic survived its most perilous years—the experimental years—because of dedicated efforts by individuals, not because it had a built-in guarantee of success or a path free from obstacles.

Our case for peace, based on justice, is as sound as was John Marshall's for the Constitution and the Union. And it will be as successful—if we present it before the bar of world opinion with the same courage and dedicated conviction that he brought to his mission.

In our communities we can, each according to his capacity, promote comprehension of what this Republic must be—in strength, in understanding, in dedication to principle—if it is to fulfill its role of leadership for peace.

In the search for justice, we can make our system an ever more glorious example of an orderly government devoted to the preservation of human freedom and man's individual opportunities and responsibilities.

No matter how vigorously we propose and uphold our individual views in domestic problems, we can present abroad a united front in all that concerns the freedom and security of the Republic, its dedication to a just and prosperous peace.

Above all, conscious of the towering achievements manifest in the Republic's history under the Constitution, assured that no human problem is beyond solution given the will, the perseverance and the strength—each of us can help arouse in America a renewed and flaming dedication to justice and liberty, prosperity and peace among men.

So acting, we shall prove ourselves—lawyers and laymen alike—worthy heirs to the example and spirit of John Marshall. Like him in his great mission, we shall succeed.

NOTE: The President's opening words referred to Loyd Wright, President of the American Bar Association, Chief Justice Warren, and Claude Pepper, former U.S. Senator from Florida. The President spoke in Independence Hall at 2:30 p.m.

211 ¶ Statement by the President Concerning New York Meeting of the United Nations Subcommittee on Disarmament.
August 29, 1955

OF THE actual decisions reached at Geneva, the first to be put to practical test is the decision to renew talks on limitations of armaments.

Today, in New York City, the Subcommittee of the United Nations Disarmament Committee is meeting to continue these discussions, pursuant to a directive from the four heads of government issued at their final session at Geneva.

I sincerely trust that the Subcommittee meeting will be marked by the same spirit of frankness and cooperation which typified the meetings at Geneva. If this is so, then I am sure that the Subcommittee work, in the end, can produce practical results that should lead to an easing of the tensions and the heavy burdens of armament that the world is presently carrying.

NOTE: This statement was released at Lowry Air Force Base, Denver, Colo.

212 ¶ Statement by the President: Labor Day.
September 5, 1955

THIS DAY is set aside, in our country, for America to salute the men and women who with their heads, hands and hearts produce the wealth of the Nation.

All of us are proud that the working men and women of our land labor in freedom and dignity, with efficiency and enthusiasm, at the jobs of their choice, in whatever community they wish, and receive fair compensation for their efforts.

We can also be proud that the individual human beings who make up this great labor force come from all races, all religions, and all national origins. They work on farms, in factories, in stores, in mines and in offices. They work on land and on sea and in the air.

In honoring the Nation's workers today, we reaffirm our devotion to the Nation itself—which over the years and decades, American workmen have built.

NOTE: This statement was released at Lowry Air Force Base, Denver, Colo.

213 ¶ Remarks at the Breakfast Meeting of Republican State Chairmen, Denver, Colorado. *September* 10, 1955

THANK YOU very much, gentlemen. This is a special group and of course I feel especially honored at the privilege of meeting you. I understand that you are just new graduates, and I must say, in a way, it's the strangest kind of commencement exercise for me to attend, although I have made a number of commencement addresses.

What strikes me is this: governmental service is the temporary privilege of some people. But what you are doing is exercising the inherent right and performing the basic duties of citizenship. Every citizen owes it to himself and his country to participate individually, or of course through a political organization, in making certain that our country goes in the direction that conforms to his ideals and hopes for that government—for that country.

Now, if you will forgive me, instead of jumping into farm problems and Geneva problems, and things of that kind, which are discussed interminably, I am going to talk just a little bit of philosophy this morning—political philosophy. That is because of a very deep and abiding belief that if a political party is not held together by a common faith, a common conviction, in certain fundamentals, then it is not a true political party but it is merely a conspiracy to gain power.

If we are not held together by a cause, then we are not making of ourselves an agency to help the United States of America. It is merely another form of gaining distinction for ourselves, to get ourselves a pat on the back, and to appear important.

Now, the text I am going to take is one with which you are completely familiar. You have all used it a thousand times, but whether or not we have stopped to think sufficiently of what it means is another story.

Lincoln concluded his Gettysburg address: ". . . that government of the people, by the people and for the people shall not perish from the earth."

The first thing I want to bring out is that he recognized that the possibility of this type of government perishing is always with us, and it is still with us.

The experiment in free government that was started by our Founding Fathers is still going on, and it will go on to the end of time, because the law of change is the law of life. No established philosophy or doctrine set up in 1737 could possibly apply in its detail today as it did then. It will be the same a hundred years hence.

"Of the people." Just exactly what do you think of when you say "government of the people"?

I think, in a simple sort of way, we could say, "of the people" doesn't mean a government of farmers, of labor bosses, of smart politicians, of businessmen, or of anybody else. It means a government of all types and classes of people, regardless of race or color or religion or everything else that tends to separate us in our social and ordinary lives. It means a government which, in its whole constitution, its whole concept and its aims, takes in the thoughts, the purposes, the ideals, the aspirations and the problems of today and 165 years ago.

And "by the people." "By the people" really means that every individual is participating in that government. Remember, Lincoln defined this government in three ways: of, by and for, implying that if the people did not exercise their right to govern, it shall perish from the earth.

In the national elections, something like a little over 50 percent of all qualified electors vote and in State and local elections, I am told that it is frequently as low as 25 percent.

Well, government by the people would seem to be not flourishing as well as it should. Some politician some years ago said that bad officials are elected by good voters who do not vote.

If we are going to have government by the people, then the man who is trying to exercise his rights and duties as a citizen makes certain that others are voting—not only in order to promote the fortunes of his own political life, but to make sure that this type of government shall not perish from the earth.

Now, what did he mean by "for the people"?

It seems to me here is one of the tall riddles of free government. "For the people." We have seen the phrase tortured by demagogic types to mean that an over-wise and over-busy governmental bureaucracy takes over all the functions of living. They say, "Now go on, boys, do just what you are told and we will take care of the 165 million people." And they tortured the General Welfare Clause of the Constitution.

I don't believe that is what Lincoln meant at all. If we are for the people, which means for the individual as such, we go first to the ten first amendments of the Constitution—to the Bill of Rights. That was written for the people. That Bill of Rights does not guarantee to each of us a profitable living. It guarantees to each of us an equal opportunity with all others to earn our living for ourselves and for our families, and to protect our future.

We could discuss further what we mean by "for the people," but I refer to another quotation of Lincoln's which was generally to this effect: the function of government is to do for the people what the individual cannot do at all, or do so well for himself, and in all those things which the individual can do for himself the government ought not to interfere.

Now I think today that is as good a presentation of the Republican case as I know how to make.   It puts it in terms and in words that all of us not only understand, but which we can make others understand.

In attempting to summarize the philosophy of the Republican Party I, myself, have sometimes used such phrases as moderate progressive and dynamic conservative, because we want to be known for what we are, the party of progress.   And if we are the party of progress, we must be the party of peace and prosperity, because this is implicit in the term "progress."   But I don't believe that you can sloganize the kind of honest philosophy that the Republican Party is trying to promote in the United States.   If we can live by that philosophy, however, then I think we have proved our worthiness to be the instrument through which the people of the United States carry on the job of government—of the people, by the people, and for the people.   And representative government shall not perish from the earth.

We have a great cause for which to fight.   Possibly this manner of cause, something in which you believe, is deeper with an old soldier than it is with some.   In the military life you are required to study whole campaigns, the careers of leaders—how did they think, how did they produce the things they wanted?

One man who always attracted me because of his military career, rather than anything else, was old Cromwell.   Cromwell's Army had the sternest and toughest discipline of any army that I know of in the world.   It has been the belief that if you had that kind of discipline, you couldn't have enthusiasm.   But he had it. He sent his Roundheads into battle singing hymns and chopping off the heads of cavaliers.   Why?   Because they believed in something.   He told them, by golly, if you are going to fight under the Roundheads you will go straight to heaven; and whatever your desires were, you got them.   He taught them to believe in something.

Now, what I am trying to get at is how do we get hold of something that we believe in so much that it shines in our faces every time we say it to anybody else?

It is not only what we believe. It is what we believe we live for. We say "for God and country." Our country was organized and defined, when you come down to it, on a very fervent and firm basic religious faith. Our founding documents maintained the only way you could explain our form of government was because "man was endowed by his Creator." On this principle our cause is founded.

How do we convince the people that we are for a cause? How do we go about this thing, believing in it as fervently as we do? How do we get the people to accept it and put into power the people who will exemplify and practice that kind of doctrine?

Well now, again you will have to let me go back to the military. After all, I have been in it much more than I have the political. Before every great battle, the commander gets together his corps commanders. This group here this morning numbers forty-eight. I suppose it would be about comparable to the number of corps commanders I had, finally, in the European campaign.

Now, to the corps commanders, the commander explains his plans. Everybody is indoctrinated. It is supposed to be a very useful performance.

But gentlemen, could you imagine a battle—and some of you here in this room were probably in the very campaigns of which I am talking—if the commanders all knew everything about what was going to be done, and they were all doing it, and they were all dedicated, and it started on down from there and finally got down to where there wasn't a corporal in the whole business that knew his job? You will forgive me for using military terms. Getting this information through the ranks is the corps commander's job.

Now, in volunteering for the work you have undertaken, you have undertaken one of the highest forms of duty which an American citizen performs. You are also taking on the tough job, just like a corps commander in battle, of making sure that his organization is ready to carry the fight right down on through. In your case, that means from the state chairman to the district chairman and the precinct chairman and all the workers in the ranks—and to each individual.

Unless you can take the fervor that you have, and carry it back to your State, and conduct the same effective campaign schools there—make sure that the spirit and know-how is going right on down through—it is all in vain. If you do the job right, it is government by the people. Let's emphasize people, not just us, not just a bunch of politicians seeking office. By the people.

So the object in the organization of a political party comes down to: how can I get to the last man living in my block, my apartment house? How can I get to him? Well, if you can get to him with your conviction, with your belief, with your fervor, with the leadership that you have exhibited by getting where you are today in this organization, you can win any election in the country. You can go down and reach that 50 percent of people who do not vote and get them to believe in some of the things that you believe in your own heart. The thing is done.

And incidentally, while I have been forbidden to mention this subject by your Chairman, I will bring up for a moment the question of one man and one man's value.

Now, I just want to point out to you that I greatly appreciated your telegram, particularly where you said, "I like Ike more than ever." May I return the compliment and say that when I see these faces before me, I like the Republican Party more than ever.

But we don't believe for a minute that the Republican Party is so lacking in inspiration, high quality personnel, and leadership that we are dependent on one man. We don't believe it for a minute.

Now as long as we have a man in the leadership position, why of course, as a party, we are going to be loyal, we are going to help in the fight.

But humans are frail—and they are mortal. Finally, you never pin your flag so tightly to one mast that if a ship sinks you cannot rip it off and nail it to another. It is sometimes good to remember that.

So I suggest that as a party everybody on down the line pledge to get a new recruit, a youngster, and make him a member of the party. Now, if you will carry that idea far enough, making each party member a vote-seeker as well as a voter, you have got elected a President of the United States.

The job of getting people really wanting to do something is the essence of leadership. And one of the things a leader needs occasionally is the inspiration he gets from the people he leads. The old tactical textbooks say that the commander always visits his troops to inspire them to fight. I for one soon discovered that one of the reasons for my visiting the front lines was to get inspiration from the young American soldier. I went back to my job ashamed of my own occasional resentments or discouragements, which I probably—at least I hope I concealed them.

The young American in action is something to inspire anybody. If you get these young men of zeal and vigor, pep and tireless energy, get them on your side and get them to going, you just have to keep a light rein on them, you don't have to use a spur or whip.

Let me give you a very quick application of this principle of getting young recruits. If you get a recruit my age, I am lucky if I can vote in two presidential elections. But if you get a recruit at 21, he can vote for you in 12 or 15.

Now gentlemen, I know you have discussed the problems—domestic and foreign—of the times. They are important. The National Committee will continue to give you literature that analyzes and shows what the Administration is trying to do, working with the leadership in the Congress, to bring these things about. All those things will be coming to you. That is ammunition for your guns, to show that you are working for the people, and that the party is of the people, and you are trying to get that kind of thing done by the people.

But underneath it all, just remember that the cause for which you are working is: to make certain that government is to do for the people those things which they cannot do themselves, or so well do, but we are not going to interfere with those things which are the proper province of the individual. With your other ammunition, you have got something that you can carry to the voters with a grin on your face. And for heaven's sake, don't forget the value of a grin! Pessimism never won a battle.

One more point: there is no such thing as a hopeless State, or a hopeless district. They are Americans, aren't they?

The harder the fight in your State, in your district—wherever it is—the harder you ought to fight. You don't go into a battle and say to one division or one corps, "Oh, we don't care if you fight. Just stand there. It's all right. We know it's pretty tough stuff over there." You get everybody to operate for a common objective.

If you just increase the Republican vote by, let us say, 15 percent over what it was before in these difficult localities, you make the Republican party that much more respected there, and you increase the prospects of State victories.

So I just ask each one, don't believe in political defeatism. We have got a positive program, to develop, exploit, exemplify, the philosophy that Lincoln taught us. That is the positive thing. That means not merely in Kansas, or Pennsylvania, or Colorado, or anywhere else—but throughout the U.S.A.

Again, gentlemen, I refer to the telegram you sent me, and your expression of confidence.

To fail to say that I am complimented by such action on your part, fail to say that I am grateful, would be inexcusable. Of course I am. Any American would like to think that he has the confidence of his fellow Americans when he is trying to do a tough job. But, again I say, this country, this party, is not only big—it overshadows every individual and any individual in it.

We must set as a goal the extra 15 percent of recruits that we need—and are going to have—to make this party a perpetual agency for carrying out the kind of doctrine that Lincoln taught us, for the benefit of our children and all our grand-children.

I overlooked one thought: your attention to the character and quality of your candidates in every district. I mean not only Presidents and Vice Presidents, particularly—but gubernatorial, senatorial, congressional candidates—right on down.

Did you ever stop to think how important it is to a man to know who his councilman is going to be, or the type of man running for mayor? If the councilman is a personable and fine fellow, with a lot of vigor and ability, and you get him out where people can see him, I would say that that would be a reinforcing and an implementation of your leadership that would be most effective in the State and national contests.

Thank you very much.

NOTE: The President spoke at the Brown Palace Hotel, Denver, Colo., at 8:40 a.m.

214 ¶ Telegram to the President of the United States Chamber of Commerce on Assistance Given Flood Disaster Areas. *September* 12, 1955

Mr. Boyd Campbell
President of the Chamber of Commerce
of the United States
Washington, D.C.

Thank you very much for writing me about the actions taken by the Chamber of Commerce of the United States to assist in alleviating the damage caused by the recent floods in the northeastern United States.

The generous response of Americans in all walks of life to appeals for assistance in this catastrophe has been most heartwarming. It is additionally gratifying to know that American businesses and industries, acting individually and through trade associations, plan still further assistance to their associates in the flooded areas so that their return to normal activity may be hastened, and their tremendous losses may be quickly overcome.

Such a demonstration of goodwill and cooperation will not only provide evidence of the fine spirit underlying our economic system but will also add to the very strength of that system.

I wish you all possible success in carrying out this program.

DWIGHT D. EISENHOWER

NOTE: This telegram was released at Lowry Air Force Base, Denver, Colo.

215 ¶ Statement by the President on the Occasion of the Jewish New Year.
September 16, 1955

ON THE occasion of the Jewish New Year I extend greetings to all Americans of the Jewish faith.

I hope that your observance will renew in each of you a devotion to the cause of peace and a determination to help advance the welfare of your fellow men in accordance with the ancient spiritual and moral teachings of your religion. To people of every persuasion these teachings are a continuing guide in the search for justice and good will among nations and a better life for men, women, and children everywhere in the world.

DWIGHT D. EISENHOWER

NOTE: This statement was released at Lowry Air Force Base, Denver, Colo.

216 ¶ Message to President Ruiz Cortines on the Anniversary of the Independence of Mexico.
September 16, 1955

His Excellency
Senor Don Adolfo Ruiz Cortines
President of the United Mexican States

It gives me pleasure on this anniversary of the Independence of the United Mexican States to convey to Your Excellency and to the people of Mexico my sincere good wishes and felicitations as well as those of the people of the United States.

DWIGHT D. EISENHOWER

NOTE: This message was released at Lowry Air Force Base, Denver, Colo.

217 ¶ Message Prepared for the Conference on Fitness of American Youth.　*September* 18, 1955

To Participants of the Conference on Fitness of American Youth:

Your willingness to participate in this Conference shows that you share my concern about the fitness of our American youth. It is certain that we can and should do more than we are now doing to help our young people become physically fit and therefore better qualified, in all respects, to face the requirements of modern life.

I very much appreciate your interest. Your conference deliberations will help guide the efforts of all of us who are interested in improving the total fitness of all our children and youth.

DWIGHT D. EISENHOWER

NOTE: This message was prepared for inclusion in the program for the President's Conference on Fitness of American Youth, scheduled to be held September 27–28 at Lowry Air Force Base, Denver, Colo.

Earlier, on September 17, the White House released a list of 139 persons who had been invited to attend the Conference.

On September 25 the White House, on behalf of the Vice President who was Chairman of the Conference, announced its postponement.

The message and announcements were released at Lowry Air Force Base, Denver, Colo.

EDITOR'S NOTE:

The President suffered a heart attack early in the morning of September 24 while staying at the home of Mrs. Eisenhower's mother, Mrs. John Sheldon Doud, in Denver, Colo.

Information concerning the President's illness was made available at Fitzsimons Army Hospital usually by oral statements by Press Secretary James C. Hagerty or by Assistant Press Secretary Murray Snyder.

During the President's illness, Vice President Nixon presided over the meetings of the Cabinet and the National Security Council. Members of the Cabinet and other officials made frequent trips to Denver to consult with the President.

The President's first official act following the onset of his illness was the initialing on September 30 of two lists of recess appointments of foreign service officers. His recovery was without complication and on November 11 he was able to fly back to Washington. From that city he went to his farm at Gettysburg, Pa., to continue his convalescence. On November 22 the President attended his first Cabinet meeting following his illness. This was held at Camp David, the Presidential camp in the Catoctin Mountains of Maryland.

218 ¶ Message Opening the United Community Campaigns of America. *October 2, 1955*

[Recorded on tape and film]

My Fellow Citizens:

My talk has to do with a strictly domestic matter. Between now and Thanksgiving Day the United Community Campaigns of America will be held. In one town the campaign may be called the United Community Chest; in another, the United Fund or the United Crusade. The names differ, but the one word and the one purpose that all have in common is "united."

The campaigns are united in support of some twenty-one thousand voluntary health, welfare and youth agencies—including the USO, and in many cities, the Red Cross and national causes such as Heart, Cancer and Crippled Children. They ask your help, not through twenty-one thousand separate competitive appeals, but through one annual appeal in each city. Together they constitute the biggest single voluntary cause in our nation.

In addition to the many health services they support, these United Community agencies help social scientists study the cause and cure of family break-downs that wreck homes, hurt children, waste life. They work to prevent and thus to end the plague of juvenile delinquency—and adult delinquency too, may I add. And they constantly wage war against the virus of prejudice, bigotry and inhumanity. They are doing their job the united way because man is a united being. Such an appeal calls for a united response.

So, when the volunteer campaigner knocks at our doors and at our hearts, I urge that we all unite to give him a neighborly welcome.

Thank you very much.

NOTE: This message, recorded before the President's hospitalization, was broadcast over radio and television at 7:55 p.m.

219 ¶ Letter to the Columbus Citizens' Committee in New York City.   *October 11, 1955*

[Released October 11, 1955. Dated September 15, 1955]

To the Columbus Citizens' Committee:

The memory of Christopher Columbus—a common heritage of the Old and New World—is even in the Atomic Age a source of inspiration to all who, under God, would search the unknown and advance the frontiers of human knowledge for the betterment of mankind. Out of courage, perseverance in purpose and unshakable confidence in his principles, he fashioned a new age in human history.

Those same qualities today can strengthen the men and women of the United States and of all freedom-loving countries in the search for prosperity with fair opportunity, for peace with justice. If we are courageous and persevering and confident, dedicated in mission and decent in purpose, as was Columbus, we too shall build a new and better world for human living.

DWIGHT D. EISENHOWER

NOTE: This letter was sent to the Committee, which was holding its annual dinner at the Waldorf-Astoria Hotel in New York City on October 11. It was released at Lowry Air Force Base, Denver, Colo.

220 ¶ Letter to Nikolai Bulganin, Chairman, Council of Ministers, U.S.S.R.   *October* 12, 1955

[Released October 12, 1955. Dated October 11, 1955]

Dear Mr. Chairman:

I wish to thank you for your letter of September 19, 1955 about my Geneva proposal of July 21 that we exchange information about military establishments and permit reciprocal aerial inspection over our two countries.

You raise a good many questions, and I shall not be able to reply to them until the doctors let me do more than at present. In any event, a full reply calls for preliminary work by my advisers and this is actively under way.

Let me now say, however, that I am encouraged that you are giving such full consideration to my Geneva proposal. I hope that we can agree on it, not as a cure-all, but, as I said at Geneva, to show a spirit of non-aggressiveness on both sides and so to create a fresh atmosphere which would dispel much of the present fear and suspicion. This, of itself, would be worthwhile. It would, I believe, make it more possible to make progress in terms of comprehensive plans for inspection, controls and reductions of armament, which will satisfy the high hopes of our peoples, and indeed of all the world.

I have not forgotten your proposal having to do with stationing inspection teams at key points in our countries, and if you feel this would help to create the better spirit I refer to, we could accept that too.

With best wishes,

Sincerely,

Dwight D. Eisenhower

NOTE: Mr. Bulganin's letter of September 19, released by the White House on September 23, is published in the Department of State Bulletin (vol. 33, p. 644). The President's July 21 proposal at Geneva appears as Item 166, above.

This letter was released at Lowry Air Force Base, Denver, Colo.

221 ¶ Statement by the President on Observance of Farm-City Week. *October* 17, 1955

I HAVE proclaimed October 23–29 as Farm-City Week for 1955 in response to requests from the numerous farm, service, and business organizations and of private industry.

It is a source of deep satisfaction to me personally that there is such broad interest in a national observance dedicated to strengthening ties and increasing understanding between the people of our farms and cities. Farmers and city dwellers alike recognize the interdependence of all of us in our free society. Our reliance upon each other is so much a part of our established daily living that we have come to accept it as a matter of course.

Farm-City Week presents an opportunity for public recognition of the vital role agriculture plays in providing an abundance of food and fiber for our fast-growing population. At the same time, this observance will focus attention upon the great contribution of labor, industry and commerce to the increasing efficiency of agriculture and to the continuing development of our total economy.

I strongly urge full participation in Farm-City Week activities as a national tribute to this important and effective partnership.

DWIGHT D. EISENHOWER

NOTE: This statement was released at Lowry Air Force Base, Denver, Colo.

222 ¶ Letter to Governor Roberts of Rhode Island on the Recommendations of the New England Governors' Conference.
October 18, 1955

[Released October 18, 1955. Dated October 17, 1955]

Dear Governor Roberts:

I appreciate your letters and the resolutions of the New England Governors' Conference. At the outset I want to reaffirm the determination of the entire Administration to assist the States and people of the Northeast in developing adequate protections against future flood and hurricane losses.

Aside from the resolution concerning establishment of atomic reactor generating plants in New England, about which I shall write you a separate letter, I shall discuss below for your convenience each of the Governors' recommendations and the status of our efforts concerning them.

First, the Governors recommend that $1,500,000 of emergency funds be made immediately available to accelerate the planning of certain authorized flood control structures. For some weeks we have been striving to do exactly this but still lack the needed Congressional concurrences to permit it. These efforts are continuing, with the cooperation of Members of the New England Congressional Delegation. The Administration shares the Governors' hope that this matter can be successfully resolved. Certainly all that can be done to that end is being done.

Second, the Conference recommends a $3,400,000 supplemental appropriation for fiscal year 1956 to start construction of authorized flood control projects on which planning has been completed. The amount of funds the Administration will recommend for this purpose will be affected by the success or failure of attempts to secure the Congressional concurrences mentioned above, but I assure the Governors that in January such a supplemental request will be submitted to the Congress. Detailed studies of this matter are already well under way in the affected Government agencies.

Third, it is urged that $100,000 be provided in supplemental 1956 funds for studies of possible new flood construction projects in New England. This matter, too, is far along in governmental processes. Funds therefor will be recommended to the Congress.

Fourth, the Governors recommend that $34,300,000 be requested of the Congress in the 1957 budget to accelerate flood control construction. It is too early to give a figure, but you can count on our recommending additional funds for this purpose in the 1957 budget. The size of this item in the budget will also be affected by the results of our efforts to obtain the Congressional concurrences mentioned above.

Fifth, the Governors urge the Administration to include $12,453,000 in the 1957 budget for construction of navigation and beach erosion projects. This item would appear to be less critically needed than the others mentioned, but it is undergoing careful examination and will unquestionably receive attention in the 1957 budget.

Sixth, the Governors urge $200,000 more in 1956 to expand and expedite the authorized hurricane survey for the New England States. I can assure you that additional funds will be recommended for this purpose in both the 1956 and 1957 budgets.

Seventh, the Governors recommend that the Secretary of Commerce organize the resources of his Department in support of

Federal disaster insurance. Some weeks ago this matter was taken under close scrutiny. It is now being examined by all Federal agencies concerned, under the general direction of the Bureau of the Budget and the Housing and Home Finance Agency. The Senate Banking and Currency Committee will hold hearings on this problem late this month. The Administration will present specific legislative suggestions at that time.

I am confident of your appreciation of the impossibility of setting forth specifics, either in projects or amounts of money, at this stage in the formulation of our budgetary planning. Appropriation requests, both for the rest of the fiscal year and for the 1957 fiscal year, to accelerate Corps of Engineers' flood control activities in the Northeastern States are now undergoing analysis in connection with our overall budget recommendations. These recommendations will go to the Congress in January. I will see that you are furnished the approved project list and the sums involved when these data have been prepared for Congressional submission.

Sincerely,

Dwight D. Eisenhower

The Honorable Dennis J. Roberts
Governor, State of Rhode Island
Providence, Rhode Island

P.S. The foregoing letter was prepared before the additional floods which occurred this last weekend. When the reports of the extent of the damage are in, we shall, of course, take into account whatever modifications in the above program are necessary to meet whatever emergency that now confronts us. We can well imagine how discouraging this additional disaster must be to the people in New England already so sorely afflicted.

NOTE: This letter was released at Lowry Air Force Base, Denver, Colo.

223 ¶ Letter to Governor Roberts of Rhode Island on the Establishment of Atomic Reactor Generating Plants in New England.
October 18, 1955

[Released October 18, 1955. Dated October 17, 1955]

Dear Governor Roberts:

Thank you for telling me in your letter of September 27th of the views of the New England Governors on the establishment of atomic reactor generating plants in New England. I fully appreciate their keen interest in reducing the cost of generating electric power in the New England area.

As the Atomic Energy Commission has pointed out, nuclear power will not immediately provide low cost power. The one nuclear power plant now under construction and the six others in various stages of design are experimental types and are not expected to produce power at a cost as low as a modern conventional plant. How closely their costs will approach those of conventional production of electrical energy and which of the six types of atomic power plants is the best will not be known, of course, until they have been in operation over a period of time. Justification for their construction in view of their noncompetitive costs necessarily rests upon the contribution they will make to power reactor technology.

The AEC program for the development of nuclear power plant technology was based on the expectation that industry would accept a substantial share of the responsibility and cost for the development. Invitations to industry to participate in this program were first issued in January 1955, and it was in response to this invitation that the proposal from Yankee Atomic Electric Company was submitted. Although the original Yankee proposal was unacceptable, a revised proposal has been received and will be acted upon by the Commission promptly after completion of the technical evaluation now being made.

In view of the favorable response from industry to the first invitation to submit proposals, a second invitation was issued on September 21, 1955. It provides a second means by which New England can obtain a power reactor, and I am enclosing a copy of it for your reference. A third means of obtaining a power reactor for New England would be through construction and operation by a private group without assistance from the Federal Government after applying for and receiving a license for this purpose from the AEC. Two utilities, one in New York and one in Pennsylvania, have already announced their intention of pursuing this course.

Even though nuclear power is not yet competitive, the AEC and many segments of industry believe that eventually it will be. With this in mind, it would certainly seem wise to give all reasonable encouragement to those organizations interested in advancing the development of atomic power in the New England area.

I am sure that representatives of the AEC would be glad to discuss this matter with you or with other members of the Governors' Conference, and to be of such assistance as may be appropriate.

With best wishes,

Sincerely,

DWIGHT D. EISENHOWER

NOTE: This letter was released at Lowry Air Force Base, Denver, Colo.

224 ¶ Statement by the President on the 14th Anniversary of the Civil Air Patrol.
October 19, 1955

THROUGH fourteen years the volunteers of the Civil Air Patrol, by their almost daily performance of aerial search and rescue, mercy missions and disaster relief, have added immeasurably to the safety and well-being of their fellow citizens.

Beyond that, more than fifty thousand teen age members of CAP engaged annually in its program of aviation education help answer the continuing need for alert young men and women in our Air Force and in our aviation industry.

The volunteers of the Patrol by their patriotic service, their readiness for every call, their devotion to duty have earned the gratitude of the Republic.

I heartily endorse the Civil Air Patrol and urge all of our citizens to support this worthy organization. I join with my fellow Americans in congratulating the members of CAP upon their Fourteenth Anniversary.

NOTE: This statement was released at Lowry Air Force Base, Denver, Colo.

225 ¶ Letter to the Vice President Concerning the Conference on Equal Job Opportunity.
October 22, 1955

[Released October 22, 1955. Dated October 21, 1955]

Dear Dick:

Please convey to the participants in the Conference on Equal Job Opportunity on October twenty-fifth my very best wishes.

I am keenly interested in the benefits the nation will draw from this exchange of experiences and ideas—and I will be anxious to have your report on it.

We must find ways of assuring to every American that in his search for employment he will be judged on the basis of his character and his ability, and not on the basis of his race, his religious faith, or the land from which he or his forbears came to America.

With the help of the men who will be at the Conference, I am certain we will make truly significant progress.

With warm regard,

As ever,

DWIGHT D. EISENHOWER

NOTE: The Vice President served as Chairman of the Conference, which was held at the Shoreham Hotel, Washington, D.C.

This letter was released at Lowry Air Force Base, Denver, Colo.

226 ¶ Letter to the Vice President and the Cabinet Regarding the Task of Secretary Dulles at Geneva. *October* 23, 1955

[Released October 23, 1955. Dated October 19, 1955]

Dear Dick:

I want to say a word to you, and through you to my Cabinet associates, about the task which Foster Dulles will be assuming at Geneva. As head of the American Delegation he will be carrying a heavy load of responsibility, not only as Secretary of State, but as my personal representative having my complete confidence and with whom I have continuous close understanding.

This second meeting at Geneva was one of the steps toward solving world problems which Foster and I planned together, and which we have talked over fully not only before my illness but twice since.

I hope that each one in Government will do whatever he can to make Foster's task easier. The Secretary of State must have the discretionary authority which is needed if there is to be effective negotiation and the spirit of conciliation which I have called for at that meeting. He must be the one who both at the conference table and before the world speaks with authority for our country.

With warm regard,

As ever,

DWIGHT D. EISENHOWER

NOTE: This letter was read at the Cabinet meeting at the White House on October 21. It was released at Lowry Air Force Base, Denver, Colo.

¶ 227 ¶ Statement by the President on the Foreign Ministers Meeting at Geneva. *October* 26, 1955

THREE MONTHS AGO Secretary Dulles and I, with the governmental leaders of France, Great Britain and the Soviet Union, met at Geneva. The purpose, as I said in opening that Conference, was to "create a new spirit that will make possible future solutions of problems which are within our responsibilities."

The world hopes that that Conference did in fact create that new spirit.

However, as I said to the American people on my return, the "acid test" would come when the Foreign Ministers would, in accordance with our Geneva directive, tackle concretely these problems for which our nations have responsibility and which, if unresolved, create tension and danger.

Tomorrow the four Foreign Ministers meet at Geneva to resume where we left off last July. They will seek solutions which are possible if that new spirit is real. Foremost among these measures is the reunification of Germany within a framework of European security.

Secretary Dulles and I think alike with respect to these matters. We have often discussed them and twice within the last two weeks he and I reviewed together the positions and the proposals which will be made at Geneva by the Western nations. These will be designed to promote a peace of justice, with increased security and well-being for all. They will reflect a genuine spirit of conciliation and accommodation. If the Soviet Union responds in a similar spirit, much progress can be made. That is my personal hope, as I am confident it is the hope of the American people.

We shall all of us follow with eagerness the developments at Geneva, for they will go far to demonstrate whether the "spirit of Geneva" marks a genuine change and will actually be productive of the peaceful progress for which the whole world longs.

NOTE: This statement was released at Lowry Air Force Base, Denver, Colo.

228 ¶ Message to the National Industrial Conference Board on the Peaceful Uses of Atomic Energy. *October* 27, 1955

[Released October 27, 1955. Dated October 24, 1955]

Members of the Conference:

On December 8, 1953, before the General Assembly of the United Nations, our Government pledged its determination to find ways by which the miraculous inventiveness of man shall not be dedicated to his death, but consecrated to his life. The pledge then voiced for the United States has become the law of our land.

Our progress in the field of peaceful uses of atomic energy is evident in many ways. Schools have been established for training students and professional men, including foreign nationals, in the science and technology of the atom. Atomic Energy Commission technical libraries, which have grown to tremendous size as a result of declassifying actions and which represent a vast fund of valuable information, have been distributed within the United States and to many countries abroad. The employment of radioisotopes has resulted in agricultural and industrial savings of hundreds of millions of dollars and even greater savings are promised for the future. The medical applications are increasing daily.

The establishment of an International Atomic Energy Agency now seems reasonably assured. Agreements for cooperation in the civil uses of atomic energy have been negotiated with 28 countries, and we have made available 200 kilograms of the rare isotope of uranium for use by those friendly countries in research reactors. The International Conference on the Peaceful Uses of Atomic Energy in Geneva, the largest and most important scientific gathering ever held, was initiated by the United States.

First fruit is in sight in the field of nuclear power, and with the increasing leverage of the ingenuity of American industry applied to the problem, economically competitive nuclear power will become a reality.

There is no monopoly—and we seek no monopoly—in the harnessing of the atom for man's benefit. Rather, we seek to encourage participation in that task. In particular, we want the maximum participation of American industry. Our standard of living is a product of its tools and techniques. The magnitude of the return which can be realized by the application of those same tools and techniques to the new field of atomic energy is immeasurable.

Beyond that, there are loftier implications of the potential uses of atomic energy. The book of history reflects mankind's unceasing quest for peace. What more effective contribution could be made toward true world peace than the world-wide supplanting of want with plenty?

And what finer role in world history can we wish for our nation than that we seize our opportunity to make that contribution to civilization?

Sincerely,

DWIGHT D. EISENHOWER

NOTE: This message was read at the Board's annual banquet, held at the Waldorf-Astoria Hotel in New York City, by Lewis L. Strauss, Chairman of the Atomic Energy Commission. It was released at Lowry Air Force Base, Denver, Colo.

229 ¶ Letter to President Ruiz Cortines of Mexico on the Hurricane-Flood Disaster in Tampico. *October* 28, 1955

[Released October 28, 1955. Dated October 24, 1955]

Dear Mr. President:

From my room here I have followed closely and with great anxiety the tragedy in Tampico. I am thankful that the crisis has passed and that the task of reconstruction can go forward.

I am deeply grateful, Mr. President, that you gave us the opportunity to share those dark days with you. It afforded our two peoples another opportunity to demonstrate to each other and to the world the brotherly bonds that exist between your great country and my own.

Ambassador White has informed me of your government's generous offer to reimburse the United States for expenses incident to the relief operations. It was the intention that this should be a contribution from the government and the people of the United States and an indication of our solidarity and desire to alleviate in part the distress of the Mexican people during this time of suffering. I hope that you will, therefore, be able to accept it in that spirit.

Sincerely,

DWIGHT D. EISENHOWER

NOTE: This letter to His Excellency Don Adolfo Ruiz Cortines was re- leased at Lowry Air Force Base, Denver, Colo.

230   ¶ Telegram Welcoming President Castillo-Armas of Guatemala Upon His Arrival in Washington.   *October* 31, 1955

His Excellency
Colonel Carlos Castillo-Armas
President of the Republic of Guatemala

Though my illness prevents my being in Washington to greet you, let me assure you of a most sincere welcome on behalf of the people of the United States.

I hope that your sojourn in this country will be most enjoyable and that you will have the opportunity during your visit to various parts of the United States to obtain vivid impressions of life and activities here. There will be many manifestations, I am sure, of the warm friendship that exists between our peoples.

Mrs. Eisenhower and I are indeed sorry that we cannot be in Washington today to receive you and Senora de Castillo-Armas. We sincerely hope that you both will have many pleasant memories of your visit to our country.

DWIGHT D. EISENHOWER

NOTE: This telegram, dated October 31, Denver, Colo., was presented by the Vice President to President Castillo-Armas upon his arrival in Washington.

231 ¶ Message to His Majesty Haile Selassie I on the 25th Anniversary of His Reign.
November 3, 1955

[Released November 3, 1955.   Dated November 2, 1955]

His Imperial Majesty Haile Selassie I
Emperor of Ethiopia,
Addis Ababa

The people of the United States join with me today in extending to Your Imperial Majesty heartiest congratulations on the 25th Anniversary of your accession to the throne and in sending best wishes for your continued health and happiness.

On this significant occasion it is gratifying to see the fulfillment of the confidence expressed by this Government at the time of your coronation.   Under your reign the traditional ties of friendship and mutual understanding between our two countries, as well as the sympathetic cooperation of our peoples, have indeed been strengthened, and I am confident that the mutual aspirations of our peoples will further enhance this relationship in the years to come.

DWIGHT D. EISENHOWER

NOTE: This message was released at Lowry Air Force Base, Denver, Colo.

232 ¶ Telegram on the Dedication of the International Brotherhood of Teamsters New Building. *November 3, 1955*

Mr. Dave Beck, General President
International Brotherhood of Teamsters,
Chauffeurs, Warehousemen and Helpers of America
Washington, D.C.

The International Brotherhood of Teamsters has erected in our Capital a magnificent building to serve the growing needs of a growing union. It is fitting that this structure be built in the Capital of a free Republic which accords to Labor and its representatives their equal and rightful place in its social and economic life.

Strong, dedicated, democratic trade unionism is one of the bulwarks of our American way of life. Our democracy and our economy both make possible and draw strength from free trade unions.

To the International Brotherhood of Teamsters, its officers and members, I extend my best wishes on the dedication of their new home.

DWIGHT D. EISENHOWER

NOTE: This telegram was released at Lowry Air Force Base, Denver, Colo.

233 ¶ Message to K. Voroshilov, Chairman of the Presidium of the Supreme Soviet, U.S.S.R., on National Anniversary of the Soviet Union. *November 7, 1955*

[Released November 7, 1955. Dated November 6, 1955]

ON THIS national anniversary of the Soviet Union I am happy to convey to Your Excellency and to the peoples of the Soviet

Union the best wishes of the people of the United States for progress toward a permanent and just peace.

DWIGHT D. EISENHOWER

NOTE: This message was released at Lowry Air Force Base, Denver, Colo.

234 ¶ Statement by the President on the Hostilities Between Egypt and Israel in Violation of the General Armistice Agreement. *November 9, 1955*

ALL AMERICANS have been following with deep concern the latest developments in the Near East. The recent outbreak of hostilities has led to a sharp increase in tensions. These events inevitably retard our search for world peace. Insecurity in one region is bound to affect the world as a whole.

While we continue willing to consider request for arms needed for legitimate self-defense, we do not intend to contribute to an arms competition in the Near East because we do not think such a race would be in the true interest of any of the participants. The policy which we believed would best promote the interests and the security of the peoples of the area was expressed in the Tripartite Declaration of May 25, 1950. This still remains our policy.

I stated last year that our goal in the Near East as elsewhere is a just peace. Nothing has taken place since which invalidates our fundamental policies, policies based on friendship for all of the peoples of the area.

We believe that true security must be based upon a just and reasonable settlement. The Secretary of State outlined on August 26th the economic and security contributions which this country was prepared to make towards such a solution. On that occasion I authorized Mr. Dulles to state that, given a solution of the other related problems, I would recommend that the United States join in formal treaty engagements to prevent or thwart any effort by either side to alter by force the boundaries between Israel and its Arab neighbors.

Recent developments have made it all the more imperative that a settlement be found. The United States will continue to play its full part and will support firmly the United Nations which has already contributed so markedly to minimize violence in the area. I hope that other nations of the world will cooperate in this endeavor, thereby contributing significantly to world peace.

NOTE: This statement was released at Lowry Air Force Base, Denver, Colo.

235   ¶ Remarks on Leaving Denver, Colorado. *November* 11, 1955

My friends:

Again it is time for Mrs. Eisenhower and me to say goodbye to Denver after a summer's stay.   This time we leave under somewhat unusual circumstances.   As you know, I have spent some time in the hospital.   Such a time is not wholly a loss.

Misfortune, and particularly the misfortune of illness, brings to all of us an understanding of how good people are.

To General Griffin, the staff at Fitzsimons, the medical staff, the nurses, the clinical technicians, the enlisted men—all of the people that even clean out the hospital: my very grateful thanks, because they have done so much, not only to take care of me, but to make my stay as pleasant as possible.   They are devoted people.

In the same way, here at this Post, General Sprague and his staff have taken on an additional and extra load, and have done it cheerfully and in a way to earn my eternal gratitude.

Then, Mrs. Eisenhower and I have both been touched by the volume of messages that have come in—telegrams and letters and flowers and gifts.   And finally we have been especially grateful for the knowledge that over this country and over the world friends have sent up their prayers for a sick person.

So I leave with my heart unusually filled with gratefulness, to Denver, to the people here, to the locality—in fact to everyone who has been so kind.

And I hope that those people who have sent in messages—and Mrs. Eisenhower has not been able to reach them all; she did her best—that they will know, through this little talk, that we are eternally thankful to them.

Goodbye and good luck.

NOTE: The President spoke at the airport, Lowry Air Force Base, Denver, Colo., at 8:44 a.m. In his remarks the President referred to Maj. Gen. Martin E. Griffin, Commanding General of Fitzsimons Army Hospital, and Maj. Gen. John T. Sprague, Commander of Lowry Air Force Base.

236 ¶ Remarks Upon Arrival at the Washington National Airport. *November 11, 1955*

President Hoover, Mr. Vice President, my very dear friends:

I am deeply honored that so many of you should come down to welcome Mrs. Eisenhower and me back to Washington. It has been a little longer stay than we had planned, but the circumstances you will understand.

I am happy that the doctors have given me at least a parole if not a pardon, and I expect to be back at my accustomed duties, although they say I must ease my way into them and not bulldoze my way into them.

To each of you who have come down, of course, we would like to speak personally and thank you for the honor you have done us.

That is impossible, and so, possibly in just saying thank you, we are grateful, you will understand what we would like to do and you will let the wish take the place of the deed.

Thank you very much.

NOTE: The President spoke at 4:03 p.m. The Vice President's remarks of welcome follow:

Mr. President:

The members of the Cabinet, the members of the Diplomatic Corps and Members of Congress, and the residents of the Washington area that you see before you, are just a small indication of the joy and inspiration your return to Washington has brought to the people of the United States and the people throughout the world.

I know that I express the sentiments in their hearts when I say welcome back and Godspeed in the days ahead.

237　¶ Remarks Upon Arrival in Lincoln Square, Gettysburg, Pennsylvania.　*November 14, 1955*

Mr. Burgess, Mrs. Weaver, Patty, and my future permanent neighbors, I hope:

Of course, Mrs. Eisenhower and I feel deeply honored that you should turn out today to welcome us to this area where we expect to make our home and which has been so long a part of the Eisenhower family's life.

In fact, I think that my wife decided back in 1918, before many of you were born, that this was going to be our home upon retirement, but she did not give me her decision until later than that.

In any event, I am just as delighted as she that you are the people who are going to be our neighbors, God willing.

And to each of you who has come out this morning, to each of the school children who along the way have waved these little flags or his hand, or called a greeting, our very deep thanks. We are truly grateful to all of you.

Goodbye.

NOTE: The President spoke at 1:00 p.m. His opening words "Mr. Burgess, Mrs. Weaver, Patty" referred to William G. Weaver, Burgess of Gettysburg, Mrs. Weaver, and their daughter, Patricia.

238 ¶ Letter to Mrs. Martin P. Durkin on the Death of Her Husband. *November 14, 1955*

Dear Mrs. Durkin:

The word of Martin's death is deeply distressing to me, as it must be to all those who had the privilege of friendship and association with him over the years. His career was marked by an unfaltering devotion to high ideals and to the service of his fellowmen. He will be greatly missed by those who knew him.

Martin's dedication to his religious faith and to the welfare of his fellowman made his life both exemplary and purposeful. He was a good and distinguished American.

Mrs. Eisenhower joins me in extending our deepest sympathy to you and your family.

Sincerely,
DWIGHT D. EISENHOWER

NOTE: Mr. Durkin served as Secretary of Labor from January 21 to September 10, 1953.

239 ¶ Message to Rabbi Abba Hillel Silver on the Near East Situation. *November 15, 1955*

I AM GLAD to comply with your request to send a message to the meeting which you are addressing this evening, as I know of your great concern about the recent developments in the Near East which disturb all of us.

A threat to peace in the Near East is a threat to world peace. As I said the other day, while we continue willing to consider requests for arms needed for legitimate self-defense, we do not intend to contribute to an arms competition in the Near East. We will continue to be guided by the policies of the Tripartite Declaration of May 25, 1950. We believe this policy best promotes the interest and security of the peoples of the area.

We believe the true and lasting security in the area must be based upon a just and reasonable settlement. It seems to me that current problems are capable of resolution by peaceful means. There is no reason why a settlement of these problems cannot be found, and when realized I would be prepared to recommend that the United States join in formal treaty engagements to prevent or thwart any effort by either side to alter by force the boundaries upon which Israel and its immediate neighbors agree.

The need for a peaceful settlement becomes daily more imperative. The United States will play its full part in working toward such a settlement and will support firmly the United Nations in its efforts to prevent violence in the area. By firm friendship towards Israel and all other Nations in the Near East, we shall continue to contribute to the peace of the world.

DWIGHT D. EISENHOWER

NOTE: Rabbi Silver informed the President that he was to address a mass rally at Madison Square Garden in New York City on November 15, at which many civic, religious, and labor organizations would participate to express concern over the situation. The Rabbi added: "I know that they would welcome a word from you as coming not only from the Chief Executive of our beloved country but as the foremost spokesman of international justice, freedom and peace in the world today."

The Rabbi's telegram of November 14 and the President's reply were released at Gettysburg, Pa.

In the second paragraph the President referred to his statement of November 9 (see Item 234, above).

240   ¶ Message to the Sultan of Morocco on the Anniversary of His Accession to the Throne. *November 18, 1955*

His Cherifian Majesty Sidi Mohammed ben Youssef
Sultan of Morocco, Rabat

On the anniversary of your accession to the Throne, it gives me pleasure to send to Your Majesty and to the people of Morocco greetings from the people of the United States. It also gives me particular satisfaction to recall the good and friendly relations between your country and mine which began in the early days of our own history.

May your reign open new vistas for that community of purpose which has contributed so much to the greatness of Morocco, and restore the peace and prosperity which the United States so deeply desires for all the inhabitants of your country.

DWIGHT D. EISENHOWER

NOTE: The Sultan's reply, released on November 30, follows:

We are very touched by the noble sentiments that you have kindly expressed in the name of the people of the United States. We are happy to note that the time-honored friendship of our two countries remains intact. We hope to see established in Morocco an era of liberty, that liberty for which your people and you yourself have never ceased to work and which is the best guarantee of a durable peace.

MOHAMMED BEN YOUSSEF

The messages were released at Gettysburg, Pa.

241 ¶ Message to King Haakon VII of Norway on the 50th Anniversary of His Reign. *November 24, 1955*

[Released November 24, 1955. Dated November 17, 1955]

Dear King Haakon:

On the fiftieth anniversary of your reign it gives me pleasure, on behalf of the people of the United States, to send to Your Majesty cordial felicitations and best wishes. The close relationship which we in this country enjoy with the people of Norway helps us understand how much this anniversary means to them. We share in their rejoicing.

It is indeed inspiring to contemplate the wise and steadfast influence which Your Majesty has exerted for half a century.

Your courageous leadership has won for you great esteem both at home and abroad.

Please accept this expression of my hope for your good health and of my warmest regard.

Sincerely,

DWIGHT D. EISENHOWER

His Majesty Haakon VII
King of Norway
Oslo, Norway

NOTE: This message was released at Gettysburg, Pa.

242 ¶ Remarks for the White House Conference on Education. *November 28, 1955*

[Recorded on film and tape]

IT IS indeed an honor to have this opportunity to address, even by indirect method, you men and women of the White House Conference on Education. You come from every one of our States and our Territories. By being here you are focusing attention on a grave national problem. That problem is the losing race between the number of classrooms and qualified teachers we have on the one hand, and, on the other, the increasing population of school age.

Ten years ago the guns were stilled and the war was ended. Very naturally, our country, like all others, found itself in a state of great confusion. Many problems were lost sight of as we turned our attention to preserving the peace, to establishing international organizations for that purpose. We took care of many other problems that were directly incidental to the war.

Much has happened in those ten years. We have seen the bright hopes for peace not fully fulfilled certainly, but we have seen our Nation grow stronger economically, militarily, stronger intellectually and, we believe, spiritually.

Through this period confusion has gradually been disappearing. We have had a chance to clarify our thinking and to look at most of our national problems with a good hard look.

One of the factors that has come forcibly to our attention is that in the last ten years our population has increased by 26 million souls. During that great increase a similar increase in the number of schoolrooms and qualified teachers available for teaching our young has not come about. So we are faced today with the grave problem of providing a good education for American youth.

In such a problem as this we know, of course, that many facilities are lacking—many things have to be done. There are, likewise, many conflicting opinions as to how to provide these things. This is only natural. In such a problem that is so nationwide in scope, everybody has opinions and is perfectly ready to express them, and not all of these opinions ever agree in a democracy.

But there are two points, I think, on which we all agree.

The first thing is that the education of our young should be free. It should be under the control of the family and the locality. It should not be controlled by any central authority. We know that education, centrally controlled, finally would lead to a kind of control in other fields which we don't want and will never have. So we are dedicated to the proposition that the responsibility for educating our young is primarily local.

At the same time we know that everybody must have a good education if they are properly to discharge their functions as citizens of America.

And so we come to the heart of this whole problem. We want good facilities on the one hand, and we know that there are many areas in which people cannot afford to build the schools, to provide the facilities that the populations of that particular area need.

If we depend too much on outside help, too much on the Federal Government, we will lose independence and initiative. But if the Federal Government doesn't step in with leadership and with providing credit and money where necessary, there will be a lack of schools in certain important areas. And this cannot be allowed.

So this is a problem again where the private citizen, the locality, the State and the Federal Government all have a function to perform, all have a responsibility to meet—always in conformity with those two basic truths that education must be free and it must be good.

There are no easy solutions, and I don't expect this Conference to find any easy solutions. But I do know this: when sensible Americans—men and women—sit down together to discuss a problem in the hope of achieving a solution that is good for the whole Nation, something sensible comes out. We don't have crackpot ideas. We don't have doctrinaire opinions or solutions.

So we want a solution that is good for all, and all of us want to help in the proper way.

This Conference of yours, of course, has been preceded by State and community conferences all over the Nation. Some of you participated in them. Much good has come out of it. You, by meeting here, continue the work of those conferences. You begin to crystallize the solutions that they have proposed and suggested and will try to bring them together so that the good of the whole Nation may be met.

You have an arduous schedule ahead of you. But I particularly like the idea I have heard that you are going to break yourselves up into small groups so that every phase and facet of this problem will be thoroughly discussed among you and so that nothing will be glossed over, nothing will be handled in generalities. We will get down to specific things.

So all I can say further is: I am deeply grateful to each of you for participating in this Conference, for helping in the solution of this problem. I am grateful to all of those in the community and State conferences that took place ahead of this one. I am perfectly certain that I speak for every American in expressing their thanks, along with my own, as you take up this task.

NOTE: On November 23 the President drove from his farm to Gettysburg College where his remarks were recorded for the Conference. The remarks were released at Gettysburg on the 28th.

243 ¶ Statement by the President on Observance of Safe Driving Day.   *November* 30, 1955

ALL OVER the United States tomorrow, Americans will join in a great National effort to save lives.   The occasion will be the second nationwide "S–D Day"—Safe Driving Day.

The immediate objective of S–D Day is to have twenty-four hours without a single traffic accident.   The long-range, and more important objective is to impress upon all of us the necessity for safe driving and safe walking every day of the year.

The need is obvious and urgent.   Last year, an American man, woman or child was killed in traffic every fifteen minutes.   Someone was injured every twenty-five seconds.   And, this year, the record is worse: More people are dying; more are injured and crippled.

This tragic situation concerns every State, every community, every American.   Actual experience has demonstrated that traffic accidents can be greatly reduced by proven, year-round safety programs, when these programs have year-round public support.

S–D Day is directed to the development of that kind of support. Literally millions of Americans are participating, through local, state and national organizations, cooperating with the President's Committee for Traffic Safety.   This is a volunteer group, appointed by me, to stimulate permanent, effective safety programs in every community.

We know that we cannot solve the traffic accident problem in one day, but we can—and must—start doing a better job.   I appeal, then, to every American to help demonstrate tomorrow that we can—by our own, personal efforts—reduce accidents on our streets and highways. Having shown that we can do so on one day, let us all, as good citizens, accept our responsibility for safety every day in the future.

DWIGHT D. EISENHOWER

NOTE: This statement was released at Gettysburg, Pa.

244 ¶ Letter Accompanying Medallion for Presentation to Sir Winston Churchill on His 81st Birthday. *November 30, 1955*

[Released November 30, 1955. Dated November 26, 1955]

Dear Winston:

This medallion, struck to commemorate your eighty-first birthday, is a timely recognition both of your lifelong friendship toward the United States and of the incalculable debt owed you by all mankind for your unfaltering defense of peace with justice, and the freedom of men.

The English-speaking peoples—and the entire world—are the better for the wisdom of your counsel, for the inspiration of your unflagging optimism and for the heartening example of your shining courage. You have been a towering leader in the quest for peace, as you were in the battle for freedom through the dark days of war.

In that light, the medallion is a token of America's enduring gratitude. But more than that, it sharpens in our minds today the eternal faith that the forces of evil cannot triumph over men whose courage is many times fortified by dedication to human freedom, to human rights, to the God-guided destiny of free men.

Warm sentiment is mingled with gratitude as I send this medallion, provided by American friends of yours, to commemorate your birthday. Millions of my countrymen join me in tribute to you on this anniversary and in best wishes for long and happy years ahead.

With warm regard,

As ever,

DWIGHT D. EISENHOWER

NOTE: This letter was released at Gettysburg, Pa.

The presentation was made in England by Ambassador Winthrop W. Aldrich. The face of the gold medallion bears a representation of Sir Winston's head and shoulders, as taken from the President's portrait of him. The following citation is inscribed on the reverse, together with a design of clasped hands flanked by British and United States shields:

"Presented to Sir Winston Spencer Churchill by President Dwight D. Eisenhower on behalf of his millions of admiring friends in the United States for courageous leadership and in recognition of his signal services to the defense of freedom in which cause his country and the United States have been associated in both peace and war."

The medallion was designed by Gilroy Roberts, head sculptor and engraver of the United States mint.

245 ¶ Telephone Broadcast to the AFL–CIO Merger Meeting in New York City. *December 5, 1955*

Mr. Meany, Mr. Schnitzler, members of the Executive Council, Delegates to this Convention and ladies and gentlemen of the AFL-CIO everywhere in America:

You of organized labor and those who have gone before you in the union movement have helped make a unique contribution to the general welfare of the Republic—the development of the American philosophy of labor. This philosophy, if adopted globally, could bring about a world, prosperous, at peace, sharing the fruits of the earth with justice to all men. It would raise to freedom and prosperity hundreds of millions of men and women—and their children—who toil in slavery behind the Curtain.

One principle of this philosophy is: the ultimate values of mankind are spiritual; these values include liberty, human dignity, opportunity and equal rights and justice.

Workers want recognition as human beings and as individuals— before everything else.   They want a job that gives them a feeling of satisfaction and self-expression.   Good wages, respectable working conditions, reasonable hours, protection of status and security; these constitute the necessary foundations on which you build to reach your higher aims.

Moreover, we cannot be satisfied with welfare in the aggregate; if any group or section of citizens is denied its fair place in the common prosperity, all others among us are thereby endangered.

The second principle of this American labor philosophy is this: the economic interest of employer and employee is a mutual prosperity.

Their economic future is inseparable.   Together they must advance in mutual respect, in mutual understanding, toward mutual prosperity.   Of course, there will be contest over the sharing of the benefits of production; and so we have the right to strike and to argue all night, when necessary, in collective bargaining sessions.   But in a deeper sense, this surface struggle is subordinate to the overwhelming common interest in greater production and a better life for all to share.

The American worker strives for betterment not by destroying his employer and his employer's business, but by understanding his employer's problems of competition, prices, markets.   And the American employer can never forget that, since mass production assumes a mass market, good wages and progressive employment practices for his employee are good business.

The Class Struggle Doctrine of Marx was the invention of a lonely refugee scribbling in a dark recess of the British Museum. He abhorred and detested the middle class.   He did not forsee that, in America, labor, respected and prosperous, would constitute—with the farmer and businessman—his hated middle class. But our second principle—that mutual interest of employer and employee—is the natural outgrowth of teamwork for progress, characteristic of the American economy where the barriers of class do not exist.

The third principle is this: labor relations will be managed best when worked out in honest negotiation between employers and unions, without Government's unwarranted interference.

This principle requires maturity in the private handling of labor matters within a framework of law, for the protection of the public interest and the rights of both labor and management. The splendid record of labor peace and unparalleled prosperity during the last 3 years demonstrates our industrial maturity.

Some of the most difficult and unprecedented negotiations in the history of collective bargaining took place during this period, against the backdrop of non-interference by Government except only to protect the public interest, in the rare cases of genuine national emergency. This third principle, relying as it does on collective bargaining, assumes that labor organizations and management will both observe the highest standards of integrity, responsibility, and concern for the national welfare.

You are more than union members bound together by a common goal of better wages, better working conditions, and protection of your security. You are American citizens.

The roads you travel, the schools your children attend, the taxes you pay, the standards of integrity in Government, the conduct of the public business is your business as Americans. And while all of you, as to the public business, have a common goal—a stronger and better America—your views as to the best means of reaching that goal vary widely, just as they do in any other group of American citizens.

So in your new national organization, as well as in your many constituent organizations, you have a great opportunity of making your meetings the world's most effective exhibit of democratic processes. In those meetings the rights of minorities holding differing social, economic, and political views must be scrupulously protected and their views accurately reflected. In this way, as American citizens you will help the Republic correct the faulty, fortify the good, build stoutly for the future, and reinforce the most cherished freedoms of each individual citizen.

This country has long understood that by helping other peoples to a better understanding and practice of representative government, we strengthen both them and ourselves. The same truth applies to the economic field. We strengthen other peoples and ourselves when we help them to understand the workings of a free economy, to improve their own standards of living, and to join with us in world trade that serves to unite us all.

In the world struggle, some of the finest weapons for all Americans are these simple tenets of free labor. They are again: man is created in the Divine image and has spiritual aspirations that transcend the material; second, the real interests of employers and employees are mutual; third, unions and employers can and should work out their own destinies. As we preach and practice that message without cease, we will wage a triumphant crusade for prosperity, freedom, and peace among men.

To close, it is fitting that we let our hearts be filled with the earnest prayer that, with the help of a kind Providence, the world may be led out of bitterness and materialism and force into a new era of harmony and spiritual growth and self-realization for all men. Thank you very much.

NOTE: The President spoke at 2:30 p.m. from Gettysburg.

The meeting was held in the 71st Regimental Armory in New York City. The President's opening words "Mr. Meany, Mr. Schnitzler" referred to George Meany and William F. Schnitzler, President and Secretary-Treasurer, respectively, of the AFL–CIO.

The President's remarks were released at Gettysburg.

246 ¶ Statement by the President on Early Mailing of Christmas Gifts and Greetings.
December 10, 1955

OUR CHRISTMAS MAIL this year will be the heaviest in the history of the Post Office. To all the world, this will be evidence of the spirit which animates us in this season of peace and good will.

The men and women of the Post Office Department, I am sure, will meet our challenge to their efficiency in the traditional spirit of the postal service. Once again they will deliver every Christmas package, letter and card, mailed on time, by Christmas Day. We can help them by mailing early. Then, our gifts, our messages of cheer and Christmas greetings will reach our friends and loved ones to make the Holiday a joyous and happy time.

And, by mailing early, we will help give hundreds of thousands of our fellow Americans, the men and women of the Post Office, a pleasant, joyful Christmas—free from the turmoil of last-minute mail pressures.

DWIGHT D. EISENHOWER

247 ¶ White House Statements Following Meetings With Republican Leaders of the Senate and the House of Representatives.
December 12, 1955

THE PRESIDENT met today in the Cabinet Room with the Republican leaders of the Senate and the House of Representatives.

General preliminary discussions were held on many of the domestic programs which will be submitted by the Administration to the Congress in the State of the Union and other special messages at the 1956 Session.

A general discussion of foreign policy, mutual aid and national defense programs will be held tomorrow when the President meets with the Legislative Leaders of both parties.

This morning the main subjects discussed were the Budget, school construction, highways, water resources and statehood for Alaska and Hawaii.

The Secretary of the Treasury and the Director of the Budget outlined the fiscal plans for the 1957 Budget as well as the projected receipts and expenditures for the 1956 Budget. The Secretary and the Director were hopeful that with increasing economies and no loss of existing revenues a balance in the 1956 Budget could be attained in June without cutting down in any way on defense and national security plans of the United States.

The Secretary of Health, Education, and Welfare next discussed a series of proposals concerning his Department. These proposals included Social Security modifications, increased health coverage, additional Federal grants for medical research and plans for assuring the construction of additional schoolrooms, to clear up the backlog of a 200,000-room deficiency in the nation.

The Secretary of the Treasury and the Secretary of Commerce then joined in a discussion of recommendations for a highway construction bill. It was agreed that there was an urgent need for the Congress to pass at the 1956 Session a workable highway program to build up the nation's roads.

The Under Secretary of the Interior outlined and then joined in a discussion of proposals for a nationwide water resources program.

At the conclusion of the morning session the leaders were guests at a luncheon given at the Mayflower Hotel by the Chairman of the Republican National Committee.

The meeting will reconvene this afternoon at two o'clock. Among the subjects on the agenda are: farm legislation, amendments to immigration legislation, civil rights, labor legislation, postal rates, housing and area redevelopment programs.

———

At the afternoon session the Secretary of Agriculture outlined a suggested program for assisting the farmers of the nation.

The leaders discussed in detail the suggestions and while no final decisions were reached today, the leaders expressed approval of the aims of the major recommendations of the program which will supplement programs already in effect. They also stated their belief that the final farm recommendations, when submitted by the President to the Congress, would win widespread support from farmers and farm organizations throughout the country. Both the Executive and Legislative leaders agreed that enactment of the legislative proposals in the farm program will be of top priority in the next session.

The Attorney General next presented a series of proposed amendments to the immigration laws.

Other subjects discussed at the afternoon session were:

1. Civil Rights—The Attorney General
2. Postal Rates—The Postmaster General
3. Labor Legislation—The Secretary of Labor
4. Slum Clearance and Housing—The Administrator of the Housing and Home Finance Agency
5. Personnel Legislation—The Chairman of the Civil Service Commission

At the conclusion of the meeting the President personally thanked the leaders for their cooperation and their constructive suggestions made during the day on subjects under discussion for the 1956 legislative program which the Administration will present to the Congress.

248　¶ White House Statement Following Bipartisan Conference on Foreign Affairs and National Defense.　*December* 13, 1955

THE PRESIDENT met today with the leaders of both political parties in the Senate and the House of Representatives for a bi-partisan conference on the problems of foreign affairs and national defense which will be submitted to the 1956 Congress.

Subjects under discussion included foreign affairs, the national defense budget, mutual security appropriations, the program of the United States Information Agency, policies on the question of disarmament and the Organization for Trade Cooperation.

At the start of the meeting the President thanked the leaders for accepting his invitation to discuss these subjects.　He pointed out that he desired to discuss them on a bi-partisan basis with the leaders of the legislative branch of the government and to receive their observations and suggestions prior to the opening of the Congress.

The Secretary of State presented a review of world conditions since the Foreign Ministers' Meeting at Geneva.　He said that his department placed special emphasis on the economic aspects of foreign policy particularly in view of the stepped-up Soviet campaign in this field in Southeast Asia and the Middle East. He also urged approval by the Congress of American participation in the Organization for Trade Cooperation.

The Secretary of Defense reviewed with the leaders the program of the Defense establishment of the United States and the forced levels which must be maintained to protect the nation against attack and to assure the maintenance of peace in this Atomic Age.

The Director of the International Cooperation Administration outlined the aspects of mutual security including mutual military support and economic and technical assistance for our allies and friends.

The President discussed the program of the United States Information Agency. The President and the Deputy Director of the Agency stressed the necessity for expanding the Agency's program to present America's proposals for peace to all the peoples of the world.

The Special Assistant to the President for Disarmament Planning discussed in detail proposals for disarmament particularly those phases dealing with the President's "Open Sky" recommendation. He pointed to the overwhelming vote taken yesterday at the United Nations as an indication of world-wide support and interest in our country's pursuit of world peace.

A general discussion was held after each subject was presented.

The President asked me to add one further thing directly from him:

"I want to give my thanks and my very real gratitude to the leaders on both sides of the aisle in the Senate and the House of Representatives for the very great contribution they have made and are making to true bi-partisanship."

249 ¶ Statement by the President: Bill of Rights Day. *December* 14, 1955

[Released December 14, 1955. Dated December 12, 1955]

BILL OF RIGHTS DAY ranks in the forefront of our days of commemoration. On this day, the people of America remember and honor the passage of the Bill of Rights—the first ten Amendments to the Constitution.

By the Bill of Rights our people are guaranteed the most precious of liberties: freedom of speech, press and religion; the right peaceably to assemble and to petition the Government; freedom from unreasonable search and seizure and the right of privacy; judicial safeguards of life, liberty and property; the right to a fair trial and protection against excessive punishment. These rights, indispensable to our happiness and security, reaffirm our belief in the dignity of the individual.

On this day I hope that citizens throughout our land will renew in their hearts and minds a devotion to these freedoms and a determination to defend them against all forms of attack. Let us also highly resolve to continue to strive for a peaceful world in which all mankind will share them.

DWIGHT D. EISENHOWER

250 ¶ Remarks Broadcast for the Pageant of Peace Ceremonies in Washington. *December* 18, 1955

My fellow Americans at home and across the seas, my fellow men and women of every nation:

For hundreds of millions of us, Christmas symbolizes our deepest aspirations for peace and for goodwill among men.

For me, this particular Christmas has a very special meaning, and has brought to me, really, new understandings of people.

During the past three months my family and I have received literally thousands—tens of thousands of messages. Each of these has borne a sentence of good wishes and goodwill for health and happiness to us both. It has been heartwarming evidence that human understanding and human sympathy can surmount every obstacle—even those obstacles that some governments sometimes seem to raise in the attempt to divide us.

Now the free world is just coming to the close of a very significant year, one in which we have worked hard and sometimes effectively for peace. Now the facts of today, of course, do not measure up to the high hopes of the free world, the hopes by which we have lived and which we have long entertained. But this Christmas is, nevertheless, brighter in its background and its promise for the future than any we have known in recent years.

I think it is even better than last year, and you will remember that Christmas was the first one in many years that was not marred by the tragic incidents of war.

Now peace is the right of every human being. It is hungered for by all of the peoples of the earth. So we can be sure that tonight in the fullness of our hearts and in the spirit of the season, that as we utter a simple prayer for peace we will be joined by the multitudes of the earth.

Those multitudes will include rulers as well as the humblest citizens of lands; the great and the meek; the proud and the poor; the successful and the failures; the dispirited and the hopefuls.

Now each of those prayers will of course differ according to the characteristics and the personality of the individual uttering it, but running through every single one of those prayers will be a thought something of this kind:

May each of us strive to do our best to bring about better understanding in the world. And may the infinite peace from above live with us and be ours forever, and may we live in the confident hope that it will come.

And so it is tonight in that hope, which must never die from the earth, which we must cling to and cherish and nurture and work for, that I light the National Community Christmas Tree at the Pageant of Peace in Washington.

To each of you—wherever you may be—from Mrs. Eisenhower and me: a very Merry Christmas!

NOTE: The President spoke at 5:10 p.m. over radio and television from Gettysburg College just before lighting, by remote control, the National Community Christmas Tree in Washington.

Appendix A—White House Press Releases, 1955

NOTE: Includes releases covering matters with which the President was closely concerned, except announcements of Presidential personnel appointments and approvals of legislation with which there was no accompanying statement.

Releases relating to Proclamations and Executive Orders have not been included. These documents are separately listed in Appendix B.

For list of Press and Radio Conferences, see subject index under "News Conferences."

January   Subject

1 Memorandum concerning the Government Employees Incentive Awards Program

3 Statement by the President on the death of President Remon of Panama

5 Letter to the Secretary of Defense on national security requirements

6 Annual message to the Congress on the State of the Union

6 Special message to the Senate transmitting Mutual Defense Treaty with Republic of China

8 Letter accepting resignation of James C. Worthy, Assistant Secretary of Commerce

10 Special message to the Congress on foreign economic policy

10 Message to the Congress transmitting the President's first semiannual report on activities under the Agricultural Trade Development and Assistance Act

10 Message to the Congress transmitting report on inclusion of escape clauses in trade agreements

11 Special message to the Congress on Federal personnel management

11 Special message to the Congress on postal pay and rates

January   Subject

13 Remarks at luncheon meeting of the Association of American Colleges

13 Special message to the Congress on national security requirements

13 Special message to the Congress on career incentives for military personnel

13 Letter to the President of the Senate and to the Speaker of the House of Representatives approving certain Virgin Islands Corporation activities

13 Cablegram to Dr. Albert Schweitzer on his 80th birthday

13 Letter accepting resignation of John Slezak, Under Secretary of the Army

14 Message to the Congress transmitting the fourth annual report of the National Science Foundation

14 Statement by the President on U.N. negotiations with Communist China for release of American airmen and other personnel

17 Annual budget message to the Congress

20 Annual message presenting the economic report to the Congress

20 Letter to Representative Auchincloss, on the anniversary of the President's inauguration

January   Subject

22 White House statement on appointment of Howard Pyle as Administrative Assistant to the President

22 White House statement regarding a special message to the Congress regarding U.S. policy for the defense of Formosa

23 Special message to the Congress regarding U.S. policy for the defense of Formosa

25 Letter from President Heuss of Germany

25 Remarks on receiving statue presented by Ambassador Krekeler on behalf of the German people

26 Special message to the Senate transmitting a convention on Great Lakes fisheries

26 White House announcement of resignation of Thomas E. Stephens, Secretary to the President, and the following appointments: Bernard M. Shanley, as Secretary to the President; Gerald D. Morgan, as Counsel to the President; and Fred A. Seaton, as Administrative Assistant to the President

26 Toasts of the President and the President of Haiti

27 White House statement following discussions with the National Security Council and others concerning the deployment of air and naval forces in the Formosa area

27 White House statement concerning tariff on imports of hatters' fur

29 Statement by the President upon signing Joint Resolution on defense of Formosa

31 Special message to the Congress on a health program

February   Subject

3 Message recorded for the New York USO defense fund dinner

6 Message to the Boy Scouts of America

7 Letter to the Governors concerning uniform State legislation on absentee voting rights of members of the armed services

7 White House statement announcing forthcoming visit of the Prime Minister of Australia

7 Letter to the Acting Chairman of the Civil Aeronautics Board, on the West Coast-Hawaii case

8 Special message to the Congress concerning Federal assistance in school construction

8 Letter accepting resignation of Neil H. Jacoby, member of the Council of Economic Advisers

8 Message to nationwide meetings in support of the campaign for Radio Free Europe

9 Message to meetings of the nationwide clinical conference on heart ailments

10 White House statement on requests for supplemental appropriations for the legislative, judicial, and executive branches, and the District of Columbia

17 Remarks at luncheon meeting of Republican National Committee and Republican National Finance Committee

18 Exchange of messages between the President and the President of the Republic of China

19 Letter to Emil Sandstrom, League of Red Cross Societies, on completion of the flood relief program in Europe

20 Remarks recorded for the "Back to God" program of the American Legion

864

Appendix A

February   *Subject*

22 Special message to the Congress regarding a national highway program

22 Letter extending greetings to the Brotherhood Dinner of the National Conference of Christians and Jews

23 Exchange of messages between the President and the Shah of Iran

24 Remarks at the annual breakfast for Masonic leaders

24 Letter to Nelson Lee Smith, Federal Power Commissioner, concerning his request that he not be considered for reappointment

26 White House statement: Report on energy supplies and resources policy

28 Message to the inter-American investment conference held in New Orleans

28 Letter to Oscar B. Ryder on his retirement from the U.S. Tariff Commission

28 Remarks recorded for the opening of the Red Cross campaign

March

1 Letter accepting resignation of John C. Hughes, U.S. Permanent Representative to the North Atlantic Council

2 Message to the Pope on his 79th birthday

3 Letter to the Chief of State of Viet-Nam

4 Statement by the President concerning offer of food supplies to Albania

4 Special message to the Congress on extension of the Renegotiation Act

5 Letter to Gen. Omar N. Bradley, Chairman, President's Commission on Veterans' Pensions

March   *Subject*

7 Remarks to Distinguished Service Cross recipients and commanders who participated in seizure of Remagen Bridge

8 Letter accepting resignation of Robert Cutler, Special Assistant to the President for National Security Affairs

8 White House statement concerning rejection by Albania of food supplies

10 Remarks to students attending the International School of Nuclear Science and Engineering, Argonne National Laboratory

10 Message to the Prime Ministers of the seven nations signatory to the protocols establishing the Western European Union

11 White House statement regarding forthcoming visit of the Prime Minister of Australia

11 Letter accepting resignation of Raymond A. Spruance, ambassador to the Philippines

14 Message to the Congress transmitting the seventh semiannual report on the mutual security program

16 Letter to George A. Garrett, President, Federal City Council, concerning the redevelopment of Southwest Washington

17 Memorandum to the President: Report of the Presidential Advisory Committee to consider an additional Washington airport

19 Statement by the President announcing appointment of Harold Stassen as Special Assistant to the President for disarmament studies

22 Remarks at annual Washington conference of the Advertising Council

865

Appendix A

March *Subject*

24 White House statement concerning import restrictions on walnuts

24 White House statement concerning investigation of tariff on hatters' fur

25 Remarks to representatives of American voluntary societies cooperating in the U.S. escapee program

28 Joint statement following discussions with the Prime Minister of Italy

28 White House statement regarding U.S. Antarctica expedition in connection with IGY 1957–58

31 Citation to accompany the award of the Medal of Freedom to Robert Cutler, Special Assistant to the President

April

1 Statement by the President on the death of Joseph Pulitzer and Robert R. McCormick

1 Letter to the President of the Senate and to the Speaker of the House of Representatives regarding the Inter-American Highway

2 Letter accepting resignation of Samuel W. Anderson, Assistant Secretary of Commerce for International Affairs

5 Statement by the President on the retirement of Sir Winston Churchill, Prime Minister of the United Kingdom

6 Statement by the President on the appointment of Anthony Eden as Prime Minister of the United Kingdom

7 Memorandum to the Director of the Office of Defense Mobilization relating to the Buy American Act

8 White House statement announcing a study of Presidential office space by Robert Heller and Associates of Cleveland

April *Subject*

9 White House announcement of the President and Mrs. Eisenhower's Easter plans

9 White House statement regarding investigation of cheese imports

11 Remarks to the Easter Egg Rollers on the south grounds of the White House

11 Statement by the President on the mutual security program

12 Remarks at The Citadel, Charleston, S.C.

13 Letter to Chairman, Joint Committee on Atomic Energy, on proposed agreement for cooperation with NATO on atomic information

13 White House statement announcing settlement of a labor dispute between airlines and their employees

14 Special message to the Congress on U.S. membership in proposed organization for trade cooperation

16 Telegram to Senator Thurmond saluting James F. Byrnes as a great American

17 Letter to Secretary Dulles regarding transfer of affairs of the Foreign Operations Administration to Department of State

17 Statement by Secretary of State following his discussion of foreign relations with the President

18 White House announcement of report of the Presidential Advisory Committee on Transport Policy and Organization

18 Statement by the President on the death of Albert Einstein

20 Special message to the Congress on the mutual security program

866

Appendix A

April   Subject

22 White House statement on the forth-coming visit of the Permanent Repre-sentatives of the North Atlantic Council

22 Citation presented to Dr. Jonas E. Salk and accompanying remarks

22 Citation presented to the National Foundation for Infantile Paralysis and accompanying remarks

25 Address at annual luncheon of the As-sociated Press, New York City

26 Letter to Harvey S. Firestone, Jr., upon accepting Honorary Chairman-ship of the USO

27 Special message to the Congress con-cerning a program for low income farmers

28 Remarks to the Committee for a Na-tional Trade Policy

30 Remarks at cornerstone-laying cere-mony for the AFL building

May

2 Remarks at annual meeting of the U.S. Chamber of Commerce

2 Special message to the Congress on United States participation in the In-ternational Finance Corporation

2 Citation and remarks at presentation to Field Marshal Pibulsonggram of Thailand of the Legion of Merit, De-gree of Chief Commander

2 Remarks at the Governors' Conference dinner

3 Statement by the President on approv-ing proposed agreement with Turkey for cooperation in the peaceful uses of atomic energy

May   Subject

3 White House statement following the approval of the proposed agreement with Turkey for cooperation in the peaceful uses of atomic energy

5 Letter to the President of the Senate and to the Speaker of the House of Representatives on revision of the Philippine trade agreement

6 White House announcement of the resignation of Norman Armour, Am-bassador to Guatemala, and the selec-tion of Edward J. Sparks as his suc-cessor

6 Letter accepting resignation of Nor-man Armour, Ambassador to Guate-mala

6 Remarks at the dedication of the Washington Hebrew Congregation Temple

9 White House announcement of U.S. delegation to World Health Assembly, Mexico City

9 White House statement announcing forthcoming visit of Prime Minister U Nu of Burma

10 Remarks to the General Assembly of the Organization of World Touring and Automobile Clubs

10 Remarks at the Republican Women's National Conference

10 White House statement concerning the authority of the Secretary of State to arrange for a summit conference

10 White House statement concerning mission of Gen. J. Lawton Collins to Viet-Nam and the arrival of Am-bassador G. Frederick Reinhardt in Viet-Nam

11 Statement by the President concerning conferences on education

Appendix A

May   *Subject*

11 White House announcement of appointments to the USO and nominations to the Board of Governors

11 White House statement concerning tariff on imports of bicycles

12 Message recorded for use in conjunction with observance of Armed Forces Day

13 White House announcement of nomination of Gen. Maxwell D. Taylor as Army Chief of Staff, and the appointment of Gen. Lyman L. Lemnitzer to the commands relinquished by General Taylor

15 Message to the President of Austria on the signing of the treaty restoring Austrian independence

17 White House statement announcing the President's forthcoming visit to Vermont, New Hampshire, and Maine

17 Television report to the President by the Secretary of State following his European visit

18 Memorandum to Federal agencies directing participation in a national civil defense exercise

19 Veto of postal field service compensation bill

20 Letter to the Chairman, Tariff Commission, on imports of rye

23 Remarks to the President's Committee on the Employment of the Physically Handicapped

23 Remarks at a dinner sponsored by the District of Columbia Republican Women's Finance Committee

24 Remarks to the National Association of Radio and Television Broadcasters

25 Letter to the Chairman, Civil Aeronautics Board, regarding the States-Alaska case

May   *Subject*

26 White House statement concerning requests for supplemental appropriations

26 Message to the Congress transmitting conventions and recommendations adopted at Geneva by ILO conference

26 Remarks at dedication of the Armed Forces Institute of Pathology, Walter Reed Medical Center

27 Special message to the Congress recommending amendments to the Refugee Relief Act

27 Citation and remarks at presentation of the National Security Medal to J. Edgar Hoover

27 White House announcement of designation of Nat B. King as U.S. Deputy Representative on U.N. Economic and Social Council

27 Letter accepting resignation of H. Struve Hensel, Assistant Secretary of Defense for International Security Affairs

27 Statement by the President on safe driving

31 Statement by the President on the polio vaccine situation

31 White House statement concerning agreements with Brazil and Colombia for cooperation in the peaceful uses of atomic energy

June

1 Special message to the Senate transmitting Austrian State Treaty

1 White House statement announcing allocation of funds for wind erosion area

3 Remarks on acceptance of a Palestinian "Lamp of Freedom" from the United Jewish Appeal

868

Appendix A

June   *Subject*

3 Veto of bill for relief of Kurt Glaser

4 Letter appointing Robert Cutler as Consultant to the National Security Council

6 Remarks at the United States Military Academy alumni luncheon, West Point, N.Y.

7 Address at the graduation ceremonies, United States Military Academy, West Point, N.Y.

10 Statement by the President upon signing the Postal Field Service Compensation Act

11 Address at the centennial commencement of Pennsylvania State University

14 Joint statement following discussions with Chancellor Adenauer of Germany

14 Letter accepting resignation of Charles F. Willis, Jr., Assistant to The Assistant to the President

15 Statement by the President on proposed agreements with Belgium, Canada, and the United Kingdom for cooperation in the civil uses of atomic energy

16 Letter accepting resignation of Preston Hotchkis, U.S. Representative to UNESCO

18 Letter to William Randolph Hearst, Jr., regarding his appointment to the President's Committee for Traffic Safety and its Advisory Council

18 Letter to T. S. Petersen requesting him to serve on the President's Committee for Traffic Safety

20 Address at tenth anniversary meeting of the United Nations, San Francisco, Calif.

June   *Subject*

21 Remarks to National Association of Television and Radio Farm Directors

21 Remarks to the National 4–H conference

21 Statement by the President upon signing the Trade Agreements Extension Act

22 Letter accepting resignation of Robert T. Stevens, Secretary of the Army

22 Memorandum to Federal agencies on the Community Chest Campaign

22 Remarks at Vermont State Dairy Festival, Rutland, Vt.

23 Remarks at a breakfast for Vermont women representatives of dairy and agricultural organizations, Chittenden, Vt.

23 Remarks at State Capitol, Concord, N.H.

23 Remarks at Belknap Lodge Picnic Grounds, Laconia, N.H.

24 Remarks at Lincoln High School, Lincoln, N.H.

24 Remarks at ceremonies commemorating the discovery of the Old Man of the Mountain, Franconia Notch, N.H.

25 Remarks at Lancaster, N.H.

25 Remarks at Jefferson, N.H.

25 Remarks at Hansen Ski Jump area, Berlin, N.H.

26 Letter to Helen Keller on her 75th birthday

27 Remarks at fawn presentation ceremonies, Rangeley, Maine

27 Remarks at Skowhegan Fairgrounds, Skowhegan, Maine

27 Remarks at Dow Air Force Base, Bangor, Maine

June   Subject

27 White House statement following the President's conference with Secretary of State

28 Remarks on presentation of the Distinguished Service Medal to General Ridgway, and accompanying citation

28 Message to the Congress transmitting final report of the Commission on Intergovernmental Relations

29 Letter from Prime Minister U Nu of Burma

29 White House statement concerning Adolphe Wenzell's connection with the Dixon-Yates contract

30 White House statement on reports of the Boards of Visitors to the U.S. Military and Naval Academies

30 White House statement releasing letter from Chairman of the TVA to Director of the Budget Bureau regarding Memphis power plant

July

1 Veto of bill to prohibit publication by the U.S. Government of predictions as to apple prices

1 White House announcement of U.S. delegation to the U.N. conference on the peaceful uses of atomic energy in Geneva

1 White House announcement of U.S. delegation to the Geneva heads of government conference

1 White House statement regarding invitation to the President of Guatemala to visit the United States

3 Joint statement following discussions with the Prime Minister of Burma

7 White House statement regarding an evaluation of relocation activities by ODM Director

July   Subject

8 White House statement concerning the Secretary of State's remarks on the Soviet Communist system

8 White House statement on continuing review by Director of the Budget of the responsibility for Memphis power needs

8 Letter from Allen Whitfield requesting withdrawal of his nomination for membership on the Atomic Energy Commission

9 White House statement announcing assignment of Everett F. Morrow as Administrative Officer for the Special Projects Group, Executive Office of the President

11 Letter accepting resignation of Robert B. Anderson, Deputy Secretary of Defense

12 White House statement following bipartisan meeting on the forthcoming 4-power conference in Geneva

12 Message to the Congress transmitting the second semiannual report under the Agricultural Trade Development and Assistance Act

12 Remarks to the American Field Service students

12 White House statement following the President's conference with Edgar Dixon and Paul O. Canaday

13 Letter accepting the resignation of Mrs. Oveta Culp Hobby, Secretary of Health, Education, and Welfare

13 Remarks following the acceptance of the resignation of Secretary Hobby

13 Letter to Secretary Wilson marking the third anniversary of Operation Skywatch

13 Special message to the Congress upon signing the Department of Defense Appropriation Act

Appendix A

July   Subject

14 Letter from the Attorney General regarding the Department of Defense Appropriation Act

15 Message to the Congress transmitting the ninth annual report on United States participation in the United Nations

15 Statement by the President upon signing the Public Works Appropriation Act

15 Statement by the President upon signing act providing for a highway bridge across Lake Texoma

15 Statement by the President upon signing bill for relief of the Highway Construction Company

15 Letter to the Chairman, House Committee on Ways and Means, concerning U.S. membership in the Organization for Trade Cooperation

15 Radio and television address to the American people prior to departure for Geneva

16 Remarks at the Keflavik Airport, Iceland

16 Remarks upon arrival at the airport in Geneva

18 Opening statement at the Geneva conference

20 Remarks at the research reactor building, Palais des Nations, Geneva

20 Letter accepting resignation of Roger Lewis, Assistant Secretary of the Air Force

21 Statement by the President on disarmament presented at the Geneva conference

22 White House statement announcing signing of proclamation carrying out the protocol of terms of accession by Japan to GATT

July   Subject

22 Statement by the President on East-West contacts, Geneva

22 Memorandum to Federal agencies on the United Fund and Community Chest campaigns

22 Letter to Prime Minister Maung Nu concerning the gift of the Burmese people

23 White House announcement of the U.S. delegation to the Tenth Session of the United Nations General Assembly

23 Closing statement at the final meeting of the Geneva conference

23 Remarks on leaving Geneva

23 Statement by the President upon signing bill concerning mineral claims filed on public lands

24 Remarks at Washington National Airport on returning from Geneva

25 White House statement following bipartisan meeting on the Geneva conference

25 Radio and television address to the American people on the Geneva conference

28 Remarks at the ceremony marking the issuance of the Atoms for Peace stamp

28 Statement by the President on Congressional action regarding a nationwide system of highways

29 White House statement regarding plans for launching earth satellites

August

1 Statement by the President regarding release of United States airmen by Communist China

871

Appendix A

August   Subject

1 Special message to the Congress recommending changes in act relating to construction of irrigation systems on Federal projects by local agencies

1 Letter accepting resignation of Harold E. Talbott, Secretary of the Air Force

2 Remarks to members of the Bull Elephants Club

2 Statement by the President upon signing the Mutual Security Appropriation Act

3 Letter accepting resignation of Orme Lewis, Assistant Secretary of the Interior

3 Citation and remarks at presentation of the Medal of Freedom to Robert B. Anderson

3 Statement by the President upon signing bill relating to the Red River flood control project

4 Letter to the Treasurer of the United States appointing her chairman of the Interdepartmental Savings Bond Committee

4 Memorandum to Federal agencies concerning the voluntary payroll savings plan for purchase of U.S. savings bonds

4 Citation accompanying the Distinguished Service Medal presented to Adm. Robert B. Carney

5 Memorandum to the Chairman, Tariff Commission, requesting cancellation of hearing on tree nut imports

6 Memorandum of Disapproval of bill concerning term of office of Subversive Activities Control Board members

6 Exchange of letters between the President and Chancellor Adenauer of Germany on the Geneva conference

August   Subject

8 Message to the United Nations conference on the peaceful uses of atomic energy at Geneva

9 Statement by the President upon signing the Reserve Forces Act of 1955

9 Letter accepting resignation of Edward F. Howrey, Chairman of the Federal Trade Commission

10 Statement by the President upon signing bill authorizing salary payment to an interim appointee to the Atomic Energy Commission

11 Letter concerning retirement of Ernest H. Van Fossan, Judge of the Tax Court of the United States

11 Statement by the President upon signing the Housing Amendments of 1955

12 Statement by the President on the death of Ambassador John E. Peurifoy and his son

12 Memorandum of Disapproval of bill for relief of E. J. Albrecht Company

12 Memorandum of Disapproval of bill to change the military record of Stephen Swan Ogletree

12 Memorandum of Disapproval of bill amending the Internal Revenue Code of 1954

12 Memorandum of Disapproval of bill to reconvey to former owners certain lands acquired for reservoir projects in Texas

12 Memorandum of Disapproval of bill for the relief of Fred P. Hines

12 Memorandum of Disapproval of bill to amend the Civil Service Retirement Act

12 Statement by the President upon signing bill amending the Agricultural Trade Development and Assistance Act

Appendix A

August   *Subject*

12 Letter to Maj. Gen. John S. Bragdon appointing him as Special Assistant to the President

13 Exchange of messages between the President and Chancellor Adenauer on the Air Force disaster in Germany

13 White House statement announcing Presidential approval of FCDA delegation No. 3 to Departments of Commerce and Interior

14 Memorandum of Disapproval of bill extending the domestic minerals purchase programs

14 Statement by the President upon signing bill concerning public transit services in the District of Columbia

17 Letter accepting resignation of Archie A. Alexander, Governor of the Virgin Islands

17 Letter accepting resignation of Harold Shantz, Minister to Rumania

19 Letter to Chairman of Senate Finance and House Ways and Means Committees on tariff on bicycle imports

20 Letter accepting resignation of Maj. Gen. Glen E. Edgerton, President, Export-Import Bank of Washington

22 Remarks on the hurricane-flood disaster in the northeastern States

23 Remarks following a meeting with the Governors of flood-stricken States at Bradley Field, Hartford, Conn.

23 Exchange of messages between the President and Her Majesty Queen Elizabeth II on the flood disaster

23 White House statement announcing forthcoming visit of the Vice President to the Near East and Africa

24 Address at the annual convention of the American Bar Association, Philadelphia, Pa.

August   *Subject*

24 Exchange of messages between the President and the Prime Minister of the United Kingdom on the flood disaster

24 Exchange of messages between the President and the President of Italy on the flood disaster

24 Exchange of messages between the President and the Prime Minister of Italy on the flood disaster

24 Exchange of messages between the President and the King of the Belgians on the flood disaster

24 Exchange of messages between the President and the Acting Chancellor of Germany on the flood disaster

29 Statement by the President concerning New York meeting of the U.N. subcommittee on disarmament

September

2 White House statement concerning dried fig imports

5 Statement by the President: Labor Day

6 Letter accepting resignation of Charles R. Hook, Jr., Deputy Postmaster General

8 Letter to Judge Orie L. Phillips regarding his retirement from regular active service from the U.S. Court of Appeals

9 White House statement announcing elevation of the legations of the United States and Luxembourg to the status of embassies

9 White House statement on import quotas on oats and barley

10 Remarks at the breakfast meeting of Republican State Chairmen, Denver, Colo.

873

September   Subject

12 Telegram to the President of the U.S. Chamber of Commerce on assistance given flood disaster areas

16 Statement by the President on the occasion of the Jewish New Year

16 Message to President Ruíz Cortines on the anniversary of the independence of Mexico

17 White House statement listing persons invited to attend the President's Conference on Fitness of American Youth

18 Message prepared for the Conference on Fitness of American Youth

23 Letter from Nikolai Bulganin, Chairman, Council of Ministers, U.S.S.R.

25 White House statement regarding recognition by the United States of the new Government of Argentina

25 White House announcement of postponement of the President's Conference on Fitness of American Youth

26 White House announcement concerning scheduled meetings of the National Security Council and the Cabinet

29 Messages from the President of the National Council of Uruguay, the King of Nepal, and the Prime Minister of Burma on the President's illness

30 White House statement following Cabinet meeting on the conduct of foreign and domestic affairs during the President's absence

October

1 White House statement regarding the forthcoming visit of President Castillo Armas of Guatemala

2 Message opening the United Community Campaigns of America

October   Subject

11 Letter to the Columbus Citizens' Committee in New York City

12 Letter to Nikolai Bulganin, Chairman, Council of Ministers, U.S.S.R.

15 Letter accepting resignation of T. Coleman Andrews, Commissioner of Internal Revenue

15 White House statement concerning Small Business Administration disaster loan funds for hurricane disaster areas

17 Statement by the President on observance of Farm-City Week

18 Letter to Governor Roberts of Rhode Island on the recommendations of the New England Governors' Conference

18 Letter to Governor Roberts of Rhode Island on establishment of atomic reactor generating plants in New England

19 Statement by the President upon the 14th anniversary of the Civil Air Patrol

21 White House statement regarding the President's report to the Congress on lend-lease operations

22 Letter to the Vice President concerning the Conference on Equal Job Opportunity

23 Letter to the Vice President and the Cabinet regarding the task of Secretary Dulles at Geneva

25 Letter accepting resignation of J. Haden Alldredge, member, Interstate Commerce Commission

26 Statement by the President on the foreign ministers meeting at Geneva

27 White House statement on tung oil import quota

Appendix A

October   Subject

27 Message to the National Industrial Conference Board on the peaceful uses of atomic energy

28 Letter to the President of Mexico on the hurricane-flood disaster in Tampico

31 Telegram welcoming the President of Guatemala upon his arrival in Washington

November

1 Letter accepting resignation of Frank L. Roberts, Chairman of the Renegotiation Board

3 Message to His Majesty Haile Selassie 1 on the 25th anniversary of his reign

3 Telegram to Dave Beck on the dedication of the International Brotherhood of Teamsters new building

7 Message to K. Voroshilov, Chairman of the Presidium of the Supreme Soviet, U.S.S.R., on national anniversary of the Soviet Union

8 White House statement regarding presentation of letters of credence by listed ambassadors

9 Statement by the President following the outbreak of hostilities in the Near East

10 Letter accepting resignation of Bernard M. Shanley, Appointment Secretary to the President

11 Remarks on leaving Denver, Colo.

11 Remarks upon arrival at the Washington National Airport

14 Remarks upon arrival in Lincoln Square, Gettysburg, Pa.

14 Letter to Mrs. Martin P. Durkin on the death of her husband

November   Subject

14 White House statement announcing receipt of letters of credence from Ambassador Romulo of the Philippines and Ambassador Urrutia-Holguin of Colombia

15 White House statement on the privacy of the President during his convalescent period

15 Message to Rabbi Abba Hillel Silver on the Near East situation, for delivery at New York City rally

18 Message to the Sultan of Morocco on the anniversary of his accession to the throne

22 Letter accepting resignation of Lothair Teetor, Assistant Secretary of Commerce for Domestic Affairs

22 White House statement concerning recess appointment of Frederick H. Mueller as Assistant Secretary of Commerce for Domestic Affairs

24 Message to King Haakon VII of Norway on the 50th anniversary of his reign

25 Letter accepting resignation of Hugh W. Cross, member, Interstate Commerce Commission

28 Remarks to the White House Conference on Education

29 Letter accepting resignation of John J. Forbes, Director of the Bureau of Mines

30 Message from the Sultan of Morocco

30 Statement by the President on observance of Safe Driving Day

30 White House statement concerning the third Washington conference of mayors and other city officials

30 Letter accompanying medallion for presentation to Sir Winston Churchill on his 81st birthday

875

Appendix A

December   Subject

5 Telephone broadcast to the AFL–CIO merger meeting in New York City

6 Letter accepting resignation of Morehead Patterson, U.S. representative for international atomic energy negotiations

10 Letter accepting resignation of Frederic B. Lee, Administrator of Civil Aeronautics

10 Statement by the President on early mailing of Christmas gifts and greetings

12 White House statements following meetings with Republican leaders of the Senate and the House of Representatives

13 White House statement following bipartisan conference on foreign affairs and national defense

December   Subject .

14 Statement by the President: Bill of Rights Day

18 Remarks broadcast for the Pageant of Peace Ceremonies in Washington

19 Letter accepting resignation of Nelson A. Rockefeller, Special Assistant to the President

23 Letter accepting resignation of H. Brian Holland, Assistant Attorney General in charge of Tax Division

24 Letter accepting resignation of James A. McConnell, Assistant Secretary of Agriculture and member of the Board of Directors, Commodity Credit Corporation

30 White House statement following reported remarks by Mr. Khrushchev on the Christmas messages of the President and the Secretary of State to the peoples of Eastern Europe

Appendix B—Presidential Documents Published in the Federal Register, 1955

PROCLAMATIONS

No.	Date 1955	Subject	20 F.R. page
3080	Jan. 1	Fixing terminal date respecting service in the Armed Forces entitling persons to certain veterans' benefits and services, preferences, and other assistance	173
3081	Feb. 21	Armed Forces Day, 1955	1171
3082	Feb. 23	Determining 4,4-Diphenyl-6-Dimethylamino-3-Hexanone to be an opiate	1263
3083	Feb. 24	Red Cross Month, 1955	1263
3084	Mar. 9	Modification of restrictions on imports of peanuts	1549
3085	Mar. 17	National Farm Safety Week, 1955	1653
3086	Mar. 25	Cancer Control Month, 1955	2009
3087	Mar. 25	World Trade Week, 1955	2009
3088	Mar. 31	Pan American Day and Pan American Week, 1955	2103
3089	Mar. 31	Excluding certain lands from the Glacier Bay National Monument and adding a portion thereof to the Tongass National Forest—Alaska	2103
3090	Apr. 5	United Nations Day, 1955	2297
3091	Apr. 28	Loyalty Day, 1955	2945
3092	May 5	Mother's Day, 1955	3147
3093	Apr. 26	Child Health Day, 1955	3179
3094	May 10	National Maritime Day, 1955	3245
3095	May 16	Further modification of restrictions on imports of peanuts	3491
3096	May 24	Prayer for Peace, Memorial Day, 1955	3783
3097	June 1	Flag Day, 1955	3925
3098	June 1	Citizenship Day, 1955	3925
3099	June 25	Carrying out the supplementary agreement with Switzerland	4561

Appendix B

No.	Date 1955	Subject	20 F.R. page
3100	June 29	Further modification of trade-agreement concession on alsike clover seed	4699
3101	June 29	Imposing a quota on imports of rye, rye flour, and rye meal	4701
3102	July 13	John Marshall Bicentennial Month	5089
3103	July 15	Modification of restrictions on imports of shelled filberts	5219
3104	July 23	Death of Cordell Hull	5337
3105	July 22	Carrying out the protocol of terms of accession by Japan to the General Agreement on Tariffs and Trade and for other purposes	5379
3106	Aug. 2	Fire Prevention Week, 1955	5671
3107	Aug. 5	Revocation of Proclamation No. 2626 of October 11, 1944, relating to service courts of friendly foreign forces within the United States	5805
3108	Aug. 18	Modification of trade agreement concessions and adjustment in rates of duty with respect to bicycles	6113
3109	Aug. 19	Constitution Week, 1955	6209
3110	Aug. 25	Veterans Day, 1955	6309
3111	Aug. 27	Termination of Ecuadoran trade agreement proclamation	6485
3112	Sept. 1	American Education Week, 1955	6543
3113	Sept. 3	National Employ the Physically Handicapped Week, 1955	6603
3114	Sept. 24	General Pulaski's Memorial Day, 1955	7319
3115	Oct. 10	Columbus Day, 1955	7717
3116	Oct. 11	Thanksgiving Day, 1955	7801
3117	Oct. 17	Termination of Guatemalan trade agreement proclamation	7925
3118	Oct. 17	Farm-City Week	7925
3119	Oct. 18	National Olympic Day, 1955	7955
3120	Oct. 18	National Day of Prayer, 1955	7977
3121	Dec. 8	United Nations Human Rights Day, 1955	9327

EXECUTIVE ORDERS

| 10585 | Jan. 1 | Termination of combatant activities in Korea and waters adjacent thereto; designation of date | 17 |

878

Appendix B

No.	Date 1955	Subject	20 F.R. page
10586	Jan. 13	Designation of certain officers to act as Secretary of the Treasury	361
10587	Jan. 13	Trading With the Enemy Act; administration of section 32(h) .	361
10588	Jan. 14	President's Commission on Veterans' Pensions; establishment of	361
10589	Jan. 15	Creation of the Quetico-Superior Committee; amendment of Executive Order No. 6783 of June 30, 1934	385
10590	Jan. 18	President's Committee on Government Employment Policy: establishment of	409
10591	Jan. 20	Olesen, Otto K.; waiving the age requirements for permission to compete in the competitive civil-service examination for the position of postmaster at Los Angeles, California	481
10592	Jan. 21	Delegating certain functions of the President respecting school-construction assistance; amendment of Executive Order No. 10524 of March 31, 1954	509
10593	Jan. 27	Authorizing the Director of the Office of Defense Mobilization to perform additional functions of the President; amendment of Executive Order No. 10296, as amended	599
10594	Jan. 31	Selective Service Regulations; amendment of	735
10595	Feb. 7	Panama Canal and the Canal Zone; amendment of Executive Order No. 9746 of July 1, 1946, relating thereto	819
10596	Feb. 15	Reservation of source material in certain lands owned by the United States; revocation of Executive Order No. 9908 of December 5, 1947	1007
10597	Feb. 15	Provision for the restoration of certain lands at Kaakaukukui, Honolulu, Hawaii, to the jurisdiction of the Territory of Hawaii and transfer of title thereto to the Territory	1007
10598	Feb. 28	Establishing the Operations Coordinating Board; amendment of Executive Order No. 10483	1237
10599	Mar. 14	Snyder, Hon. A. Cecil; designation to act, under certain circumstances, as Judge of the United States District Court for the District of Puerto Rico during the year 1955	1569
10600	Mar. 15	"Legion of Merit"; amendment of Executive Order No. 9260 of October 29, 1942	1569
10601	Mar. 21	Administration of commodity set-aside	1761
10602	Mar. 23	Designation of the Secretary of the Interior as the representative of the President to approve the obligation and expenditure of certain moneys by the government of the Virgin Islands . .	1795

Appendix B

No.	Date 1955	Subject	20 F.R. page
10603	Apr. 19	Providing for the restoration of possession, use, and control of certain lands reserved for military purposes to the Territory of Hawaii and transfer of title to such lands to the Territory; amendment of Executive Order No. 10309	2645
10604	Apr. 22	Operation of vending stands on Federal property by blind persons; delegating to the Director of the Bureau of the Budget the authority of the President to approve regulations relating thereto	2747
10605	Apr. 22	Prescribing regulations governing the payment of basic allowances for subsistence to members of the uniformed services; amendment of Executive Order No. 10119 of March 27, 1950	2747
10606	May 3	Tax returns (income, excess-profits, declared-value excess-profits, capital-stock, estate, and gift); inspection by the Senate Committee on Government Operations	3017
10607	May 3	Tax returns (income, excess-profits, declared-value excess-profits, capital-stock, estate, and gift); inspection by the Committee on Government Operations, House of Representatives	3017
10608	May 5	United States authority and functions in Germany	3093
10609	May 7	Delegating to the Secretary of State authority to appoint alternate United States Commissioners to the Caribbean Commission	3147
10610	May 9	Mutual Security and related functions; administration of	3179
10611	May 11	Civil Defense Coordinating Board; establishment of and definition of duties	3245
10612	May 11	Restoring certain lands reserved for military purposes to the jurisdiction of the Territory of Hawaii	3246
10613	May 16	Establishing the Clemency and Parole Board for War Criminals; amendment of Executive Order No. 10393 of September 4, 1952	3455
10614	May 25	General-average contributions in connection with the transportation of certain baggage and household goods and effects of military and civilian personnel of the United States; regulations governing the payment of	3699
10615	June 17	Certain carriers represented by the Eastern, Western, and Southeastern Carriers' Conference Committees and certain of their employees; creation of an emergency board to investigate a dispute	4315

Appendix B

No.	Date 1955	Subject	20 F.R. page
10616	June 21	Officer Personnel Act of 1947, as amended; suspension of certain provisions which relate to officers of the Marine Corps of the grade of brigadier general	4435
10617	June 28	Officer Personnel Act of 1947; suspension of the operation of certain provisions applicable to the retirement of colonels of the Regular Army	4671
10618	June 28	Prescribing regulations relating to the right of members of the uniformed services to incentive pay for the performance of hazardous duty required by competent orders; amendment of Executive Order No. 10152	4671
10619	June 29	Individual income tax returns; inspection by the Department of Health, Education, and Welfare	4673
10620	July 1	Tax returns (income, excess-profits, declared-value excess-profits, capital-stock, estate, and gift); inspection by the Senate Committee on the Judiciary	4759
10621	July 1	Delegation of certain functions of the President to the Secretary of Defense	4759
10622	July 1	Railway Express Agency, Inc., and certain of its employees; creation of an emergency board to investigate a dispute . . .	4762
10623	July 23	Salary differentials and allowances for officers and employees of the Foreign Service serving outside the United States; amendment of certain provisions of Executive Orders No. 10000 and No. 10011, as amended	5297
10624	July 28	Department of Agriculture, service abroad; regulations relating to personnel assigned thereto	5445
10625	Aug. 2	Foreign aid functions; further providing for the administration of	5571
10626	Aug. 4	Interdepartmental Committee for Voluntary Payroll Savings Plan for the Purchase of United States Savings Bonds; establishment of	5671
10627	Aug. 5	Tax returns (income, excess-profits, declared-value excess-profits, capital-stock, estate, and gift); inspection by the Committee on Un-American Activities, House of Representatives .	5741
10628	Aug. 5	Uniform Code of Military Justice; restoring limitations upon punishments for violations of Articles 82, 85, 86(3), 87, 90, 91 (1) and (2), 113, and 115	5741
10629	Aug. 13	Authorizing enlistments in the Ready Reserve of the Army Reserve and Marine Corps Reserve	5911

Appendix B

No.	Date 1955	Subject	20 F.R. page
10630	Aug. 13	New York Central System, Lines East, and certain of its employees; creation of an emergency board to investigate a dispute	5911
10631	Aug. 17	Code of Conduct for Members of the Armed Forces of the United States	6057
10632	Aug. 19	Officer Personnel Act of 1947, as amended; suspension of certain provisions which relate to the promotion of officers of the Medical Corps and Dental Corps of the Navy	6115
10633	Aug. 19	Airspace reservation over the Las Vegas Project, Las Vegas, Nevada; establishment of	6209
10634	Aug. 25	Aid in reconstruction, rehabilitation and replacement of facilities which are destroyed or damaged by a major disaster and which are required for national defense; provision for loans	6433
10635	Sept. 1	Pennsylvania Railroad and certain of its employees; creation of an emergency board to investigate a dispute	6485
10636	Sept. 16	Regulations governing additional compensation and credit granted certain employees of the Federal Government serving outside the United States; amendment of Executive Order No. 10000 of September 16, 1948	7025
10637	Sept. 16	Delegating to the Secretary of the Treasury certain functions of the President relating to the United States Coast Guard . .	7025
10638	Oct. 10	Strategic and critical materials; authorizing the Director of the Office of Defense Mobilization to order release from stock piles in the event of an attack upon the United States	7637
10639	Oct. 10	United States Foreign Service Fees; amendment of the Tariff .	7717
10640	Oct. 10	The President's Committee on Employment of the Physically Handicapped	7717
10641	Oct. 26	Appointments to overseas positions; amendment of Civil Service Rules by addition of Rule VIII	8137
10642	Oct. 26	Employment in Canal Zone; suspension of certain statutory provisions	8137
10643	Nov. 7	Albany Port District Railroad and other carriers and certain of their employees; creation of an emergency board to investigate disputes	8359
10644	Nov. 7	Bulgarian, Hungarian, and Rumanian property; administration of Title II of the International Claims Settlement Act of 1949, as amended, relating to the vesting and liquidation thereof . .	8363

Appendix B

No.	Date 1955	Subject	20 F.R. page
10645	Nov. 22	State of Michigan; amendment of Executive Order No. 9 of January 17, 1873, to permit an officer or employee of the Federal Government to hold the office of Member of the State Board of Agriculture	8681
10646	Nov. 22	Federal Voting Assistance Act of 1955; designation of the Secretary of Defense to coordinate and facilitate actions required to discharge Federal responsibilities	8681
10647	Nov. 28	Defense Production Act of 1950, as amended; provision for the appointment of certain persons thereunder	8769
10648	Dec. 8	Restoration of certain lands comprising portions of the Fort Ruger Military Reservation to the jurisdiction of the Territory of Hawaii	9287
10649	Dec. 28	Regulations relating to certain travel time of members of the uniformed services called to active duty in excess of thirty days; amendment of Executive Order No. 10153	10095

PRESIDENTIAL DOCUMENTS OTHER THAN PROCLAMATIONS AND EXECUTIVE ORDERS

July 22 Letter: Trade Agreement; Carrying out the Protocol of Terms of Accession by Japan to the General Agreement on Tariffs and Trade and for other purposes 5383

Aug. 22 Letter: Trade Agreement; Carrying out the Protocol of Terms of Accession by Japan to the General Agreement on Tariffs and Trade and for other purposes 6211

Oct. 3 Letter: Trade Agreement; Carrying out the Protocol of Terms of Accession by Japan to the General Agreement on Tariffs and Trade and for other purposes 7801

Appendix C—Presidential Reports to the Congress, 1955

Subject	Published	Sent to the Congress	Date of White House release
Public Law 480 (83d Cong.):			
First Semiannual Report	H. Doc. 62	Jan. 10	Jan. 10
Second Semiannual Report	H. Doc. 216	July 12	July 12
Escape Clauses—report on the inclusion of escape clauses in existing trade agreements	H. Doc. 64	Jan. 10	Jan. 10
Panama Canal Company and the Canal Zone Government:			
Second Annual Report		Jan. 17	. . . .
Third Annual Report		May 19	. . . .
Saint Lawrence Seaway Development Corporation	H. Doc. 71	Jan. 14 (S)	. . . .
		Jan. 17 (H)	. . . .
Commodity Credit Corporation	H. Doc. 73	Jan. 14 (S)	. . . .
		Jan. 17 (H)	. . . .
Foreign Service Retirement and Disability Fund .	H. Doc. 70	Jan. 14 (S)	. . . .
		Jan. 17 (H)	. . . .
Corregidor Bataan Memorial Commission . . .	H. Doc. 72	Jan. 14 (S)	. . . .
		Jan. 17 (H)	. . . .
National Science Foundation, Fourth Annual Report	H. Doc. 74	Jan. 14 (S)	. . . .
		Jan. 17 (H)	. . . .
Economic Report of the President	H. Doc. 31	Jan. 20	Jan. 20
National Advisory Committee for Aeronautics, Fortieth Annual Report	S. Doc. 1	Jan. 27	. . . .
National Advisory Council on International Monetary and Financial Problems:			
October 1, 1953, to June 30, 1954	H. Doc. 85	Feb. 8	. . . .
July 1 to December 31, 1954	H. Doc. 194	June 22	. . . .

Appendix C

Subject	Published	Sent to the Congress	Date of White House release
United States Civil Service Commission	H. Doc. 13	Feb. 16 (H) Feb. 18 (S)	. . . .
National Capital Housing Authority	. . . . .	Feb. 23	. . . .
Railroad Retirement Board	H. Doc. 28	Mar. 10	. . . .
Mutual Security Program:			
For the 6 months ended December 31, 1954 . .	H. Doc. 97	Mar. 14	Mar. 14
For the 6 months ended June 30, 1955	H. Doc. 226	Aug. 25	. . . .
Report on the Federal-Aid Highway Act of 1954 entitled "Public Utility Relocation Incident to Highway Improvement"	H. Doc. 127	Apr. 5	. . . .
Development of Agriculture's Human Resources .	H. Doc. 149	Apr. 27 (H) Apr. 28 (S)	Apr. 27
Report of the Office of Alien Property, Department of Justice	. . . . .	June 6	. . . .
Final Report of the Commission on Intergovernmental Relations	H. Doc. 198	June 28	. . . .
United States Participation in the United Nations, Ninth Annual Report	H. Doc. 166	July 15	July 15
Lend Lease Operations, Thirty-sixth Report . .	H. Doc. 221	Oct. 21	. . . .

Appendix D—Rules Governing This Publication

[Reprinted from the Federal Register, vol. 24, p. 2354, dated March 26, 1959]

TITLE 1—GENERAL PROVISIONS

Chapter I—Administrative Committee of the Federal Register

PART 32—PUBLIC PAPERS OF THE PRESIDENTS OF THE UNITED STATES

PUBLICATION AND FORMAT

Sec.
32.1 Publication required.
32.2 Coverage of prior years.
32.3 Format, indexes, ancillaries.

SCOPE

32.10 Basic criteria.
32.11 Sources.

FREE DISTRIBUTION

32.15 Members of Congress.
32.16 The Supreme Court.
32.17 Executive agencies.

PAID DISTRIBUTION

32.20 Agency requisitions.
32.21 Extra copies.
32.22 Sale to public.

AUTHORITY: §§ 32.1 to 32.22 issued under sec. 6, 49 Stat. 501, as amended; 44 U.S.C. 306.

PUBLICATION AND FORMAT

§ 32.1 *Publication required.* There shall be published forthwith at the end of each calendar year, beginning with the year 1957, a special edition of the FEDERAL REGISTER designated "Public Papers of the Presidents of the United States."

Each volume shall cover one calendar year and shall be identified further by the name of the President and the year covered.

§ 32.2 *Coverage of prior years.* After conferring with the National Historical Publications Commission with respect to the need therefor, the Administrative Committee may from time to time authorize the publication of similar volumes covering specified calendar years prior to 1957.

§ 32.3 *Format, indexes, ancillaries.* Each annual volume, divided into books whenever appropriate, shall be separately published in the binding and style deemed by the Administrative Committee to be suitable to the dignity of the office of President of the United States. Each volume shall be appropriately indexed and shall contain appropriate ancillary information respecting significant Presidential documents not published in full text.

SCOPE

§ 32.10 *Basic criteria.* The basic text of the volumes shall consist of oral utterances by the President or of writings subscribed by him. All materials selected for inclusion under these criteria must also be in the public domain by virtue of White House press release or otherwise.

§ 32.11 *Sources.* (a) The basic text of the volumes shall be selected from the official text of: (1) Communications to

886

the Congress, (2) public addresses, (3) transcripts of press conferences, (4) public letters, (5) messages to heads of state, (6) statements released on miscellaneous subjects, and (7) formal executive documents promulgated in accordance with law.

(b) Ancillary text, notes, and tables shall be derived from official sources only.

FREE DISTRIBUTION

§ 32.15 *Members of Congress.* Each Member of Congress shall be entitled to one copy of each annual volume upon application therefor in writing to the Director.

§ 32.16 *The Supreme Court.* The Supreme Court of the United States shall be entitled to twelve copies of the annual volumes.

§ 32.17 *Executive agencies.* The head of each department and the head of each independent agency in the executive branch of the Government shall be entitled to one copy of each annual volume upon application therefor in writing to the Director.

PAID DISTRIBUTION

§ 32.20 *Agency requisitions.* Each Federal agency shall be entitled to obtain at cost copies of the annual volumes for official use upon the timely submission to the Government Printing Office of a printing and binding requisition (Standard Form No. 1).

§ 32.21 *Extra copies.* All requests for extra copies of the annual volumes shall be addressed to the Superintendent of Documents, Government Printing Office, Washington 25, D.C. Extra copies shall be paid for by the agency or official requesting them.

§ 32.22 *Sale to public.* The annual volumes shall be placed on sale to the public by the Superintendent of Documents at prices determined by him under the general direction of the Administrative Committee.

*   *   *   *   *

ADMINISTRATIVE COMMITTEE OF
THE FEDERAL REGISTER,
WAYNE C. GROVER,
Archivist of the United States,
Chairman.
RAYMOND BLATTENBERGER,
The Public Printer,
Member.
WILLIAM O. BURTNER,
Representative of the Attorney
General, Member.

Approved March 20, 1959.
WILLIAM P. ROGERS,
Attorney General.
FRANKLIN FLOETE,
Administrator of General Services.
[F.R. Doc. 59–2517; Filed, Mar. 25, 1959;
8:45 a. m.]

INDEX

[References are to items except as otherwise indicated]

Abel, Elie, 47, 62, 81, 90, 95
Accidents
  Aircraft
    Troop transport, Germany, 204
    U.S. plane in Bering Sea, 146
  Highway traffic, 39, 243
    Statement on safe driving, 111
Acreage allotments, 90
Acreage controls, 4, 17 (p. 150)
Adams, Francis L., 146 and ftn. (p. 658)
Adams, Sherman, 131, 133, 134, 135
  News conference remarks on, 119, 146, 176
Adamy, Clarence G., 51 n.
Addresses, remarks, or messages to national groups
  Advertising Council, 58
  AFL cornerstone-laying ceremony, 245
  American Bar Association, 210
  American Legion, 38
  Associated Press, 79
  Association of American Colleges, 11
  Boy Scouts of America, 28
  4–H Club, 128
  Masonic breakfast, 43
  National Association of Radio and Television Broadcasters, 105
  National Association of Television and Radio Farm Directors, 127
  National Conference of Christians and Jews, 40
  Republican National Committee, 35
  Republican Women's National Conference, 94
  United Service Organizations, 27
  U.S. Chamber of Commerce, 85
  White House Conference on Education, 242

Addresses, remarks, or messages at presentation ceremonies
  Acceptance of citation by United Jewish Appeal, 115
  Acceptance of fawn, 141
  Acceptance of honorary degrees, 70, 121
  Acceptance of statue, Laboring Youth, 22
  Citation to National Foundation for Infantile Paralysis, 78
  Citation to Dr. Salk, 77
  Medal to Robert B. Anderson, 183
  Medal to Adm. Carney, 188
  Medal to J. Edgar Hoover, 110
  Medal to Field Marshal Pibulsonggram, 87
  Medal to Gen. Ridgway, 144
  Medallion to Winston Churchill, 244
Addresses or remarks on commemorative or dedicatory occasions
  AFL cornerstone-laying ceremony, 84
  Armed Forces Institute of Pathology, dedication, 108
  Old Man of the Mountain, 150th anniversary of discovery, 136
  U.N. tenth anniversary meeting, 126
  Washington Hebrew Congregation Temple, 92
Adenauer, Konrad
  Invitation to visit U.S.S.R., 119
  Joint statement with, 122
  Letter, 190
  Message, 204
  Visit to United States, 119
Adkins, Bertha, 94
Advertising Council, 96
  Conference, remarks, 58

Index

Advisory Committee on Government Operations, 74

Aerial inspection. *See* Disarmament

Aeronautical research, 17 (p. 92)

Aeronautics, National Advisory Committee for, 17 (p. 170)

AFL, 41
  Cornerstone-laying ceremonies, remarks, 84

AFL–CIO, merger, 47
  Remarks, 245

Africa
  Assistance, 17 (p. 130), 76
  World War II campaign, 10

Afro-Asian conference. *See* Bandung conference of Asian-African countries

Agreements, international. *See* International agreements

Agricultural Marketing Act amendment, veto, 147

Agricultural research, 17 (pp. 94, 155)

Agricultural surpluses, 4, 7
  Approval of amendment to Public Law 480, 202
  Budget message, 17 (pp. 103, 130, 152, 153)
  News conference remarks, 90
  Rice, 148
  Sale for foreign currencies, 76

Agricultural Trade Development and Assistance Act, 76
  Amendment, approval, 202
  Reports, 7, 150

Agriculture, 4, 6, 221
  Budget message, 17 (pp. 93, 94, 148–155)
    Table, 17 (p. 151)
  News conference remarks, 33, 90
  Soviet Union, 33

Agriculture, Department of, 147
  Budget message, 17 (pp. 144, 155)
  Ladejinsky, Wolf, 10, 18

Agriculture, Secretary of (Ezra Taft Benson), 90 ftn. (p. 475), 127
  Low income farmers, 15-point program, 82
  News conference remarks on, 10, 18

Agronsky, Martin, 90, 95, 149, 185

Aiken, Sen. George D., 131

Air Coordinating Committee, 17 (p. 169)

Air Defense Command, 13, 17 (p. 116)

Air Force, 50
  Accident to troop transport, Germany, 204
  Budget message, 17 (pp. 113, 114, 117)
  Personnel strength, 3

Air Force, Secretary of the (Harold E. Talbott), 90, 112, 119, 176, 185

Air Force Academy, remarks on establishment, 117

Air navigation facilities, 17 (p. 92)

Air pollution, 25

Air power, Soviet, 100

Air power, U.S., 100
  See also Military strength, U.S.

Aircraft, military
  Accident to U.S. troop transport, Germany, 204
  Bering Sea U.S. plane accident, 146
  Bombers, 3, 149
    B–36 bombers, 100, 112
    B–52 bombers, 100
  Budget message, 17 (pp. 116, 117, 121)
  News conference remarks, 100, 112, 146, 149
  Nuclear, 17 (p. 121)
  Soviet, 112

Aircraft industry dispersal, comment on, 90

Airlines
  Alaska Airlines, 106
  Northwest Airlines, 30, 33
  Pacific Northern Airlines, 106
  Pan American World Airways, 30, 33
  Subsidies, 17 (p. 169), 30, 33, 106

Index

Airmen, U.S., prisoners in Communist China, 4, 16, 148
News conference remarks, 18, 41, 62, 81, 112, 176
Release of, 112, 179
U.N. action on, 156
Airports, Federal aid, 146
Alabama, Sen. Lister Hill, 33
Alaska, statehood, 4, 247
News conference remarks, 56, 95
Alaska Airlines, certification, 106
Albania, offer of food supplies, statement, 49
Albert, Irene, 90
Albrecht, E. J., Co., relief of, disapproval, 196
Aldrich, Winthrop W., 244 n.
Allen, Ethan, 131
Alsop, Joseph, 119
Alsop, Stewart, 119
American Bar Association
Address, 210
News conference remarks, 47, 112
American Federation of Labor, 41
Cornerstone-laying ceremonies, remarks, 84
American Field Service students, remarks, 151
American Heritage Foundation, 32 n.
American Legion, 119, 169
Americanism program, remarks, 38
American Medical Association, 34 n.
Action on polio vaccine, 112, 113
American Republics, 76
See also American States, Organization of; Inter-American; Latin America; *specific countries*
American Revolution, 10
American Society of Newspaper Editors, 79, 99 n.
American States, Organization of
Costa Rican dispute, action on, 10

American States—Continued
Guatemalan situation, 156
News conference remarks, 10, 26
U.S. contributions to, 76
Amtorg, 10
AMVETS, 169
Anderson, Sen. Clinton P.
Letter on NATO cooperation re atomic information, 71
News conference remarks on, 10
Anderson, Dillon, 146 ftn. (p. 644)
Anderson, Robert B., Medal of Freedom, citation, 183
Antarctic, mission of U.S.S. *Atka*, 47
Anti-segregation amendments to legislation, 119
Anti-trust study, 56
Appeasement, 79
News conference remarks, 26, 100
Apple price predictions, prohibition of Government publication, veto, 147
Appointments
Bragdon, Maj. Gen. John S., Special Assistant to the President, 203
Hearst, William Randolph, Jr., Committee for Traffic Safety, 124
Petersen, T. S., Committee for Traffic Safety, 125
President's Commission on Veterans Pensions, 51
Stassen, Harold E., Special Assistant to the President, 57
Appropriations
Department of Defense Appropriation Act, 1956, 155
Mutual Security Appropriation Act, 182
Public Works Appropriation Act, 157
Approval of acts of Congress, statements or messages. *See* Legislation, statements or messages upon approval
Arab-Israeli dispute and hostilities, 76, 239
Statement, 234

Index

[References are to items except as otherwise indicated]

Arab States, refugees, 17 (p. 131)
Arends, Repr. Leslie C., 41
Argentina, atomic research agreement, 121
Argonne National Laboratory, foreign students, remarks, 53
Armed forces, U.S., 4
  Absentee voting rights, 29
  Code of conduct, 207
  Decline in re-enlistment rate, 13
  Housing, 4, 13, 17 (p. 118)
  In Formosa area, 21, 24 n.
  In Germany, 119
  Letter to Secretary Wilson re, 3
  Medical Corps, 108
  Milk program for, 17 (p. 152)
  News conference remarks, 26, 119, 149
  Reduction, 26, 119
  Reserve bill, 90, 100, 119, 146, 149, 176, 192
  Reserve program, 3, 4, 12, 17 (p. 91)
  Tachen Islands, 36
  See also Military personnel
Armed forces, U.S.S.R., 119
Armed Forces Day, message, 97
Armed Forces Institute of Pathology, dedication remarks, 108
Arms limitation and reduction, 4
  Statement at Geneva, 164
  Western European Union, 54
  See also Disarmament
Army
  Budget message, 17 (pp. 112–114, 116)
  Modernization, 4
  Reduction in, 119
Army, Chief of Staff (Gen. Matthew B. Ridgway), award of Distinguished Service Medal, 144
Army, Department of the, 3
Army, Secretary of the (Robert T. Stevens), resignation, rumor of, 33
Arrowsmith, Marvin L., 10, 18, 26, 33, 41, 47, 56, 59, 62, 81, 90, 95, 100, 112

Arts, Federal Advisory Commission on, proposed, 4
Asgeirsson, Asgeir, exchange of greetings, 162
Asia, South Asia, and Southeast Asia, 4, 99, 248
  Assistance, 17 (pp. 123, 129, 130), 41, 47, 48, 69, 76
  Bandung conference, 26
  Colombo Plan for economic development, 76
  Joint statement with Prime Minister Nu, 148
  News conference remarks, 18, 26, 41, 47
  See also specific countries
Associated Press, address, 79
Association of American Colleges, remarks, 11
Atka, U.S.S., Antarctic mission, 47
Atomic attack, highways for evacuation purposes, 39
Atomic energy, 17 (pp. 108, 119)
Atomic Energy Agency, International. See International Atomic Energy Agency
Atomic Energy Commission, 79, 89, 123, 146 ftns. (pp. 646, 658), 223
  Appropriations, 157
  Argonne National Laboratory, 53
  Budget message, 17 (pp. 119, 121, 143, 161, 162)
  "Effects of High-Yield Nuclear Explosions," 41, 56
  Filling of vacancy, 62, 119
  Libby, Willard F., 89 n., 191 n.
  News conference remarks, 10, 41, 56, 62, 119
  Salary payment to interim appointee, 193
  Technical libraries, 228
Atomic Energy Commission, Chairman (Lewis L. Strauss), 10, 53, 177, 228 n.
  Geneva conference on atomic energy, 191

Index

[References are to items except as otherwise indicated]

Atomic energy for peaceful uses, 4, 53 n.,
121, 126
  Budget message, 17 (p. 91)
  Fissionable materials for, 79, 156, 164,
  165
    See also Uranium
  Geneva conference (1955), 100, 123,
  149, 156, 176, 177 n., 228
    Message, 191
  International agreements on civil uses.
    See International agreements
  Merchant ship exhibit, 79
  Message to National Industrial Confer-
  ence Board, 228
  News conference remarks, 59, 81, 100,
  146, 149, 176
  President's address at United Nations
  (1953), 191
  Remarks in Geneva, 165
  U.N. activities, 156
    See also International Atomic Energy
    Agency
Atomic power projects. *See* Power projects
Atomic reactors. *See* Reactors
"Atoms for Peace" postage stamp, remarks
  on issuance, 177
Attorney General (Herbert Brownell, Jr.),
  110 n.
  News conference remarks on, 81, 149
  Opinion on Department of Defense
  Appropriation Act, 155
Atwood, Frank, 127
Auchincloss, Repr. James C., letter, 20
Augusta, Ga., 1 n., 26 ftn. (p. 231), 71 n.,
  72 n., 73 n., 74 n.
Austria
  Ambassador Llewellyn E. Thompson,
  146 ftn. (p. 644)
  Exchange visitor, Kurt Glaser, 116
  Koerner, Theodor, 98
  News conference remarks, 81, 100
  Neutralization, 100
  Vienna, 81, 95, 98 n., 114

Austrian State Treaty, 99
  Message to President Koerner upon
  signing, 98
  News conference remarks, 59, 81, 95, 100
  Transmittal to Senate, 114
Automation, comment on, 56
Automobile industry, threatened strike, 112
Automobiles, excise tax on, 41
Aviation, 17 (pp. 169, 170)
Awards and citations
  Citation by United Jewish Appeal, 115
  Distinguished Service Medal
    Adm. Carney, 188
    Gen. Ridgway, 144
  Honorary degrees, 70, 121
  Legion of Merit, Field Marshal Pibul-
  songgram, 87
  Medal of Freedom, Robert B. Anderson,
  183
  Medallion, Winston Churchill, 244
  National Foundation for Infantile Pa-
  ralysis, 78
  National Security Medal, J. Edgar
  Hoover, 110
  Salk, Dr. Jonas E., 77

Bandung conference of Asian-African
  countries, 26 and ftn. (p. 231)
Bangkok, Thailand
  SEATO conference, 41
  Trade fair (1954), 6
Bangor, Maine, remarks at Dow Air Force
  Base, 143
Bao Dai, letter, 48
Barnes, Stanley N., 56
Bartelt, Edward F., 187
Bartlett, Charles L., 146, 149
Bass, Repr. Perkins, 139
Baudouin I, 208 n.
Bayar, Celal, 89
Beach, Comdr. Edward L., 183, 188
Beck, Dave, telegram, 232

[References are to items except as otherwise indicated]

Beckley, Harold, death of, 62

Belgium, 54 n., 112 ftn. (p. 548)
  Agreement with U.S. on civil uses of atomic energy, 123
  Baudouin I, 208 n.

Bell, Repr. John J., 95

Bennett, Sen. Wallace F., 119

Benson, Ezra Taft. *See* Agriculture, Secretary of

Bering Sea, U.S. plane accident, 146

Berlin
  Assistance, 76
  News conference remarks, 33

Berlin, N.H., remarks at Hansen Ski Jump area, 139

Big Dam Foolishness (Peterson), 56

Big Four Conference. *See* Heads of state and governments, meeting

Bill of Rights, news conference remarks, 56, 59

Bill of Rights Day, statement, 249

Bingham, Hiram, 10

Bipartisan action, 185
  Foreign affairs and national defense, 248
  Report on Geneva heads of government conference, 174

Blair, William M., 62, 90, 95, 119, 176

Blind persons,
  Medical care, 25
  Services of Post Office Department, 9

Bluecher, Franz, 208 n.

Blumenthal, Hermann, 22 n.

Bohlen, Charles E., 146 ftn. (p. 644)

Bolivia, assistance, 17 (p. 129), 76

Bombers. *See* Aircraft, military

Bombs
  News conference remarks, 33, 41, 47, 56
  See also Nuclear tests; Nuclear Weapons

Bonaparte, Napoleon, 59, 118

Bonds, U.S. savings, 186, 187

Boston Tea Party, 92

Bowie, Robert R., 146 ftn. (p. 644)

Boy Scout Week, 28

Boy Scouts of America, message, 28

Bradley, Gen. Omar N., 135
  Letter, 51

Bragdon, Maj. Gen. John S., appointment as Special Assistant to the President, 203

Brandt, Raymond P., 26, 41, 47, 56, 59, 62, 81, 95

Brazil, 112 ftn. (p. 548)
  Atomic research agreement, 121
  Rio de Janeiro, 4

Bricker, Sen. John W., 59

Bricker amendment, comment on, 59, 81

Bridges, Sen. Styles, 134, 135, 139

British Empire Service League, 119

Broadcasts to the American people. *See* Messages to the American people

Bronk, Detlev W., 191 n.

Brooks, Repr. Overton, 100

Brosio, Manlio, 61

Brotherhood Week, 40

Brown, John R., 112

Brown Swiss Dairy Cattle Association, remarks, 131

Brownell, Herbert, Jr. *See* Attorney General

Brownell, Samuel M., 96

Brucellosis control, 17 (p. 155)

Brussels Treaty, 54

Bryan, Maj. Gen. Blackshear M., 117, 118

Buddhist Synod, 148

Budget, Bureau of the, 222
  Dixon-Yates contract, 146, 149
  Employment of Adolphe Wenzell, 146 and ftn. (pp. 657, 658)

Budget, Bureau of the, Director (Rowland R. Hughes), 74, 90 ftn. (p. 475), 146 ftns. (pp. 646, 657)
  News conference remarks on, 56, 176

Index

[References are to items except as otherwise indicated]

Budget (1956), 247
  Annual message, 17
    Tables, 17 (pp. 89, 90, 96, 102–105, 107, 110, 111, 115, 123, 127, 135, 140, 142, 146, 151, 157, 165, 166, 178, 180, 184)
  News conference remarks, 18, 41, 112
Budget (1957), 247
Budget policies, 17 (pp. 88, 89)
Bulganin, Nikolai A., 161, 164, 166 n.
  Letter, 220
  News conference remarks on, 62, 95, 146, 185
Bull Elephants Club, remarks, 181
Bunker Hill, Battle of, 118
Burd, Laurence H., 18, 33, 41, 62, 81, 90, 95, 112, 149
Burma
  Gift to children of U.S. veterans, 169
  Nu (U), 146, 148, 169
  Rangoon, 148
Business loans, 17 (pp. 176, 177)
Buy American Act
  Applicability to spun silk yarn for cartridge cloth, 155
  Memorandum, 67
Byrd, Sen. Harry F., 81, 90 ftn. (p. 471)
Byrnes, James F., 73

Caesar, Julius, 118
Caffery, Jefferson, 47
Cain, Harry P., criticism of Government employee security program, 18
California
  Knowland, Sen. William F., 26, 41, 59
  San Francisco, 47, 81, 112, 126, 131, 156
Calumet-Sag Waterway, Ill., 17 (p. 169)
Cambodia, assistance, 17 (p. 129)
Camp David, editor's note, p. 822
Camp Feldafing, 115 n.
Campbell, Boyd, letter, 214
Campbell, Joseph, Comptroller General, 62

Canada, 43, 112 ftn. (p. 548)
  Agreement with U.S. on civil uses of atomic energy, 123
  Highways to, 39
Canal Zone, inter-American highway, 64
Canali, Paolo, 61
Candidacy for second term, comment on, 10, 47, 56, 62, 146, 149, 185
CAP. See Civil Air Patrol
Capetown, South Africa, visit of U.S.S. Midway, 18
Capital Transit Co., termination of franchise, 206
Capitol Hill Club, message, 20
Caracas, Venezuela, conference in, 4
Career incentives for military personnel, 17 (pp. 91, 109)
Carignan, Norman, 10
Carlson, Sen. Frank, 62
Carmichael, Leonard, 22
Carney, Adm. Robert B.
  Comment on, 62
  Distinguished Service Medal, citation, 188
Castillo Armas, Carlos, telegram, 230
Castillo Armas, Senora, 230
Cater, S. Douglass, Jr., 26, 119
Cathey, Sam M., 103
Census Bureau, 17 (p. 148)
Central America. See Latin America
Central Intelligence Agency, 59
Chamber of Commerce, U.S., action on flood disaster, letter, 214
Charleston, S.C., remarks at The Citadel, 70
Chi-Com. See China, Communist
Chiang, Joseph, 56, 81, 176
Chiang Kai-shek
  Exchange of messages, 36
  News conference remarks on, 18, 26, 47
Chicago, Ill., 47
  Governors Conference (1955), 90

Chief Justice of the United States (Earl Warren), 210
  On Bill of Rights, 56, 59
Children
  Health program, 25
  Of U.S. veterans, gift from Burma, 169
  Orphans, recommendations under Refugee Relief Act, 109
Children's Bureau, 25
Children's Fund, U.N., 76, 156
China, Communist, 21
  Aggression in North Korea, 185
  Formosa Strait situation. *See* Formosa (Taiwan) Strait situation
  News conference remarks, 18, 33, 41, 47, 59, 62, 81, 112, 176, 185
  Peiping, 16
  Soviet Union, relations with, 33
  U.S. airmen, prisoners in, 4, 16, 18, 41, 62, 81, 148, 176
    Release of, 112, 179
    U.N. action on, 156
  U.S. negotiations with, 176, 185
China, Republic of
  Assistance, 17 (p. 129), 21
  Chiang Kai-shek, 18, 26, 36, 47
  Invasion of mainland, question of, 47
  Military assistance, 76
  Mutual Defense Treaty, 4, 5, 21, 35
  News conference remarks, 18, 26, 47, 81
  See also Formosa (Taiwan); Formosa (Taiwan) Strait situation
Chinese overseas, question of return to mainland, 56
Chittenden, Vt., remarks to women representatives of dairy and agricultural organizations, 132
Christmas mail, statement, 246
Christmas Tree, National Community, 250
Churchill, Winston
  Comment on, 47

Churchill, Winston—Continued
  Medallion, presentation letter, 244
  Retirement as Prime Minister of United Kingdom, statement, 65
CIA. *See* Central Intelligence Agency
Citadel, The, commencement remarks, 70
Citations. *See* Awards and citations
Citizens Commission for the Public Schools, National, 96
Civil Aeronautics Administration, 146
Civil Aeronautics Board
  Budget message, 17 (p. 169)
  Chairman, filling of position, 10
  States-Alaska case, 106
  West Coast-Hawaii case, 30, 33
Civil Aeronautics Board, Chairman (Ross Rizley), letter, 106
Civil Air Patrol, 14th anniversary, statement, 224
Civil benefits, budget message, 17 (pp. 96, 101–103)
  Table, 17 (p. 103)
Civil defense, 4
  Budget message, 17 (pp. 119, 175)
  News conference remarks, 56, 112, 149
  Test exercise
    Memorandum, 101
    Relocation of Federal agencies (Operation Alert), 149 and ftn. (p. 672)
Civil Defense Administration. *See* Federal Civil Defense Administration
Civil Defense Administrator (Val Peterson), 209
Civil rights, 247
  Public school education. *See* Integration, public schools
Civil Service Commission
  Budget message, 17 (p. 181)
  Government employees incentive awards program, 1
Civil Service Retirement Act, amendment, disapproval, 201

Index

Civil service retirement fund, 17 (pp. 96, 106)

Clague, Ewan, 18

Claims and relief acts, 17 (p. 183)

Clark, Mayor Joseph, on civil defense, 56

Clark, Gen. Mark W., 70

Clark, Robert E., 18, 26, 33, 41, 47, 59, 62, 81, 90, 100, 112, 146, 176, 185

Class struggle doctrine of Karl Marx, 245

Clay, Gen. Lucius D., 39, 146

Clements, Sen. Earle C., 33

Clinchy, Everett R., 40

Coast Guard, 17 (p. 169)

Code of conduct for members of armed forces, statement, 207

Coexistence, comment on use of term, 26

Cole, Benjamin R., 26, 47, 81

Collective bargaining, 245

Collective security, 3, 4
  See also North Atlantic Treaty Organization; Organization of American States; Southeast Asia Treaty Organization

Colleges and universities
  Association of American Colleges, 11
  Citadel, The, 70
  Columbia University, 62, 151
  Gettysburg College, 242 n., 250 n.
  Housing, 17 (pp. 174, 175)
  Pennsylvania State University, 121, 149
  University of Louisville, International Center, 116
  University of Michigan, 113 n.
  University of Pittsburgh, 11 n.

Collins, Gen. J. Lawton, 48, 81

Collins, Seaborn P., Jr., 119

Colombia, 112 ftn. (p. 548)
  Atomic research agreement, 121

Colombo Plan Consultative Group, 76

Colorado
  Denver, 207 n., 208, 211 n., 212 n., 213 n., 214 n., 215 n., 216 n., 217 n.,

Colorado—Continued
  219 n., 220 n., 221 n., 222 n., 223 n., 224 n., 225 n., 226 n., 227 n., 228 n., 229 n., 230 n., 231 n., 232 n., 233 n., 234 n., 235
  Editor's note on President's illness, p. 822
  Millikin, Sen. Eugene D., 81

Colorado River (Upper) Basin, development project, 4, 56

Columbia University, 151

Columbus, Christopher, 219

Columbus Citizens' Committee, letter, 219

Commemorative or dedicatory occasions. *See* Addresses or remarks on commemorative or dedicatory occasions

Commerce, Secretary of, 222

Commerce, Secretary of (Sinclair Weeks), 39 n., 90 ftn. (p. 475), 137
  European visit, 59

Commerce and manpower, budget message, 17 (pp. 163–178)
  Table, 17 (pp. 165, 166)

Commissary and post exchange privileges, 100

Commission on Fine Arts, proposed, 17 (p. 141)

Commission on Intergovernmental Relations, 4
  Civil defense recommendations, 149
  News conference remarks, 47, 146, 149
  Report, 145

Commission on Organization of the Executive Branch of the Government, recommendations. *See* Hoover Commission recommendations

Commission on Veterans' Pensions
  Budget message, 17 (p. 134)
  Letter, 51

Committee on Energy Supplies and Resources Policy (Flemming Committee), report, 33 and ftn. (p. 259), 41, 56

Committee on Government Operations, 74

Committee on Minerals Policy, 17 (p. 163)

Committee on a National Highway Program (Clay Committee), 4, 146
  Report, 39

Committee for a National Trade Policy, remarks, 83

Committee on Poliomyelitis Vaccine, National Advisory, 81, 90

Committee on Retirement Policy for Federal Personnel, report, 17 (p. 181)

Committee for Traffic Safety, 111, 243
  Hearst, William Randolph, Jr., letter re appointment, 124
  Petersen, T. S., letter re appointment, 125

Committee on Transport Policy and Organization, report, 33, 62, 90 and ftn. (p. 475)

Committee for the White House Conference on Education, 96

Commodity Credit Corporation, 17 (pp. 126, 130, 149, 150, 152, 155)

Communiques, comment on, 146

Communism, 13, 35, 43, 48, 57, 58, 64, 79, 85, 94, 99, 175
  News conference remarks, 26, 81, 119

Communist aggression and expansion, 4, 12, 21, 24
  Budget message, 17 (p. 129)
  Economic offensive, 6

Communist bloc, 4
  U.S. trade with, 18
  See also Satellite countries; *specific countries*

Communist imperialism, 4

Community Chest campaign, 130

Comptroller General (Joseph Campbell), 62

Concord, N. H., remarks, 133

Conduct of Government officials, 176

Conference on Equal Job Opportunity, letter, 225

Conference on Fitness of American Youth, message, 217

Conflict of interest case, Gen. W. W. White, 185

Congress, letters to Members of
  Anderson, Sen. Clinton P., NATO cooperation re atomic information, 71
  Cooper, Repr. Jere, Organization for Trade Cooperation, 160
  President of the Senate
    Inter-American highway, 64
    Philippine trade agreement revision, 91
    Virgin Islands Corporation, 14
  Speaker of the House of Representatives
    Inter-American highway, 64
    Philippine trade agreement revision, 91
    Virgin Islands Corporation, 14

Congress, messages to
  Agricultural Trade Development and Assistance Act (P.L. 480, 83d Cong.), reports, 7, 150
  Austrian State Treaty ratification, 114
  Budget message, 17
  Commission on Intergovernmental Relations, report, 145
  Department of Defense Appropriation Act, 155
  Economic report, 19
  Federal personnel management, 8
  Foreign economic policy, 6
  Formosa Strait situation, 21
  Health program, 25
  Highway program, 39
  ILO conventions and recommendations, 107
  International Finance Corporation, U.S. participation in, 86
  Low income farmers, 82
  Military personnel, 13
  Mutual Defense Treaty, U.S.-China, 5
  Mutual security program, 76

Congress, messages to—Continued
  National security, 12
  Organization for Trade Cooperation,
    U.S. membership, 72
  Postal pay and rates, 9
  Reclamation projects, approval of act,
    180
  Refugee Relief Act, recommendations,
    109
  Renegotiation Act, extension, 50
  School construction, 31
  State of the Union, 4
  United Nations, U.S. participation, re-
    port, 156
  Vetoes
    Apple price predictions, prohibition of
      Government publication, 147
    Glaser, Kurt, relief of, 116
    Postal field service compensation bill,
      102
Congress, reports to, list, Appendix C, p.
  884
Congress, reports to, messages transmitting
  Agricultural Trade Development and
    Assistance Act (Public Law 480,
    83d Cong.), 7, 150
  Commission on Intergovernmental Re-
    lations, 145
  Economic report, 19
  United Nations, U.S. participation, 156
Congressional support of program
  News conference remarks, 41, 95, 185
  Priority list, 146
Congressmen, comment on pay raise and
  term of office, 47
Connecticut, Hartford, 209
Conservation of natural resources, 4
  Budget message, 17 (pp. 155–163)
  Mineral lands, 172
Constitution, U.S., 40, 70, 81, 118, 131,
  145, 155, 249
Construction starts, 157
Consumer spending, 4, 18, 19

Continental Shelf, Outer, 17 (p. 162)
Contracts, Government, extension of Re-
  negotiation Act, 50
Controls, Government economic, comment
  on, 18, 26, 112, 146
Conversations between officials and ad-
  visers, comment on investigation of,
  149
Coolidge, Calvin, 131
Cooper, Repr. Jere, 90 ftn. (p. 471)
  Letter, 160
Cooper Dam and Reservoir, Texas, ap-
  proval, 184
Coosa River, Ala., 4
Copper industry, labor dispute, 176
Corporate taxes, 4, 6, 41
  Budget message, 17 (pp. 87, 97, 98)
Corps of Engineers
  Budget message, 17 (pp. 158–160, 168)
  Flood control, 222
Corsi, Edward, 62
Cost of living, 41, 119
Costa Rica, conflict in, 10
Cotton
  Acreage allotments, 90
  Exports, 6, 185
Cotton, Sen. Norris, 139
Cougar project, Oreg., 17 (p. 158)
Council of Economic Advisers, 4, 19
Council on Foreign Economic Policy, 76
Courts, Federal
  Circuit Court of Appeals, Fourth, filling
    of vacancy, 149, 176
  Circuit Court of Appeals, Fifth, nomi-
    nation of John R. Brown, 112
  News conference remarks, 47, 112, 149,
    176
  Northern Texas court, filling of vacancy,
    47
  U.S. District Courts, school integration
    cases, 149
Craig, Mrs. May, 10, 18, 26, 41, 81, 95,
  112, 146, 149, 176

[References are to items except as otherwise indicated]

Crippled children, 25

Cromley, Allan W., 146

Cromwell, Oliver, 213

Crusade for Freedom campaign, 32
  Participation of newspaper boys, 79

Cuba, independence, 69

Currencies, foreign, 6
  Sale of agricultural commodities for, 17
    (p. 130), 76

Curry, Ralph, 47

Curtice, Harlow, 111, 124, 125

Customs administration, simplification, 6

Cutter, John L., 59, 81, 90

Cutter Laboratories, licensing to produce
  Salk vaccine, 95

Dallas, Tex., 10

Daniel, Sen. Price, 47

Darrison, F. Gibson, 181 n.

Davis, Repr. Glenn R., 56

Dear, Joseph A., 149

Debt, national
  Budget message, 17 (pp. 99–101, 106,
    183, 184)
  News conference remarks, 33

Declaration of Independence, 40, 136

DeCoursey, Brig. Gen. Elbert, 108

Dedicatory occasions. *See* Addresses or remarks on commemorative or dedicatory occasions

Defense, Department of, 3, 24 n., 74, 207 n.
  Appropriation Act (1956), 155
  Budget message, 17 (pp. 91, 107, 111,
    119, 121, 169, 183)
    Table, 17 (p. 115)
  Information, release of, 81
  News conference remarks, 81, 176, 185
  White, Gen. W. W., Staff Director of
    Petroleum Logistics, 176, 185
  See also Joint Chiefs of Staff

Defense, national. *See* National security

Defense, Secretary of, 12
  Review of National Guard programs, 192

Defense, Secretary of (Charles E. Wilson),
  29, 71 n., 90 ftn. (p. 475), 108
  Letters to, 3, 154
  News conference remarks on, 18, 81
  On trade with Communist bloc, 18

Defense Advisory Committee on Prisoners
  of War, report, 207 n.

Defense establishment, 12, 248
  Expenditures, reduction of, 4

Defense Mobilization, Office of, Director
  (Arthur S. Flemming), 90 ftn. (p.
  475), 119
  Civil defense report, 149 ftn. (p. 672)
  Memorandum, 67

Defense procurement, 26, 76, 95

Defense production, 17 (pp. 175, 176)

Defense Production Act, extension, 4, 17
  (p. 175), 112

Defense spending, reduction, 19

Defense support. *See* Military assistance
  and defense support

Deficit spending, comments on, 18, 41

Definitive Treaty of Peace of 1783, 81

Delaware River channel, dredging of, 17
  (p. 168), 18

Democratic leaders, consultation on proposed legislation, comment on, 26

Denfeld, Adm. Louis E., 112

Denmark, atomic research agreement, 121

Dentists, induction, 12

Denver, Colo., 207 n., 208, 211 n., 212 n.,
  213 n., 214 n., 215 n., 216 n., 217 n.,
  219 n., 220 n., 221 n., 222 n., 223 n.,
  224 n., 225 n., 226 n., 227 n., 228 n.,
  229 n., 230 n., 231 n., 232 n., 233 n.,
  234 n.
  Editor's note on President's illness, p. 822
  Remarks on departure, 235

Dependent children, 25

Depressed areas (chronic unemployment),
  56

Detroit, Mich., automobile industry,
  threatened strike, 112

Index

[References are to items except as otherwise indicated]

"Development of Agriculture's Human Resources," report on problems of low
income farmers, 82

Dewey, Thomas E., 10, 56

Diem, Ngo Dinh, 48, 81

Disabled persons, 25

Disability compensation for Government
employees, 4
Budget message, 17 (p. 106)

Disarmament, 94, 164, 166
Aerial inspection (open skies) proposal,
166, 175, 176, 185, 220, 248
Arms limitation, and reduction, 4, 41,
166, 211
Exchange of information on military
establishments, 164, 166, 176, 185,
220
Letter to Nikolai Bulganin, 220
News conference remarks, 33, 41, 47, 62,
95, 146, 149, 176, 185
Soviet proposal (1955), 95, 156

Disarmament, Special Assistant to the
President on. *See* Stassen, Harold E.

Disarmament Commission and subcommit-
tee, U.N., 57, 156, 166
London meeting, 41
Soviet disarmament plan, 95
New York meeting, statement, 211
News conference remarks, 41, 95, 185

Disaster insurance, 222

Disaster relief, 4, 95, 208 n.
Budget message, 17 (p. 175)

Disasters, natural
Drought, 4, 95
Floods. *See* Floods

Dispersal of U.S. industry, 90
Commission to study, comment on proposal, 119

Displaced persons, 115 n.

Distinguished Service Cross recipients, remarks, 52

Distinguished Service Medal
Presentation to Adm. Carney, 188
Presentation to Gen. Ridgway, 144

District of Columbia
Budget message, 17 (pp. 182, 183)
Police force, 149
Public transportation bill, approval, 206
Redevelopment of Southwest Washing-
ton, 55
Republican Women's Finance Commit-
tee, remarks, 104
Self-government, 4
Transit strike, 149, 176, 206
Unemployment compensation, 4

Dixon, Edgar, 149 ftn. (p. 669)

Dixon-Yates contract
News conference remarks, 26, 41, 56,
146 and ftn. (p. 646), 149, 176
White House releases, 146 ftn. (pp. 657,
658), 149 ftn. (p. 669)

Doctors, induction, 12

Dodge, Joseph M., 74, 176

Dollar, sound, 4
News conference remarks, 41, 119, 185

Donovan, Robert J., 18, 33, 81, 90, 100,
112, 185

Donovan, William J., 51 n.

Doud, Mrs. John Sheldon, editor's note on
President's illness, p. 822

Drought, relief for, 4, 95

Drummond, Roscoe, 18, 26, 33, 41, 81, 119

Dulles, John Foster. *See* State, Secretary
of

Dunnigan, Alice A., 18

Durkin, Martin P., death of, letter, 238

Durkin, Mrs. Martin P., letter, 238

Dwinell, Gov. Lane, 133, 135, 136, 139

Eagle Gorge Reservoir, Wash., 17 (p. 160)

East-West contacts, 175, 176
Statements at Geneva conference, 164,
167

Index

[References are to items except as otherwise indicated]

East-West trade, 100
Easter egg rollers, remarks, 68
Economic Advisers, Council of, 4, 19
Economic assistance, 76
  Asia, statement, 69
  Budget message, 17 (pp. 91, 92)
  Letter to Secretary of State, 74
  News conference remarks, 47
  U.N. program, contributions to, 126
  See also Foreign assistance; Mutual security program
Economic policy, foreign, 72
  Message, 6
Economic report to the Congress (1954), reference to, 19
Economic report to the Congress (1955), 19
Economy, farm. *See* Farm economy
Economy, national, 3, 4, 12, 19, 20, 128
  Budget message, 17 (p. 87)
  News conference remarks, 18, 41, 56, 81, 119, 185
EDC. *See* European Defense Community
Edelweiler, Germany, 204 n.
Eden, Anthony, 208 n.
  Appointment as Prime Minister of United Kingdom, statement, 66
  Comment on, 41
Education, 4, 11, 121
  Budget message, 17 (pp. 94, 140–148)
    Table, 17 (p. 142)
  Federal aid for, 31, 33, 47, 119
    See also School construction
  News conference remarks, 33, 47, 95, 119
  School construction. *See* School construction
  State and community conferences on, 33, 95, 96
  White House Conference, 17 (pp. 141, 147)
Education, Commissioner of (Samuel M. Brownell), 96

Education, Office of, 31
  Budget message, 17 (pp. 141, 148)
Education, White House Conference on (1955), 31, 96
  News conference remarks, 18, 33, 95
  Remarks, 242
Educational exchange program, 4
  Less developed areas, 17 (p. 132)
Egan, Charles E., 62, 112, 149
Egypt, 4, 18, 234
  Assistance, 17 (p. 130)
  See also Arab-Israeli dispute and hostilities
Einstein, Albert, death of, statement, 75
Eisenhower, Dwight D., personal reminiscences
  Member of board on establishment of Air Force Academy, 117
  Military experiences
    Gas warfare, World War I, 118
    Pantelleria, capture of, 59
    World War II, 4, 22, 59, 100
  Patton, Gen. George S., 81
  Study of wage-price controls, 26
  Suggestion re presidency, 10
  V–E Day, 81
  Visit to Soviet collective farm, 47
  West Point, 70, 118
  Work week, 84
  Yalta conference, 59
  Zhukov, Marshal Georgi, 33
Eisenhower, Mrs. Dwight D., 20, 23 n., 42, 45, 61, 63, 68, 88, 90, 133, 152, 163, 195, 230, 235, 236, 237, 238, 250
Editor's note on President's illness, p. 822
Eisenhower, Milton S., 10, 121
Election campaign (1952), remarks on the budget, quoted, 18
Election campaign (Congressional, 1954), 10
Election campaign (1956), comment on, 10, 47

Index

[References are to items except as otherwise indicated]

Electoral college, 47

Elizabeth II, 208 n.

Emory, Alan S., 10, 26, 33, 41, 47, 56, 62, 90, 100, 146, 176

Employees, Government, 8, 186, 187

Employment, 4, 19
  Conference on Equal Job Opportunity, 225
  News conference remarks, 119, 185

Employment of the Physically Handicapped, President's Committee on the, remarks, 103

Empress of Britain, 146

Energy Supplies and Resources Policy, President's Advisory Committee on (Flemming Committee), report, 33 and ftn. (p. 259), 41, 56

Engineers, Corps of, 4
  Budget message, 17 (pp. 158–160, 168)
  Construction starts, 157
  Flood control, 222

Enterprise system, 19
  Abroad, 76

Escapees. *See* Refugees and escapees

Esso Export Corp., 176, 185

Ethiopia, Haile Selassie I, 231

Europe
  Flood relief (1954), 37, 47, 49
  Western European Union, 54, 61, 100
  See also specific countries

European Advisory Commission, meeting in London (1944), 59

European Defense Community, 54
  News conference remarks, 41, 62

European Migration, Intergovernmental Committee for, 17 (p. 131), 76

European recovery program, 76

European security, 175

European Union. *See* Western European Union

Evins, Repr. Joe L., 112

Exchange of persons, 17 (p. 132)

Exchange of students, 4

Exchange visitors, 116

Excise taxes. *See* Taxes

Executive orders, 67, 74 n., 186, 187, 192 n., 207 n.
  List, Appendix B, p. 877

Export-Import Bank, 86
  Budget message, 17 (pp. 128, 129)
  Loans to Latin American countries, 76

Exports, 79
  Agricultural commodities, 4, 6, 7, 72
    Cotton, 6, 185
    Wheat, 6, 17 (p. 152)

Far East
  Budget message, 17 (p. 112)
  See also Asia, South Asia, and Southeast Asia

Farm, the President's, 127

Farm-City Week, statement, 221

Farm Credit Administration, 147
  Budget message, 17 (p. 153)

Farm economy, 4, 62, 127, 128
  Budget message, 17 (pp. 150–153)

Farm program, 127, 247
  Budget message, 17 (p. 103)
  News conference remarks, 18, 62, 90

Farmers, low-income, 4
  Message, 82

Farmers Home Administration, 17 (pp. 149, 153)

Faure, Edgar, 170 n.

Fawn, gift to the President, 141

FBI. *See* Federal Bureau of Investigation

Federal Advisory Commission on the Arts, proposed, 4

Federal aid to States
  Airports, 146
  Budget message, 17 (pp. 94, 103, 106, 167)
  Education, 31, 33, 47, 119
  Health program, 25

Index

[References are to items except as otherwise indicated]

Federal aid—Continued
  Highway programs, 17 (p. 167), 39, 146
  Hospital and health center construction,
    17 (p. 94)
  Public assistance, 17 (p. 103)
  School construction. *See* School con-
    struction
Federal Bureau of Investigation, 4, 17 (pp.
  95, 182)
Federal Bureau of Investigation, Director
  (J. Edgar Hoover), National Security
  Medal, citation, 110
Federal City Council of Washington, D.C.,
  55
Federal Civil Defense Administration, 17
  (p. 119)
Federal Communications Commission, 41
Federal Home Loan Bank Board, inde-
  pendent agency, 194
Federal Housing Administration, 17 (pp.
  171, 172), 26
Federal Mediation and Conciliation Serv-
  ice, 95
Federal National Mortgage Association, 17
  (pp. 166, 172, 173)
Federal personnel. *See* Government em-
  ployees
Federal personnel management, message,
  8
Federal Power Commission, 4
  Adams, Francis L., 146 and ftn. (p. 658)
  News conference remarks on, 10, 33
Federal Republic of Germany. *See* Ger-
  many
Federal Reserve Board, 81
Federal Reserve System, 19
Federal Savings and Loan Insurance Cor-
  poration, 194
Federal-State-local governmental respon-
  sibilities, 4, 19, 31, 43, 242
  Budget message, 17 (pp. 93, 94, 140,
    147, 156, 158, 161)

Federal–State–local—Continued
  Civil defense, 149
  Flood prevention, 17 (p. 94)
  News conference remarks, 18, 33, 47, 149
  Report of Commission on Intergovern-
    mental Relations, 145
Federal Trade Commission
  Kern, William C., 95
  Mead, James M., 95
Fellows, Harold E., 105
Fenton, Brig. Gen. Chauncey L., 117
Fernsworth, Lawrence, 47, 62, 100
Finney, Nat S., 10, 18, 26, 33, 59, 90, 112,
  149
Firestone, Harvey S., Jr., letter, 80
First Boston Corporation, 146
First War Powers Act of 1941, title II, ex-
  tension, 4
Fish and wildlife resources, 4
Fissionable materials for peaceful uses, 79,
  156, 164, 165
  See also Uranium
Fitzgerald, Rufus H., 11 n.
Fitzsimons Army Hospital, 235
  Editor's note on President's illness, p. 822
Flanders, Sen. Ralph E., 131, 149
Flemming, Arthur S. *See* Defense Mobili-
  zation, Director, Office of
Flood control and prevention
  Budget message, 17 (pp. 94, 156–160)
  Letter to Gov. Roberts, 222
Flood relief, Europe (1954), 37, 47, 49
Floods
  Northeastern States, 208, 209, 210, 214,
    222
  Tampico, Mexico, 229
Florida, 210 n.
  Smathers, Sen. George A., 62
Folliard, Edward T., 10, 18, 26, 33, 47, 56,
  59, 81, 112, 146, 149, 176, 185
Folsom, Marion B., rumor of appointment
  as Secretary of Health, Education, and
  Welfare, 112

Index

[References are to items except as otherwise indicated]

Food and Drug Administration, 25
Forced Labor, U.N. Ad Hoc Committee on, 156
Ford Motor Co., 119
Foreign affairs, 185
  Bipartisan meeting on, 248
  Budget message, 17 (pp. 126–132)
    Table, 17 (p. 127)
Foreign assistance, 4, 248
  Africa, 17 (p. 130), 76
  Asia and Southeast Asia, 17 (pp. 123, 129, 130), 41, 47, 48, 69, 76
  Bolivia, 17 (p. 129), 76
  Cambodia, 17 (p. 129)
  China, Republic of, 17 (p. 129), 21
  Egypt, 17 (p. 130)
  Germany, 17 (p. 124), 76
  Greece, 76
  Guatemala, 17 (p. 129), 76
  Haiti, 23 n.
  India, 17 (p. 129)
  Iran, 17 (p. 130), 76
  Israel, 17 (p. 130)
  Jordan, 17 (p. 130)
  Korea, 17 (pp. 104, 124, 129)
  Laos, 17 (p. 129)
  Latin America, 17 (pp. 129, 130), 76
  Lebanon, 17 (p. 130)
  Less developed countries, 6
  Libya, 17 (p. 130)
  Middle East, 17 (pp. 125, 130)
  News conference remarks, 41, 47, 119
  Spain, 76
  Turkey, 76
  Viet-Nam, 17 (p. 129), 48
  Yugoslavia, 76, 119
  See also Economic assistance; Military assistance and defense support; Mutual security program; Technical assistance to less developed countries

Foreign currencies, 6
  Sale of agricultural surpluses for, 17 (p. 130), 76
Foreign economic policy, 72
  Message, 6
Foreign Economic Policy, Council on, 76
Foreign ministers meetings
  Geneva conference (1955), 170, 185, 226
    Statement re, 227
  Vienna (1955), 95
Foreign Operations Administration,
  Flood relief for Europe, 49
  Ladejinsky, Wolf, 10, 18
  News conference remarks, 10, 18, 62
  Termination in 1955, 76
  Transfer of functions, 62, 74
Foreign Operations Administration, Director (Harold E. Stassen), 57, 60 n., 94
  News conference remarks on, 10, 47, 62, 146, 185
  Visit to New Delhi, 47
Foreign service, 47
  Budget message, 17 (p. 126)
  Improvements, 17 (p. 132)
  Pay adjustments, 8
Foreign students, atomic studies in U.S., 165
Forest resources, 4
Forests, national, 17 (pp. 162, 163)
Formosa (Taiwan)
  Defense treaty and Joint Resolution on, 21, 26, 47, 62
  Joint Resolution, approval, 24
  Military Assistance Advisory Group (MAAG), 90
  News conference remarks, 18, 26, 33, 47, 62, 81, 90, 185
  U.S. armed forces in, 21, 24 n.
  U.S. military base, comment on, 90
  Visit of Secretary Dulles, 47

Index

[References are to items except as otherwise indicated]

Formosa (Taiwan) Strait situation
Message to Congress, 21
News conference remarks, 18, 26, 33, 41, 59, 62, 81, 90, 100, 112
U.N. truce, comment on proposal, 18
U.S.-Communist China negotiations, 81
U.S.-Soviet Union negotiations, 90
Forrestal, James V., 117
Fort Knox, 52
4–H Club, remarks, 128
France, 54 n.
Faure, Edgar, 170 n.
Paris agreements. See Paris agreements
Francis, Dr. Thomas, Jr., 112, 113
Franconia Notch, N.H., remarks at 150th anniversary of discovery of Old Man of the Mountain, 136
Franklin, Benjamin, 121
Frantz, Harry W., 26
Freudenheim, Milton B., 81, 119, 146, 185
Friedman, Milton, 56
Fryingpan-Arkansas project, Colo., 17 (p. 159)
Fund-raising campaigns
Crusade for Freedom, 79
Radio Free Europe, 32
Red Cross, 45
United Community Campaigns, 168, 218
United Service Organizations, 27

Garrett, George A., letter, 55
Gas bill, 146
Gas industry, report on, 56
Gas warfare, World War I, 118
Gasoline excise tax on, 41
General Agreement on Tariffs and Trade, 6, 72
Tariff concessions, textiles, 149
General Armistice Agreement in Middle East, violation of, statement, 234
General Services Administration, 17 (p. 179)
Geneva, 37 n., 168 n., 169 n.

Geneva, research reactor, 100
Remarks, 165
Geneva conferences
Atomic energy (1955), 100, 123, 149, 156, 176, 177 n., 228
Message, 191
Foreign ministers (1955), 170, 185, 226
Statement re, 227
French-Communist negotiations on Indochina (1954), 119
Heads of governments (1955), 99, 118, 126, 146, 149, 162, 176, 190, 210, 227
Bipartisan meeting on, 174
Broadcast prior to departure, 161
Broadcast report on, 175
Closing statement, 170
Delegation, U.S., 146 ftn. (p. 644)
East-West contacts, statement, 167
Opening statement, 164
Remarks on arrival at Geneva airport, 163
Remarks on departure, 171
Remarks on return from Geneva, 173
International Labor Organization (1955), 107, 119
News conference remarks, 100, 119, 146, 149, 176, 185
U.S.-Communist China ambassadorial talks, 176
George, Sen. Walter F., 26, 59, 62, 112, 185
Georgia
Augusta, 1 n., 26 ftn. (p. 231), 71 n., 72 n., 73 n., 74 n.
George, Sen. Walter F., 26, 59, 62, 112, 185
Thomasville, 33
Vinson, Repr. Carl, 149
Germany, 210
Adenauer, Konrad, 119, 190, 204
Joint statement with, 122

906

Index

[References are to items except as otherwise indicated]

Germany—Continued
  Assistance, 17 (p. 124), 76
  Berlin, 33, 76
  Bluecher, Franz, 208 n.
  Edelweiler, 204 n.
  Gift to the President, 22
  Heuss, Theodor, 22
  Krekeler, Heinz L., 22
  NATO, membership in, 4, 99
  News conference remarks, 33, 41, 59, 62, 90, 112, 119
  Paris agreements on, 41, 54, 59, 62, 164
  Reunification, 59, 112, 122, 164, 175, 190, 227
  U.S. Air Force transport accident, 204
  U.S. armed forces in, 119
  World War II, 22
Gettysburg, Pa., 239 n., 240 n., 241 n., 242 n., 243 n., 244 n., 245 n.
  Editor's note, p. 822
  President's farm, 127
  Remarks in Lincoln Square, 237
Gettysburg College, 242 n., 250 n.
Glaser, Kurt, immigration status, 116
Gompers, Samuel, pledge to Woodrow Wilson, 84
Gonzales, Donald J., 90, 176
Government employees
  Disability compensation, 4, 17 (p. 106)
  Health insurance, 4
    Group insurance, 8
  Incentive awards program, 1
  Old-age and survivors insurance, 4
  Overseas personnel, 8
  Pay, 4, 8, 59
  Payroll savings plan, 186, 187
  Retirement, 4, 17 (pp. 96, 106, 145, 181, 182)
  Security program, 10
  Training, 8
  Travel allowances, 8

Government employees—Continued
  Unemployment compensation, 17 (p. 182)
Government Employees Incentive Awards Program, 1
Government employment, security program, 18, 41, 81, 146
Government officials, conduct of, 176
Government Operations, Advisory Committee on, 74
Governmental responsibility, division of, 4
Governors, letter to, 29
Governors' Conference, New England (1955), 222, 223
Governors' Conference (1954), Lake George, N.Y., 4, 39, 90
Governors' Conference (1955), Washington, D.C., 90
  Remarks, 88
Grandchild, the President's, vaccination against polio, 113
Graves, William, 119
Greece, 4
  Assistance, 76
Green Peter-White Bridge project, Oreg., 17 (p. 158)
Griffin, Charles, 133 n.
Griffin, Maj. Gen. Martin E., 235
Gronchi, Giovanni, 208 n.
Ground Observer Corps, 154
Group Life Insurance Act, 4
Guaranteed wage, 119
Guatemala, 18
  Assistance, 17 (p. 129), 76
  Castillo Armas, Carlos, 230
  U.S. position in U.N. Security Council, 156
Guizado, Jose Ramon, 2
Gurney, Chan, letter, 30

H-Bomb. *See* Hydrogen bomb

Index

Haakon VII, 50th anniversary of reign, letter, 241

Hagerty, James C., 10, 18, 26, 33, 41, 47, 56, 59, 62, 81, 90, 95, 100, 112, 119, 146 and ftn. (p. 644), 149, 176, 185
 Editor's note, p. 822

Haile Selassie I, 25th anniversary of reign, message, 231

Haiti, Paul E. Magloire, 23

Hall, George H., 33, 100

Hall, Leonard W., 47, 247

Hall, Robert, 47

Halvorson, Alf, 139

Hammarskjold, Dag, 179
 Meeting with Secretary Dulles, 18
 Negotiations with Communist China on release of prisoners, 4, 18, 156
 Statement re, 16

Handicapped persons, President's Committee on Employment of the Physically Handicapped, remarks, 103

Harding, Warren G., 18

Harkness, Richard, 146

Harlan, John Marshall, nomination to Supreme Court, comment on, 26

Harriman, E. Roland, 208, 209

Harriman, W. Averell, 90

Harsch, Joseph C., 10, 33, 47, 59, 62

Hartford, Conn., remarks on flood disaster, 209

Hawaii
 Air carriers, West Coast-Hawaii Case, 30, 33
 News conference remarks, 33, 56, 95
 Statehood, 4, 56, 95, 247

Hawley, Paul R., 51 n.

Hayden, Jay G., 47, 90

Hayden, Martin S., 18, 90, 100, 112, 146

Heads of state and governments, meetings
 Congressional delegation, question of, comments on, 59, 95, 112
 Geneva. See Geneva conferences

Heads of state—Continued
 Joint statement with Chancellor Adenauer on, 122
 News conference remarks, 59, 62, 81, 95, 100, 112, 119, 146, 149
 Paris (1951), 59
 Paris (1952), 62

Heads of state and governments, messages. See Messages to heads of state and governments

Health, Education, and Welfare, Department of, 4, 25, 81

Health, Education, and Welfare, Secretary of (Mrs. Oveta Culp Hobby), 77 n., 78, 79, 96
 Appraisal by the President, 100
 Budget message, 17 (pp. 141, 144, 145)
 Indian health services, 17 (pp. 144, 145)
 Poliomyelitis vaccine program, 113
 News conference remarks on, 18, 100, 112, 119
 Resignation
  Comment on rumor of, 100, 112
  Letter, 152
  Remarks, 153

Health, National Institutes of, 17 (p. 143)

Health insurance, 4
 Budget message, 17 (p. 143)
 Group, for Government employees, 8
 Reinsurance program, 25

Health of the President
 Editor's note on illness, p. 822
 Remarks on return from Denver, 236

Health program, 25, 247
 Budget message, 17 (pp. 94, 140–148)
  Table, 17 (p. 142)
 Indians, 17 (pp. 144, 145)

Hearst, William Randolph, Jr.
 Interview of Molotov, comment on, 26
 Letter, 124

Heart disease, conference on, message, 34

Index

[References are to items except as otherwise indicated]

Herling, John, 18, 47, 56, 81, 95, 112, 119, 149, 176
Heuss, Theodor, 22
Hightower, John M., 81, 90
Highway, Inter-American, 59, 64
Highway Construction Co. of Ohio, Inc., relief of, 159
Highway safety, Safe Driving Day, 243
Highway system, interstate, 4, 19, 39
   Administration by authority or corporation, 185
   Budget message, 17 (p. 92)
Highways, 39, 247
   Budget message, 17 (p. 167)
   News conference remarks, 26, 33, 62, 90, 146, 185
Higley, Harvey V., Chairman, Community Chest campaign, 130
Hill, Sen. Lister, 33
Hiner, Louis C., 41
Hines, Fred P., disability claim, 200
Hitler, Adolph, 57
Hobby, Mrs. Oveta Culp. *See* Health, Education, and Welfare, Secretary of (Mrs. Oveta Culp Hobby)
Hobby, William P., 152
Hollister, John B., 74 n.
   Comment on, 90
Home Loan Bank Board, Federal, independent agency, 194
Hong Kong, arrival of four airmen from Communist China, 112
Hoover, Herbert, Jr., 94
Hoover, Herbert, President, 4, 236
   News conference remarks re, 33
Hoover, J. Edgar, National Security Medal, citation, 110
Hoover Commission recommendations, 4
   News conference remarks, 41, 90, 100
   Paperwork reduction, 41
Horner, Garnett D., 33, 41, 47, 56, 90, 100, 176

Hospitals and medical care facilities, 17 (pp. 94, 138, 139), 25
Housing, 4, 247
   Budget message, 17 (pp. 118, 136, 171–175)
   College, 17 (pp. 174, 175)
   Military, 4, 13, 17 (p. 118)
   News conference remarks, 18, 176
   Public, 4, 17 (p. 174), 176, 194
   Veterans, 17 (pp. 136, 173, 174)
   See also Urban renewal
Housing bill, 185
   Amendments of 1955, approval, 194
Housing and Home Finance Agency, 222
   Budget message, 17 (p. 174)
   Home Loan Bank Board, made independent agency, 194
Howley, Gen. Frank, 62
Hughes, Rowland R. *See* Budget, Director of the (Rowland R. Hughes)
Humphrey, George M. *See* Treasury, Secretary of the (George M. Humphrey)
Humphrey, Sen. Hubert H., comment on, 26
Hydroelectric power projects, 17 (pp. 158–161)
Hydrogen bomb, 41, 47, 56

Icebreaker, U.S.S. *Atka,* 47
Iceland, Asgeir Asgeirsson, 162
Illinois
   Arends, Repr. Leslie C., 41
   Chicago, 47
   Lemont, 53 n.
   Peoria, 18
ILO. *See* International Labor Organization
Immigration laws, 4, 247
Immigration and Naturalization Service, 4
   Budget message, 17 (p. 182)

Index

[References are to items except as otherwise indicated]

Imports, 72
  Oil, comment on, 33, 81
  Spun silk yarn, restrictions, 155
Inauguration, ceremonies commemorating second anniversary, 20
Incentive awards for Government employees, 1
Incentives, career, for military personnel, 17 (pp. 91, 109)
Income taxes, 41
India
  Assistance, 17 (p. 129)
  Nehru, Jawaharlal, 119
  New Delhi, 47
Indiana, Sen. William E. Jenner, 10
Indians
  Citizenship, 100
  Health services, 17 (pp. 144, 145)
  Lands and resources, 17 (p. 162)
  Welfare of, 4, 100
Indochina, 12, 105
  News conference remarks, 18, 41, 47, 119
Indonesia, Bandung conference, 26
Industrial capacity, U.S., 3
Industrial Conference Board, National, message, 228
Industrial safety, 17 (p. 177)
Industry, dispersal of, comment on, 90, 119
Infantile Paralysis, National Foundation for
  Citation, 78
  Vaccination program, 112, 113
Inflation, comment on, 41, 47, 185
Information
  Directed to Iron Curtain countries, 17 (p. 131)
  East-West exchange, 167
  News conference remarks, 10, 59, 62, 81, 146
  Yalta documents, 59
Information Agency. See United States Information Agency

Information program, 4
Inland Waterways Corporation, sale of, 17 (p. 92)
Institute of Inter-American Affairs, 76
Insurance
  Disability, 4, 17 (p. 106)
  Disaster, 222
  Group Life Insurance Act, 4
  Health, 4, 8, 17 (p. 143), 25
  Military personnel, 17 (p. 145)
  Mortgage, 17 (p. 172), 19
  Old-age and survivors, 4, 17 (pp. 94, 140, 141, 143–146)
  Unemployment, 17 (pp. 136, 176, 177, 182), 19, 56, 112, 119
  Veterans, 17 (pp. 136–138)
    Table, 17 (p. 140)
Integration, public schools, comment on, 119, 149
Inter-American Affairs, Institute of, 76
Inter-American Highway, 59
  Letter to Vice President and Speaker, 64
Inter-American Investment Conference, message, 44
Interdepartmental Committee for the Voluntary Payroll Savings Plan for the Purchase of United States Savings Bonds
  Letter to Chairman, 186
  Memorandum, 187
Interest expenditures, 17 (pp. 95, 101, 183, 184)
  Table, 17 (p. 184)
Interest rates, 17 (pp. 96, 106)
Intergovernmental Committee for European Migration
  Budget message, 17 (p. 131)
  U.S. support of, 76
Intergovernmental Relations, Commission on, 4
  Civil defense recommendations, 149
  News conference remarks, 47, 146, 149
  Report, 145

Index

[References are to items except as otherwise indicated]

Interior, Department of the
  Federal property in Virgin Islands, 14
  Indian health services, 17 (p. 144)
Interior, Secretary of the, 14
Internal Revenue Code of 1954, disapproval of amendment, 198
Internal Revenue Service, 17 (p. 179)
International agreements (1955)
  Austrian State Treaty, 59, 81, 95, 98, 99, 100, 114
  Civil uses of atomic energy, 228
    U.S.-Belgium, Canada, United Kingdom, 123
    U.S.-NATO, 71
    U.S.-Turkey, 89, 112
  Manila Pact (Southeast Asia Defense Treaty), 4
  News conference remarks, 41, 59, 81, 112
  Paris agreements, 41, 54, 59, 62, 164
  Southeast Asia Collective Defense Treaty, 5, 35
  U.S.-China, Mutual Defense Treaty, 5, 21, 35
International Atomic Energy Agency, proposed, 17 (p. 119), 59, 79, 121, 156, 228
International Bank for Reconstruction and Development, 6, 72, 156
  Budget message, 17 (p. 128)
  Loans to Latin American countries, 76
  Memorandum on International Finance Corporation, 86
  Wenzell, Adolphe H., 146 and ftn. (pp. 657, 658)
International Brotherhood of Teamsters, 232
International Cooperation Administration, letter to Secretary of State re, 74
International Cooperation Administration, Director (John B. Hollister), 90

International Finance Corporation, 6, 44, 156
  Budget message, 17 (p. 128)
  U.S. participation in, message, 86
International Geophysical Year, 47 ftn. (p. 308)
  Budget message, 17 (p. 148)
International Labor Organization, 156
  Conventions and recommendations, message, 107
  Geneva conference (1955), 119
International Monetary Fund, 72
International School of Nuclear Science and Engineering, foreign students, remarks, 53
International trade. See Trade, international
Investments abroad, 4, 6, 76
  Budget message, 17 (pp. 128, 132)
  Less developed areas, 17 (p. 128)
Iran, 4, 18, 35, 76
  Assistance, 17 (p. 130)
  Pahlavi, Mohammad Reza, 42
Iron Curtain, 81
Irrigation, 17 (pp. 156–159)
Irwin, Donald, 26
Isotopes, radioactive, 121
Israel
  Assistance, 17 (p. 130)
  Atomic research agreement, 121
Israeli-Arab dispute and hostilities, 76, 239
  Statement, 234
Italy, 4, 18, 54 n.
  Ambassador Clare Boothe Luce, 61
  Atomic research agreement, 121
  Brosio, Manlio, 61
  Gronchi, Giovanni, 208 n.
  Martino, Gaetano, 61
  Paris agreement, ratification of, 62
  Scelba, Mario, joint statement, 61
  Segni, Antonio, 208 n.
Izvestia, postal ban, 59

Index

[References are to items except as otherwise indicated]

Jefferson, N.H., remarks to postmasters, 138
Jefferson, Thomas, 94, 105
Jenkins, Martin D., 51 n.
Jenner, Sen. William E., 10
Jewell, Ingrid M., 59
Jewish New Year, statement, 215
Johnson, Alice F., 56
Johnson, Gov. Joseph B., 131
Johnson, Sen. Lyndon B., 81, 90 ftn. (p. 471), 146
Johnson, U. Alexis, 176
Johnston, Clement D., 85 n.
Joint Chiefs of Staff, 3
    Review of National Guard programs, 192
    Ridgway, Gen. Matthew B., 26
Joint Chiefs of Staff, Chairman (Adm. Arthur W. Radford), 56, 81
Joint statements with heads of state and governments
    Burma, Prime Minister Nu, 148
    Germany, Chancellor Adenauer, 122
    Italy, Prime Minister Scelba, 61
Jordan, assistance, 17 (p. 130)
Judd, Repr. Walter H., 33
Judges, pay raise, 47
Judiciary, Federal, 112
    See also Courts, Federal
Justice, Department of, 112
    Anti-trust study, 56
    Barnes, Stanley N., 56
    Immigration laws, 4
    Internal Security Division, 4
    News conference remarks on, 10, 18, 56, 112
    Security cases, 18
    Tompkins, William F., 10
    See also Attorney General
Juvenile delinquency, 4, 25

Kansas, Sen. Frank Carlson, 62
Kefauver, Sen. Estes, 146, 149

Keflavik, Iceland, remarks at airport, 162
Keller, Helen, letter, 140
Kennon, Gov. Robert F., 88
Kenton, John E., 81, 146, 176
Kentucky, Sen. Earle C. Clement, 33
Kern, William C., 95
Kerr, Walter, 90, 95, 100, 112, 119
Keyserling, Leon H., 47
Khrushchev, Nikita S., 95, 146
    On summit conference, 149
Knebel, Fletcher, 47, 176
Knowland, Sen. William F., 26, 41, 59
Koerner, Theodor, message, 98
Korea, 12, 18, 21
    Assistance, 17 (pp. 104, 124, 129)
Korea, North, 185
Korean Armistice, 16
Korean war, 12, 13, 35, 57, 118
    News conference remarks, 10, 18, 26, 59
    North Korean prisoners of war, 18
Krekeler, Heinz L., 22
Kuh, Frederick, 41, 59

Labor, Department of
    Budget message, 17 (p. 177)
    Clague, Ewan, 18
Labor, Secretary of (James P. Mitchell), 107
    ILO conference, 119
    News conference remarks on, 18, 90, 119, 176
Labor Day, statement, 212
Labor disputes
    Automobile industry, comment on, 112
    Copper industry, 176
    Louisville and Nashville Railroad strike, 90, 95
    Role of Government, 90, 112, 119, 149, 176
    Southern Bell Telephone Co., and employees, 90, 95
    Transit strike, Washington, D.C., 149, 176, 206

Index

Labor legislation (1956), 247

Labor-management relations, 4, 245

Labor organizations
AFL cornerstone-laying ceremony, 84
AFL–CIO, 47, 245
International Brotherhood of Teamsters, 232

Laconia, N.H., remarks, 134

Ladejinsky, Wolf, comment on, 10, 18, 56

Lamb, Edward O., 41

Lamp of Freedom, gift to the President, 115

Lancaster, N.H., remarks, 137

Land, Frank S., 43 n.

Land resources
Budget message, 17 (pp. 158–163)
Indian lands, 17 (p. 162)

Laos, assistance, 17 (p. 129)

Larsen, Roy E., 96

Latin America, 18, 35, 43
Assistance, 17 (pp. 129, 130), 76
See also specific countries

Lausanne, Switzerland, question of summit conference in, 112, 119

Lawrence, William H., 10, 47, 59, 90, 95, 100, 119, 146, 149

Laycook, L. G., 26

Leach, Paul R., 59

League of Red Cross Societies, 37, 49

Lebanon
Assistance, 17 (p. 130)
Atomic research agreement, 121

Legion of Merit, presentation to Field Marshal Pibulsonggram, 87

Legislation, domestic, meeting of Republican Congressional leaders on, 247

Legislation, extraneous amendments, comment on, 149

Legislation, priority list, 146

Legislation, statements or messages upon approval
Agricultural Trade Development and Assistance Act, amendment, 202

Legislation—Continued
Department of Defense Appropriation Act, 1956, 155
District of Columbia public transportation, 206
Highway bridge across Lake Texoma, 158
Highway Construction Co. of Ohio, Inc., relief of, 159
Housing Amendments, 194
Joint Resolution on Formosa, 24
Materials Act of 1947, amendments, 172
Mutual Security Appropriation Act, 182
Postal Field Service Compensation Act, 120
Public Works Appropriation Act, 157
Reclamation projects, 180
Red River flood control project, 184
Reserve Forces Act, 192
Salary payment to interim appointee, AEC, 193
Trade Agreements Extension Act of 1955, 129

Legislation, Vetoes and Memorandums of Disapproval
Apple price predictions, prohibition of Government publication, 147
Civil Service Retirement Act, amendment, 201
Internal Revenue Code of 1954, amendment, 198
Minerals purchase programs, extension, 205
Ogletree, Stephen Swan, change of military record, 197
Postal field service compensation bill, 102
Reconveyance to former owners of certain reservoir project lands in Texas, 199

Legislation, Vetoes and Memorandums of Disapproval—Continued

Relief of

Albrecht, E. J., Co., 196

Glaser, Kurt, 116

Hines, Fred P., 200

Subversive Activities Control Board, term of office, 189

Legislative recommendations, messages and letters. *See* Congress, messages to; Congress, letters to Members of

Leisure, use of, 121

Lemont, Ill., 53 n.

Leonard, Lt. Gen. John W., 52

Leviero, Anthony H., 149

Libby, Willard F., 89 n., 191 n.

Libraries, AEC technical, in United States and abroad, 228

Libya, assistance, 17 (p. 130)

Life expectancy of man, 121

Lilly, Eli, & Co., 100

Lincoln, Abraham, 35, 121, 126, 181, 213

Lincoln, G. Gould, 146

Lincoln, N.H., remarks, 135

Liquor excise tax, 41

Lodge, Henry Cabot, Jr. (U. S. Representative to U.N.), 156

Loftus, Joseph A., 10, 18

London disarmament conference. *See* Disarmament Commission and subcommittee, U.N.

Lord, Mrs. Oswald B., 156

Louisiana

Brooks, Repr. Overton, 100

Kennon, Gov. Robert F., 88

New Orleans, 44

Louisville and Nashville Railroad strike, 90, 95

Low-income housing, 4

Lowe, Herman A., 112

Luce, Mrs. Clare Boothe, meeting with Prime Minister Scelba, 61

Luxembourg, 54n.

MAAG. *See* Military Assistance Advisory Group

Maas, Gen. Melvin J., 103

MacArthur, Douglas II, 146 ftn. (p. 644)

Magistrati, Massimo, 61

Magloire, Paul E., exchange of toasts, 23

Magloire, Mrs. Paul E., 23

Maine

Bangor, 143

Muskie, Gov. Edmund S., 142, 143

Parmachenee Lake, 140 n.

Payne, Sen. Frederick G., 142

Rangeley, 141

Skowhegan, 142

Smith, Sen. Margaret Chase, 47, 95, 142

Malenkov, Georgi M., 33, 95

Manila, 4

Manila Pact. *See* Southeast Asia Collective Defense Treaty

Marine Corps

Budget message, 17 (pp. 112, 113, 117)

Decline in reenlistment rate, 13

Federal property in Virgin Islands, 14

Maritime Administration, 79

Markel, Hazel, 146

Markham Ferry project, Okla., 4, 17 (p. 158)

Marshall, Gen. George C., 135

Marshall, John, Bicentennial, 210

Martial law proclaimed during civil defense test exercise, 149

Martin, I. Jack, 181

Martin, Paul, 10

Martino, Gaetano, 61

Marx, Karl, doctrines, 146, 245

Masonic breakfast, remarks, 43

Massachusetts, Repr. John W. McCormack, 95, 146

Materials Act of 1947, amendment, 172

Matsu, 26, 62, 90, 112

McCarren-Walter Immigration Act, 56

Index

[References are to items except as otherwise indicated]

McClendon, Sarah, 10, 18, 26, 33, 41, 47, 56, 59, 62, 81, 90, 95, 100, 112, 119, 146, 149, 176, 185

McCormack, Repr. John W., 95, 146

McCormick, Robert R., death of, statement, 63

McElroy, Neil H., Chairman, White House Conference on Education, 95, 96

McGrath, William L., 119

McLean, Robert, 79

McNeil, Marshall, 56

Mead, James M., 95

Meany, George, 84, 245

Medals, remarks or messages on presentation or acceptance
Distinguished Service Medal
Adm. Carney, 188
Gen. Ridgway, 144
Legion of Merit, Field Marshal Pibulsonggram, 87
Medal of Freedom, Robert B. Anderson, 183
Medallion, Winston Churchill, 244
National Security Medal, J. Edgar Hoover, 110

Medical care
Cost of, 25
For military dependents, 4, 13

Medical research, 247

Mediterranean Sea, 4

Memorandums of Disapproval
Civil Service Retirement Act, amendment, 201
Internal Revenue Code of 1954, amendment, 198
Minerals purchase programs, extension, 205
Ogletree, Stephen Swan, change of military record, 197
Reconveyance to former owners of certain reservoir project lands in Texas, 199

Memorandums of Disapproval—Con.
Relief of
Albrecht, E. J., Co., 196
Hines, Fred P., 200
Subversive Activities Control Board, term of office, 189
See also Veto Messages

Memorandums to heads of Federal agencies
Civil defense exercise, 101
Community Chest campaign, 130
Government Employees Incentive Awards Program, 1
Payroll Savings Plan, 187
United Community campaign, 168

Memphis, Tenn., power projects in area, 56, 146, 149
See also Dixon-Yates contract

Mental health, 25

Merchant, Livingston T., 61, 146 ftn. (p. 644)

Merchant marine, 17 (pp. 167, 168)

Merchant ship, nuclear-powered, 79, 121
News conference remarks, 81, 112, 146
World tour proposed, 146

Merrow, Repr. Chester E., 139

Messages to the American people
Geneva conference
Broadcast prior to departure, 161
Broadcast report on, 175

Messages to the Congress. See Congress, messages to

Messages to heads of state and governments
Austria, President Koerner, 98
Burma, Prime Minister Nu, 169
China, Republic of, President Chiang Kai-shek, 36
Ethiopia, Emperor Haile Selassie I, 231
Germany, Chancellor Adenauer, 190, 204

915

Index

[References are to items except as otherwise indicated]

Messages to heads of state and governments—Continued
Guatemala, President Castillo Armas, 230
Iran, Shah Mohammad Reza Pahlavi, 42
Mexico, President Ruiz Cortines, 216, 229
Morocco, Sultan Mohammed ben Youssef, 240
Norway, King Haakon VII, 241
U.S.S.R., Premier Bulganin, 220
Vatican City State, Supreme Pontiff Pius XII, 46
Viet-Nam, Chief of State, Bao Dai, 48
Western European Union, Prime Ministers of member nations, 54
Mexican farm workers, 17 (p. 177)
Mexico
Ambassador Francis White, 229
Highways to, 39
Ruiz Cortines, Adolfo, 216, 229
Tampico flood relief, 229
Michigan, Detroit, 112
Middle East and Near East, 4, 18, 248
Assistance, 17 (pp. 125, 130)
Message to Rabbi Silver, 239
Statement, 234
Tripartite Declaration (1950), 234, 239
See also specific countries
Middle South Utilities Co., 149 ftn. (p. 669)
Midway, visit to Capetown, South Africa, 18
Migratory farm workers, Mexican, 17 (p. 177)
Military Assistance Advisory Group, Formosa, 90
Military assistance and defense support, 76
Budget message, 17 (pp. 123–125, 128–130)
Letter to Secretary of State, 74

Military assistance—Continued
News conference remarks, 10, 90, 119
See also Foreign assistance; Mutual security program
Military personnel
Career incentives, 17 (pp. 91, 109)
Commissary and post exchange privileges, 100
Discussion of war plans, comment on, 62
Doctors and dentists, induction, 12
Insurance, 17 (p. 145)
Letter to Secretary Wilson, 3
Pay, 4, 13, 59
Retirement, 4, 17 (p. 145)
Survivor benefits, 4, 13, 17 (p. 134)
Turnover, message, 13
Military procurement. See Defense procurement
Military strength, U.S., 4, 10, 12
Letter to Secretary Wilson, 3
Milk programs
Armed forces, 17 (p. 152)
Schools, 17 (p. 144)
Millikin, Sen. Eugene D., 81
Milne, Edward J., 18, 100, 119, 149, 176
Mineral lands, approval of bill restricting multiple use, 172
Mineral resources, 4
Budget message, 17 (p. 163)
Minerals Policy, Committee on, 17 (p. 163)
Minerals purchase programs, extension, disapproval, 205
Minimum wage, 4, 19
Extension of coverage, 81, 112
News conference remarks, 26, 81, 90, 119, 149, 176
Minnesota
Humphrey, Sen. Hubert H., 26
Judd, Repr. Walter H., 33
Thye, Sen. Edward J., 33

Index

[References are to items except as otherwise indicated]

Missiles, 149
Nike, 17 (p. 116)
Mississippi Valley Generating Co., 149 ftn.
(p. 669)
Mitchell, James P. *See* Labor, Secretary of
Mohammed ben Youssef, message, 240
Mollenhoff, Clark R., 10, 18, 26, 33, 41,
59, 62, 81, 95, 146, 149, 176, 185
Molotov, Vyacheslav M., 26, 33, 146
Monroe, Marvin E., 181n.
Morgan, Edward P., 41, 59, 81, 90, 95,
100, 112, 149, 176
Morgan, Gerald D., 56, 181
Morocco, Mohammed ben Youssef, 240
Morris, John D., 18
Morse, Sen. Wayne, 100
Mortgage Association, Federal National,
17 (pp. 166, 172, 173)
Mortgage insurance, 19
Budget message, 17 (p. 172)
Moscow Declaration on Austria (1943),
114
Mountbatten, Vice Adm. Louis, 119
"Mudslinging," comment on, 62
Munroe, Pat, 56, 100, 146
Muskie, Gov. Edmund S., 142, 143
Mutual Security Appropriation Act, ap-
proval, 182
Mutual security program, 57, 76, 146
Budget message, 17 (pp. 91, 97, 104, 108,
122, 123, 128–130)
Table, 17 (p. 123)
Letter to Secretary of State, 74
Statement, 69
See also Economic assistance; Military
assistance and defense support;
Technical assistance to less devel-
oped countries

Napoleon Bonaparte, 59, 118
Narcotics, international control, 4
National Advisory Committee for Aero-
nautics, 17 (p. 170)

National Advisory Committee on Polio-
myelitis Vaccine, 81, 90, 113
National Association of Radio and Tele-
vision Broadcasters, remarks, 105
National Association of Television and
Radio Farm Directors, remarks, 127
National Bureau of Standards, 17 (p. 148)
National Citizens Commission for the Pub-
lic Schools, 96
National Community Christmas Tree and
Pageant of Peace, 250
National Conference of Christians and
Jews, letter, 40
National debt. *See* Debt, national
National economy. *See* Economy, na-
tional
National Foundation for Infantile Paral-
ysis
Citation, 78
Vaccination program, 112, 113
National groups. *See* Addresses, remarks,
or messages to national groups
National Guard, 12, 119, 192
National Industrial Conference Board,
message, 228
National Institutes of Health, 17 (p. 143)
National Mediation Board, 112
National parks, 4, 17 (p. 163)
National product, 4, 19, 39, 41, 79
National School Boards Association, 96
National Science Foundation, 17 (p. 148)
National security, 4, 12, 13, 67, 81
Bipartisan meeting on, 248
Budget message, 17 (pp. 91, 97, 104,
107–126)
Tables, 17 (pp. 104, 110)
Letter to Secretary Wilson, 3
National Security Council, 24 n., 57, 76,
119
Editor's note, p. 822
National Security Medal, presentation to
J. Edgar Hoover, 110

Index

[References are to items except as otherwise indicated]

National Security Training Mission, 12
National Zoological Park, 141 n.
NATO. *See* North Atlantic Treaty Organization
Natural gas bill, 146
Natural resources
 Budget message, 17 (pp. 93, 155–163)
  Table, 17 (p. 157)
 Conservation, 4, 17 (pp. 155–163), 172
 For land, minerals, water, etc., *see specific resources*
Nautilus, U.S.S., 81
 Budget message, 17 (p. 121)
Navigation aids and facilities, 17 (pp. 168, 169)
Navy, 17 (pp. 112, 113, 117)
Navy, Department of the, 3, 13
 Federal property in Virgin Islands, 14
Nazism, 115, 163
Near East. *See* Middle East and Near East
Neely, Sen. Matthew M., 81, 185
Nehru, Jawaharlal, 119
Netherlands, 54 n.
Neutrality
 Austria, 100
 Germany, joint statement with Chancellor Adenauer on, 122
 Satellite countries, comment on, 119
New Delhi, India, 47
New Hampshire
 Bass, Repr. Perkins, 139
 Berlin, 139
 Bridges, Sen. Styles, 134, 135, 139
 Concord, 133
 Cotton, Sen. Norris, 139
 Dwinell, Gov. Lane, 133, 135, 136, 139
 Franconia Notch, 136
 Jefferson, 138
 Laconia, 134
 Lancaster, 137
 Lincoln, 135
 Merrow, Repr. Chester E., 139

New Jersey, Repr. James C. Auchincloss, 20
New Mexico, Sen. Clinton P. Anderson, 10, 71
New Orleans, La., Inter-American Investment Conference, 44
New York
 New York City, 27, 79, 219, 228 n., 239 n., 245
 Niagara power project, 10
New York Bar Association, 18
News conferences
 Censorship, 26
 First TV and newsreel recording, editor's note, 18 (p. 185)
News conferences, the President's
 January 12 (No. 57), 10
 January 19 (No. 58), 18
 February 2 (No. 59), 26
 February 9 (No. 60), 33
 February 23 (No. 61), 41
 March 2 (No. 62), 47
 March 16 (No. 63), 56
 March 23 (No. 64), 59
 March 30 (No. 65), 62
 April 27 (No. 66), 81
 May 4 (No. 67), 90
 May 11 (No. 68), 95
 May 18 (No. 69), 100
 May 31 (No. 70), 112
 June 8 (No. 71), 119
 June 29 (No. 72), 146
 July 6 (No. 73), 149
 July 27 (No. 74), 176
 August 4 (No. 75), 185
Newsmen, disclosure of sources of information at Congressional hearings, 10
Newspaper Editors, American Society of, 79, 99 n.
Newspaperboys, participation in Crusade for Freedom campaign, 79
Niagara power project, 10

Nike missiles, 17 (p. 116)

Norman, Jack, 26

North Atlantic Council, 54

    Perkins, George W., U.S. Permanent Representative, 71

North Atlantic Treaty, 54

North Atlantic Treaty Organization, 3, 54, 72, 144, 162, 175

    Atomic information, agreement for co-operation regarding, 71

    German membership in, 4, 99

    Joint statement with Prime Minister Scelba on, 61

Northwest Airlines, certification, 30, 33

Norway, Haakon VII, 241

Nu (U)

    Joint statement with President, 148

    Letter, 169

    News conference remarks on, 146

Nuclear aircraft, 17 (p. 121)

Nuclear power projects. *See* Power projects

Nuclear-powered ships. *See* Ships

Nuclear reactors. *See* Reactors

Nuclear Science and Engineering, International School of, foreign students, remarks, 53

Nuclear tests

    AEC report on effects of, 41, 56

    Ban on, 41

    Fallout. *See* Radioactive fallout

    Pacific (1954), 56

    Soviet, 185

Nuclear war, 33, 79, 175

Nuclear weapons, 4, 166

    Budget message, 17 (p. 109)

    News conference remarks, 10, 33, 41, 47, 56, 59, 149

    Soviet, 33, 47

    Strategic and tactical, 10, 56

    See also Bombs; Disarmament; Nuclear tests

Nurses, training programs, 25

Oak Ridge, Tenn., self-government, 17 (p. 121)

O'Brien, John C., 18

Occupational safety, 4

O'Connor, Basil, 78

Office, government, indiscretion in use of, 176

Office of Coordinator of Public Works Planning, proposed, 19

Offshore procurement contracts, 76

Ohio, Sen. John W. Bricker, 59

Oil

    Imports, 33, 81

    In Iran, 76

Old-age and survivors insurance, 4

    Budget message, 17 (pp. 94, 140, 141, 143–146)

Old Man of the Mountain, 150th anniversary of discovery, remarks, 136

Old River Control project, La., 17 (p. 160)

Older persons

    Effects of inflation, 41

    Medical care, 25

    News conference remarks, 41, 119

Open skies proposal. *See* Disarmament

Operation Alert (1955). *See* Civil defense

Operation Skywatch, 3rd anniversary, letter to Secretary Wilson, 154

Oregon, Sen. Wayne Morse, 100

Organization of American States

    Action on Costa Rican dispute, 10

    Guatemalan situation, 156

    News conference remarks, 10, 26

    U.S. contributions, 76

Organization for Trade Cooperation

    U.S. membership proposed, 129, 160, 248

    Message, 72

Organization of World Touring and Automobile Clubs, General Assembly, remarks, 93

Index

[References are to items except as otherwise indicated]

Orphans, recommendations under Refugee Relief Act, 109
Overseas personnel, Federal, 8

Pacific Charter, 4
Pacific Northern Airlines, certification, 106
Pacific Proving Ground, nuclear tests (1954), 56
Pageant of Peace, remarks, 250
Pahlavi, Mohammad Reza, message, 42
Pakistan, 4
Palestine, development of water resources, 76
Pan American Highway, 93
Pan American World Airways, certification, 30, 33
Panama
  Guizado, Jose Ramon, 2
  Remon, Jose Antonio, 2
Panama Canal Zone, Inter-American highway, 64
Pantelleria, capture of, 59
Paperwork management program, comment on proposal, 41
Paperwork reduction, Hoover Commission recommendations, 41
Paris, heads of government meeting (1951), 59
Paris agreements (1955), 54, 164
  News conference remarks, 41, 59, 62
  Ratification by France and Italy, comment on, 62
Parke, Davis & Co., 100
Parks, monuments, and historic sites, national, 4, 17 (p. 163)
Parmachenee Lake, Maine, 140 n.
Passamaquoddy Bay hydroelectric power survey, 17 (p. 161)
Patton, Gen. George S., 81
Pay
  Congressmen, 47
  Government employees, 4, 8, 59
  Judges, 47

Pay—Continued
  Military personnel, 4, 13, 59
  Postal employees, 4, 9, 59, 90, 100
    Approval of Postal Field Service Compensation Act, 120
    Veto of bill, 102
  See also Wages
Payne, Ethel, 26
Payne, Sen. Frederick G., 142
Payroll Savings Plan
  Letter to Mrs. Priest, Chairman of Committee, 186
  Memorandum on, 187
Peaceful uses of atomic energy. See Atomic energy for peaceful uses
Peiping, China, 16
Penghu (Pescadores) Islands, 18, 21, 24 n., 33
Pennsylvania
  Gettysburg, 237, 239 n., 240 n., 241 n., 242 n., 243 n., 244 n., 245 n.
    Editor's note, p. 822
  Philadelphia, 56, 210
  Walter, Repr. Francis E., 59, 62
  Water drainage in anthracite coal region, 17 (p. 163)
Pennsylvania State University
  Atomic reactor, 121
  Commencement address, 121
  News conference remarks on, 149
Peoria, Ill., campaign remarks (1952), 18
Pepper, Claude, 210
Pericles, Age of, 121
Perkins, George W., 71
Personnel management, Federal, 8
Pescadores (Penghu) Islands, 18, 21, 24 n., 33
Petersen, Theodore S., 51 n.
  Letter, 125
Peterson, Elmer, Big Dam Foolishness, 56
Peterson, Val, 209
Petitpierre, Max, 163

Index

[References are to items except as otherwise indicated]

Peurifoy, Daniel, death of, statement, 195
Peurifoy, John E., death of, statement, 195
Peurifoy, Mrs. John E. 195
Philadelphia, Pa., 210
  Mayor Joseph Clark, on civil defense, 56
Philippines
  Independence, 69
  Manila, 4
  Trade agreement revision, letter, 91
Phillips, Cabell, 10, 81
Phleger, Herman, 146 ftn. (p. 644)
Physically Handicapped, President's Committee on, remarks, 103
Pibulsonggram, Field Marshal, Legion of Merit, citation, 87
Pierce, Franklin, 85, 92 n.
Pierre, Henri, 100
Pius XII
  Message, 46
  News conference remarks on, 47
Police force, Washington, D.C., handling of transit emergency, 149
Poliomyelitis, citation to National Foundation for Infantile Paralysis, 78
Poliomyelitis vaccine, 79
  Citation to Dr. Jonas E. Salk for development of, 77
  Distribution, 78, 90, 112, 113
  News conference remarks, 81, 90, 95, 100, 112, 119
  Statement, 113
Poliomyelitis Vaccine, National Advisory Committee on, 81, 90, 113
Poliomyelitis Vaccine Evaluation Center, University of Michigan, 113 n.
Politics, comment on, 112
Porter, H. J. (Jack), 47
Post exchange and commissary privileges, 100
Post Office Department
  "Atoms for Peace" postage stamp, 177
  Budget message, 17 (pp. 103, 164, 171)
  Christmas mail, 246

Post Office Department—Continued
  Postal field service compensation bill, veto, 102
  Seizure of copies of *Izvestia* and *Pravda*, 59
Postal deficit, 4, 9
  Budget message, 17 (p. 103)
Postal employees
  Pay, 4, 9, 59, 90, 100
    Approval of Postal Field Service Compensation Act, 120
    Veto of pay bill, 102
  Uniforms for, 9
Postal rates, 4, 9, 247
  Budget message, 17 (pp. 93, 103, 171)
  Commission on, 9, 17 (p. 171)
  Increase, 17 (pp. 103, 171)
Postal services, 9
  Budget message, 17 (pp. 170, 171)
Postmaster General (Arthur E. Summerfield), 9, 90 ftn. (p. 475), 102, 138, 177
Postmasters, New Hampshire conference, remarks, 138
Power projects, 4
  Budget message, 17 (pp. 91, 93, 120, 121, 156–161)
  Hydroelectric, 17 (pp. 158–161)
  Memphis, Tenn., area, 56, 146, 149
    See also Dixon-Yates contract
  News conference remarks, 10, 33, 56, 146, 149
  Niagara project, 10
  Nuclear, 17 (pp. 91, 120, 121), 228
    Abroad, 121
    New England, 223
  TVA Fulton steam plant, 56, 149
Pravda, postal ban, 59
Presentation ceremonies, addresses, remarks, or messages. *See* Addresses, remarks, or messages at presentation ceremonies

Presidency, comment on the President's first two years in office, 18, 112

President of the Senate. *See* Vice President

Presidential Advisory Committee on Transport Policy and Organization, report, 33, 62, 90 and ftn. (p. 475)

Presidential Documents published in the Federal Register (1955), Appendix B, p. 877

Presidential reports to the Congress, list, Appendix C, p. 884

President's Advisory Committee on Energy Supplies and Resources Policy (Flemming Committee), report, 33 and ftn. (p. 259), 41, 56

President's Advisory Committee on a National Highway Program (Clay Committee), 4, 146
Report, 39

President's Commission on Veterans' Pensions
Budget message, 17 (p. 134)
Letter, 51

President's Committee on the Employment of the Physically Handicapped, remarks, 103

President's Committee for Traffic Safety, 111, 243
Letter to William Randolph Hearst, Jr., re appointment, 124
Letter to T. S. Petersen re appointment, 125

President's Conference on Fitness of American Youth, message, 217

Preston, Dickson J., 56

Price freeze, 26

Price predictions on apples, prohibition of Government publication, veto, 147

Price supports, 62, 90, 127
Budget message, 17 (pp. 93, 94, 103, 106, 150–153)

Price and wage controls, 112, 146
See also Controls, Government economic

Prices, farm. *See* Farm economy

Priest, Mrs. Ivy Baker, 187
Letter, 186

Priest Rapids project, Wash., 4, 17 (p. 158)

Prisoners of war, code of conduct, 207

Prisoners of War, Defense Advisory Committee on, report, 207 n.

Private enterprise. *See* Enterprise system

Proclamation of martial law during civil defense text exercise, 149

Proclamations, list, Appendix B, p. 877

Proctor, Mrs. Mortimer R., 132

Procurement, military. *See* Defense procurement

Property, Federal, 17 (pp. 95, 179–181)

Public assistance
Budget message, 17 (pp. 103, 143, 144)
Medical care, 25

Public health programs, 25
Budget message, 17 (pp. 142, 143)

Public Health Service, 17 (p. 142), 25, 119

Public Health Service, Surgeon General (Leonard A. Scheele), 95, 112, 113, 119

Public Health Service Commissioned Corps, survivor benefits, 25

Public housing, 4, 176, 194
Budget message, 17 (p. 174)

Public lands
Budget message, 17 (pp. 162, 163)
Highways, 39
Mining claims, restrictions, 172

Public Roads, Bureau of, 39

Public works, 4
Appropriation Act, approval, 157

Public Works, Office of Coordinator, proposed, 4, 19
Appointment of Maj. Gen. John S. Bragdon as coordinator, 203

Index

[References are to items except as otherwise indicated]

Pulitzer, Joseph, death of, statement, 63

Queen Mary, S.S., 42 n.
Quemoy, 21
  News conference remarks, 26, 62, 90, 112

Rabb, Maxwell M., 181
Rabi, I. I., 191 n.
Radar screen. *See* Warning systems
Radford, Adm. Arthur W., 56, 81
Radiation, peaceful uses, 121
Radio Free Europe, 32
Radio liberation, 81
Radio and Television Broadcasters, National Association, remarks, 105
Radio and television farm directors, remarks, 127
Radioactive fallout
  AEC report, comment on, 41, 56
  News conference remarks, 33
Radioisotopes, uses of, 228
Railroad, Louisville and Nashville, strike, 90, 95
Railroad retirement benefits, 17 (p. 145)
Rangeley, Maine, remarks at fawn presentation ceremonies, 141
Rangoon, Burma, Buddhist Synod, 148
Rankine, Paul S., 26
Rayburn, Repr. Sam. *See* Speaker of the House of Representatives
Reactors, 228
  Geneva installation, 100
  Industrial power, 17 (p. 121)
  International agreements for use of, 89, 121, 123, 165
  Merchant ship, 79
  Naval vessels, 17 (p. 121)
  New England, 223
  Nuclear, 17 (p. 143)
  Pennsylvania State University, 121
Reading, the President's
  Big Dam Foolishness (Peterson), 56
  West Point Plebe (Reeder), 117

Reclamation, Bureau of
  Budget message, 17 (pp. 158–160)
  Construction starts, 157
Reclamation projects, 4, 180
Reconstruction Finance Corporation, 17 (pp. 92, 176)
Records management, 17 (pp. 179–181)
  See also Information
Red Cross, 210
  Campaign, remarks, 45
  Flood relief in the Northeast, 208, 209
Red Cross Societies, League of, 37, 49
Red Feather campaign. *See* Community Chest campaign
Red River flood control project, approval, 184
Reeder, Red, *West Point Plebe,* 117
Refugee Relief Act, 109
  Budget message, 17 (p. 131)
Refugees and escapees, 76, 81
  Admission, 17 (p. 131)
  American voluntary societies cooperating in escapee program, remarks, 60
  Arab, 17 (p. 131)
  Message to Congress, 109
  U.N. program, 17 (p. 131), 156
Relocation exercises, Federal. *See* Civil defense
Remagen Bridge, remarks to participants in seizure of, 52
Remagen Bridgehead, Society of the, 52
Remon, Jose Antonio, assassination, statement, 2
Remon, Senora, 2
Renegotiation Act, extension, 50
Reorganization Act, extension, 4
Reports to the Congress. *See* Congress, reports to
Reports to the President
  Committee on Energy Supplies and Resources Policy, comment on, 33, 41, 56

Index

[References are to items except as otherwise indicated]

Reports to the President—Continued
  Federal agency relocation exercise, 149
    ftn. (p. 672)
  Low income farmers, problems of, 82
  President's Advisory Committee on a
    National Highway Program, 39
  Secretary Dulles
    European visit, 99
    ILO conventions and recommenda-
      tions, 107
    Mutual Defense Treaty with China, 5
Republican National Committee
  Chairman (Leonard W. Hall), 47, 247
  Remarks to, 35
Republican National Convention (1956),
    10, 47
Republican National Finance Committee,
  remarks, 35
Republican Party, comment on, 35
Republican State chairmen, remarks to,
    213
Republican Women's Finance Committee
  of the District of Columbia, remarks,
    104
Republican Women's National Conference,
  remarks, 94
Research
  Aeronautical, 17 (p. 92)
  Agricultural, 17 (pp. 94, 155)
  Medical, 247
  Scientific, 19
Research and development, military, 4, 17
  (p. 118)
Reserve forces bill, 176
  Approval, 192
  News conference remarks, 90, 100, 119,
    146, 149
  Segregation rider, 119
Reserve program, armed forces, 3, 4, 12
  Budget message, 17 (p. 91)
  White House release, 192 n.

Reservoir projects, Texas, reconveyance of
  certain reservoir project lands to
  former owners, 199
Resignation, Mrs. Oveta Culp Hobby
  Letter, 152
  Remarks, 153
Reston, James B., 47, 59, 81, 95, 100, 112,
    119, 146, 149
Retaliatory power in case of attack, 3
Retirement
  Federal personnel, 4, 17 (pp. 96, 106,
    145, 181, 182)
  Military personnel, 4, 17 (p. 145)
  Railroad employees, 17 (p. 145)
Retirement Policy for Federal Personnel,
  Committee on, report, 17 (p. 181)
Reynolds, James A., 95
Rhode Island, Gov. Dennis J. Roberts, 222,
    223
Rhodes scholars appointed from West
  Point (1955), 117
Rice, agricultural surpluses, 148
Richards, Robert W., 90
Richland, Wash., self-government, 17 (p.
    121)
Ridder, Walter T., 59
Ridgway, Gen. Matthew B.
  Distinguished Service Medal, citation,
    144
  News conference remarks on, 26
Ridgway, Mrs. Matthew B., 144 n.
Ridgway, Matthew B., Jr., 144 n.
Riggs, Robert L., 33
Rio de Janeiro, conference in, 4
River basin development, 17 (pp. 156–
    161)
Rivers and harbors, 17 (pp. 168, 169)
Rizley, Ross, letter, 106
Roberts, Chalmers M., 10, 18, 26, 33, 41,
    47, 59, 62, 90, 95, 100, 119, 146, 149,
    185
Roberts, Gov. Dennis J., letters, 222, 223

Index

[References are to items except as otherwise indicated]

Roberts, Gilroy, 244 n.
Robertson, Walter S., 81
Rocky Beach project, Wash., 17 (p. 158)
Roosevelt, Franklin D., 78
Rosenwald, William, 115 n.
Roth, Robert, 56, 119
Rubber plants, synthetic, sale of, 17 (p. 92)
Rubber producing facilities disposal, 17 (p. 175)
Ruiz Cortines, Adolfo
  Letter to, 229
  Message, 216
Rules governing this publication, Appendix D, p. 886
Rural electrification, 17 (pp. 153, 154)
Rural Electrification Administration, 17 (p. 153)
Rural telephones. *See* Telephone service, rural
Rutland, Vermont, remarks at Dairy Festival, 131

SACLANT. *See* Supreme Allied Command Atlantic
Safe driving, statements, 111, 243
Saigon, Viet-Nam, 48
St. Lawrence Seaway, 47
  Budget message, 17 (pp. 164, 168)
Salk, Dr. Jonas E., 78, 79, 113
  Citation, 77
Salk vaccine. *See* Poliomyelitis vaccine
Salpeter, A. E., 26, 90
San Francisco, Calif., 126, 131
  News conference remarks, 47, 81, 112, 146
  U.N. 10th anniversary meeting, 81, 112, 146, 156
Sandstrom, Emil, letter, 37
Sarnoff, David, recommendations on cold war strategy, 95
Satellite countries, Soviet, 12, 33, 37 n., 119, 146, 175

Satellite countries, Soviet—Continued
  Information program, 17 (p. 131)
Satellite, earth, 47 ftn. (p. 308)
Savings bonds, U.S., payroll savings plan, 186, 187
Scelba, Mario, joint statement, 61
Scelba, Signora, 61
Scheele, Leonard A., 95, 112, 113, 119
Scheibel, Kenneth M., 10, 33, 47, 81, 90, 112, 149
Scherer, Ray L., 10, 62, 81, 95, 100, 112, 119, 146, 176
Schnitzler, William F., 245
School Boards Association, National, 96
School construction, 19, 247
  Anti-segregation amendment to bill, 149
  Budget message, 17 (p. 147)
  Message to Congress, 31
  News conference remarks, 18, 33, 47, 119, 149
School integration. *See* Integration, public schools
School milk program, 17 (p. 144)
Schools. *See* Education; Integration, public schools
Schorr, Daniel L., 10, 47, 59, 62
Schurman, Wilbur M., 137 n.
Schwartz, Lloyd M., 26, 33, 56, 81, 90, 112, 119, 176
Schweitzer, Dr. Albert, cablegram, 15
Science, use for military purposes, 3
Science Foundation, National, 17 (p. 148)
Scientific research, 19
Seawolf, U.S.S., 17 (p. 121)
SEATO. *See* Southeast Asia Treaty Organization
Securities and Exchange Commission, 146
  Intervention by Sherman Adams, comment on, 176
Security clearance cases
  Ladejinsky, Wolf, 10, 56
  News conference remarks, 10, 18, 56, 81
  U.S. employees of United Nations, 156

[References are to items except as otherwise indicated]

Security program for Government employment, comment on, 10, 18, 26, 41, 81, 146

Segni, Antonio, 208 n.

Selective Service System, extension, 4, 12

Sentner, David P., 26, 81, 112, 149, 185

Separation of legislative, executive, and judicial powers, 155

Shackford, Roland H., 47

Shannon, Donald H., 90

Shannon, William V., 26

Shinkman, Paul A., 146

Ships
  Empress of Britain, 146
  Merchant marine, 17 (pp. 167, 168)
  Naval, 17 (p. 117)
  Nuclear-powered
    Merchant ship, 79, 81, 112, 121, 146
    U.S.S. *Nautilus,* 17 (p. 121), 81
    U.S.S. *Seawolf,* 17 (p. 121)
  S.S. *Queen Mary,* 42 n.
  Subsidies, 17 (pp. 92, 167, 168)
  U.S.S. *Atka,* icebreaker, 47
  U.S.S. *Midway,* 18

Shutt, Charles E., 41, 56, 59, 90, 95, 100, 146, 149, 185

Silk yarn for cartridge cloth, 155

Silver, Rabbi Abba Hillel, message, 239

Sims, Edward H., 149

Skowhegan, Maine, remarks, 142

Slevin, Joseph R., 81, 90, 185

Slum clearance, 194, 247
  Budget message, 17 (pp. 171, 172)

Small Business Act of 1953, extension, 4

Small Business Administration, 4, 208 n.
  Loans, 17 (p. 176)

Small business taxes, 4

Smathers, Sen. George A., 62

Smith, Kingsbury, interview of Molotov, 26

Smith, Sen. Margaret Chase, 142
  News conference remarks on, 47, 95

Smith, Merriman, 10, 18, 26, 33, 41, 47, 56, 59, 62, 95, 100, 112, 119, 146, 149, 176

Smithsonian Institution, 22 n.

Smithsonian Institution, Secretary (Leonard Carmichael), 22

Snyder, Murray, editor's note on President's illness, p. 822

Soboloff, Simon, delay in Senate confirmation, 176

Social security, 247
  Budget message, 17 (pp. 140, 141, 143–146)
  Table, 17 (p. 146)

Society of the Remagen Bridgehead, 52

Soil conservation, 17 (pp. 154, 155)

Soper, Morris A., 149

Soraya, Empress of Iran, 42

South Africa, Capetown, 18

South America. *See* Inter-American; Latin America; *specific countries*

South Carolina
  Aiken, 73
  Charleston, 70
  Thurmond, Sen. Strom, 73, 149

Southeast Asia Collective Defense Treaty, 4, 5, 35

Southeast Asia Treaty Organization, 4, 47
  Bangkok conference, 41

Southern Bell Telephone Co., strike of employees, 90, 95

Soviet Union, 12, 99, 161
  Agricultural specialists, question of U.S. visit, 47, 95
  Aircraft, 112
  Ambassador Charles E. Bohlen, 146 ftn. (p. 644)
  Amtorg, 10
  Anniversary, message, 233
  Bulganin, Nikolai A., 62, 95, 146, 161, 164, 166 n., 185
    Letter to, 220

Index

[References are to items except as otherwise indicated]

Soviet Union—Continued
Communist China, relations with, 33
Disarmament. *See* Disarmament
Economic offensive, 6
Izvestia and *Pravda*, U.S. postal ban, 59
Joint statement with Chancellor Adenauer on, 122
Khrushchev, Nikita S., 95, 146, 149
Malenkov, Georgi M., 33, 95
May Day celebrations, 95
Molotov, Vyacheslav M., 26, 33, 146
News conference remarks, 10, 33, 41, 47, 59, 62, 81, 95, 100, 112, 119, 146, 185
Nuclear tests, 185
Nuclear weapons, 33, 47
Political changes, comment on, 33, 59, 62, 146
Satellite countries, 12, 17 (p. 131), 33, 37 n., 119, 146, 175
Stalin, Joseph, 95
Trade affairs, 6
Trade with U.S., 33
U.N. activities, 156
Voroshilov, Kliment E., 233
Yugoslavia, visit of Soviet leaders, 100
Zhukov, Marshal Georgi, 33, 47, 81, 90, 95, 100, 146, 176
Spaatz, Gen. Carl, 52
Spain
Assistance, 76
Atomic research agreement, 121
Spanish-American War, 56
Military service of Stephen S. Ogletree, 197
Speaker of the House of Representatives (Sam Rayburn), 90 ftn. (p. 471)
Birthday greetings, 4
Letters
Inter-American highway, 64
Philippines trade agreement revision, 91
Virgin Islands Corporation, 14

Speaker of the House—Continued
News conference remarks on, 41, 95
On Presidential appointments, 95
Spending by Government, 4, 19
News conference remarks, 18, 41
Spivack, Robert G., 10, 26, 41, 59, 62, 95, 112, 146
Sprague, Maj. Gen. John T., 235
Squires, Paul, 181 n.
Squirrels on White House lawn, 62
S.S. *Queen Mary*, 42 n.
Stalin, Joseph, 95
Standard of living, U.S., 4, 19
Standards, Bureau of, 17 (p. 148)
Stassen, Harold E., 60 n., 94
Appointment as Special Assistant to the President, 57
News conference remarks on, 10, 47, 62, 146, 185
Visit to New Delhi, 47
State, Department of, 57, 74
Bowie, Robert R., 146 ftn. (p. 644)
Budget message, 17 (pp. 131, 132)
Corsi, Edward, 62
Delegation to 4-power conference, Geneva, 146 ftn. (p. 644)
Educational exchange program, 17 (p. 132)
Hoover, Herbert, Jr., 94
Ladejinsky case, 10
MacArthur, Douglas II, 146 ftn. (p. 644)
Merchant, Livingston, 61, 146 ftn. (p. 644)
News conference remarks, 10, 62, 81
Phleger, Herman, 146 ftn. (p. 644)
Robertson, Walter S., 81
State, Secretary of (John Foster Dulles), 26 ftn. (p. 231), 54, 94, 98 n., 126, 143, 146 ftn. (p. 644), 148, 173, 204 n.
Bangkok conference, 41

Index

[References are to items except as otherwise indicated]

State, Secretary of—Continued
Bipartisan meeting on Geneva conference of heads of state, 174
Geneva conferences (1955)
Foreign ministers, 226, 227
Heads of government, 161, 175
ILO conventions and recommendations, report, 107
Letter re transfer of FOA functions, 74
Meeting with Dag Hammarskjold, 18
Meeting with Prime Minister Scelba, 61
News conference remarks on, 18, 41, 47, 59, 81, 100, 119, 146
On Middle East situation, 234
On U.S. airmen imprisoned in Communist China, 18
Refugee Relief Act, 109
Southeast Asia Collective Defense Treaty, report on, 5
TV report on European visit, 99
Comment on, 100
Visit to Asia, 100
Visit to Formosa, 47
State and community conferences on education, statement, 96
State of the Union, annual message to Congress, 4
Statehood of Alaska and Hawaii, 4, 56, 95, 247
States
Federal aid. See Federal aid to States
Governors, letter to, 29
Polio vaccine. See Poliomyelitis vaccine
See also Federal-State-local governmental responsibilities
Status of Forces agreements, 119
Stephenson, Francis M., 62, 90
Stevens, Robert T. See Army, Secretary of the
Stock market, 18, 56
Margin requirements, 81

Stockpiling of strategic and critical materials, 3, 4
Budget message, 17 (pp. 108, 122)
Strategic Air Command, 13, 17 (p. 117)
Strategic Air Force, 52 n.
Strategic and critical materials, stockpiling, 3, 4
Budget message, 17 (pp. 108, 122)
Stratemeyer, Lt. Gen. George E., 112
Strauss, Lewis L. See Atomic Energy Commission, Chairman
Strikes. See Labor disputes
Students
Atomic studies of foreign students, 53, 165
Exchange of, 4
Submarines, nuclear-powered, Nautilus and Seawolf, 17 (p. 121), 81
Subsidies, Government
Airlines, 17 (p. 169), 30, 33, 106
Ships, 17 (pp. 92, 167, 168)
Subversive Activities Control Board, tenure of office, 189
Suez, 35
Summerfield, Arthur E. See Postmaster General (Arthur E. Summerfield)
Summit meeting. See Heads of state and governments, meeting
Supreme Allied Commander Atlantic (Adm. Jerauld Wright), 100
Supreme Court, U.S.
Decision on school integration, 149
Nomination to fill vacancy, comment on, 26
Surplus agricultural commodities. See Agricultural surpluses
Survivor benefits, military personnel, 4, 13, 17 (p. 134)
Sweden, question of summit conference in, 119
Switzerland
Atomic research agreement, 121

Index

[References are to items except as otherwise indicated]

Switzerland—Continued
Geneva, 37 n., 168 n., 169 n.
Geneva conferences. *See* Geneva conferences
Lausanne, 112, 119
Petitpierre, Max, 163
Synthetic rubber plants, sale of, 17 (p. 92)

Tachen Islands, 21 36
Evacuation, 33
News conference remarks, 18, 26, 33, 47
Taiwan. *See* Formosa (Taiwan); Formosa (Taiwan) Strait situation
Talbott, Harold E. *See* Air Force, Secretary of the
Tampico, Mexico, flood relief, 229
Tariff Commission, U.S., 6
Tariffs, reduction of, 4
Tariffs and Trade, General Agreement on, 6, 72
Tariff concessions on textiles, 149
Tax returns, investigation by Congressional Committees, 90
Tax treaties, 6
Taxes
Budget message, 17 (pp. 87, 97– 99, 145)
Collection procedures, 17 (p. 145)
Corporate, 4, 6, 17 (pp. 87, 97, 98), 41
Excise, 4, 17 (pp. 87, 97, 98), 41
Income, 41
News conference remarks, 18, 41, 47, 56, 112
Reduction, 4, 18, 19, 41, 47, 112
Teachers, shortage of, 31
Teamsters, International Brotherhood of, 232
Technical assistance, U.N., 4, 76, 156
Contributions to, 126
Technical assistance to less developed countries, 4, 6, 76, 167
Budget message, 17 (p. 130)
See also Foreign assistance; Mutual security program

Telephone service, rural, 17 (pp. 153, 154)
Telephone strike, Southern Bell Telephone Co., 90, 95
Televised news conference, first, editor's note, 18 (p. 185)
Comment on, 26
Television and radio broadcasters, remarks, 105
Television and Radio Farm Directors, National Association, remarks, 127
Tennessee
Cooper, Repr. Jere, 90 ftn. (p. 471), 160
Evins, Repr. Joe L., 112
Kefauver, Sen. Estes, 146, 149
Memphis, 56, 146, 149
Oak Ridge, 17 (p. 121)
Power projects, 56
Tennessee Valley Authority
Appropriations, 157
Budget message, 17 (pp. 161, 162)
Chairman (Herbert D. Vogel), 146 ftn. (p. 646)
Dixon-Yates contract. *See* Dixon-Yates contract
News conference remarks, 26, 56, 100, 149
Steam plant, 56, 149
Tennyson, Alfred, 35
Texas
Bell, Repr. John J., 95
Cooper Dam and Reservoir, approval, 184
Dallas, 10
Daniel, Sen. Price, 47
Johnson, Sen. Lyndon B., 81, 90 ftn. (p. 471), 146
Rayburn, Repr. Sam, 4, 14, 41, 64, 90 ftn. (p. 471) 91, 95
Texas City disaster, 112
Textiles
Import quotas, 185
Tariff concessions, 149

Index

[References are to items except as otherwise indicated]

Thailand
  Ambassador John E. Peurifoy, 195
  Bangkok conference, 41
  Pibulsonggram, Field Marshal, 87
Theis, William, 18, 41, 119, 146, 185
Thomasville, Ga., 33
Thompson, John S., 51 n.
Thompson, Llewellyn E., 146 ftn. (p. 644)
Thurmond, Sen. Strom
  News conference remarks on, 149
  Telegram, 73
Thye, Sen. Edward J., 33
Tibbetts, Candy, 141
Tibbetts, Mr. and Mrs. Verde, 141 n.
Tito, Marshal, 119
Tobacco
  Excise tax on, 41
  Exports, 6
Tompkins, William F., 10
Tondreau, Aime A., 139 n.
Totalitarianism, 76
Trade, international, 4, 6, 19, 72, 79, 167
  Budget message, 17 (pp. 128, 132)
  News conference remarks, 18, 33, 41,
    100, 149
  Remarks to Advertising Council, 58
  With Communist areas, 18, 100
  With Soviet Union, 33
  See also Tariffs and Trade, General
    Agreement on; Trade Agreements
    Act
Trade Agreements Act, extension, 6, 79,
  81
  Approval, 129
  News conference remarks, 26, 41, 59
  Remarks to National Trade Policy Com-
    mittee, 83
Trade Cooperation, Organization for, 248
  U.S. membership proposed, 129, 160
    Message, 72
Trade fairs, international, 59
  Bangkok (1954), 6

Traffic accidents, 39, 243
  Statement on safe driving, 111
Traffic Safety, President's Committee for,
  111, 243
  Letter to William Randolph Hearst, Jr.,
    re appointment, 124
  Letter to T. S. Petersen re appointment,
    125
Training
  Government employees, 8
  Public health, 25
  Veterans, 17 (p. 136)
Transit strike, Washington, D.C., 149, 176
Transport Policy and Organization, Com-
    mittee on, report, 33, 62, 90 and ftn.
    (p. 475)
Transportation
  District of Columbia, 149, 176, 206
  Excise tax on, 41
  Federal policies on, 4
Travel, freedom of, 6, 167
Travel abroad by the President, 119
Travel allowances for Federal personnel, 8
Treasurer of the United States (Mrs. Ivy
    Baker Priest), 187
  Letter, 186
Treasury, Department of the, 19
  Budget message, 17 (p. 98)
  Folsom, Marion B., 112
Treasury, Secretary of the (George M.
    Humphrey), 44, 90 ftn. (p. 475)
  News conference remarks on, 33, 47
  On resignation of Mrs. Oveta Culp
    Hobby, 153
Treaties. See International agreements
  (1955)
Trieste, 18, 35
Tripartite Declaration on Middle East
  (1950), 234, 239
Truman, Harry S., President, 18, 33, 81
Trust funds, 17 (pp. 101, 106, 107, 139,
  145, 178)
  Tables, 17 (pp. 107, 178)

930

Index

[References are to items except as otherwise indicated]

Tuberculosis victims, recommendations re under Refugee Relief Act, 109

Tully, Andrew F., Jr., 18, 81, 95, 100

Turkey, 4
Agreement with U.S. on civil uses of atomic energy, 89, 112, 121
Assistance, 76

Unemployment, 4, 19
News conference remarks, 33, 119

Unemployment insurance, 19
Budget message, 17 (pp. 136, 176, 177, 182)
Government employees, 17 (p. 182)
News conference remarks, 56, 112, 119
Veterans, 17 (p. 136)

Unemployment trust fund, 17 (p. 178)

Union of Soviet Socialist Republics. *See* Soviet Union

United Community campaigns
Memorandum, 168
Statement, 218

United Defense Fund, 27

United Jewish Appeal, citation of the President, 115

United Kingdom, 4, 18, 54 n., 112 ftn. (p. 548)
Agreement with U.S. on civil uses of atomic energy, 123
Ambassador Winthrop W. Aldrich, 244 n.
British Empire Service League, 119
Churchill, Winston, 47, 65, 244
Eden, Anthony, 41, 66, 208 n.
Elizabeth II, 208 n.
Mountbatten, Vice Adm. Louis, 119

United Nations, 16, 20, 21, 24, 167, 179, 239, 248
Atomic energy for peaceful uses, 4
President's proposal for international organization (1953), 59, 121
Technical conference, Geneva, 100, 123, 149, 156, 176, 191, 228

United Nations—Continued
Disarmament. *See* Disarmament Commission and subcommittee, U.N.
Forced Labor, Ad Hoc Committee on, 156
Formosa Strait, question of action on, 18
Guatemala, meeting on, 156
Middle East situation, 234
News conference remarks, 18, 26, 33, 41, 59, 81, 100, 112, 146, 176
Refugee program, 17 (p. 131), 76, 156
Technical assistance program, 4, 17 (p. 130), 76, 126, 156
Tenth anniversary meeting, San Francisco, 81, 112, 126, 146
U.S. employees, security clearance, 156
U.S. participation, report, 156
U.S. Representative (Henry Cabot Lodge, Jr.), 156

United Nations, Secretary General (Dag Hammarskjold), 179
Meeting with Secretary Dulles, 18
Negotiations with Communist China on release of prisoners, 4, 18, 156
Statement re, 16

United Nations Charter, 4, 26, 126, 148, 156

United Nations Children's Fund, 156
U.S. contributions, 76

United Nations Educational, Scientific and Cultural Organization, 156

United Nations General Assembly
Action on detention of U.S. and U.N. prisoners, 4
Address by President (1953), 79, 156, 177 n., 228
Resolution on cooperation in peaceful uses of atomic energy (1954), 156

United Service Organizations, 130
Defense Fund Dinner, message, 27
President's acceptance of honorary chairmanship, 80

Index

[References are to items except as otherwise indicated]

United States Information Agency, 248
  Budget message, 17 (p. 131)
Universities. *See* Colleges and universities
Upper Colorado River Basin development,
  17 (p. 159)
Uranium, 121, 123
  Isotopes available for friendly countries,
    228
    Uranium 235 to Turkey, 89 n.
  Prices, 10
  See also Fissionable materials
Urban renewal, 194
  Budget message, 17 (pp. 171, 172)
  Southwest Washington, D.C., develop-
    ment, 55
U.S. Chamber of Commerce, remarks, 85
U.S. Military Academy
  Address to graduating class, 118
  Bryan, Maj. Gen. Blackshear M., Super-
    intendent, 117, 118
  President's reminiscences, 70
  Remarks to alumni, 117
USO. *See* United Service Organizations
U.S.S. *Atka,* Antarctic mission, 47
U.S.S. *Midway,* visit to Capetown, South
  Africa, 18
U.S.S. *Nautilus,* 17 (p. 121) 81
U.S.S. *Seawolf,* 17 (p. 121)
U.S.S.R. *See* Soviet Union
Utah, Sen. Wallace F. Bennett, 119

V-E Day, 10th anniversary, comment on,
  81
Van der Linden, Frank, 26, 90, 146, 176,
  185
Van Fleet, Gen. James A., 112
Van Kleffens, Eelco N., 126
Venezuela, 26
  Caracas, 4
Vermont
  Aiken, Sen. George D., 131
  Chittenden, 132

Vermont—Continued
  Flanders, Sen. Ralph E., 131, 149
  Johnson, Gov. Joseph B., 131
  Rutland, 131
Vessels. *See* Ships
Veterans
  Gift from Burma to children of U.S.
    veterans, 169
  Ogletree, Stephen Swan, 197
Veterans Administration
  Budget message, 17 (pp. 132, 136, 138,
    139, 173)
  Pay adjustments, 8
Veterans Affairs, Administrator of (Har-
  vey V. Higley), Chairman, Commu-
  nity Chest campaign, 130
Veterans benefits, 4, 51
  Budget message, 17 (pp. 94–96, 102, 106,
    132–140)
  Tables, 17 (pp. 135, 140)
Veterans of Foreign Wars, 169
Veterans housing, 17 (pp. 136, 173, 174)
Veterans' Pensions, President's Commis-
  sion on
  Budget message, 17 (p. 134)
  Letter, 51
Veto Messages
  Apple price predictions, prohibition of
    Government publication, 147
  Glaser, Kurt, relief of, 116
  Postal field service compensation bill,
    102
  See also Memorandums of Disapproval
Vice President (Richard M. Nixon), 4,
  104, 217 n., 230 n., 236
  Broadcast for Radio Liberation, 81
  Conference on Equal Job Opportunity,
    letter, 225
  Criticism of, 10
  Editor's note on President's illness, p. 822
  Inter-American highway, letter, 64
  Letters to, 14, 64, 91, 225, 226

932

Index

[References are to items except as otherwise indicated]

Vice President—Continued
  News conference remarks on, 10, 47, 59, 81, 90, 112
  Philippines trade agreement revision, letter, 91
  President's role in selection, 112
  Task of Secretary Dulles at foreign ministers conference, Geneva, letter, 226
  Virgin Islands Corporation, letter, 14
Vice Presidential nominees, comment on, 112
Vienna, 98 n., 114
  Meeting on Austrian treaty, 81, 95
Viet-Nam, 18, 81
  Assistance, 17 (p. 129), 48
  Bao Dai, 48
  Diem, Ngo Dinh, 48, 81
Viet-Nam, North, 17 (p. 130)
Vinson, Repr. Carl, 149
Virgin Islands Corporation, property management, 14
Virginia, Sen. Harry F. Byrd, 81, 90 ftn. (p. 471)
Visitors, foreign
  Castillo Armas, Carlos, 230
  Magloire, Paul, 23
  Nu (U), 148
  Pibulsonggram, Field Marshal, 87
  Soviet agriculturists, 95
  Zhukov, Marshal, question of visit, 33, 47
Vocational rehabilitation, 25
  Budget message, 17 (pp. 94, 144)
Vogel, Herbert D., 146 ftn. (p. 646)
Voluntary organizations, refugees and escapee program, 60, 76
Von Fremd, Charles S., 10, 33, 41, 47, 56, 59, 81, 90, 95, 112, 119, 146, 149, 185
Voroshilov, Kliment E., message, 233
Voting rights
  Armed forces absentee voting rights, 29
  District of Columbia, 4
  Overseas personnel, 4

WAC. See Women's Army Corps
Wage freeze, 26
Wage and price controls, 112
Wages, 4
  Guaranteed annual wage, 56, 112, 119
  Minimum, 4, 19, 26, 81, 90, 112, 119, 149, 176
  News conference remarks, 26, 56, 81, 90, 112, 119, 149, 176
  See also Pay
Waging peace, 146
Walter, Repr. Francis E., 59, 62
Walter Reed Medical Center, 108
War
  Nuclear war, 33, 79, 175
  See also Eisenhower, Dwight D., personal reminiscences; Korean War; World War I; World War II
Warning system, 17 (p. 116)
Warren, Earl. See Chief Justice of the United States
Warren, Lucian C., 95
Warren, Matthew, 56, 95
Warren, Shields, 191 n.
Washington, D.C. See District of Columbia
Washington, George, 40
  On defense posture, 56
Washington, Richland, 17 (p. 121)
Washington Hebrew Congregation Temple, dedicatory remarks, 92
Washington National Airport, 17 (p. 170)
Water conservation, 17 (pp. 154, 155)
Water pollution, 25
Water resources development, 4, 19, 247
  Budget message, 17 (pp. 158–162)
  News conference remarks, 56
  Palestine, 76
Weapons
  New, 3, 4, 81, 149
  See also Disarmament; Nuclear weapons
Weather Bureau, 17 (p. 183)

933

Index

[References are to items except as otherwise indicated]

Weather-station network, Department of Defense, 17 (p. 169)

Weaver, Patricia, 237

Weaver, Mr. and Mrs. William G., 237

Weeks, Sinclair. *See* Commerce, Secretary of

Welfare program, 17 (pp. 94, 140–148)
Table, 17 (p. 142)

Wenzell, Adolphe H., 146 and ftn. (pp. 657, 658), 149, 176

West Point. *See* U.S. Military Academy

West Point Plebe (Reeder), 117

West Virginia, Sen. Matthew M. Neely, 81, 185

Western European Union
Joint statement with Prime Minister Scelba on, 61
Message to Prime Ministers of member nations, 54
News conference remarks, 100

Wheat
Exports, 6, 17 (p. 152)
Shipment to Soviet Union, comment on proposal, 41
Surplus, 41

White, Francis, 229

White, Gen. Will W., 176, 185

White, William S., 56, 176

White House Conference on Education, 31, 96
Budget message, 17 (pp. 141, 147)
News conference remarks, 18, 33, 95
Remarks, 242

White House Office, 41
Adams, Sherman, 119, 146
Anderson, Dillon, 146 ftn. (p. 644)
Beach, Comdr. Edward L., 183
Bragdon, Maj. Gen. John S., 203
Disclosure of information by Presidential aides, 62
Dodge, Joseph M., 74

White House Office—Continued
Martin, I. Jack, 181
Morgan, Gerald D., 56, 181
Press Secretary, *See* Hagerty, James C.
Rabb, Maxwell M., 181
Snyder, Murray, editor's note, p. 822
Stassen, Harold E., 62, 146

White House releases, partial list, Appendix A. p. 863

Whitfield, Allen, nominee for AEC, 62, 119

Wildlife resources, 4

Wilson, Charles E. *See* Defense, Secretary of (Charles E. Wilson)

Wilson, Richard L., 10, 26, 56, 59, 62, 95, 119, 185

Wilson, Samuel S., 90

Wilson, Woodrow, 84, 210

Winant, John, 59

Wisconsin, Repr. Glenn R. Davis, 56

Wolfson, Norman, 181

Women in executive positions, comment on, 100

Women's Army Corps, World War II, 100, 152, 153

Wooton, Paul, 33

Workmen's compensation, 4
Budget message, 17 (p. 177)

World Bank. *See* International Bank for Reconstruction and Development

World Health Organization, 25

World Touring and Automobile Clubs, Organization of, remarks, 93

World War I, 56, 118
Cause of, 26

World War II, 4, 10, 13, 22, 29, 59, 100, 115, 166
Documents, disclosure of, 81
News conference remarks, 26
Women's Army Corps, 152, 153
See also Eisenhower, Dwight D., personal reminiscences

Index

[References are to items except as otherwise indicated]

Wright, Adm. Jerauld, 100
Wright, Loyd, 210

Yalta conference, 90
    Release of documents, 59
Yankee Atomic Electric Co., 223
Yellow fever, remarks on, 108
Youth, Republican recruitment, 35, 213
Youth fitness, conference on, 217
Yugoslavia, 4
    Assistance, 76, 119
    News conference remarks, 100, 119

Yugoslavia—Continued
    Tito, Marshal 119
    Visit of Soviet leaders, 100

Zhukov, Marshal Georgi
    Gift to the President, 33
    Geneva conference meeting, 176
    News conference remarks on, 33, 81, 90,
        95, 100, 146
    Visit to U.S., comment on, 33, 47
Zielke, George R., 47
Zoological Park, National, 141 n.

For Reference

Not to be taken from this room